Subject 44

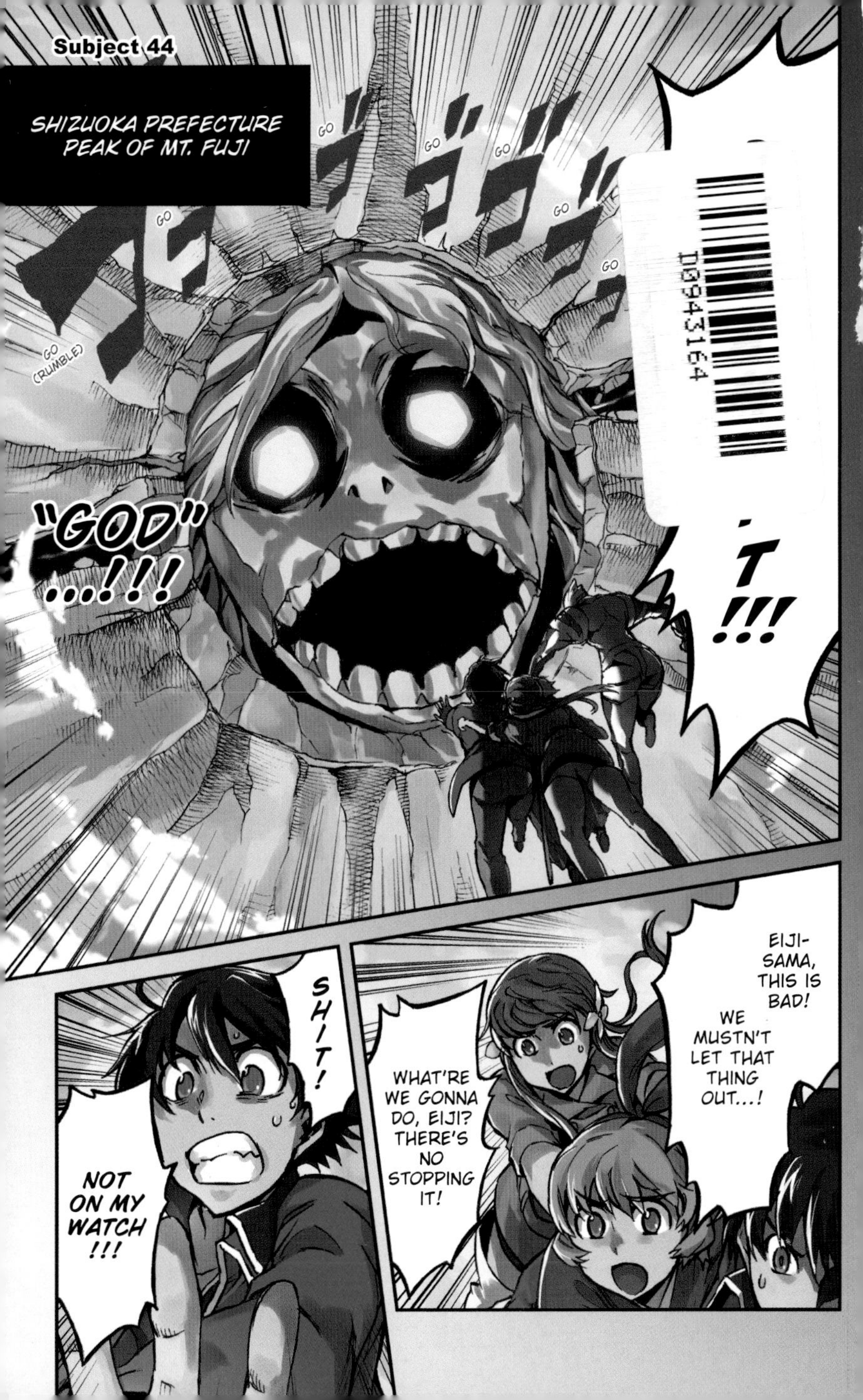
SHIZUOKA PREFECTURE
PEAK OF MT. FUJI
GO GO GO GO GO GO GO (RUMBLE)
"GOD" ...!!!
T!!!
EIJI-SAMA, THIS IS BAD!
WE MUSTN'T LET THAT THING OUT...!
WHAT'RE WE GONNA DO, EIJI? THERE'S NO STOPPING IT!
SHIT!
NOT ON MY WATCH!!!

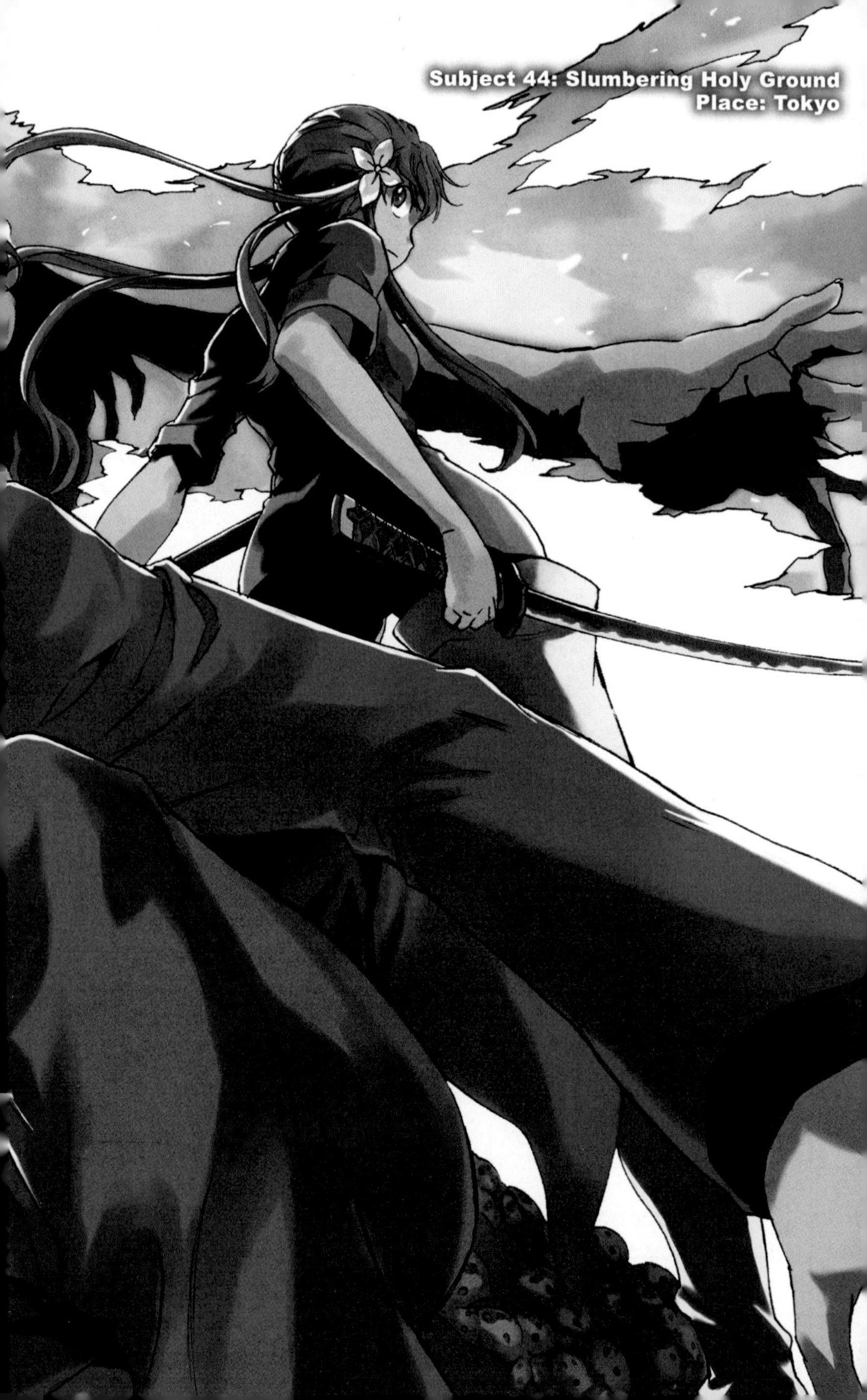
Subject 44: Slumbering Holy Ground
Place: Tokyo

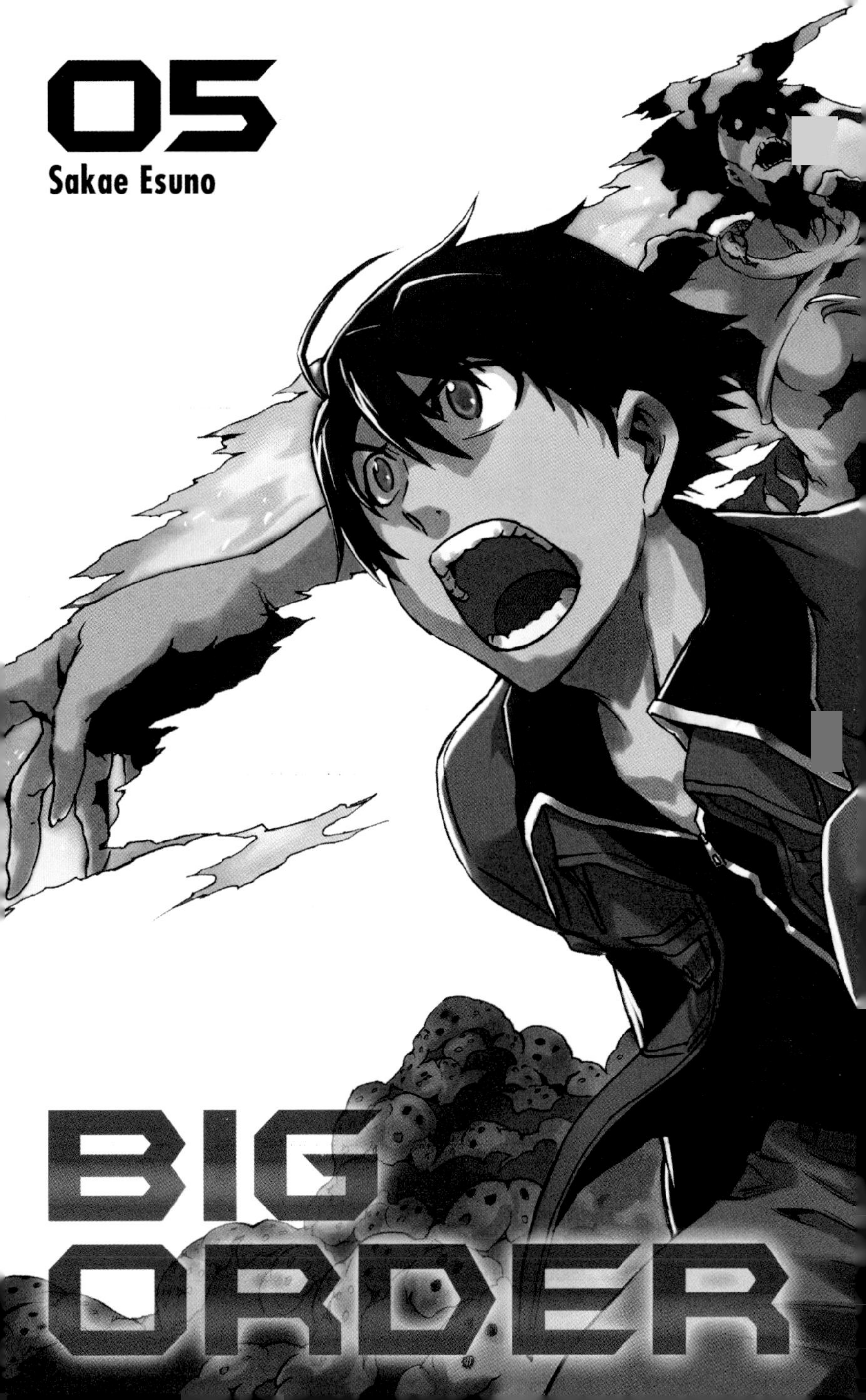
05
Sakae Esuno
BIG ORDER

BIG ORDER

I CAN'T SHIELD SENA
ANYMORE......!

Characters & Story

This story begins when the world was destroyed.

The world was brought to the verge of ruin when young Eiji Hoshimiya's wish was somehow granted. Ten years later, Eiji—now in high school—is attacked by an assassin named Rin Kurenai who knows about his past, and their battle reawakens his power. He's then set up as the enemy of the entire world as part of a scheme by the Dazaifu Government. One day, Eiji learns that his father, Gennai—a man presumed dead—is seeking to cause another Great Destruction in Kansai. He attempts to stop his father, but along the way, he learns that it was not him, but Sena who caused the Great Destruction ten years earlier. Although the scope of the Kansai destruction is minimized, it's unclear whether or not Sena survived. That is, until a despairing Eiji learns from an "irregular" Order that his sister yet lives. Sena's now intent on destroying the world, though, and she's summoned "God" to help her do it...!

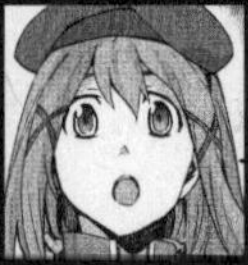

Sena Hoshimiya:
Eiji's stepsister and an Order herself. She's plotting the world's destruction and doesn't have long to live.

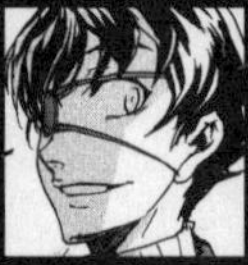

Hanzo Hatori:
Formerly one of Gennai's cunning underlings. He seems to be working with Sena now...

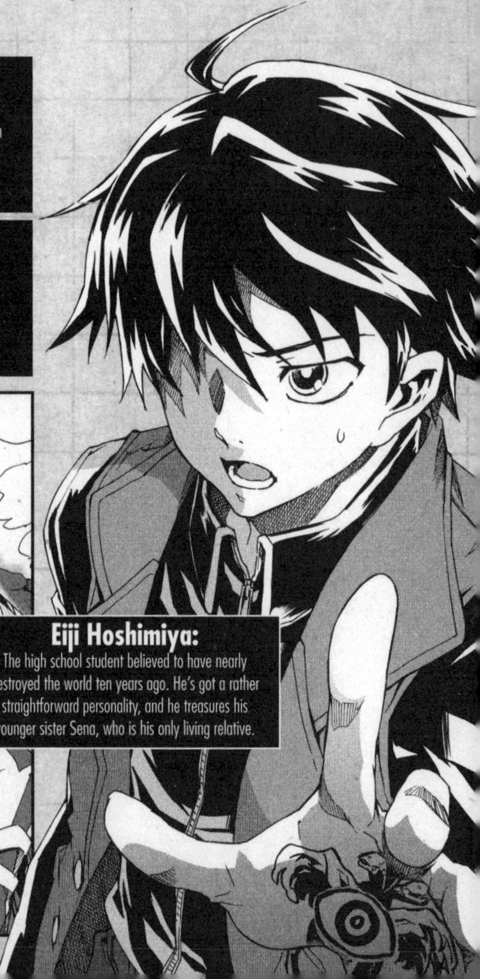

Eiji Hoshimiya:
The high school student believed to have nearly destroyed the world ten years ago. He's got a rather straightforward personality, and he treasures his younger sister Sena, who is his only living relative.

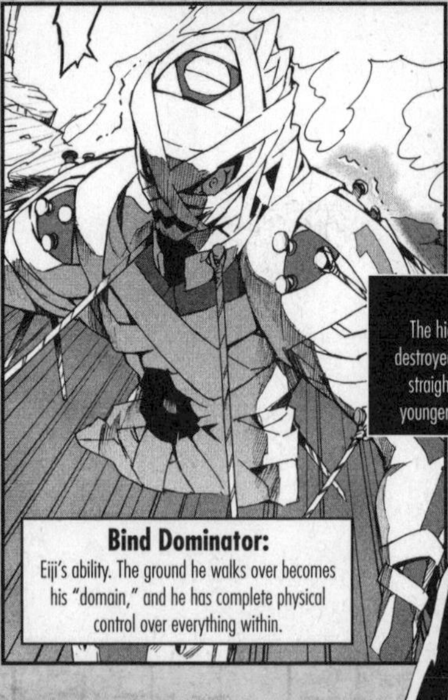

Bind Dominator:
Eiji's ability. The ground he walks over becomes his "domain," and he has complete physical control over everything within.

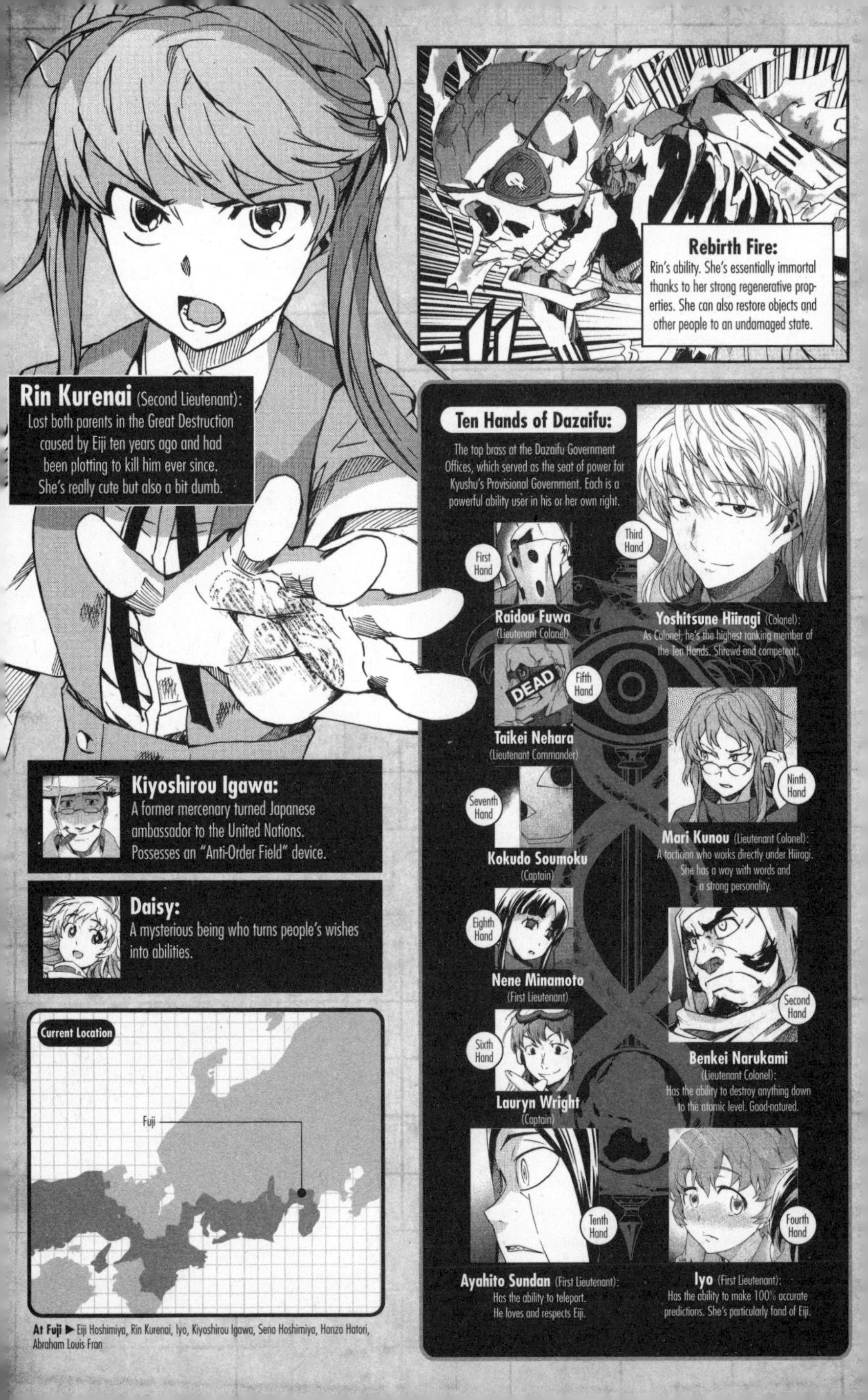
Rebirth Fire:
Rin's ability. She's essentially immortal thanks to her strong regenerative properties. She can also restore objects and other people to an undamaged state.
Rin Kurenai (Second Lieutenant):
Lost both parents in the Great Destruction caused by Eiji ten years ago and had been plotting to kill him ever since. She's really cute but also a bit dumb.
Ten Hands of Dazaifu:
The top brass at the Dazaifu Government Offices, which served as the seat of power for Kyushu's Provisional Government. Each is a powerful ability user in his or her own right.
Third Hand
Yoshitsune Hiiragi (Colonel):
As Colonel, he's the highest ranking member of the Ten Hands. Shrewd and competent.
First Hand
Raidou Fuwa
(Lieutenant Colonel)
Fifth Hand
DEAD
Taikei Nehara
(Lieutenant Commander)
Ninth Hand
Mari Kunou (Lieutenant Colonel):
A tactician who works directly under Hiiragi. She has a way with words and a strong personality.
Seventh Hand
Kokudo Soumoku
(Captain)
Eighth Hand
Nene Minamoto
(First Lieutenant)
Second Hand
Benkei Narukami
(Lieutenant Colonel):
Has the ability to destroy anything down to the atomic level. Good-natured.
Sixth Hand
Lauryn Wright
(Captain)
Tenth Hand
Ayahito Sundan (First Lieutenant):
Has the ability to teleport. He loves and respects Eiji.
Fourth Hand
Iyo (First Lieutenant):
Has the ability to make 100% accurate predictions. She's particularly fond of Eiji.
Kiyoshirou Igawa:
A former mercenary turned Japanese ambassador to the United Nations. Possesses an "Anti-Order Field" device.
Daisy:
A mysterious being who turns people's wishes into abilities.
Current Location
Fuji
At Fuji ▶ Eiji Hoshimiya, Rin Kurenai, Iyo, Kiyoshirou Igawa, Sena Hoshimiya, Hanzo Hatori, Abraham Louis Fran

BIG
ORDER

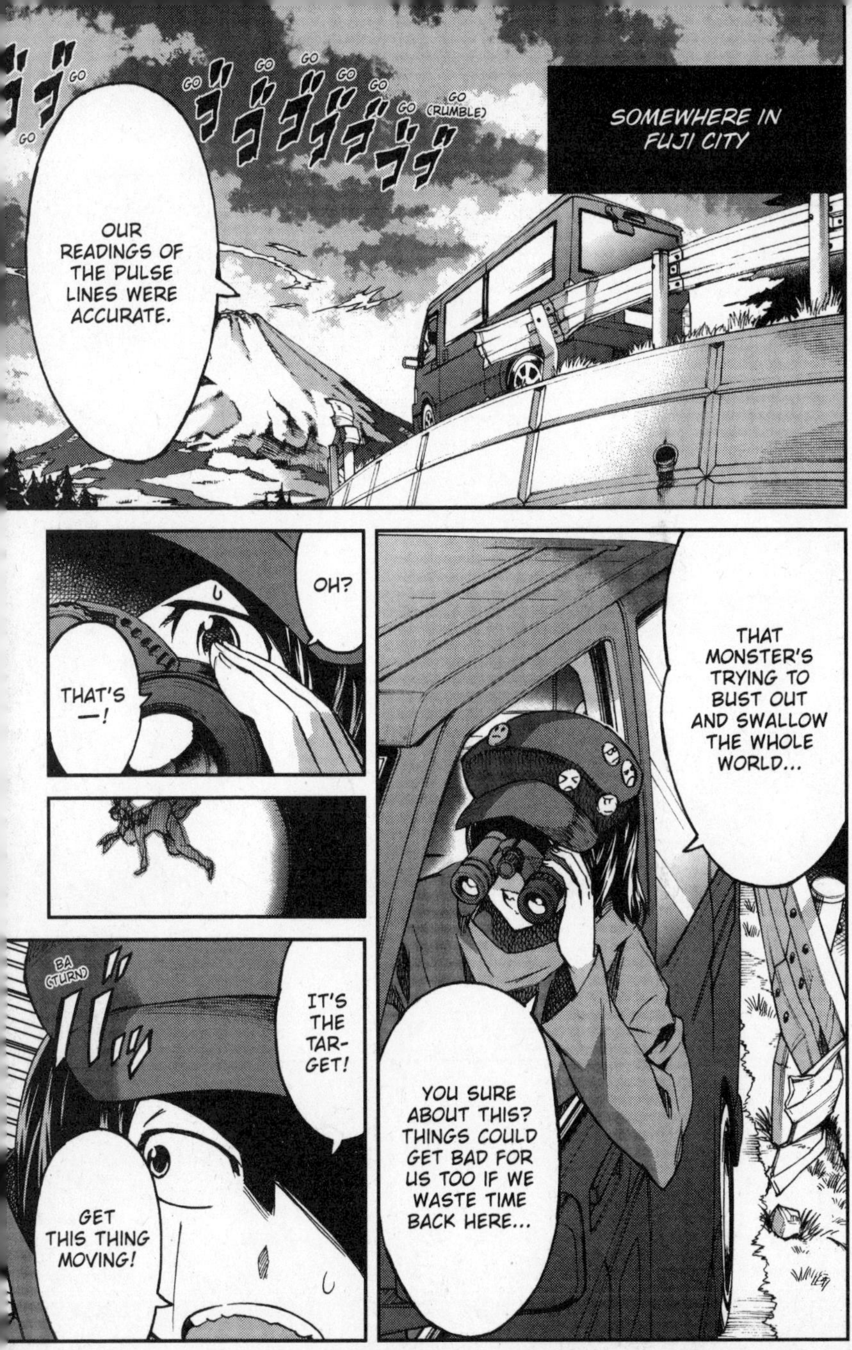
SOMEWHERE IN FUJI CITY
GO (RUMBLE)
GO
GO
GO
GO
GO
GO
GO
GO
OUR READINGS OF THE PULSE LINES WERE ACCURATE.
THAT MONSTER'S TRYING TO BUST OUT AND SWALLOW THE WHOLE WORLD...
YOU SURE ABOUT THIS? THINGS COULD GET BAD FOR US TOO IF WE WASTE TIME BACK HERE...
OH?
THAT'S—!
IT'S THE TAR-GET!
BA (TURN)
GET THIS THING MOVING!

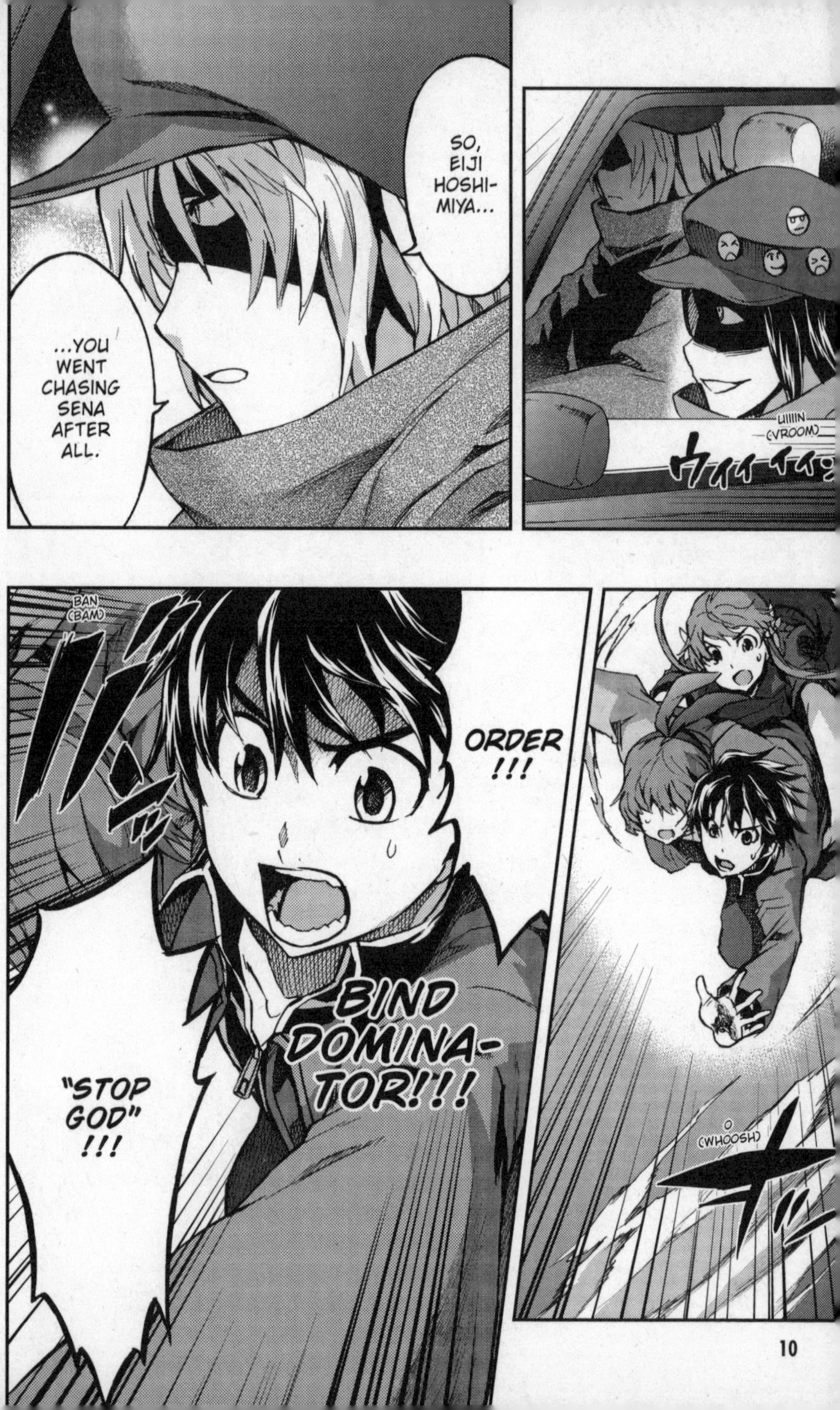
UIIIN
(VROOM)
SO, EIJI HOSHIMIYA...
...YOU WENT CHASING SENA AFTER ALL.
O
(WHOOSH)
BAN
(BAM)
ORDER!!!
BIND DOMINATOR!!!
"STOP GOD"!!!

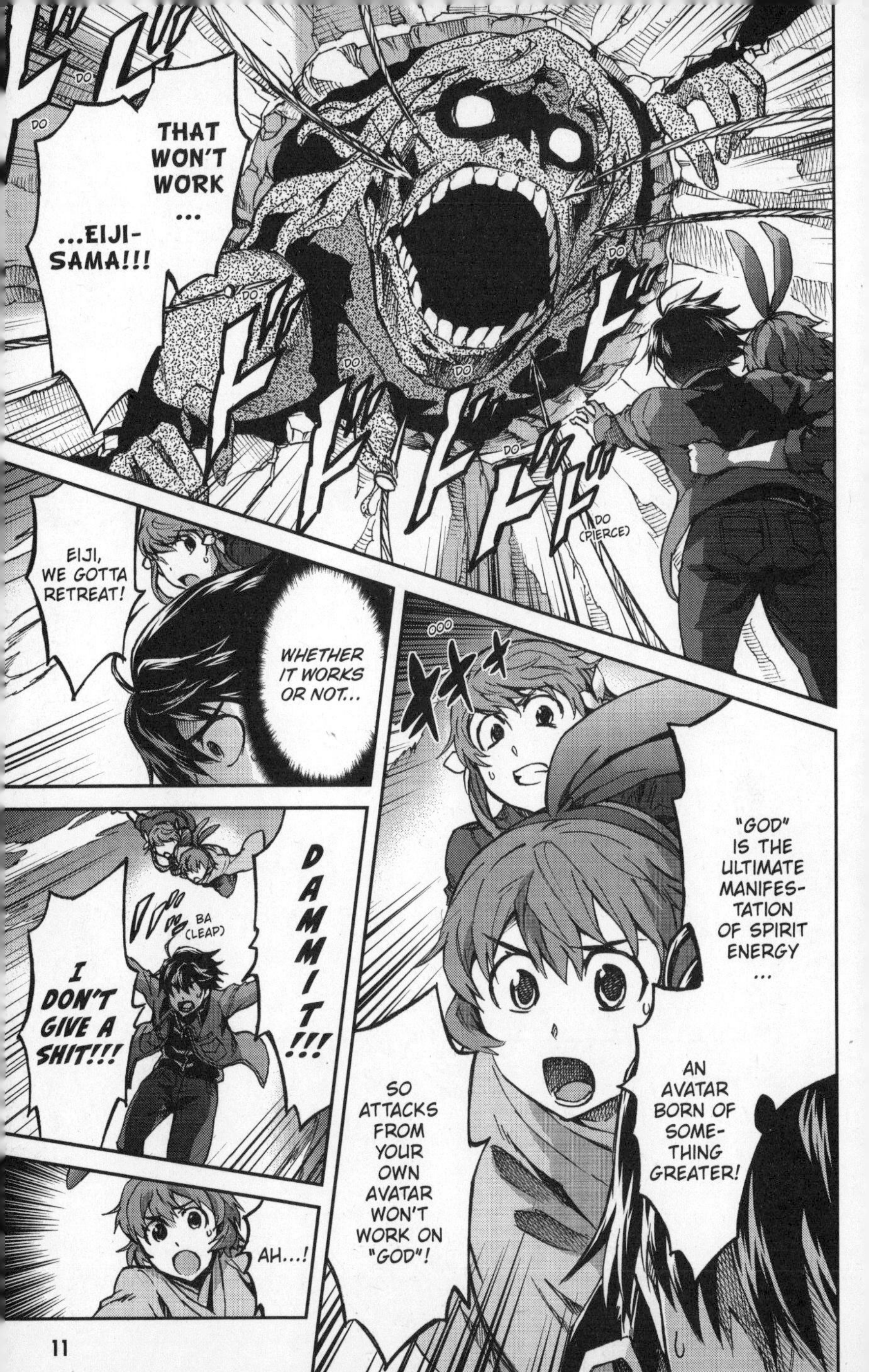
DO
DO
THAT WON'T WORK ...
...EIJI-SAMA!!!
DO
DO
DO
DO
DO
DO (PIERCE)
EIJI, WE GOTTA RETREAT!
WHETHER IT WORKS OR NOT...
BA (LEAP)
I DON'T GIVE A SHIT!!!
DAMMIT!!!
AH...!
"GOD" IS THE ULTIMATE MANIFESTATION OF SPIRIT ENERGY ...
AN AVATAR BORN OF SOMETHING GREATER!
SO ATTACKS FROM YOUR OWN AVATAR WON'T WORK ON "GOD"!

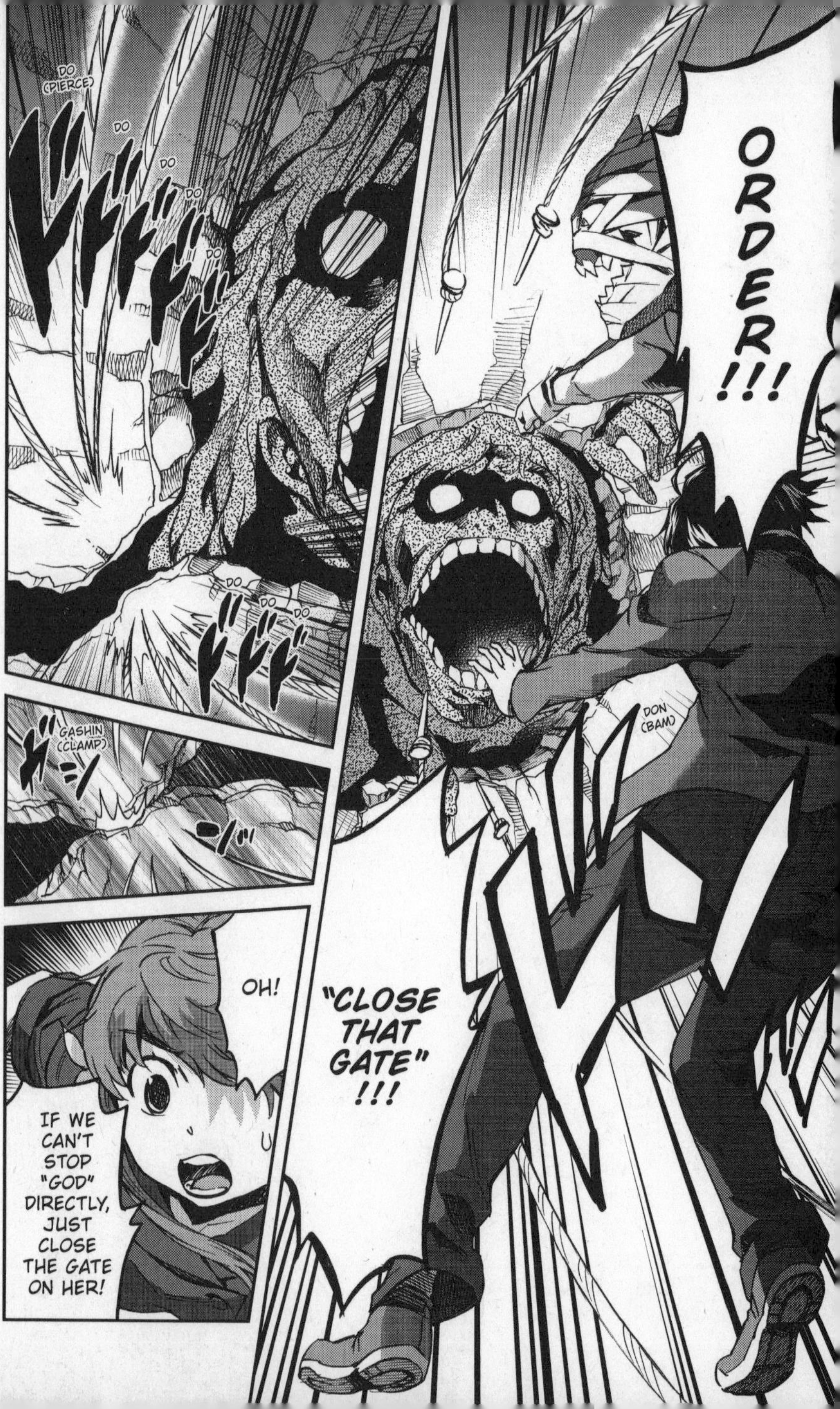
ORDER!!!
DON (BAM)
DO (PIERCE)
DO
DO
DO
DO
DO
DO
DO
GASHIN (CLAMP)
"CLOSE THAT GATE"!!!
OH!
IF WE CAN'T STOP "GOD" DIRECTLY, JUST CLOSE THE GATE ON HER!

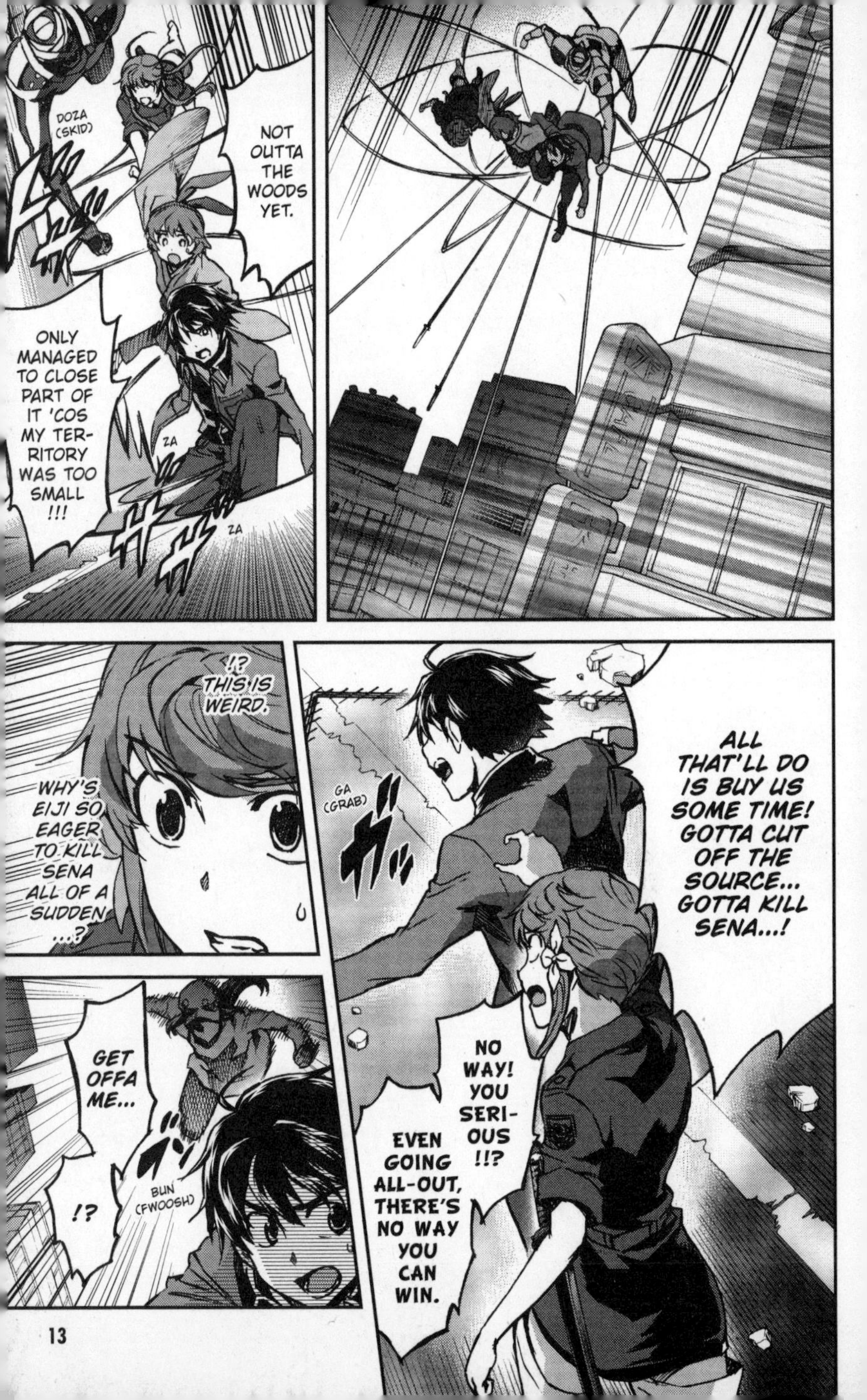
DOZA (SKID)
NOT OUTTA THE WOODS YET.
ONLY MANAGED TO CLOSE PART OF IT 'COS MY TERRITORY WAS TOO SMALL!!!
ZA
ZA
ALL THAT'LL DO IS BUY US SOME TIME! GOTTA CUT OFF THE SOURCE... GOTTA KILL SENA...!
GA (GRAB)
NO WAY! YOU SERIOUS!!?
EVEN GOING ALL-OUT, THERE'S NO WAY YOU CAN WIN.
!? THIS IS WEIRD.
WHY'S EIJI SO EAGER TO KILL SENA ALL OF A SUDDEN...?
GET OFFA ME...
BUN (FWOOSH)
!?

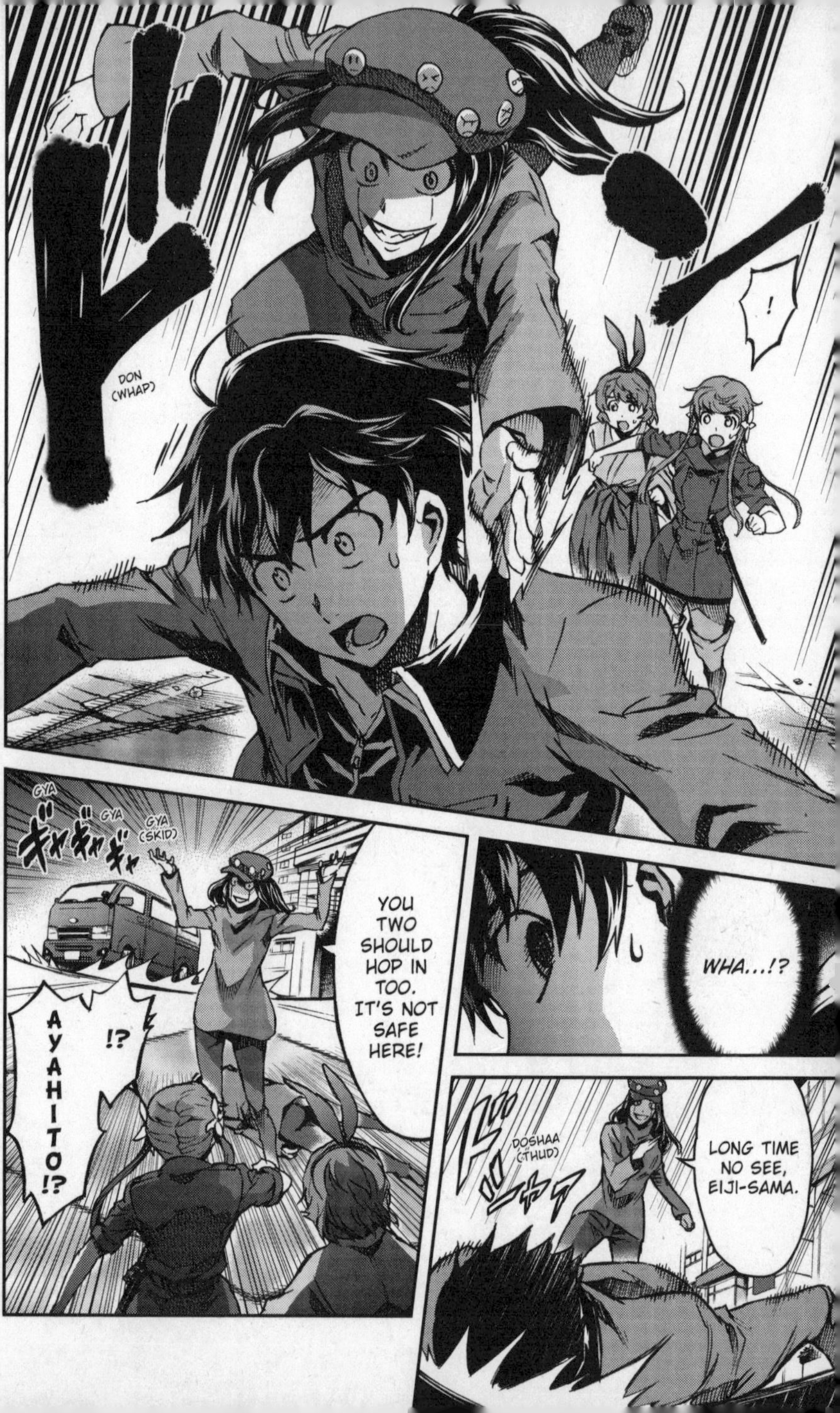
!
DON (WHAP)
WHA...!?
LONG TIME NO SEE, EIJI-SAMA.
DOSHAA (THUD)
YOU TWO SHOULD HOP IN TOO. IT'S NOT SAFE HERE!
GYA GYA GYA (SKID)
ギャギャギャ
!?
AYAHITO!?

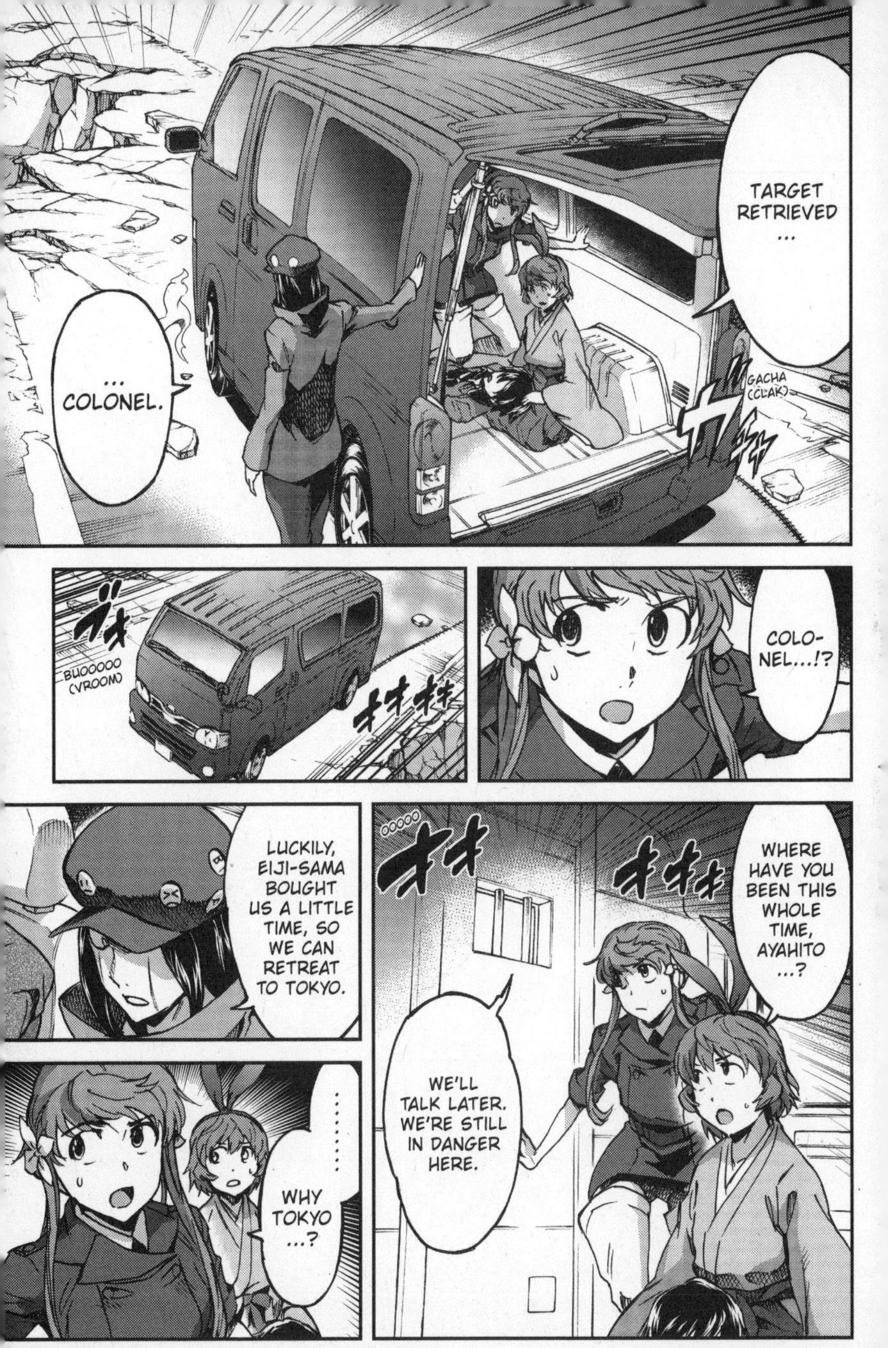
TARGET RETRIEVED ...
GACHA (CLAK)
... COLONEL.
COLO-NEL...!?
BUOOOOO (VROOM)
OOOOO
WHERE HAVE YOU BEEN THIS WHOLE TIME, AYAHITO ...?
WE'LL TALK LATER. WE'RE STILL IN DANGER HERE.
LUCKILY, EIJI-SAMA BOUGHT US A LITTLE TIME, SO WE CAN RETREAT TO TOKYO.
......
WHY TOKYO ...?

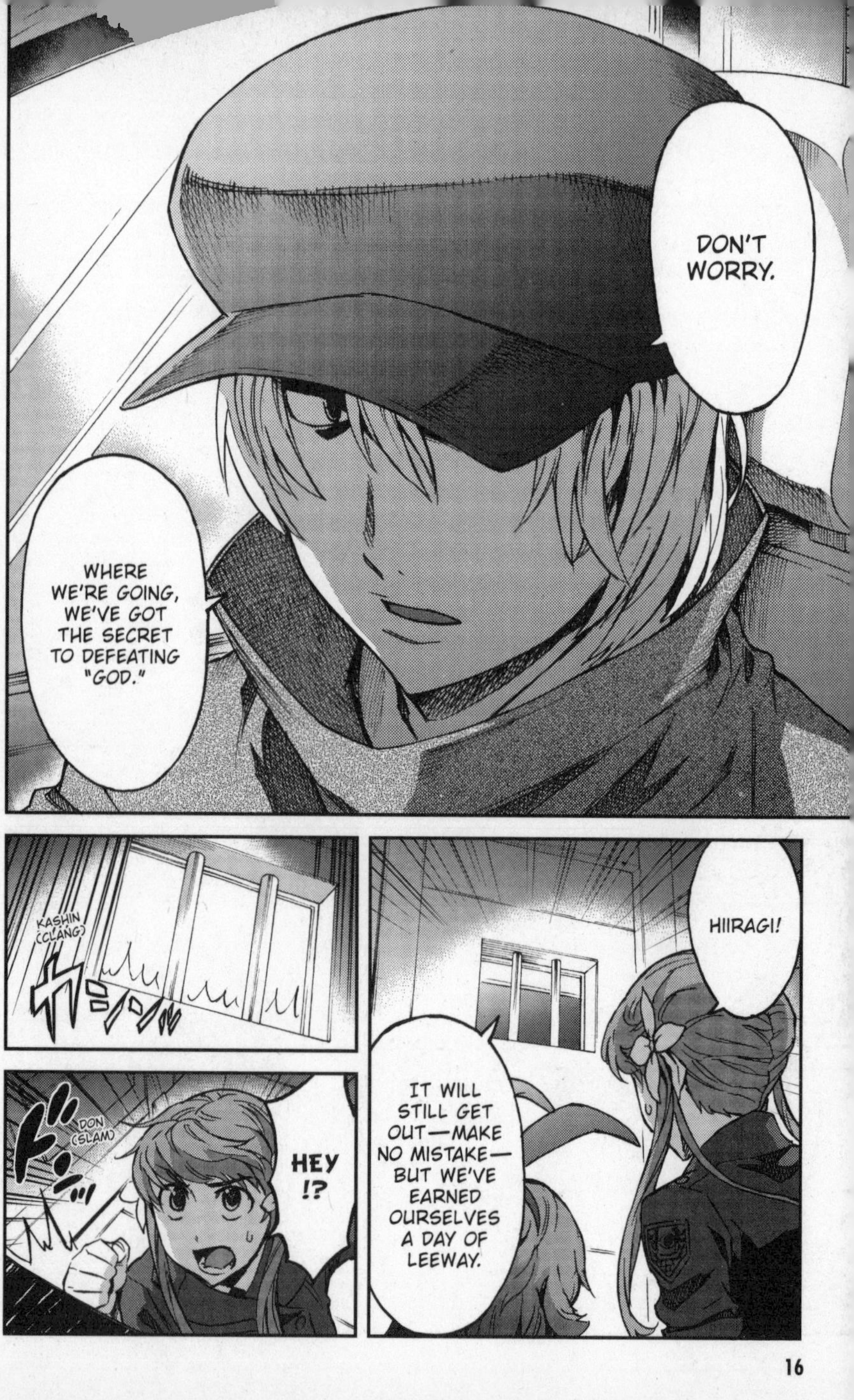
DON'T WORRY.
WHERE WE'RE GOING, WE'VE GOT THE SECRET TO DEFEATING "GOD."
HIIRAGI!
IT WILL STILL GET OUT—MAKE NO MISTAKE—BUT WE'VE EARNED OURSELVES A DAY OF LEEWAY.
KASHIN (CLANG)
DON (SLAM)
HEY !?

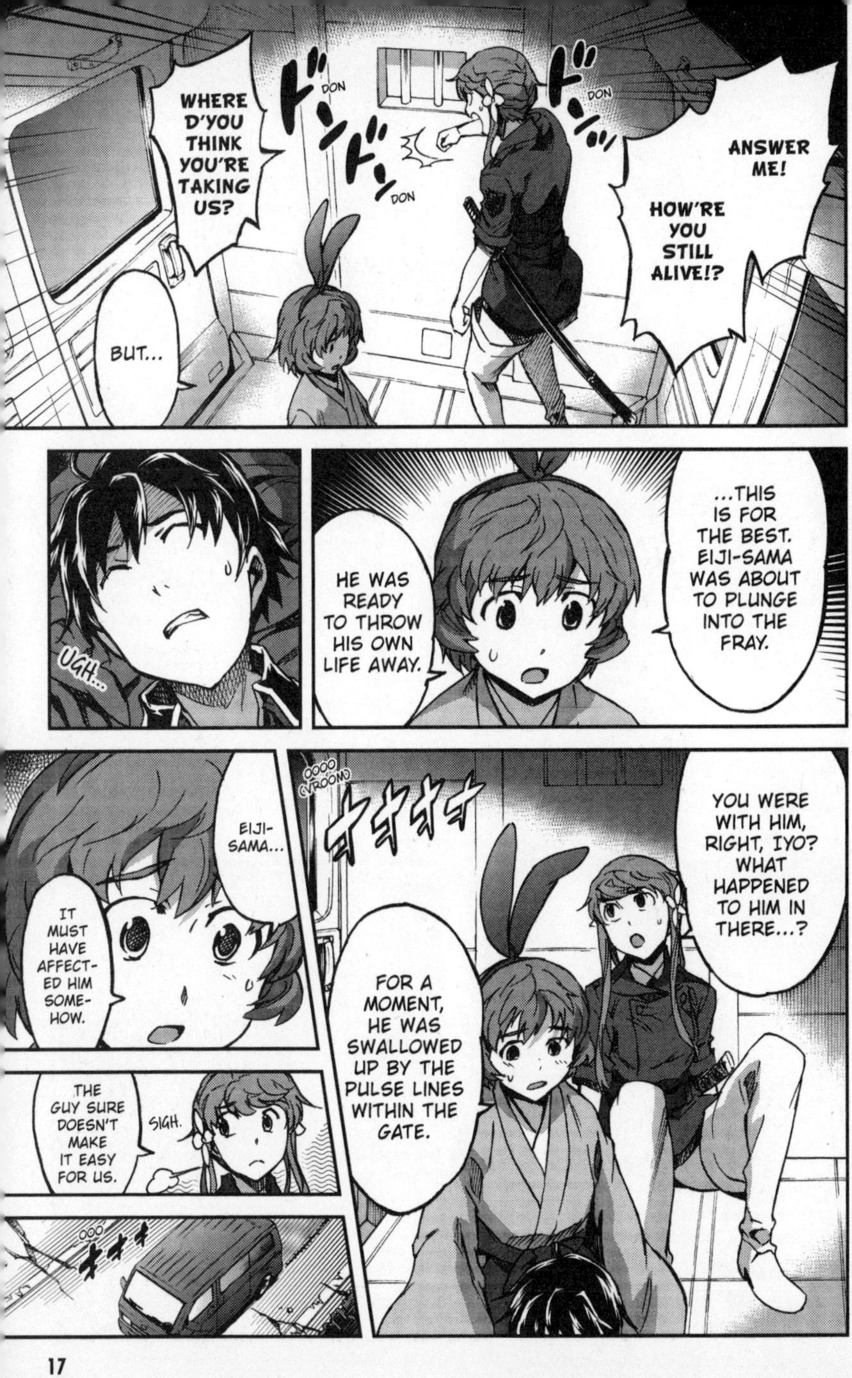
DON
ANSWER ME!
HOW'RE YOU STILL ALIVE!?
DON
DON
WHERE D'YOU THINK YOU'RE TAKING US?
BUT...
...THIS IS FOR THE BEST. EIJI-SAMA WAS ABOUT TO PLUNGE INTO THE FRAY.
HE WAS READY TO THROW HIS OWN LIFE AWAY.
UGH...
YOU WERE WITH HIM, RIGHT, IYO? WHAT HAPPENED TO HIM IN THERE...?
OOOO (VROOM)
FOR A MOMENT, HE WAS SWALLOWED UP BY THE PULSE LINES WITHIN THE GATE.
EIJI-SAMA...
IT MUST HAVE AFFECTED HIM SOMEHOW.
SIGH.
THE GUY SURE DOESN'T MAKE IT EASY FOR US.
OOO

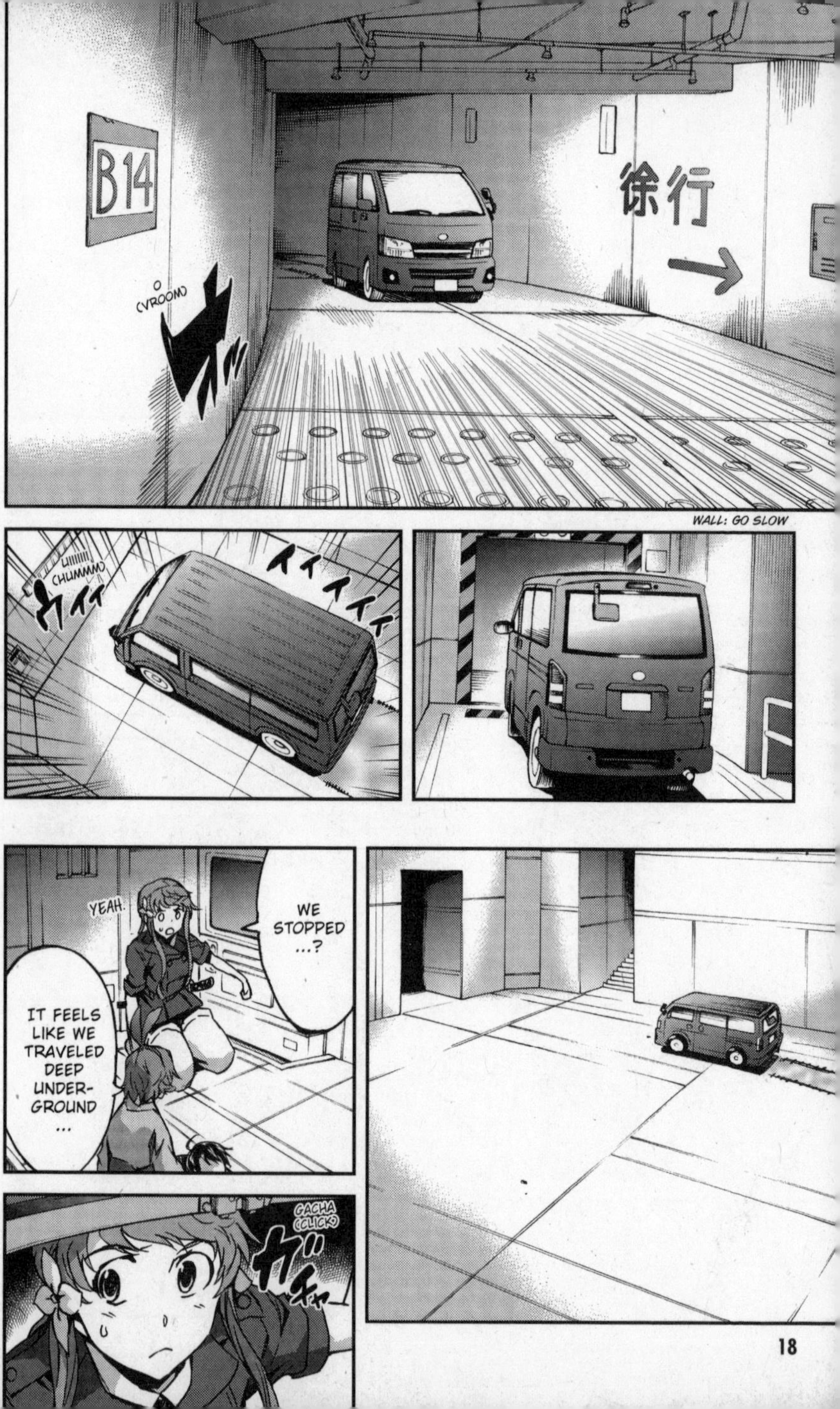
徐行
O
(VROOM)
WALL: GO SLOW
UIIIIIIII
(HUMMM)
WE STOPPED ...?
YEAH.
IT FEELS LIKE WE TRAVELED DEEP UNDER-GROUND ...
GACHA
(CLICK)

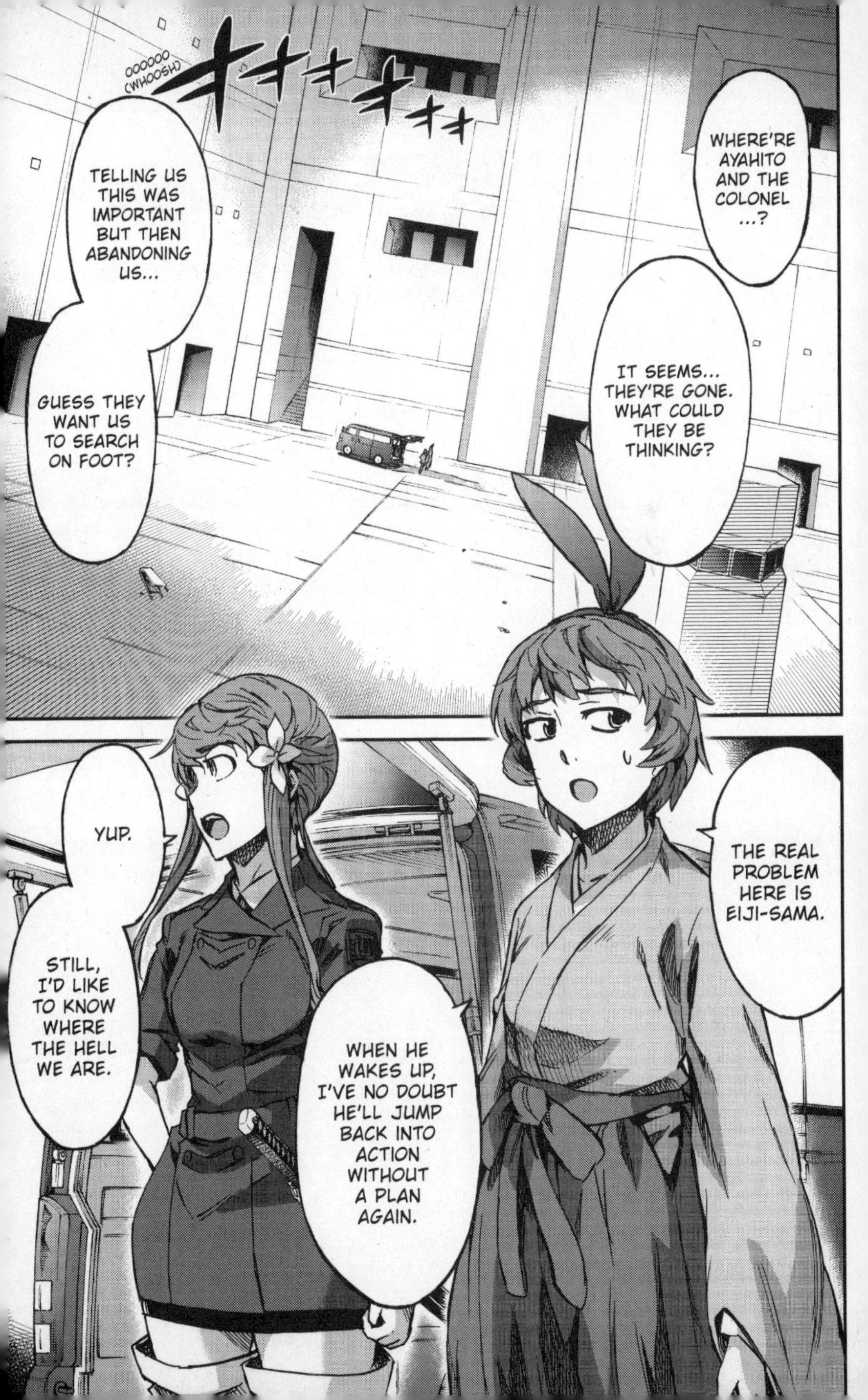
WHERE'RE AYAHITO AND THE COLONEL ...?
IT SEEMS... THEY'RE GONE. WHAT COULD THEY BE THINKING?
OOOOOO (WHOOSH)
TELLING US THIS WAS IMPORTANT BUT THEN ABANDONING US...
GUESS THEY WANT US TO SEARCH ON FOOT?
THE REAL PROBLEM HERE IS EIJI-SAMA.
WHEN HE WAKES UP, I'VE NO DOUBT HE'LL JUMP BACK INTO ACTION WITHOUT A PLAN AGAIN.
YUP.
STILL, I'D LIKE TO KNOW WHERE THE HELL WE ARE.

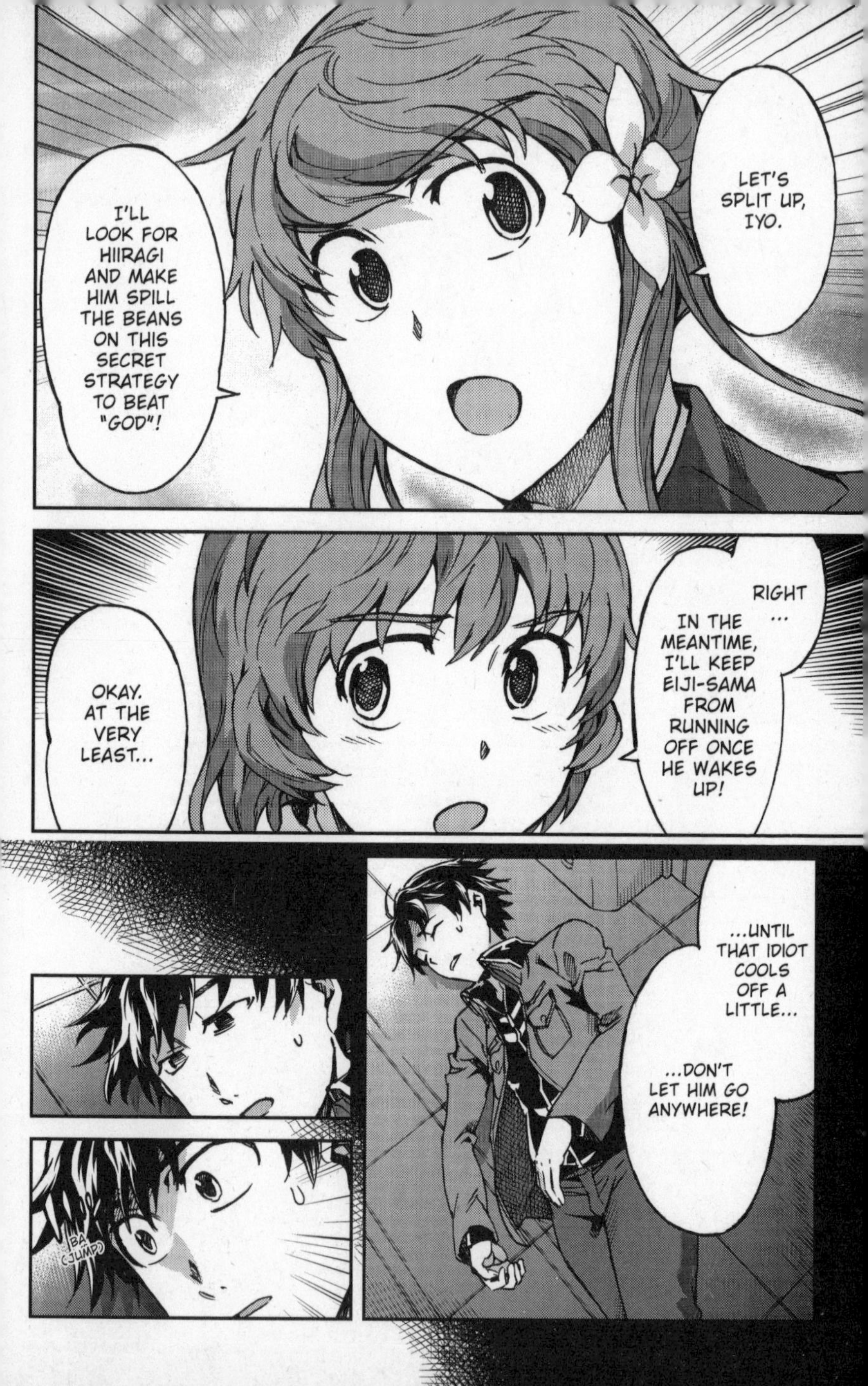
LET'S SPLIT UP, IYO.
I'LL LOOK FOR HIIRAGI AND MAKE HIM SPILL THE BEANS ON THIS SECRET STRATEGY TO BEAT "GOD"!
RIGHT...
IN THE MEANTIME, I'LL KEEP EIJI-SAMA FROM RUNNING OFF ONCE HE WAKES UP!
OKAY. AT THE VERY LEAST...
...UNTIL THAT IDIOT COOLS OFF A LITTLE...
...DON'T LET HIM GO ANYWHERE!
BA (JUMP)

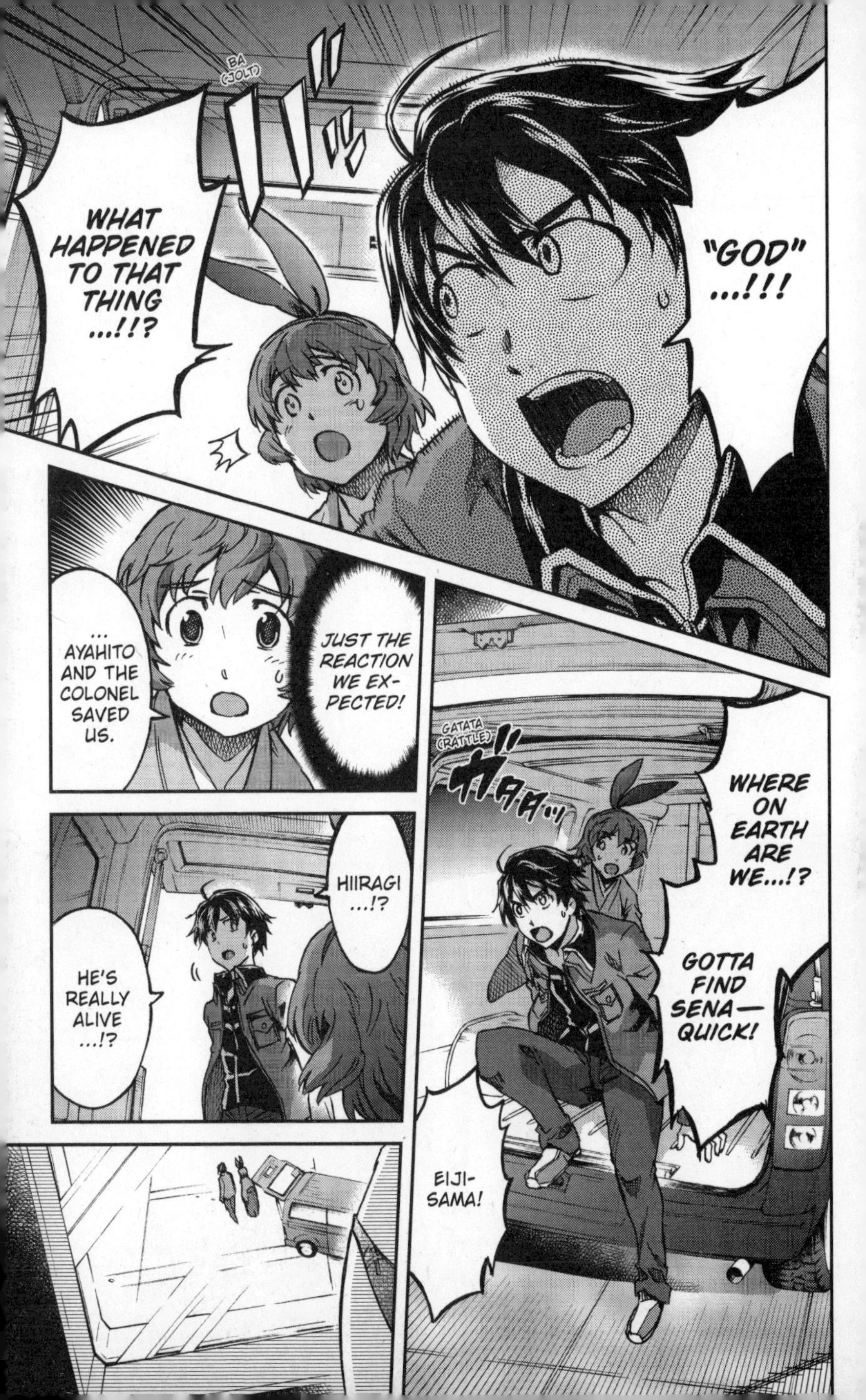
BA
(-JOLT)
"GOD" ...!!!
WHAT HAPPENED TO THAT THING ...!!?
GATATA
(RATTLE)
WHERE ON EARTH ARE WE...!?
GOTTA FIND SENA— QUICK!
EIJI-SAMA!
JUST THE REACTION WE EX-PECTED!
... AYAHITO AND THE COLONEL SAVED US.
HIIRAGI ...!?
HE'S REALLY ALIVE ...!?

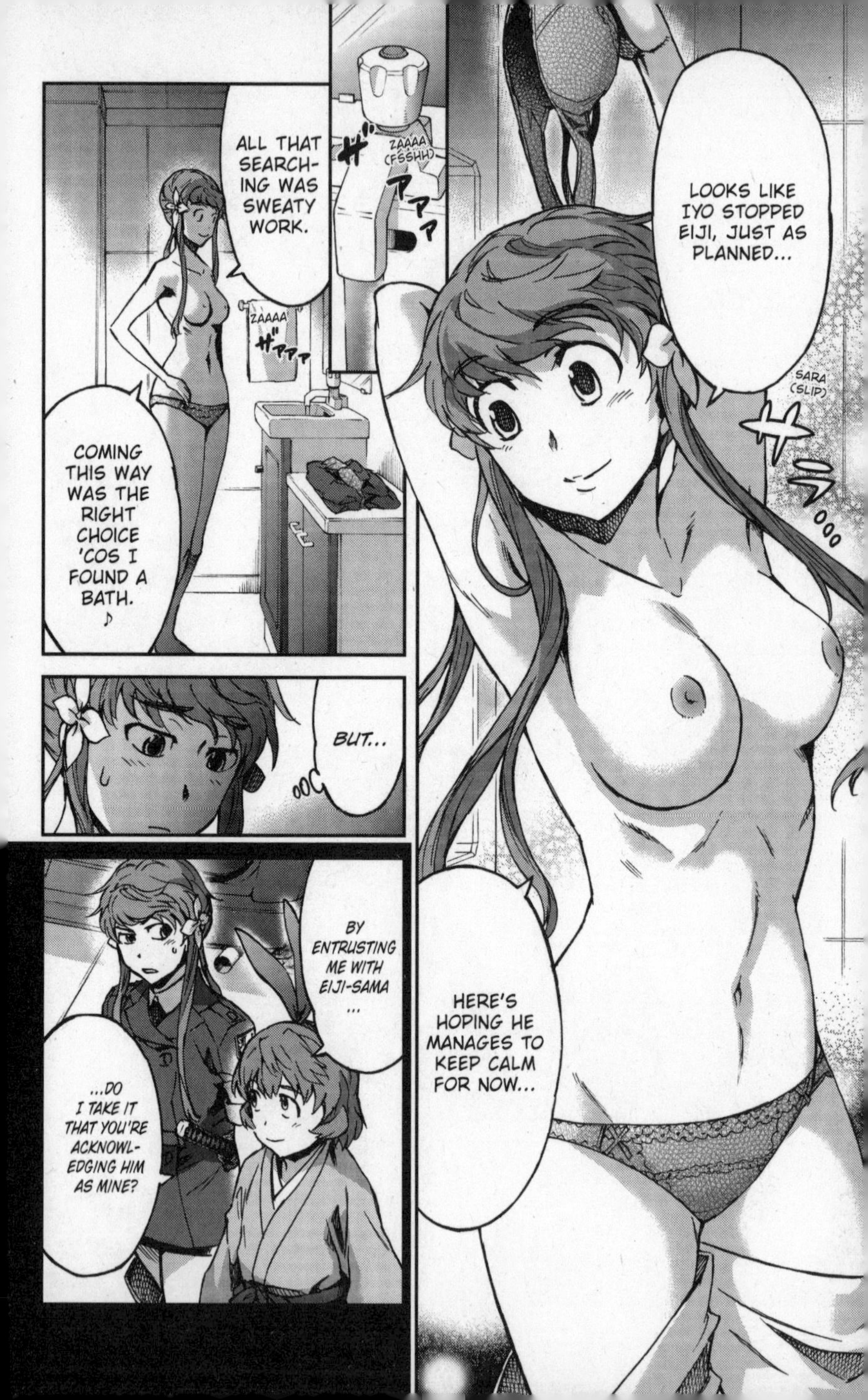
LOOKS LIKE IYO STOPPED EIJI, JUST AS PLANNED...
SARA (SLIP)
HERE'S HOPING HE MANAGES TO KEEP CALM FOR NOW...
ZAAAA (FSSHH)
ALL THAT SEARCH-ING WAS SWEATY WORK.
ZAAAA
COMING THIS WAY WAS THE RIGHT CHOICE 'COS I FOUND A BATH. ♪
BUT...
BY ENTRUSTING ME WITH EIJI-SAMA ...
...DO I TAKE IT THAT YOU'RE ACKNOWL-EDGING HIM AS MINE?

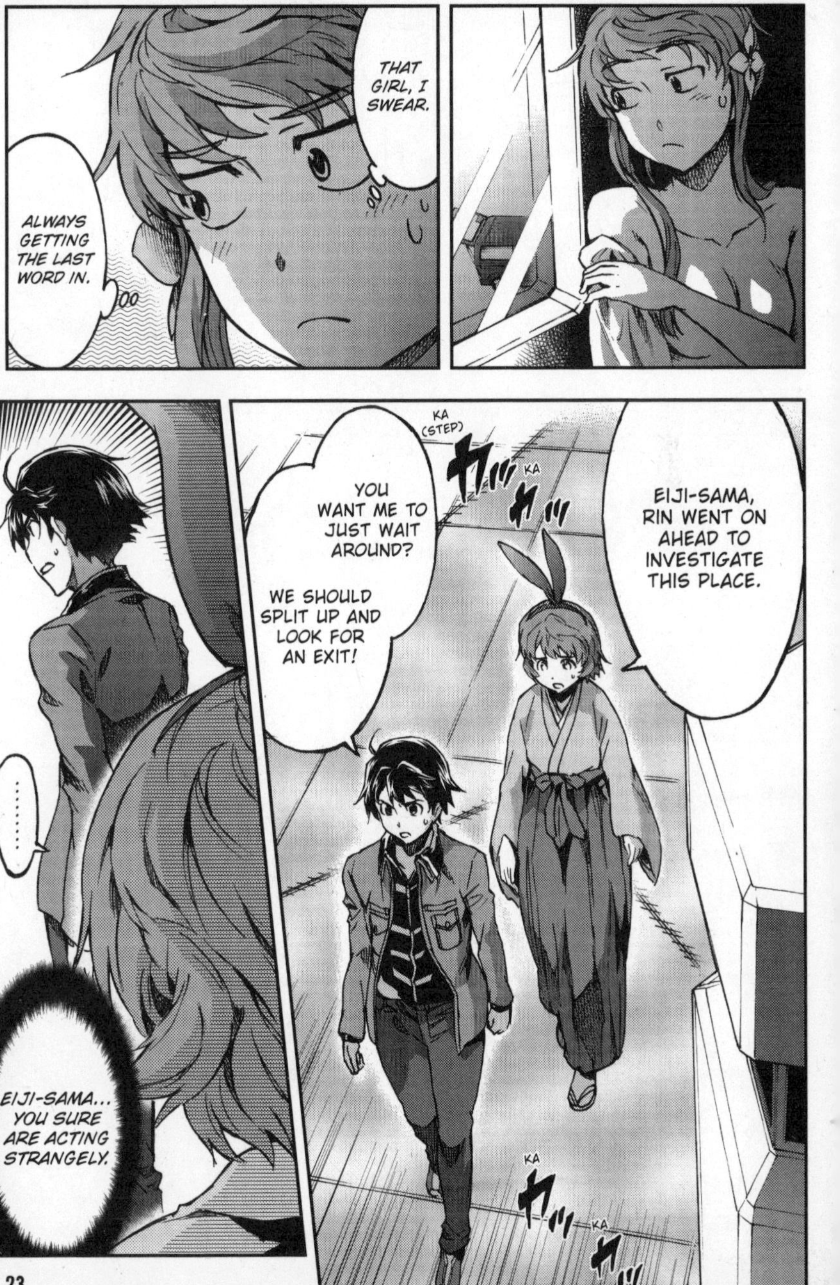
THAT GIRL, I SWEAR.
ALWAYS GETTING THE LAST WORD IN.
KA (STEP)
KA
EIJI-SAMA, RIN WENT ON AHEAD TO INVESTIGATE THIS PLACE.
YOU WANT ME TO JUST WAIT AROUND?
WE SHOULD SPLIT UP AND LOOK FOR AN EXIT!
KA
KA
......
EIJI-SAMA... YOU SURE ARE ACTING STRANGELY.

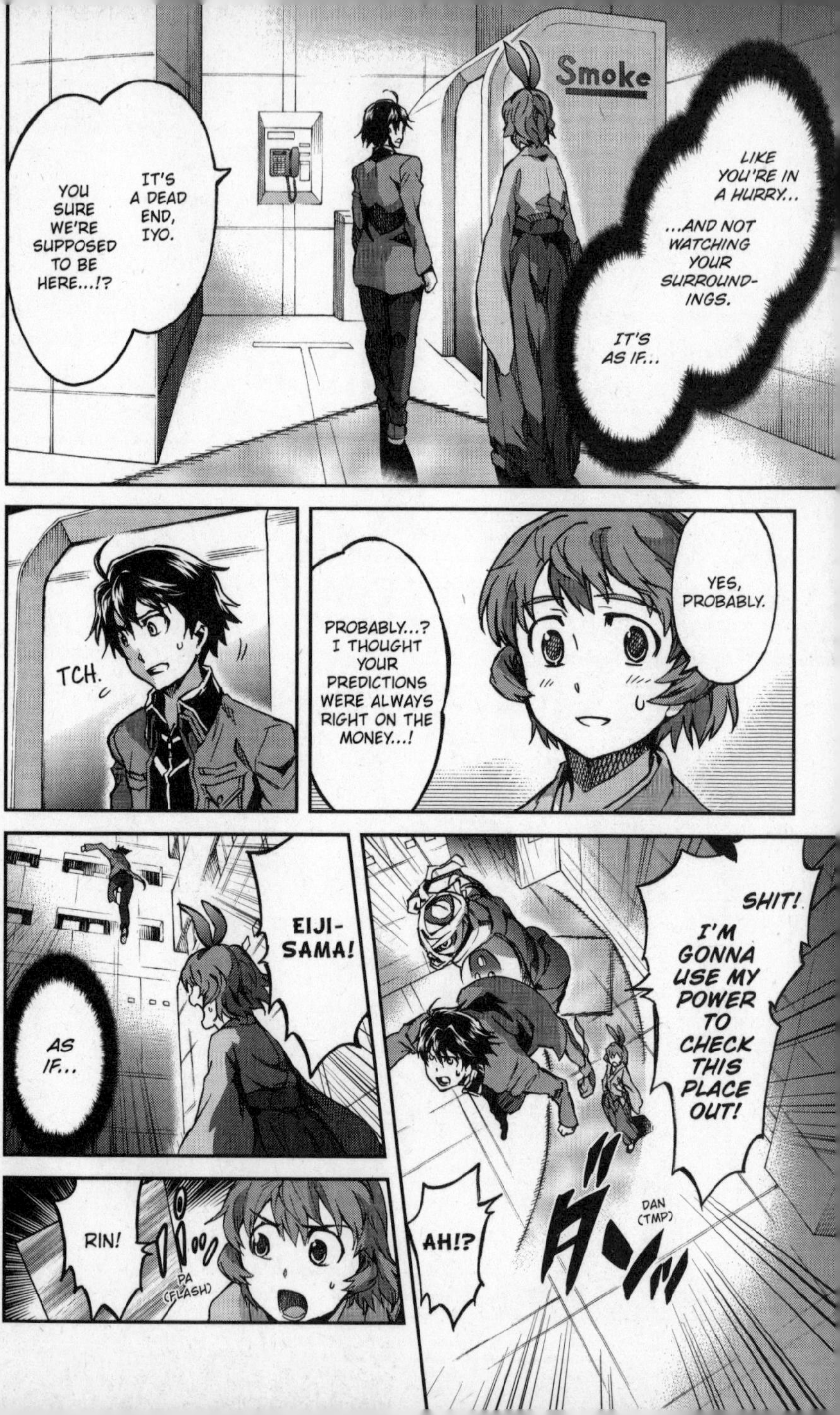

Smoke
LIKE YOU'RE IN A HURRY...
...AND NOT WATCHING YOUR SURROUNDINGS.
IT'S AS IF...
IT'S A DEAD END, IYO.
YOU SURE WE'RE SUPPOSED TO BE HERE...!?
YES, PROBABLY.
PROBABLY...? I THOUGHT YOUR PREDICTIONS WERE ALWAYS RIGHT ON THE MONEY...!
TCH.
SHIT!
I'M GONNA USE MY POWER TO CHECK THIS PLACE OUT!
DAN (TMP)
AH!?
EIJI-SAMA!
AS IF...
RIN!
PA (FLASH)

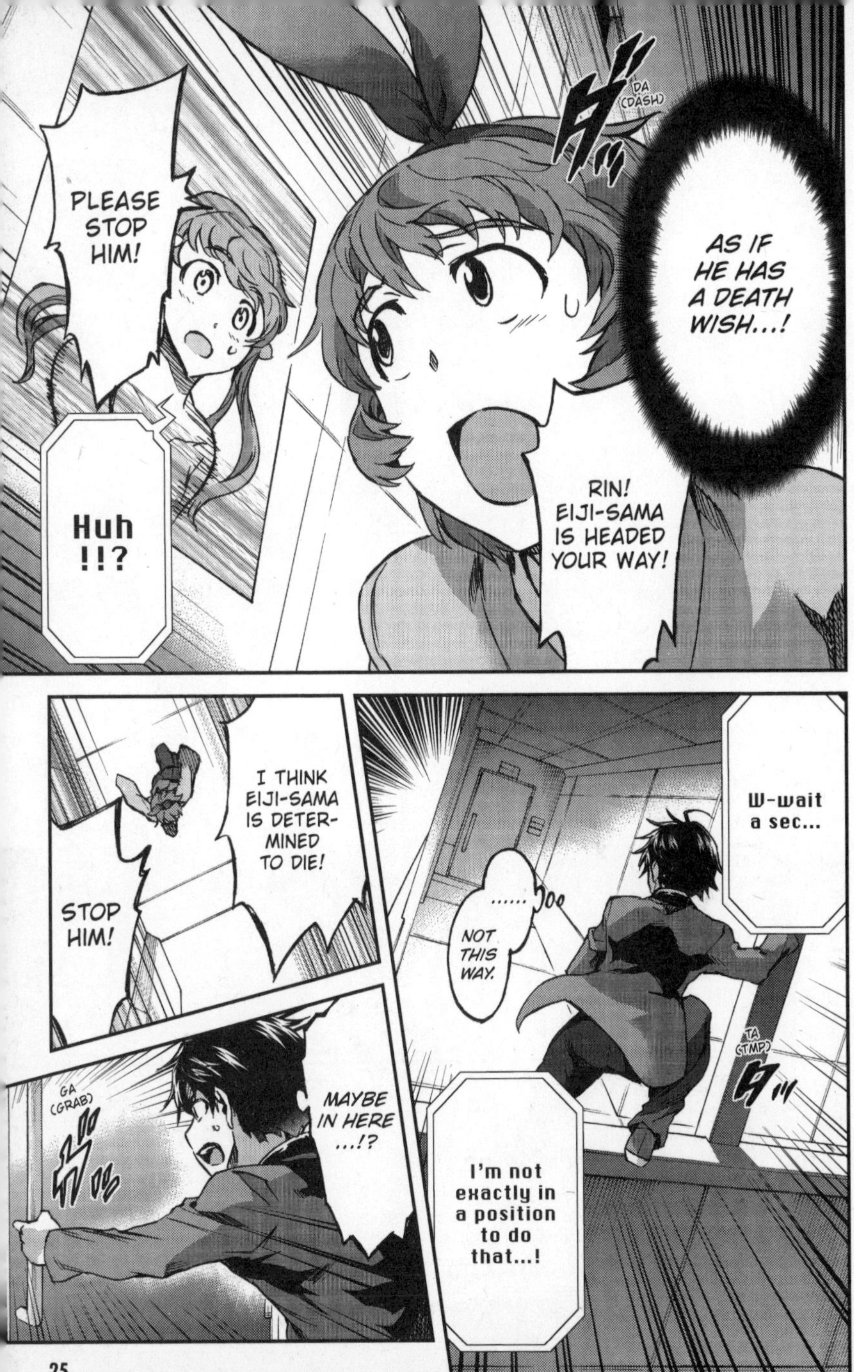
DA (DASH)
AS IF HE HAS A DEATH WISH...!
RIN! EIJI-SAMA IS HEADED YOUR WAY!
PLEASE STOP HIM!
Huh !!?
W-wait a sec...
......
NOT THIS WAY.
TA (STMP)
I'm not exactly in a position to do that...!
I THINK EIJI-SAMA IS DETERMINED TO DIE!
STOP HIM!
MAYBE IN HERE ...!?
GA (GRAB)

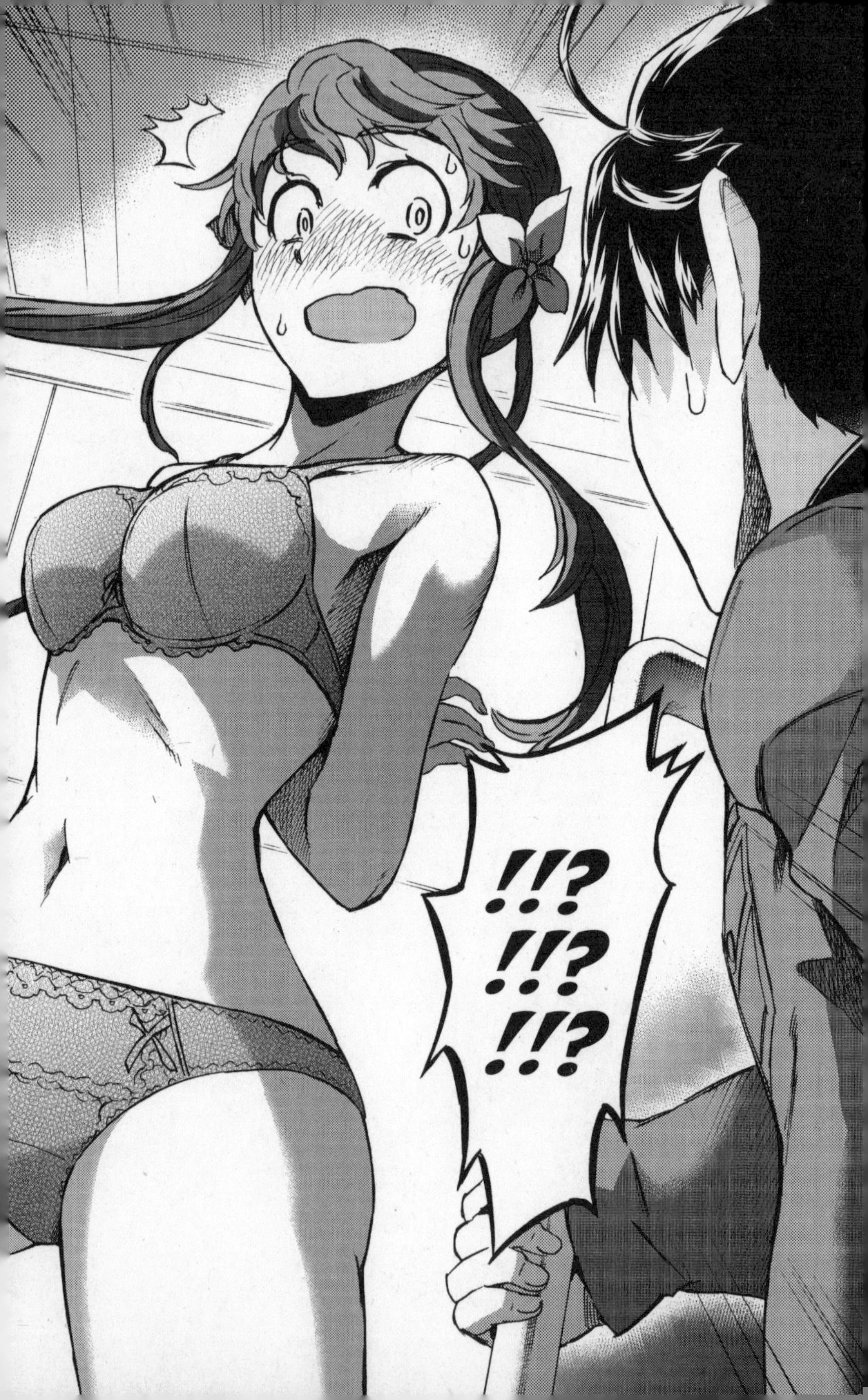
!!?
!!?
!!?

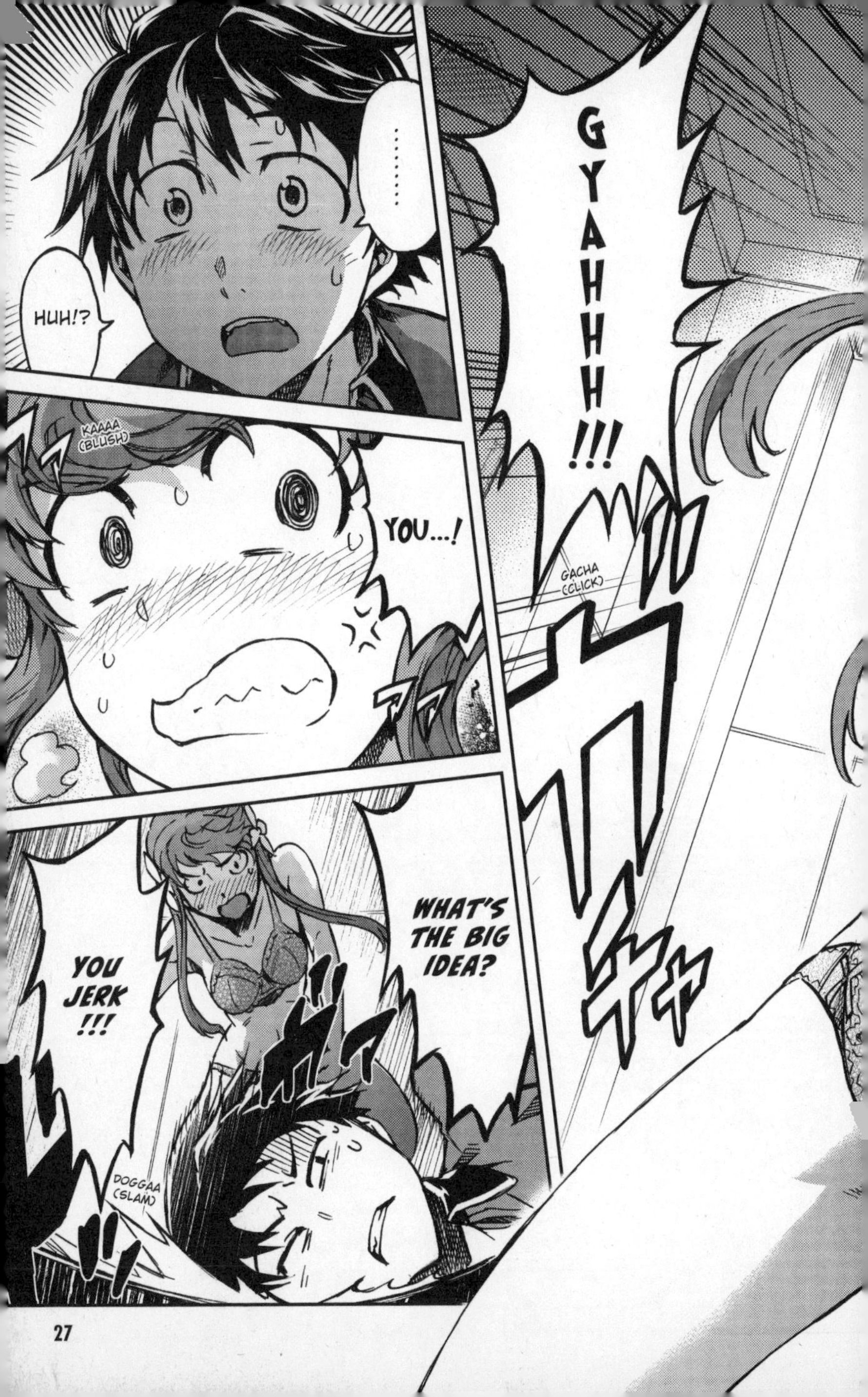

GYAHHH!!!
GACHA (CLICK)
......
HUH!?
KAAAA (BLUSH)
YOU...!
WHAT'S THE BIG IDEA?
YOU JERK!!!
DOGGAA (SLAM)

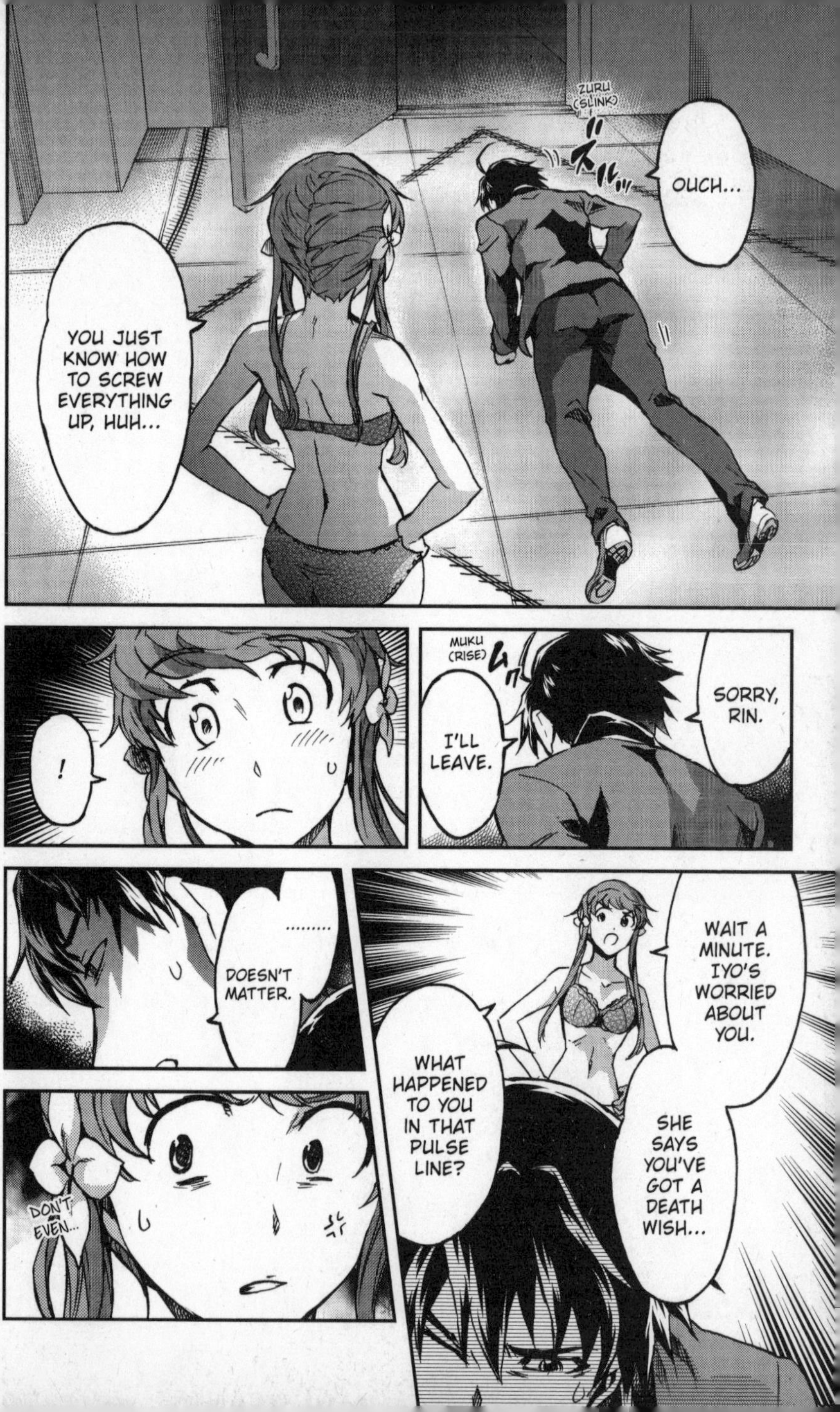
ZURU (SLINK)
OUCH...
YOU JUST KNOW HOW TO SCREW EVERYTHING UP, HUH...
MUKU (RISE)
SORRY, RIN.
I'LL LEAVE.
!
WAIT A MINUTE. IYO'S WORRIED ABOUT YOU.
SHE SAYS YOU'VE GOT A DEATH WISH...
WHAT HAPPENED TO YOU IN THAT PULSE LINE?
....
DOESN'T MATTER.
DON'T EVEN...

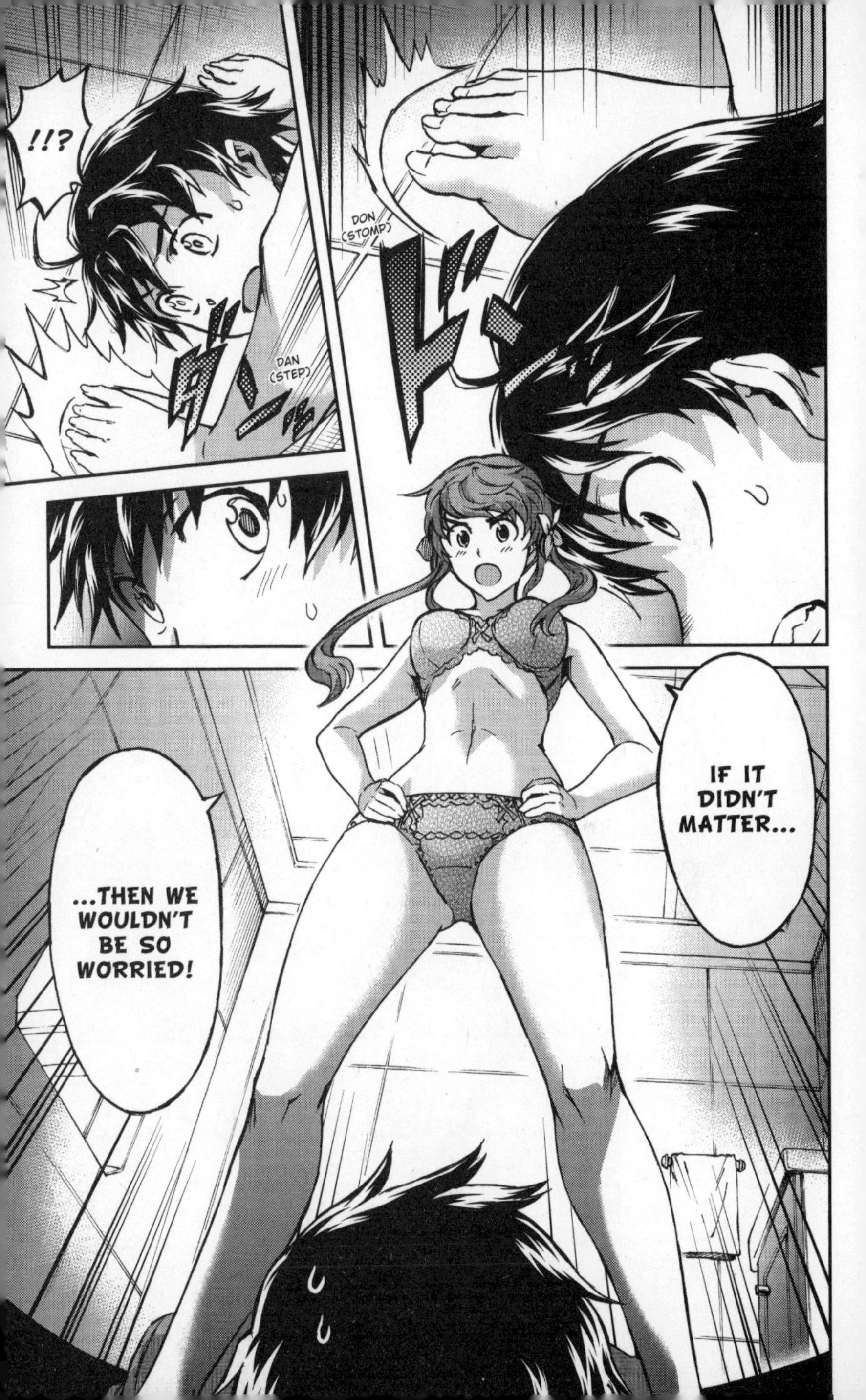
DON (STOMP)
!!?
DAN (STEP)
IF IT DIDN'T MATTER...
...THEN WE WOULDN'T BE SO WORRIED!

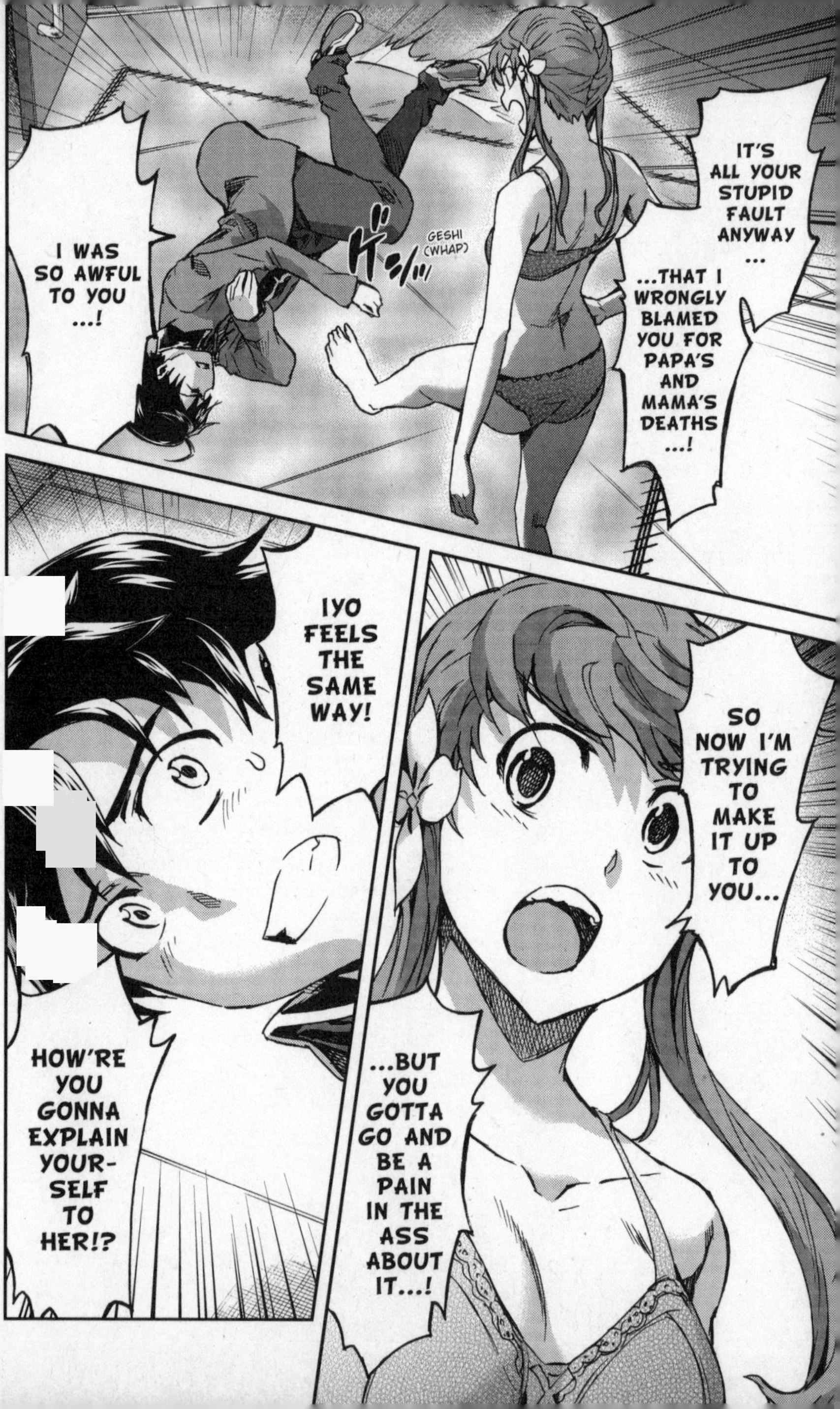
IT'S ALL YOUR STUPID FAULT ANYWAY...
...THAT I WRONGLY BLAMED YOU FOR PAPA'S AND MAMA'S DEATHS...!
GESHI (WHAP)
I WAS SO AWFUL TO YOU...!
SO NOW I'M TRYING TO MAKE IT UP TO YOU...
...BUT YOU GOTTA GO AND BE A PAIN IN THE ASS ABOUT IT...!
IYO FEELS THE SAME WAY!
HOW'RE YOU GONNA EXPLAIN YOUR-SELF TO HER!?

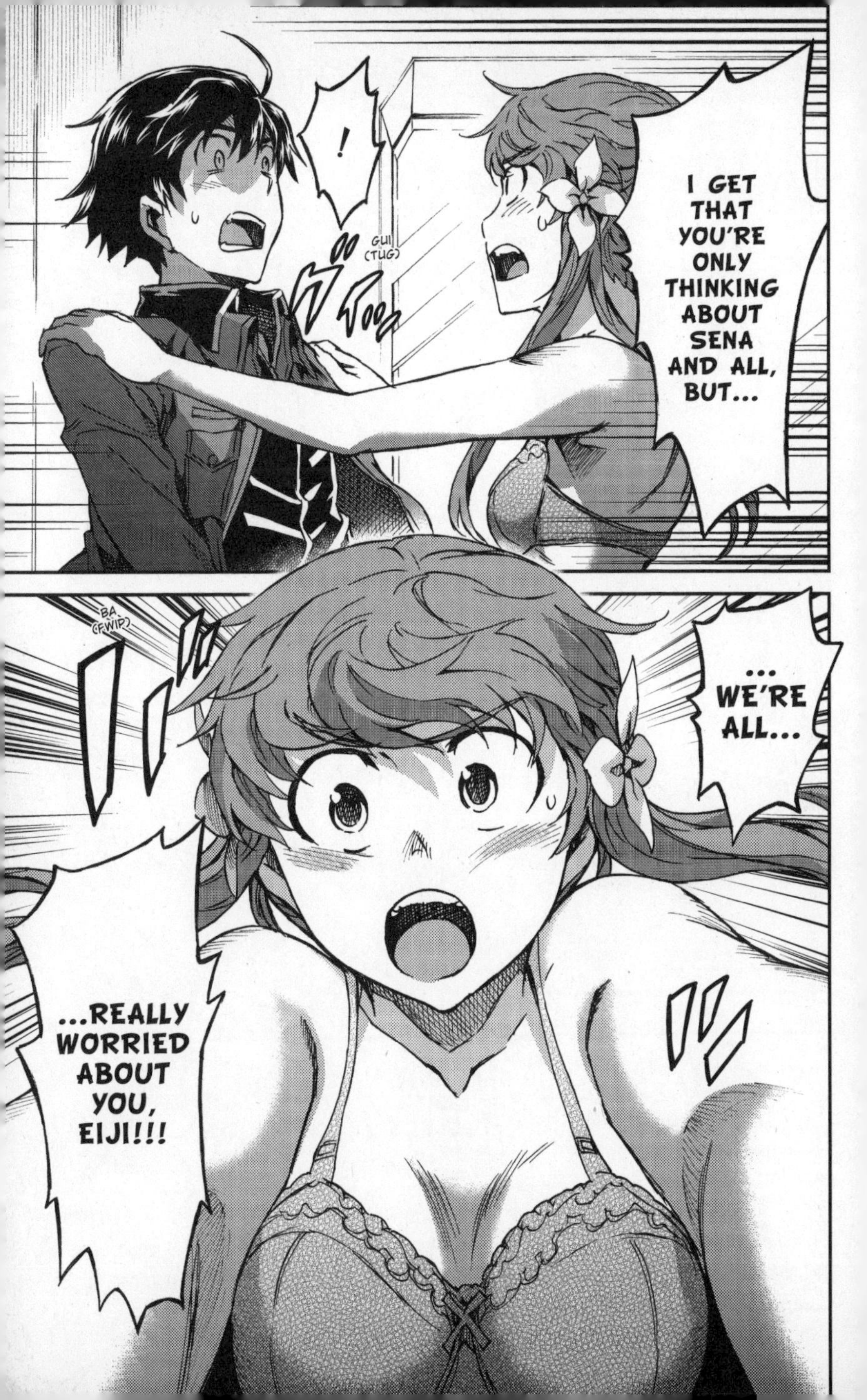
I GET THAT YOU'RE ONLY THINKING ABOUT SENA AND ALL, BUT...
!
GUI (TUG)
... WE'RE ALL...
BA (FWIP)
...REALLY WORRIED ABOUT YOU, EIJI!!!

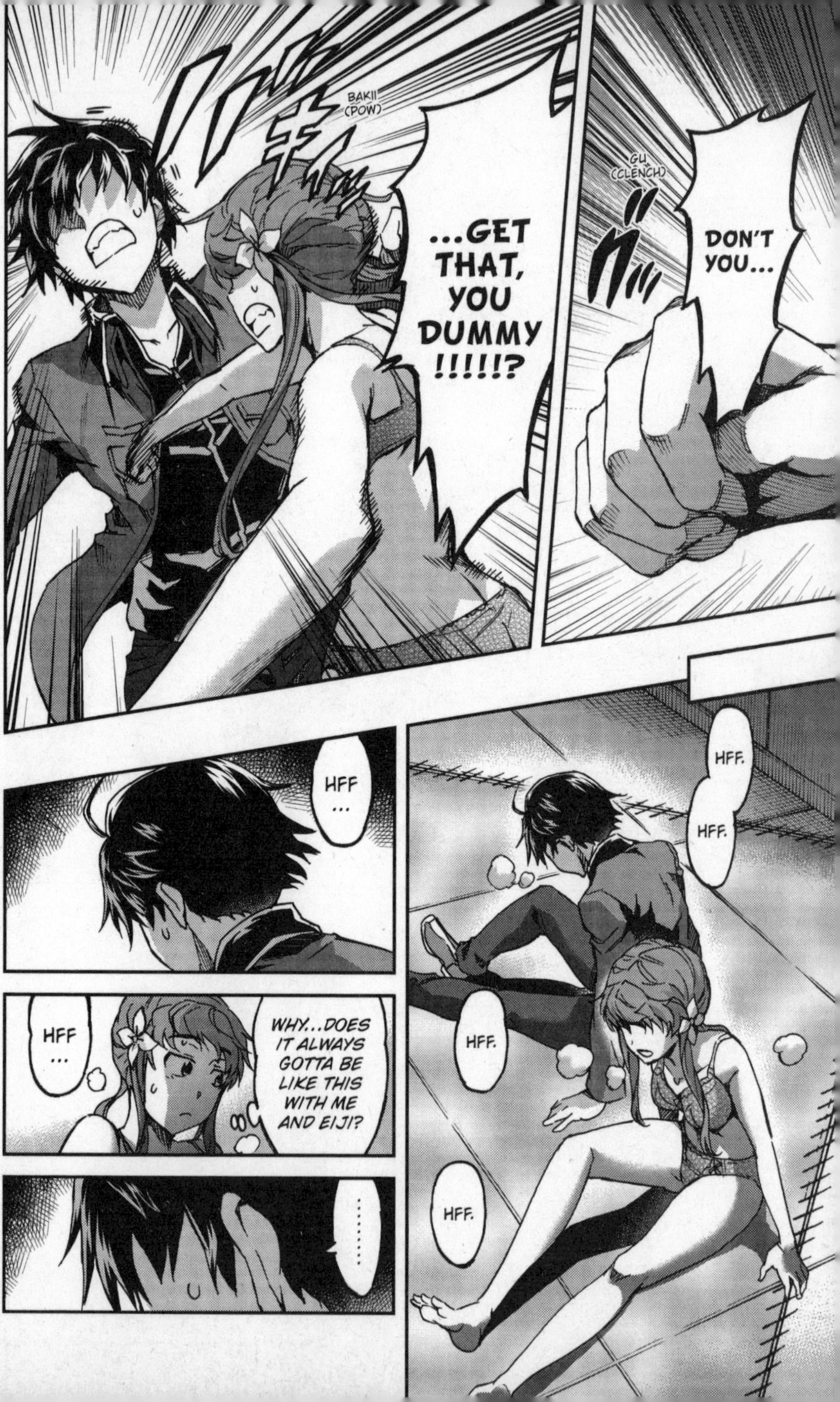

GU (CLENCH)
DON'T YOU...
BAKII (POW)
...GET THAT, YOU DUMMY !!!!!?
HFF.
HFF.
HFF.
HFF.
HFF ...
WHY...DOES IT ALWAYS GOTTA BE LIKE THIS WITH ME AND EIJI?
HFF ...
....

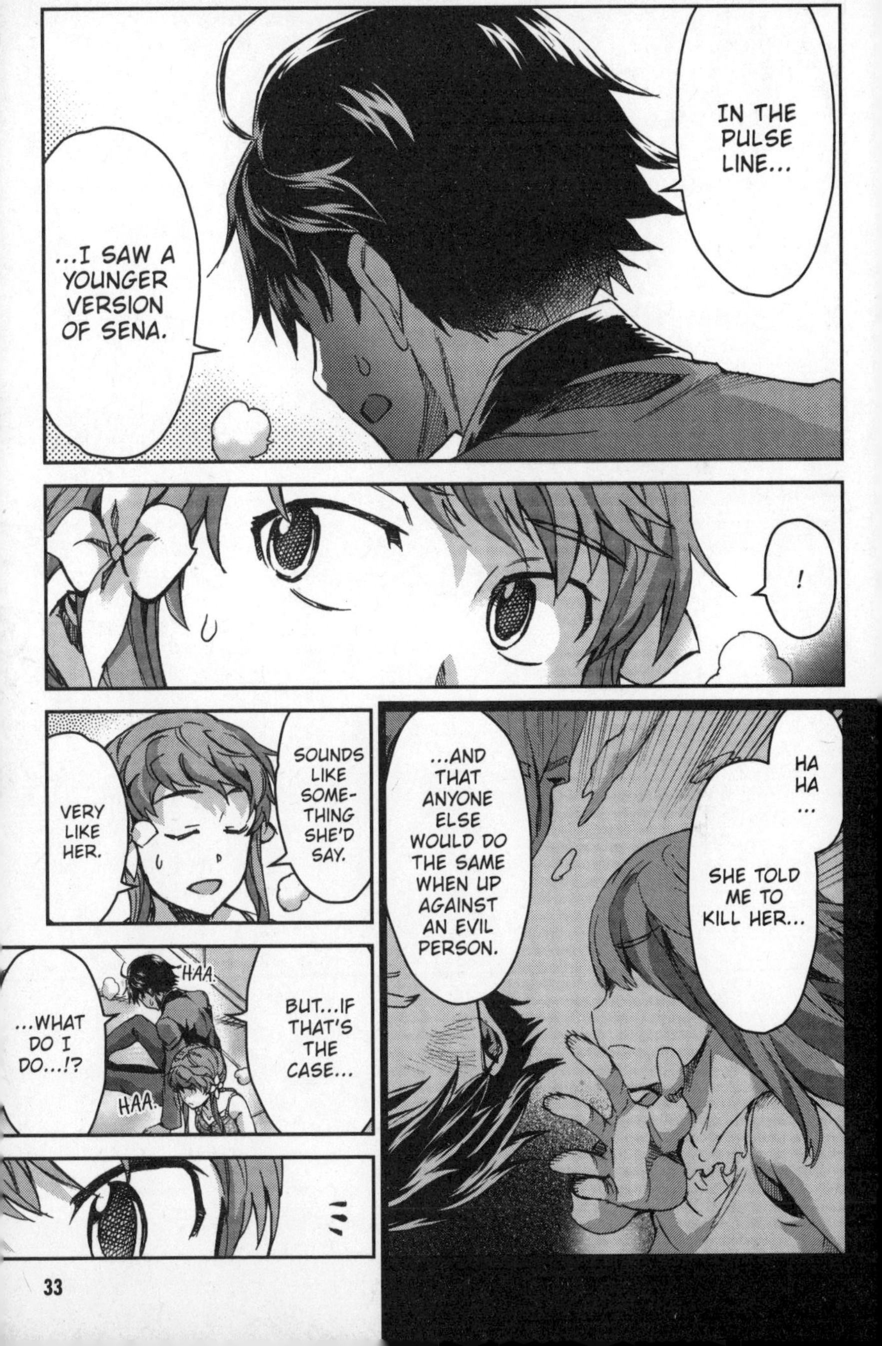
IN THE PULSE LINE...
...I SAW A YOUNGER VERSION OF SENA.
!
HA HA...
SHE TOLD ME TO KILL HER...
...AND THAT ANYONE ELSE WOULD DO THE SAME WHEN UP AGAINST AN EVIL PERSON.
SOUNDS LIKE SOME-THING SHE'D SAY.
VERY LIKE HER.
HAA.
BUT...IF THAT'S THE CASE...
...WHAT DO I DO...!?
HAA.

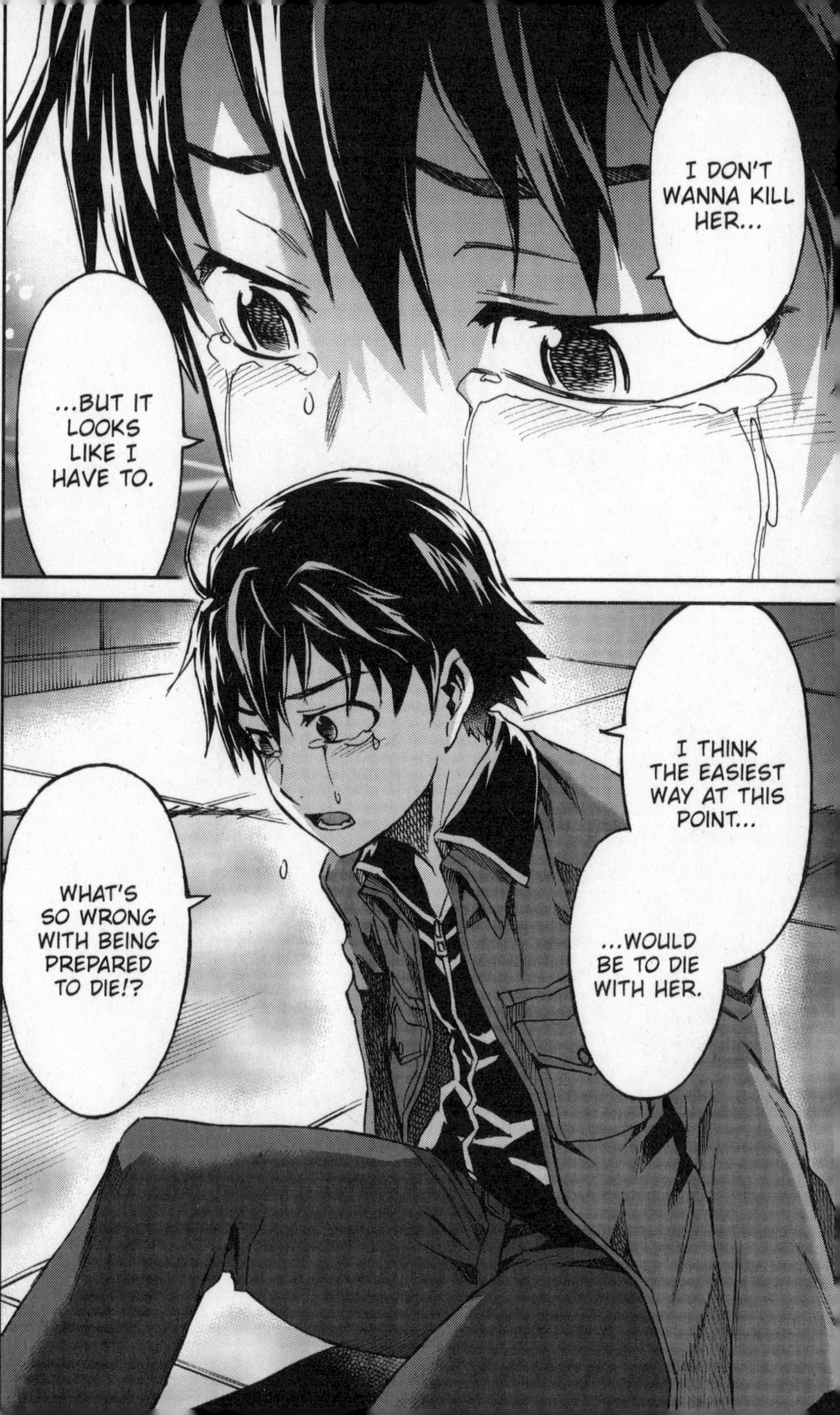
I DON'T WANNA KILL HER...
...BUT IT LOOKS LIKE I HAVE TO.
I THINK THE EASIEST WAY AT THIS POINT...
...WOULD BE TO DIE WITH HER.
WHAT'S SO WRONG WITH BEING PREPARED TO DIE!?

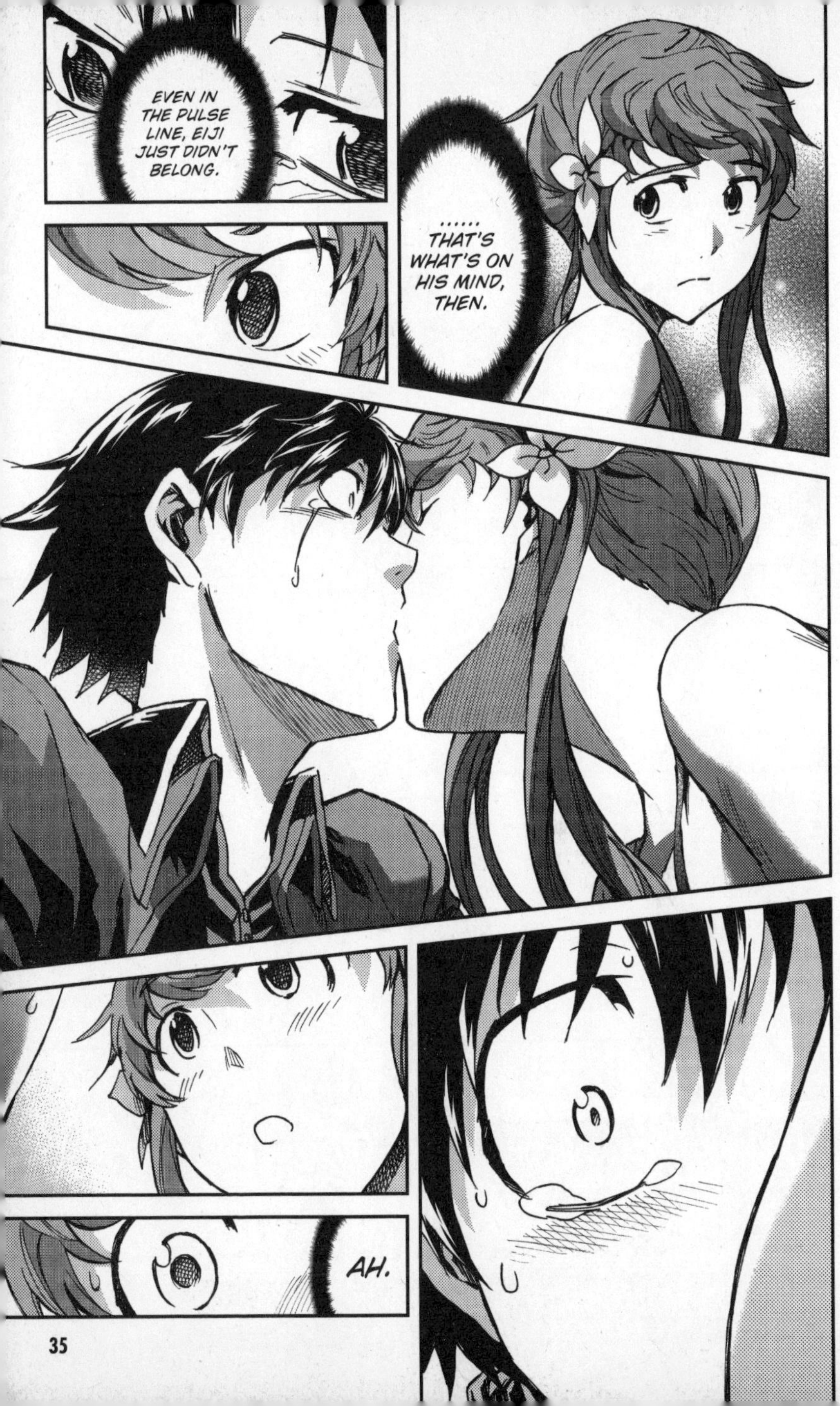

...... THAT'S WHAT'S ON HIS MIND, THEN.
EVEN IN THE PULSE LINE, EIJI JUST DIDN'T BELONG.
AH.

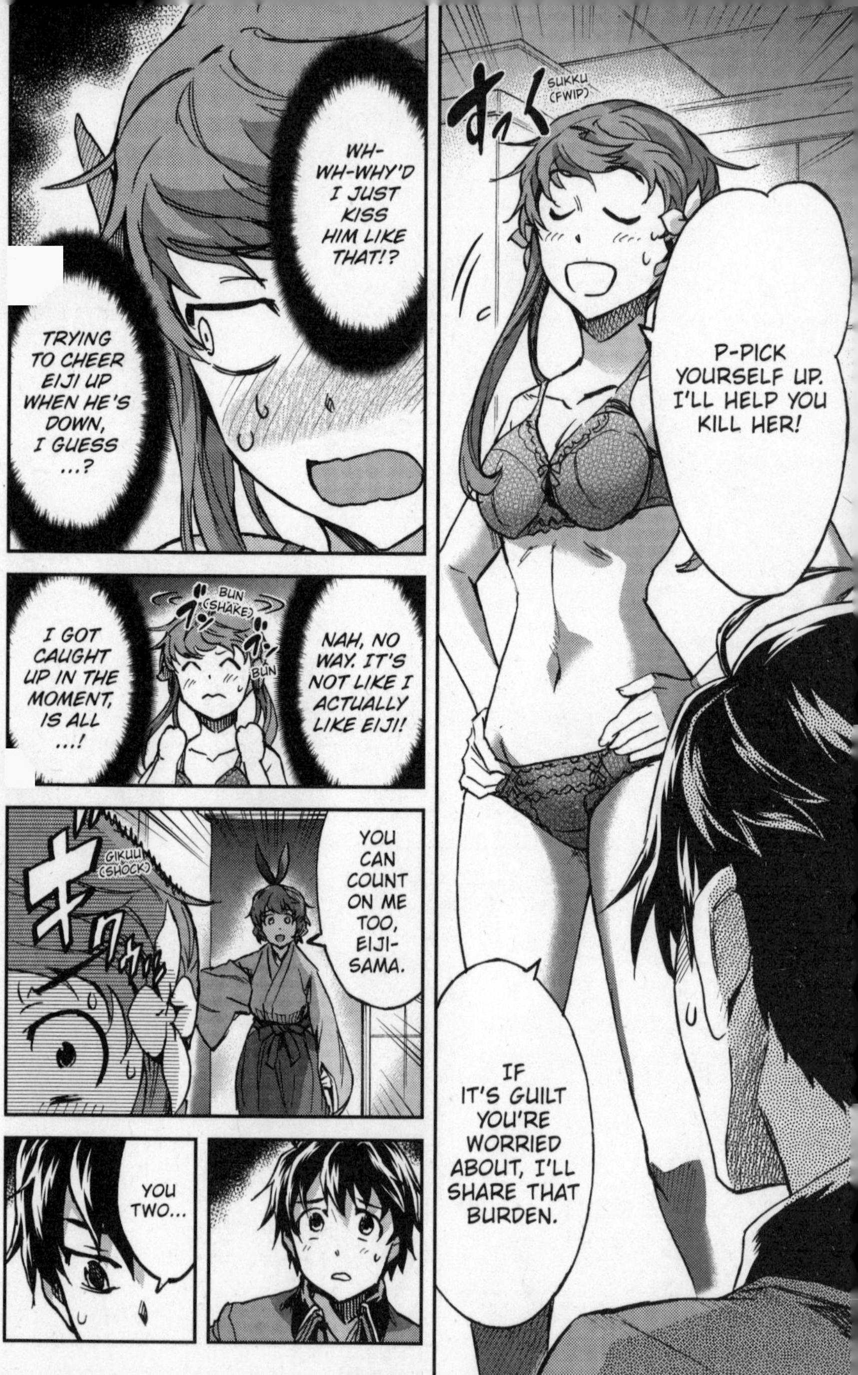
SUKKU (FWIP)
P-PICK YOURSELF UP. I'LL HELP YOU KILL HER!
IF IT'S GUILT YOU'RE WORRIED ABOUT, I'LL SHARE THAT BURDEN.
WH-WH-WHY'D I JUST KISS HIM LIKE THAT!?
TRYING TO CHEER EIJI UP WHEN HE'S DOWN, I GUESS ...?
BUN (SHAKE)
BUN
NAH, NO WAY. IT'S NOT LIKE I ACTUALLY LIKE EIJI!
I GOT CAUGHT UP IN THE MOMENT, IS ALL ...!
YOU CAN COUNT ON ME TOO, EIJI-SAMA.
GIKUU (SHOCK)
YOU TWO...

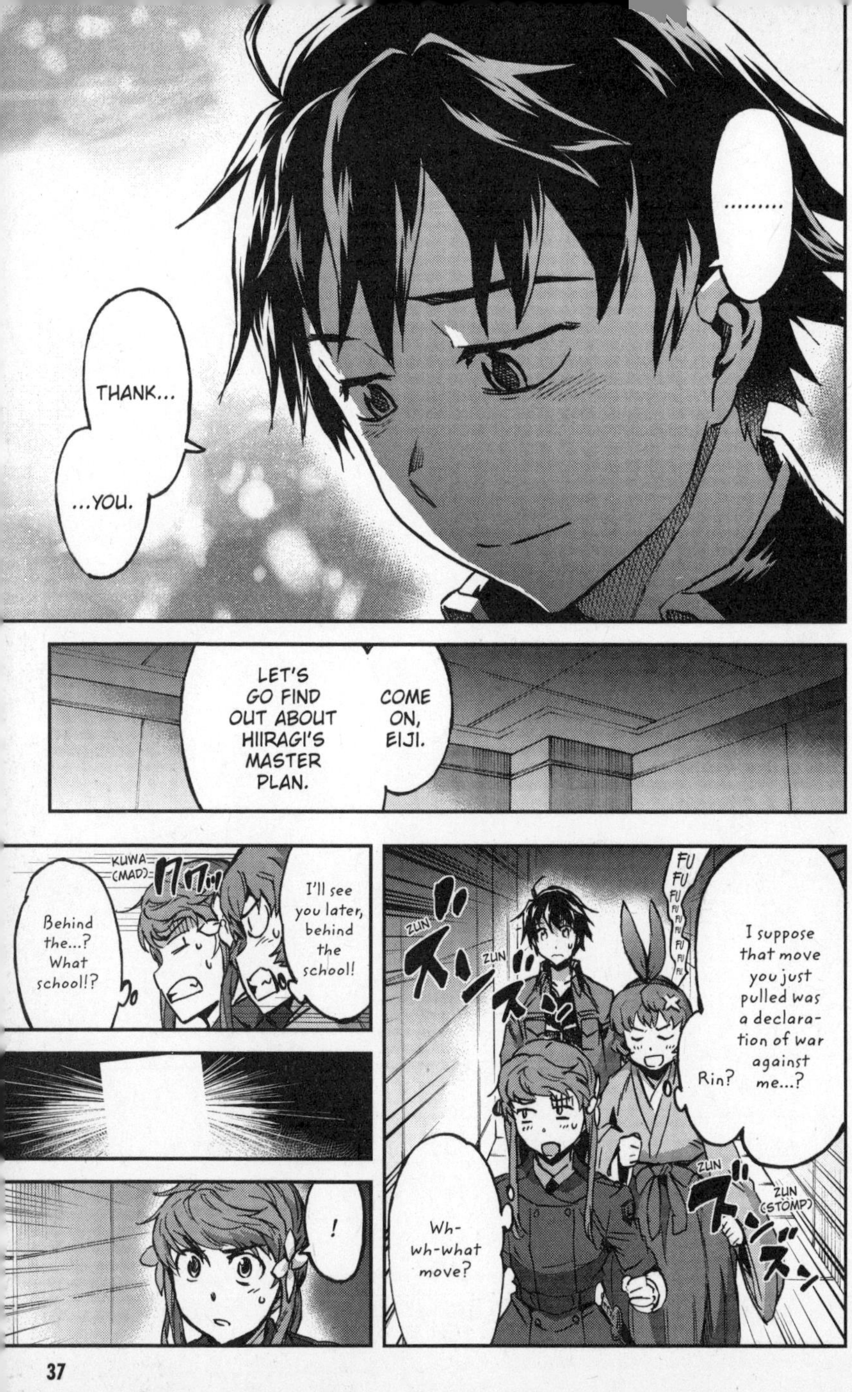
....
THANK...
...YOU.
COME ON, EIJI.
LET'S GO FIND OUT ABOUT HIIRAGI'S MASTER PLAN.
FU FU FU FU FU FU FU FU
I suppose that move you just pulled was a declaration of war against me...?
Rin?
ZUN
ZUN
Wh-wh-what move?
ZUN
ZUN (STOMP)
I'll see you later, behind the school!
KUWA (MAD)
Behind the...? What school!?
!

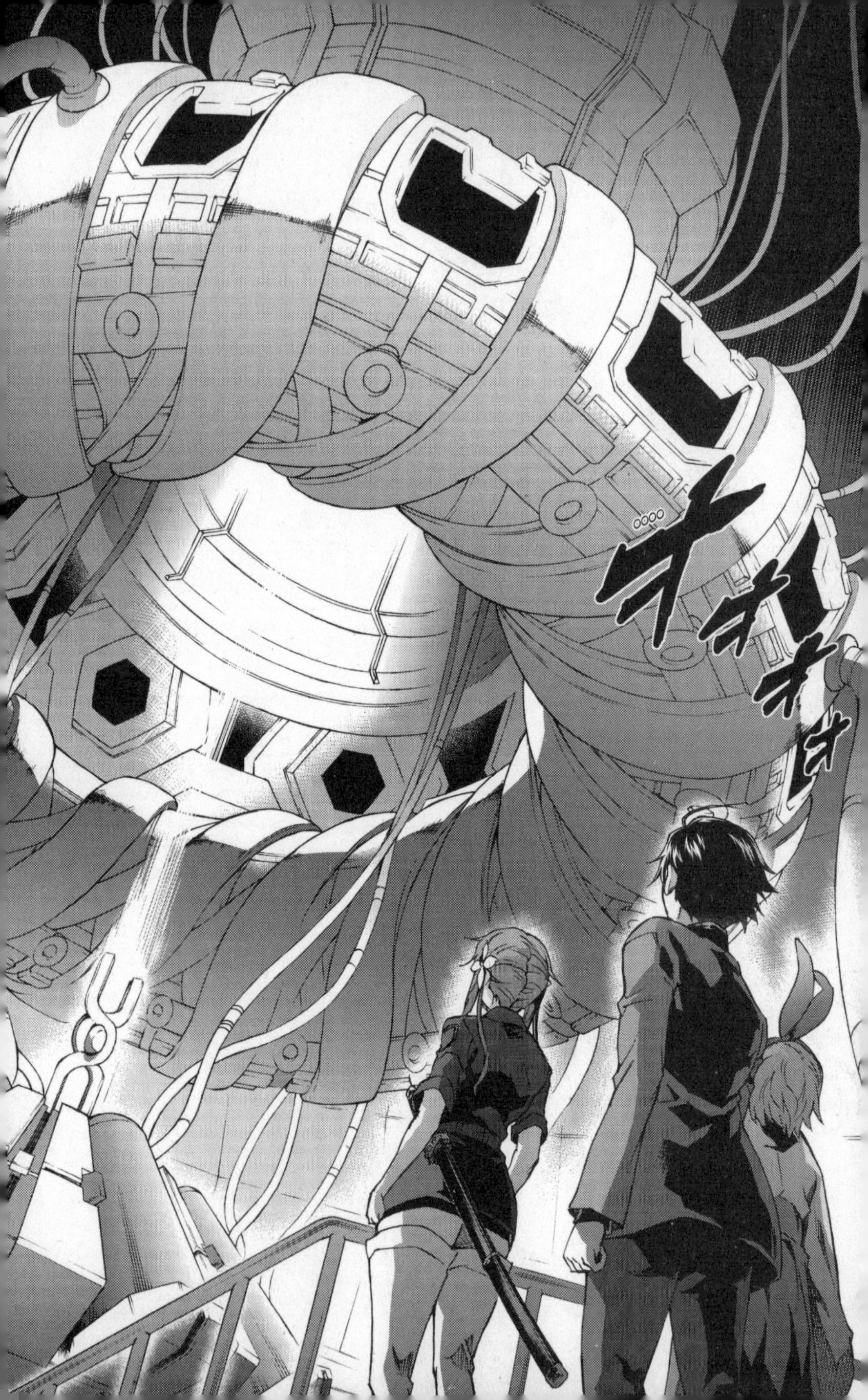
オォォォ

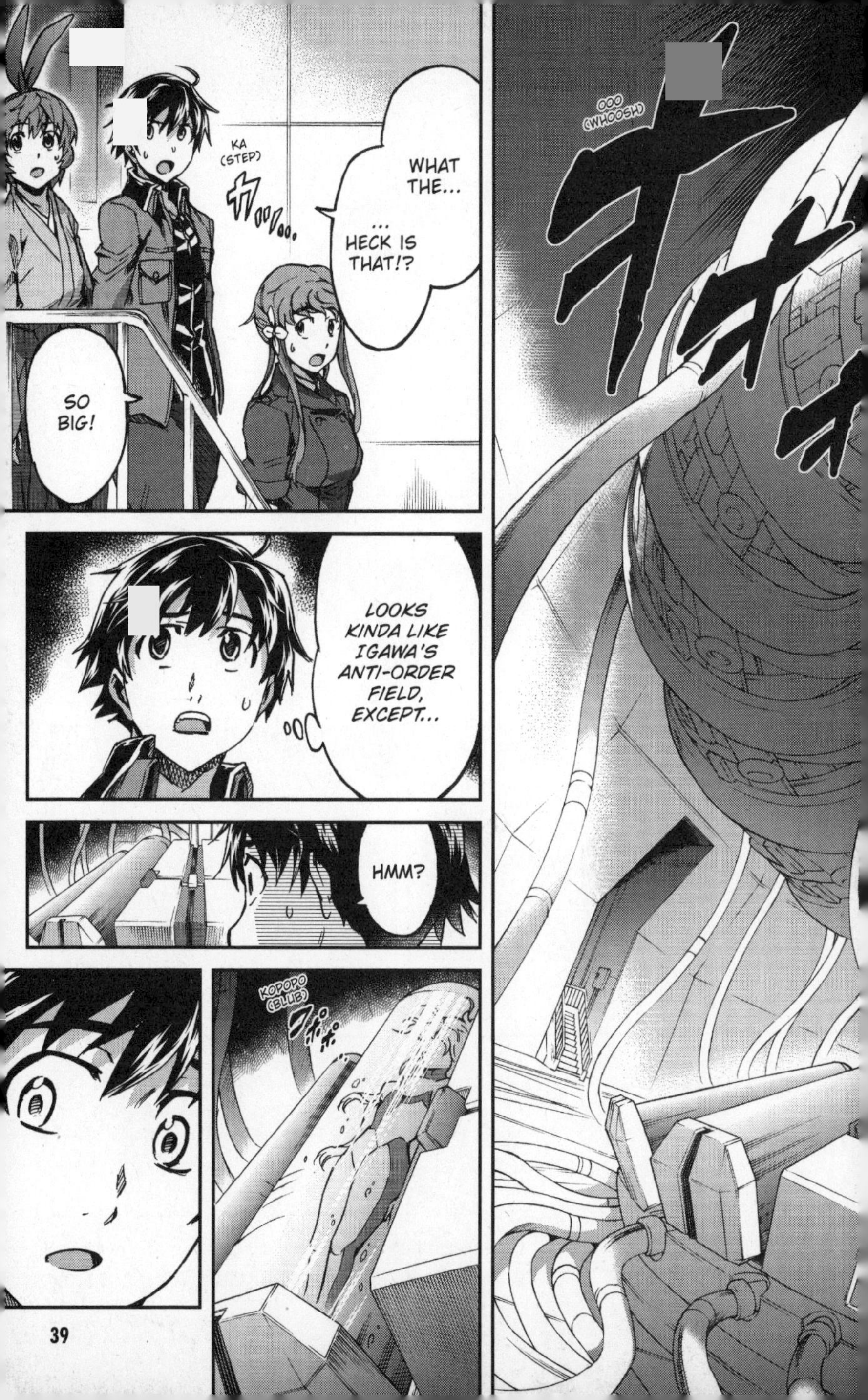
OOO (WHOOSH)
WHAT THE...
... HECK IS THAT!?
KA (STEP)
SO BIG!
LOOKS KINDA LIKE IGAWA'S ANTI-ORDER FIELD, EXCEPT...
HMM?
KOPOPO (BLUB)

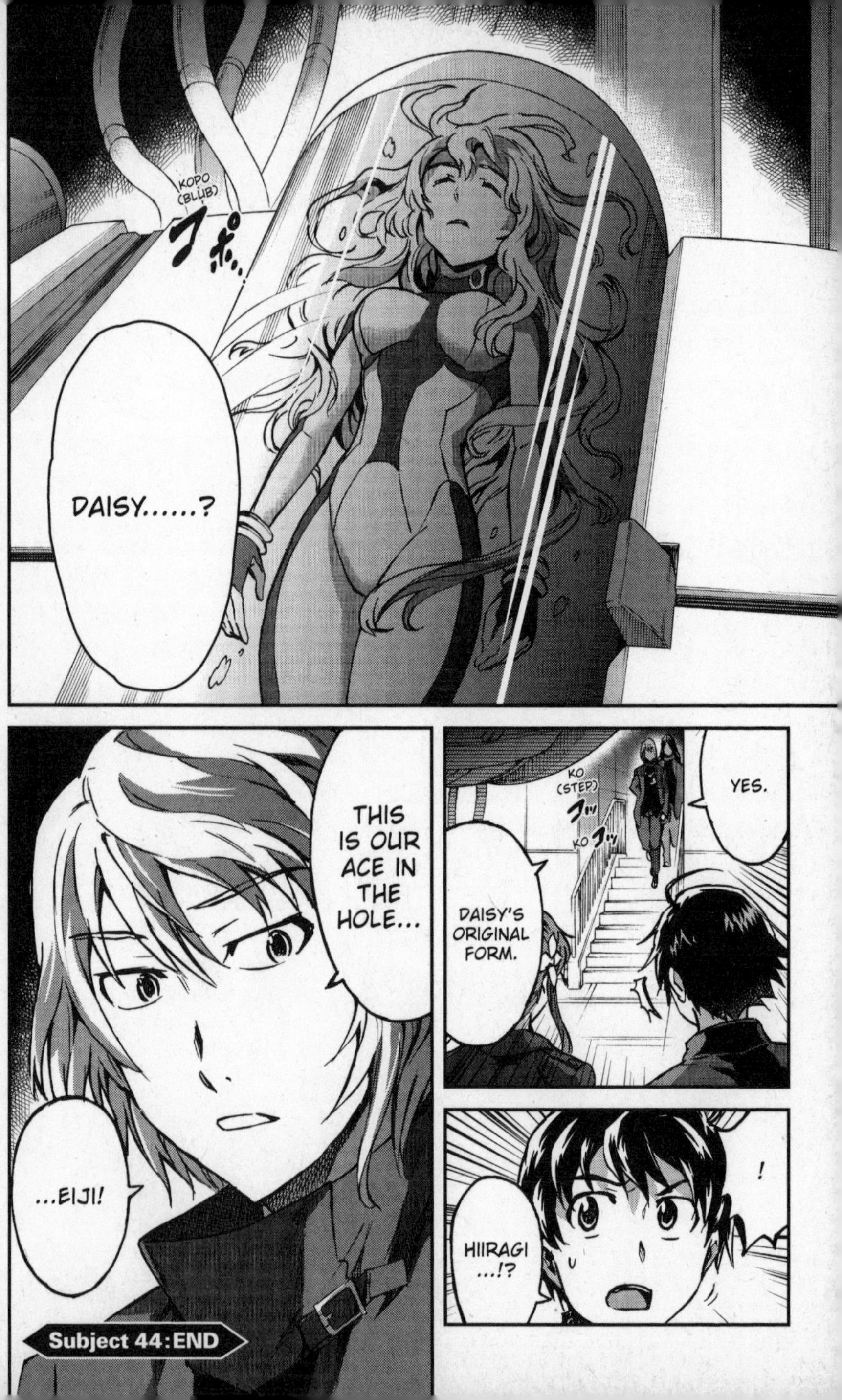
KOPO (BLUB)
DAISY......?
YES.
KO (STEP)
KO
DAISY'S ORIGINAL FORM.
!
HIIRAGI ...!?
THIS IS OUR ACE IN THE HOLE...
...EIJI!
Subject 44: END

⋙ Big Order World

A world where those who've had their "wishes" transformed into "abilities" call the shots.
The average citizen knows nothing of Gennai's plans or the Orders he created.

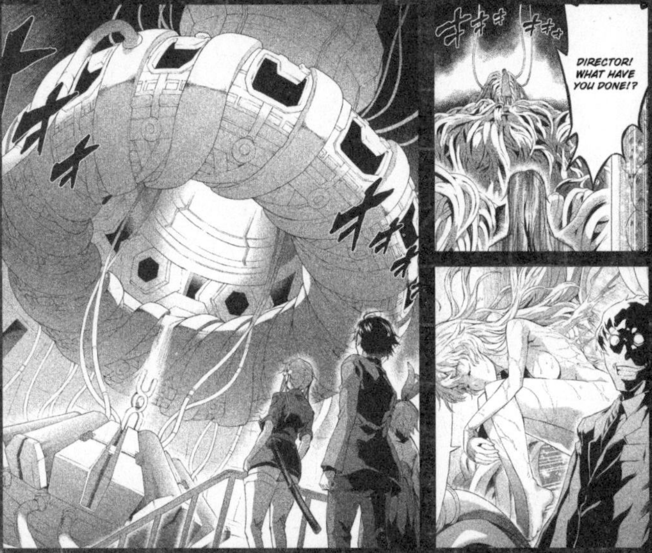
DIRECTOR! WHAT HAVE YOU DONE!?

Daisy (Desire Accessible Information System) + Supermassive Coil

Daisy was created by Eiji's father, Gennai, to serve as the human interface for accessing the spirit world. Her original body was hidden away deep underground in Hoshimiya Institute Laboratory #1. The Daisy that Eiji and the others have interacted with up until this point is a mere projection—a literal UI for inputting people's wishes. Daisy receives wishes and sends them directly to the coil while also opening a small gate connected to it. As Daisy inputs wishes and the coils transforms them into abilities, they serve as two halves of the whole. Sena and "God" currently share a similar relationship, although "God"'s transformative power is superior by far.

BIG
ORDER

Subject 45

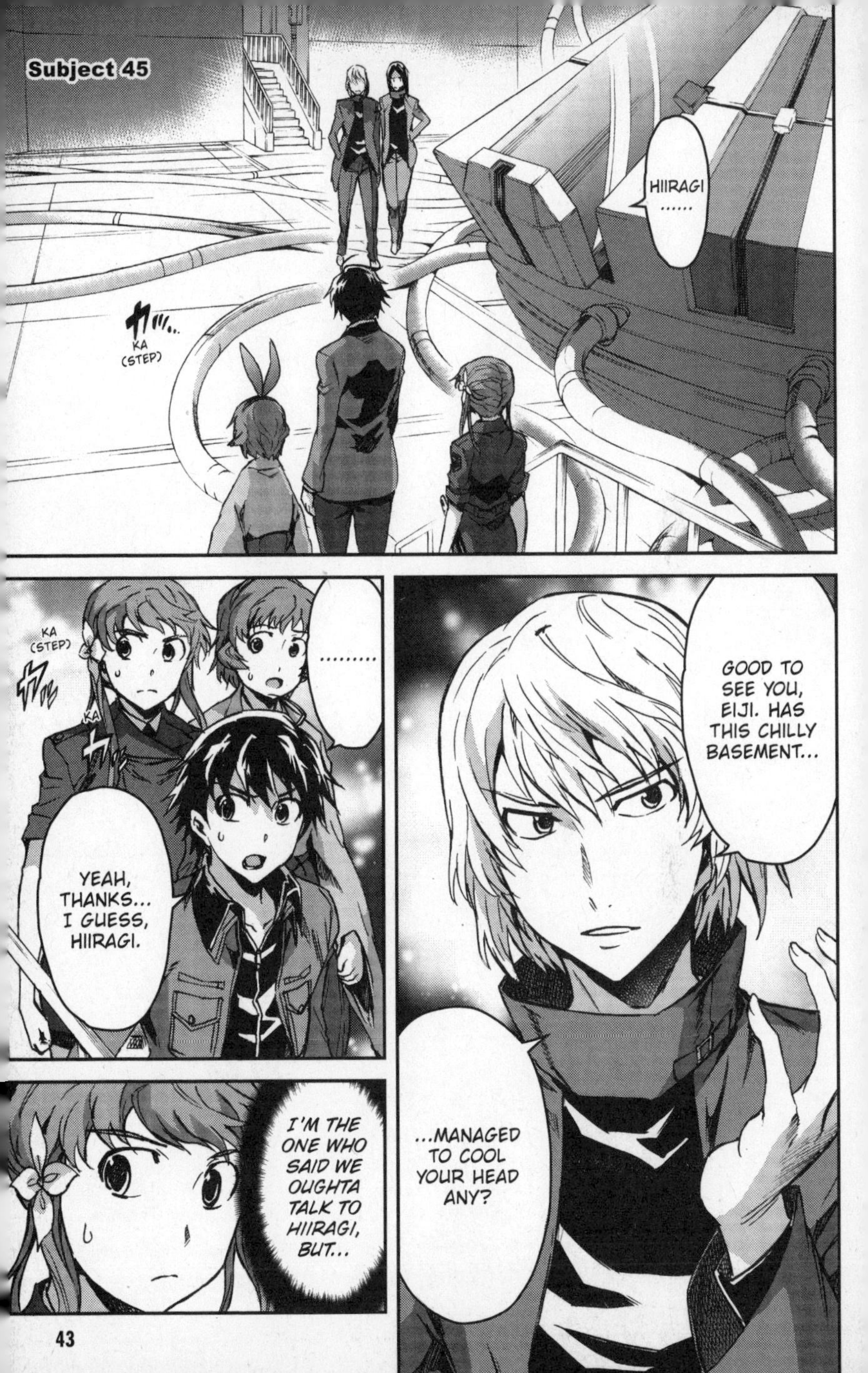
HIIRAGI ......
KA (STEP)
GOOD TO SEE YOU, EIJI. HAS THIS CHILLY BASEMENT...
...MANAGED TO COOL YOUR HEAD ANY?
....
KA (STEP)
YEAH, THANKS... I GUESS, HIIRAGI.
I'M THE ONE WHO SAID WE OUGHTA TALK TO HIIRAGI, BUT...

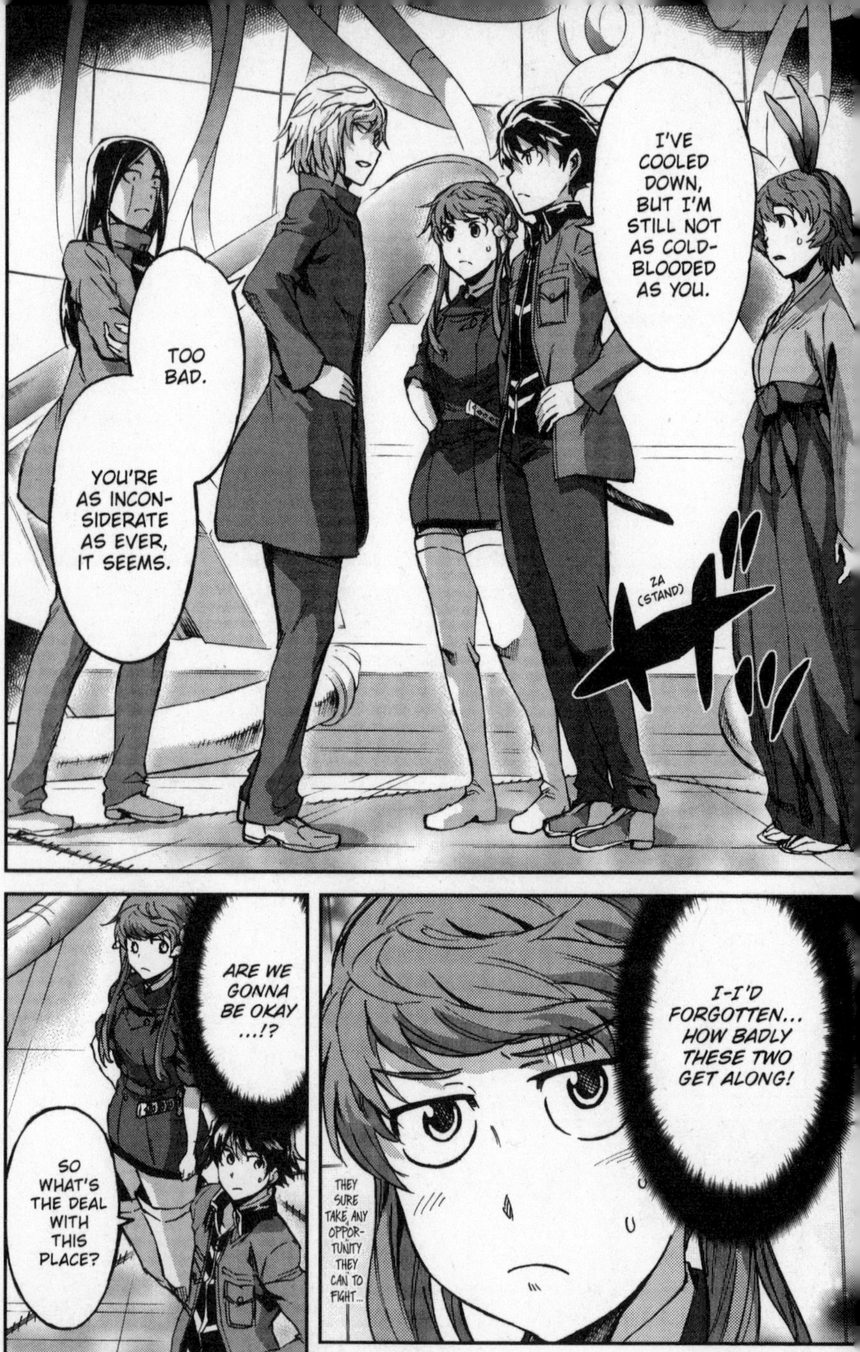
I'VE COOLED DOWN, BUT I'M STILL NOT AS COLD-BLOODED AS YOU.
ZA (STAND)
TOO BAD.
YOU'RE AS INCONSIDERATE AS EVER, IT SEEMS.
I-I'D FORGOTTEN... HOW BADLY THESE TWO GET ALONG!
THEY SURE TAKE ANY OPPORTUNITY THEY CAN TO FIGHT...
ARE WE GONNA BE OKAY ...!?
SO WHAT'S THE DEAL WITH THIS PLACE?

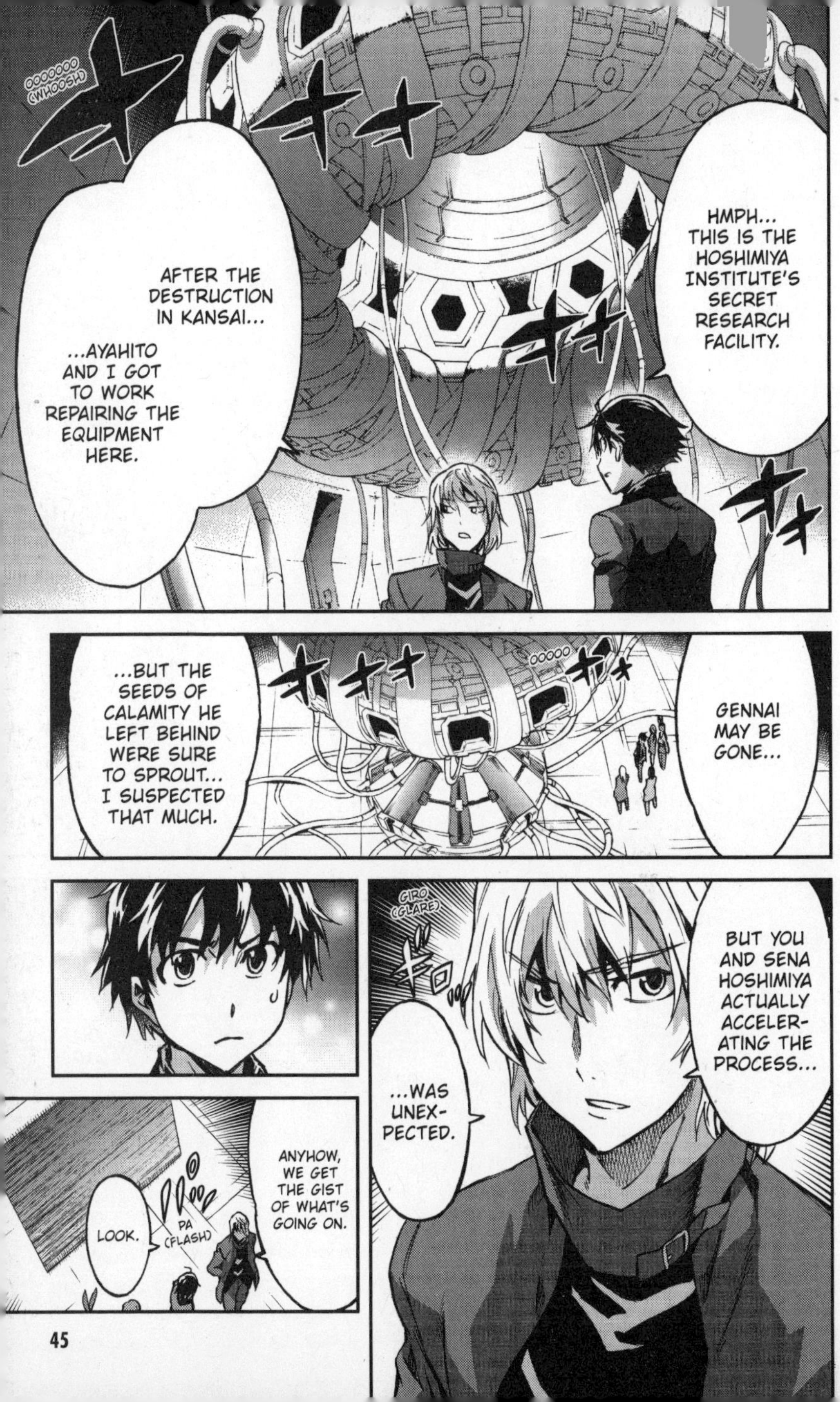
OOOOOOO (WHOOSH)
HMPH... THIS IS THE HOSHIMIYA INSTITUTE'S SECRET RESEARCH FACILITY.
AFTER THE DESTRUCTION IN KANSAI...
...AYAHITO AND I GOT TO WORK REPAIRING THE EQUIPMENT HERE.
OOOOO
GENNAI MAY BE GONE...
...BUT THE SEEDS OF CALAMITY HE LEFT BEHIND WERE SURE TO SPROUT... I SUSPECTED THAT MUCH.
GIRO (GLARE)
BUT YOU AND SENA HOSHIMIYA ACTUALLY ACCELER-ATING THE PROCESS...
...WAS UNEX-PECTED.
ANYHOW, WE GET THE GIST OF WHAT'S GOING ON.
PA (FLASH)
LOOK.

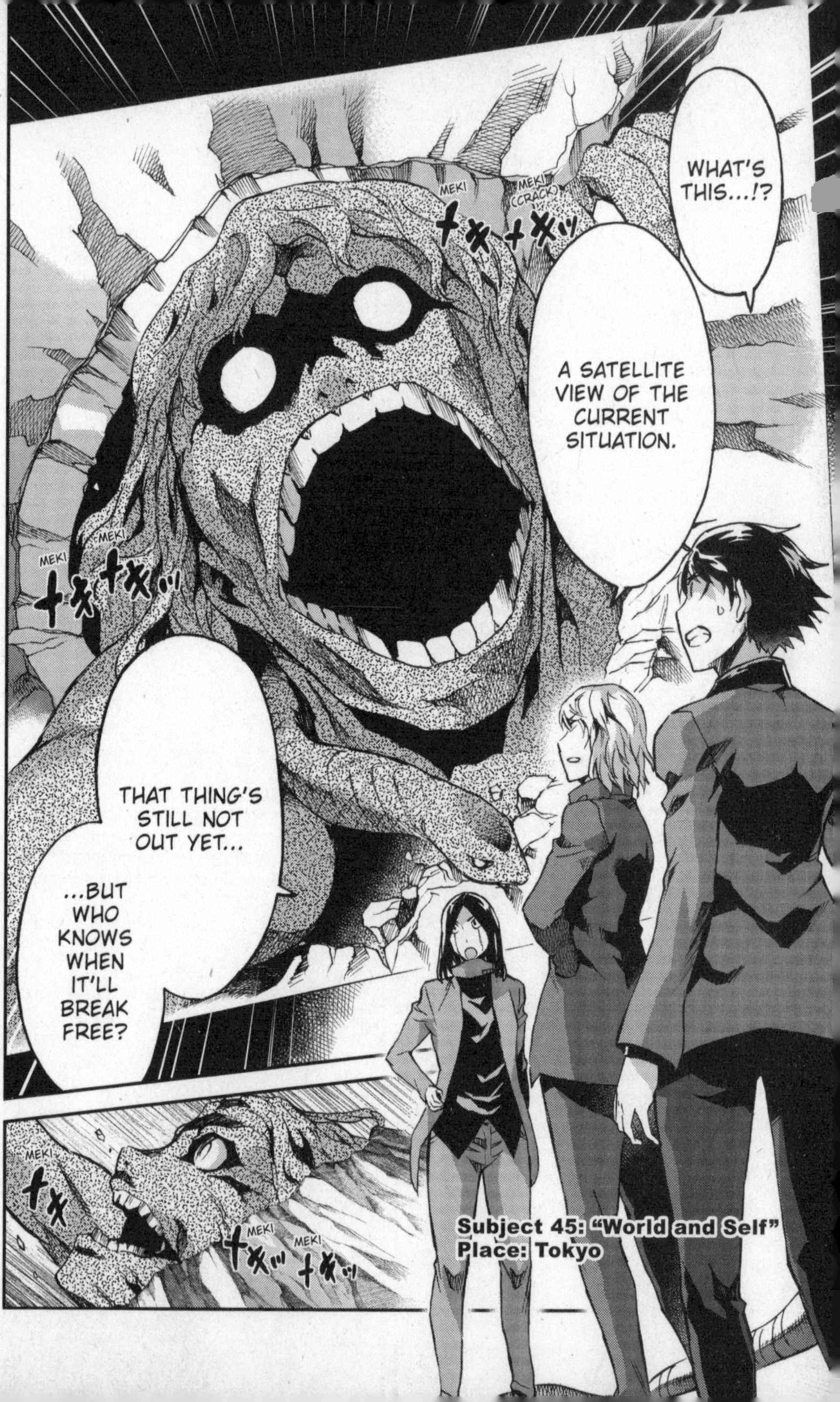
WHAT'S THIS...!?
MEKI MEKI (CRACK)
A SATELLITE VIEW OF THE CURRENT SITUATION.
MEKI MEKI
THAT THING'S STILL NOT OUT YET...
...BUT WHO KNOWS WHEN IT'LL BREAK FREE?
Subject 45: "World and Self"
Place: Tokyo
MEKI MEKI
MEKI

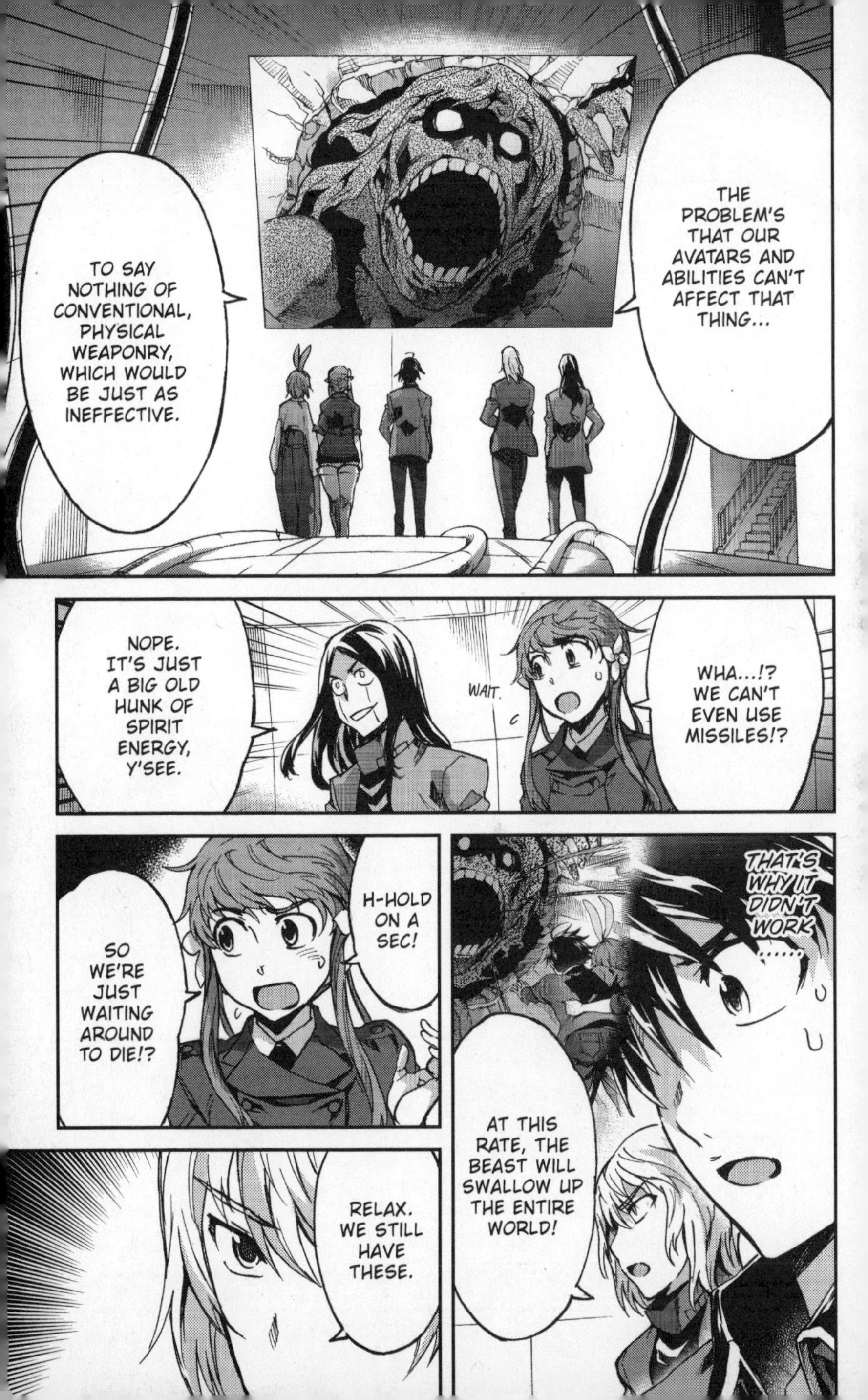
THE PROBLEM'S THAT OUR AVATARS AND ABILITIES CAN'T AFFECT THAT THING...
TO SAY NOTHING OF CONVENTIONAL, PHYSICAL WEAPONRY, WHICH WOULD BE JUST AS INEFFECTIVE.
WHA...!? WE CAN'T EVEN USE MISSILES!?
WAIT.
NOPE. IT'S JUST A BIG OLD HUNK OF SPIRIT ENERGY, Y'SEE.
THAT'S WHY IT DIDN'T WORK......
AT THIS RATE, THE BEAST WILL SWALLOW UP THE ENTIRE WORLD!
H-HOLD ON A SEC!
SO WE'RE JUST WAITING AROUND TO DIE!?
RELAX. WE STILL HAVE THESE.

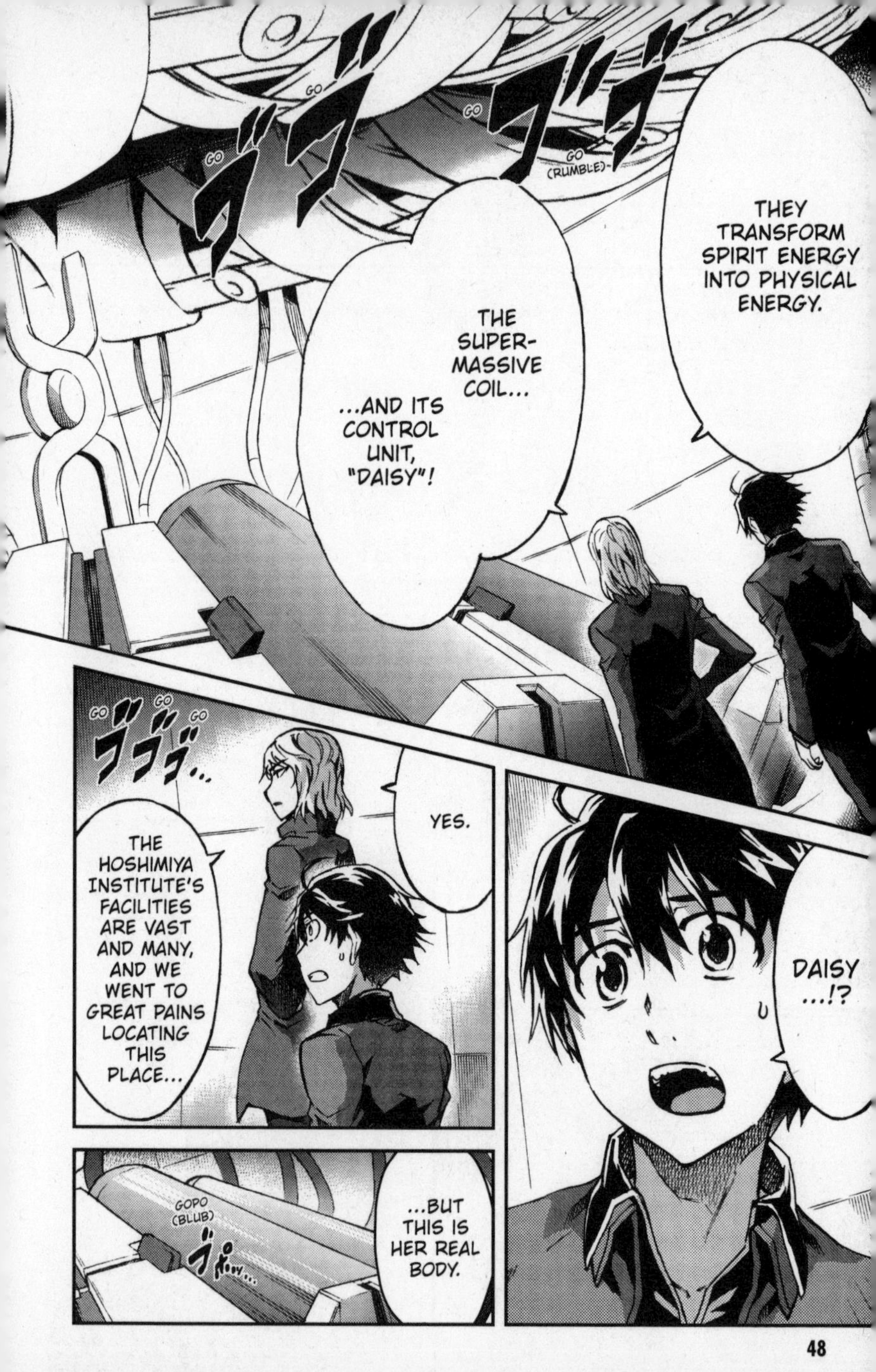
GO
GO
GO
GO
(RUMBLE)
THEY TRANSFORM SPIRIT ENERGY INTO PHYSICAL ENERGY.
THE SUPER-MASSIVE COIL...
...AND ITS CONTROL UNIT, "DAISY"!
DAISY ...!?
GO GO GO
YES.
THE HOSHIMIYA INSTITUTE'S FACILITIES ARE VAST AND MANY, AND WE WENT TO GREAT PAINS LOCATING THIS PLACE...
...BUT THIS IS HER REAL BODY.
GOPO (BLUB)

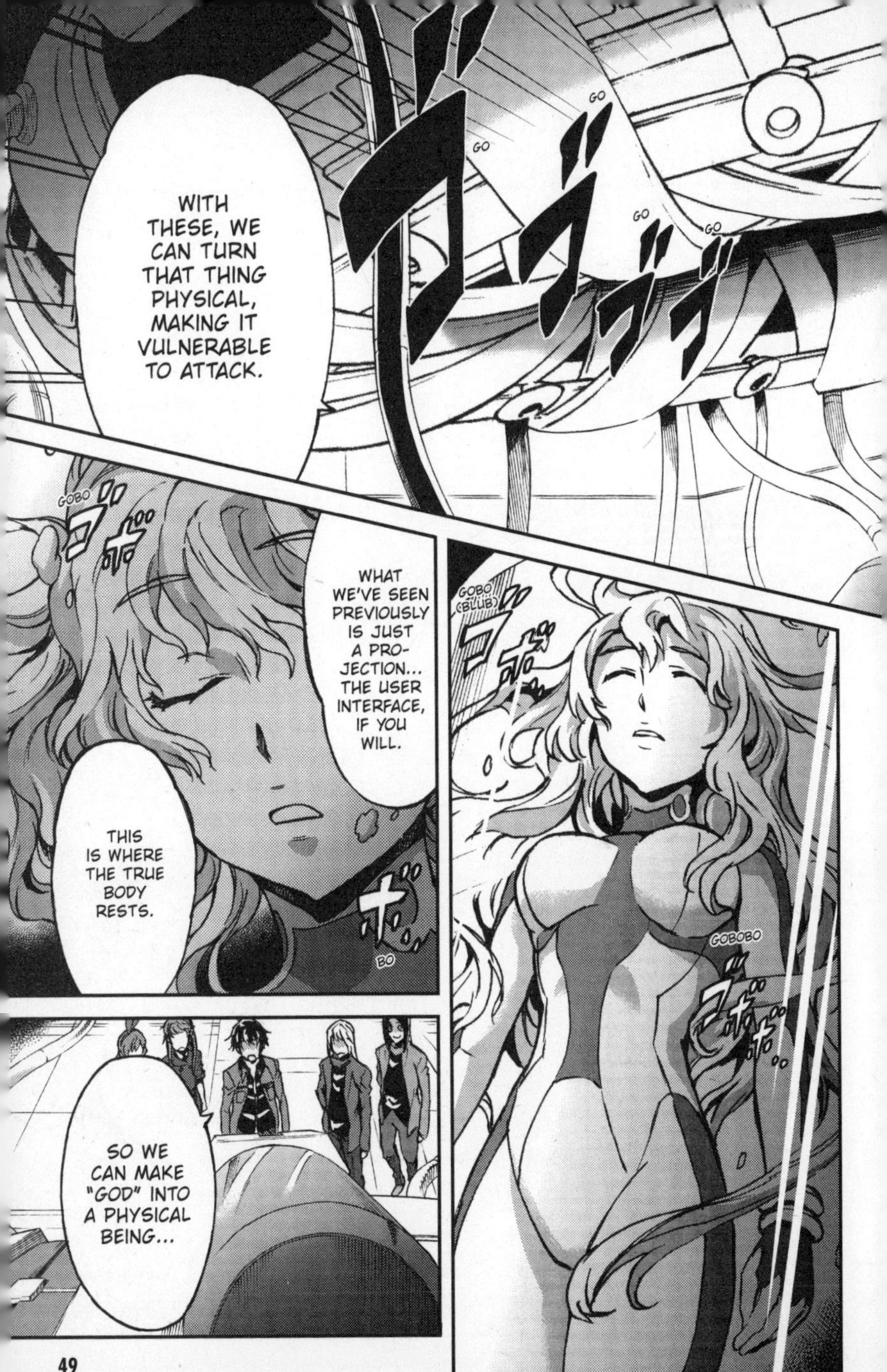
GO
GO
GO
GO
WITH THESE, WE CAN TURN THAT THING PHYSICAL, MAKING IT VULNERABLE TO ATTACK.
GOBO (BLUB)
GOBOBO
GOBO
WHAT WE'VE SEEN PREVIOUSLY IS JUST A PRO-JECTION... THE USER INTERFACE, IF YOU WILL.
THIS IS WHERE THE TRUE BODY RESTS.
BO
SO WE CAN MAKE "GOD" INTO A PHYSICAL BEING...

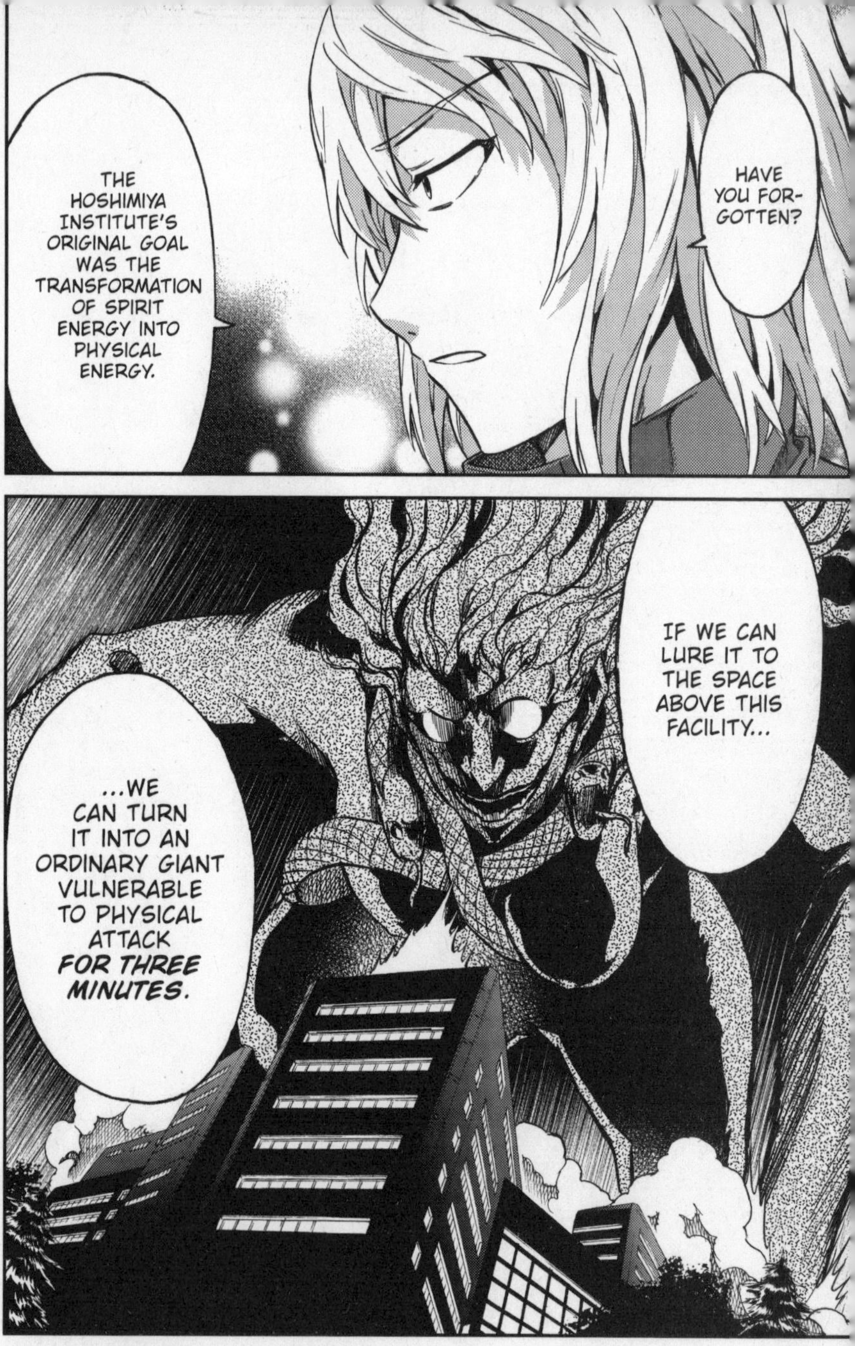
HAVE YOU FOR-GOTTEN?
THE HOSHIMIYA INSTITUTE'S ORIGINAL GOAL WAS THE TRANSFORMATION OF SPIRIT ENERGY INTO PHYSICAL ENERGY.
IF WE CAN LURE IT TO THE SPACE ABOVE THIS FACILITY...
...WE CAN TURN IT INTO AN ORDINARY GIANT VULNERABLE TO PHYSICAL ATTACK *FOR THREE MINUTES*.

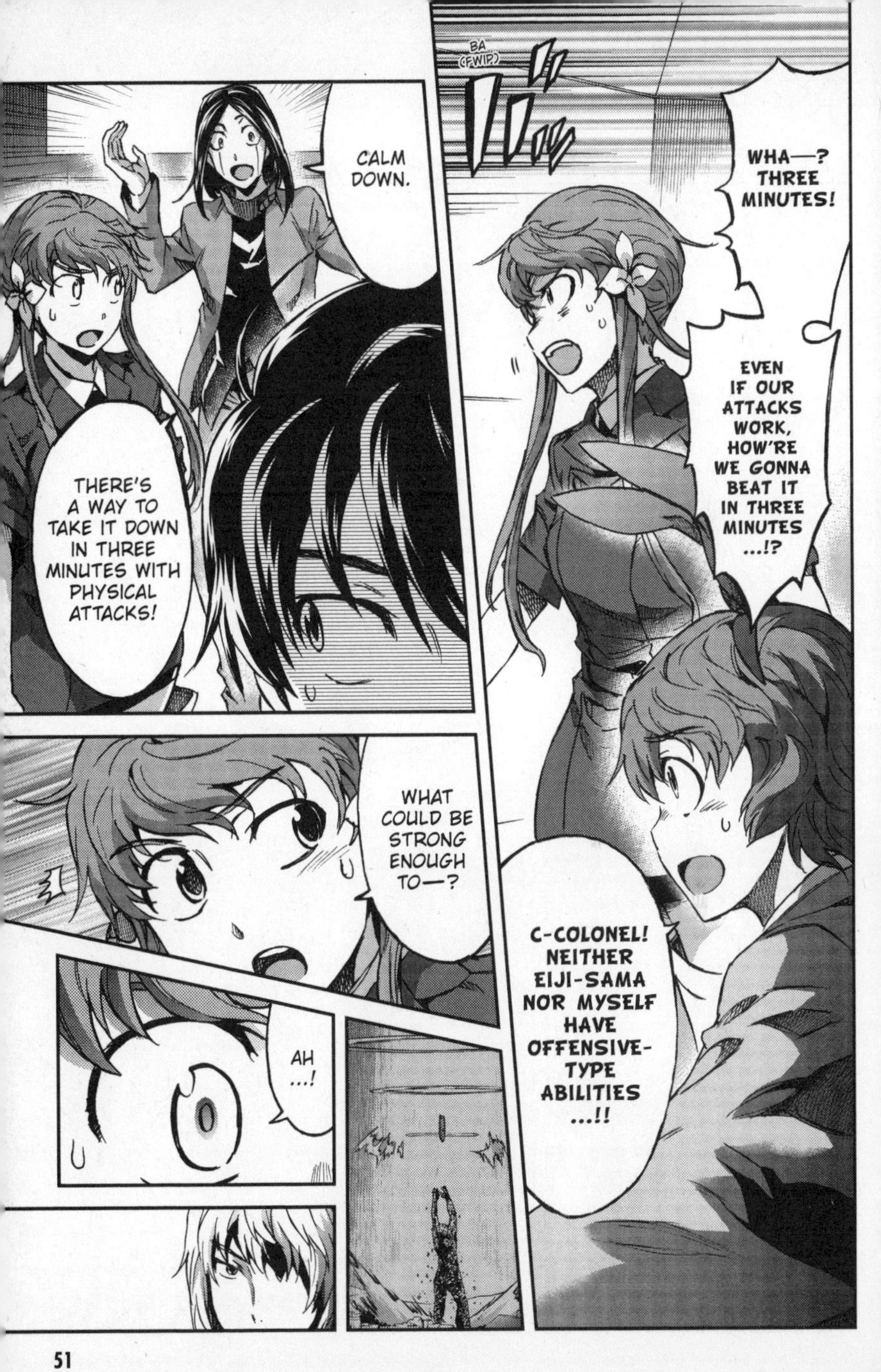
BA (FWIP)
WHA—? THREE MINUTES!
EVEN IF OUR ATTACKS WORK, HOW'RE WE GONNA BEAT IT IN THREE MINUTES ...!?
C-COLONEL! NEITHER EIJI-SAMA NOR MYSELF HAVE OFFENSIVE-TYPE ABILITIES ...!!
CALM DOWN.
THERE'S A WAY TO TAKE IT DOWN IN THREE MINUTES WITH PHYSICAL ATTACKS!
WHAT COULD BE STRONG ENOUGH TO—?
AH ...!

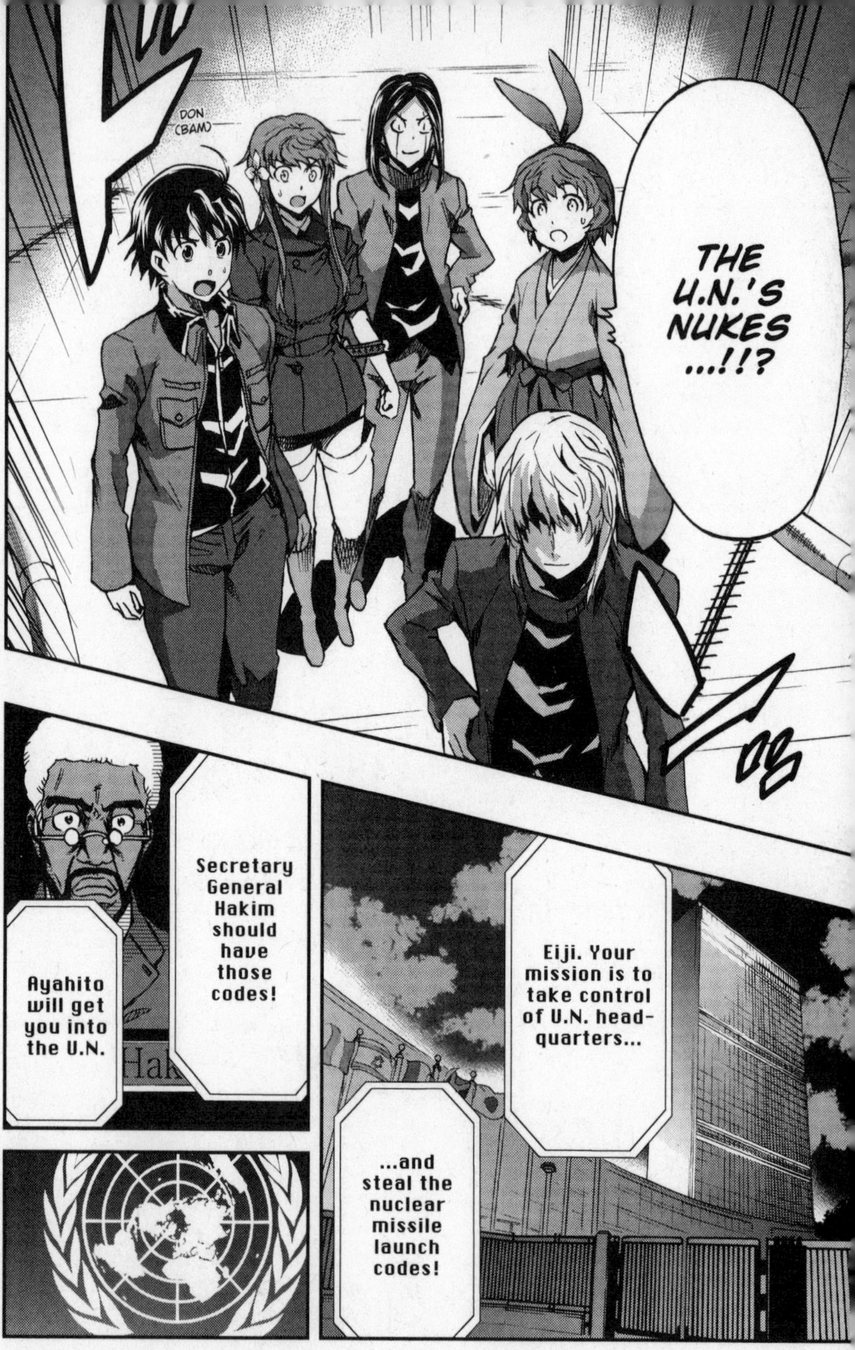
THE U.N.'S NUKES ...!!?
DON (BAM)
Eiji. Your mission is to take control of U.N. head-quarters...
...and steal the nuclear missile launch codes!
Secretary General Hakim should have those codes!
Ayahito will get you into the U.N.

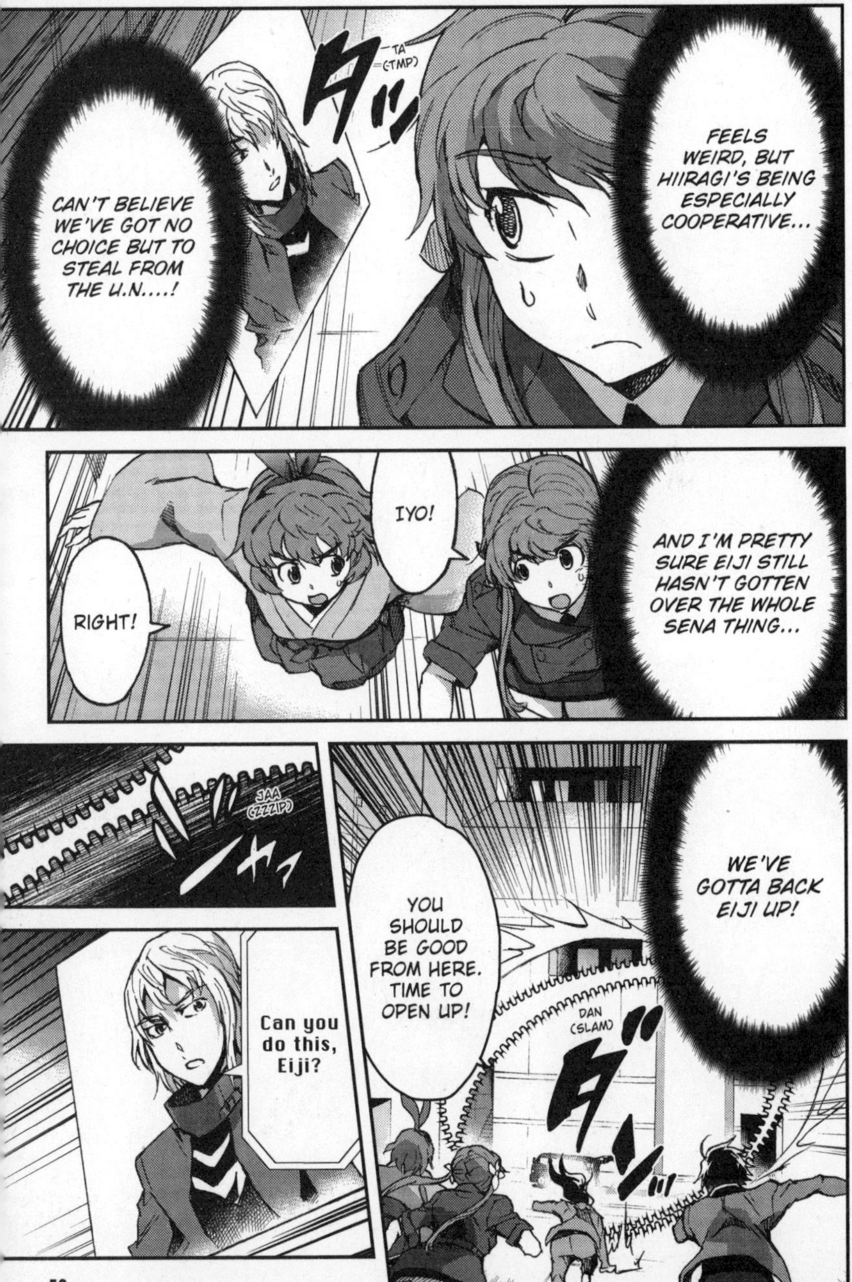
FEELS WEIRD, BUT HIIRAGI'S BEING ESPECIALLY COOPERATIVE...
TA (TMP)
CAN'T BELIEVE WE'VE GOT NO CHOICE BUT TO STEAL FROM THE U.N....!
AND I'M PRETTY SURE EIJI STILL HASN'T GOTTEN OVER THE WHOLE SENA THING...
IYO!
RIGHT!
WE'VE GOTTA BACK EIJI UP!
YOU SHOULD BE GOOD FROM HERE. TIME TO OPEN UP!
DAN (SLAM)
JAA (ZZZIP)
Can you do this, Eiji?

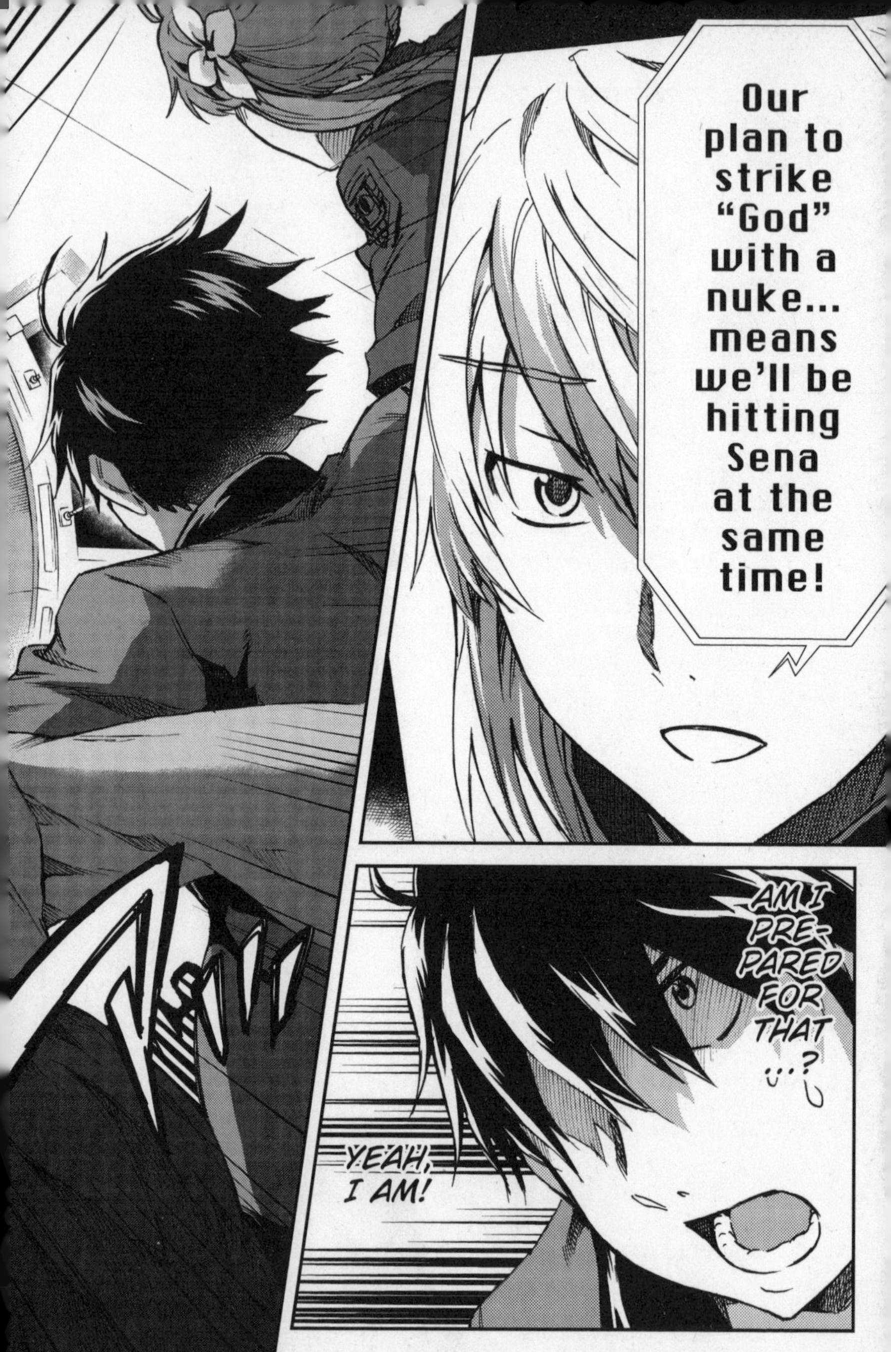
Our plan to strike "God" with a nuke... means we'll be hitting Sena at the same time!
AM I PRE-PARED FOR THAT ...?
YEAH, I AM!

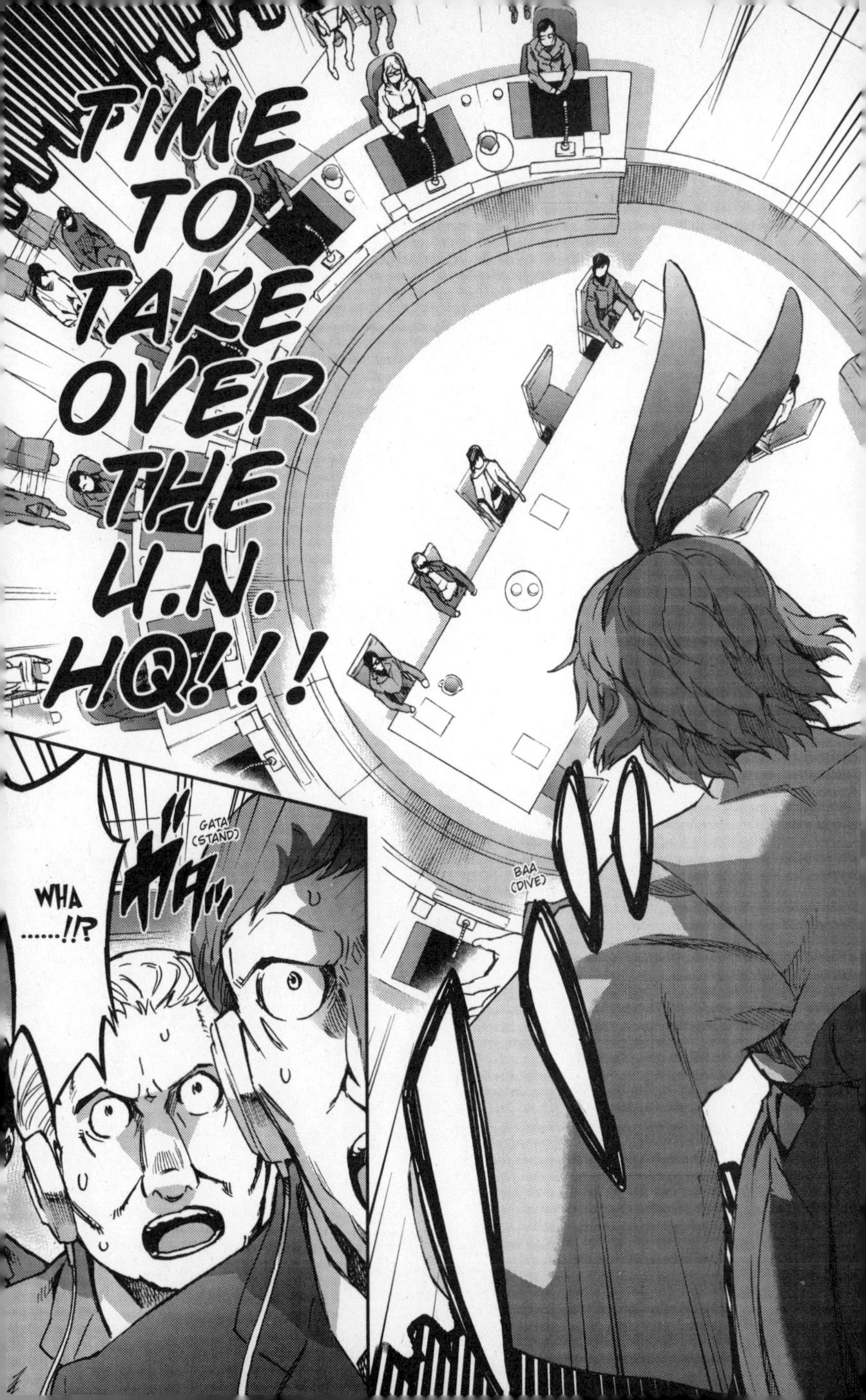
TIME TO TAKE OVER THE U.N. HQ!!!
BAA (DIVE)
GATA (STAND)
ガタッ
WHA ......!!?

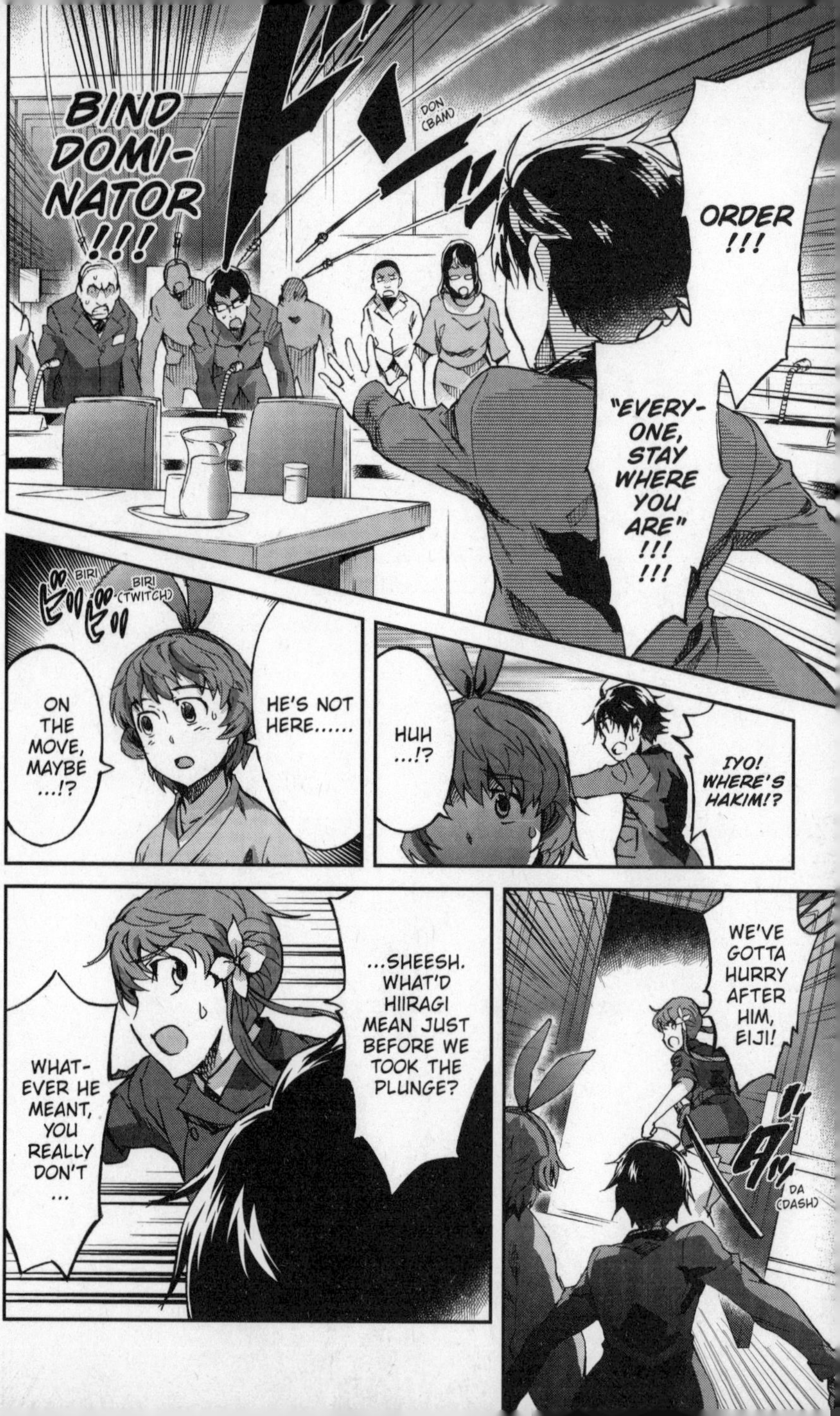
ORDER !!!
"EVERY-ONE, STAY WHERE YOU ARE" !!! !!!
DON (BAM)
BIND DOMI-NATOR !!!
IYO! WHERE'S HAKIM!?
HUH ...!?
BIRI BIRI (TWITCH)
HE'S NOT HERE......
ON THE MOVE, MAYBE ...!?
WE'VE GOTTA HURRY AFTER HIM, EIJI!
DA (DASH)
...SHEESH. WHAT'D HIIRAGI MEAN JUST BEFORE WE TOOK THE PLUNGE?
WHAT-EVER HE MEANT, YOU REALLY DON'T ...

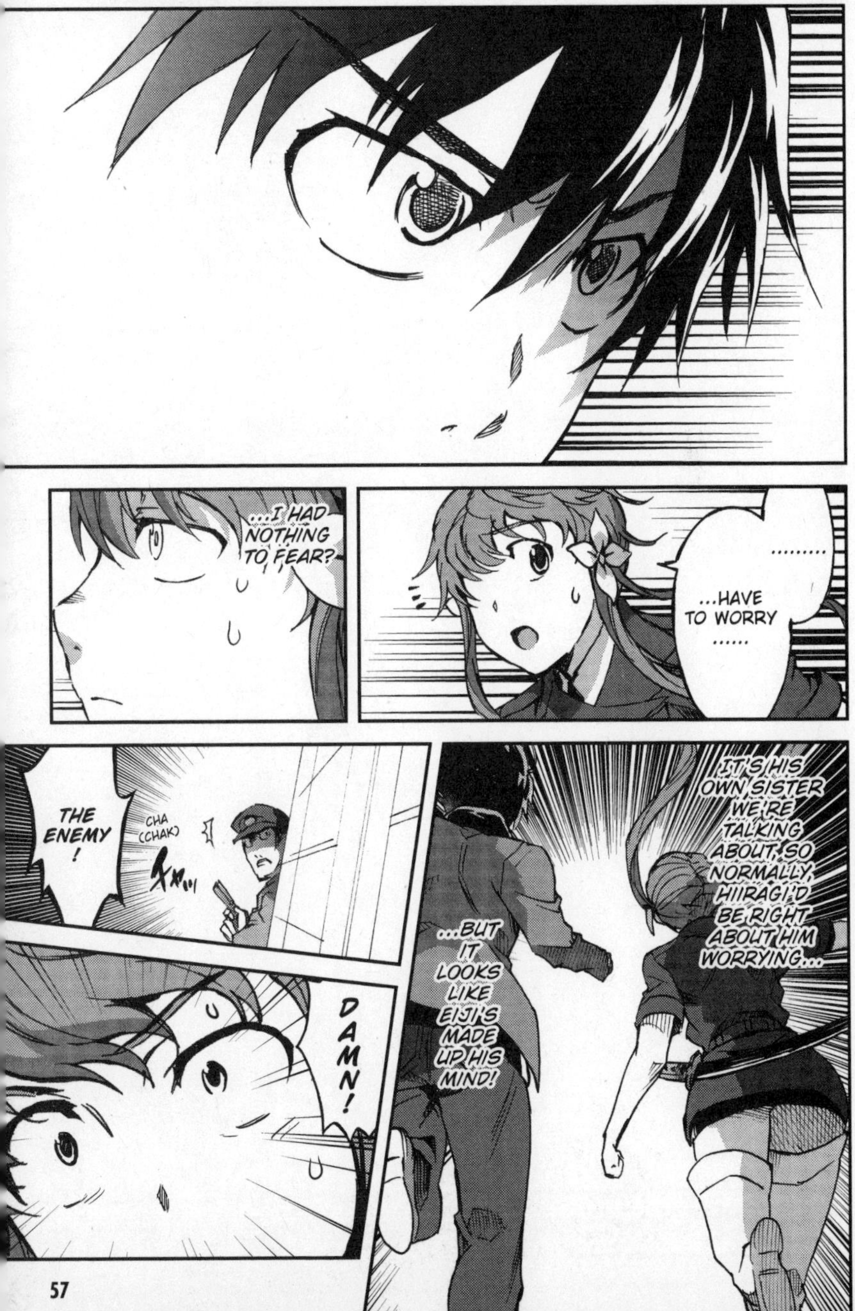
....
...HAVE TO WORRY ......
...I HAD NOTHING TO FEAR?
IT'S HIS OWN SISTER WE'RE TALKING ABOUT, SO NORMALLY, HIIRAGI'D BE RIGHT ABOUT HIM WORRYING...
...BUT IT LOOKS LIKE EIJI'S MADE UP HIS MIND!
THE ENEMY!
CHA (CHAK)
DAMN!

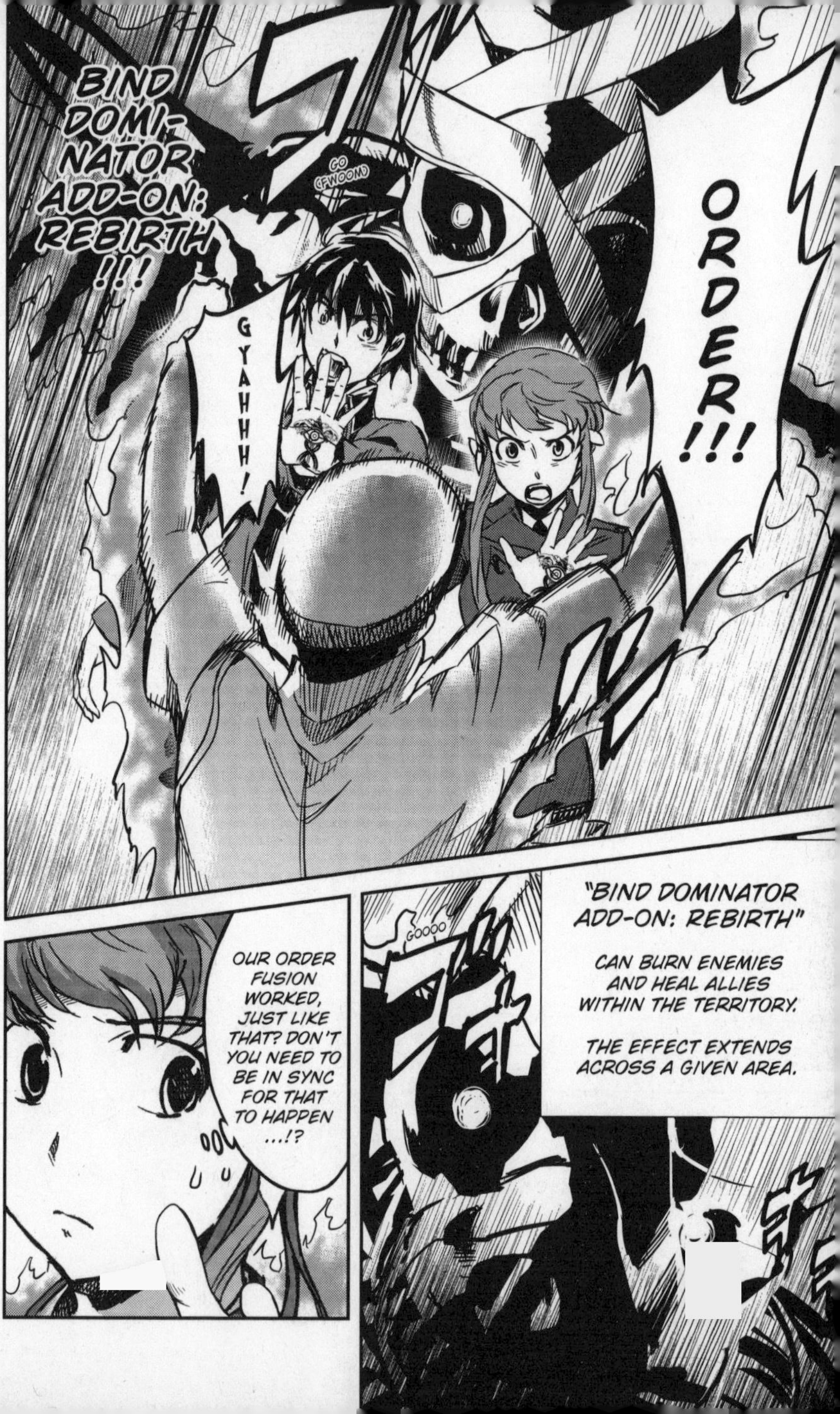
ORDER!!!
GO (FWOOM)
BIND DOMINATOR ADD-ON: REBIRTH!!!
GYAHHH!
"BIND DOMINATOR ADD-ON: REBIRTH"
CAN BURN ENEMIES AND HEAL ALLIES WITHIN THE TERRITORY.
THE EFFECT EXTENDS ACROSS A GIVEN AREA.
GOOOO
OUR ORDER FUSION WORKED, JUST LIKE THAT? DON'T YOU NEED TO BE IN SYNC FOR THAT TO HAPPEN...!?

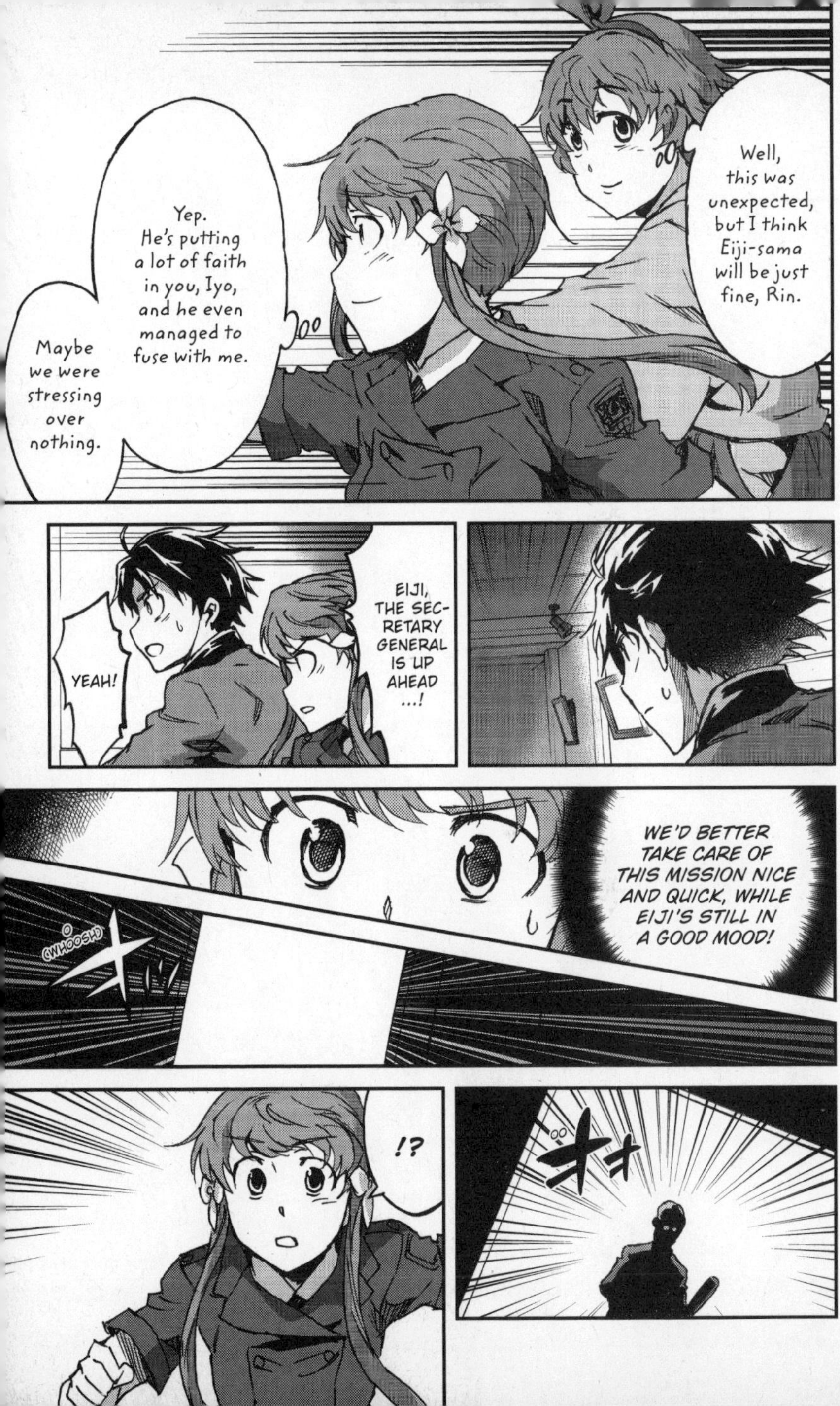
Well, this was unexpected, but I think Eiji-sama will be just fine, Rin.
Yep. He's putting a lot of faith in you, Iyo, and he even managed to fuse with me.
Maybe we were stressing over nothing.
EIJI, THE SEC-RETARY GENERAL IS UP AHEAD ...!
YEAH!
WE'D BETTER TAKE CARE OF THIS MISSION NICE AND QUICK, WHILE EIJI'S STILL IN A GOOD MOOD!
(WHOOSH)
!?

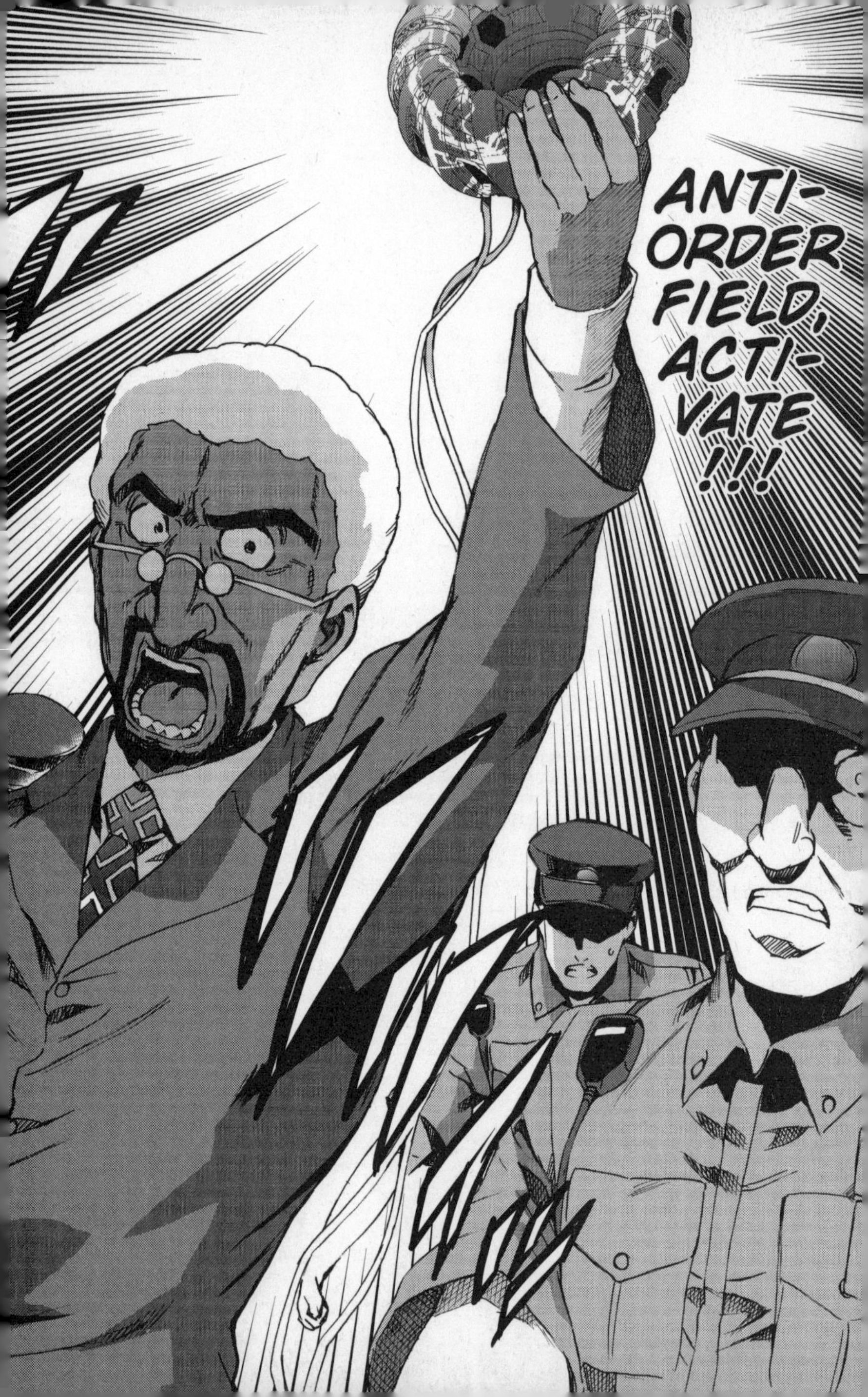
ANTI-ORDER FIELD, ACTI-VATE!!!

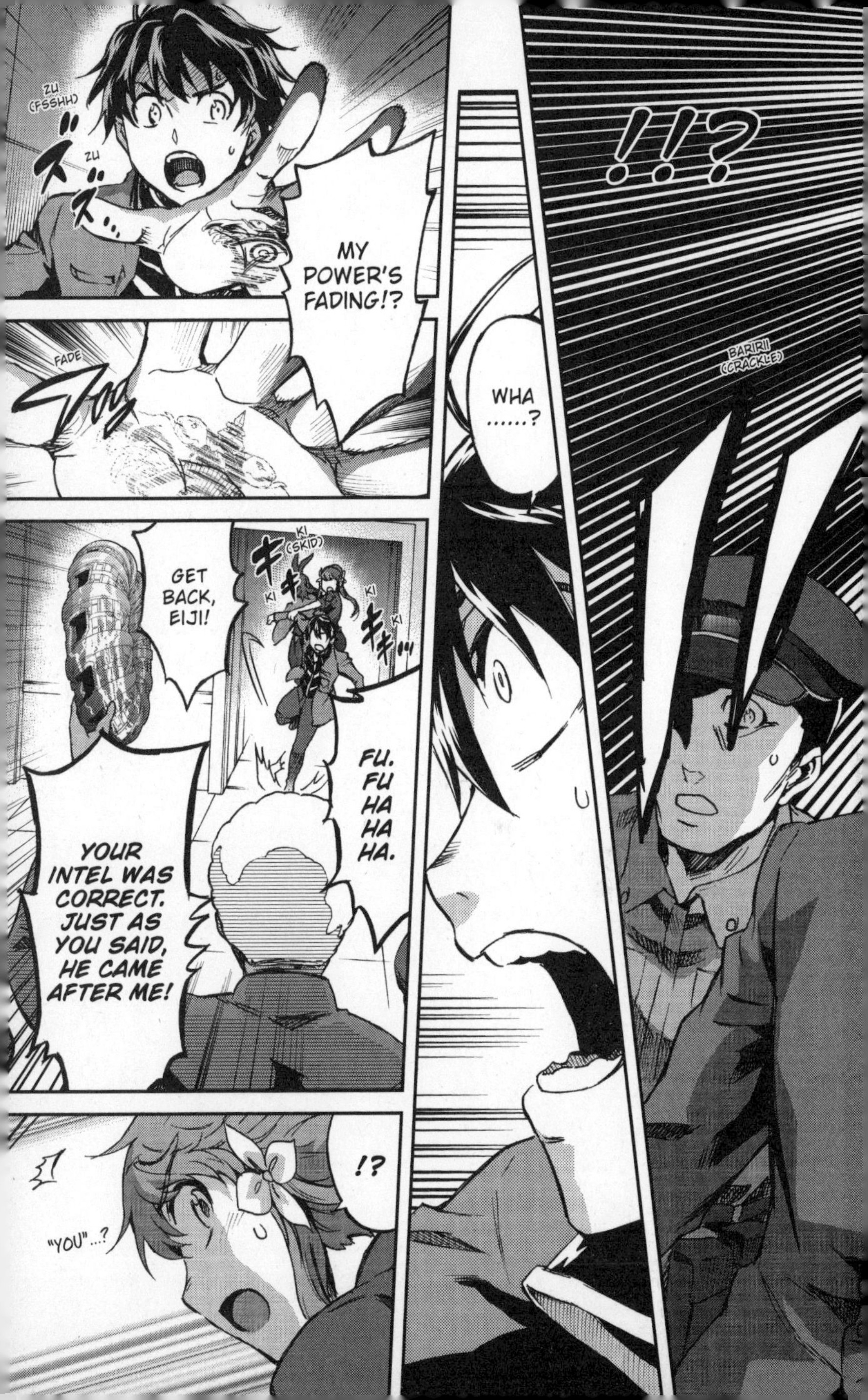
!!?
BARIRII (CRACKLE)
WHA ......?
MY POWER'S FADING!?
ZU (FSSHH)
ZU
FADE
GET BACK, EIJI!
KI (SKID)
KI
KI
KI
FU. FU HA HA HA.
YOUR INTEL WAS CORRECT. JUST AS YOU SAID, HE CAME AFTER ME!
!?
"YOU"...?

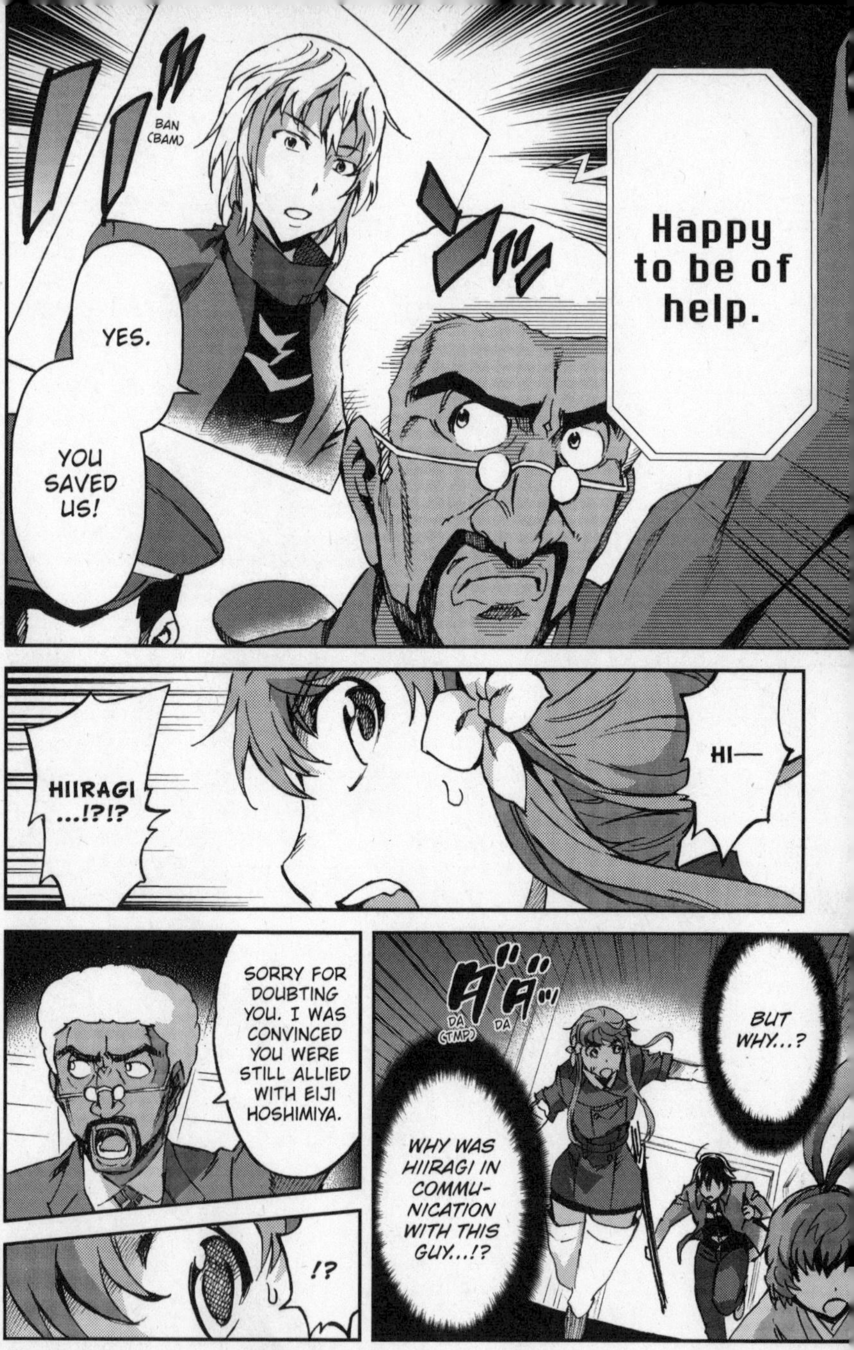
Happy to be of help.
BAN (BAM)
YES.
YOU SAVED US!
HI—
HIIRAGI ...!?!?
BUT WHY...?
DA (TMP) DA
WHY WAS HIIRAGI IN COMMUNICATION WITH THIS GUY...!?
SORRY FOR DOUBTING YOU. I WAS CONVINCED YOU WERE STILL ALLIED WITH EIJI HOSHIMIYA.
!?

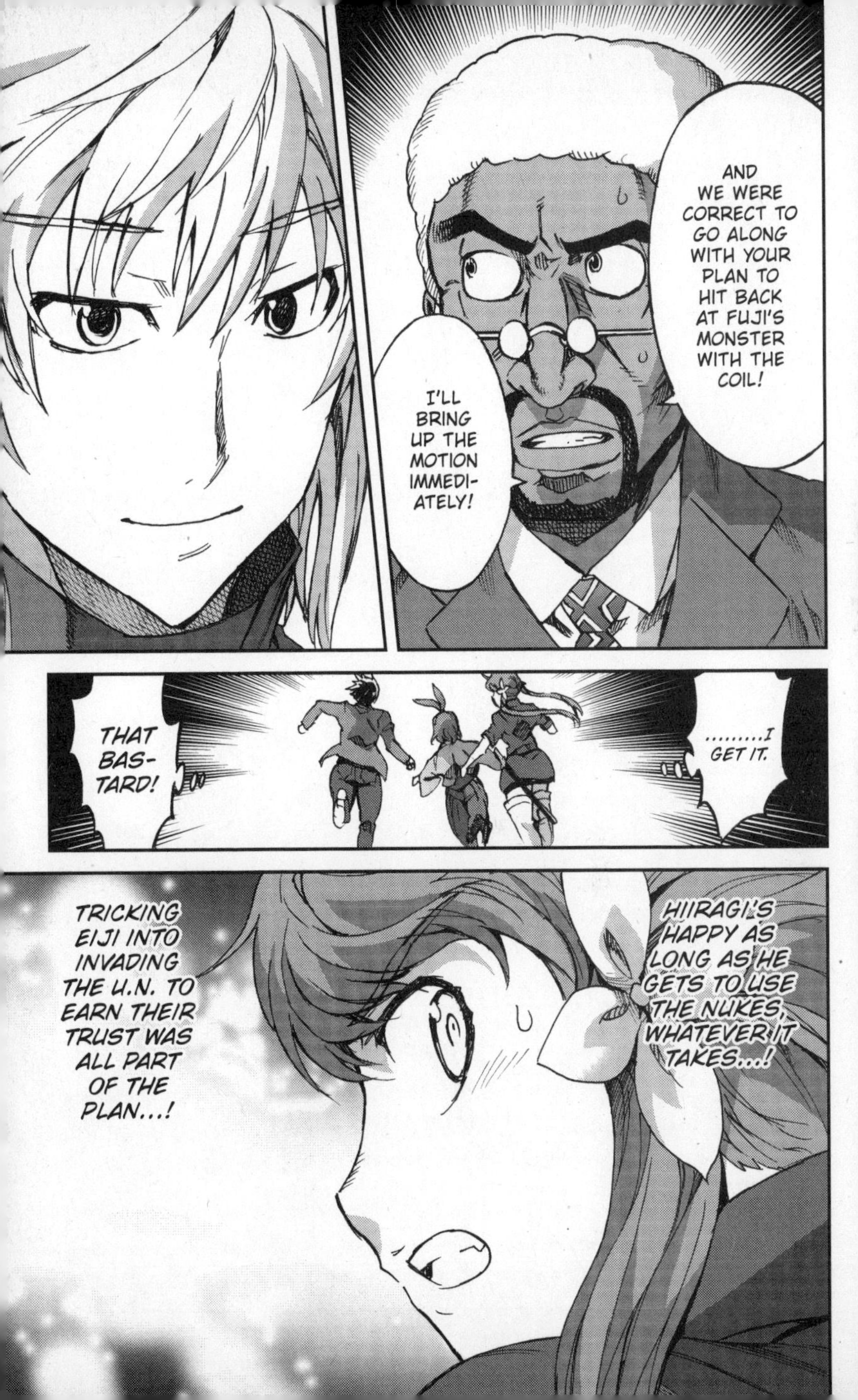
AND WE WERE CORRECT TO GO ALONG WITH YOUR PLAN TO HIT BACK AT FUJI'S MONSTER WITH THE COIL!
I'LL BRING UP THE MOTION IMMEDI-ATELY!
.........I GET IT.
THAT BAS-TARD!
HIIRAGI'S HAPPY AS LONG AS HE GETS TO USE THE NUKES, WHATEVER IT TAKES...!
TRICKING EIJI INTO INVADING THE U.N. TO EARN THEIR TRUST WAS ALL PART OF THE PLAN...!

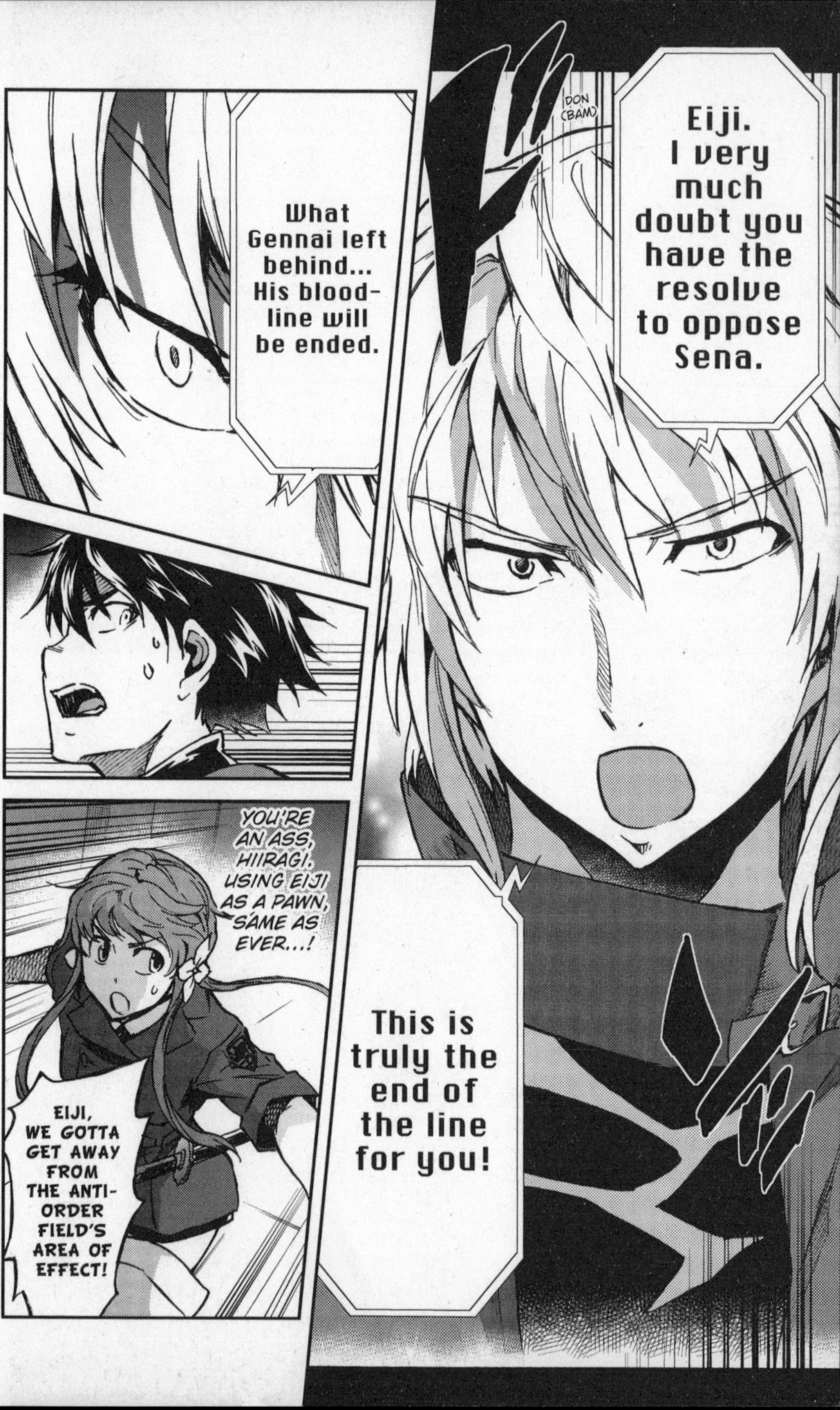
DON (BAM)
Eiji. I very much doubt you have the resolve to oppose Sena.
This is truly the end of the line for you!
What Gennai left behind... His blood-line will be ended.
YOU'RE AN ASS, HIIRAGI. USING EIJI AS A PAWN, SAME AS EVER...!
EIJI, WE GOTTA GET AWAY FROM THE ANTI-ORDER FIELD'S AREA OF EFFECT!

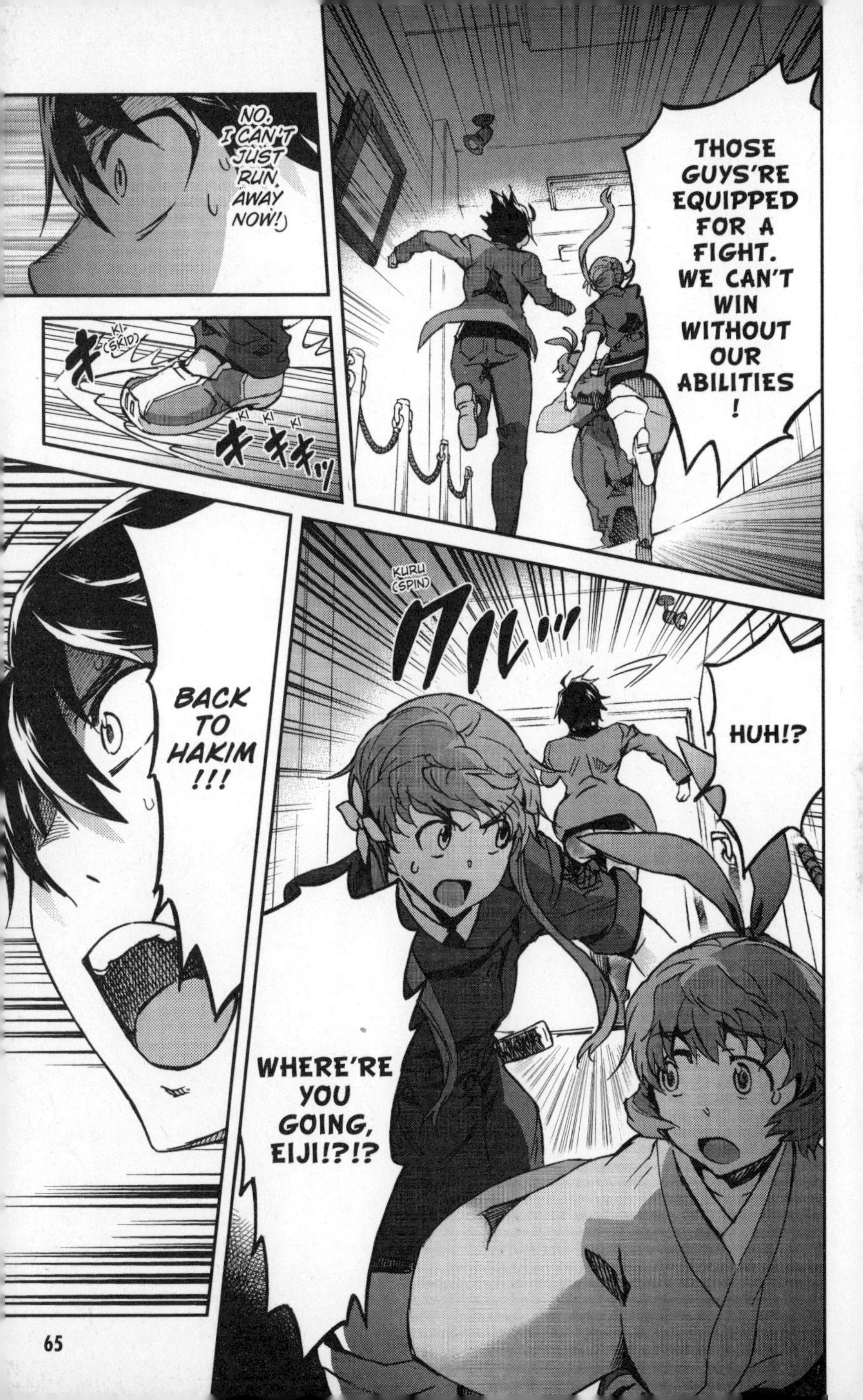
THOSE GUYS'RE EQUIPPED FOR A FIGHT. WE CAN'T WIN WITHOUT OUR ABILITIES!
NO. I CAN'T JUST RUN AWAY NOW!
KI (SKID)
KI KI KI
KURU (SPIN)
HUH!?
WHERE'RE YOU GOING, EIJI!?!?
BACK TO HAKIM!!!

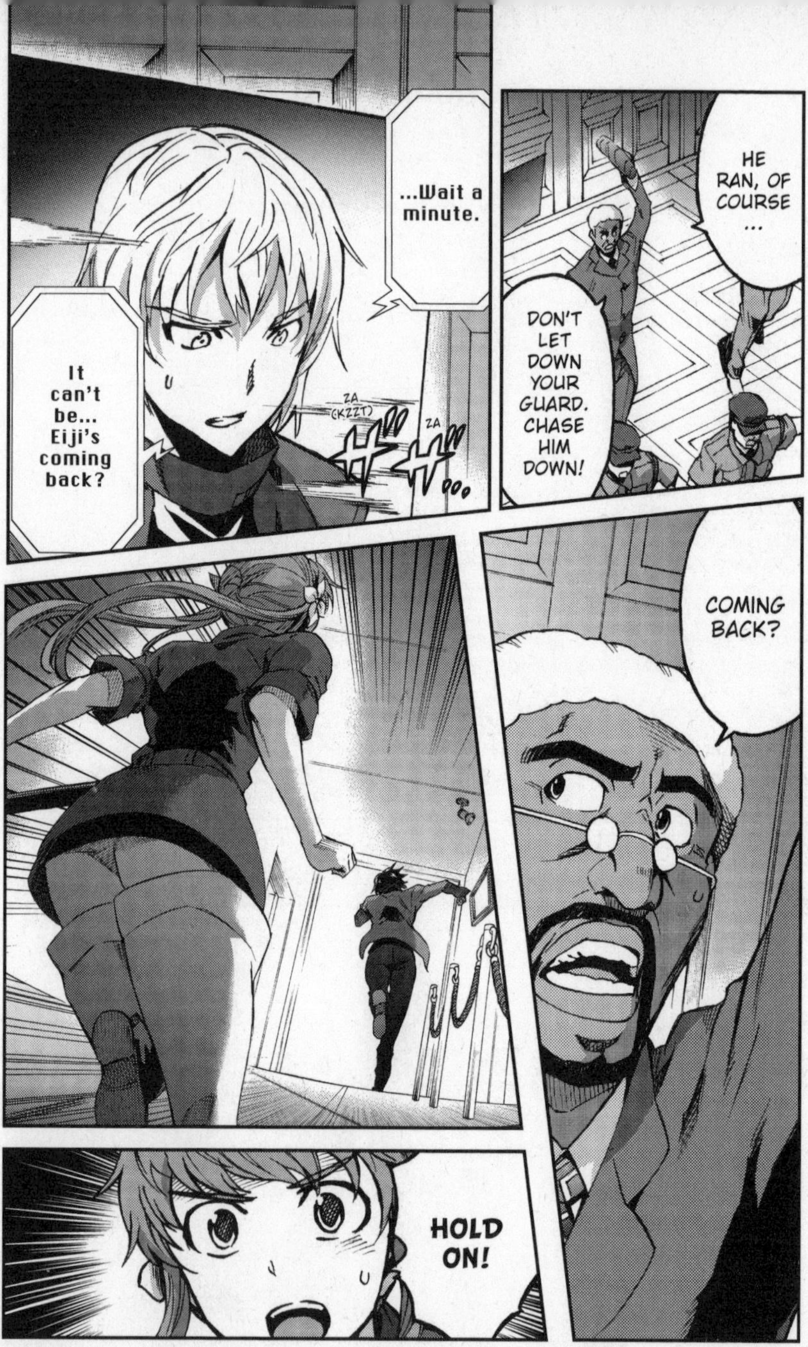
HE RAN, OF COURSE ...
DON'T LET DOWN YOUR GUARD. CHASE HIM DOWN!
...Wait a minute.
It can't be... Eiji's coming back?
ZA (KZZT)
ZA
COMING BACK?
HOLD ON!

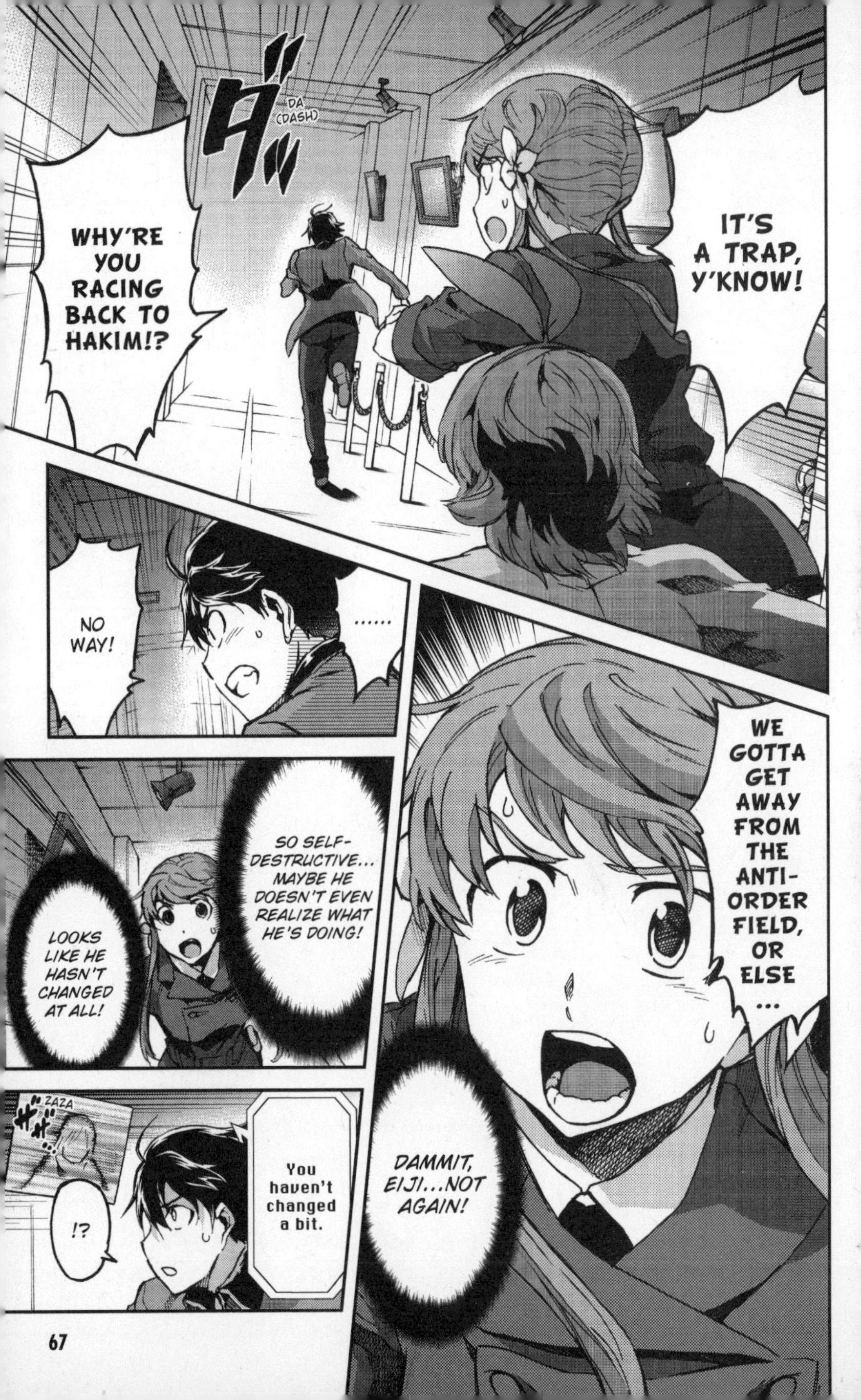
DA (DASH)
IT'S A TRAP, Y'KNOW!
WHY'RE YOU RACING BACK TO HAKIM!?
WE GOTTA GET AWAY FROM THE ANTI-ORDER FIELD, OR ELSE...
DAMMIT, EIJI...NOT AGAIN!
......
NO WAY!
SO SELF-DESTRUCTIVE... MAYBE HE DOESN'T EVEN REALIZE WHAT HE'S DOING!
LOOKS LIKE HE HASN'T CHANGED AT ALL!
ZAZA
You haven't changed a bit.
!?

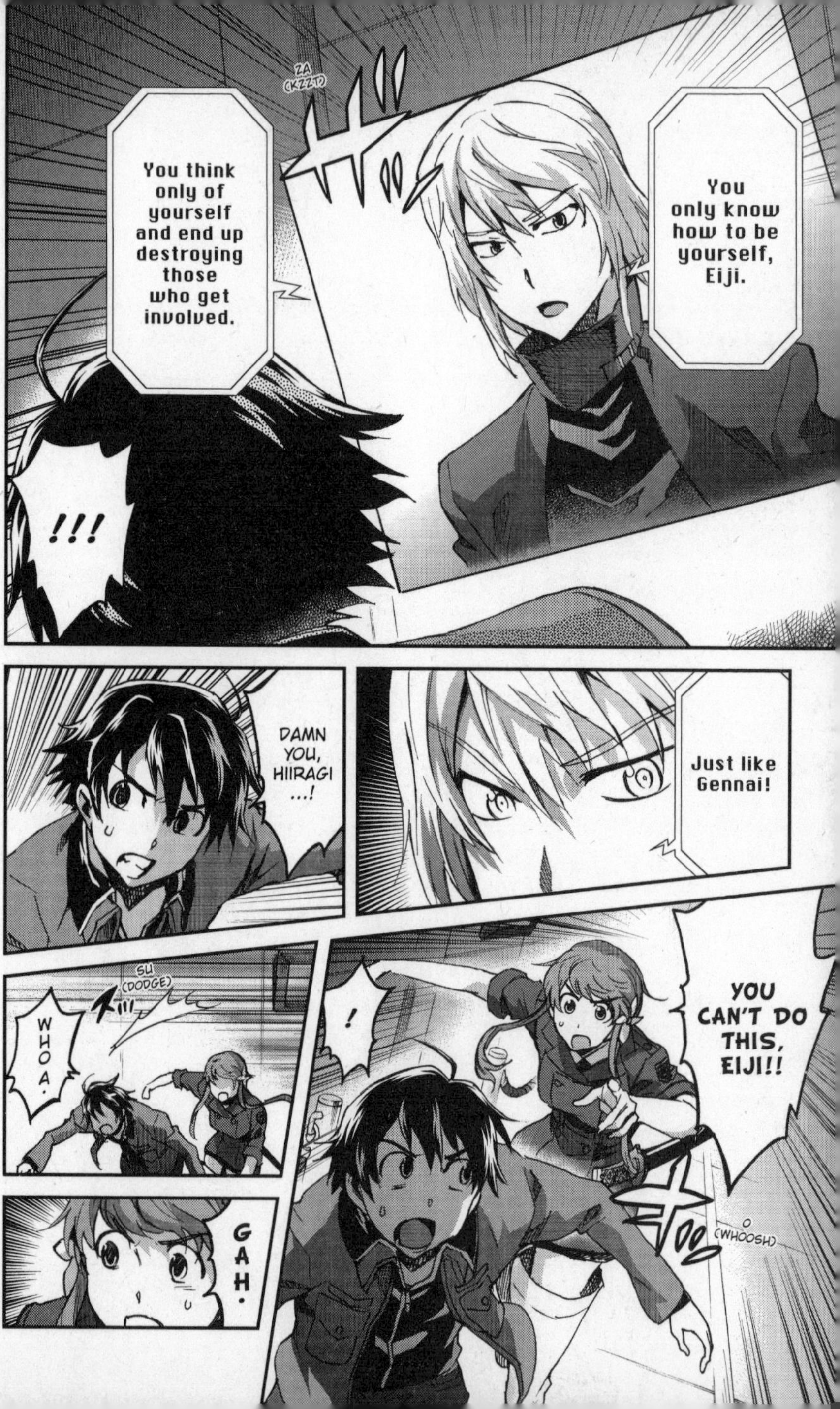
You only know how to be yourself, Eiji.
ZA (KZZT)
You think only of yourself and end up destroying those who get involved.
!!!
Just like Gennai!
DAMN YOU, HIIRAGI ...!
YOU CAN'T DO THIS, EIJI!!
!
O (WHOOSH)
SU (DODGE)
WHOA.
GAH.

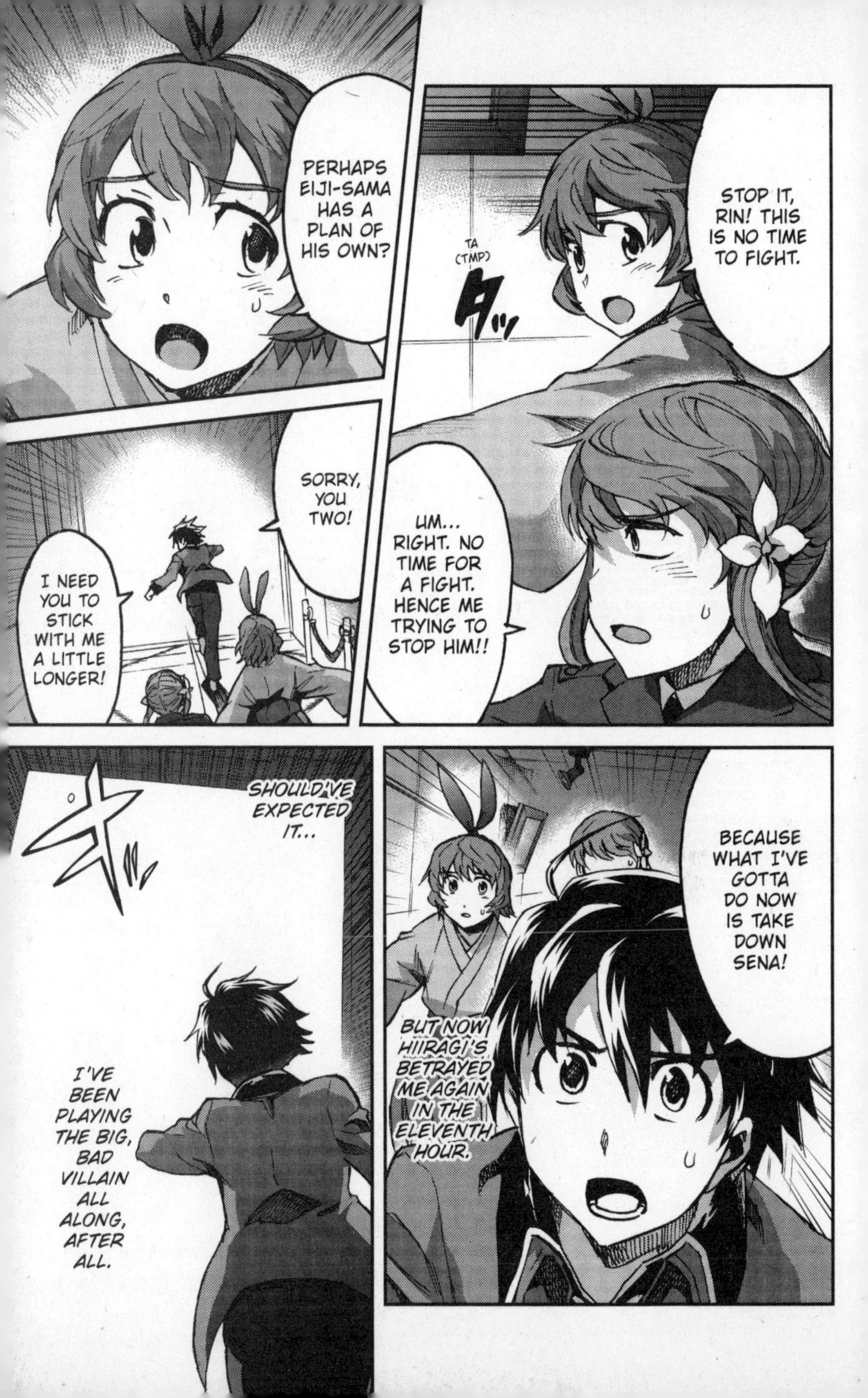
STOP IT, RIN! THIS IS NO TIME TO FIGHT.
TA (TMP)
PERHAPS EIJI-SAMA HAS A PLAN OF HIS OWN?
UM... RIGHT. NO TIME FOR A FIGHT. HENCE ME TRYING TO STOP HIM!!
SORRY, YOU TWO!
I NEED YOU TO STICK WITH ME A LITTLE LONGER!
BECAUSE WHAT I'VE GOTTA DO NOW IS TAKE DOWN SENA!
BUT NOW HIIRAGI'S BETRAYED ME AGAIN IN THE ELEVENTH HOUR.
SHOULD'VE EXPECTED IT...
I'VE BEEN PLAYING THE BIG, BAD VILLAIN ALL ALONG, AFTER ALL.

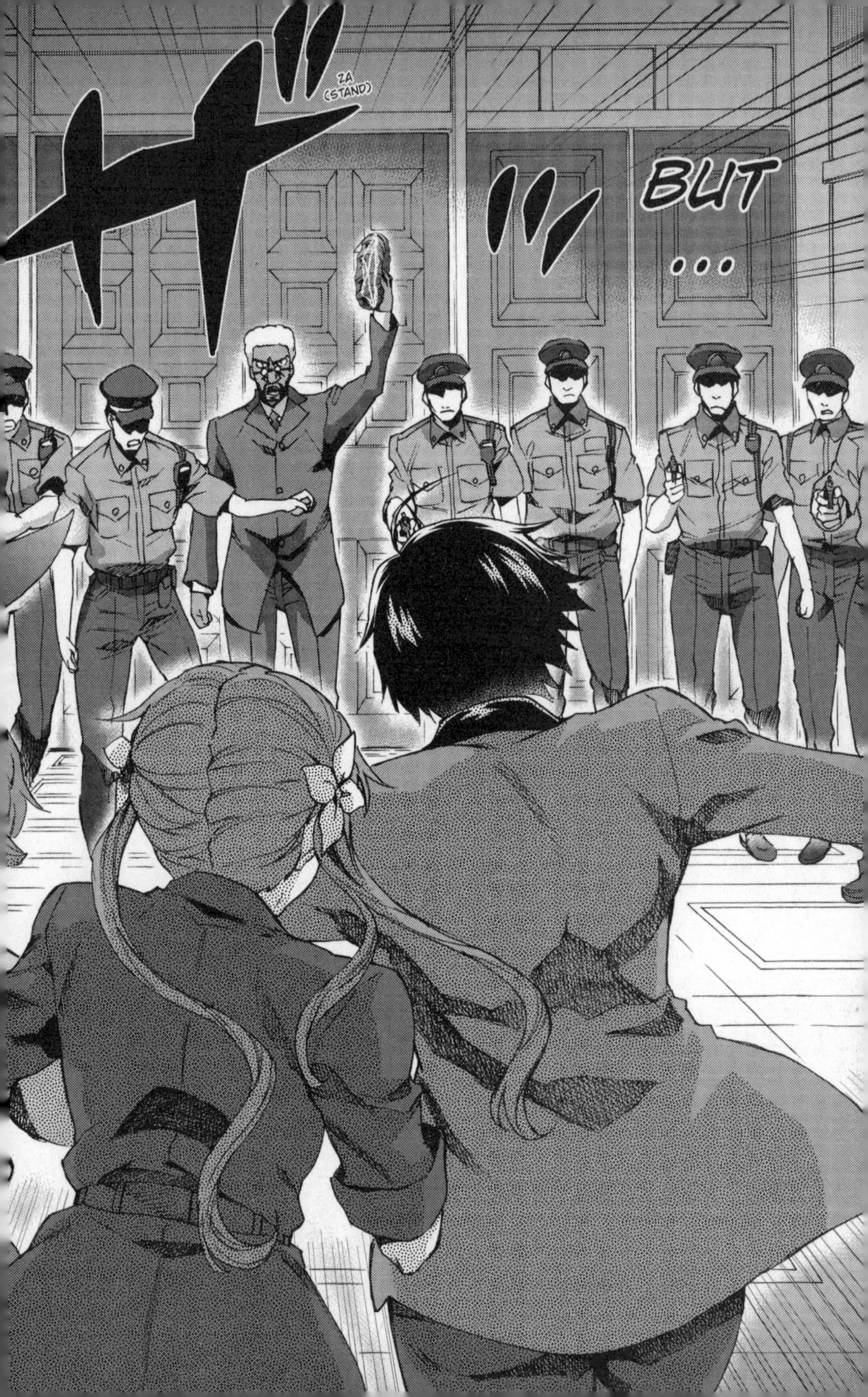
ザッ
ZA (STAND)
BUT ...

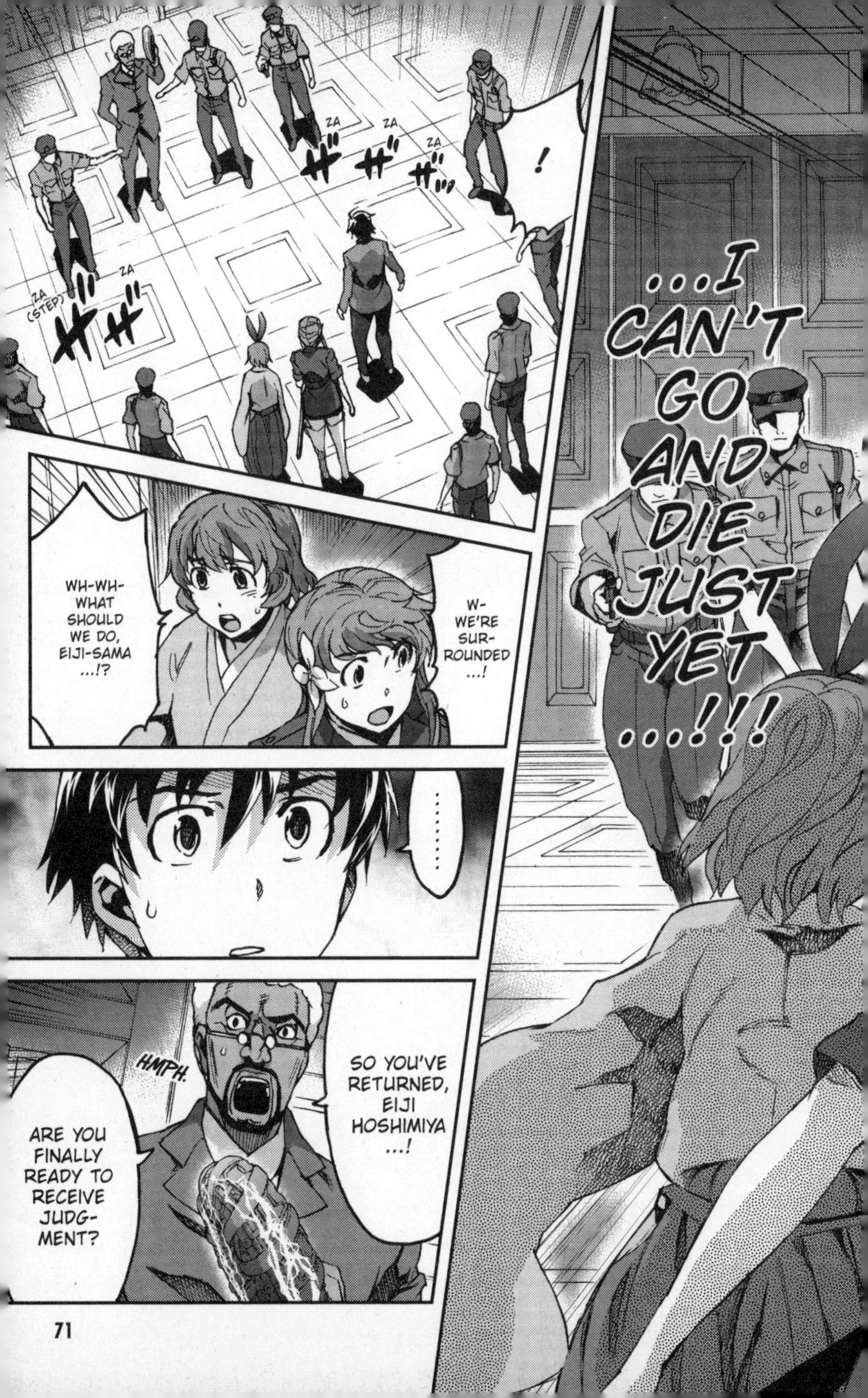
...I CAN'T GO AND DIE JUST YET ...!!!
ZA
ZA
ZA
!
ZA (STEP)
ZA
WH-WH-WHAT SHOULD WE DO, EIJI-SAMA ...!?
W-WE'RE SUR-ROUNDED ...!
....
SO YOU'VE RETURNED, EIJI HOSHIMIYA ...!
HMPH.
ARE YOU FINALLY READY TO RECEIVE JUDG-MENT?

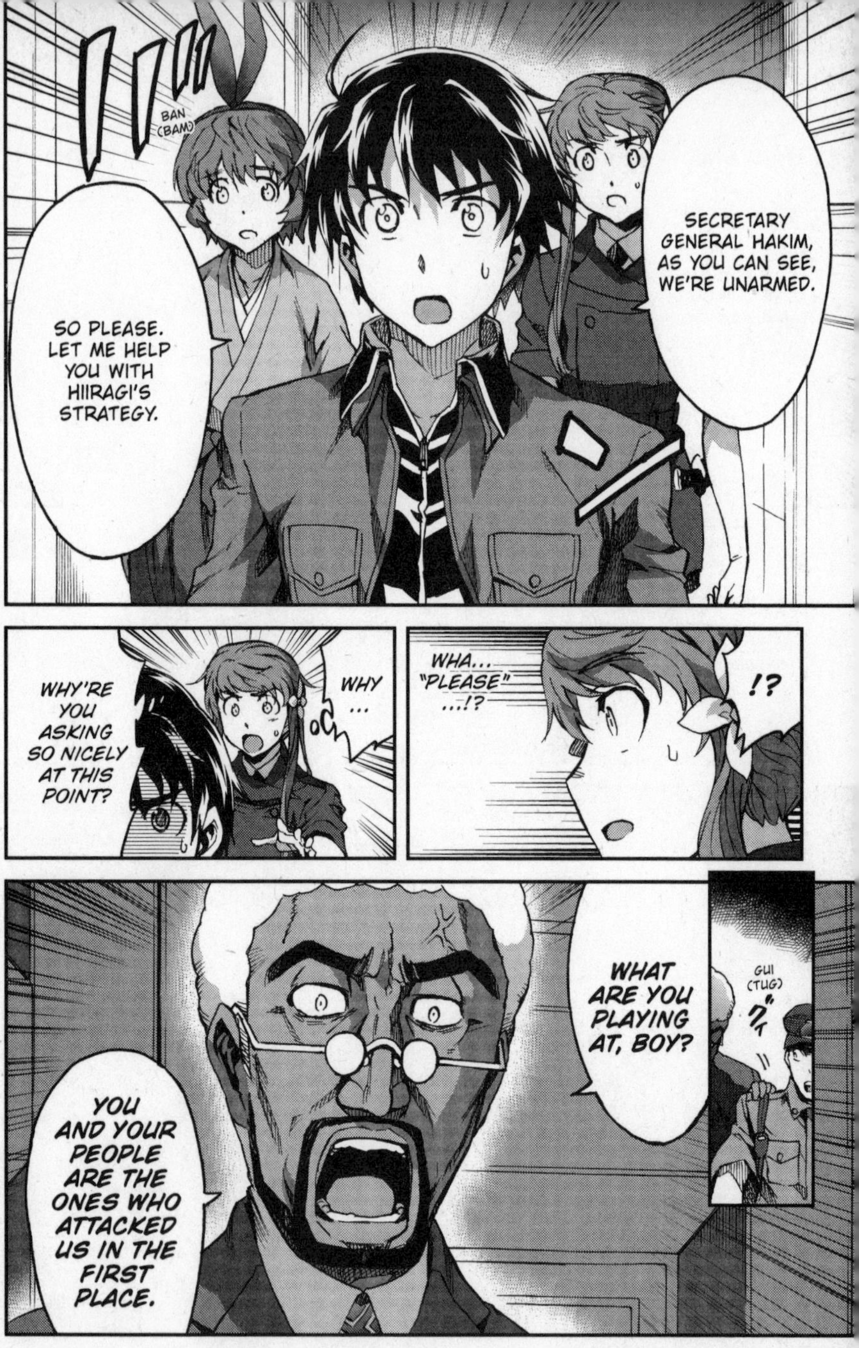
SECRETARY GENERAL HAKIM, AS YOU CAN SEE, WE'RE UNARMED.
BAN (BAM)
SO PLEASE. LET ME HELP YOU WITH HIIRAGI'S STRATEGY.
!?
WHA... "PLEASE" ...!?
WHY ...
WHY'RE YOU ASKING SO NICELY AT THIS POINT?
GUI (TUG)
WHAT ARE YOU PLAYING AT, BOY?
YOU AND YOUR PEOPLE ARE THE ONES WHO ATTACKED US IN THE FIRST PLACE.

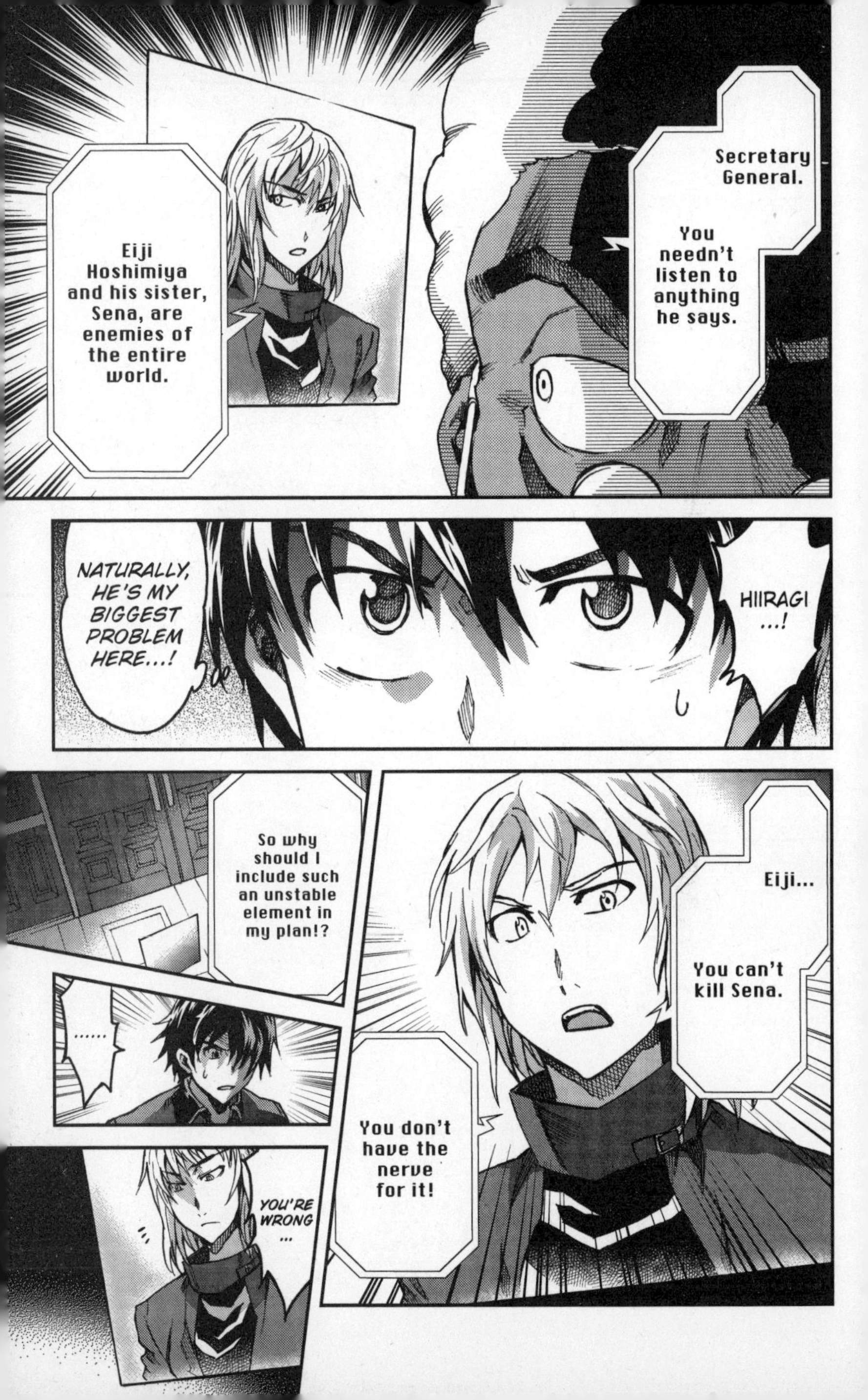
Secretary General.
You needn't listen to anything he says.
Eiji Hoshimiya and his sister, Sena, are enemies of the entire world.
HIIRAGI ...!
NATURALLY, HE'S MY BIGGEST PROBLEM HERE...!
Eiji...
You can't kill Sena.
You don't have the nerve for it!
So why should I include such an unstable element in my plan!?
......
YOU'RE WRONG ...

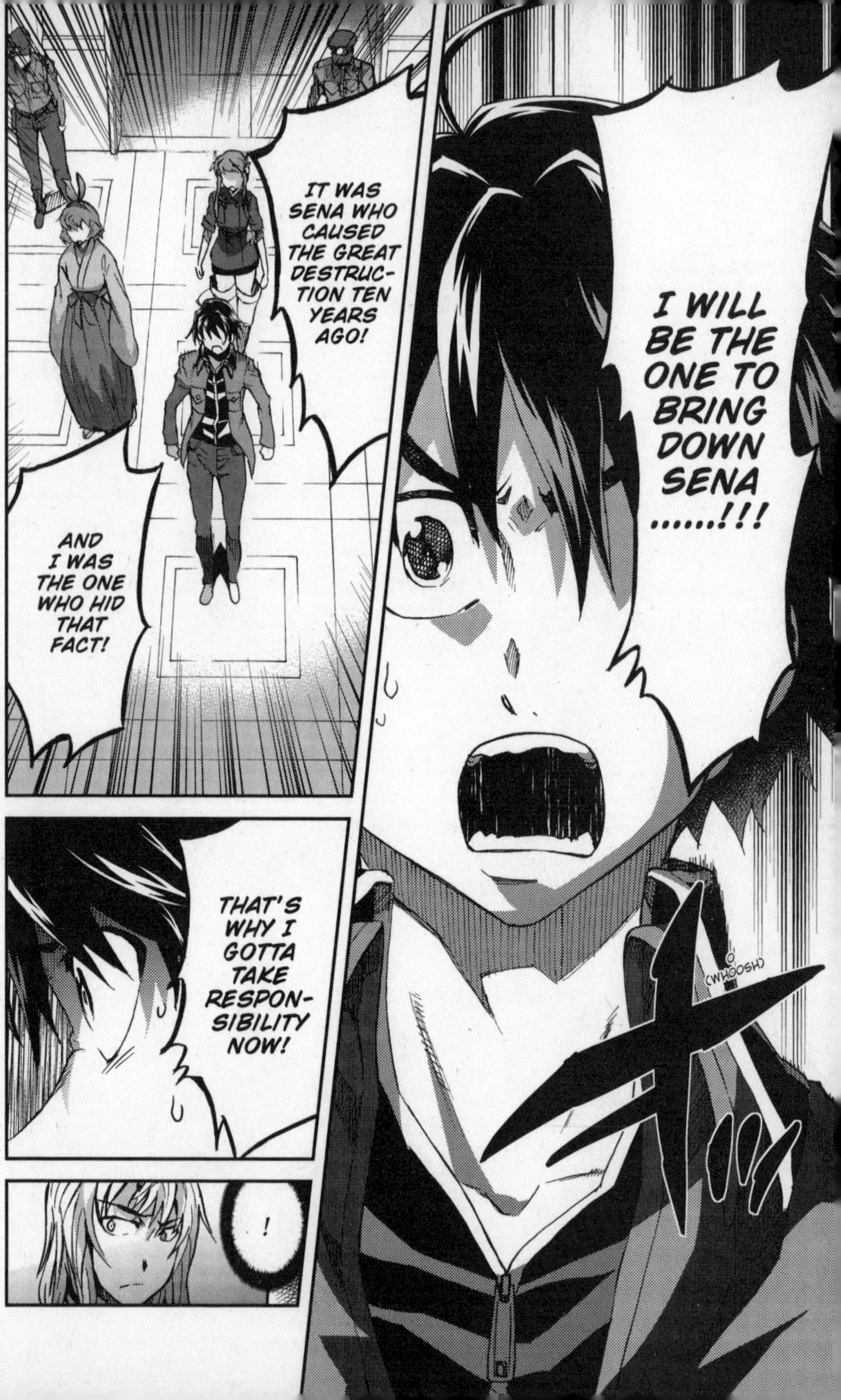
I WILL BE THE ONE TO BRING DOWN SENA......!!!
(WHOOSH)
IT WAS SENA WHO CAUSED THE GREAT DESTRUCTION TEN YEARS AGO!
AND I WAS THE ONE WHO HID THAT FACT!
THAT'S WHY I GOTTA TAKE RESPONSIBILITY NOW!
...!

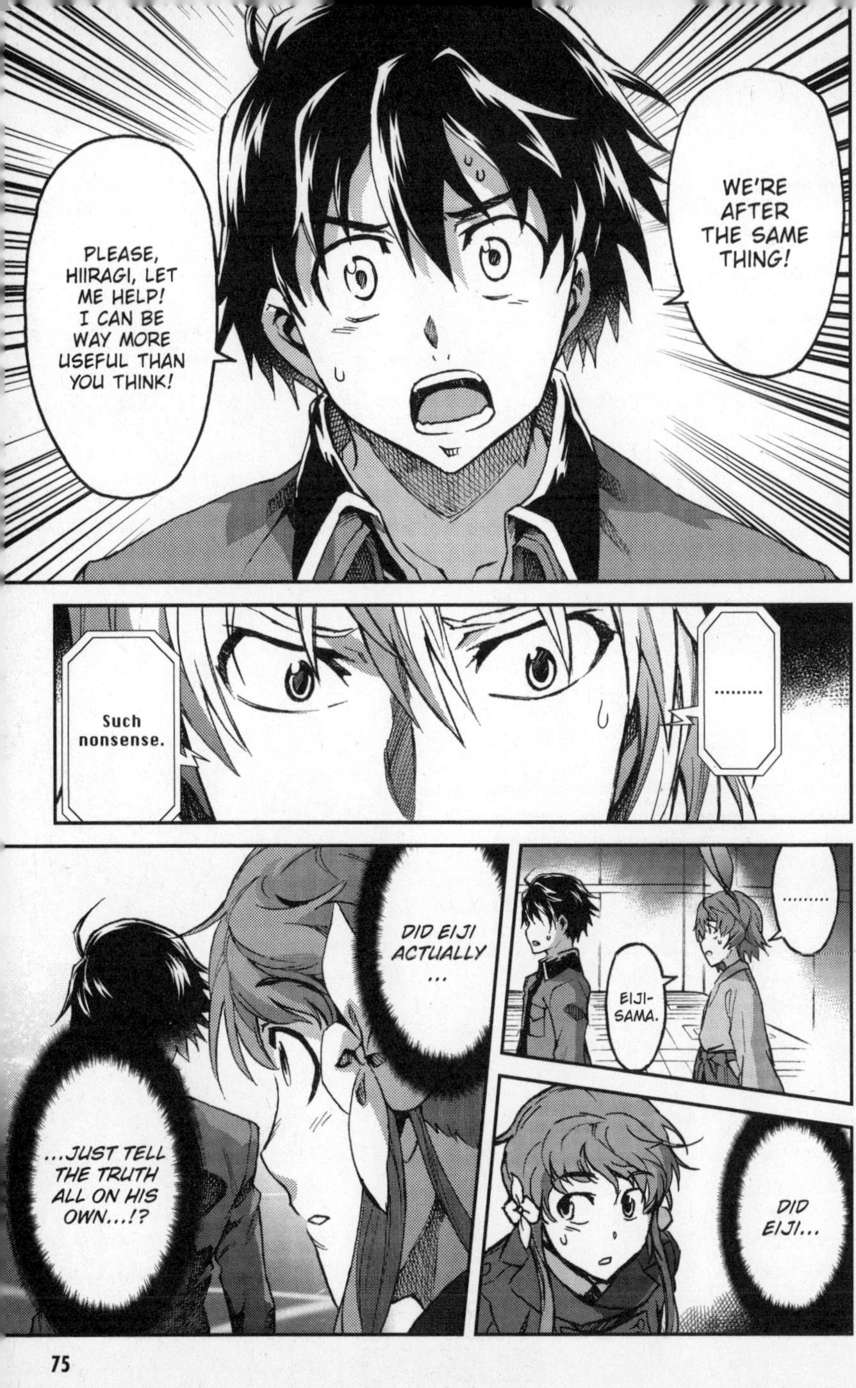
WE'RE AFTER THE SAME THING!
PLEASE, HIIRAGI, LET ME HELP! I CAN BE WAY MORE USEFUL THAN YOU THINK!
....
Such nonsense.
....
EIJI-SAMA.
DID EIJI...
DID EIJI ACTUALLY ...
...JUST TELL THE TRUTH ALL ON HIS OWN...!?

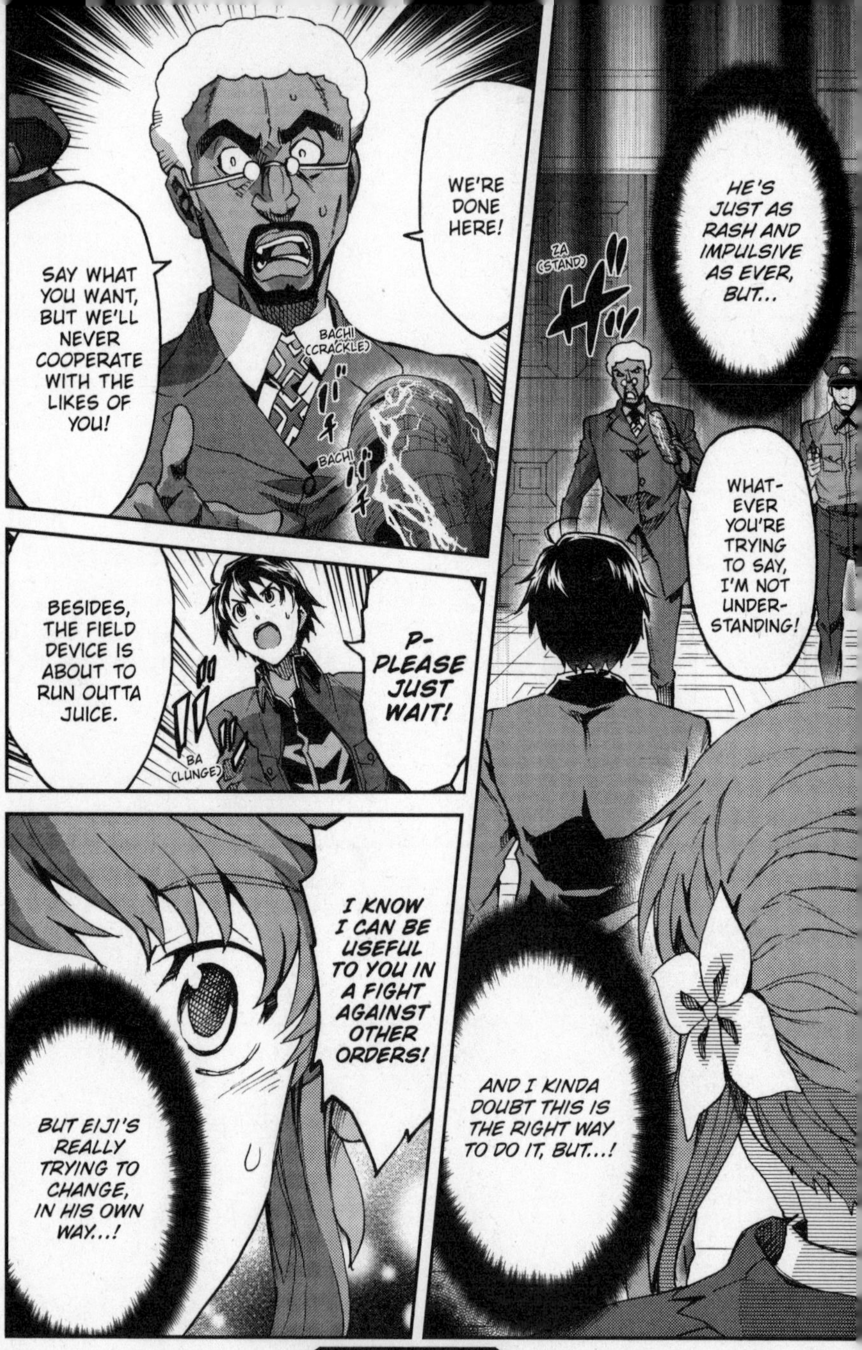
HE'S JUST AS RASH AND IMPULSIVE AS EVER, BUT...
ZA (STAND)
WHAT-EVER YOU'RE TRYING TO SAY, I'M NOT UNDER-STANDING!
AND I KINDA DOUBT THIS IS THE RIGHT WAY TO DO IT, BUT...!
WE'RE DONE HERE!
SAY WHAT YOU WANT, BUT WE'LL NEVER COOPERATE WITH THE LIKES OF YOU!
BACHI (CRACKLE)
BACHI
P-PLEASE JUST WAIT!
BESIDES, THE FIELD DEVICE IS ABOUT TO RUN OUTTA JUICE.
BA (LUNGE)
I KNOW I CAN BE USEFUL TO YOU IN A FIGHT AGAINST OTHER ORDERS!
BUT EIJI'S REALLY TRYING TO CHANGE, IN HIS OWN WAY...!

Subject 45: END

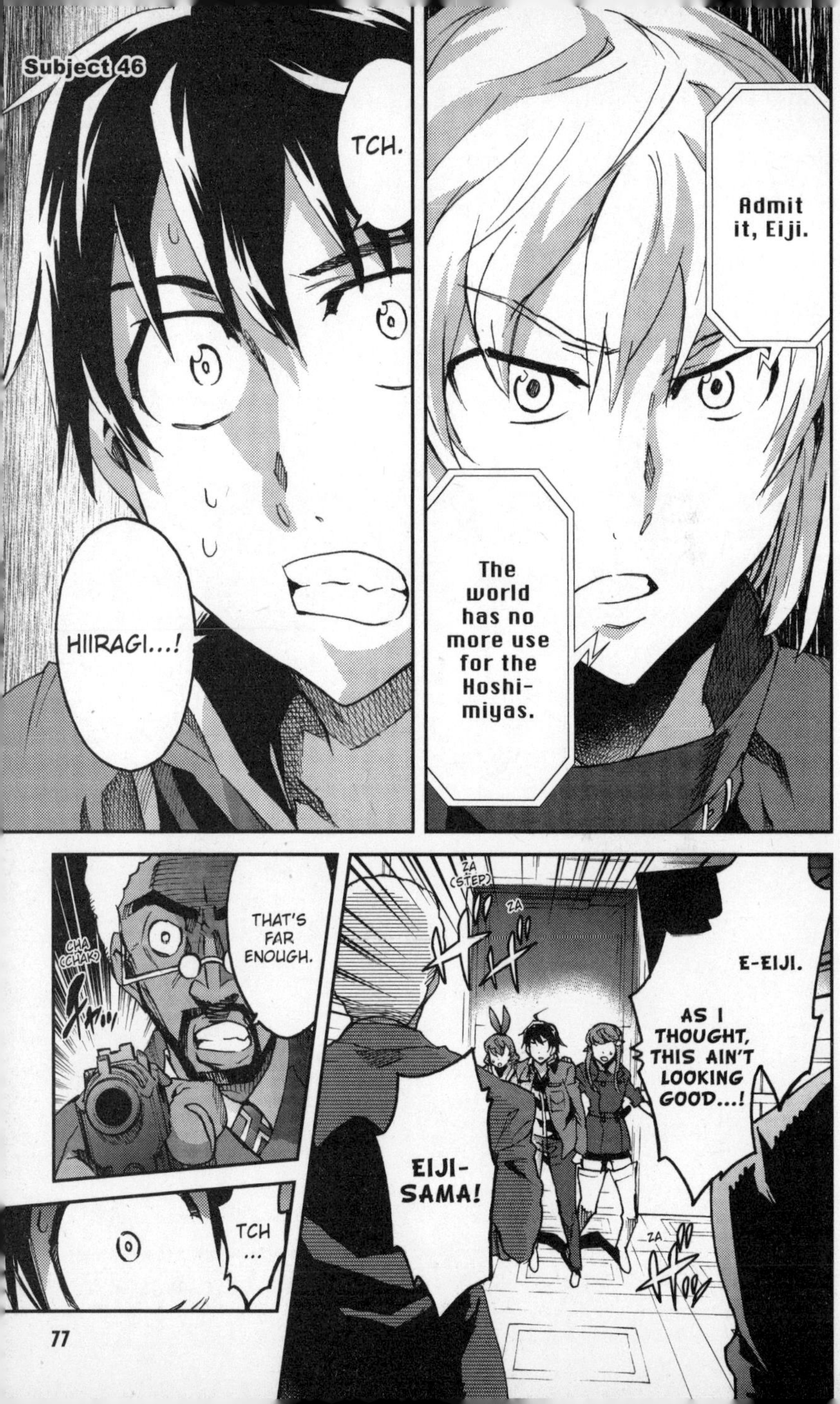
Admit it, Eiji.
The world has no more use for the Hoshimiyas.
TCH.
HIIRAGI...!
ZA (STEP)
ZA
E-EIJI.
AS I THOUGHT, THIS AIN'T LOOKING GOOD...!
EIJI-SAMA!
ZA
THAT'S FAR ENOUGH.
CHA (CHAK)
TCH ...

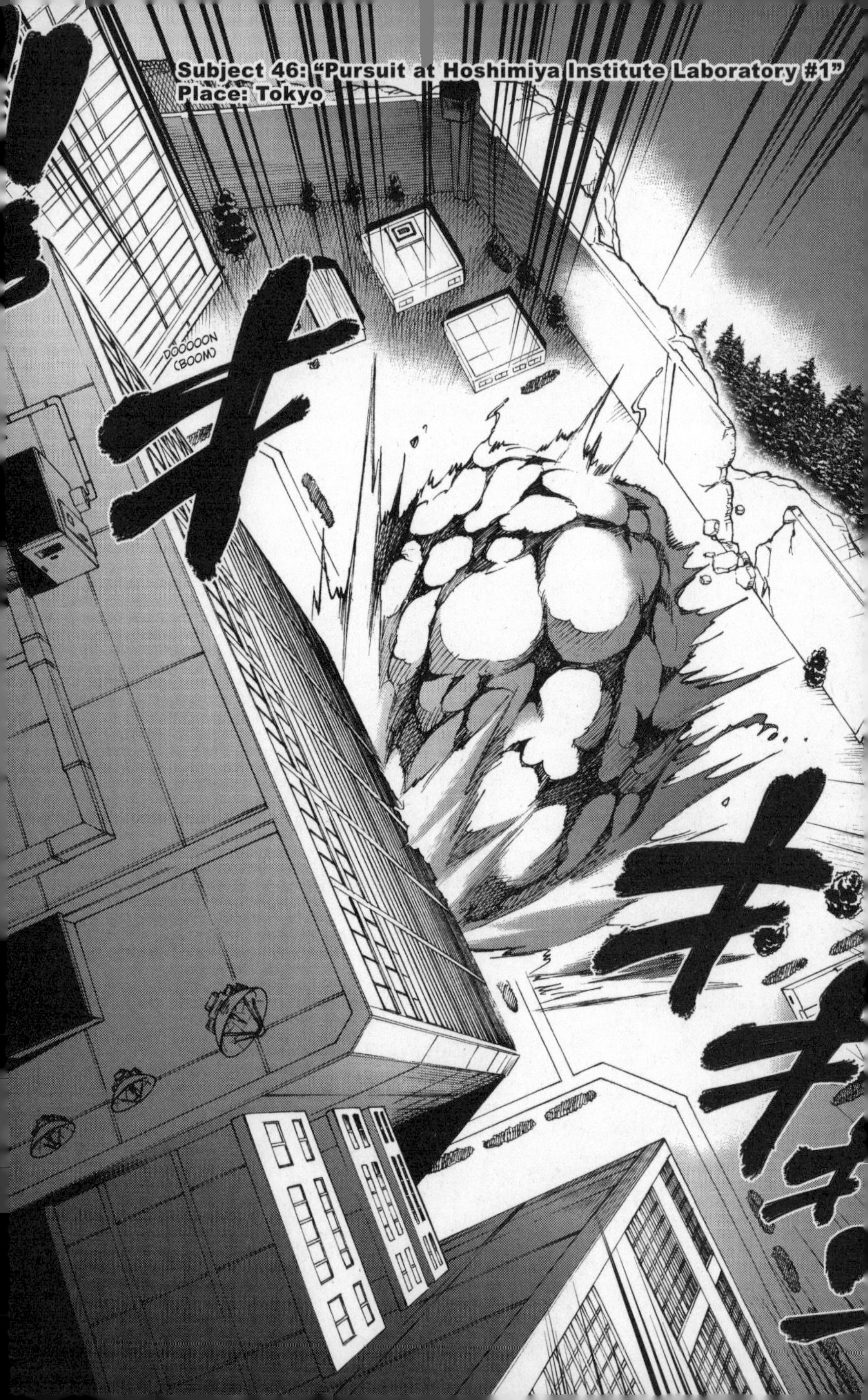
Subject 46: "Pursuit at Hoshimiya Institute Laboratory #1"
Place: Tokyo
DOOOOON
(BOOM)

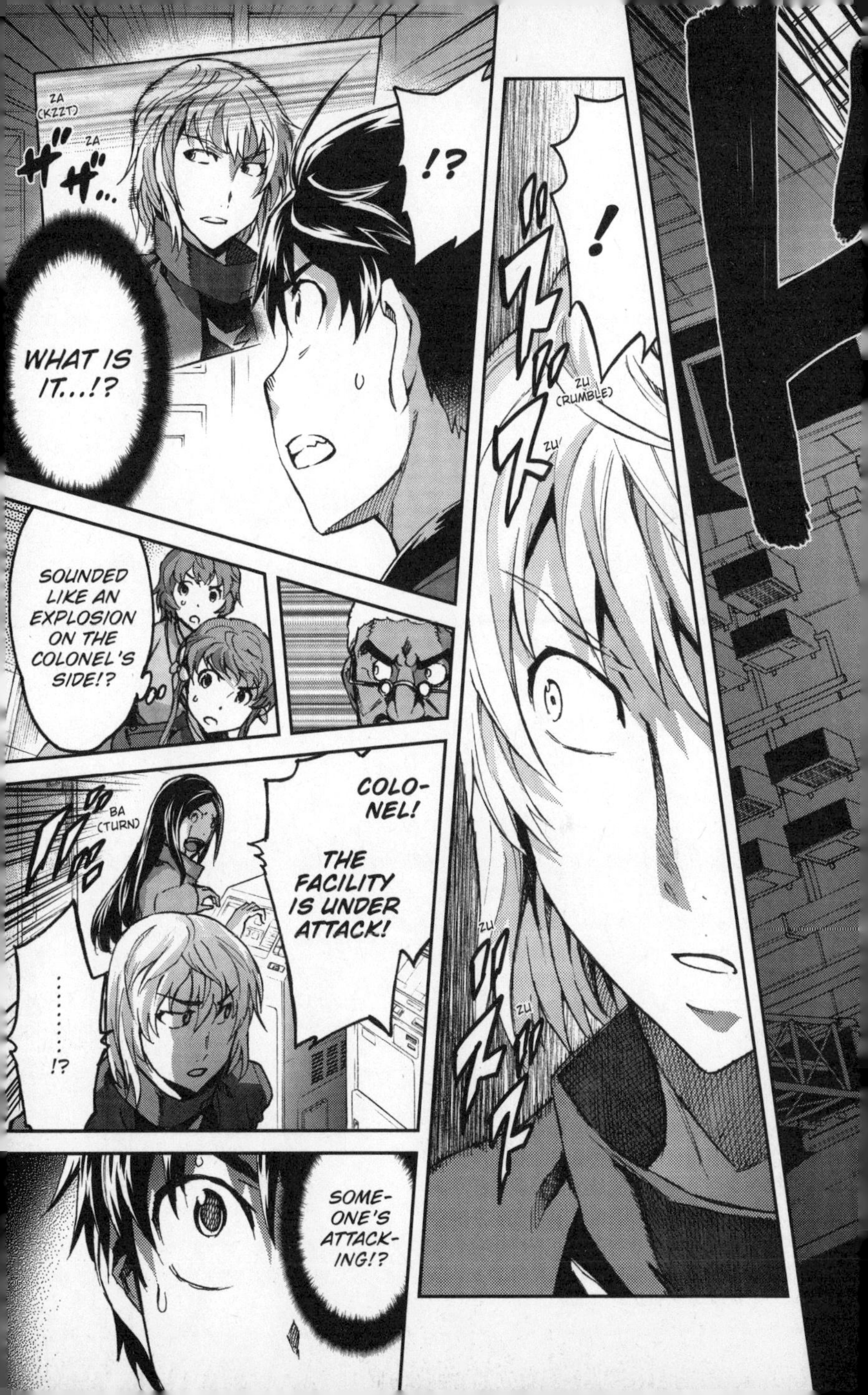
!
ZU (RUMBLE)
ZU
ZU
ZU
!?
ZA (KZZT)
ZA
WHAT IS IT...!?
SOUNDED LIKE AN EXPLOSION ON THE COLONEL'S SIDE!?
COLO-NEL!
THE FACILITY IS UNDER ATTACK!
BA (TURN)
......!?
SOME-ONE'S ATTACK-ING!?

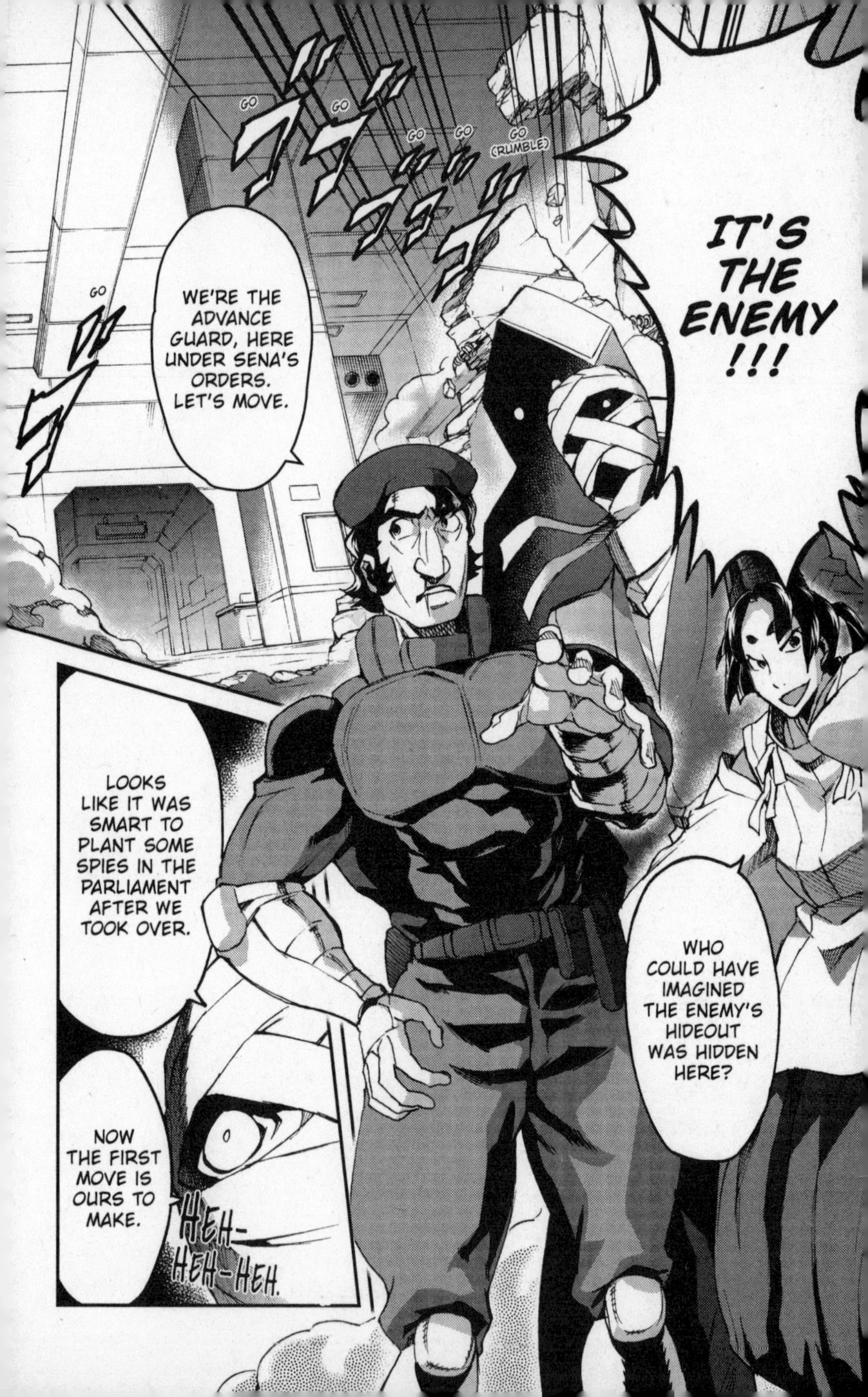
IT'S THE ENEMY!!!
GO GO GO GO GO (RUMBLE)
GO
WE'RE THE ADVANCE GUARD, HERE UNDER SENA'S ORDERS. LET'S MOVE.
WHO COULD HAVE IMAGINED THE ENEMY'S HIDEOUT WAS HIDDEN HERE?
LOOKS LIKE IT WAS SMART TO PLANT SOME SPIES IN THE PARLIAMENT AFTER WE TOOK OVER.
NOW THE FIRST MOVE IS OURS TO MAKE.
HEH-HEH-HEH.

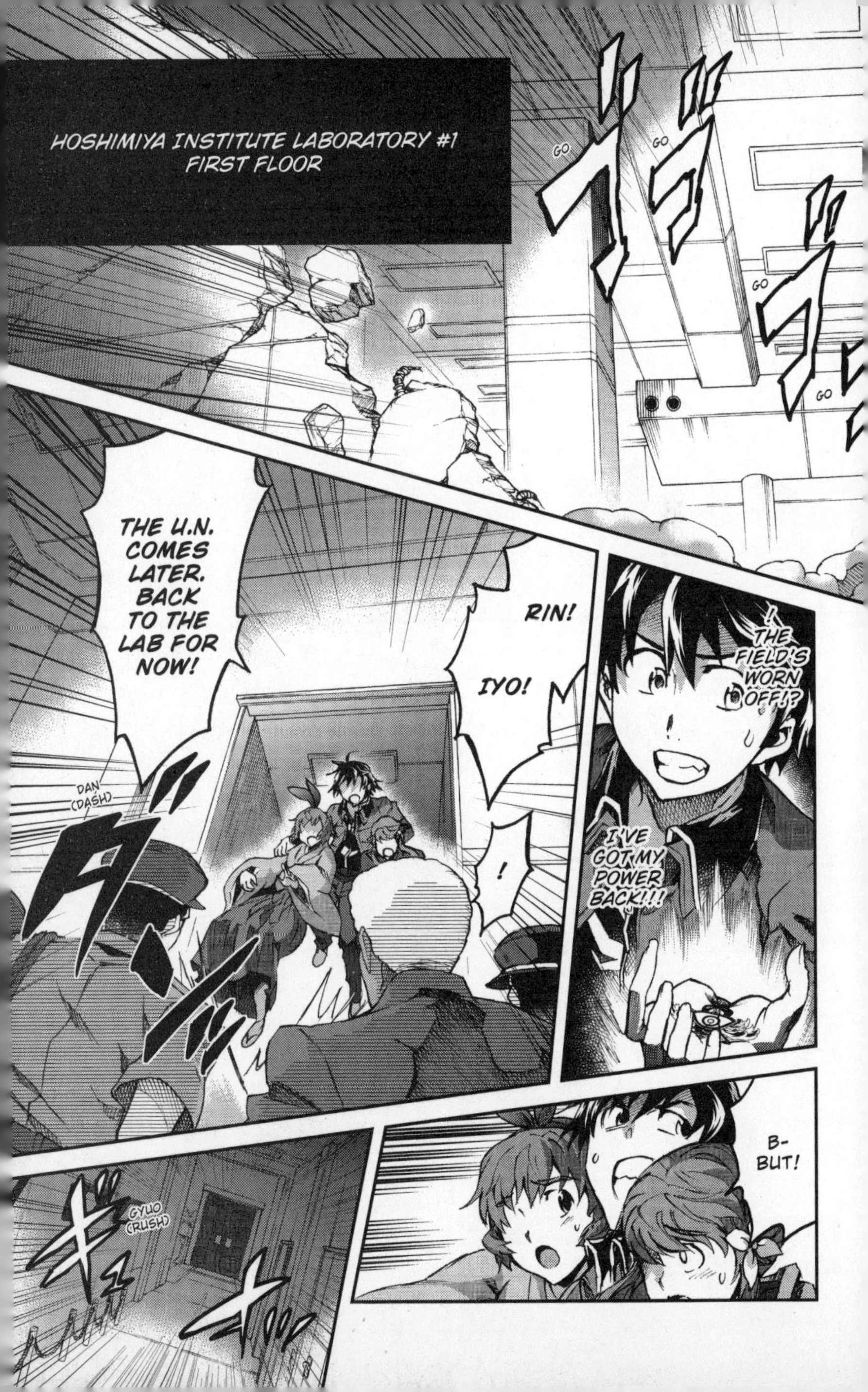
HOSHIMIYA INSTITUTE LABORATORY #1
FIRST FLOOR
GO
GO
GO
GO
! THE FIELD'S WORN OFF!?
I'VE GOT MY POWER BACK!!!
RIN!
IYO!
!
THE U.N. COMES LATER. BACK TO THE LAB FOR NOW!
DAN (DASH)
B-BUT!
GYUO (RUSH)

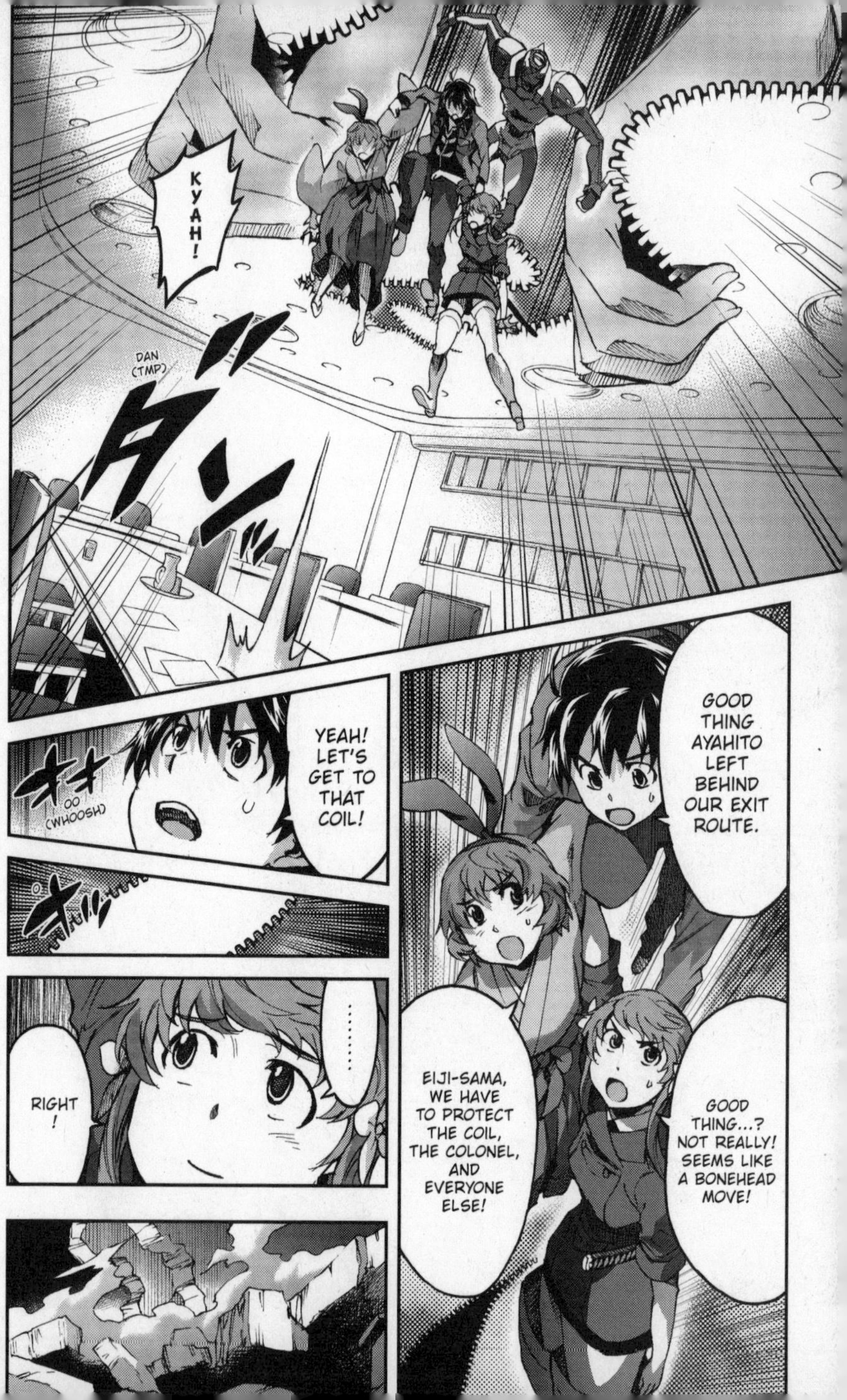
KYAH!
ダン
DAN (TMP)
GOOD THING AYAHITO LEFT BEHIND OUR EXIT ROUTE.
GOOD THING...? NOT REALLY! SEEMS LIKE A BONEHEAD MOVE!
EIJI-SAMA, WE HAVE TO PROTECT THE COIL, THE COLONEL, AND EVERYONE ELSE!
YEAH! LET'S GET TO THAT COIL!
オオ
OO (WHOOSH)
オォ
......
RIGHT!

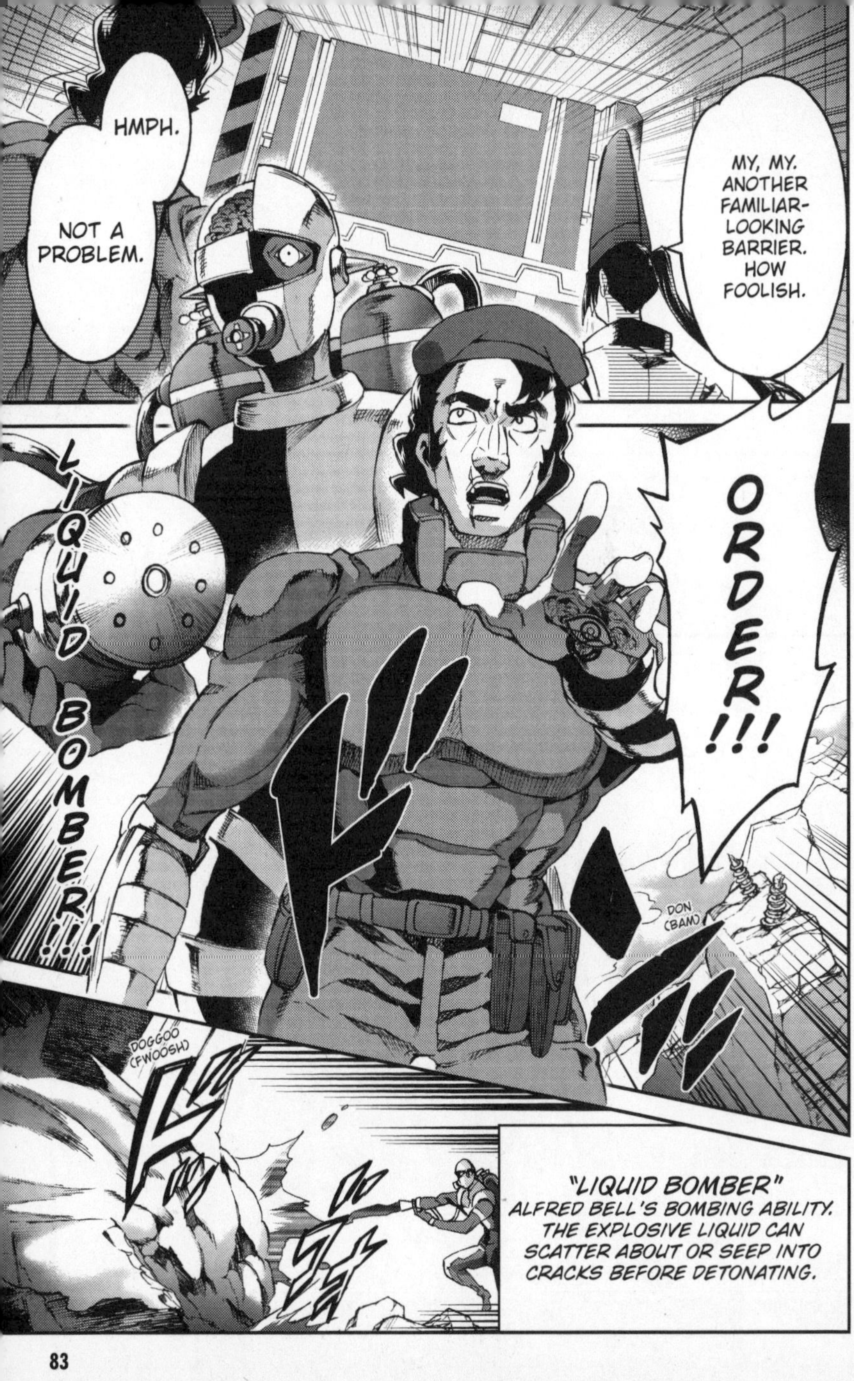
MY, MY. ANOTHER FAMILIAR-LOOKING BARRIER. HOW FOOLISH.
HMPH.
NOT A PROBLEM.
ORDER!!!
DON (BAM)
LIQUID BOMBER!!!
"LIQUID BOMBER"
ALFRED BELL'S BOMBING ABILITY. THE EXPLOSIVE LIQUID CAN SCATTER ABOUT OR SEEP INTO CRACKS BEFORE DETONATING.
DOGGOO (FWOOSH)

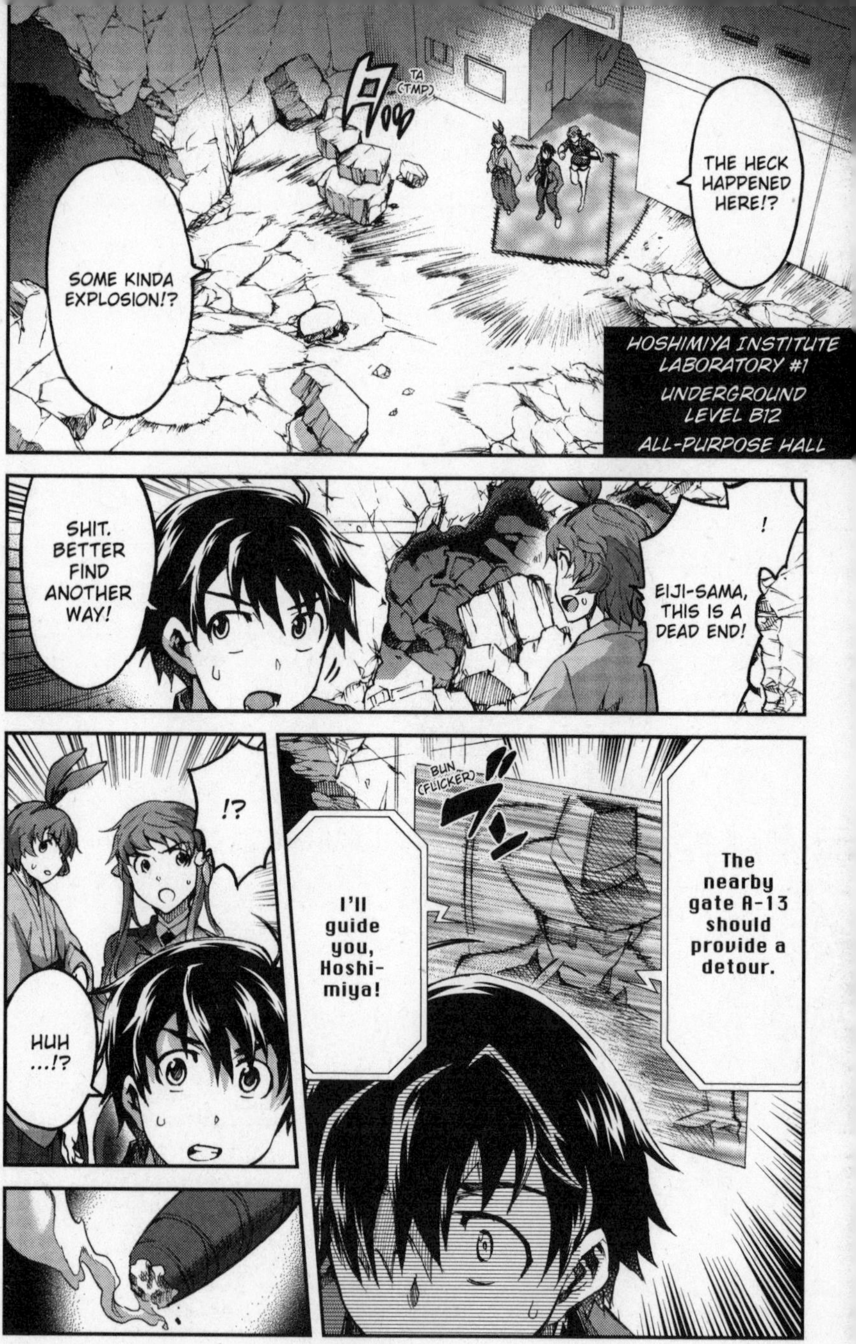
THE HECK HAPPENED HERE!?
TA (TMP)
SOME KINDA EXPLOSION!?
HOSHIMIYA INSTITUTE LABORATORY #1
UNDERGROUND LEVEL B12
ALL-PURPOSE HALL
!
EIJI-SAMA, THIS IS A DEAD END!
SHIT. BETTER FIND ANOTHER WAY!
BUN (FLICKER)
The nearby gate A-13 should provide a detour.
I'll guide you, Hoshimiya!
!?
HUH ...!?

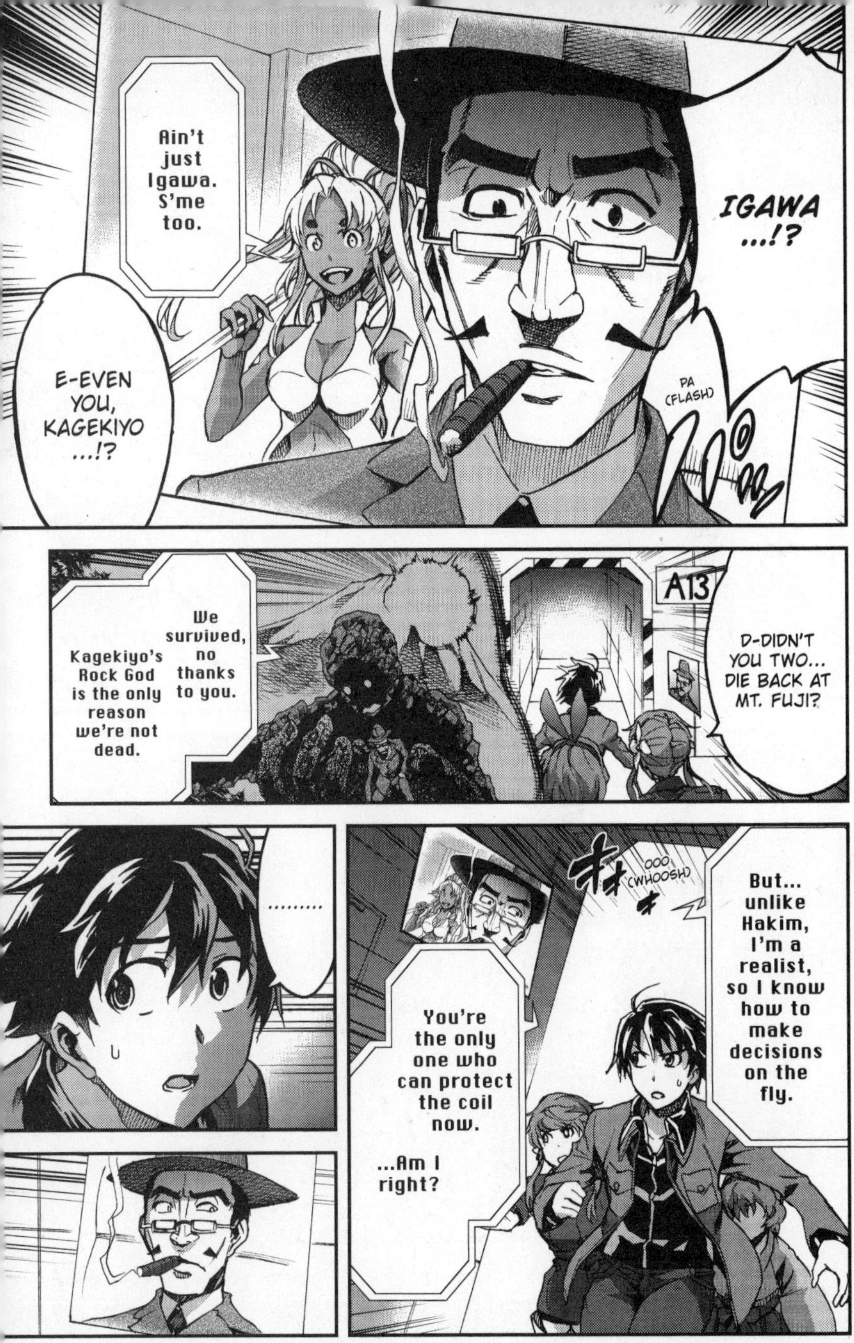
IGAWA ...!?
PA (FLASH)
Ain't just Igawa. S'me too.
E-EVEN YOU, KAGEKIYO ...!?
D-DIDN'T YOU TWO... DIE BACK AT MT. FUJI?
A13
We survived, no thanks to you.
Kagekiyo's Rock God is the only reason we're not dead.
But... unlike Hakim, I'm a realist, so I know how to make decisions on the fly.
OOO (WHOOSH)
You're the only one who can protect the coil now.
...Am I right?
....

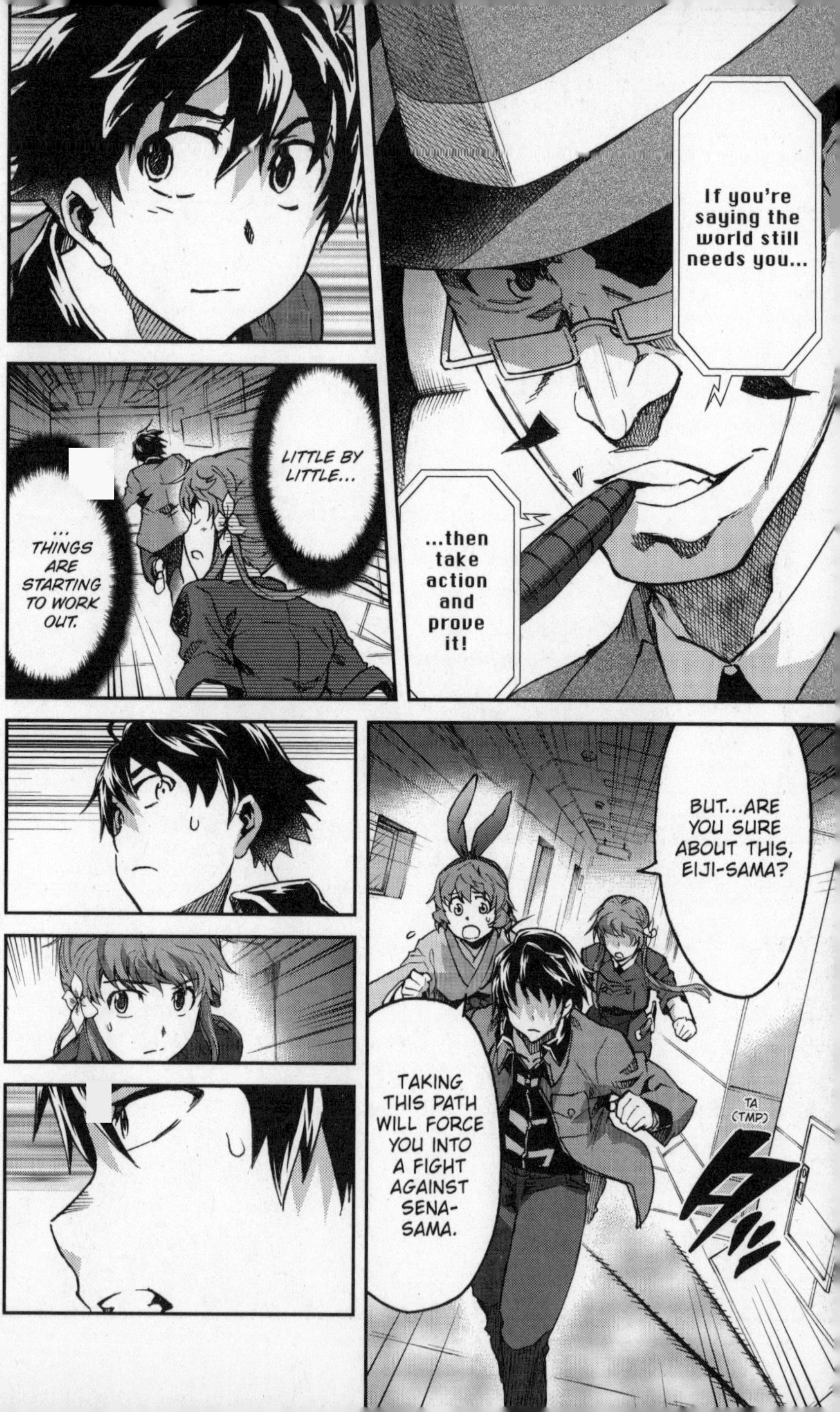
If you're saying the world still needs you...
...then take action and prove it!
LITTLE BY LITTLE...
...THINGS ARE STARTING TO WORK OUT.
BUT...ARE YOU SURE ABOUT THIS, EIJI-SAMA?
TAKING THIS PATH WILL FORCE YOU INTO A FIGHT AGAINST SENA-SAMA.
TA (TMP)

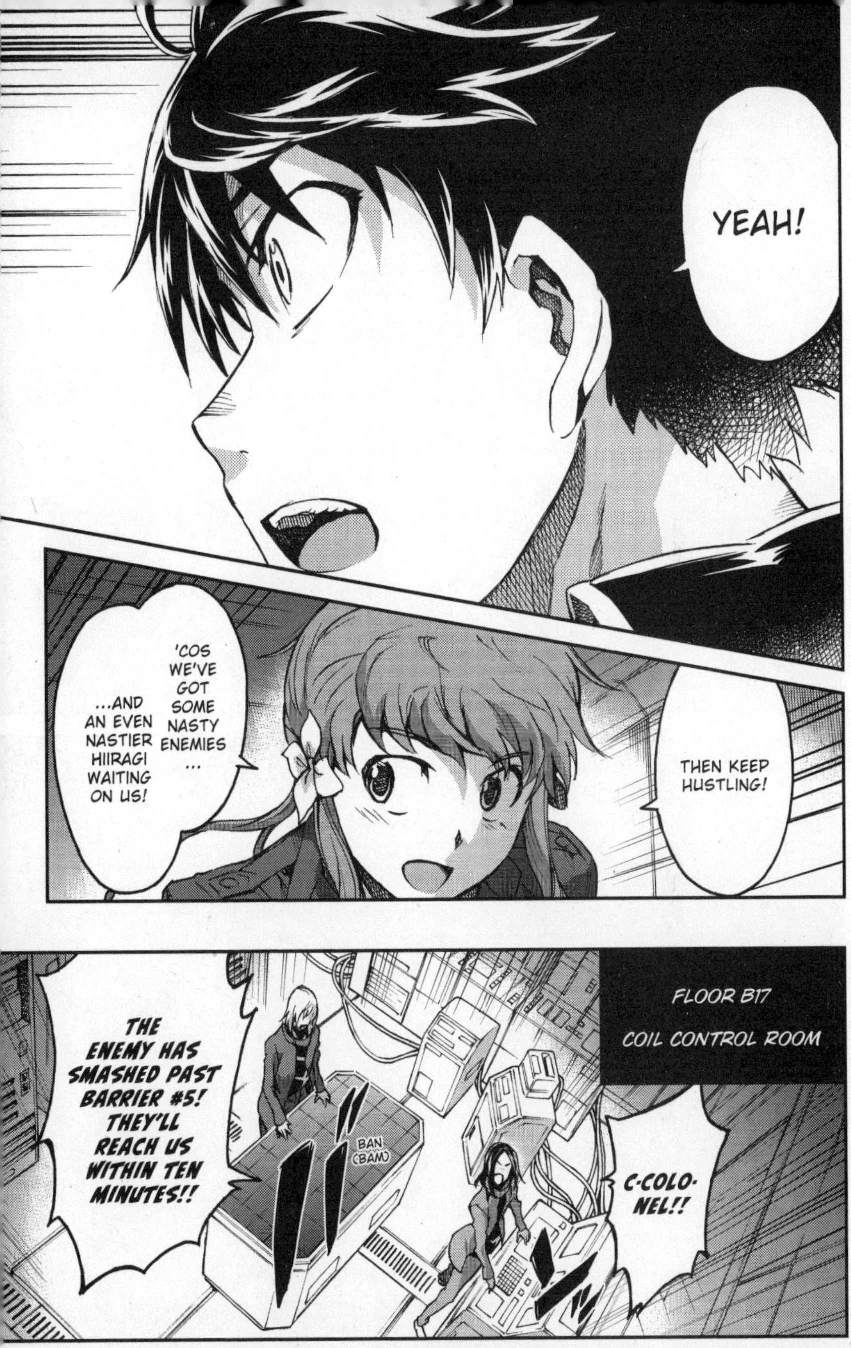
YEAH!
THEN KEEP HUSTLING!
'COS WE'VE GOT SOME NASTY ENEMIES...
...AND AN EVEN NASTIER HIIRAGI WAITING ON US!
FLOOR B17
COIL CONTROL ROOM
C-COLO-NEL!!
BAN (BAM)
THE ENEMY HAS SMASHED PAST BARRIER #5! THEY'LL REACH US WITHIN TEN MINUTES!!

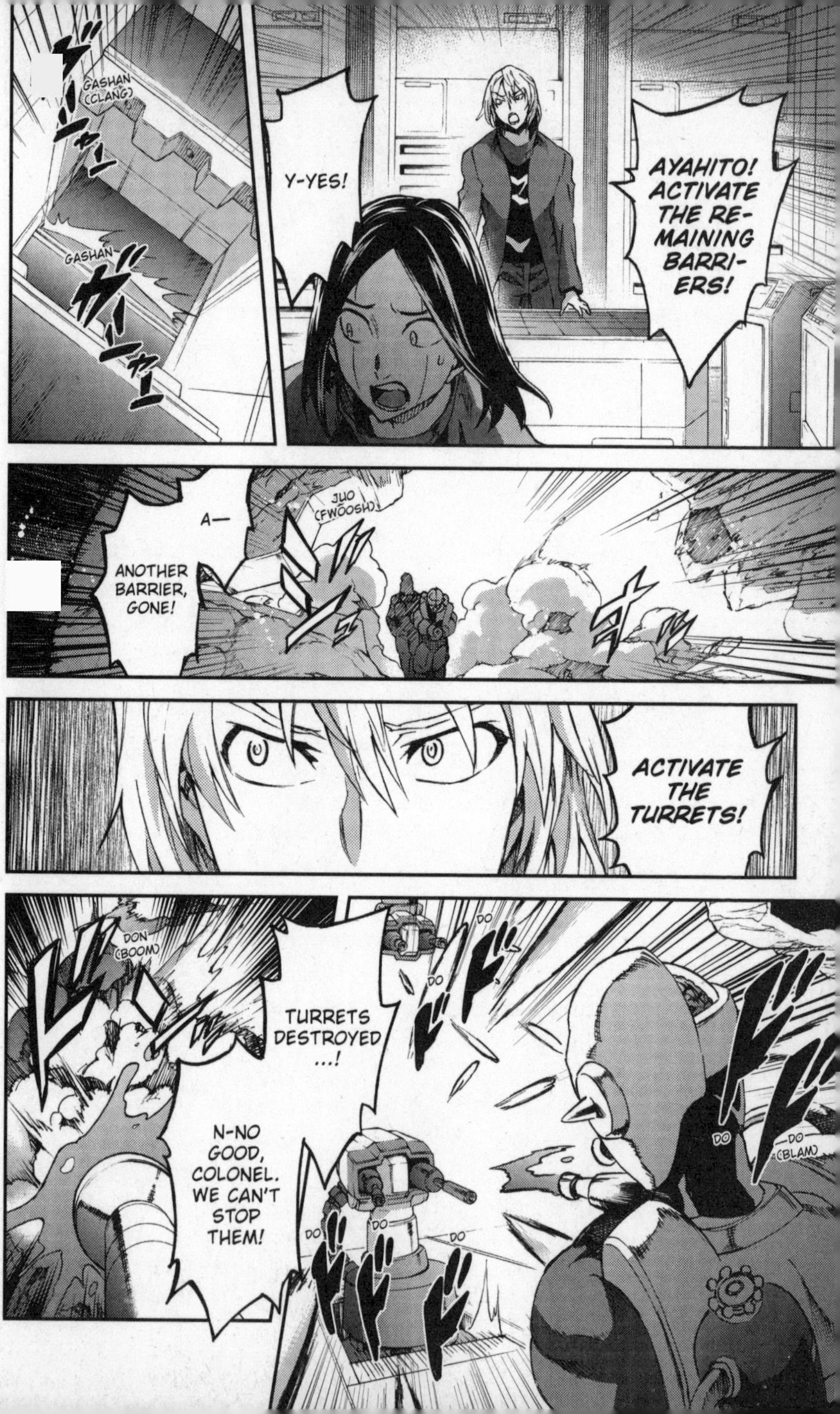
AYAHITO! ACTIVATE THE RE-MAINING BARRI-ERS!
Y-YES!
GASHAN (CLANG)
GASHAN
JUO (FWOOSH)
A—
ANOTHER BARRIER, GONE!
ACTIVATE THE TURRETS!
DO
DO
DO
DO (BLAM)
TURRETS DESTROYED ...!
N-NO GOOD, COLONEL. WE CAN'T STOP THEM!
DO
DO
DO
DON (BOOM)

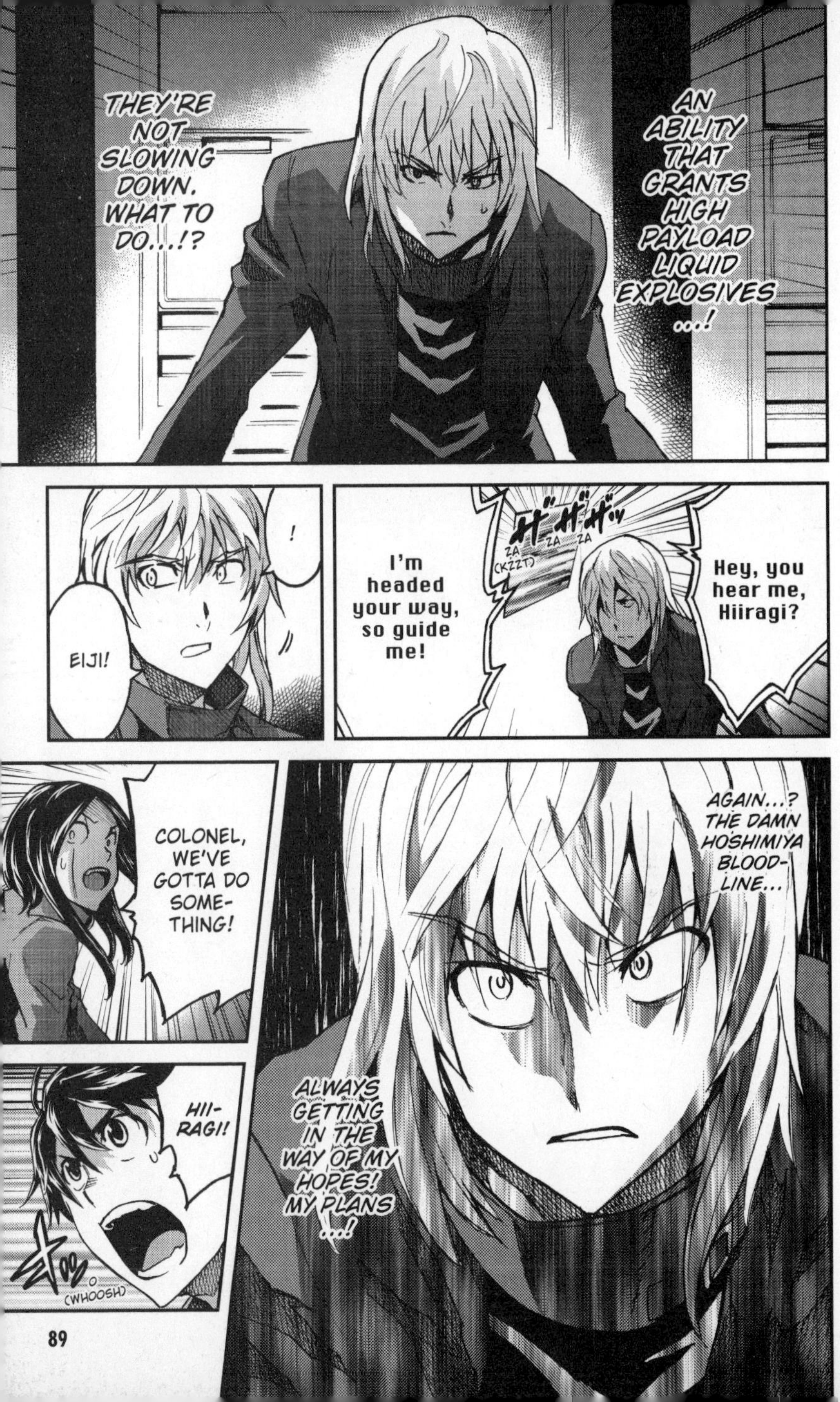
AN ABILITY THAT GRANTS HIGH PAYLOAD LIQUID EXPLOSIVES...!
THEY'RE NOT SLOWING DOWN. WHAT TO DO...!?
Hey, you hear me, Hiiragi?
ZA ZA ZA (KZZT)
I'm headed your way, so guide me!
!
EIJI!
AGAIN...? THE DAMN HOSHIMIYA BLOOD-LINE...
ALWAYS GETTING IN THE WAY OF MY HOPES! MY PLANS...!
COLONEL, WE'VE GOTTA DO SOME-THING!
HII-RAGI!
O (WHOOSH)

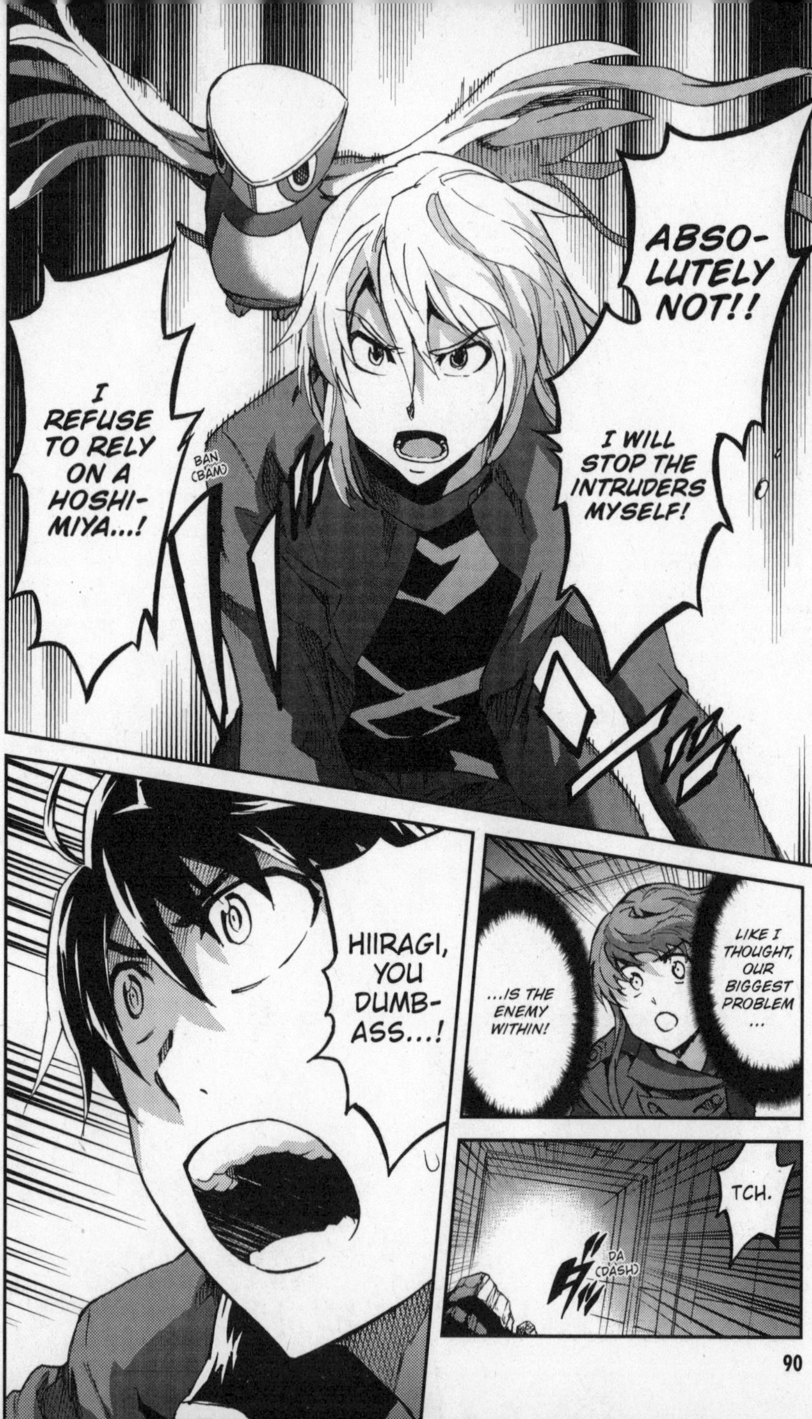
ABSO-
LUTELY
NOT!!
I WILL
STOP THE
INTRUDERS
MYSELF!
BAN
(BAM)
I
REFUSE
TO RELY
ON A
HOSHI-
MIYA...!
LIKE I
THOUGHT,
OUR
BIGGEST
PROBLEM
...
...IS THE
ENEMY
WITHIN!
TCH.
DA
(DASH)
HIIRAGI,
YOU
DUMB-
ASS...!

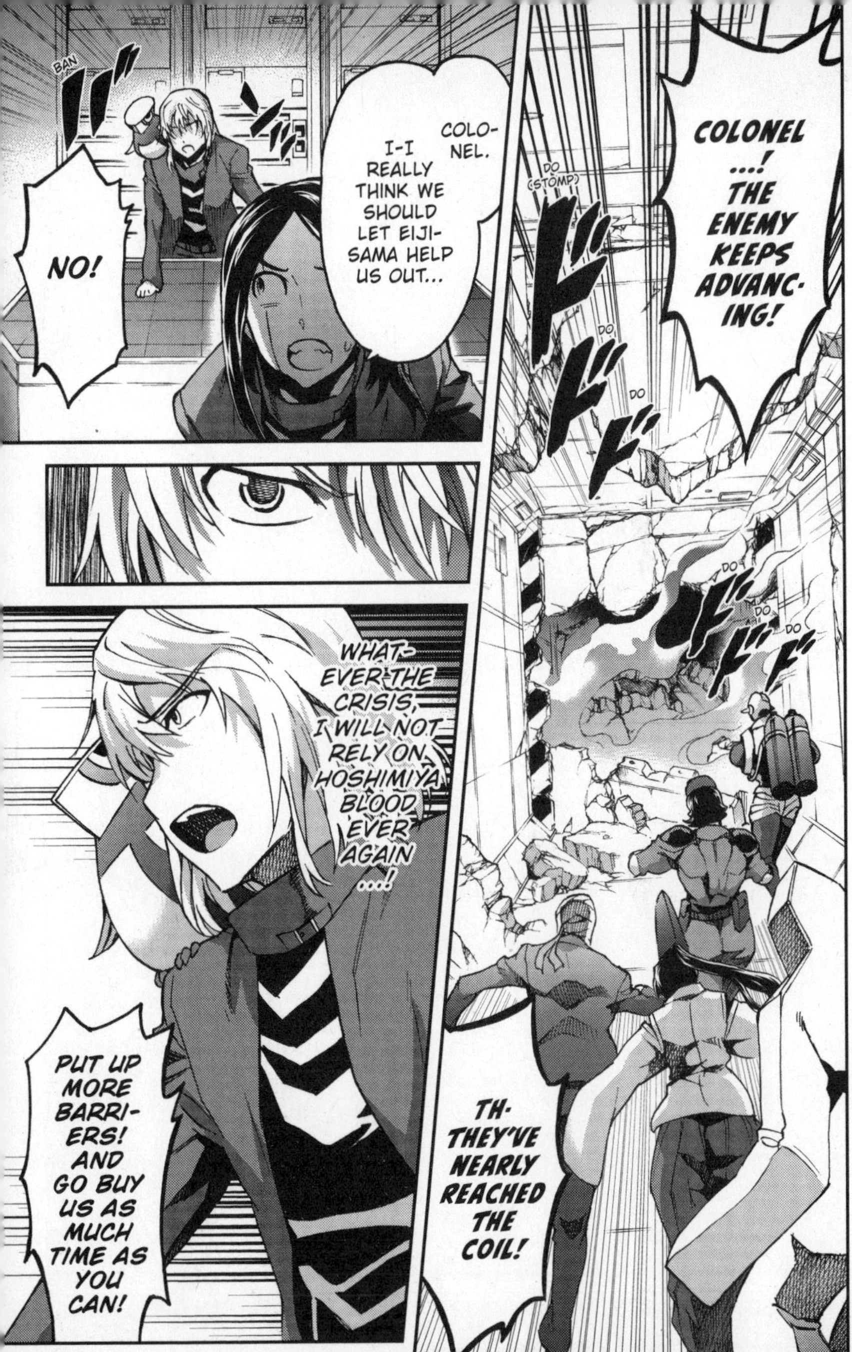
COLONEL ....! THE ENEMY KEEPS ADVANCING!
DO (STOMP)
DO
DO
DO
DO
DO
TH-THEY'VE NEARLY REACHED THE COIL!
BAN
COLONEL.
I-I REALLY THINK WE SHOULD LET EIJI-SAMA HELP US OUT...
NO!
WHATEVER THE CRISIS, I WILL NOT RELY ON HOSHIMIYA BLOOD EVER AGAIN ...!
PUT UP MORE BARRIERS! AND GO BUY US AS MUCH TIME AS YOU CAN!

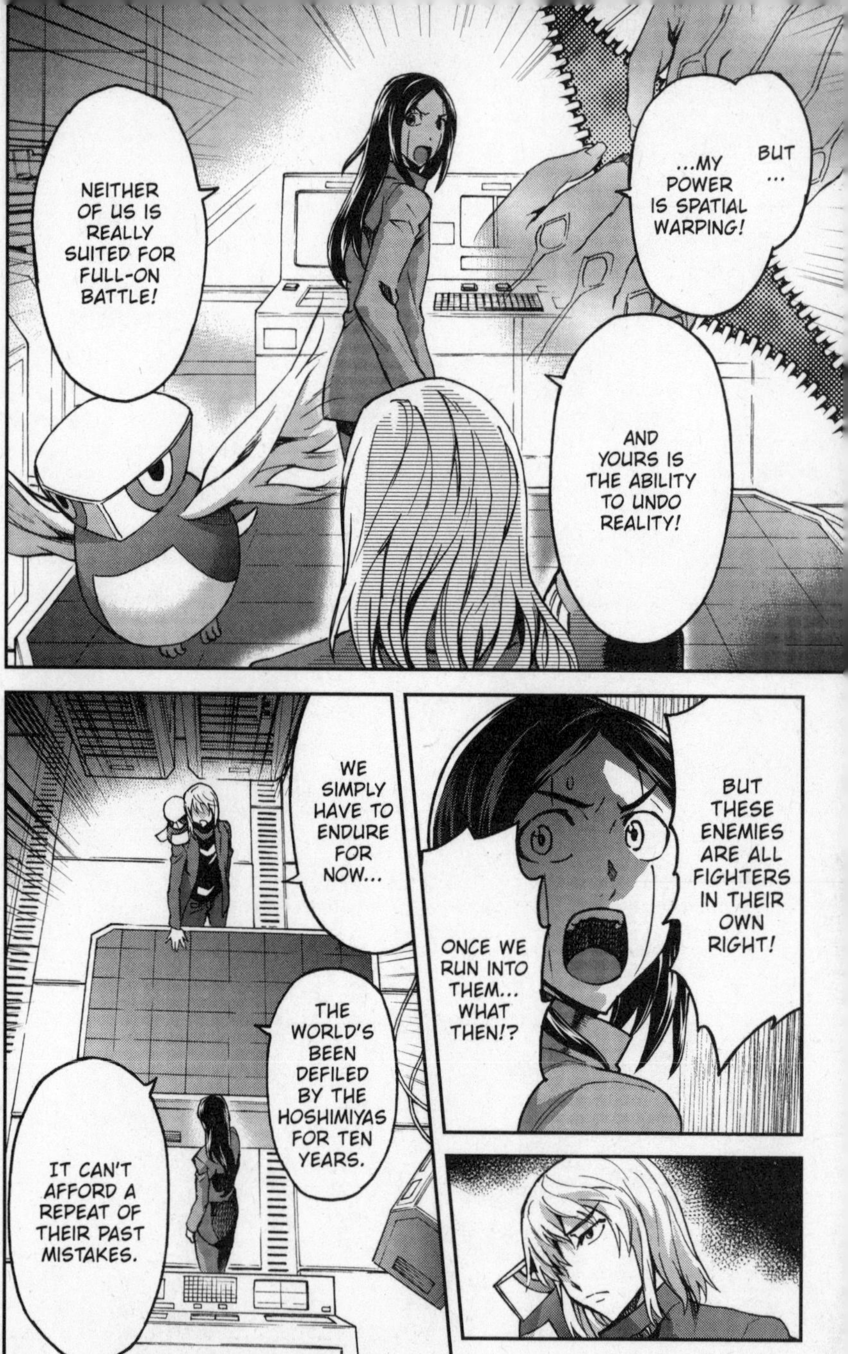
BUT... ...MY POWER IS SPATIAL WARPING!
AND YOURS IS THE ABILITY TO UNDO REALITY!
NEITHER OF US IS REALLY SUITED FOR FULL-ON BATTLE!
BUT THESE ENEMIES ARE ALL FIGHTERS IN THEIR OWN RIGHT!
ONCE WE RUN INTO THEM... WHAT THEN!?
WE SIMPLY HAVE TO ENDURE FOR NOW...
THE WORLD'S BEEN DEFILED BY THE HOSHIMIYAS FOR TEN YEARS.
IT CAN'T AFFORD A REPEAT OF THEIR PAST MISTAKES.

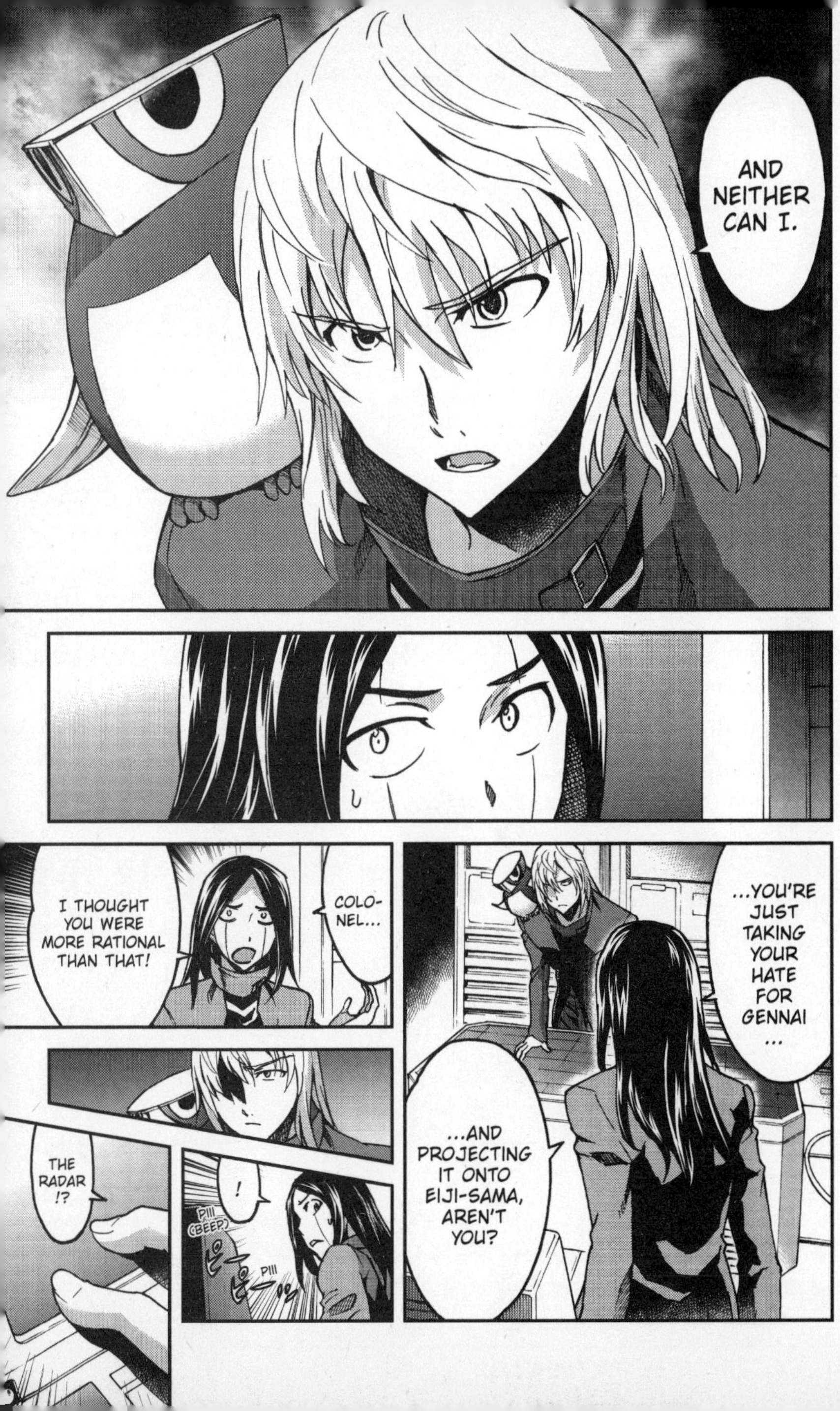
AND NEITHER CAN I.
...YOU'RE JUST TAKING YOUR HATE FOR GENNAI ...
...AND PROJECTING IT ONTO EIJI-SAMA, AREN'T YOU?
COLO-NEL...
I THOUGHT YOU WERE MORE RATIONAL THAN THAT!
!
PIII (BEEP)
PIII
THE RADAR !?

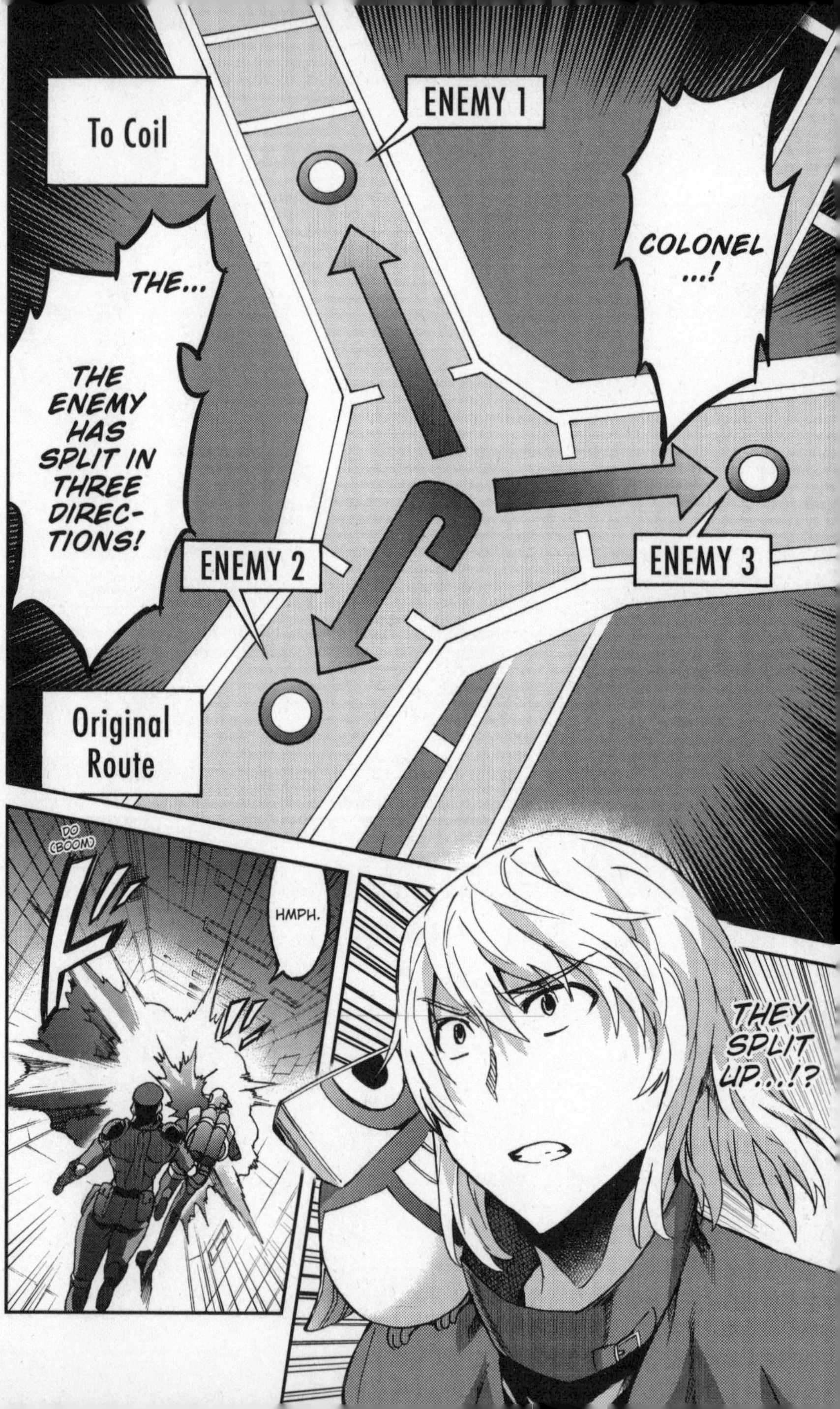
COLONEL ...!
ENEMY 1
To Coil
THE...
THE ENEMY HAS SPLIT IN THREE DIRECTIONS!
ENEMY 3
ENEMY 2
Original Route
THEY SPLIT UP...!?
HMPH.
DO (BOOM)

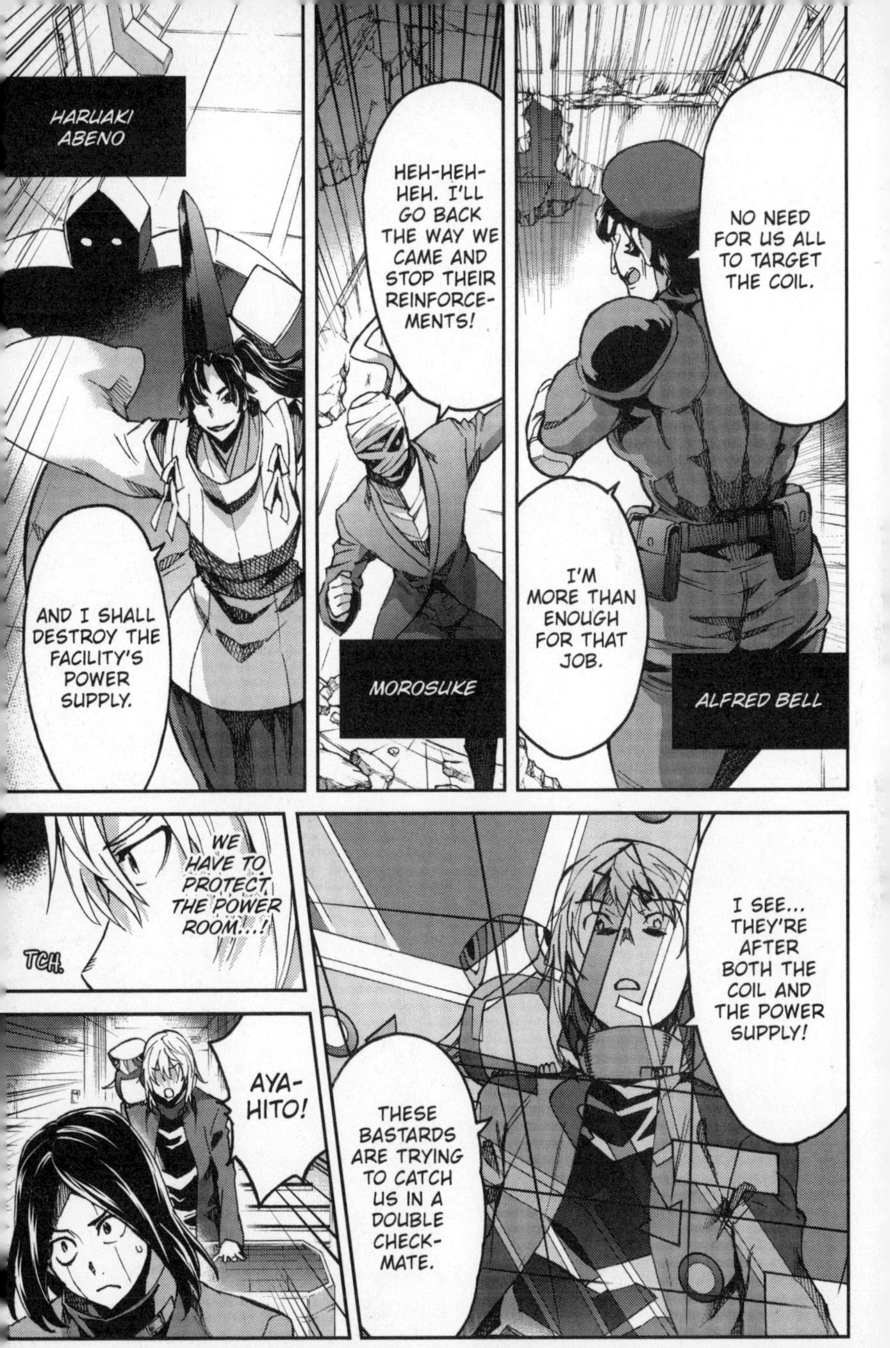
NO NEED FOR US ALL TO TARGET THE COIL.
I'M MORE THAN ENOUGH FOR THAT JOB.
ALFRED BELL
HEH-HEH-HEH. I'LL GO BACK THE WAY WE CAME AND STOP THEIR REINFORCE-MENTS!
MOROSUKE
HARUAKI ABENO
AND I SHALL DESTROY THE FACILITY'S POWER SUPPLY.
I SEE... THEY'RE AFTER BOTH THE COIL AND THE POWER SUPPLY!
THESE BASTARDS ARE TRYING TO CATCH US IN A DOUBLE CHECK-MATE.
WE HAVE TO PROTECT THE POWER ROOM...!
TCH.
AYA-HITO!

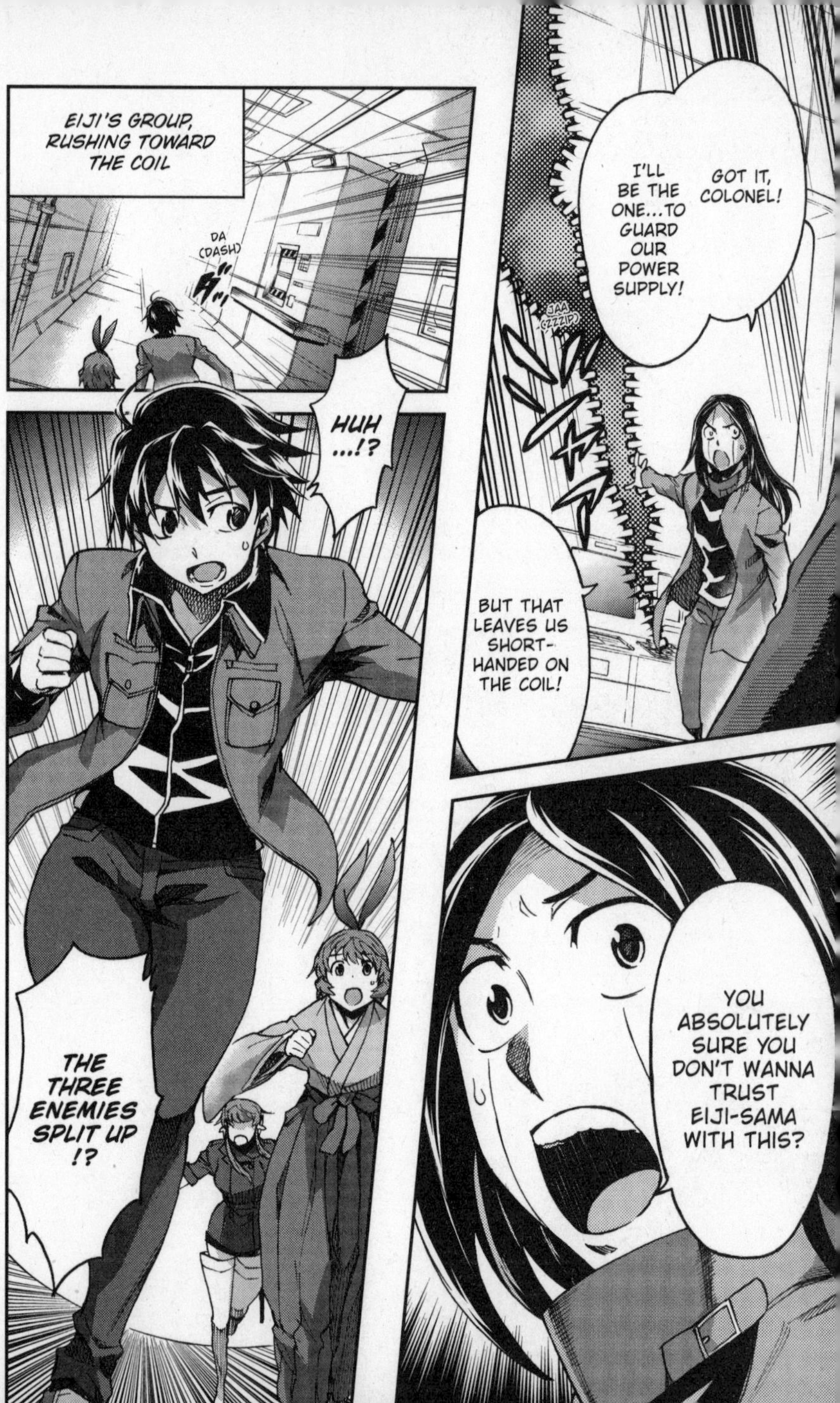
GOT IT, COLONEL!
I'LL BE THE ONE...TO GUARD OUR POWER SUPPLY!
JAA (ZZZIP)
BUT THAT LEAVES US SHORT-HANDED ON THE COIL!
YOU ABSOLUTELY SURE YOU DON'T WANNA TRUST EIJI-SAMA WITH THIS?
EIJI'S GROUP, RUSHING TOWARD THE COIL
DA (DASH)
HUH ...!?
THE THREE ENEMIES SPLIT UP !?

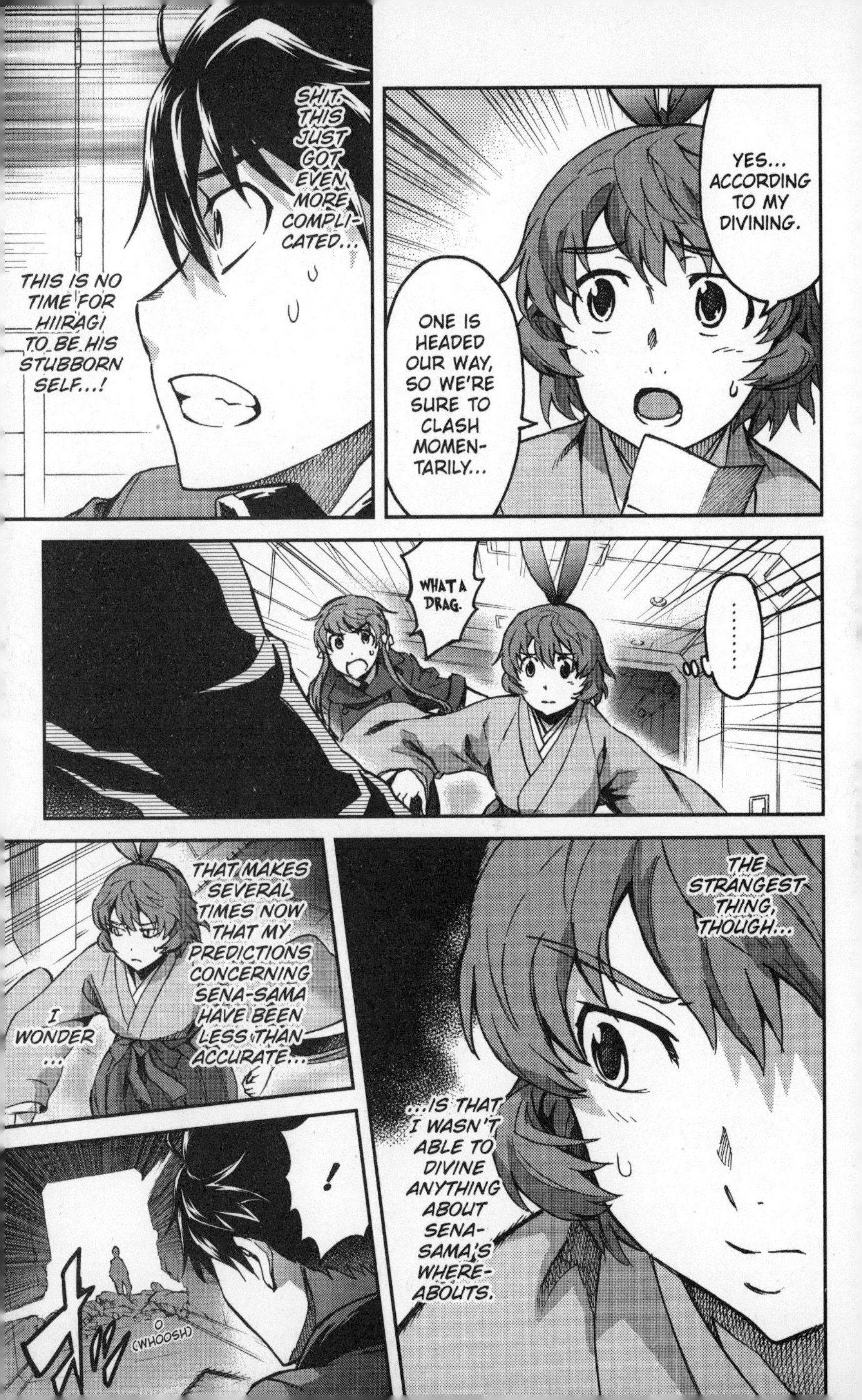
YES... ACCORDING TO MY DIVINING.
ONE IS HEADED OUR WAY, SO WE'RE SURE TO CLASH MOMENTARILY...
SHIT. THIS JUST GOT EVEN MORE COMPLICATED...
THIS IS NO TIME FOR HIIRAGI TO BE HIS STUBBORN SELF...!
......
WHAT A DRAG.
THE STRANGEST THING, THOUGH...
...IS THAT I WASN'T ABLE TO DIVINE ANYTHING ABOUT SENA-SAMA'S WHEREABOUTS.
THAT MAKES SEVERAL TIMES NOW THAT MY PREDICTIONS CONCERNING SENA-SAMA HAVE BEEN LESS THAN ACCURATE...
I WONDER...
!
O (WHOOSH)

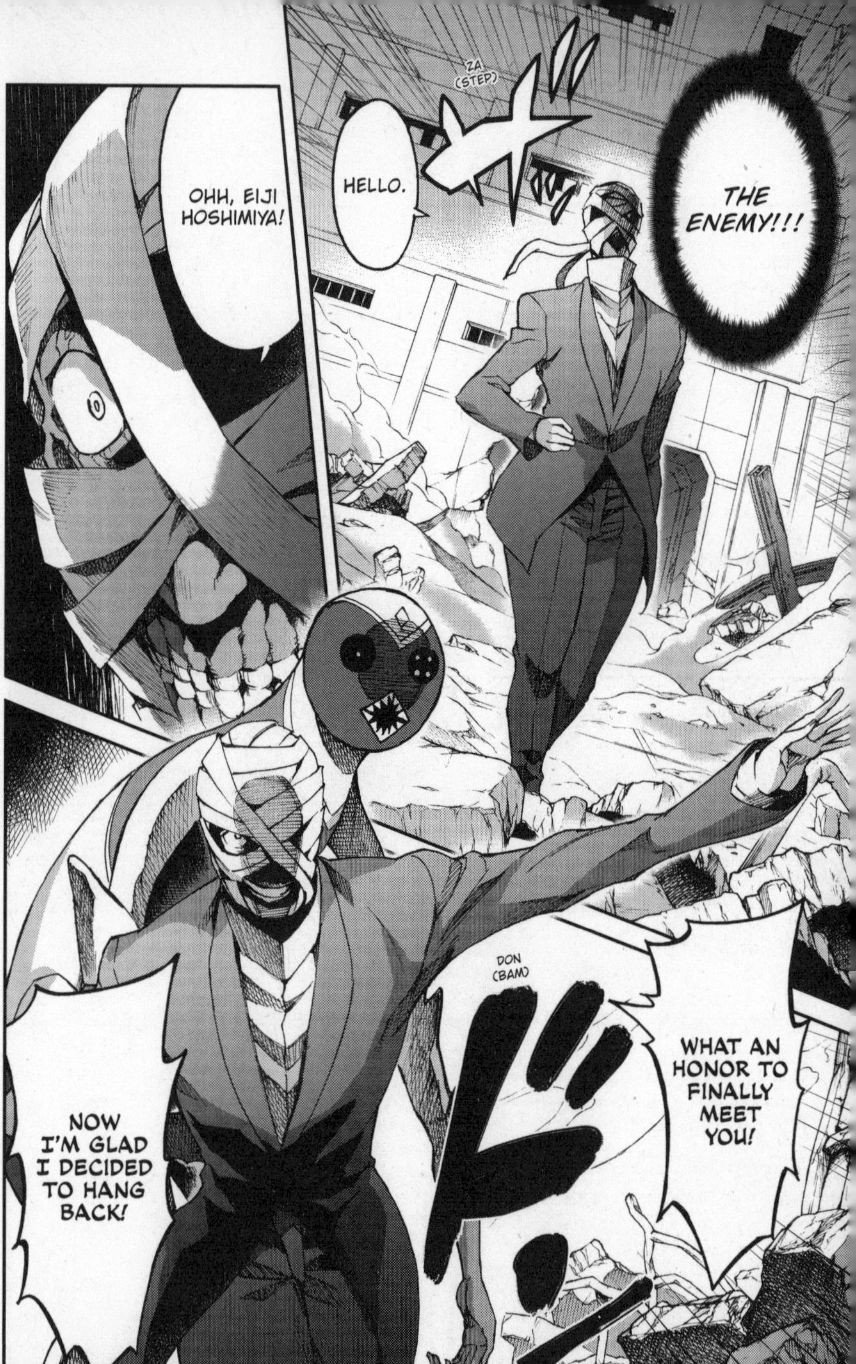
ZA (STEP)
THE ENEMY!!!
HELLO.
OHH, EIJI HOSHIMIYA!
WHAT AN HONOR TO FINALLY MEET YOU!
DON (BAM)
NOW I'M GLAD I DECIDED TO HANG BACK!

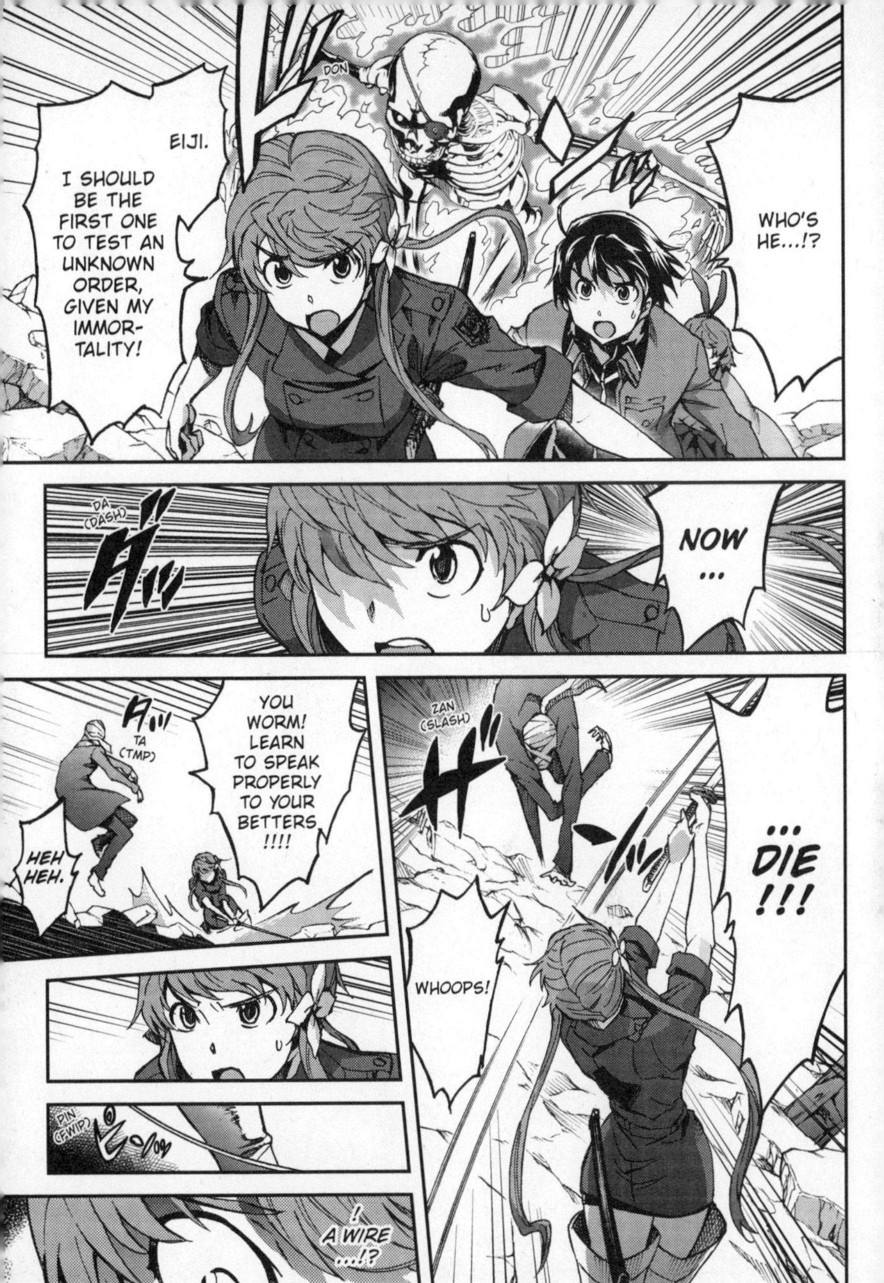
DON
WHO'S HE...!?
EIJI.
I SHOULD BE THE FIRST ONE TO TEST AN UNKNOWN ORDER, GIVEN MY IMMORTALITY!
NOW ...
DA (DASH)
ZAN (SLASH)
... DIE !!!
WHOOPS!
YOU WORM! LEARN TO SPEAK PROPERLY TO YOUR BETTERS !!!!
TA (TMP)
HEH HEH.
PIN (FWIP)
! A WIRE ...!?

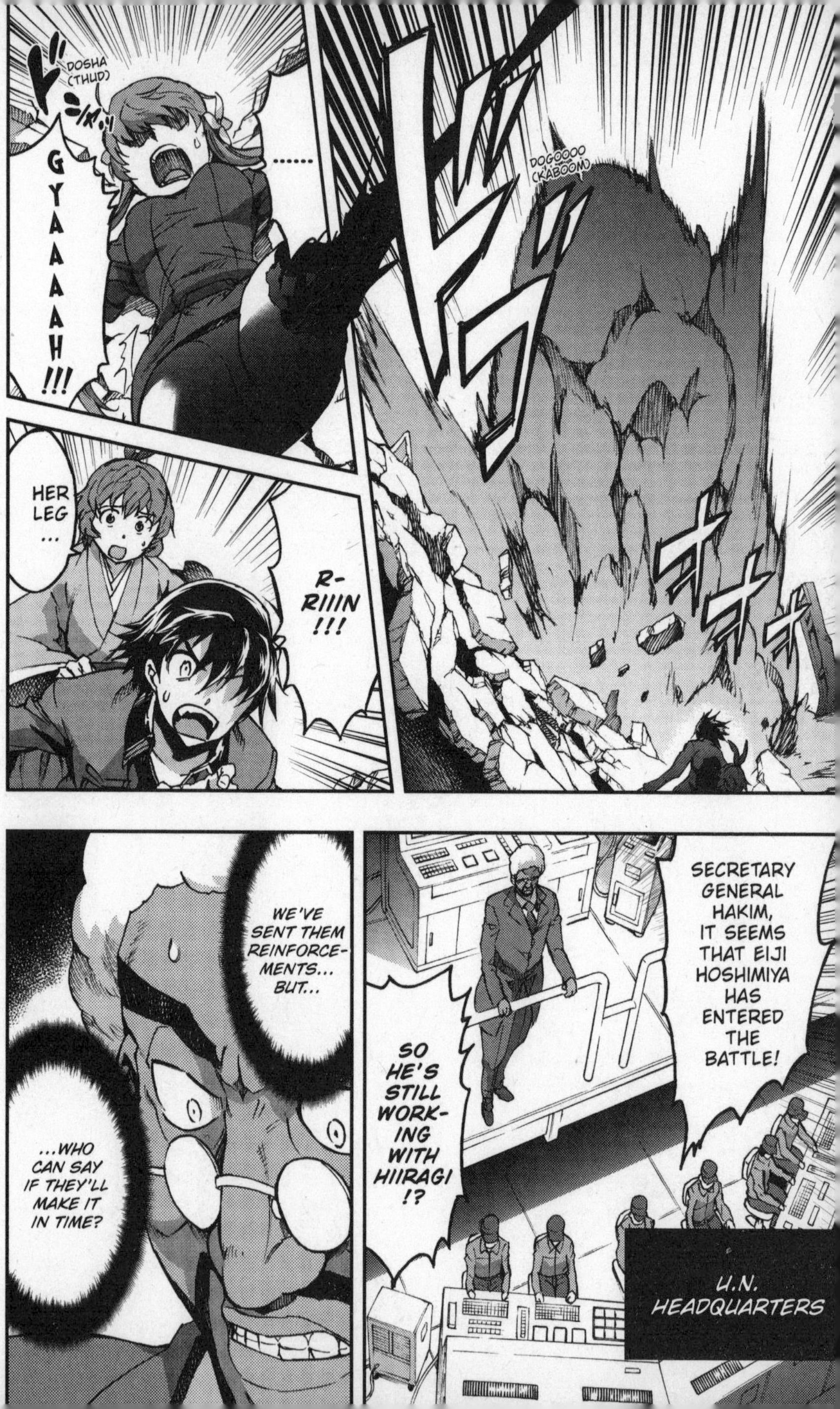

DOGOOOO (KABOOM)
DOSHA (THUD)
......
GYAAAAH!!!
HER LEG...
R-RIIIN!!!
U.N. HEADQUARTERS
SECRETARY GENERAL HAKIM, IT SEEMS THAT EIJI HOSHIMIYA HAS ENTERED THE BATTLE!
SO HE'S STILL WORKING WITH HIIRAGI!?
WE'VE SENT THEM REINFORCEMENTS... BUT...
...WHO CAN SAY IF THEY'LL MAKE IT IN TIME?

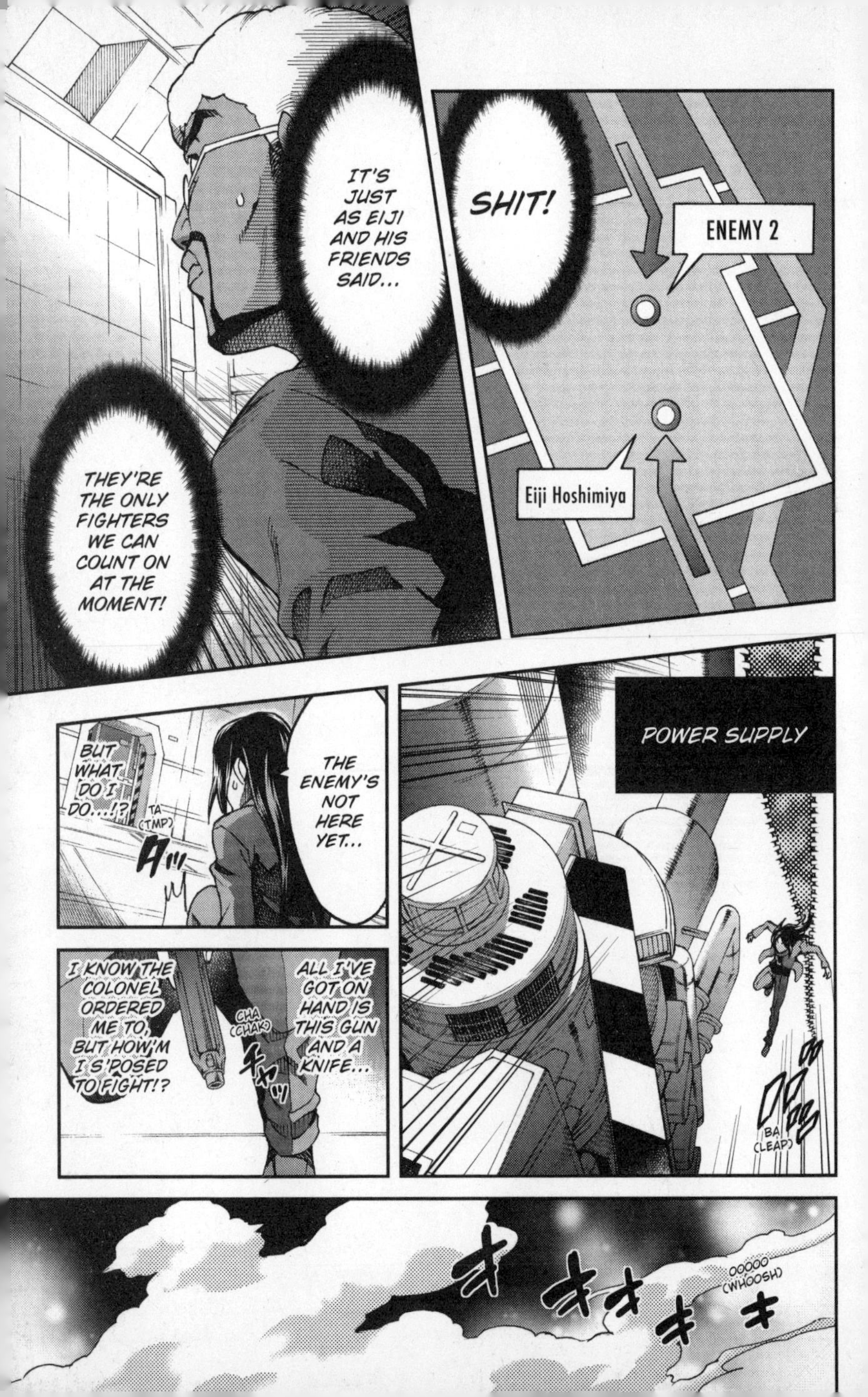
SHIT!
ENEMY 2
Eiji Hoshimiya
IT'S JUST AS EIJI AND HIS FRIENDS SAID...
THEY'RE THE ONLY FIGHTERS WE CAN COUNT ON AT THE MOMENT!
POWER SUPPLY
BA (LEAP)
THE ENEMY'S NOT HERE YET...
BUT WHAT DO I DO...!?
TA (TMP)
ALL I'VE GOT ON HAND IS THIS GUN AND A KNIFE...
I KNOW THE COLONEL ORDERED ME TO, BUT HOW'M I S'POSED TO FIGHT!?
CHA (CHAK)
OOOOO (WHOOSH)

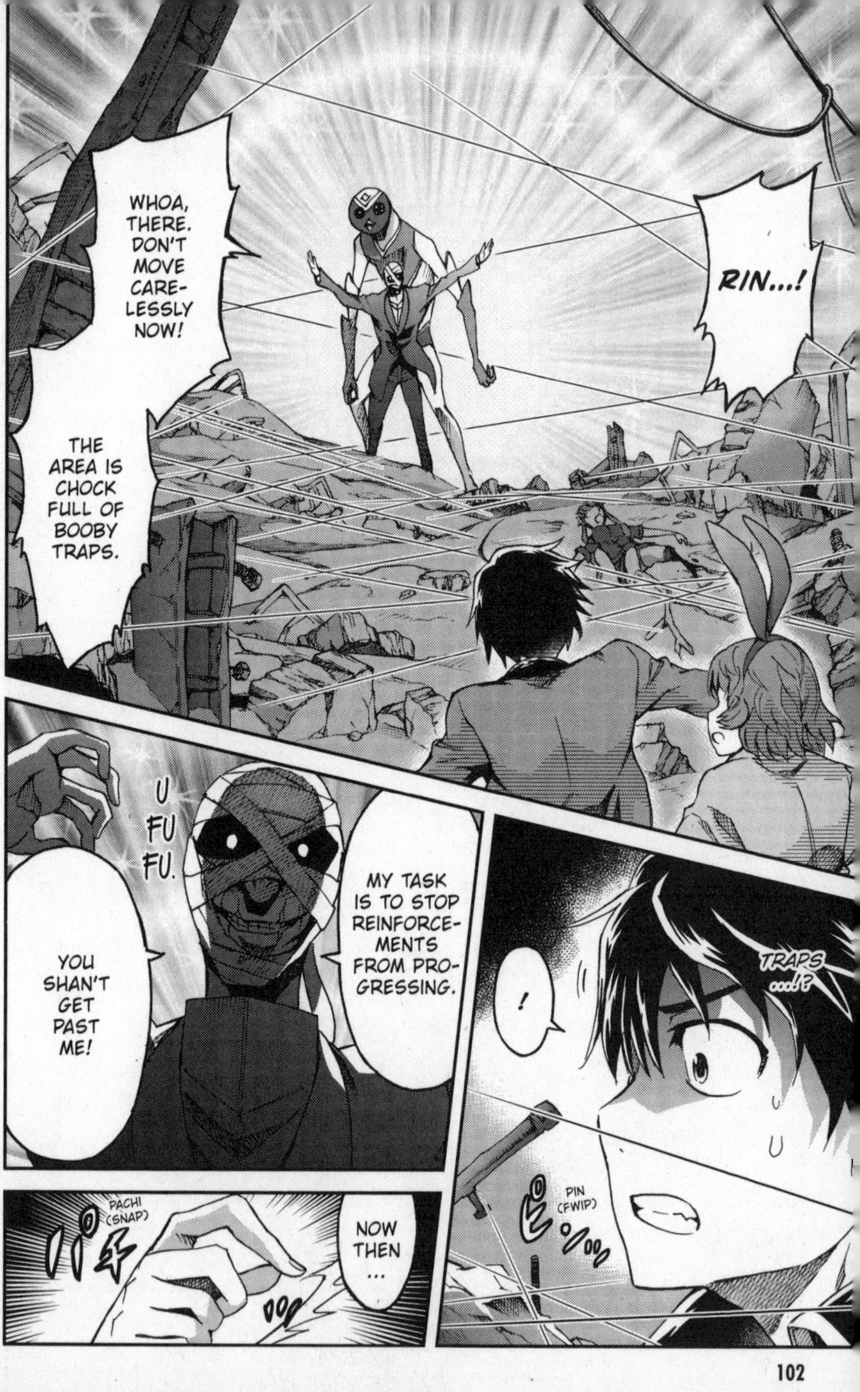
RIN...!
WHOA, THERE. DON'T MOVE CARE-LESSLY NOW!
THE AREA IS CHOCK FULL OF BOOBY TRAPS.
!
TRAPS ...!?
PIN (FWIP)
U FU FU.
MY TASK IS TO STOP REINFORCE-MENTS FROM PRO-GRESSING.
YOU SHAN'T GET PAST ME!
NOW THEN ...
PACHI (SNAP)

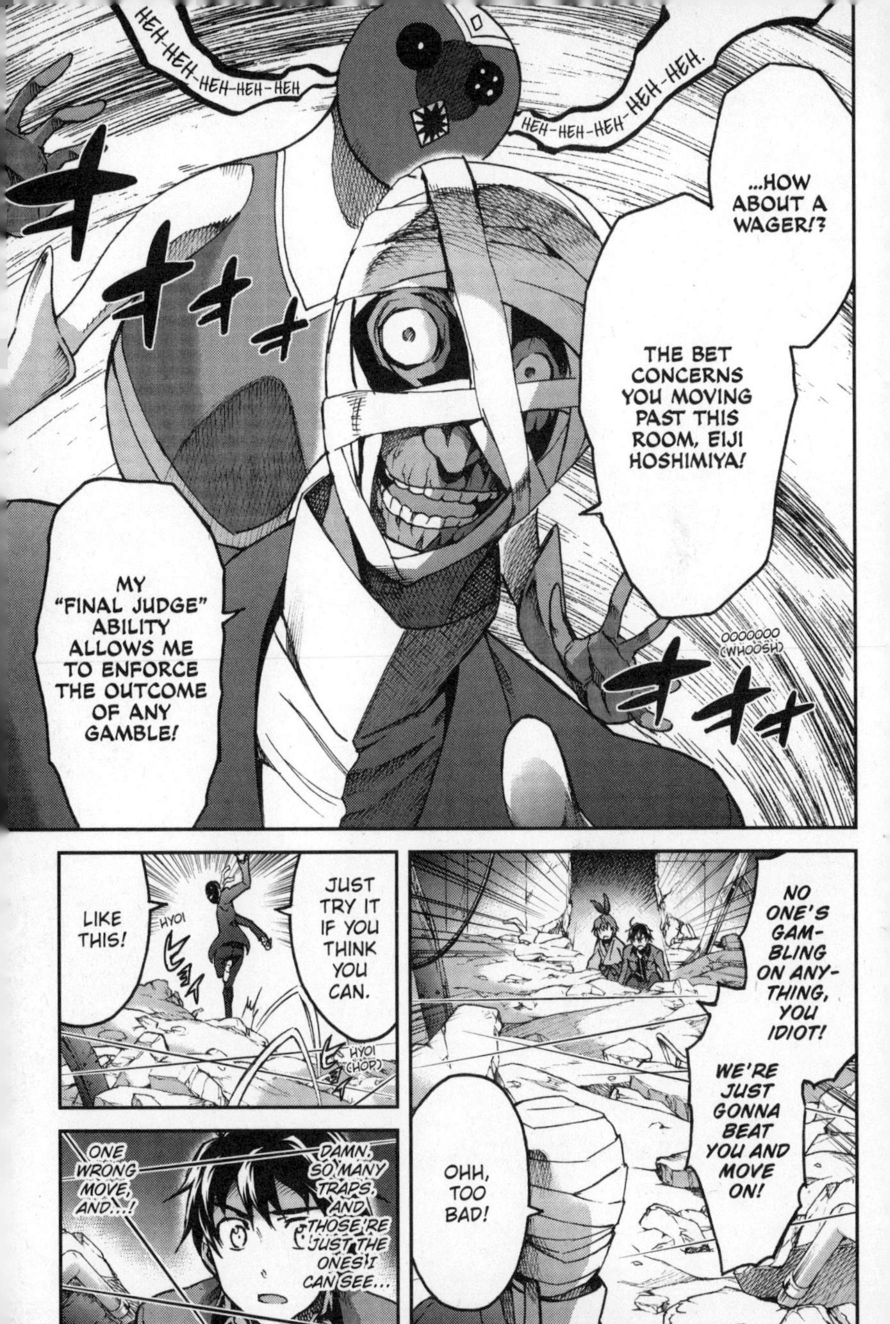
HEH-HEH-HEH-HEH-HEH.
HEH-HEH-HEH-HEH
...HOW ABOUT A WAGER!?
THE BET CONCERNS YOU MOVING PAST THIS ROOM, EIJI HOSHIMIYA!
OOOOOOO (WHOOSH)
MY "FINAL JUDGE" ABILITY ALLOWS ME TO ENFORCE THE OUTCOME OF ANY GAMBLE!
NO ONE'S GAMBLING ON ANYTHING, YOU IDIOT!
WE'RE JUST GONNA BEAT YOU AND MOVE ON!
OHH, TOO BAD!
JUST TRY IT IF YOU THINK YOU CAN.
LIKE THIS!
HYOI
HYOI (HOP)
DAMN. SO MANY TRAPS. AND THOSE'RE JUST THE ONES I CAN SEE...
ONE WRONG MOVE, AND...!

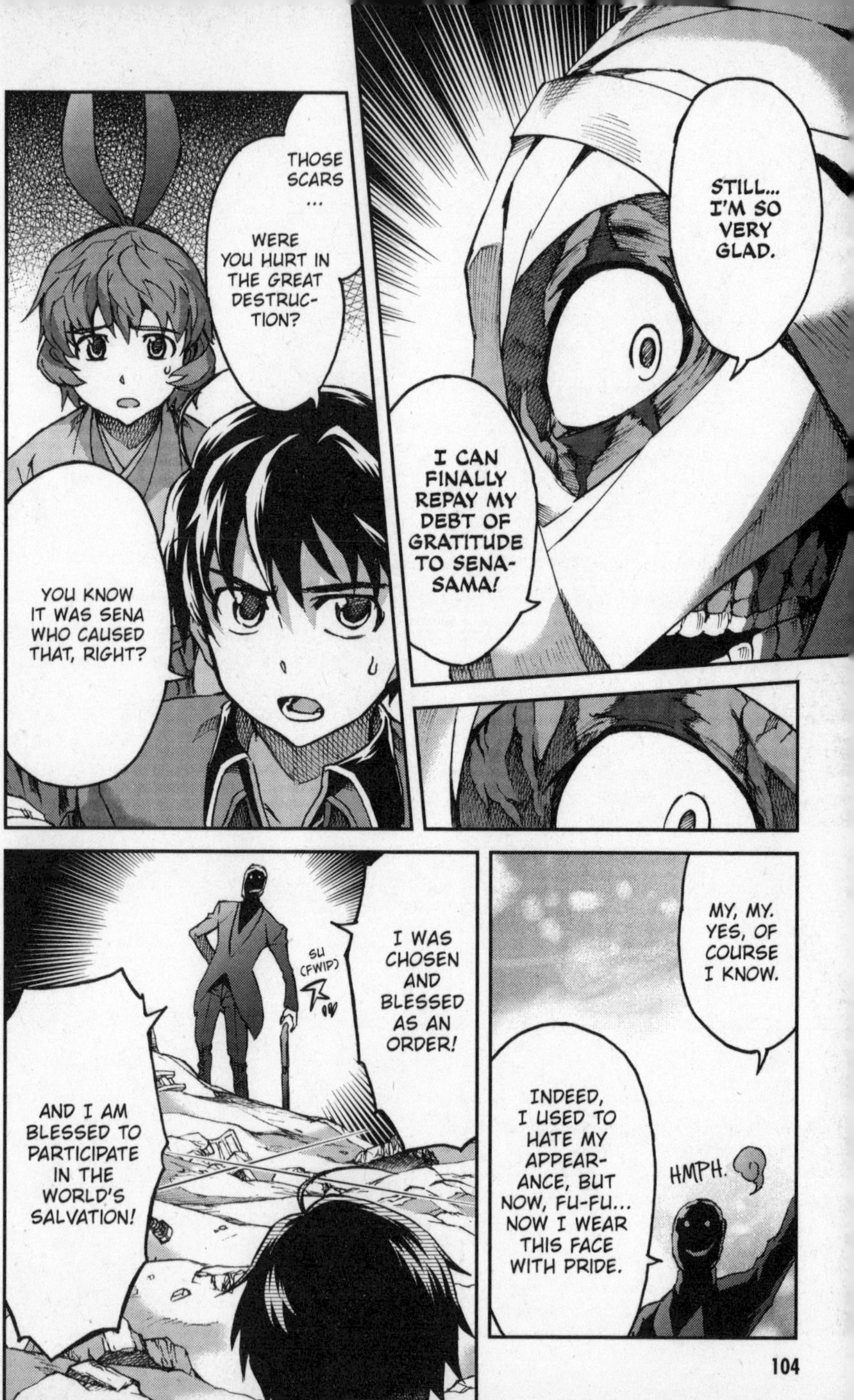
STILL... I'M SO VERY GLAD.
I CAN FINALLY REPAY MY DEBT OF GRATITUDE TO SENA-SAMA!
THOSE SCARS ...
WERE YOU HURT IN THE GREAT DESTRUC-TION?
YOU KNOW IT WAS SENA WHO CAUSED THAT, RIGHT?
MY, MY. YES, OF COURSE I KNOW.
INDEED, I USED TO HATE MY APPEAR-ANCE, BUT NOW, FU-FU... NOW I WEAR THIS FACE WITH PRIDE.
HMPH.
I WAS CHOSEN AND BLESSED AS AN ORDER!
SU (FWIP)
AND I AM BLESSED TO PARTICIPATE IN THE WORLD'S SALVATION!

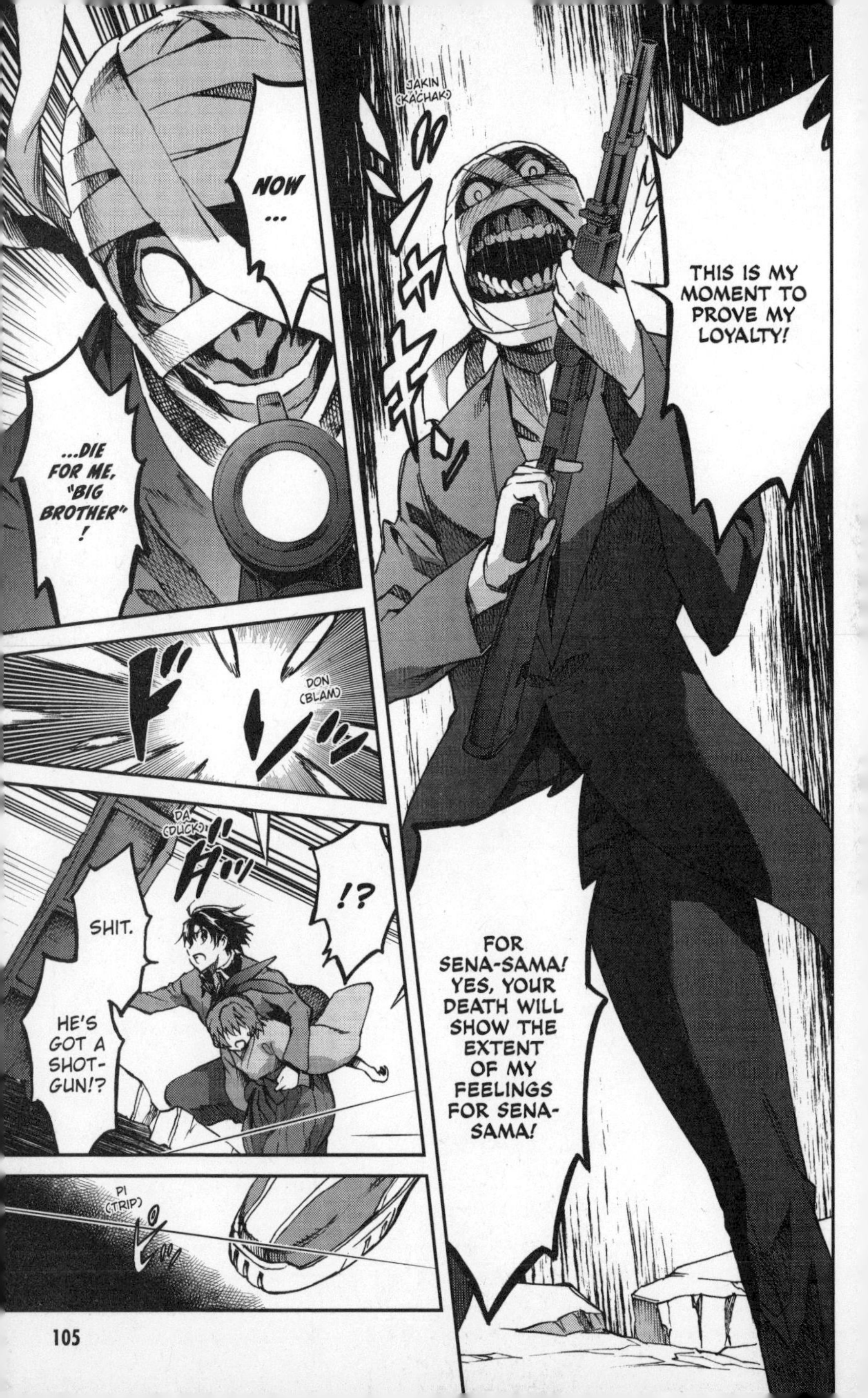
JAKIN (KACHAK)
THIS IS MY MOMENT TO PROVE MY LOYALTY!
FOR SENA-SAMA! YES, YOUR DEATH WILL SHOW THE EXTENT OF MY FEELINGS FOR SENA-SAMA!
NOW...
...DIE FOR ME, "BIG BROTHER"!
DON (BLAM)
DA (DUCK)
!?
SHIT.
HE'S GOT A SHOT-GUN!?
PI (TRIP)

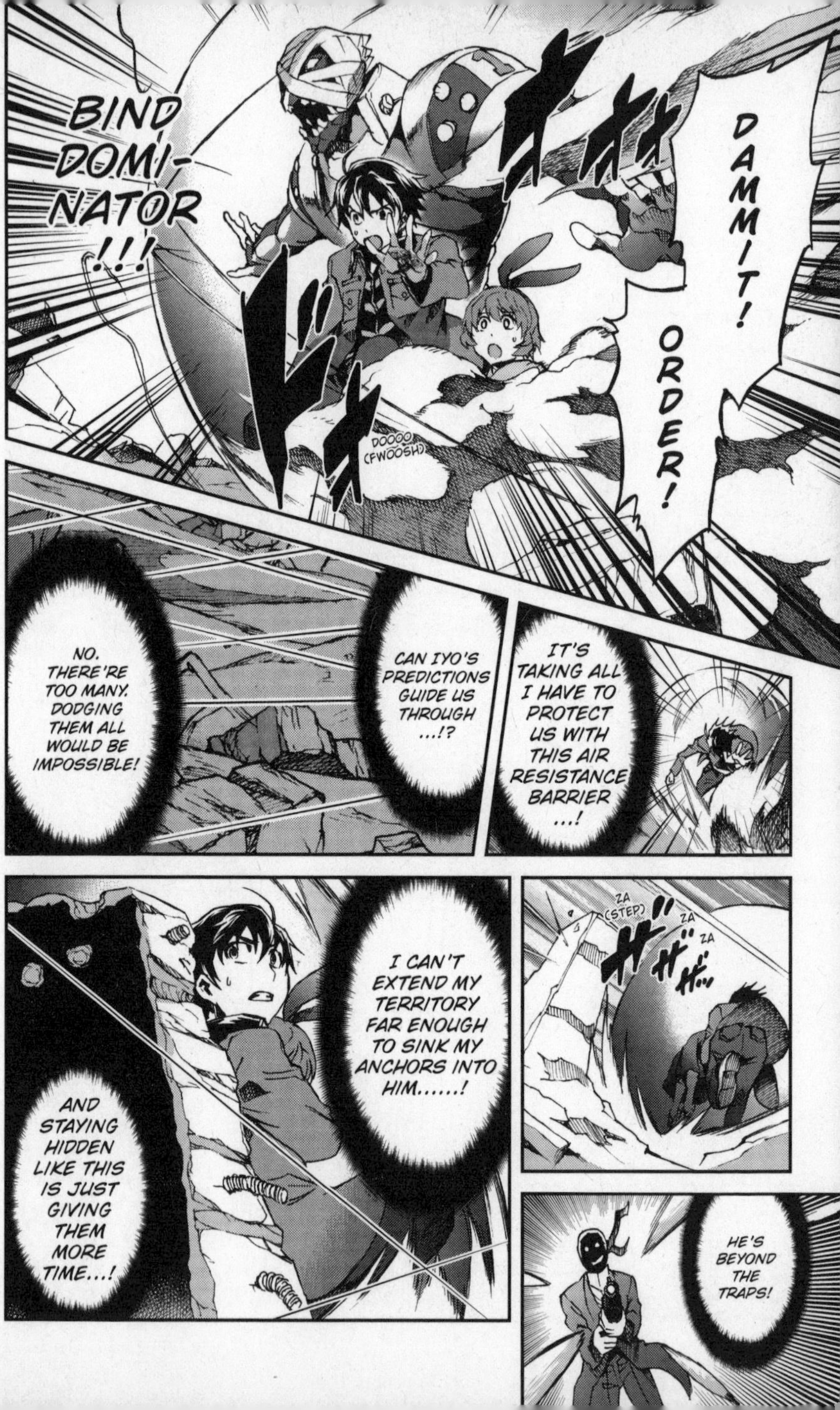
DAMMIT!
ORDER!
BIND DOMI-NATOR!!!
DOOOO (FWOOSH)
IT'S TAKING ALL I HAVE TO PROTECT US WITH THIS AIR RESISTANCE BARRIER...!
CAN IYO'S PREDICTIONS GUIDE US THROUGH...!?
NO. THERE'RE TOO MANY. DODGING THEM ALL WOULD BE IMPOSSIBLE!
ZA (STEP) ZA ZA
HE'S BEYOND THE TRAPS!
I CAN'T EXTEND MY TERRITORY FAR ENOUGH TO SINK MY ANCHORS INTO HIM......!
AND STAYING HIDDEN LIKE THIS IS JUST GIVING THEM MORE TIME...!

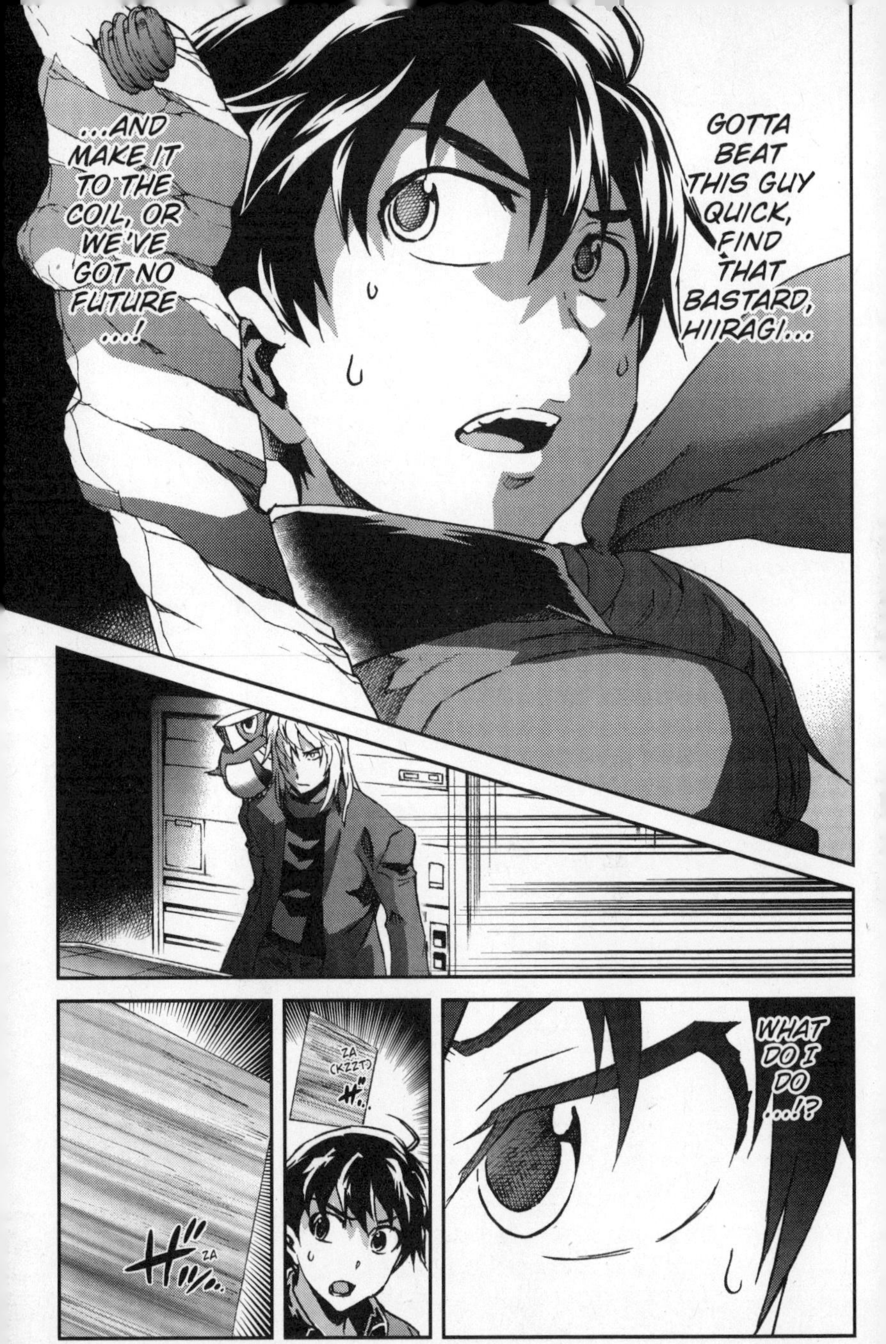
GOTTA BEAT THIS GUY QUICK, FIND THAT BASTARD, HIIRAGI...
...AND MAKE IT TO THE COIL, OR WE'VE GOT NO FUTURE...!
WHAT DO I DO...!?
ZA (KZZT)
ZA

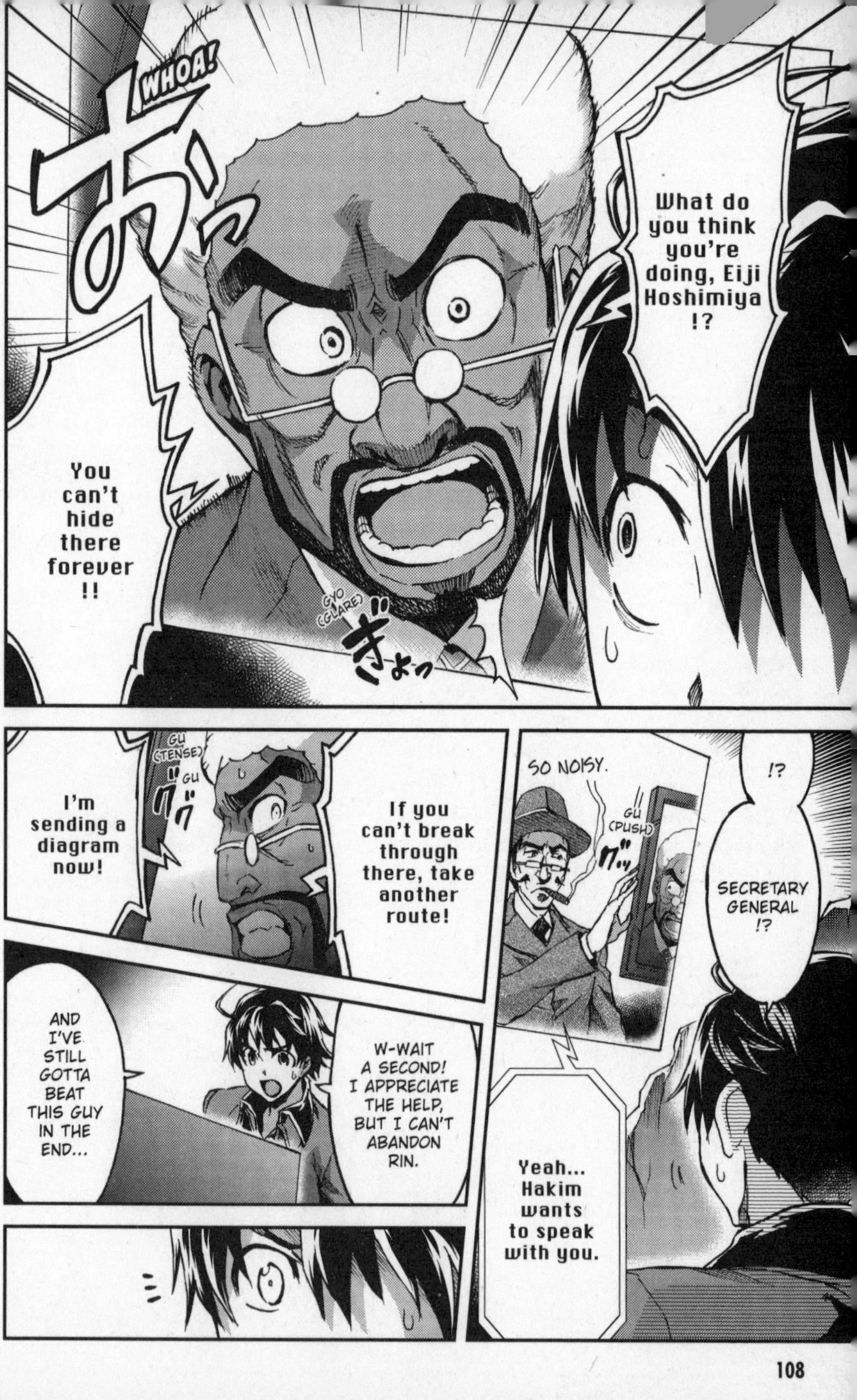
What do you think you're doing, Eiji Hoshimiya !?
WHOA!
You can't hide there forever !!
GYO (GLARE)
SO NOISY.
GU (PUSH)
!? SECRETARY GENERAL !?
Yeah... Hakim wants to speak with you.
GU (TENSE) GU
If you can't break through there, take another route!
I'm sending a diagram now!
W-WAIT A SECOND! I APPRECIATE THE HELP, BUT I CAN'T ABANDON RIN.
AND I'VE STILL GOTTA BEAT THIS GUY IN THE END...

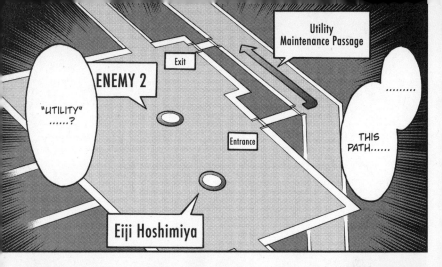

Utility
Maintenance Passage

ENEMY 2

Exit

"UTILITY"
......?

Entrance

....

THIS
PATH......

Eiji Hoshimiya

HE'S
GONE
...?

HMPH.

OOO
(WHOOSH)

PICHA
(SPLASH)

WATER
...?

THINKS
HE CAN
HIDE
IN THE
SMOKE...

...BUT THAT
WORKS OUT
SPLENDIDLY
FOR ME!

AFTER ALL,
MY GOAL WAS
SIMPLY TO
DELAY HIM!

CHORO
(OOZE)

CHORO

WHAT'S
THIS...?

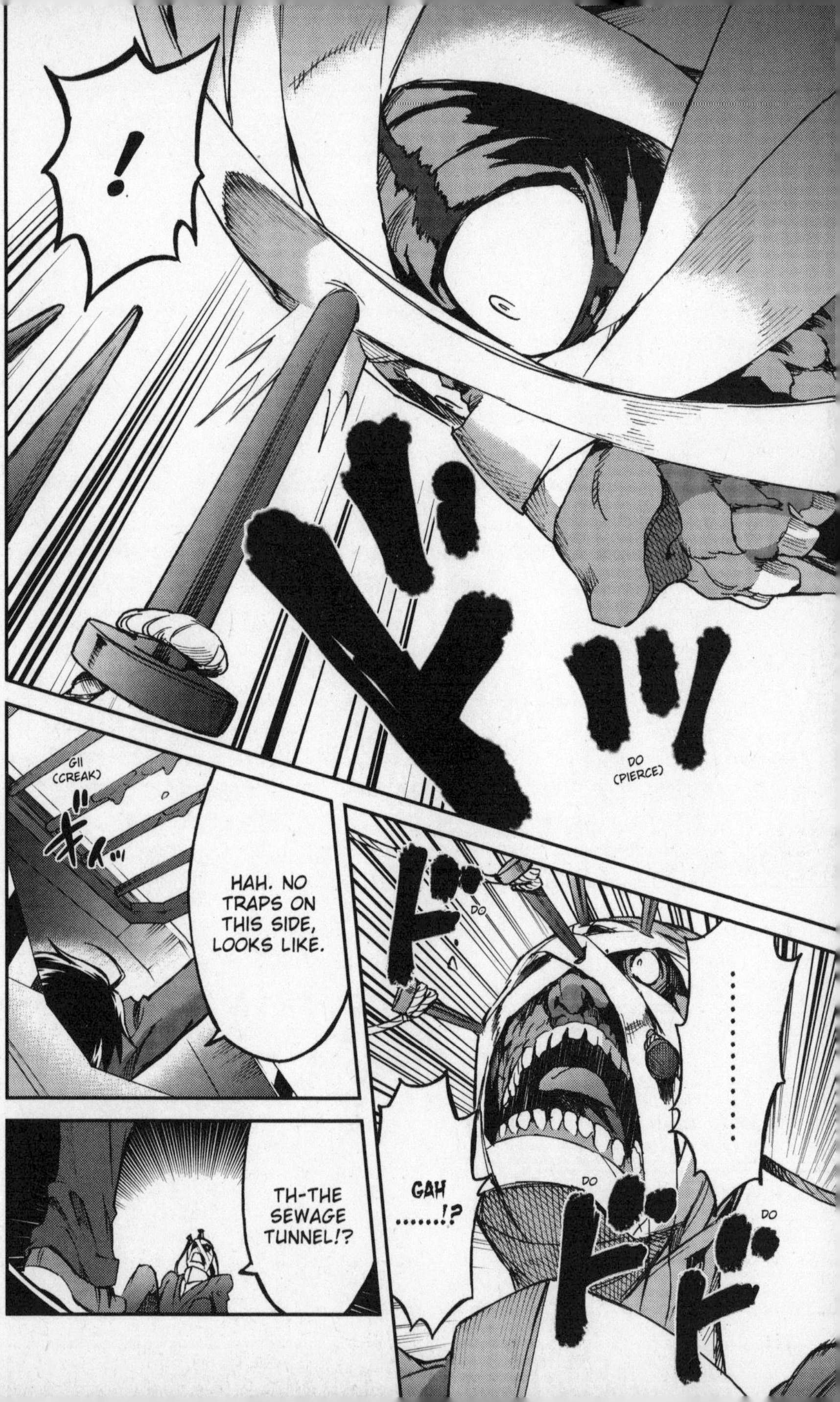
!
DO
(PIERCE)
......
DO
GAH
......!?
DO
DO
GII
(CREAK)
HAH. NO TRAPS ON THIS SIDE, LOOKS LIKE.
TH-THE SEWAGE TUNNEL!?

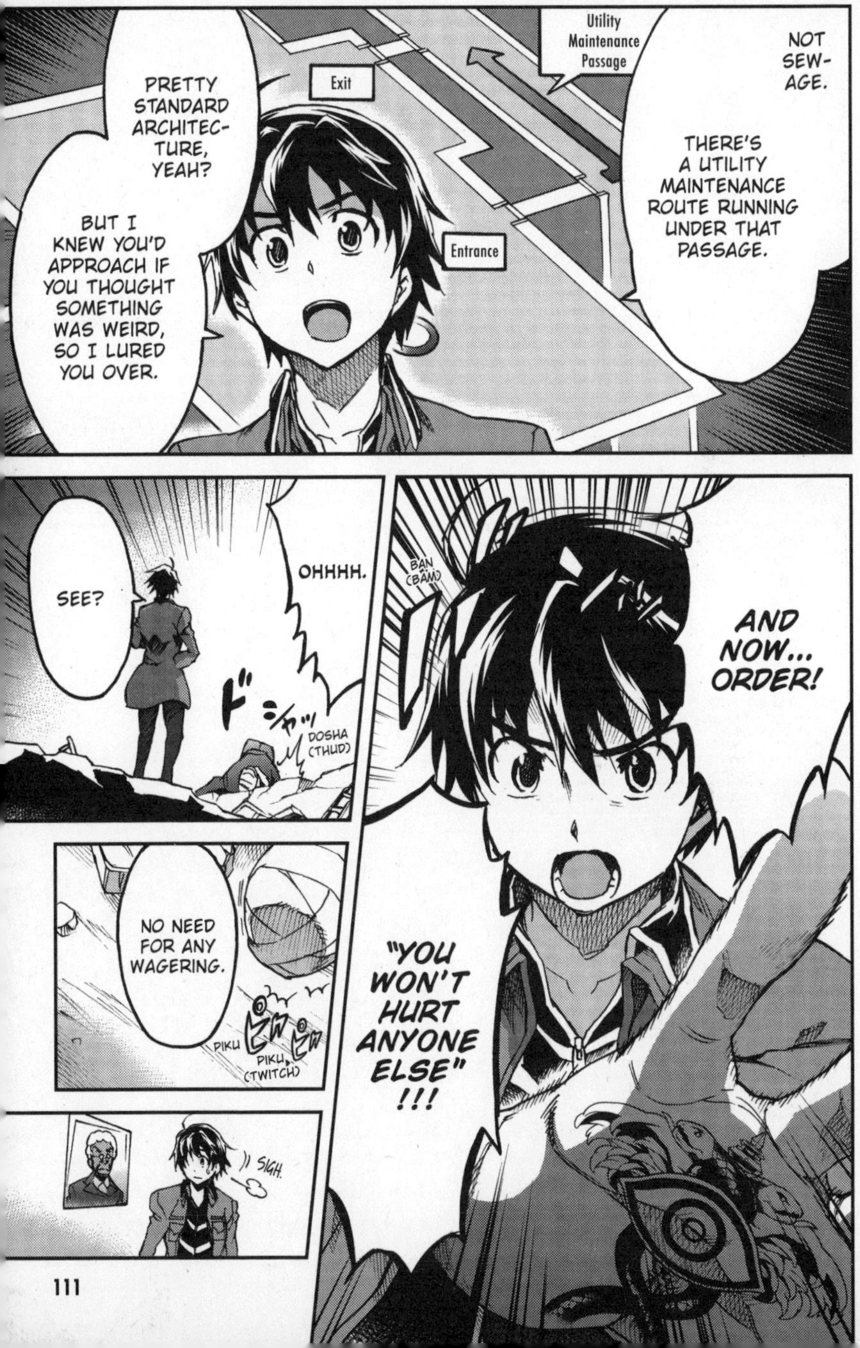
NOT SEWAGE.
THERE'S A UTILITY MAINTENANCE ROUTE RUNNING UNDER THAT PASSAGE.
Utility Maintenance Passage
Exit
Entrance
PRETTY STANDARD ARCHITECTURE, YEAH?
BUT I KNEW YOU'D APPROACH IF YOU THOUGHT SOMETHING WAS WEIRD, SO I LURED YOU OVER.
AND NOW... ORDER!
BAN (BAM)
"YOU WON'T HURT ANYONE ELSE" !!!
OHHHH.
SEE?
DOSHA (THUD)
NO NEED FOR ANY WAGERING.
PIKU PIKU (TWITCH)
SIGH.

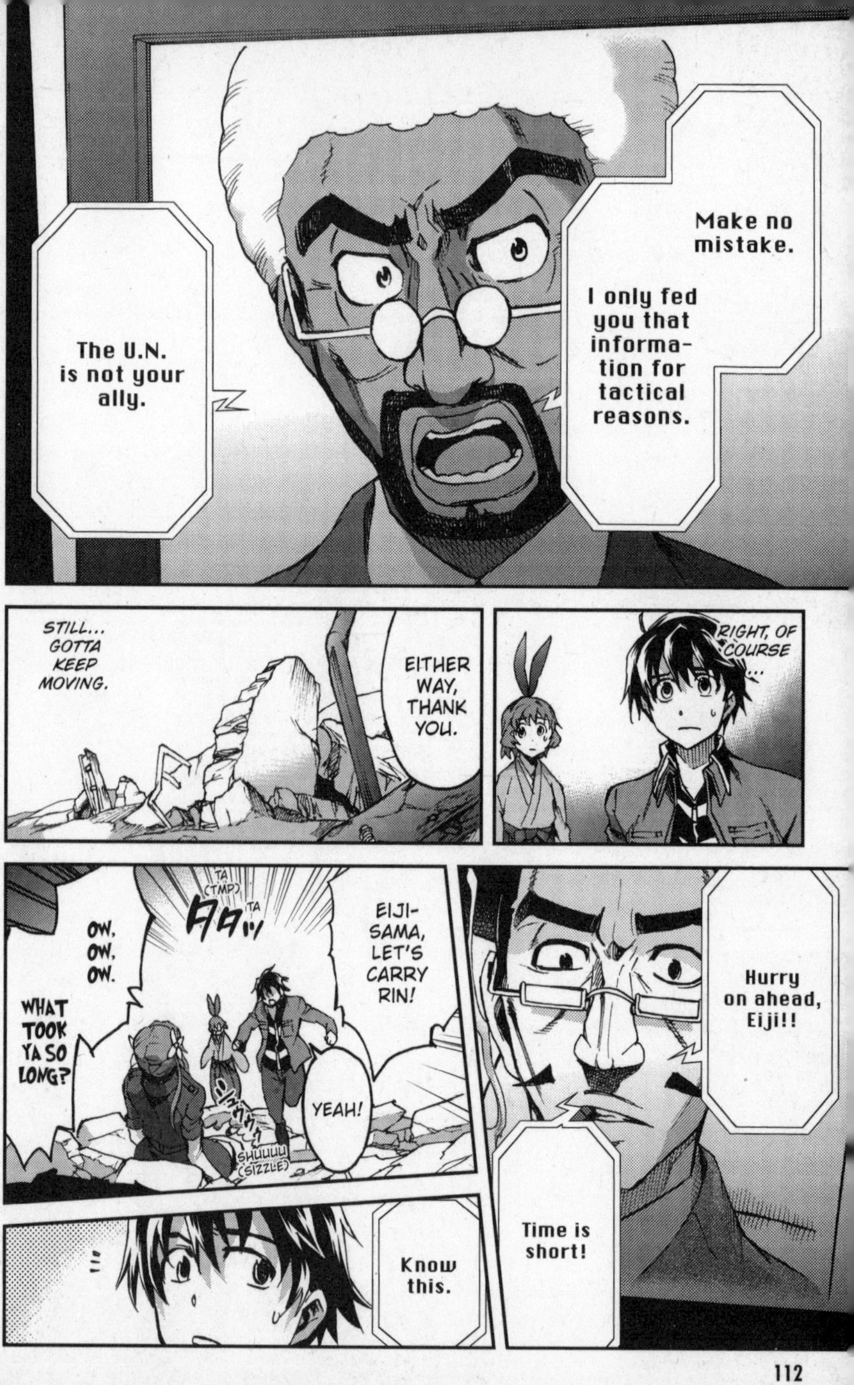
Make no mistake.
I only fed you that information for tactical reasons.
The U.N. is not your ally.
RIGHT, OF COURSE...
EITHER WAY, THANK YOU.
STILL... GOTTA KEEP MOVING.
Hurry on ahead, Eiji!!
Time is short!
EIJI-SAMA, LET'S CARRY RIN!
TA (TMP) TA
OW, OW, OW.
WHAT TOOK YA SO LONG?
YEAH!
SHUUUU (SIZZLE)
Know this.
!!

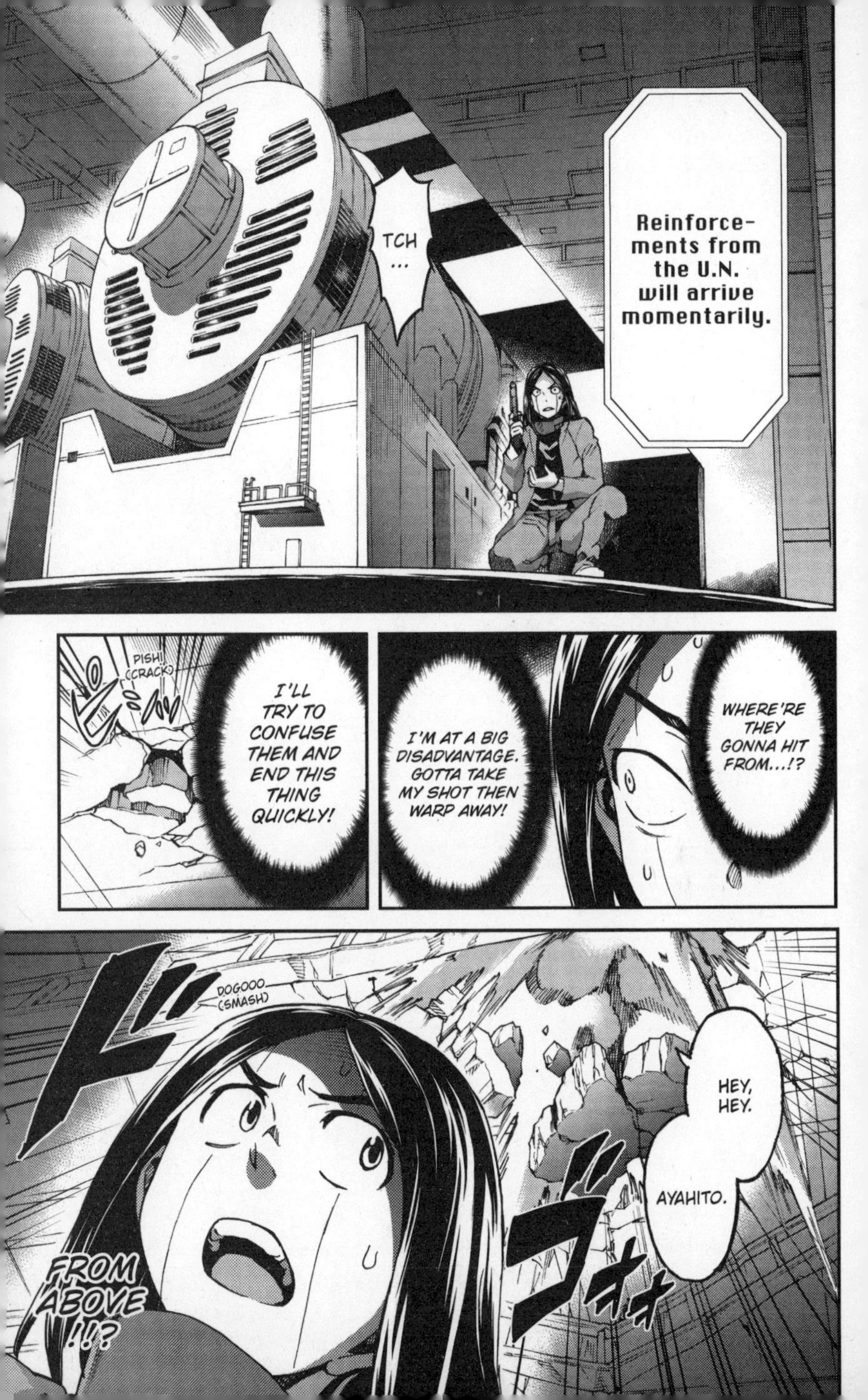

Reinforcements from the U.N. will arrive momentarily.
TCH ...
WHERE'RE THEY GONNA HIT FROM...!?
I'M AT A BIG DISADVANTAGE. GOTTA TAKE MY SHOT THEN WARP AWAY!
I'LL TRY TO CONFUSE THEM AND END THIS THING QUICKLY!
PISH! (CRACK)
HEY, HEY.
AYAHITO.
DOGOOO (SMASH)
FROM ABOVE!!?

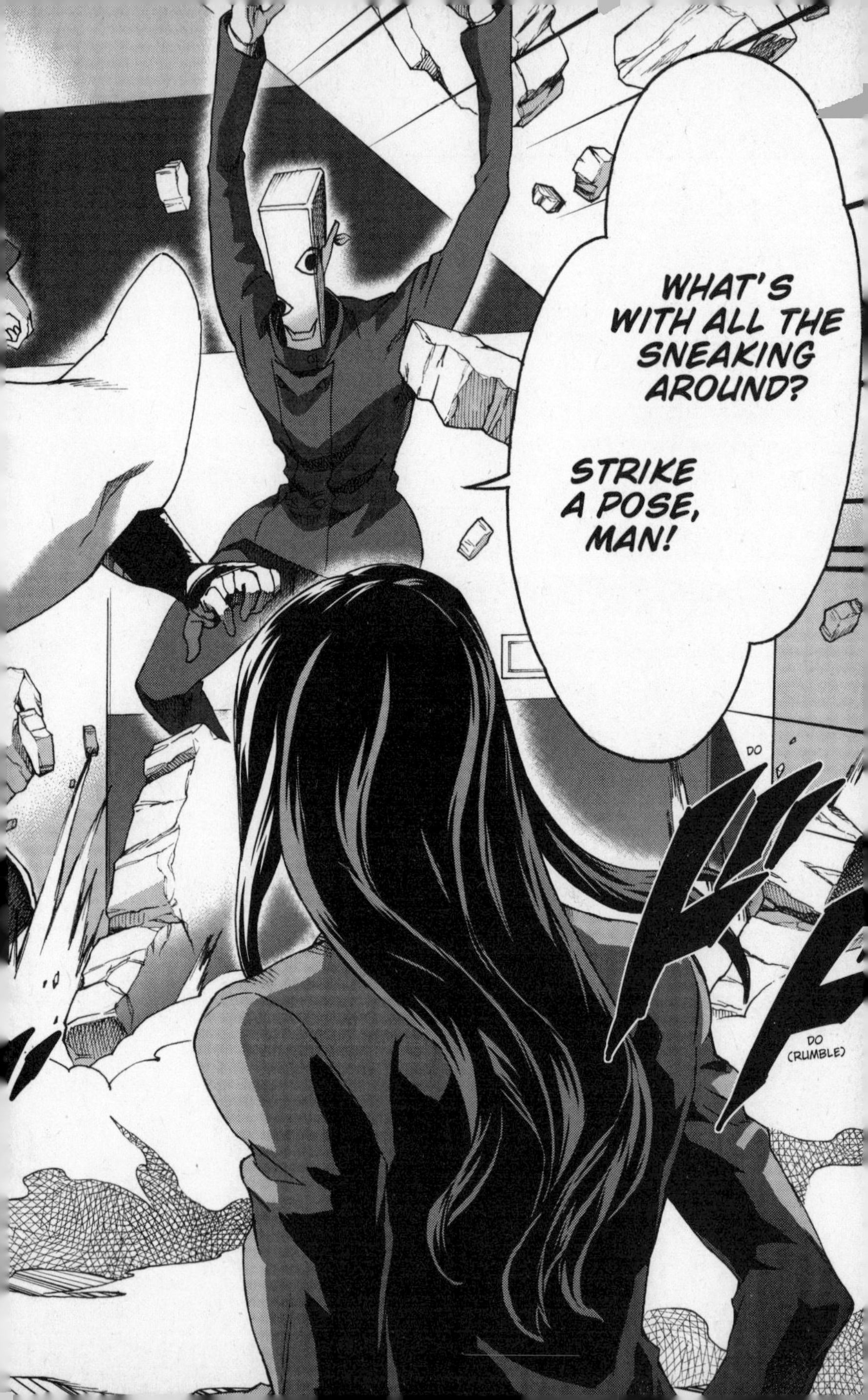
WHAT'S WITH ALL THE SNEAKING AROUND?
STRIKE A POSE, MAN!
DO
DO
(RUMBLE)

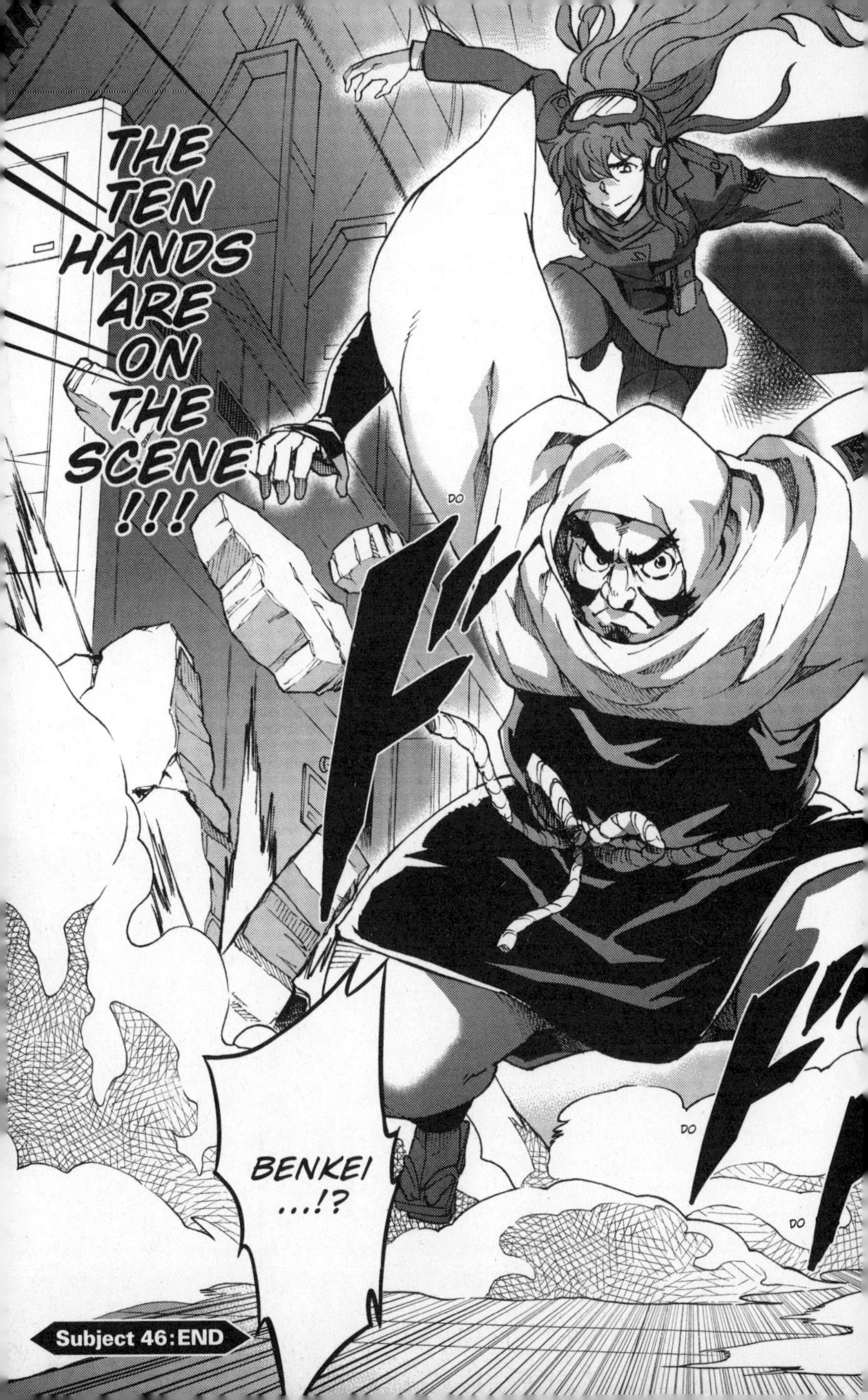
THE TEN HANDS ARE ON THE SCENE!!!
DO
BENKEI ...!?
DO
DO
Subject 46: END

BIG
ORDER

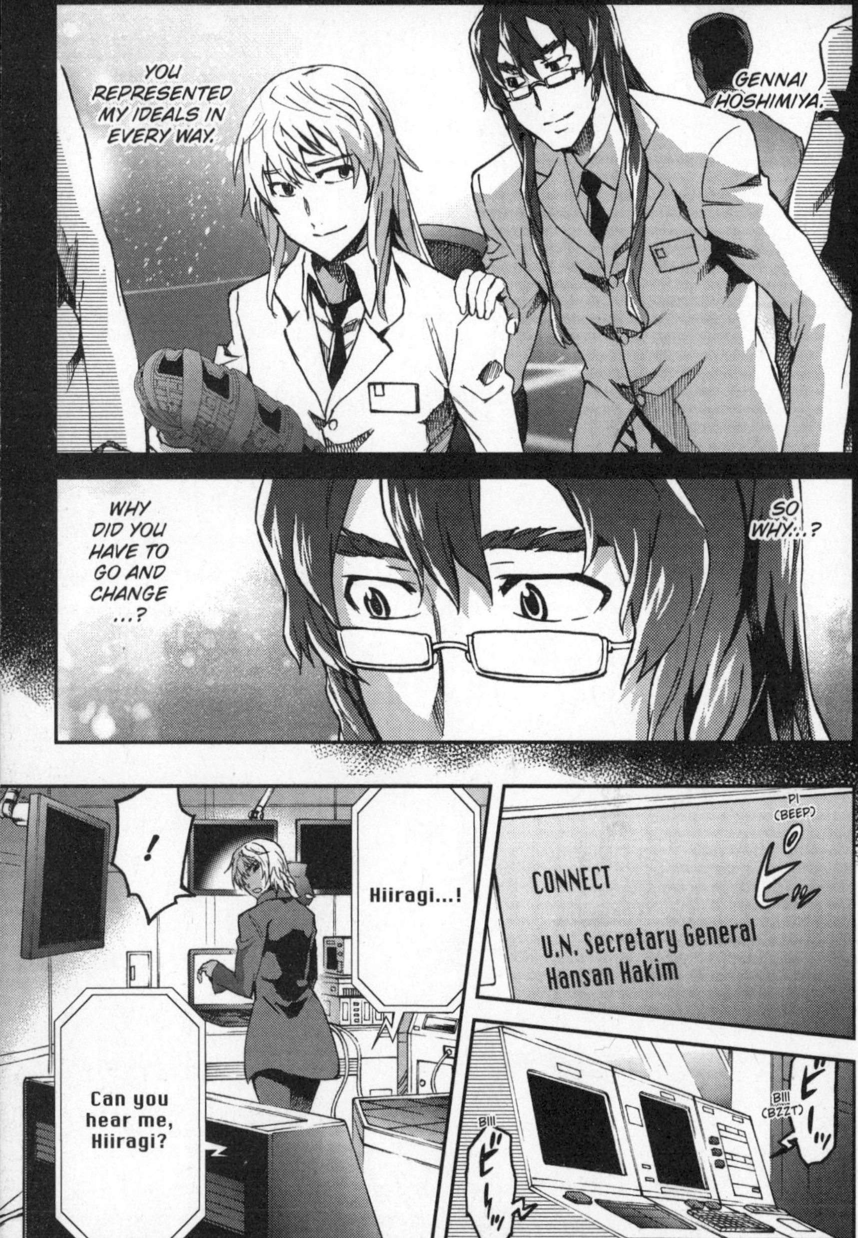
GENNAI HOSHIMIYA.
YOU REPRESENTED MY IDEALS IN EVERY WAY.
SO WHY...?
WHY DID YOU HAVE TO GO AND CHANGE ...?
PI (BEEP)
CONNECT
U.N. Secretary General Hansan Hakim
BIII (BZZT)
BIII
Hiiragi...!
!
Can you hear me, Hiiragi?

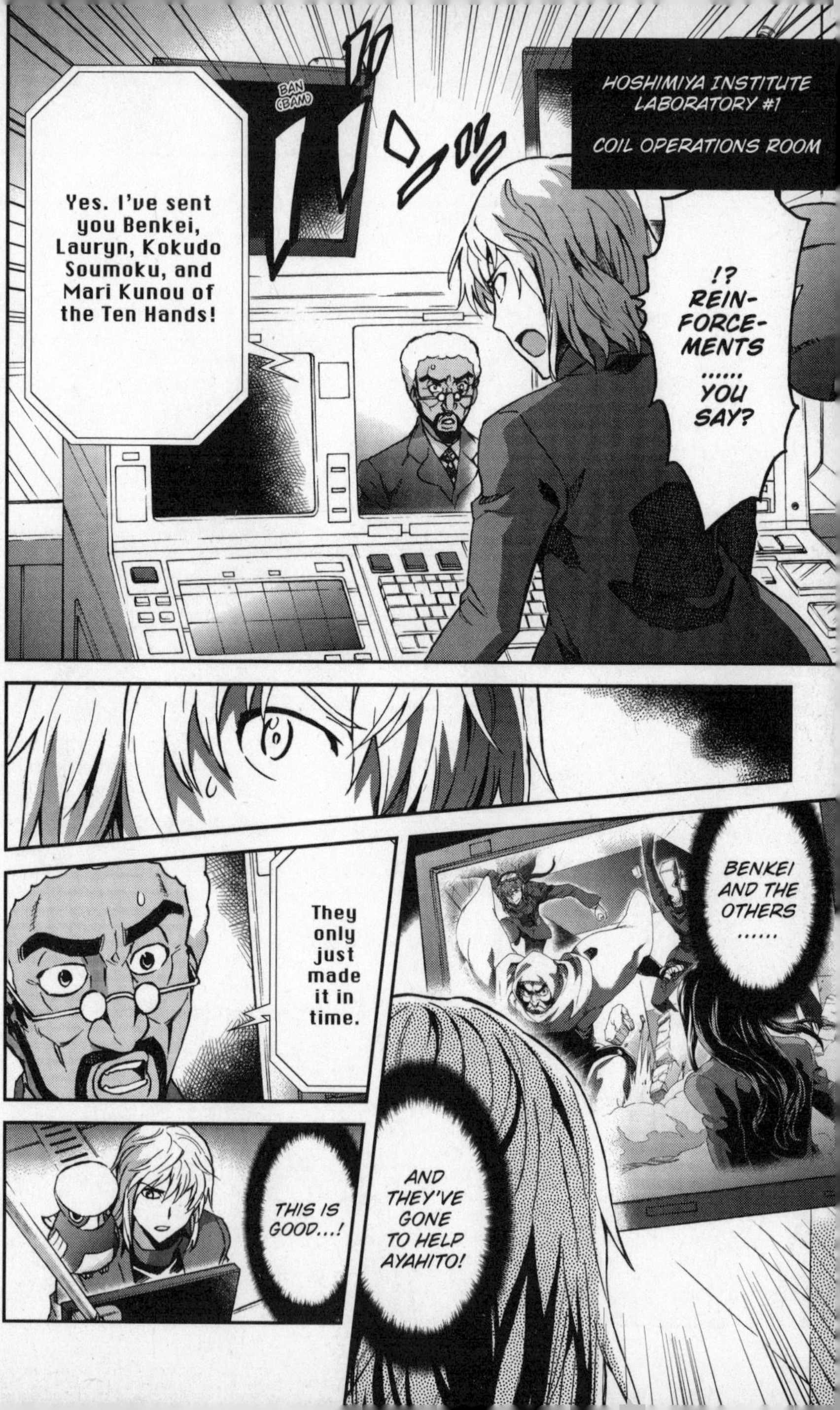
HOSHIMIYA INSTITUTE LABORATORY #1

COIL OPERATIONS ROOM
!? REIN-FORCE-MENTS ...... YOU SAY?
BAN (BAM)
Yes. I've sent you Benkei, Lauryn, Kokudo Soumoku, and Mari Kunou of the Ten Hands!
BENKEI AND THE OTHERS ......
They only just made it in time.
AND THEY'VE GONE TO HELP AYAHITO!
THIS IS GOOD...!

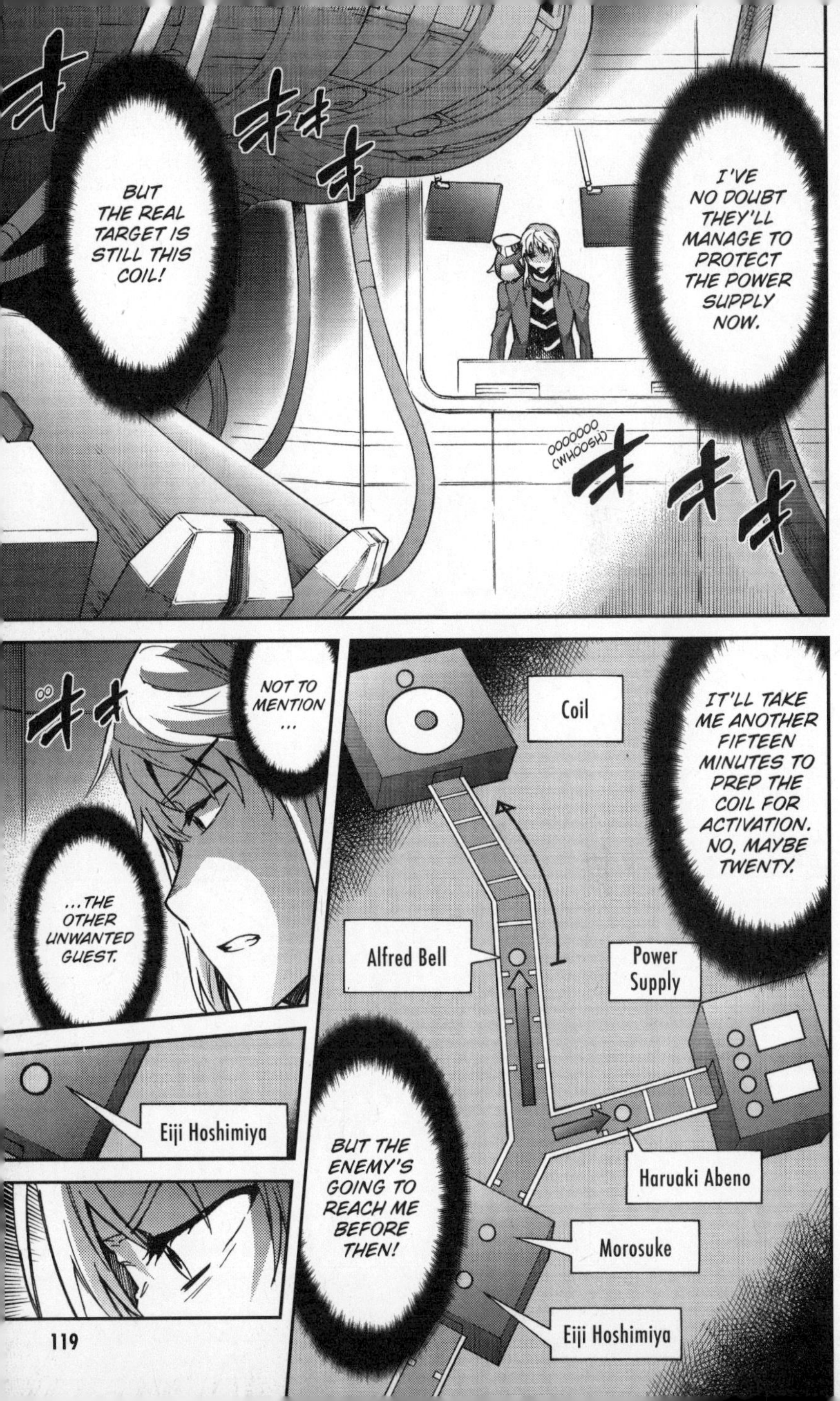
I'VE NO DOUBT THEY'LL MANAGE TO PROTECT THE POWER SUPPLY NOW.
BUT THE REAL TARGET IS STILL THIS COIL!
OOOOOOO (WHOOSH)
IT'LL TAKE ME ANOTHER FIFTEEN MINUTES TO PREP THE COIL FOR ACTIVATION. NO, MAYBE TWENTY.
Coil
Alfred Bell
Power Supply
Haruaki Abeno
Morosuke
Eiji Hoshimiya
BUT THE ENEMY'S GOING TO REACH ME BEFORE THEN!
NOT TO MENTION...
...THE OTHER UNWANTED GUEST.
Eiji Hoshimiya

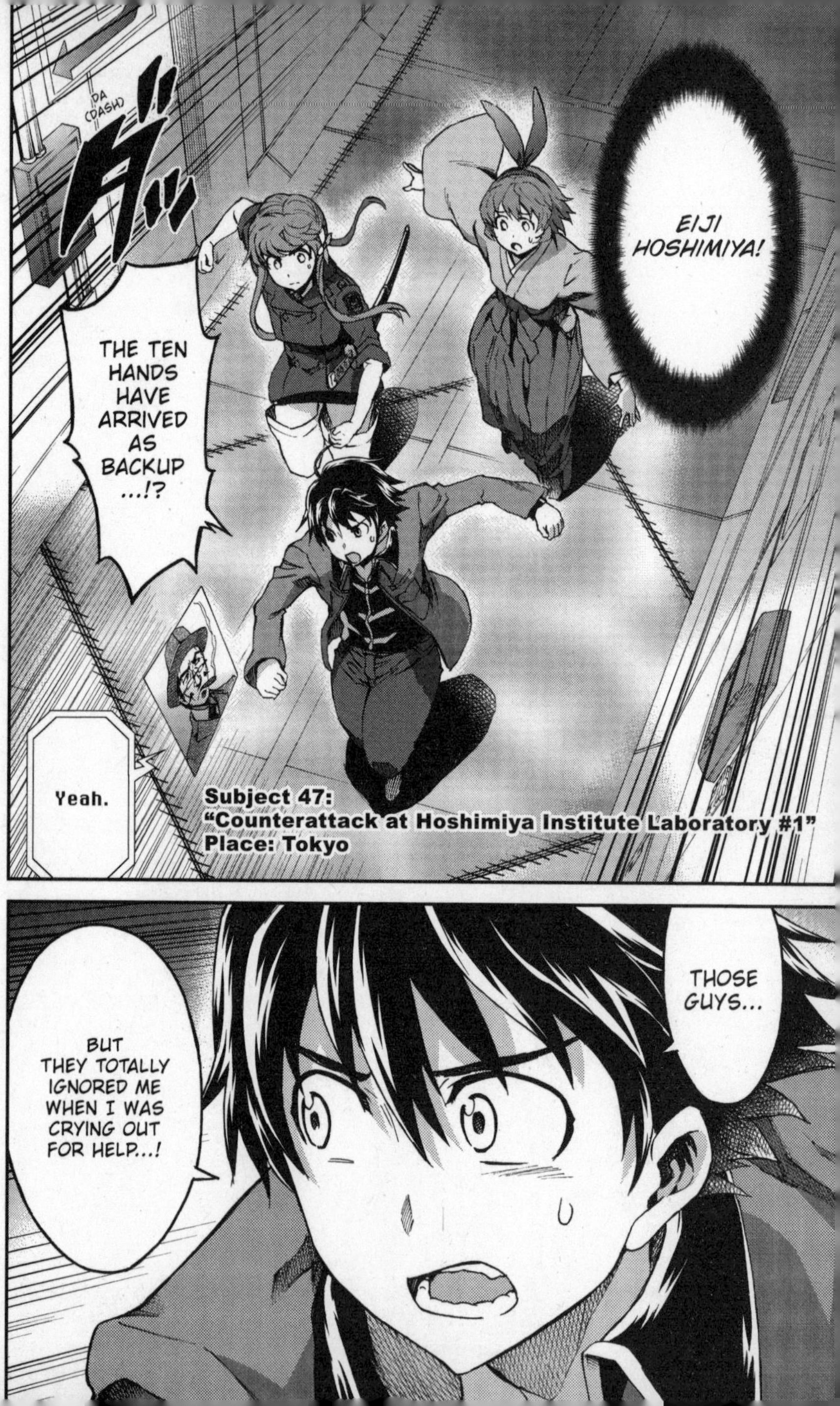
EIJI HOSHIMIYA!
DA (DASH)
THE TEN HANDS HAVE ARRIVED AS BACKUP ...!?
Yeah.
Subject 47: "Counterattack at Hoshimiya Institute Laboratory #1" Place: Tokyo
THOSE GUYS...
BUT THEY TOTALLY IGNORED ME WHEN I WAS CRYING OUT FOR HELP...!

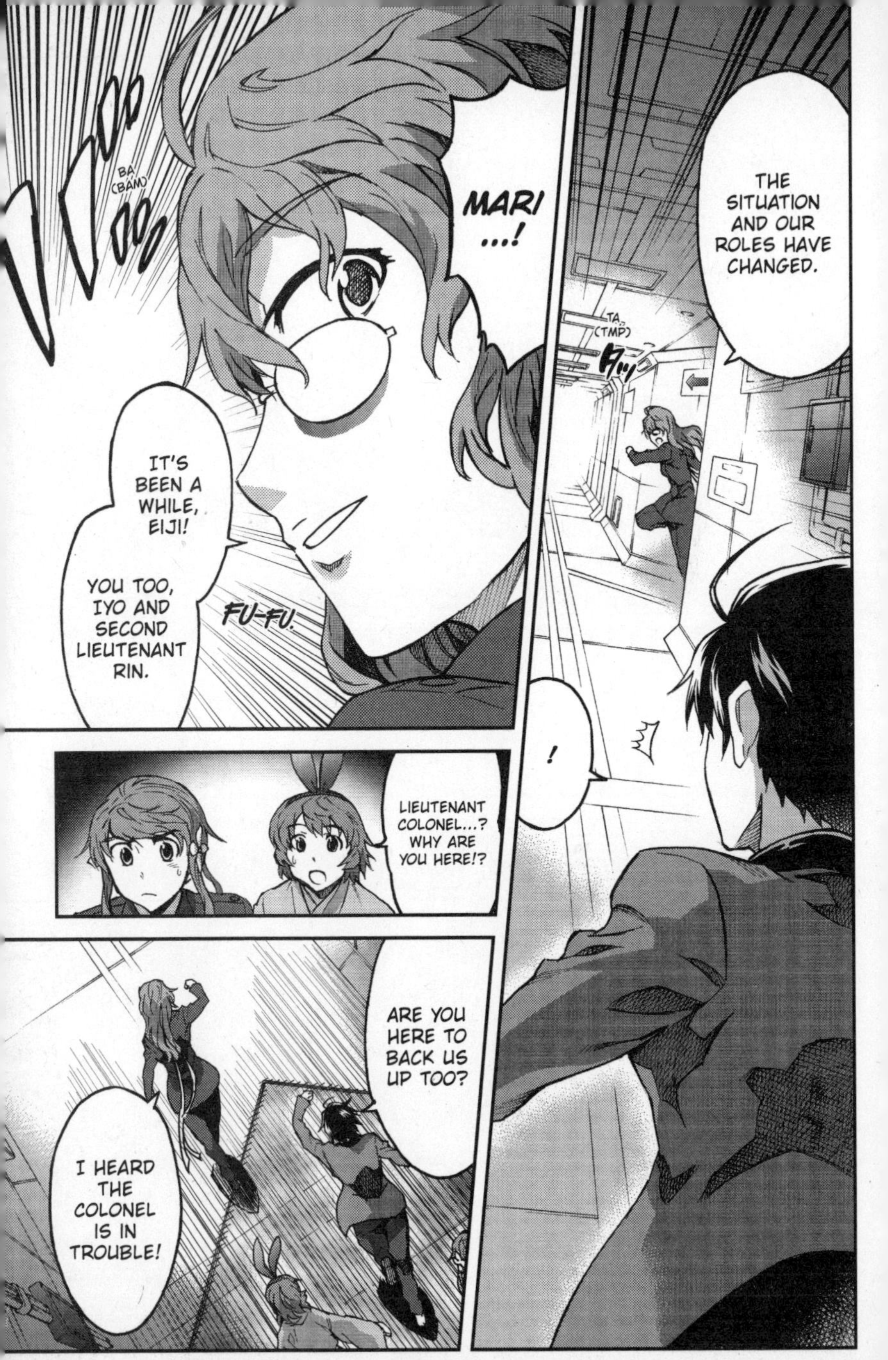
THE SITUATION AND OUR ROLES HAVE CHANGED.
TA.. (TMP)
!
BA (BAM)
MARI ...!
IT'S BEEN A WHILE, EIJI!
YOU TOO, IYO AND SECOND LIEUTENANT RIN.
FU-FU.
LIEUTENANT COLONEL...? WHY ARE YOU HERE!?
ARE YOU HERE TO BACK US UP TOO?
I HEARD THE COLONEL IS IN TROUBLE!

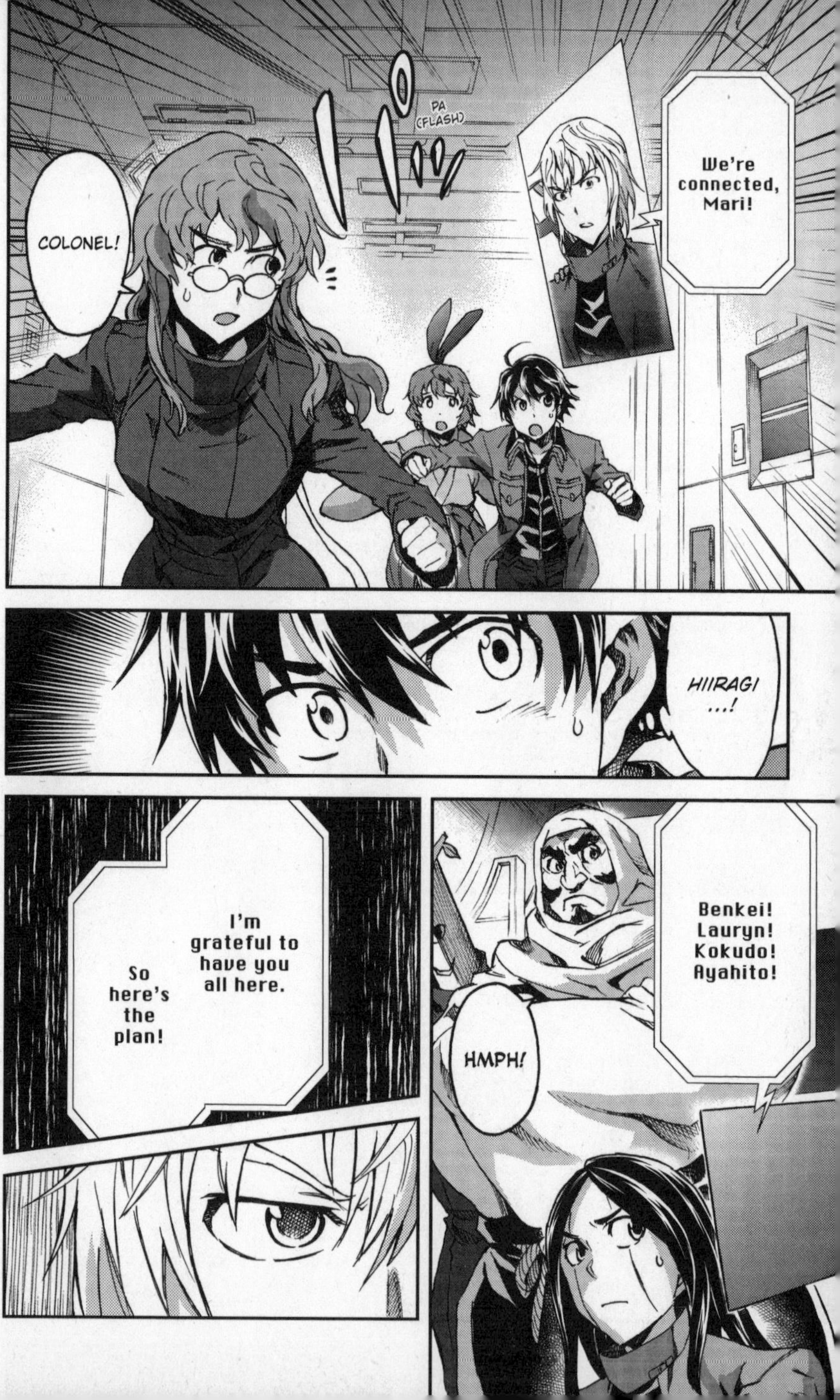
We're connected, Mari!
PA (FLASH)
COLONEL!
HIIRAGI ...!
Benkei! Lauryn! Kokudo! Ayahito!
HMPH!
I'm grateful to have you all here.
So here's the plan!

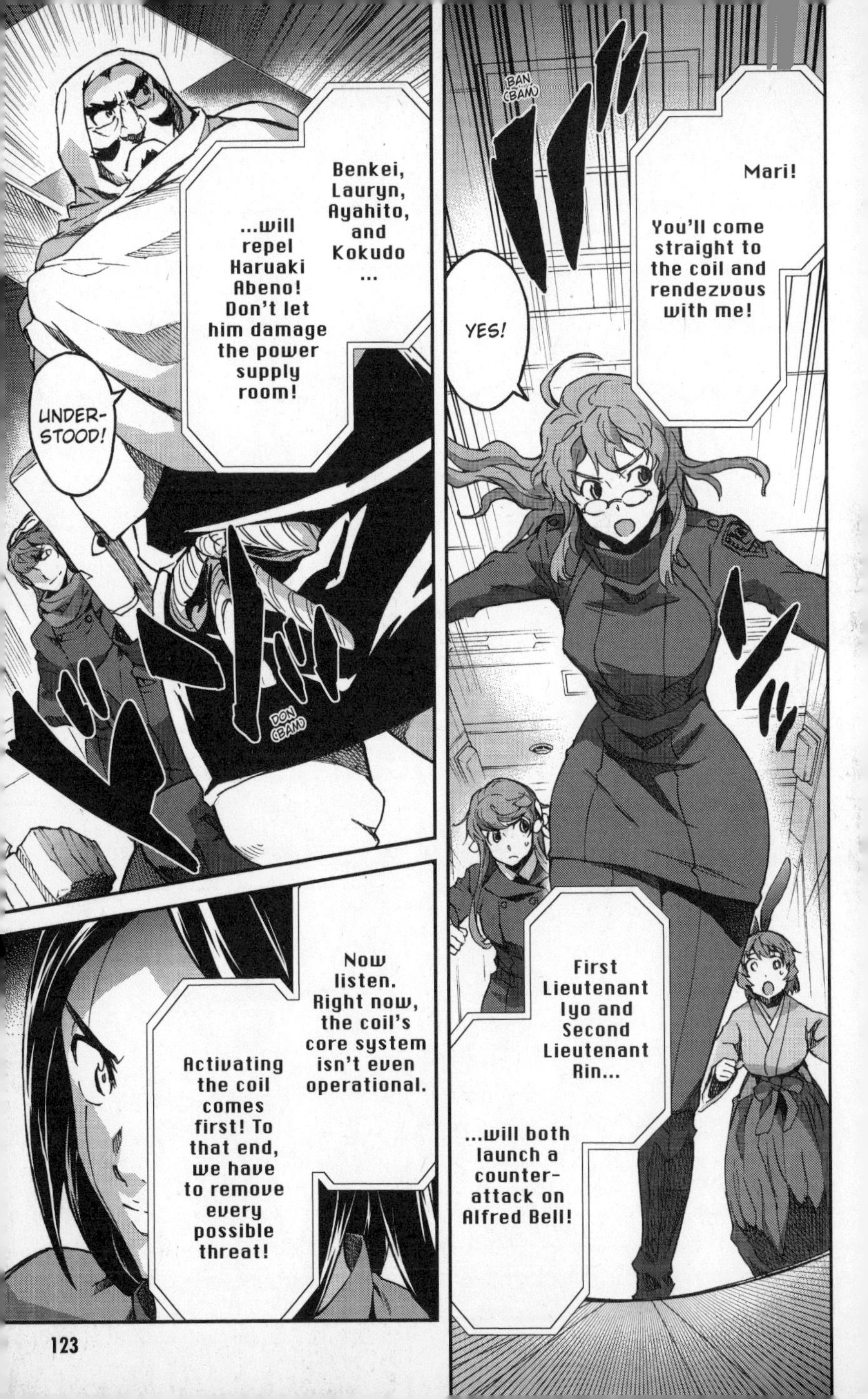
BAN (BAM)
Mari!
You'll come straight to the coil and rendezvous with me!
YES!
First Lieutenant Iyo and Second Lieutenant Rin...
...will both launch a counter-attack on Alfred Bell!
Benkei, Lauryn, Ayahito, and Kokudo ...
...will repel Haruaki Abeno! Don't let him damage the power supply room!
UNDER-STOOD!
DON (BAM)
Now listen. Right now, the coil's core system isn't even operational.
Activating the coil comes first! To that end, we have to remove every possible threat!

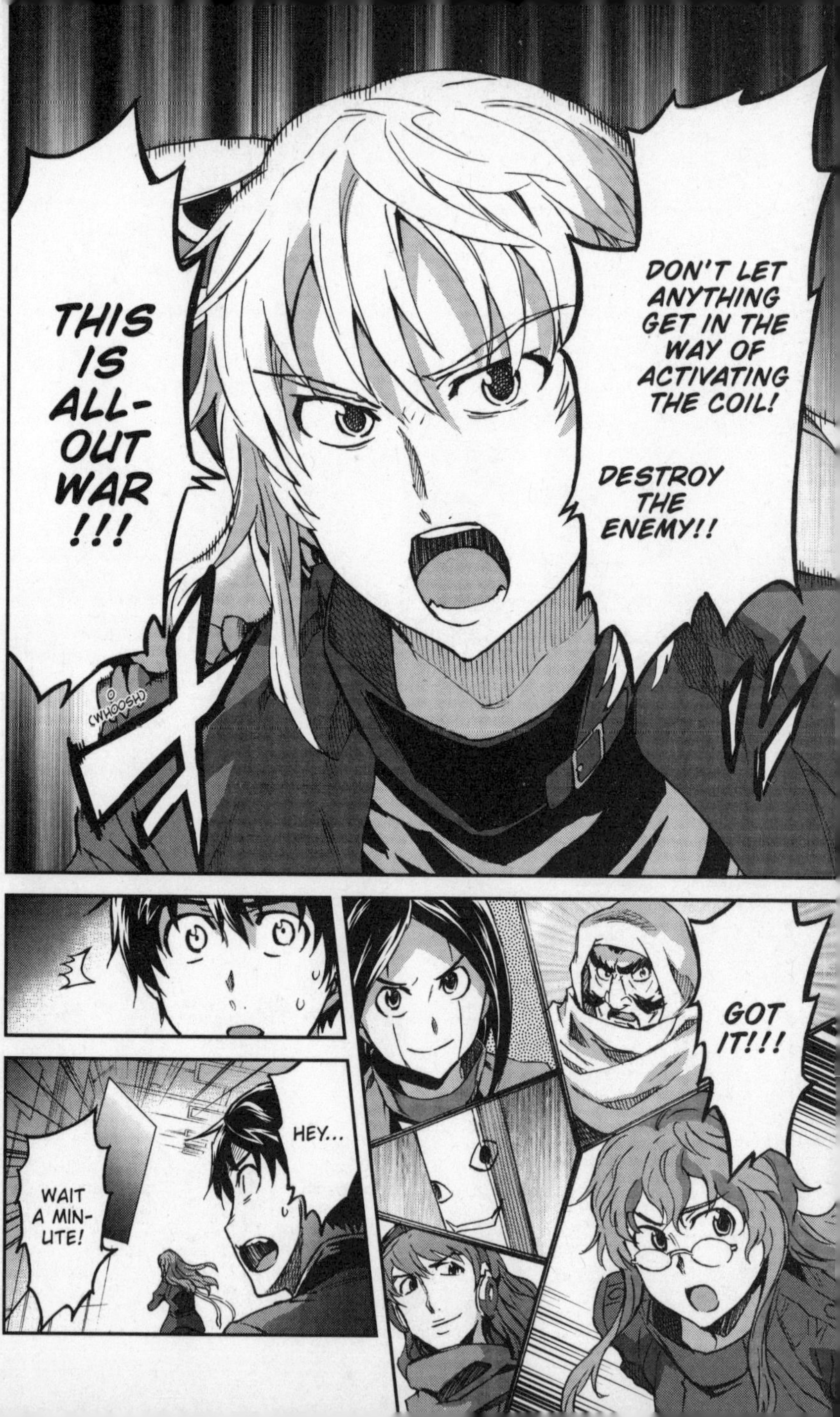
DON'T LET ANYTHING GET IN THE WAY OF ACTIVATING THE COIL!
DESTROY THE ENEMY!!
THIS IS ALL-OUT WAR!!!
(WHOOSH)
GOT IT!!!
HEY...
WAIT A MIN-UTE!

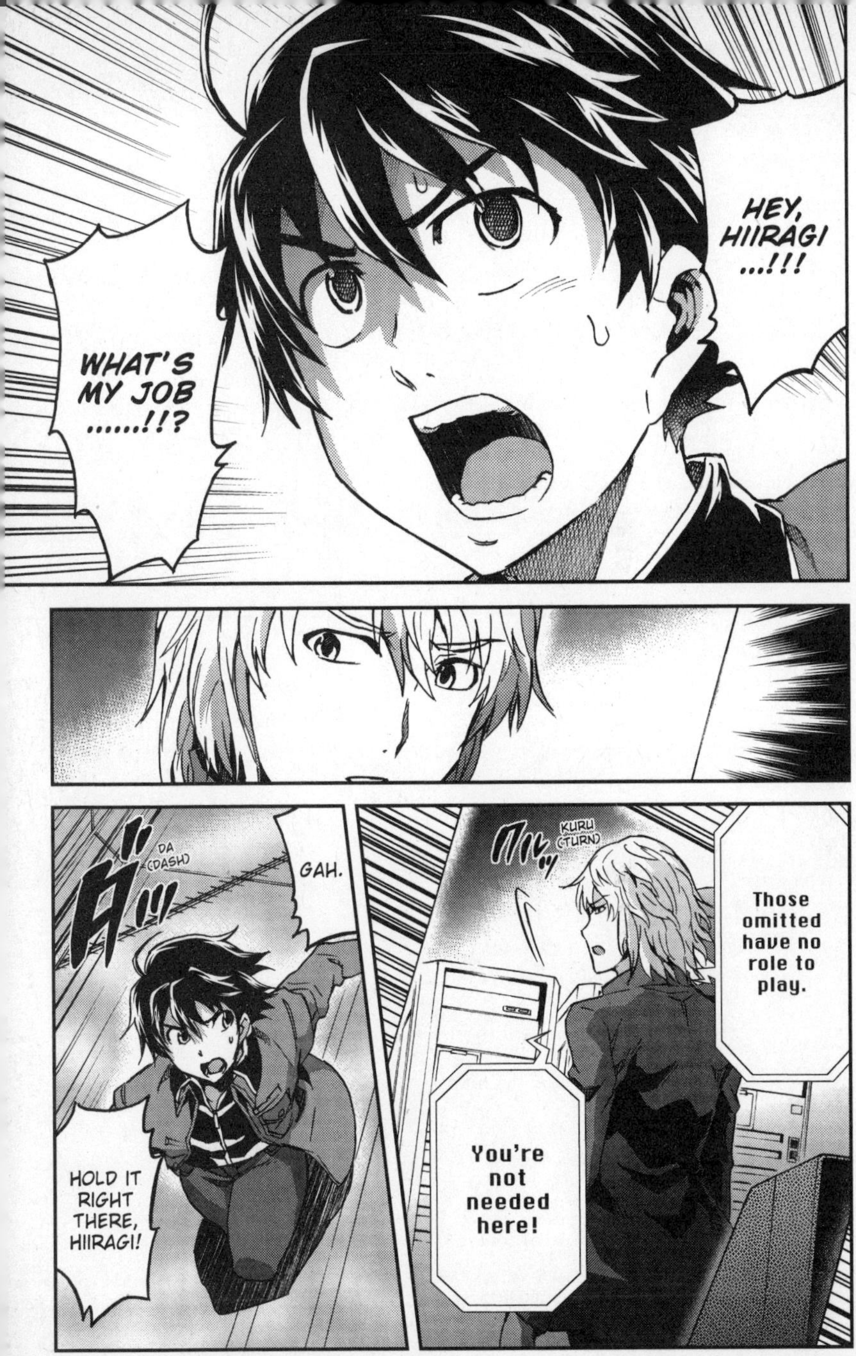
HEY, HIIRAGI ...!!!
WHAT'S MY JOB ......!!?
Those omitted have no role to play.
KURU (TURN)
You're not needed here!
GAH.
DA (DASH)
HOLD IT RIGHT THERE, HIIRAGI!

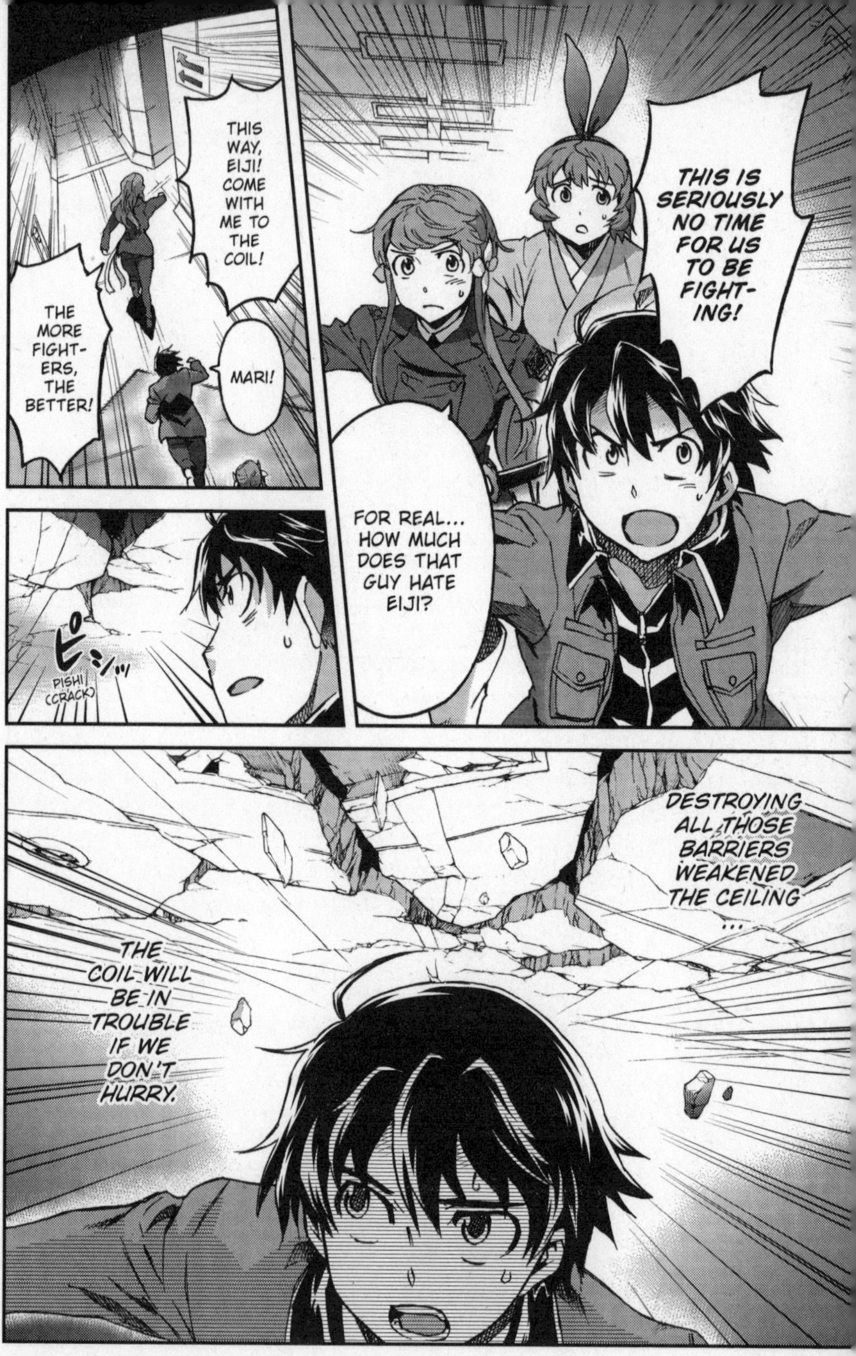
THIS IS SERIOUSLY NO TIME FOR US TO BE FIGHTING!
FOR REAL... HOW MUCH DOES THAT GUY HATE EIJI?
THIS WAY, EIJI! COME WITH ME TO THE COIL!
MARI!
THE MORE FIGHTERS, THE BETTER!
ピシッ
PISHI (CRACK)
DESTROYING ALL THOSE BARRIERS WEAKENED THE CEILING...
THE COIL WILL BE IN TROUBLE IF WE DON'T HURRY.

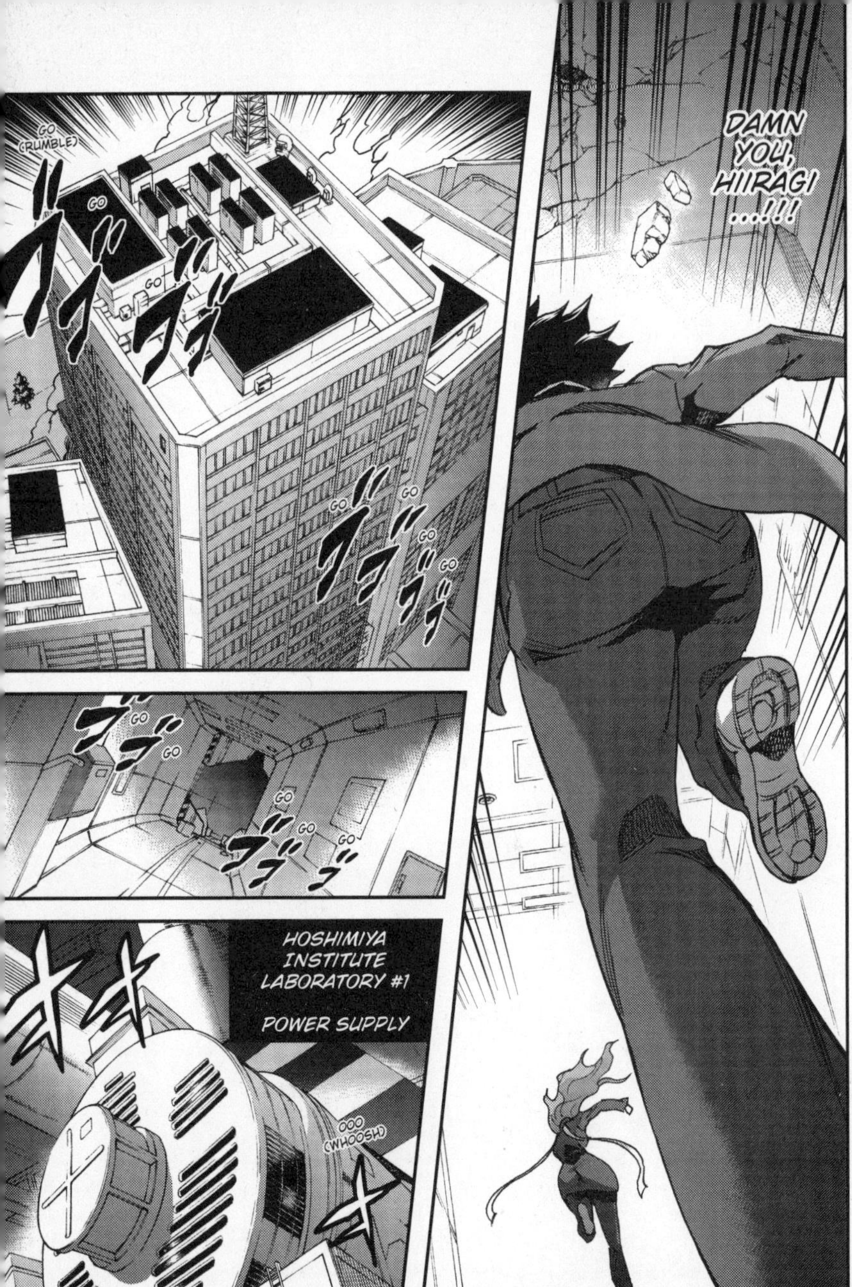
DAMN YOU, HIIRAGI ...!!!
GO (RUMBLE)
GO
GO
GO
GO
GO
GO
GO
GO
GO
GO
GO
HOSHIMIYA INSTITUTE LABORATORY #1
POWER SUPPLY
OOO (WHOOSH)

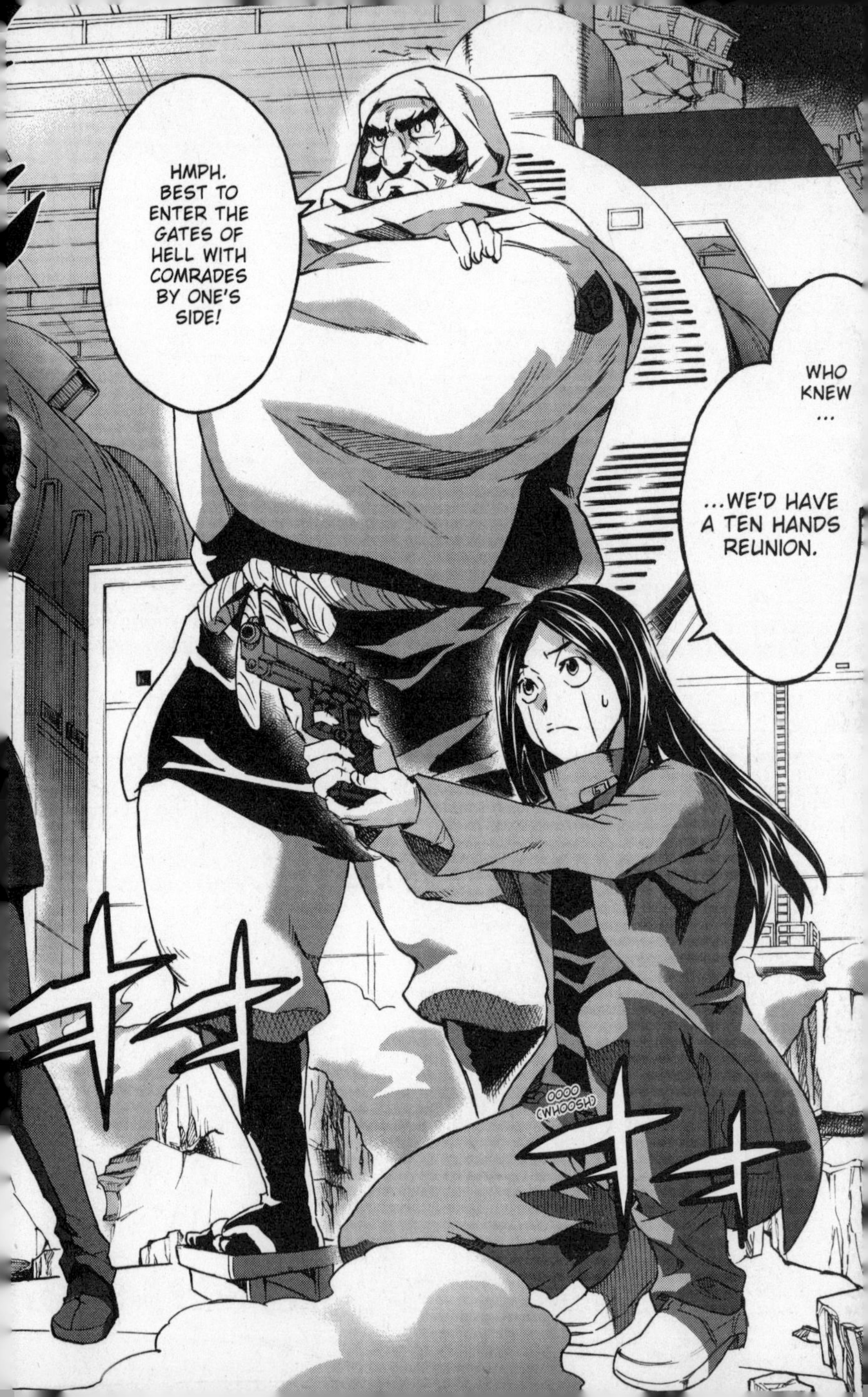
WHO KNEW ...
...WE'D HAVE A TEN HANDS REUNION.
HMPH. BEST TO ENTER THE GATES OF HELL WITH COMRADES BY ONE'S SIDE!
(WHOOSH)

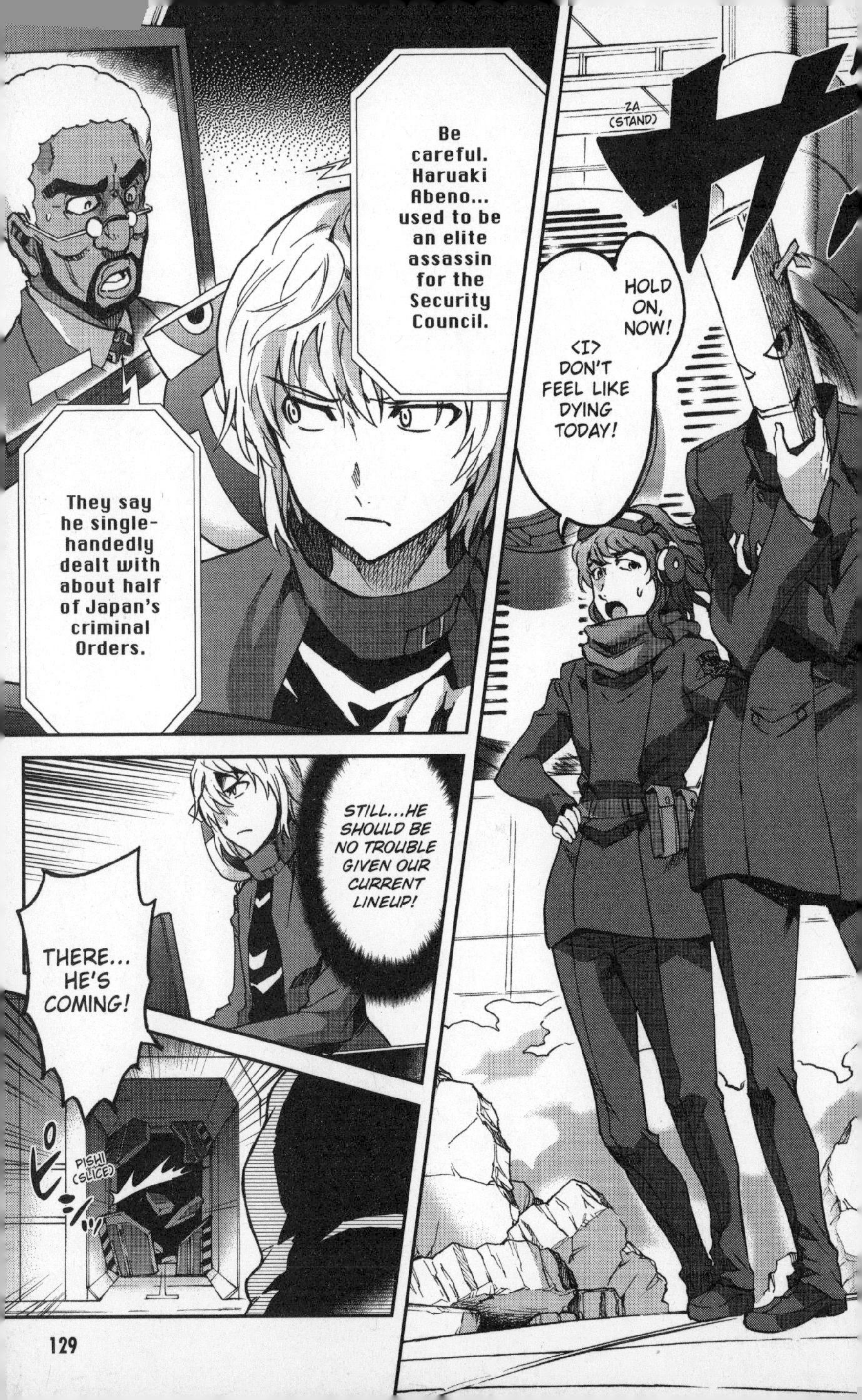
ZA
(STAND)
HOLD ON, NOW!
<I> DON'T FEEL LIKE DYING TODAY!
Be careful. Haruaki Abeno... used to be an elite assassin for the Security Council.
They say he single-handedly dealt with about half of Japan's criminal Orders.
STILL...HE SHOULD BE NO TROUBLE GIVEN OUR CURRENT LINEUP!
THERE... HE'S COMING!
PISHI
(SLICE)

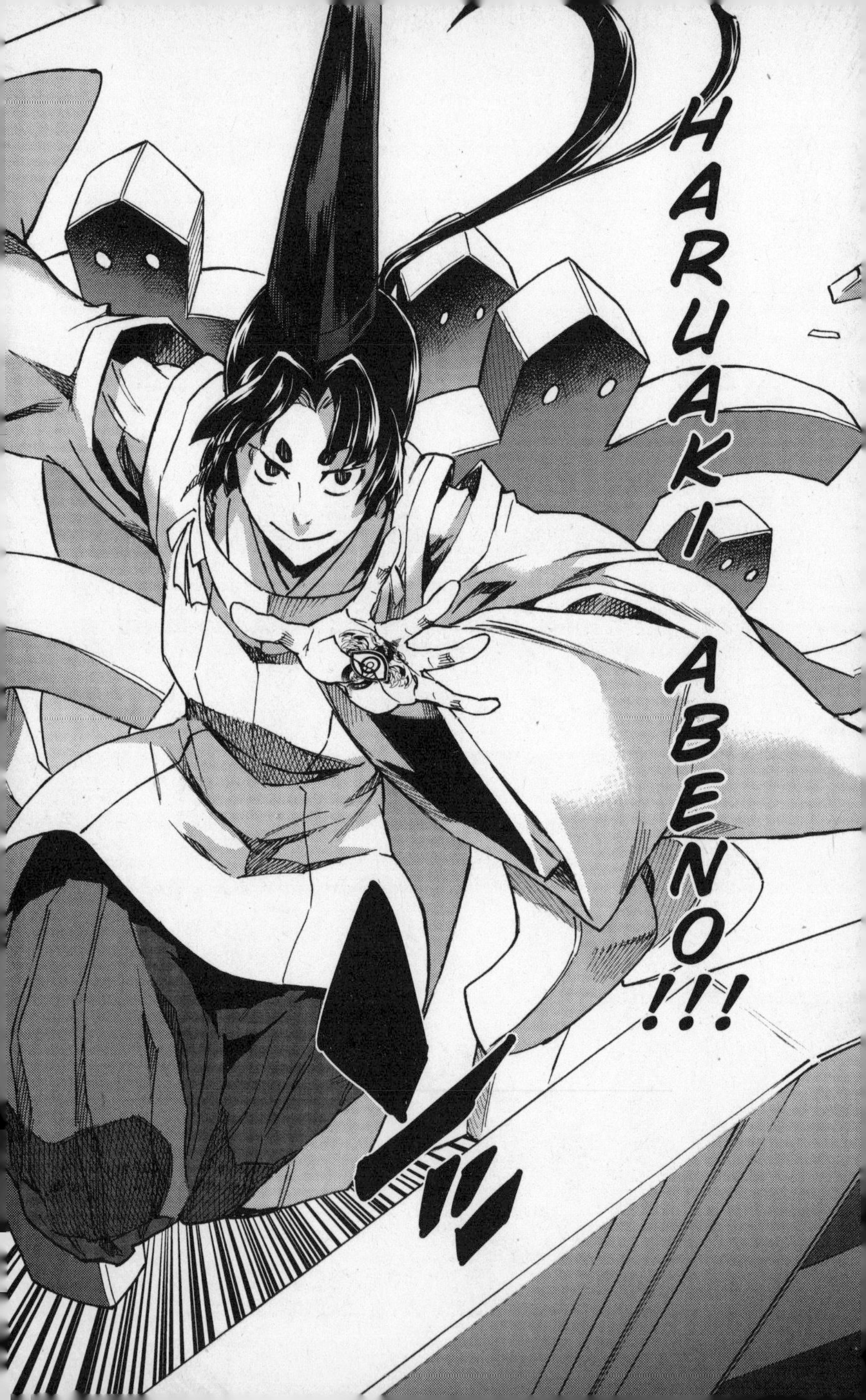
HARUAKI ABENO!!!

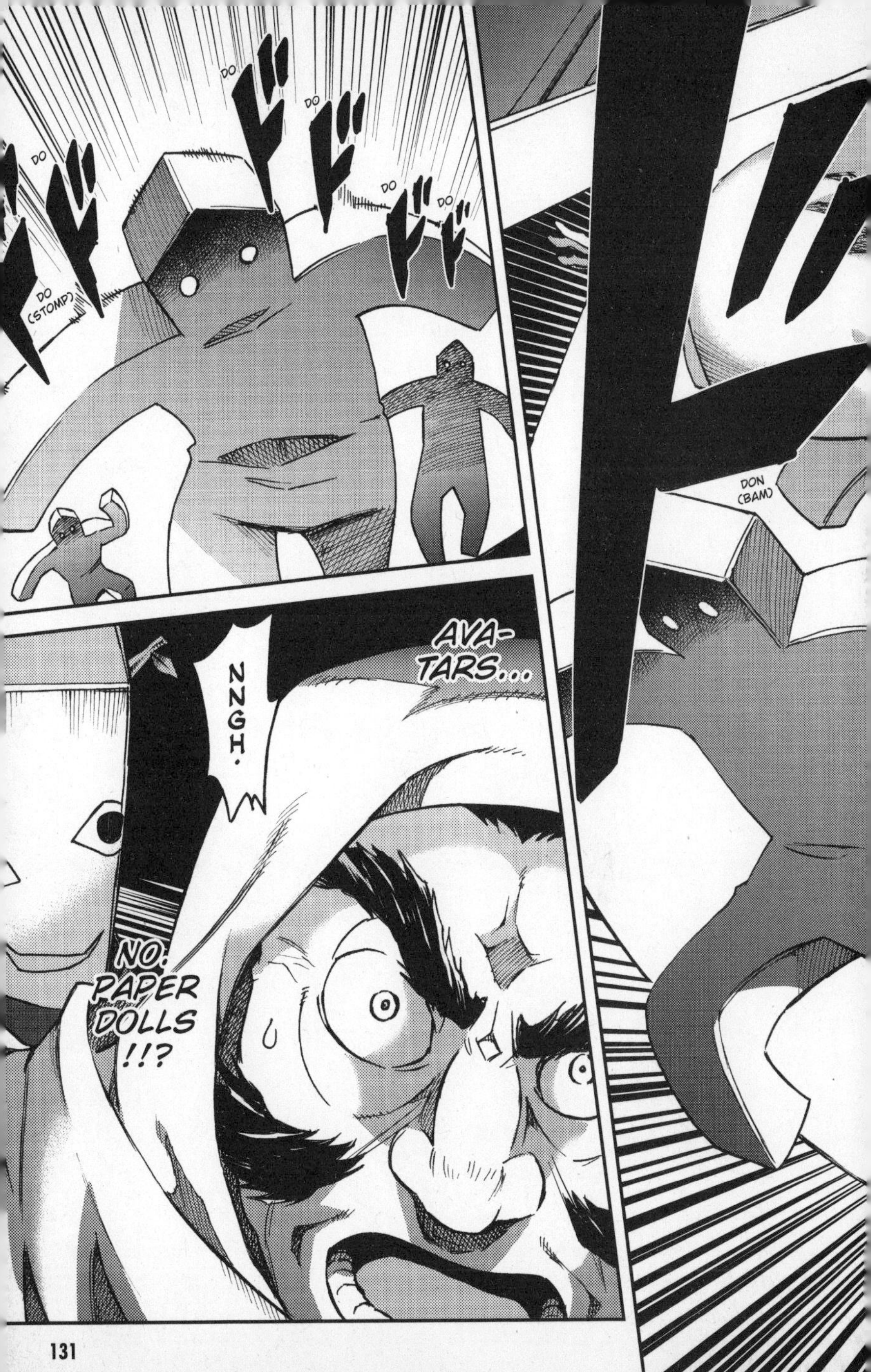
DON
(BAM)
DO
DO
DO
DO
DO
DO
(STOMP)
AVA-TARS...
NNGH.
NO. PAPER DOLLS!!?

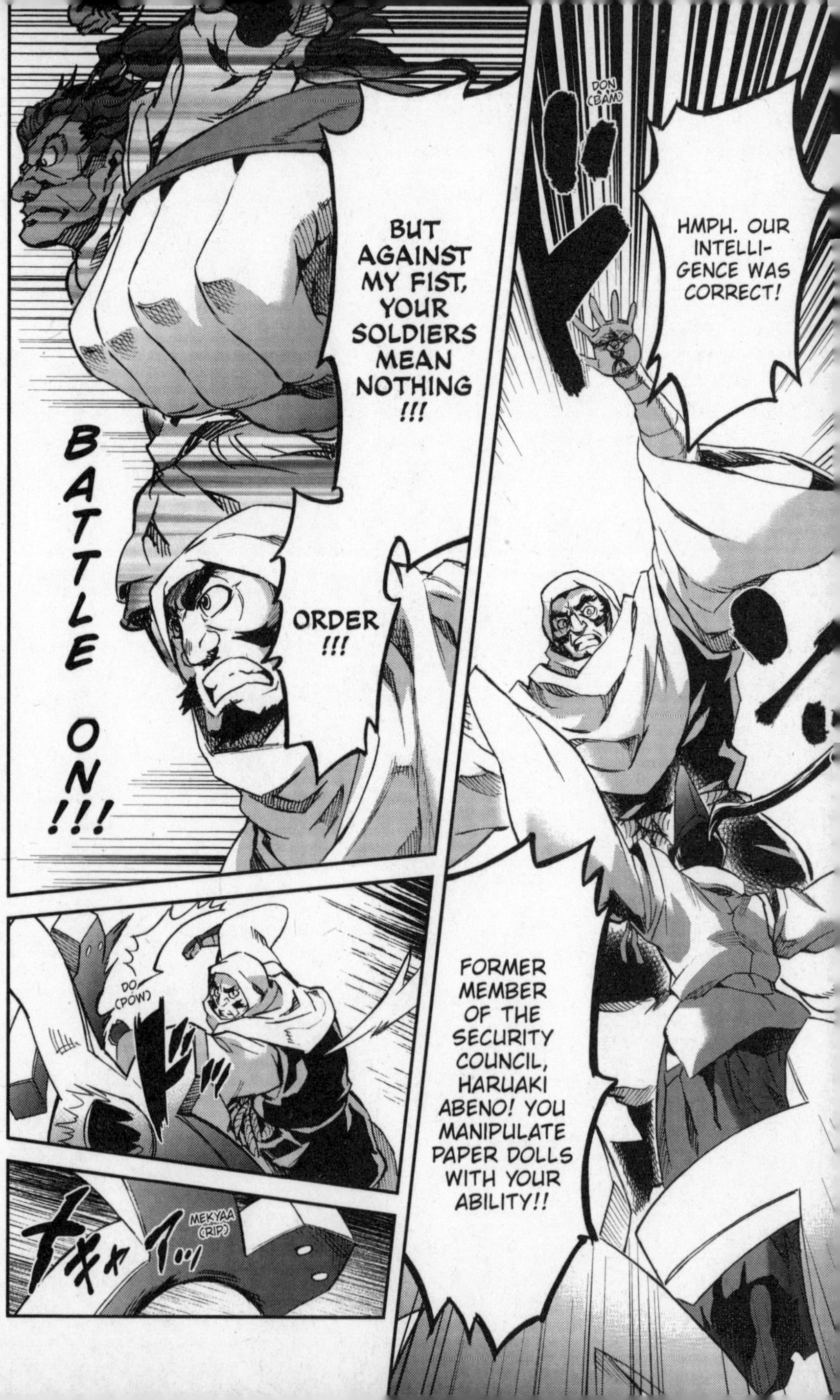
DON (BAM)
HMPH. OUR INTELLI-GENCE WAS CORRECT!
FORMER MEMBER OF THE SECURITY COUNCIL, HARUAKI ABENO! YOU MANIPULATE PAPER DOLLS WITH YOUR ABILITY!!
BUT AGAINST MY FIST, YOUR SOLDIERS MEAN NOTHING!!!
ORDER!!!
BATTLE ON!!!
DO (POW)
MEKYAA (RIP)

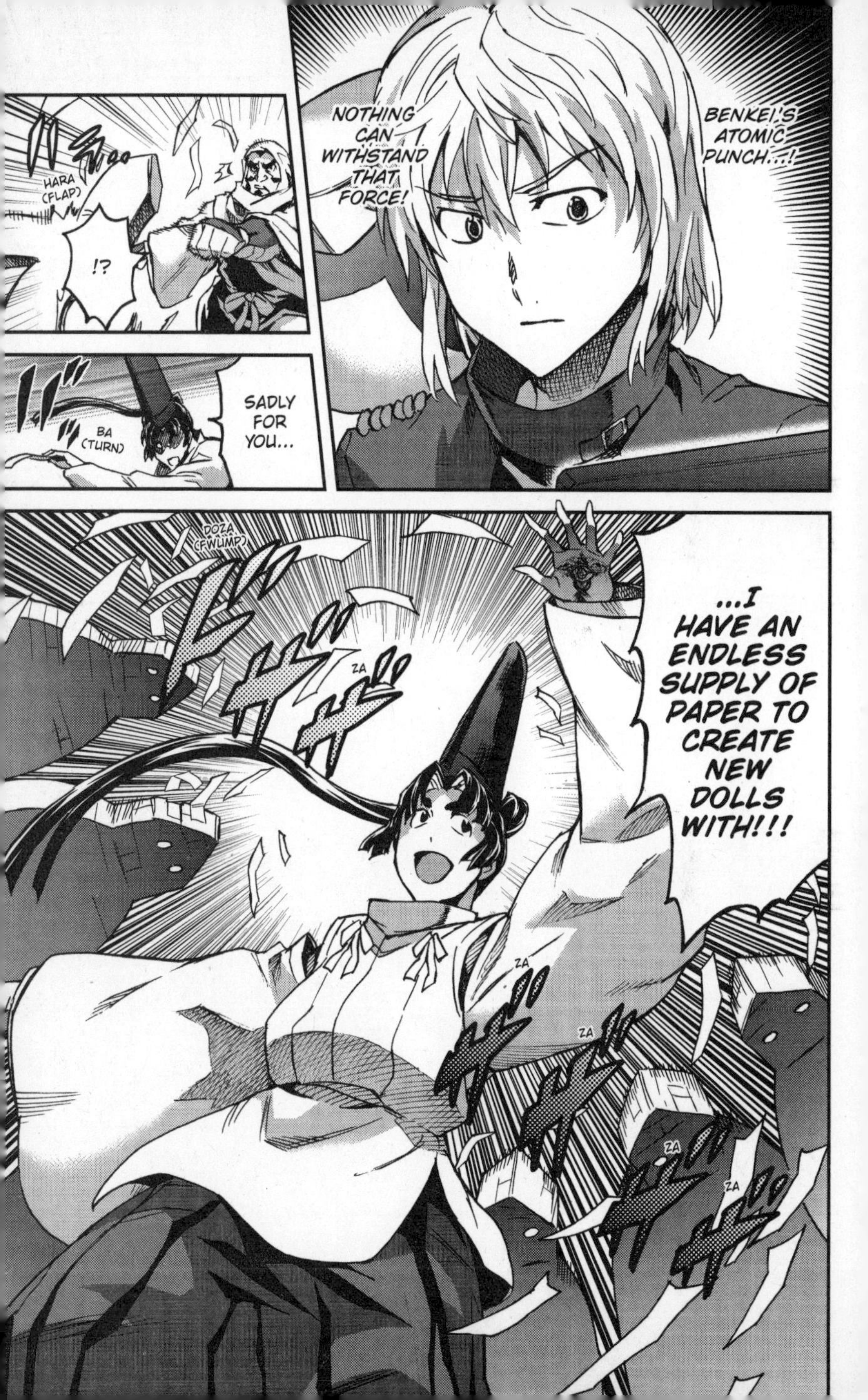
BENKEI'S ATOMIC PUNCH...!
NOTHING CAN WITHSTAND THAT FORCE!
HARA (FLAP)
!?
SADLY FOR YOU...
BA (TURN)
...I HAVE AN ENDLESS SUPPLY OF PAPER TO CREATE NEW DOLLS WITH!!!
DOZA (FWUMP)
ZA
ZA
ZA
ZA
ZA

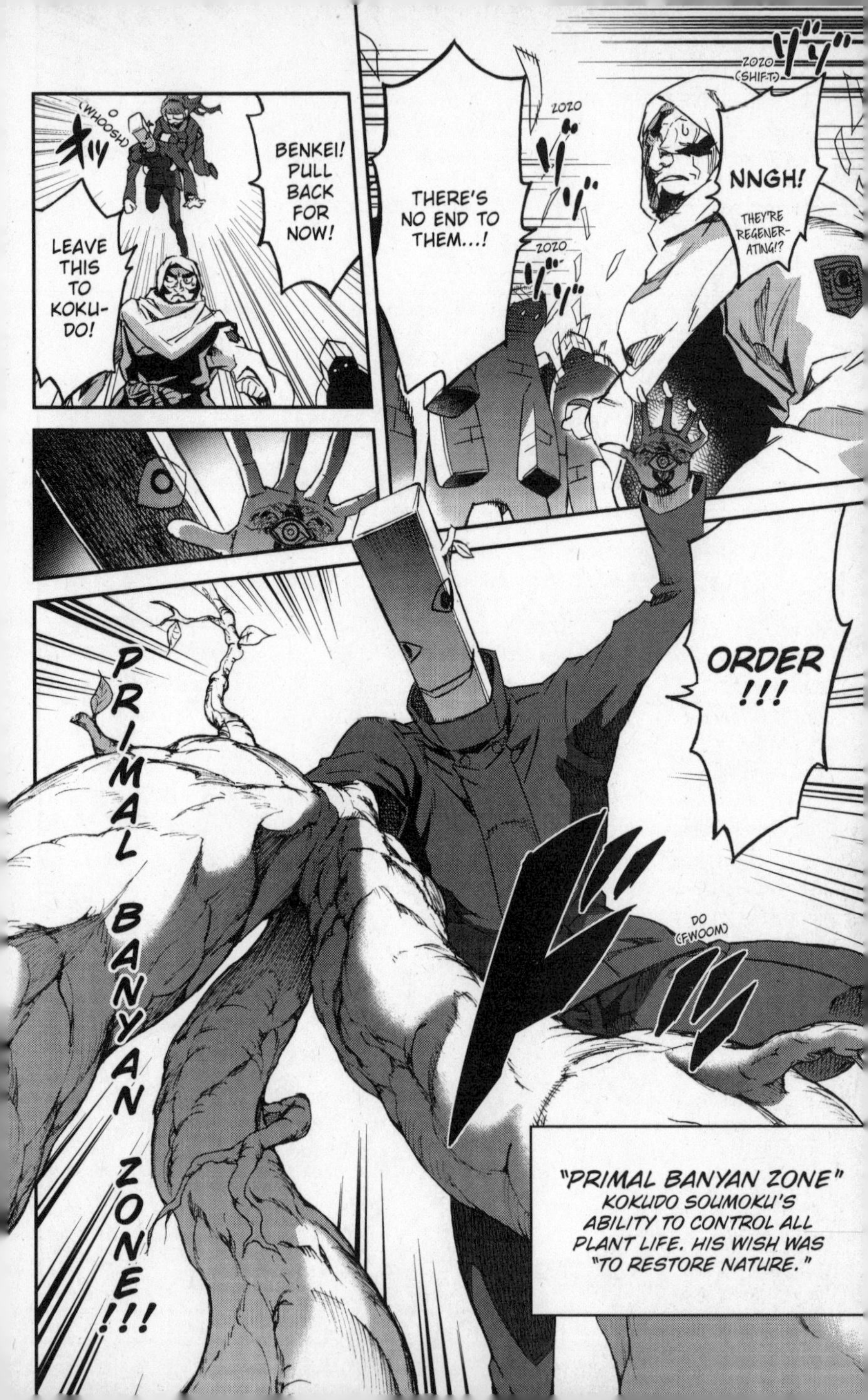
ZOZO (SHIFT-)
ZOZO
ZOZO
THERE'S NO END TO THEM...!
NNGH!
THEY'RE REGENER-ATING!?
BENKEI! PULL BACK FOR NOW!
O (WHOOSH)
LEAVE THIS TO KOKU-DO!
ORDER!!!
PRIMAL BANYAN ZONE!!!
DO (FWOOM)
"PRIMAL BANYAN ZONE" KOKUDO SOUMOKU'S ABILITY TO CONTROL ALL PLANT LIFE. HIS WISH WAS "TO RESTORE NATURE."

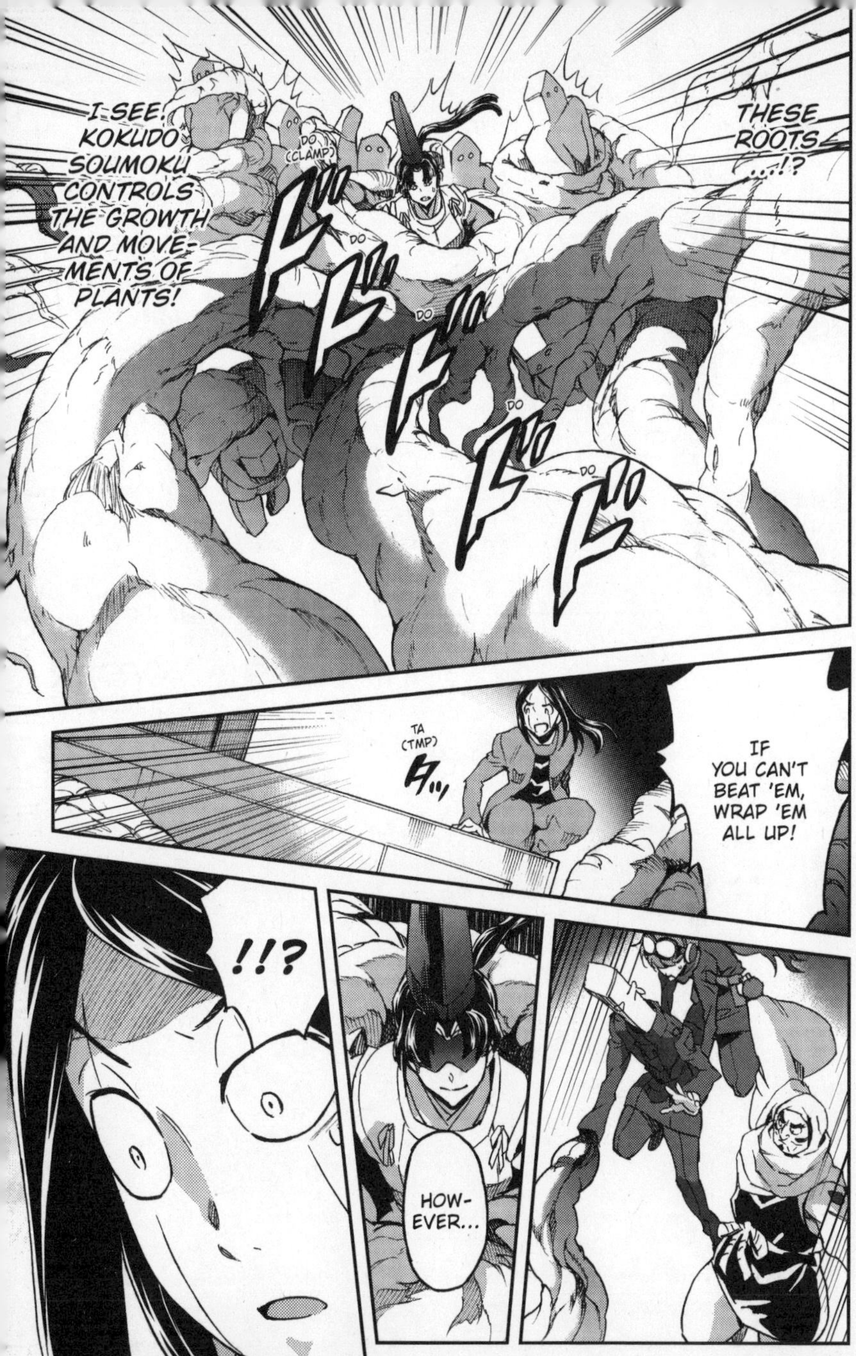
THESE ROOTS...!?
I SEE! KOKUDO SOUMOKU CONTROLS THE GROWTH AND MOVEMENTS OF PLANTS!
DO (CLAMP)
DO
DO
DO
DO
IF YOU CAN'T BEAT 'EM, WRAP 'EM ALL UP!
TA (TMP)
HOW-EVER...
!!?

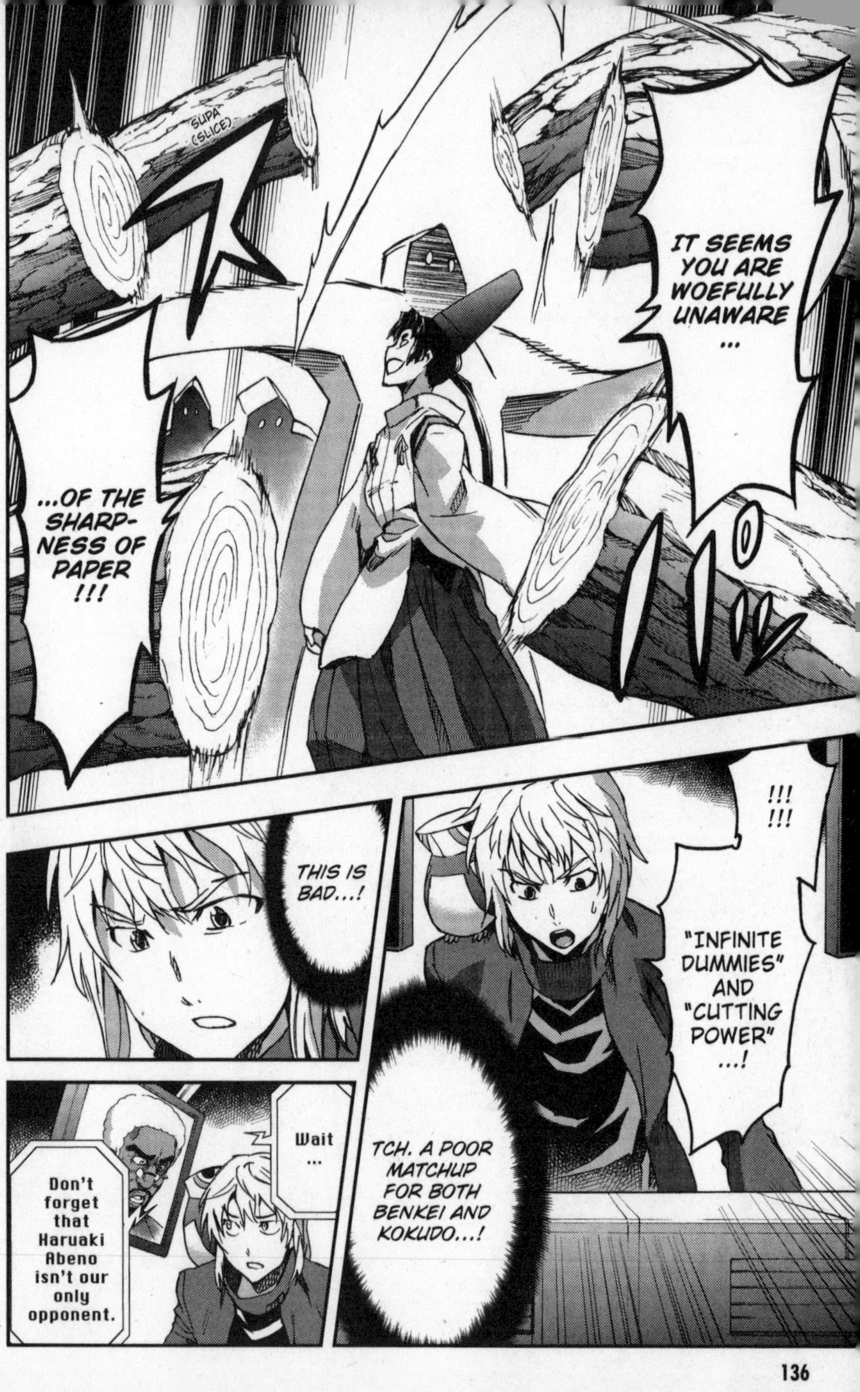
IT SEEMS YOU ARE WOEFULLY UNAWARE ...
SUPA (SLICE)
...OF THE SHARPNESS OF PAPER !!!
!!! !!!
"INFINITE DUMMIES" AND "CUTTING POWER" ...!
TCH. A POOR MATCHUP FOR BOTH BENKEI AND KOKUDO...!
THIS IS BAD...!
Wait ...
Don't forget that Haruaki Abeno isn't our only opponent.

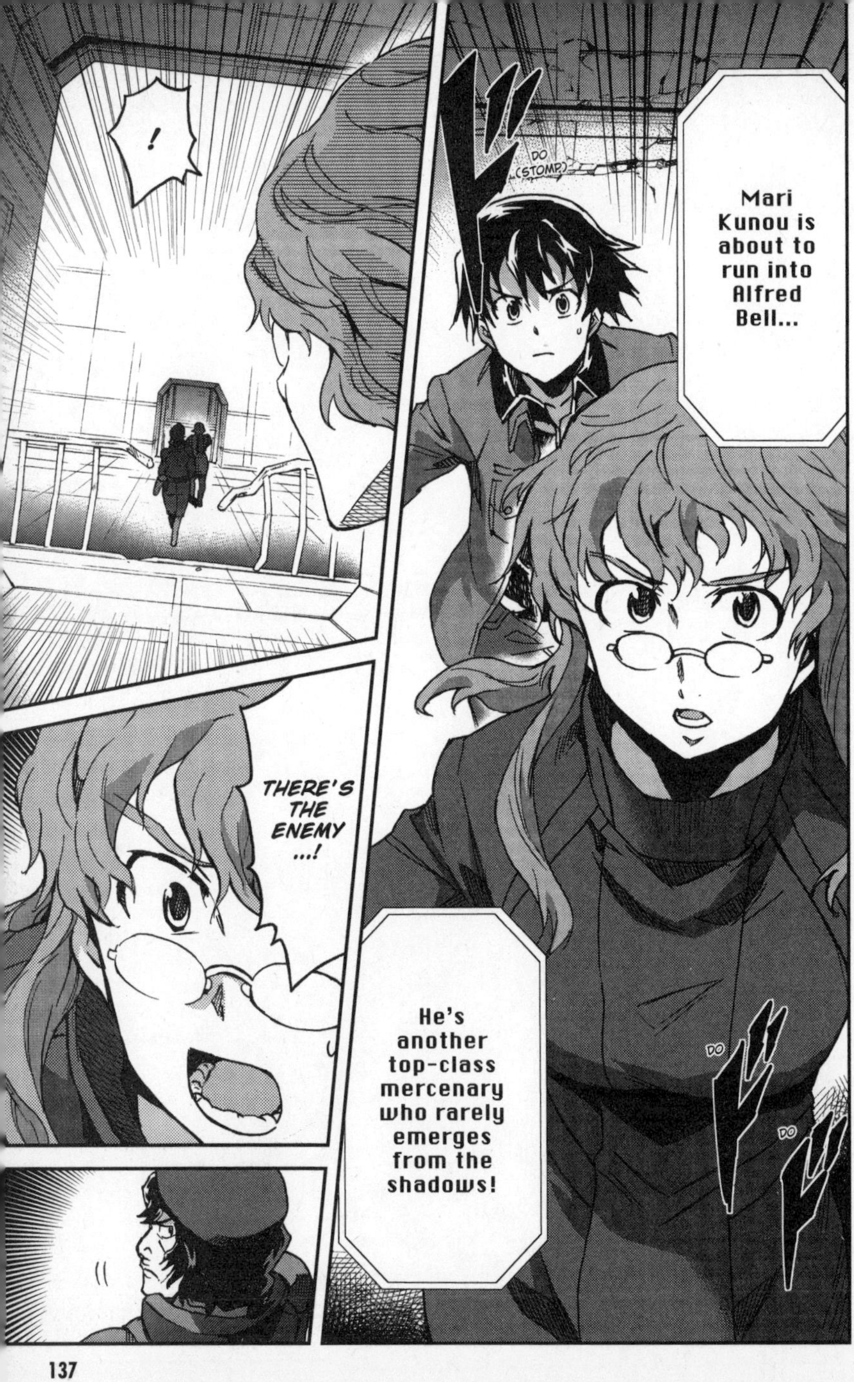
DO (STOMP)
Mari Kunou is about to run into Alfred Bell...
He's another top-class mercenary who rarely emerges from the shadows!
DO
DO
!
THERE'S THE ENEMY ...!

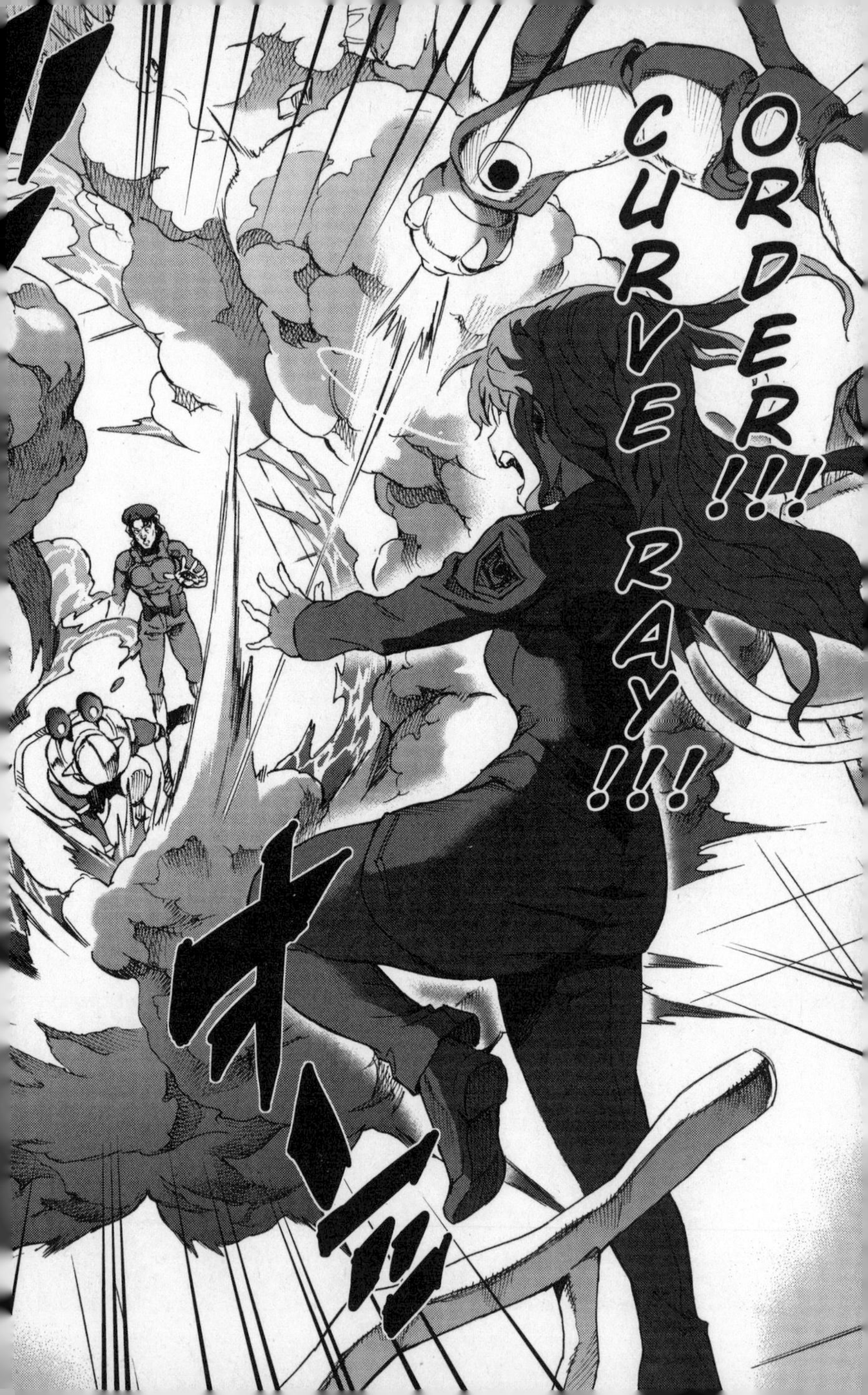
ORDER!!!
CURVE RAY!!!

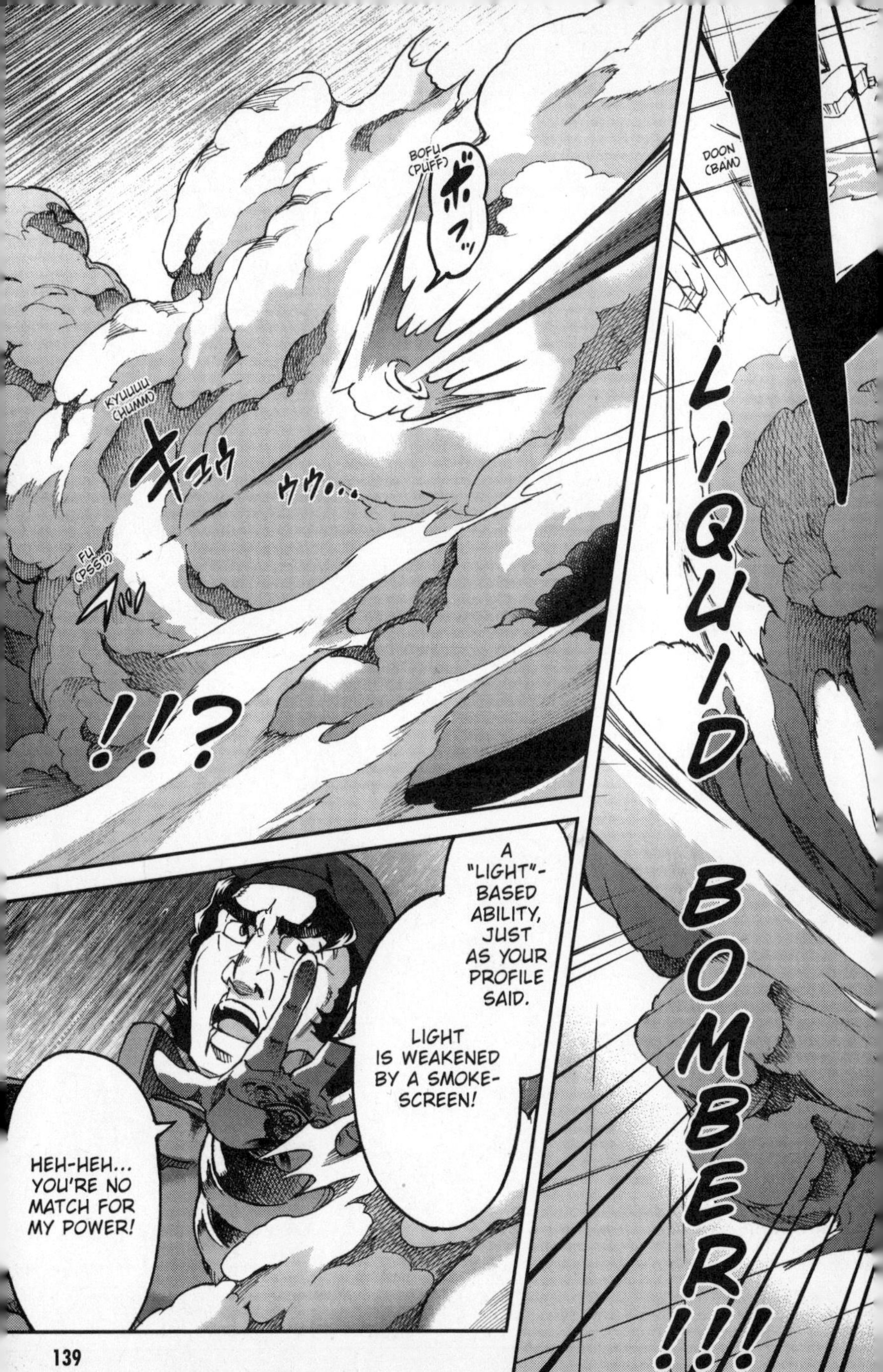
DOON (BAM)
BOFU (PUFF)
KYUUUU (HUMM)
FU (PSST)
!!?
LIQUID BOMBER!!!
A "LIGHT"-BASED ABILITY, JUST AS YOUR PROFILE SAID.
LIGHT IS WEAKENED BY A SMOKE-SCREEN!
HEH-HEH... YOU'RE NO MATCH FOR MY POWER!

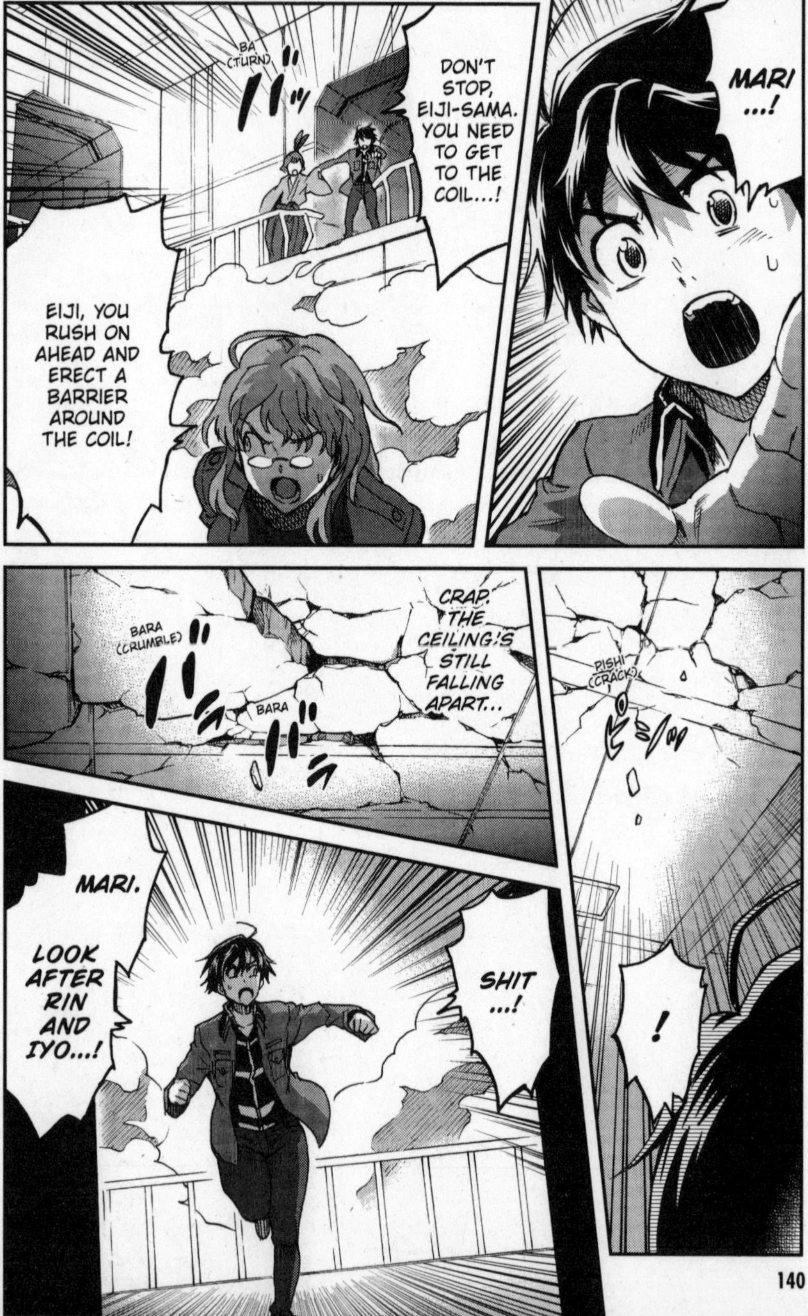
MARI ...!
BA (TURN)
DON'T STOP, EIJI-SAMA. YOU NEED TO GET TO THE COIL...!
EIJI, YOU RUSH ON AHEAD AND ERECT A BARRIER AROUND THE COIL!
PISHI (CRACK)
!
CRAP. THE CEILING'S STILL FALLING APART...
BARA (CRUMBLE)
BARA
SHIT ...!
MARI.
LOOK AFTER RIN AND IYO...!

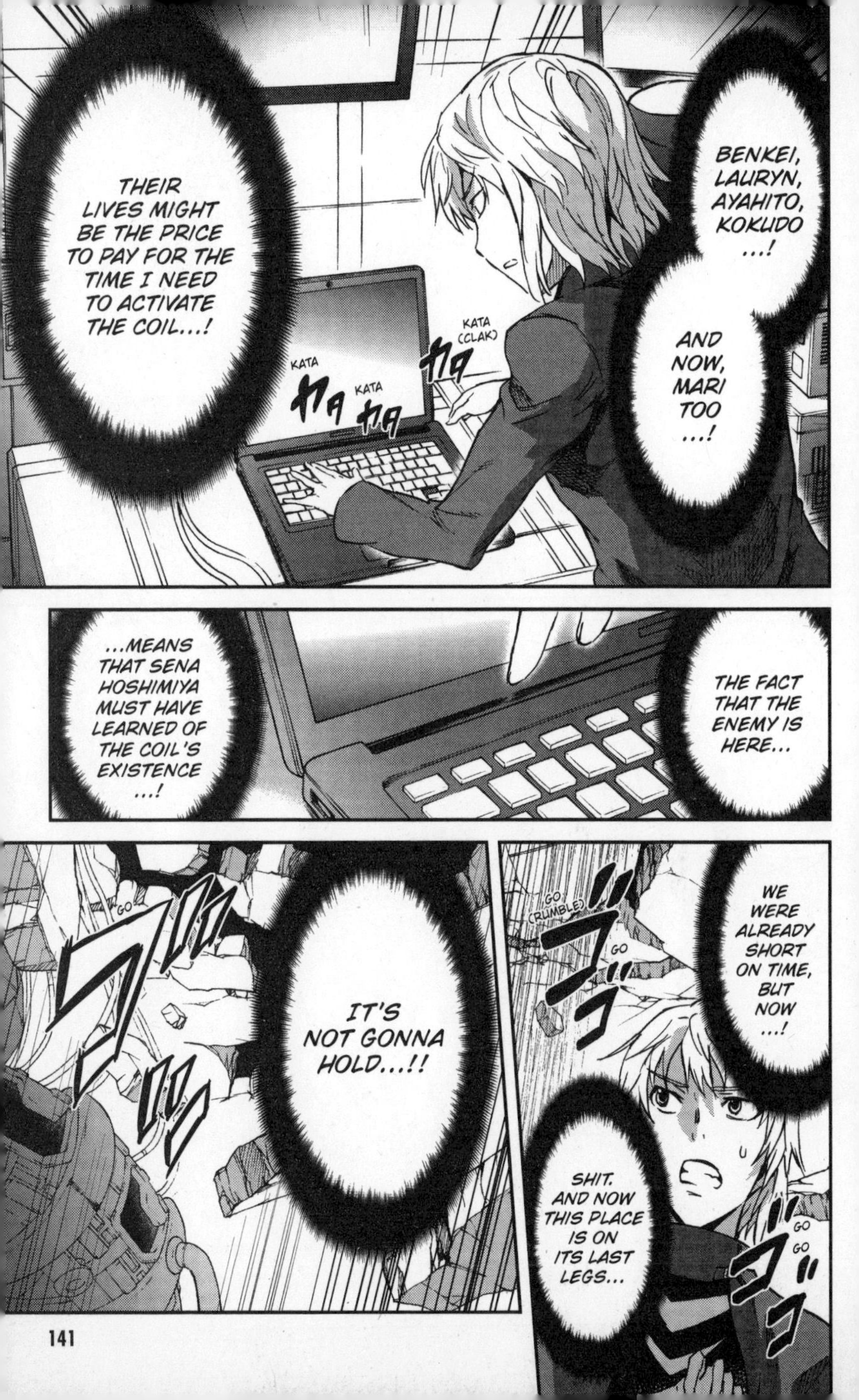
BENKEI, LAURYN, AYAHITO, KOKUDO ...!
AND NOW, MARI TOO ...!
KATA (CLAK)
KATA
KATA
THEIR LIVES MIGHT BE THE PRICE TO PAY FOR THE TIME I NEED TO ACTIVATE THE COIL...!
THE FACT THAT THE ENEMY IS HERE...
...MEANS THAT SENA HOSHIMIYA MUST HAVE LEARNED OF THE COIL'S EXISTENCE ...!
WE WERE ALREADY SHORT ON TIME, BUT NOW ...!
GO (RUMBLE)
GO
SHIT. AND NOW THIS PLACE IS ON ITS LAST LEGS...
GO
GO
IT'S NOT GONNA HOLD...!!
GO

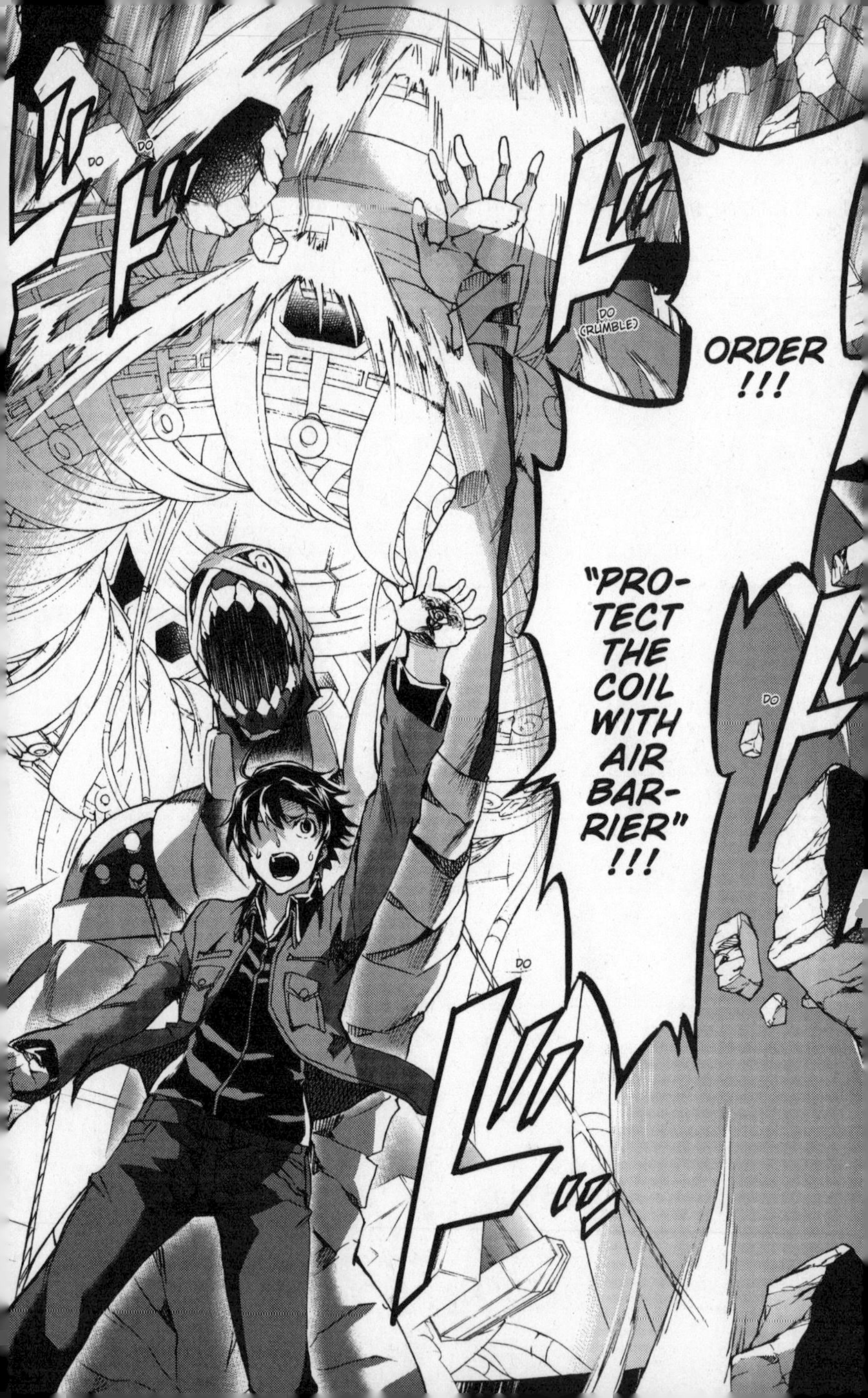
DO
DO
DO
(RUMBLE)
ORDER!!!
"PROTECT THE COIL WITH AIR BARRIER"!!!
DO
DO

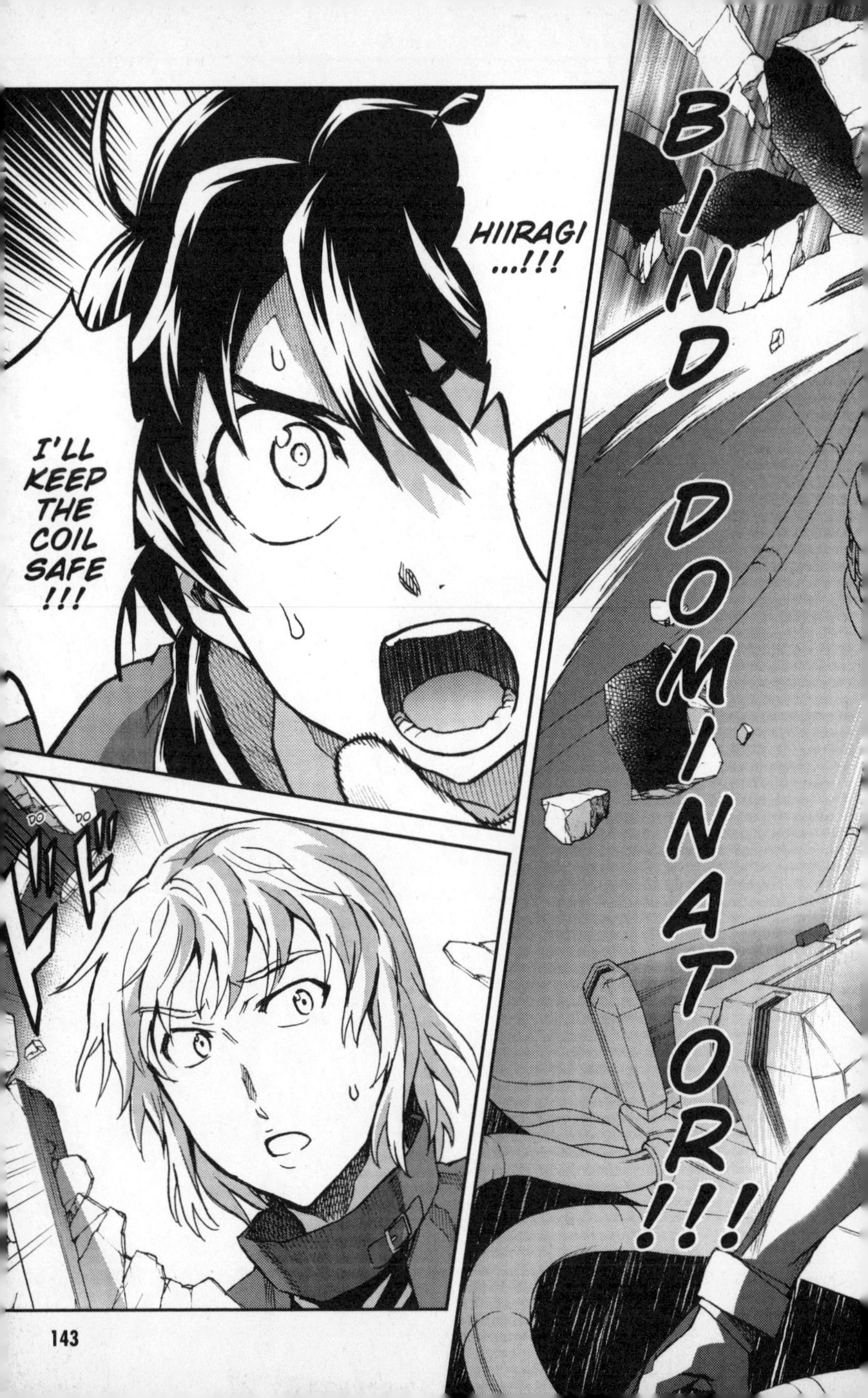
BIND DOMINATOR!!!
HIIRAGI ...!!!
I'LL KEEP THE COIL SAFE!!!
DO DO

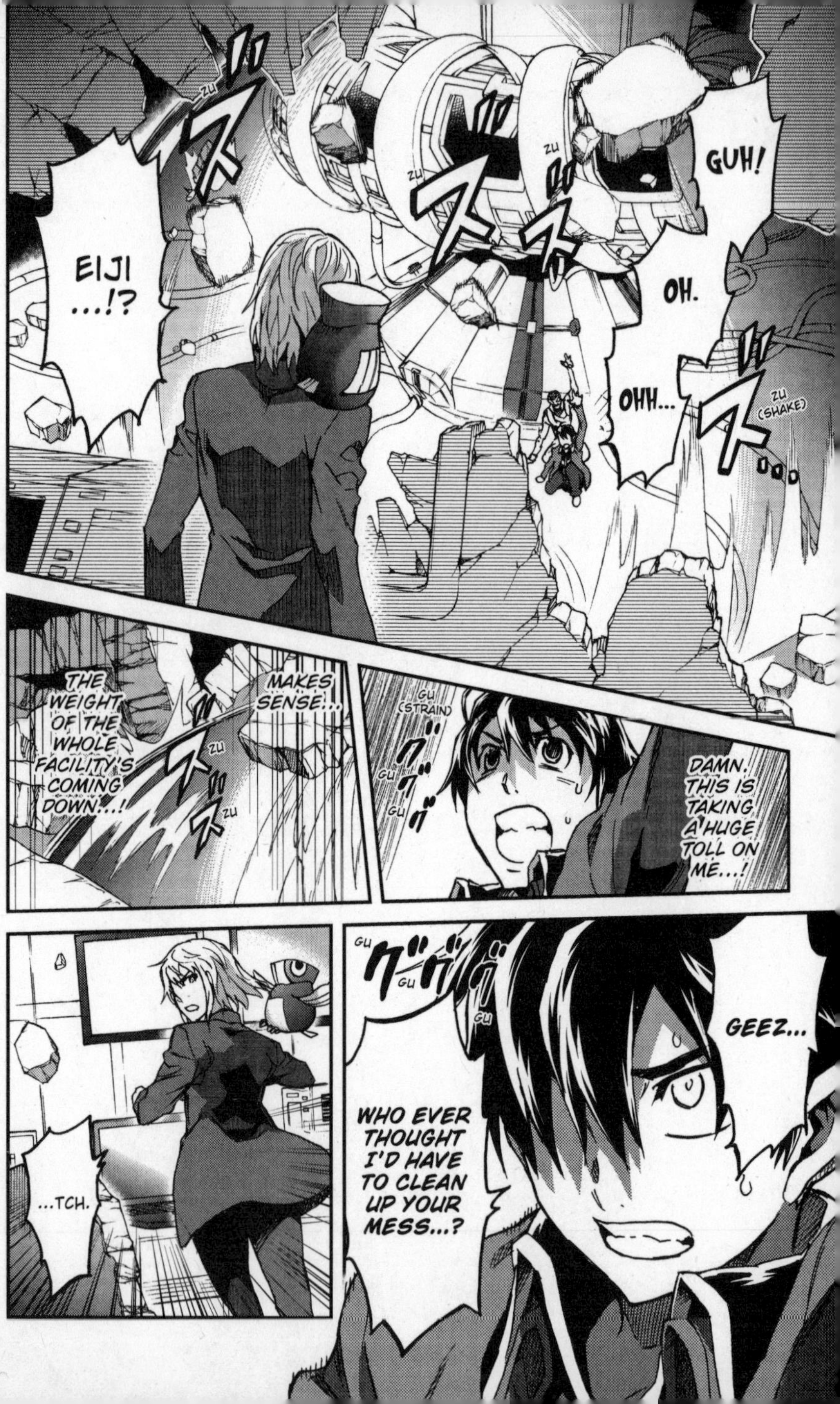
GUH!
ZU
ZU
OH.
OHH...
ZU (SHAKE)
...
EIJI ...!?
ZU
DAMN. THIS IS TAKING A HUGE TOLL ON ME...!
GU (STRAIN)
GU
GU
MAKES SENSE...
THE WEIGHT OF THE WHOLE FACILITY'S COMING DOWN...!
ZU
ZU
GU
GU
GU
GEEZ...
WHO EVER THOUGHT I'D HAVE TO CLEAN UP YOUR MESS...?
...TCH.

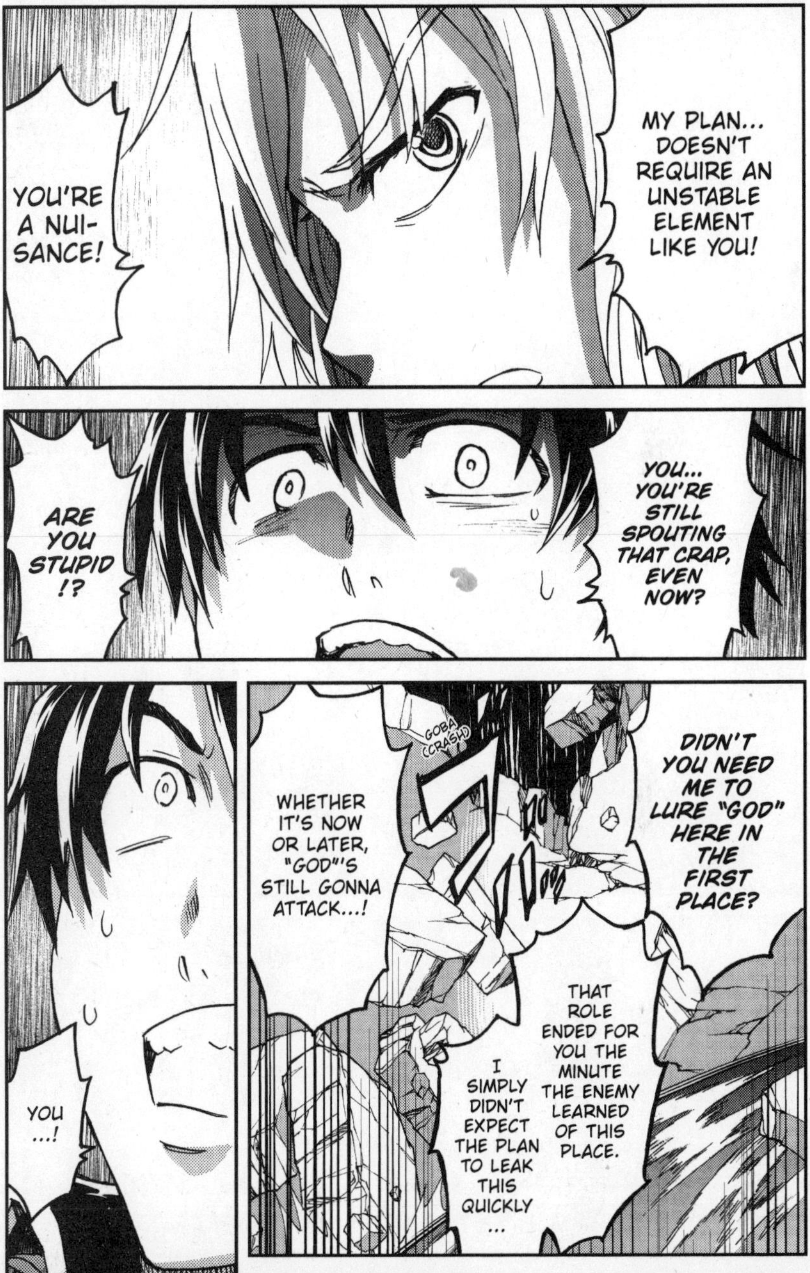
MY PLAN... DOESN'T REQUIRE AN UNSTABLE ELEMENT LIKE YOU!
YOU'RE A NUISANCE!
YOU... YOU'RE STILL SPOUTING THAT CRAP, EVEN NOW?
ARE YOU STUPID!?
DIDN'T YOU NEED ME TO LURE "GOD" HERE IN THE FIRST PLACE?
GOBA (CRASH)
WHETHER IT'S NOW OR LATER, "GOD"'S STILL GONNA ATTACK...!
THAT ROLE ENDED FOR YOU THE MINUTE THE ENEMY LEARNED OF THIS PLACE.
I SIMPLY DIDN'T EXPECT THE PLAN TO LEAK THIS QUICKLY...
YOU...!

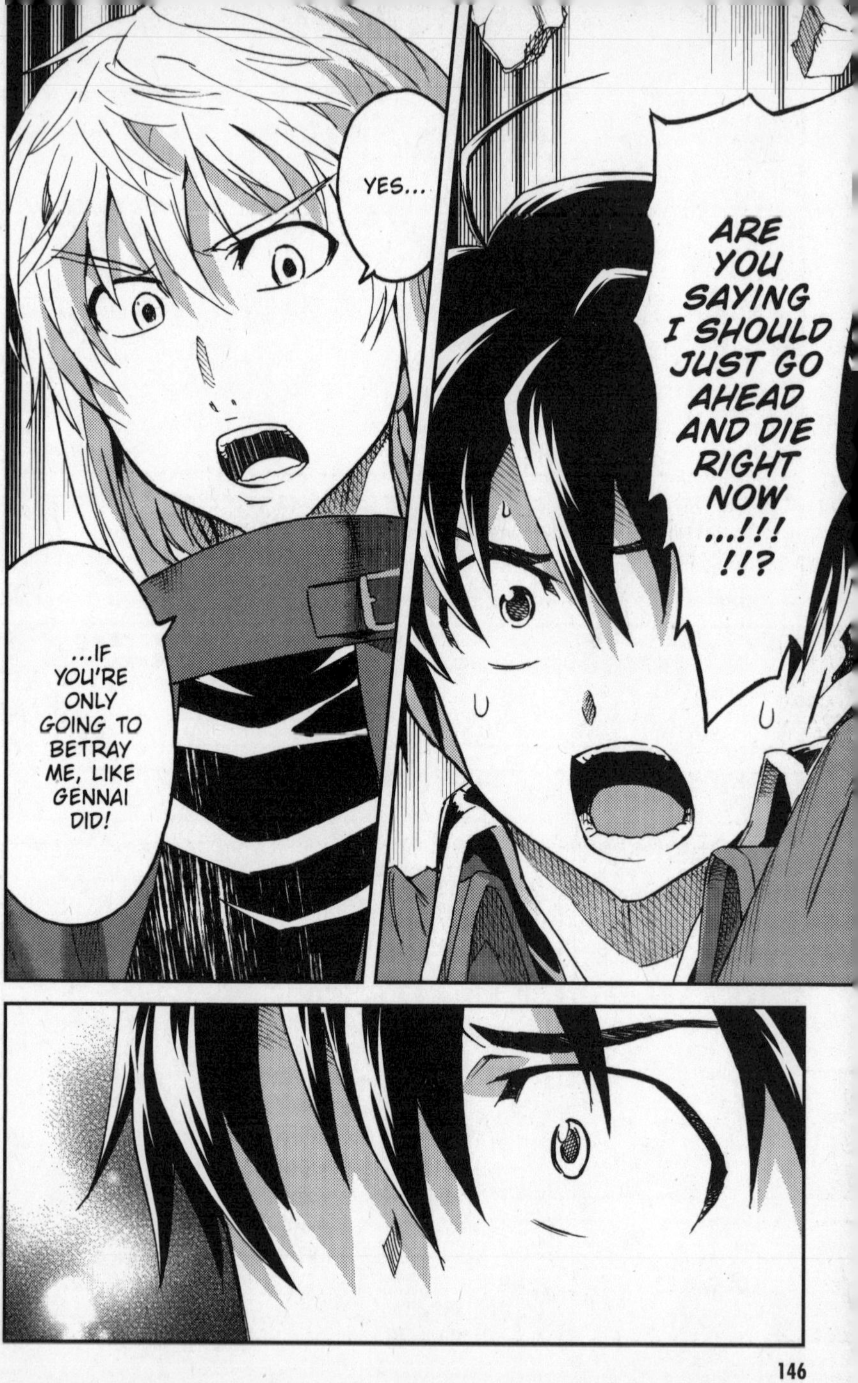
ARE YOU SAYING I SHOULD JUST GO AHEAD AND DIE RIGHT NOW ...!!! !!?
YES...
...IF YOU'RE ONLY GOING TO BETRAY ME, LIKE GENNAI DID!

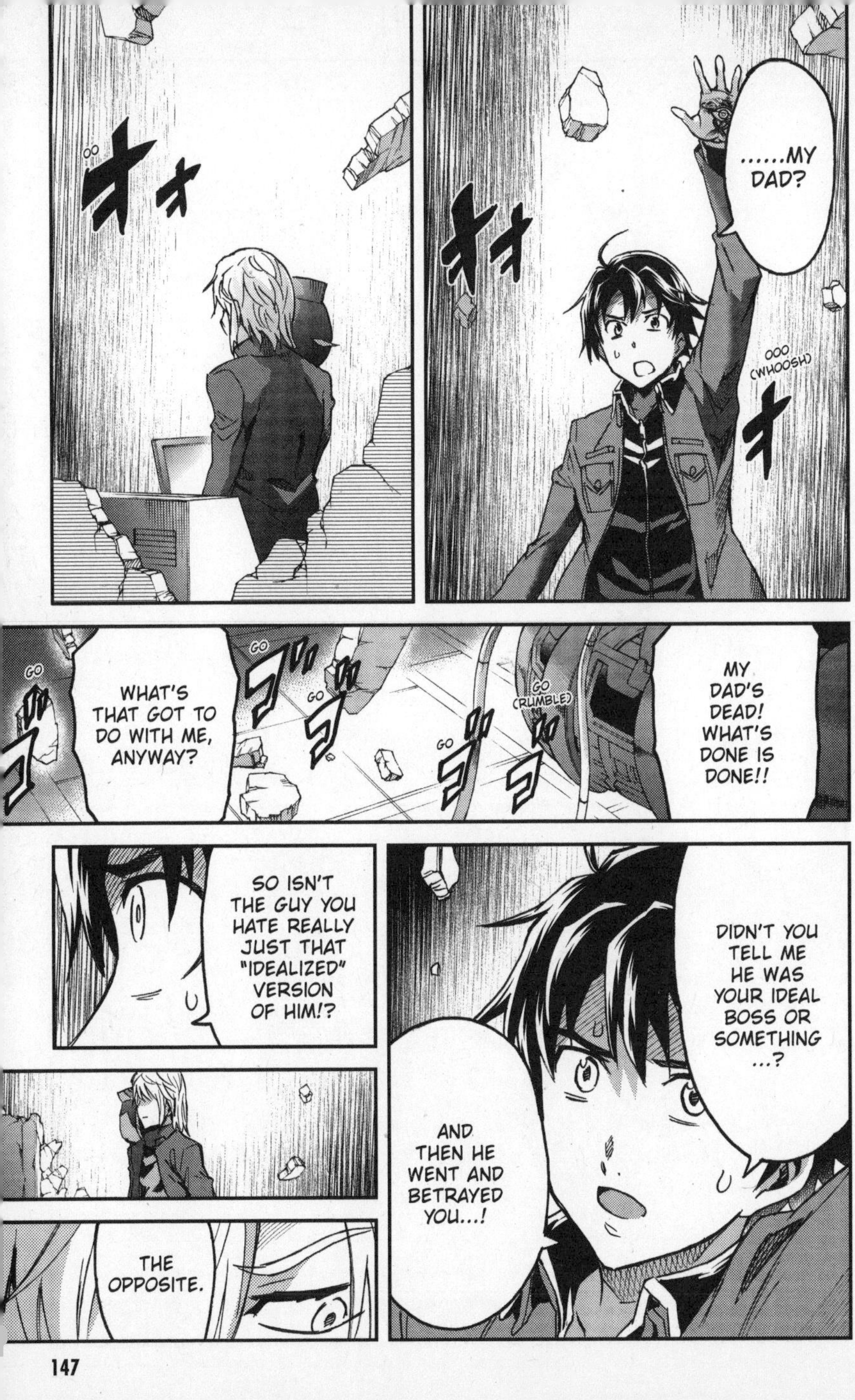
......MY DAD?
OOO (WHOOSH)
OO
MY DAD'S DEAD! WHAT'S DONE IS DONE!!
GO (RUMBLE)
GO
GO
GO
WHAT'S THAT GOT TO DO WITH ME, ANYWAY?
GO
DIDN'T YOU TELL ME HE WAS YOUR IDEAL BOSS OR SOMETHING ...?
AND THEN HE WENT AND BETRAYED YOU...!
SO ISN'T THE GUY YOU HATE REALLY JUST THAT "IDEALIZED" VERSION OF HIM!?
THE OPPOSITE.

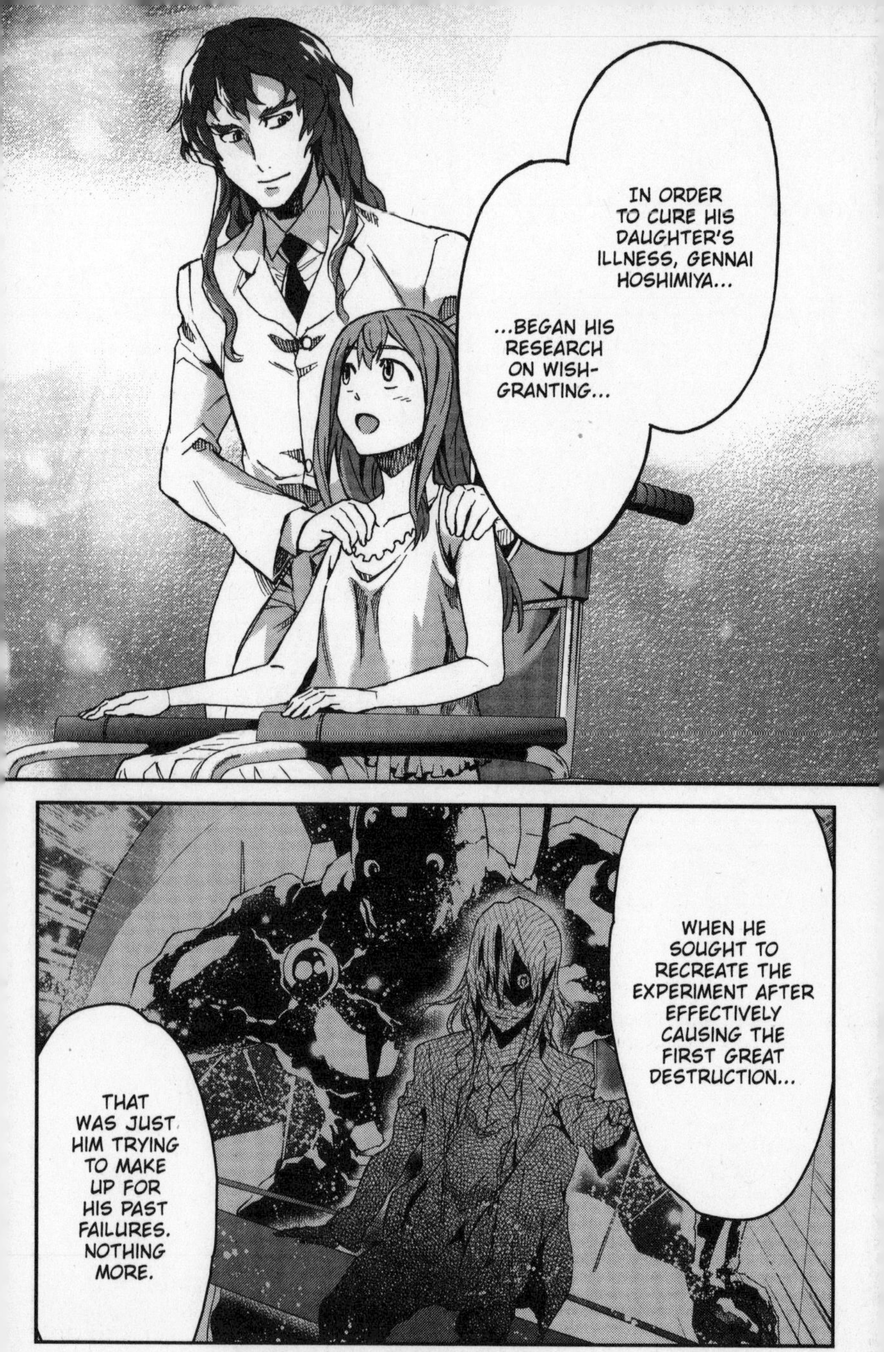
IN ORDER TO CURE HIS DAUGHTER'S ILLNESS, GENNAI HOSHIMIYA...
...BEGAN HIS RESEARCH ON WISH-GRANTING...
WHEN HE SOUGHT TO RECREATE THE EXPERIMENT AFTER EFFECTIVELY CAUSING THE FIRST GREAT DESTRUCTION...
THAT WAS JUST HIM TRYING TO MAKE UP FOR HIS PAST FAILURES. NOTHING MORE.

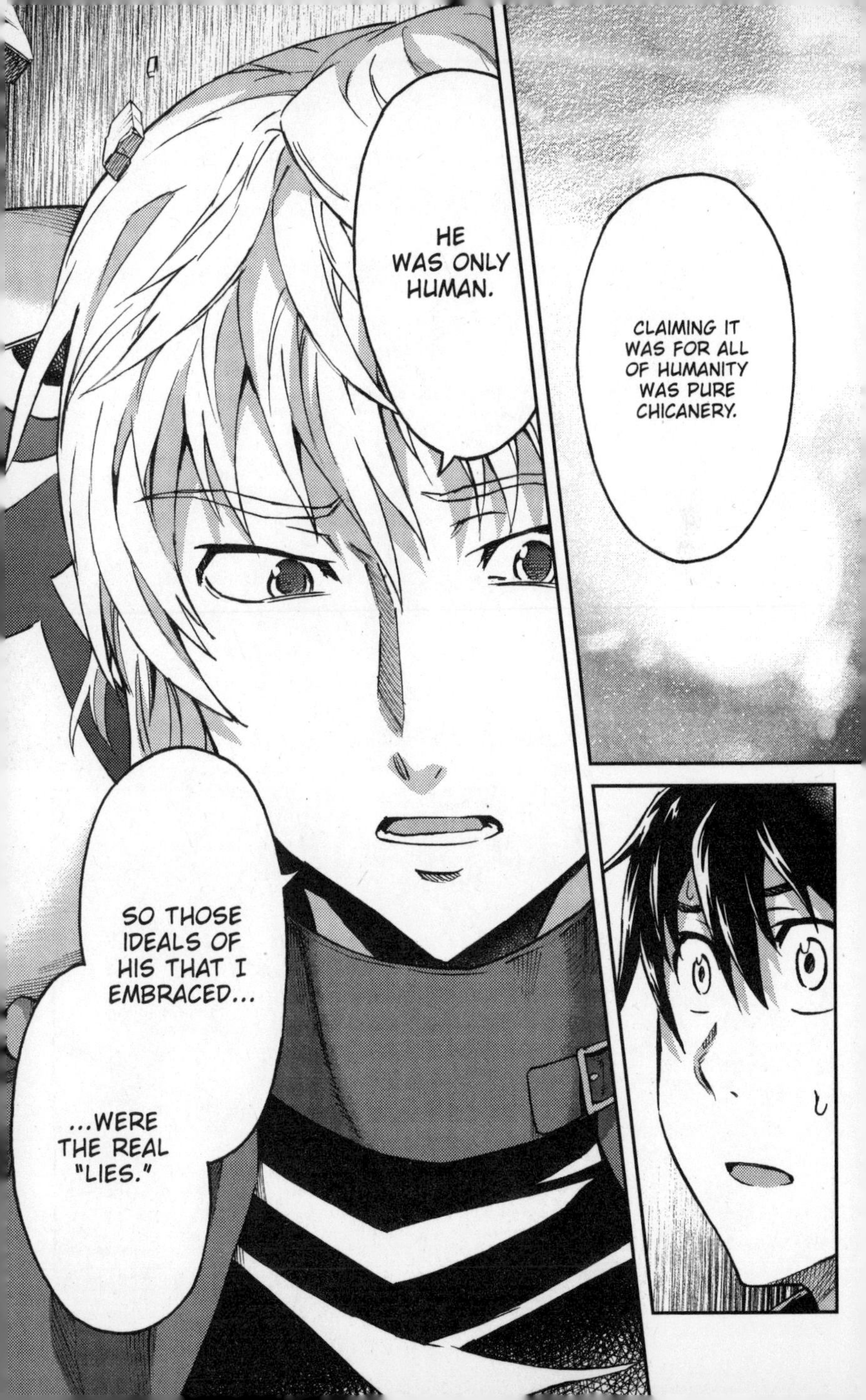

CLAIMING IT WAS FOR ALL OF HUMANITY WAS PURE CHICANERY.
HE WAS ONLY HUMAN.
SO THOSE IDEALS OF HIS THAT I EMBRACED...
...WERE THE REAL "LIES."

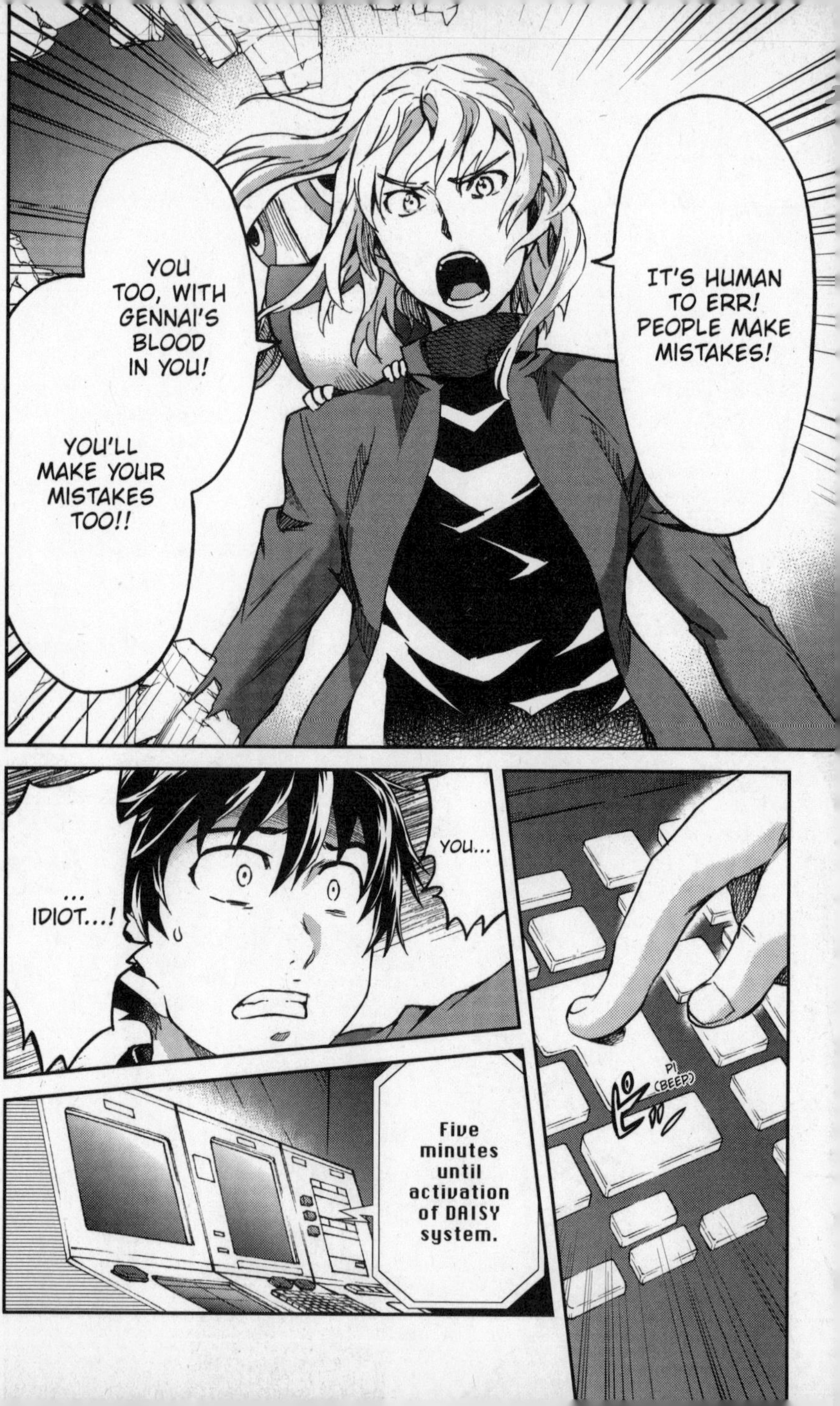
IT'S HUMAN TO ERR! PEOPLE MAKE MISTAKES!
YOU TOO, WITH GENNAI'S BLOOD IN YOU!
YOU'LL MAKE YOUR MISTAKES TOO!!
PI (BEEP)
YOU...
... IDIOT...!
Five minutes until activation of DAISY system.

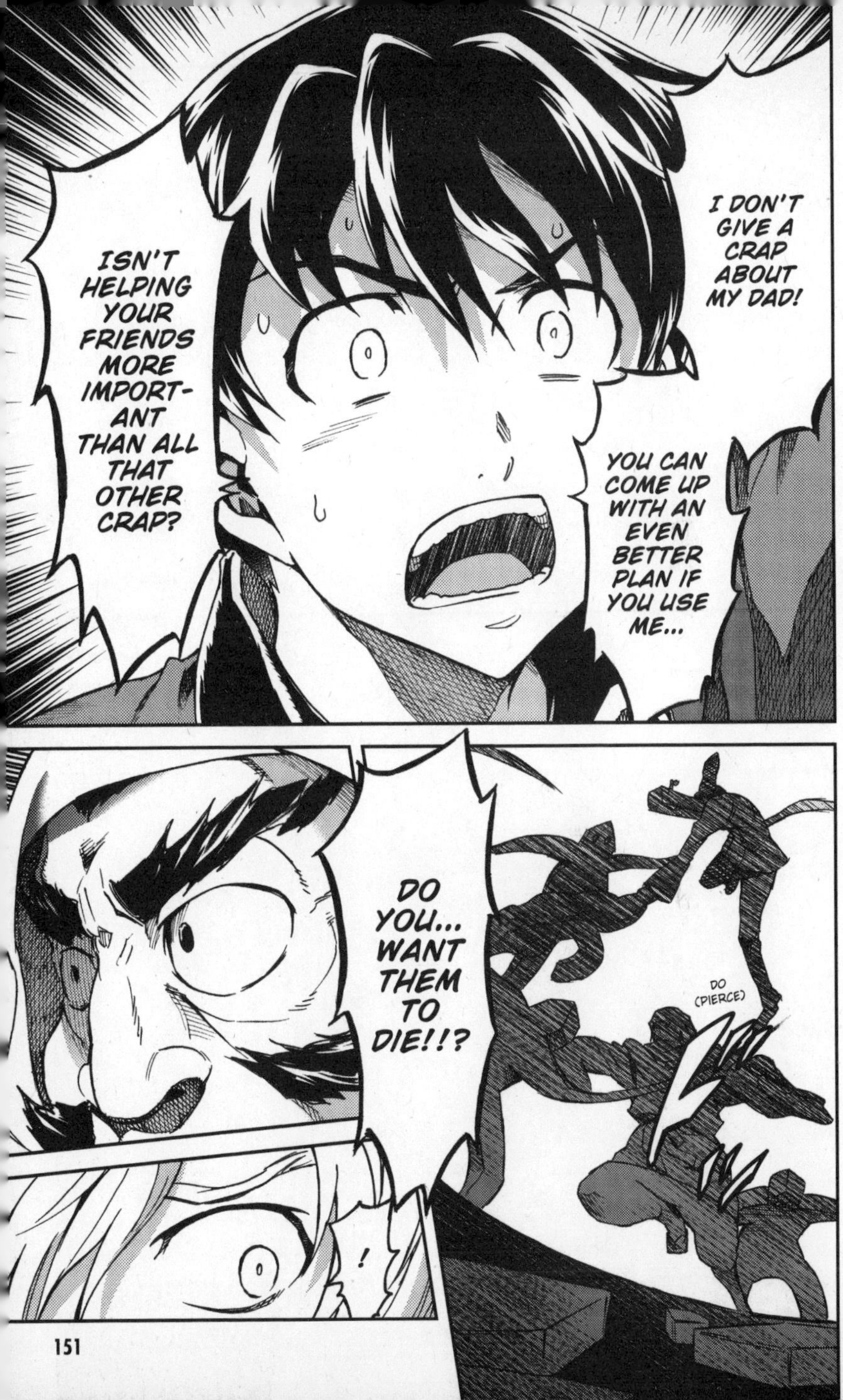
I DON'T GIVE A CRAP ABOUT MY DAD!
YOU CAN COME UP WITH AN EVEN BETTER PLAN IF YOU USE ME...
ISN'T HELPING YOUR FRIENDS MORE IMPORT-ANT THAN ALL THAT OTHER CRAP?
DO YOU... WANT THEM TO DIE!!?
DO (PIERCE)
!

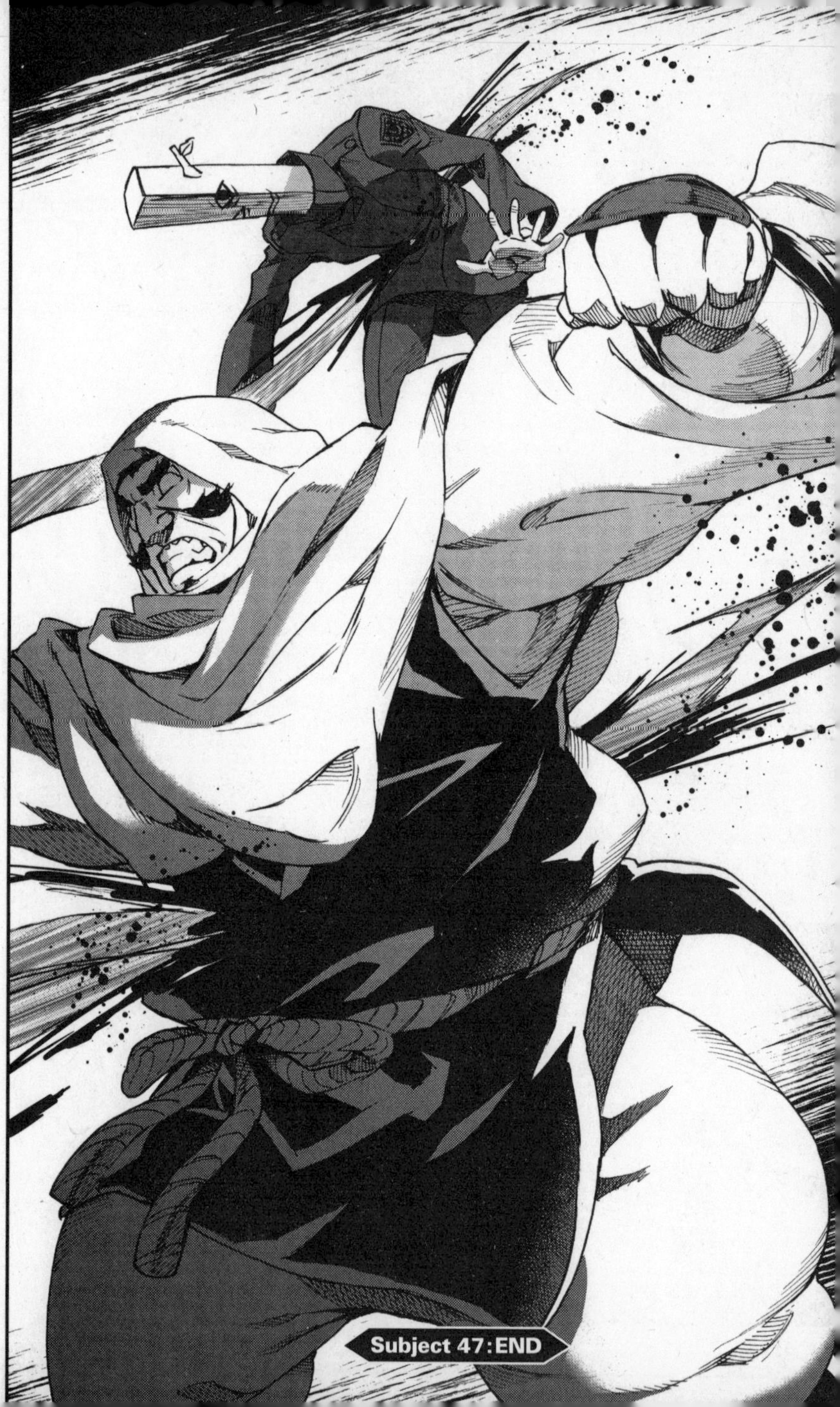
Subject 47: END

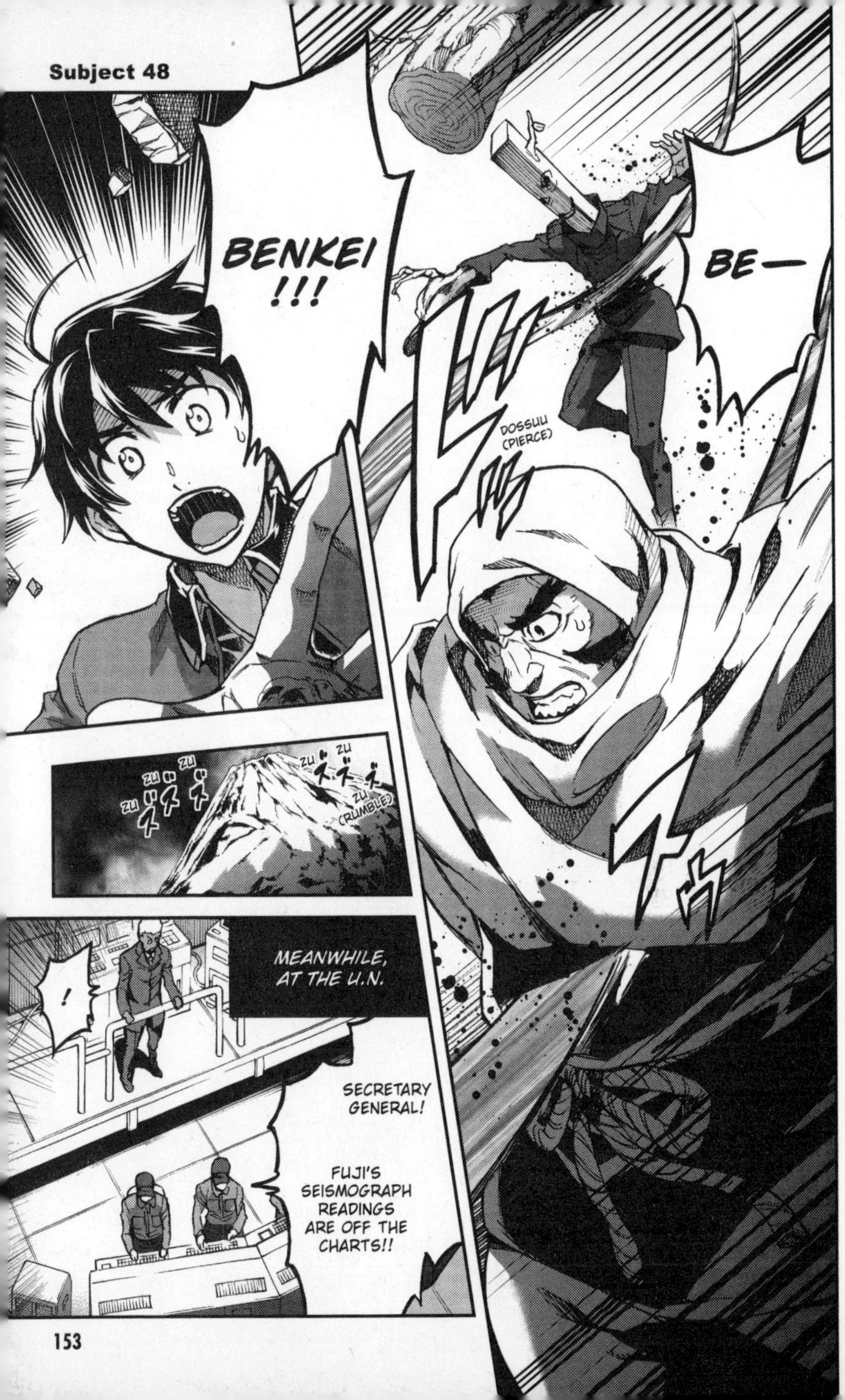
BE—
DOSSUU (PIERCE)
BENKEI!!!
ZU ZU ZU ZU ZU ZU (RUMBLE)
MEANWHILE, AT THE U.N.
!
SECRETARY GENERAL!
FUJI'S SEISMOGRAPH READINGS ARE OFF THE CHARTS!!

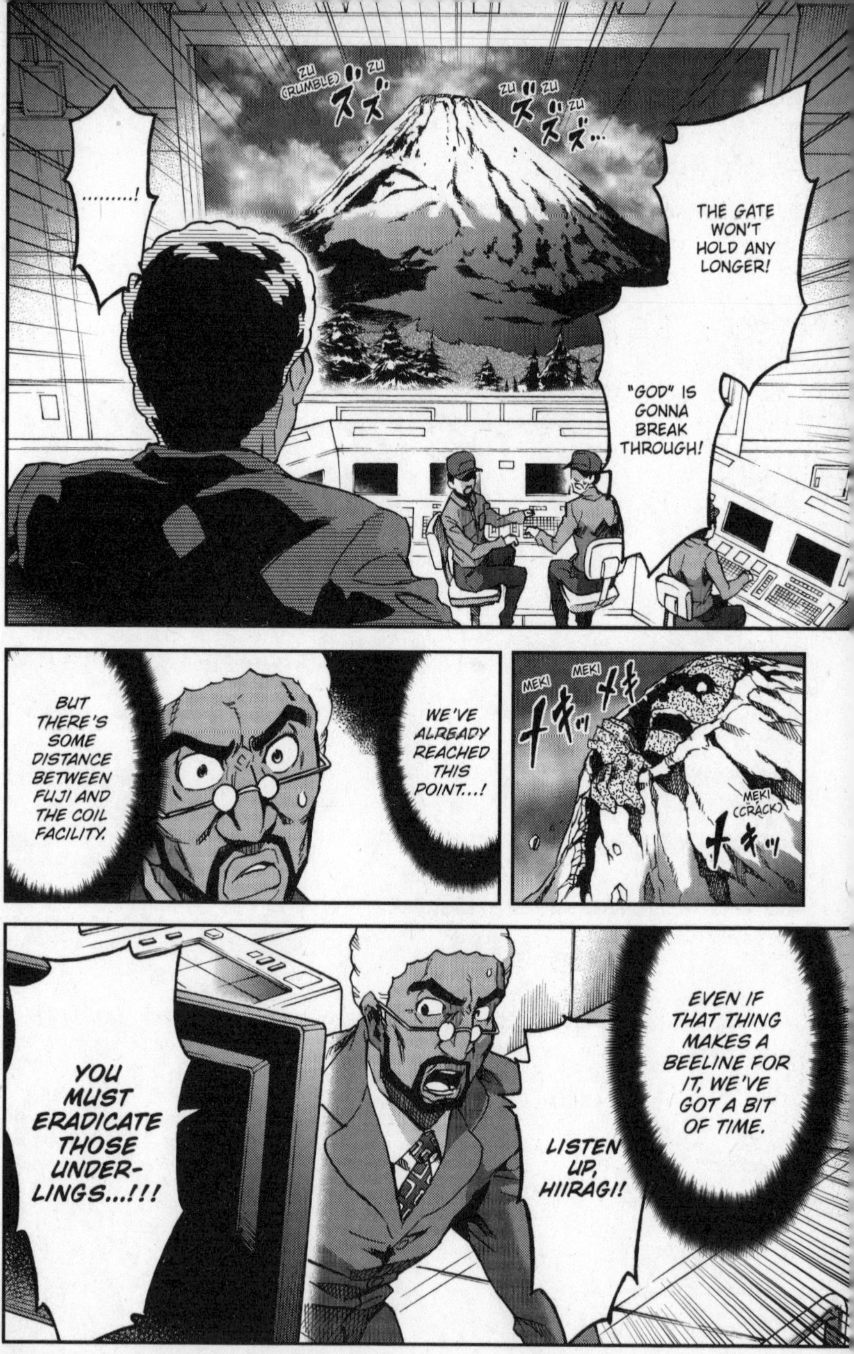
THE GATE WON'T HOLD ANY LONGER!
"GOD" IS GONNA BREAK THROUGH!
ZU ZU ZU ZU...
ZU (RUMBLE) ZU
..........!
MEKI MEKI
MEKI (CRACK)
WE'VE ALREADY REACHED THIS POINT...!
BUT THERE'S SOME DISTANCE BETWEEN FUJI AND THE COIL FACILITY.
EVEN IF THAT THING MAKES A BEELINE FOR IT, WE'VE GOT A BIT OF TIME.
LISTEN UP, HIIRAGI!
YOU MUST ERADICATE THOSE UNDER-LINGS...!!!

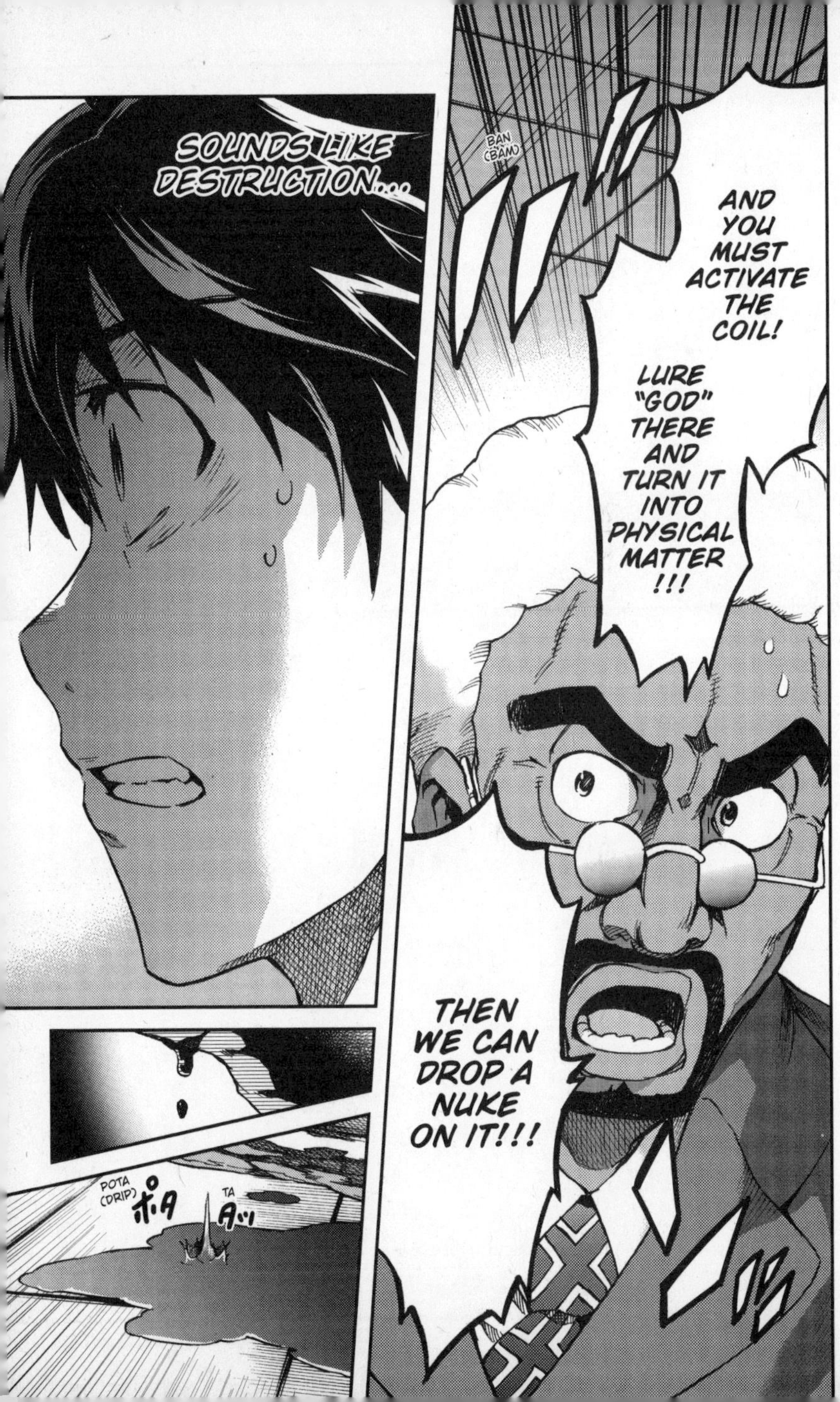
BAN (BAM)
AND YOU MUST ACTIVATE THE COIL!
LURE "GOD" THERE AND TURN IT INTO PHYSICAL MATTER!!!
THEN WE CAN DROP A NUKE ON IT!!!
SOUNDS LIKE DESTRUCTION...
POTA (DRIP)
TA

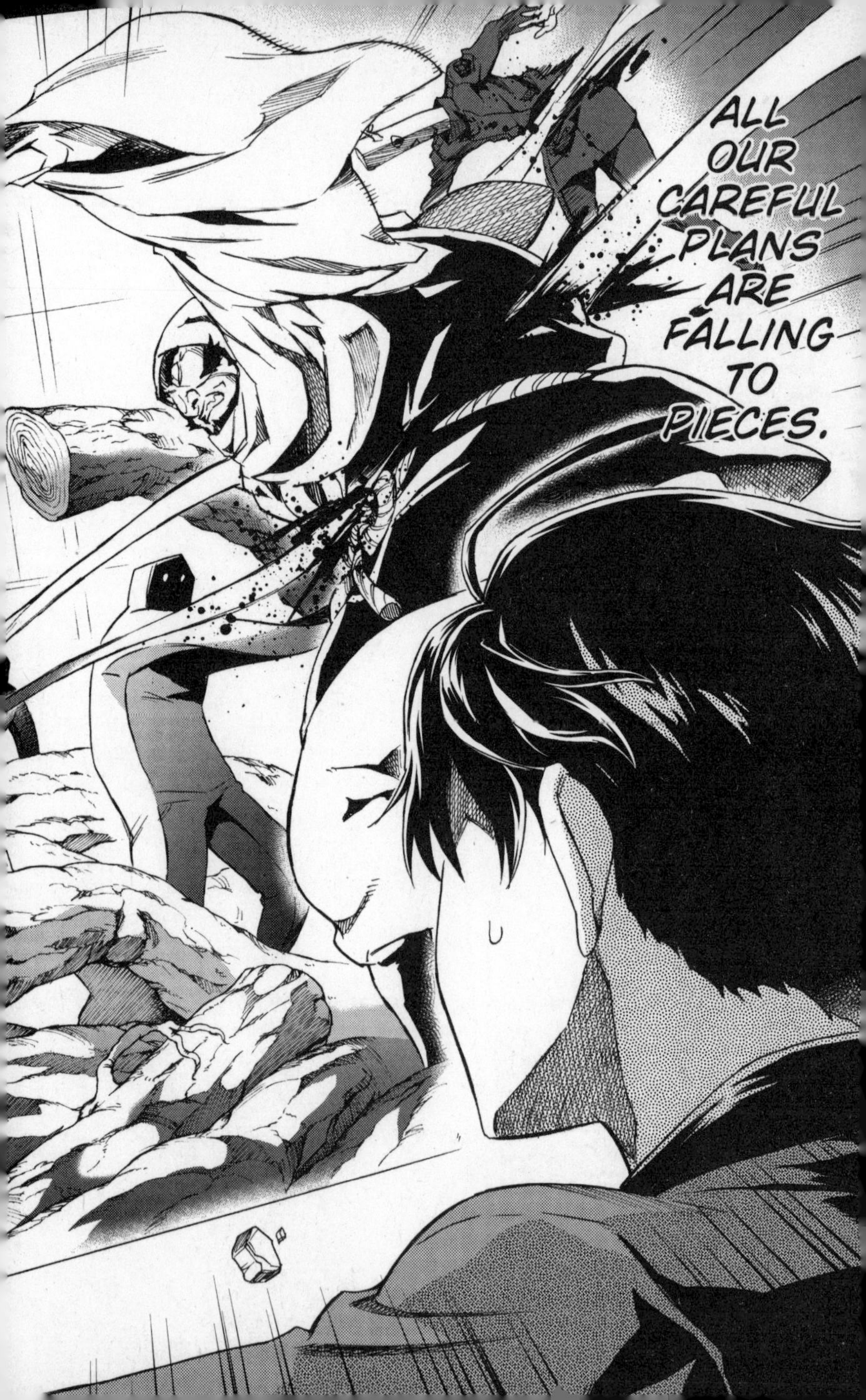
ALL OUR CAREFUL PLANS ARE FALLING TO PIECES.

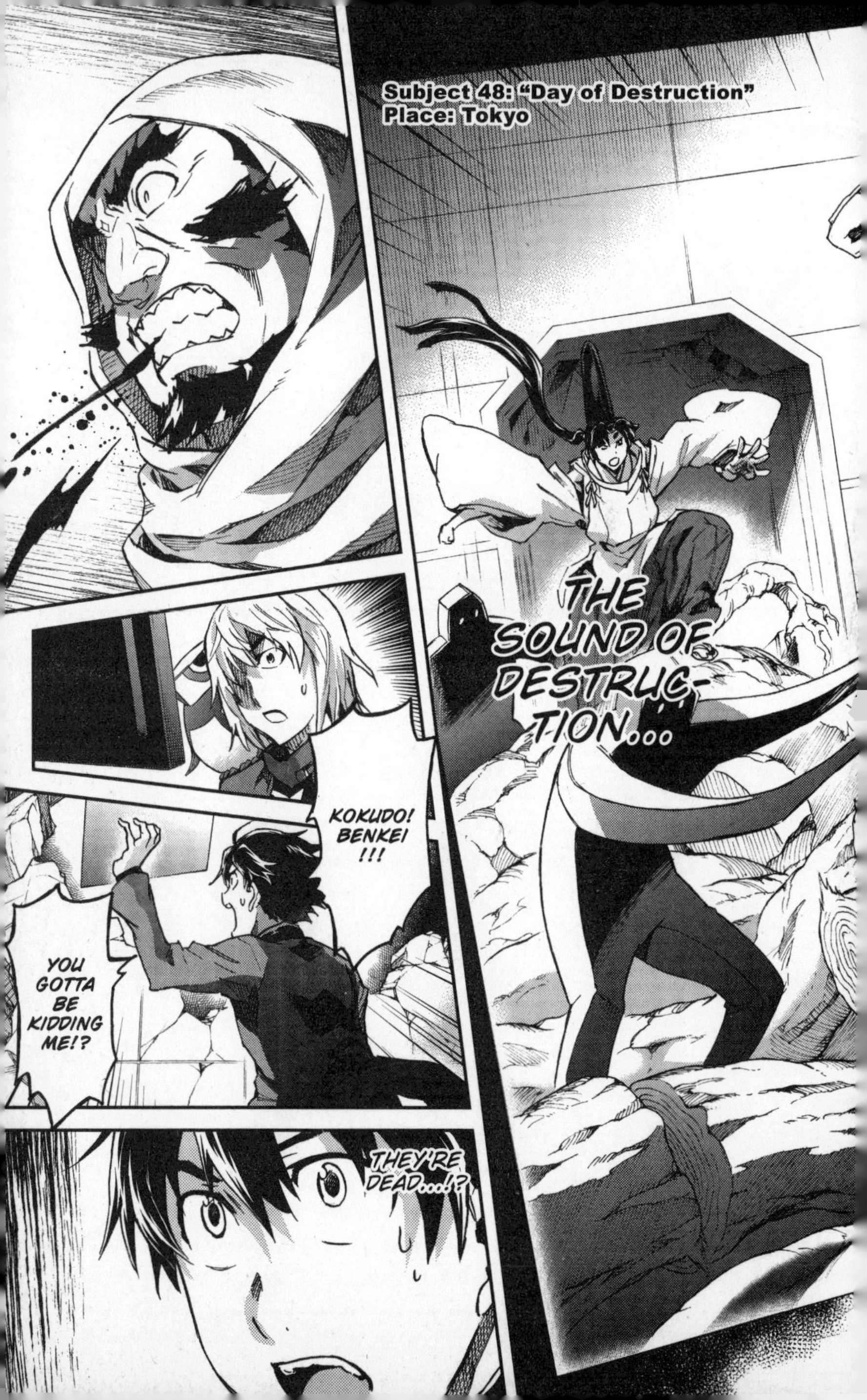
Subject 48: "Day of Destruction"
Place: Tokyo
THE SOUND OF DESTRUC-TION...
KOKUDO! BENKEI !!!
YOU GOTTA BE KIDDING ME!?
THEY'RE DEAD...!?

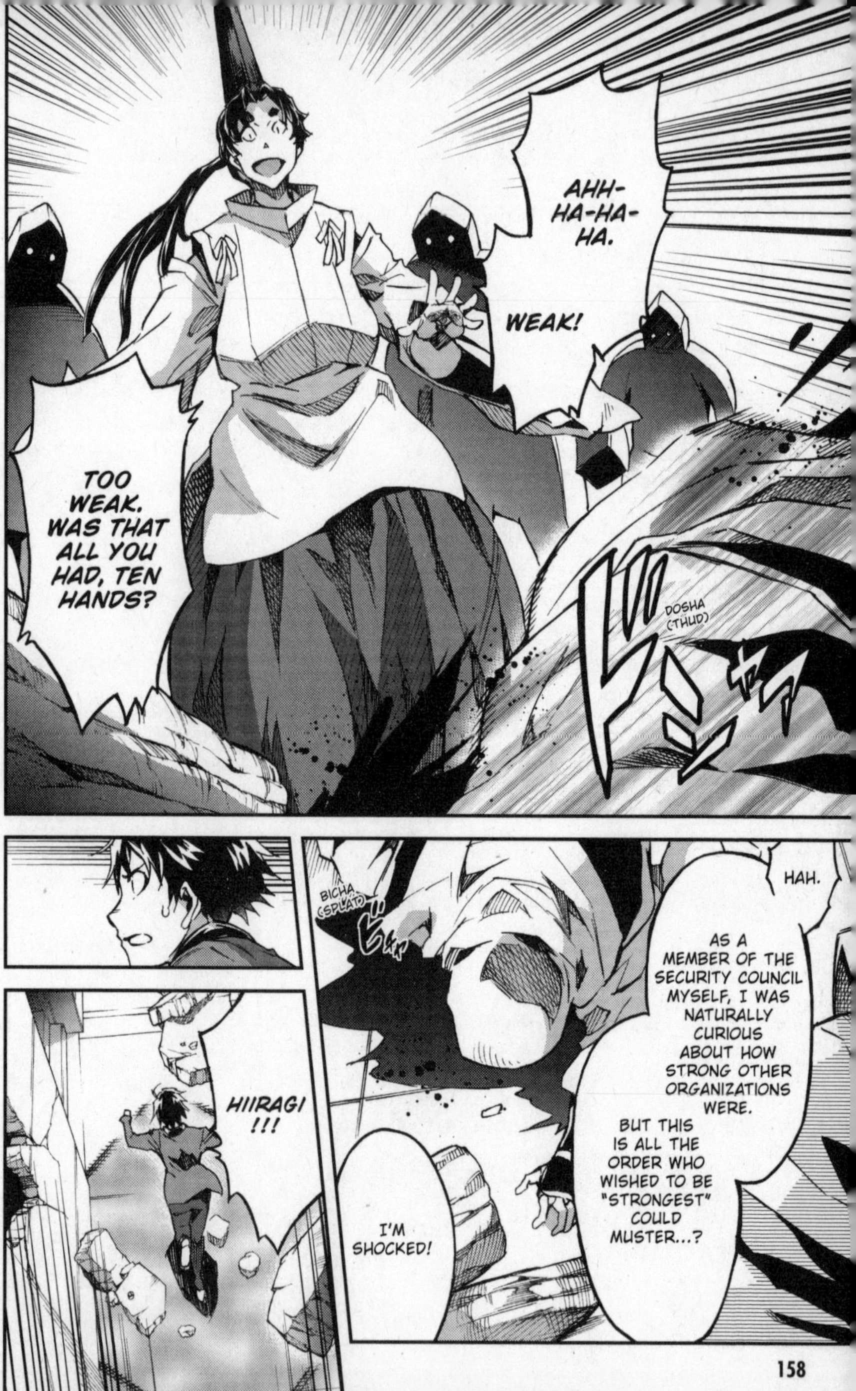
AHH-HA-HA-HA.
WEAK!
TOO WEAK. WAS THAT ALL YOU HAD, TEN HANDS?
DOSHA (THUD)
HAH.
AS A MEMBER OF THE SECURITY COUNCIL MYSELF, I WAS NATURALLY CURIOUS ABOUT HOW STRONG OTHER ORGANIZATIONS WERE.
BUT THIS IS ALL THE ORDER WHO WISHED TO BE "STRONGEST" COULD MUSTER...?
I'M SHOCKED!
BICHA (SPLAT)
HIIRAGI!!!

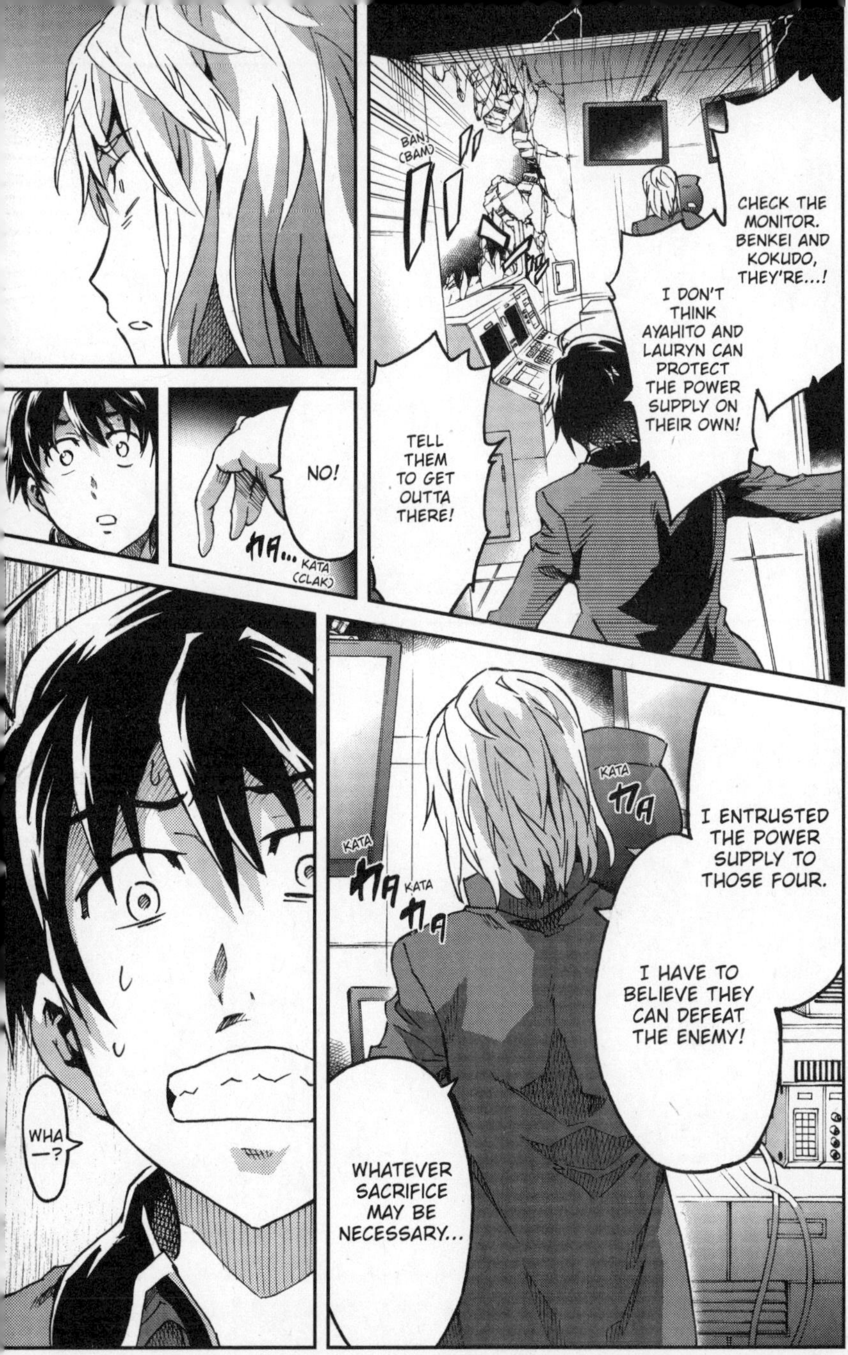
BAN (BAM)
CHECK THE MONITOR. BENKEI AND KOKUDO, THEY'RE...!
I DON'T THINK AYAHITO AND LAURYN CAN PROTECT THE POWER SUPPLY ON THEIR OWN!
TELL THEM TO GET OUTTA THERE!
NO!
KATA (CLAK)
KATA
KATA
KATA
I ENTRUSTED THE POWER SUPPLY TO THOSE FOUR.
I HAVE TO BELIEVE THEY CAN DEFEAT THE ENEMY!
WHATEVER SACRIFICE MAY BE NECESSARY...
WHA—?

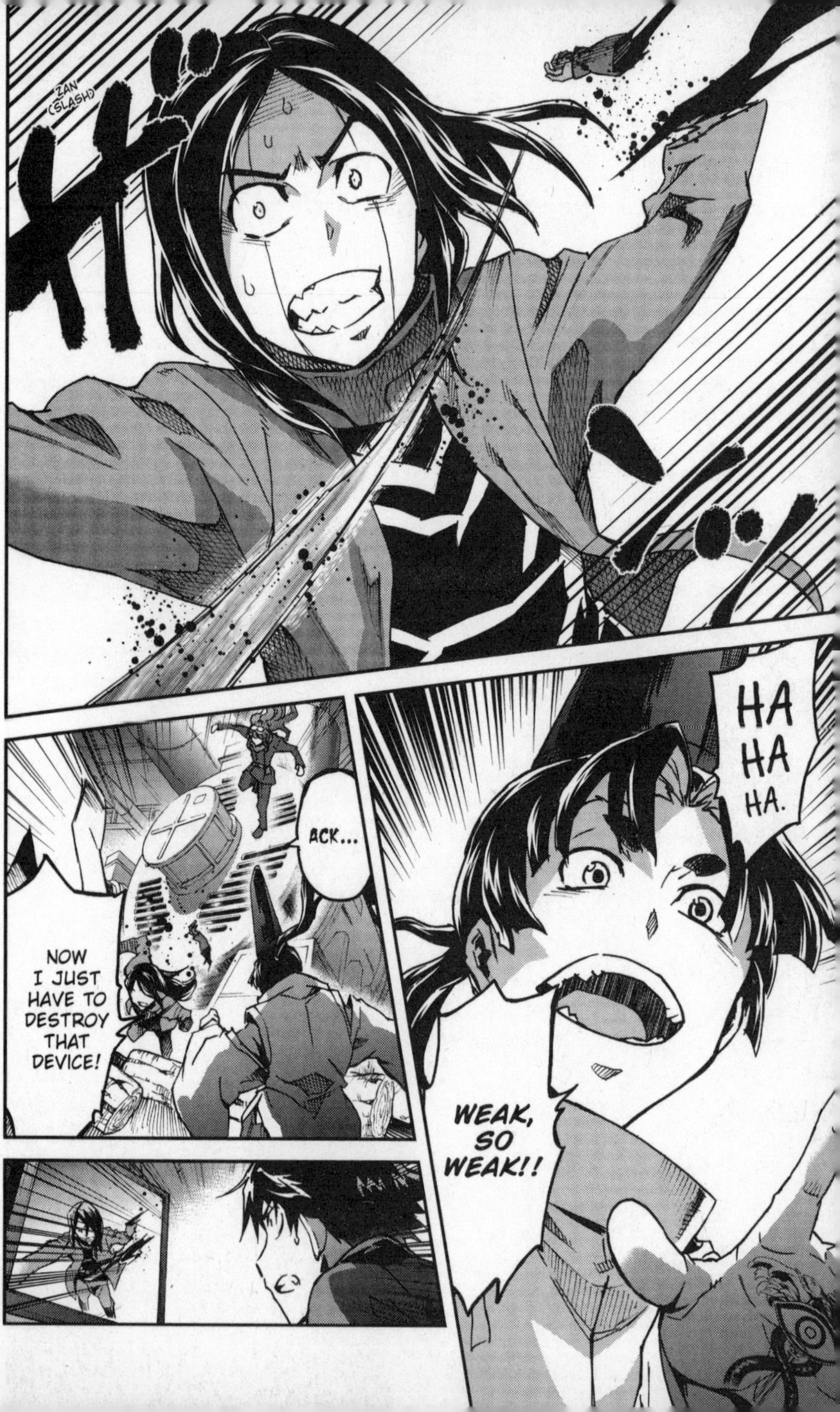
ZAN (SLASH)
HA HA HA.
WEAK, SO WEAK!!
ACK...
NOW I JUST HAVE TO DESTROY THAT DEVICE!

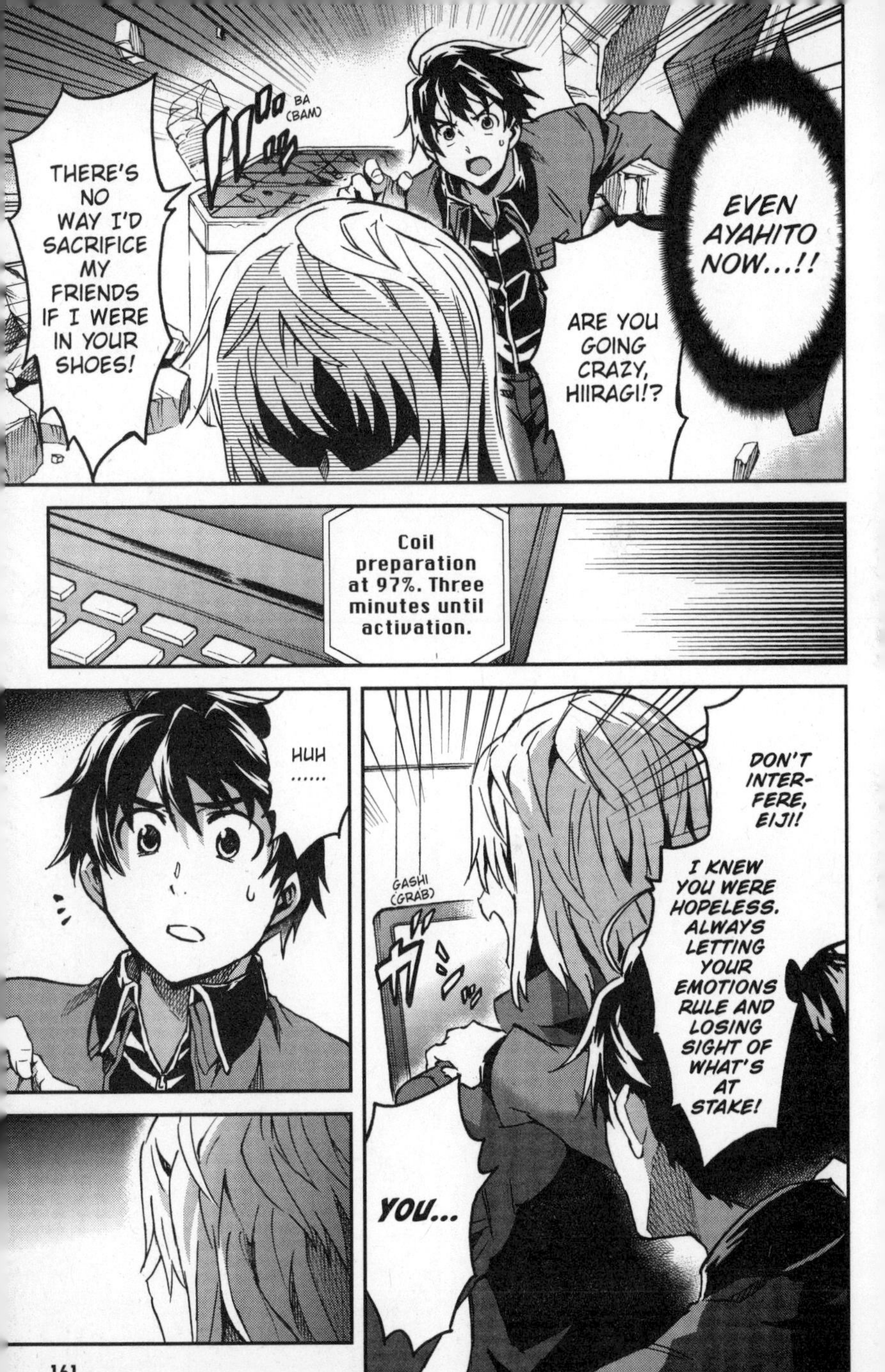
EVEN AYAHITO NOW...!!
ARE YOU GOING CRAZY, HIIRAGI!?
BA (BAM)
THERE'S NO WAY I'D SACRIFICE MY FRIENDS IF I WERE IN YOUR SHOES!
Coil preparation at 97%. Three minutes until activation.
DON'T INTER-FERE, EIJI!
I KNEW YOU WERE HOPELESS. ALWAYS LETTING YOUR EMOTIONS RULE AND LOSING SIGHT OF WHAT'S AT STAKE!
GASHI (GRAB)
YOU...
HUH ......

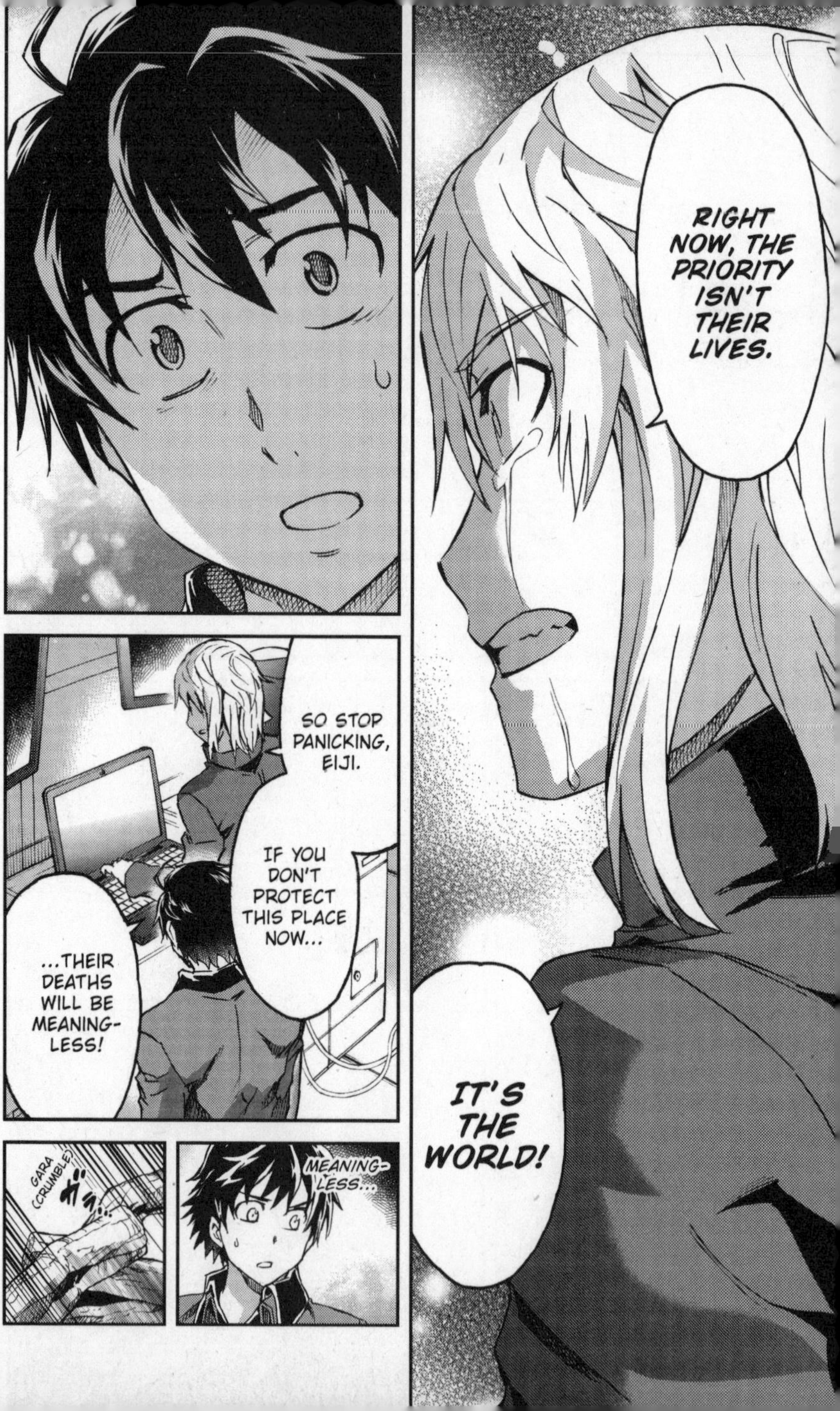
RIGHT NOW, THE PRIORITY ISN'T THEIR LIVES.
IT'S THE WORLD!
SO STOP PANICKING, EIJI.
IF YOU DON'T PROTECT THIS PLACE NOW...
...THEIR DEATHS WILL BE MEANING-LESS!
MEANING-LESS...
GARA (CRUMBLE)

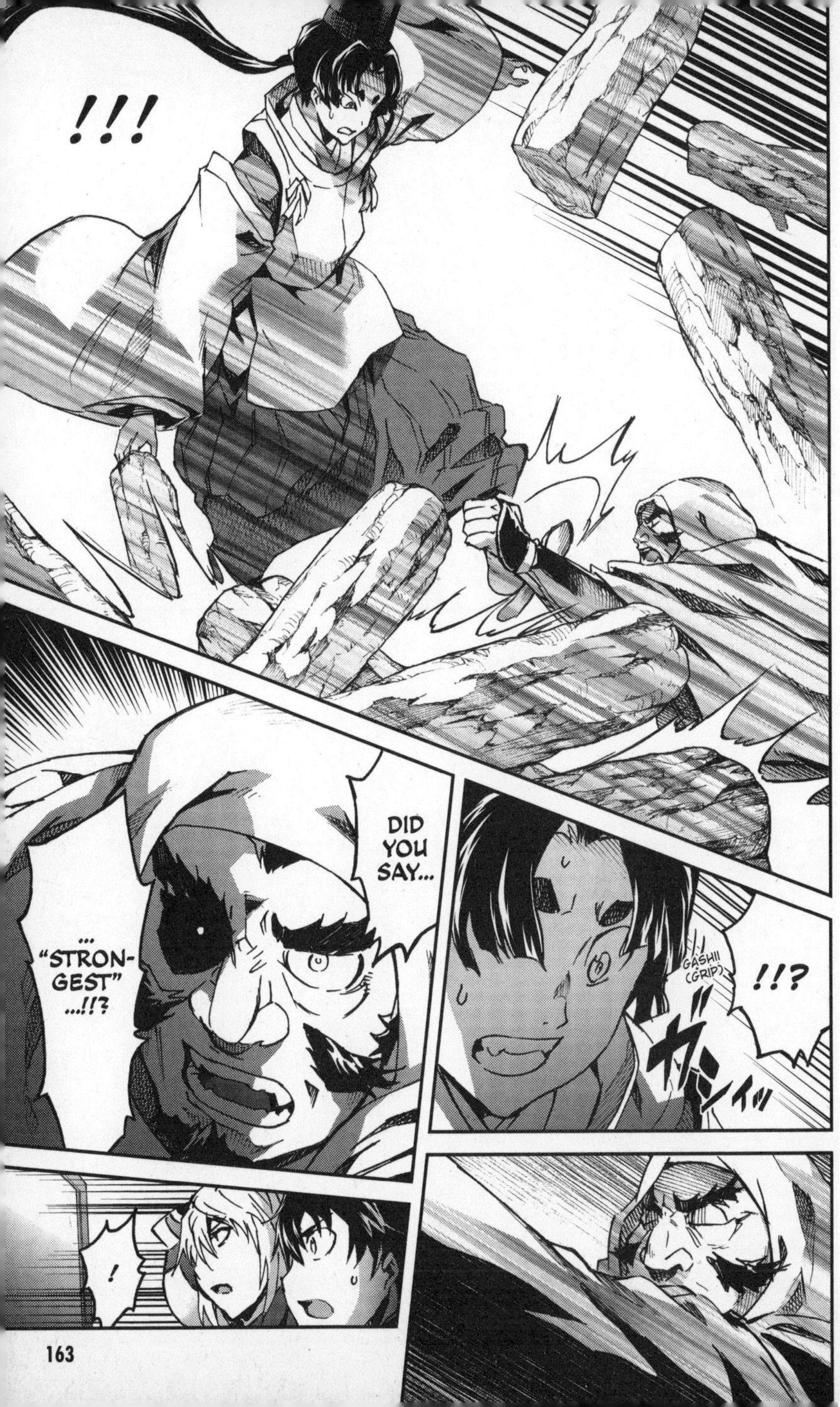
!!!
GASHI (GRIP)
!!?
DID YOU SAY...
... "STRON-GEST" ...!!?
!
!

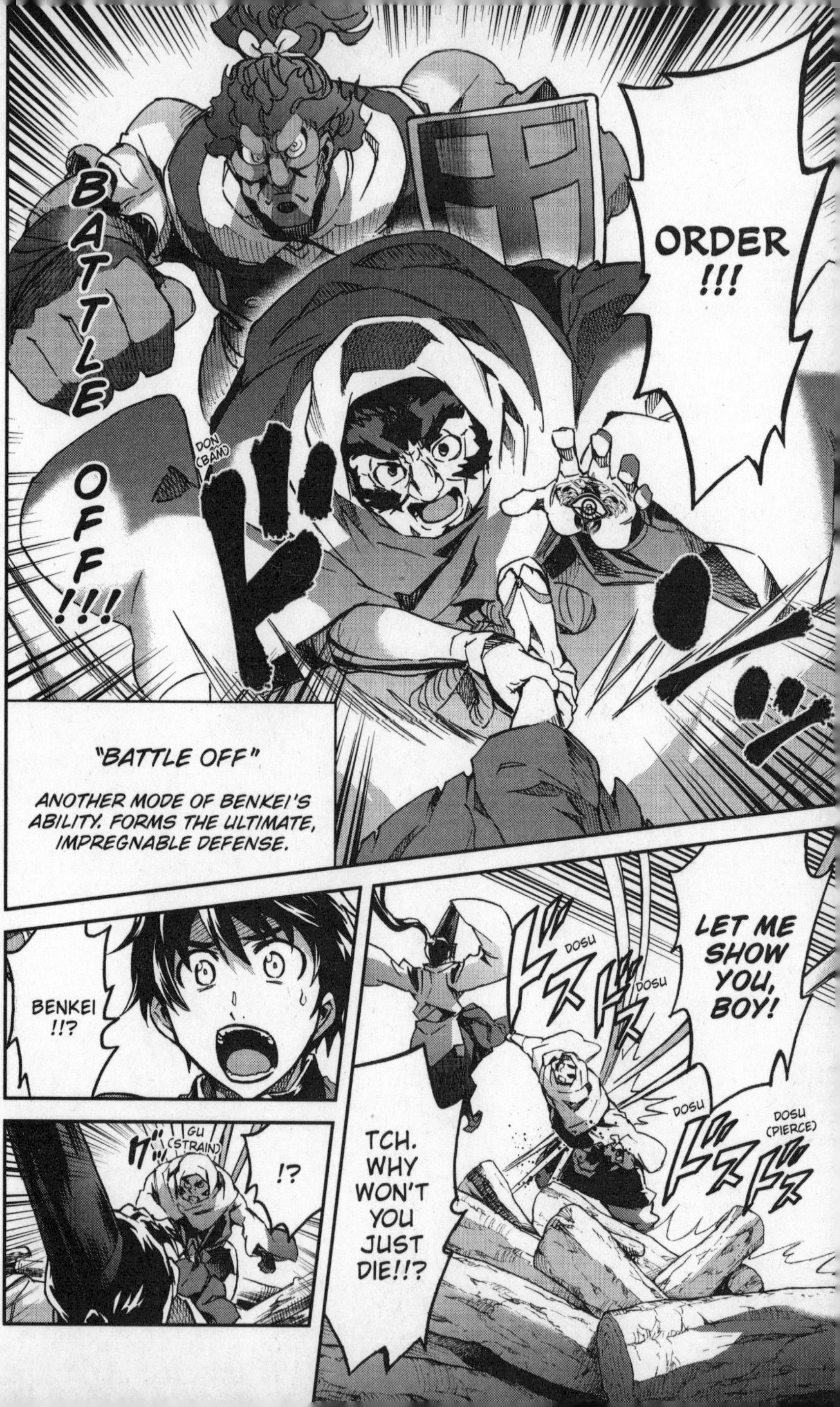
ORDER!!!
BATTLE OFF!!!
DON (BAM)
"BATTLE OFF"
ANOTHER MODE OF BENKEI'S ABILITY. FORMS THE ULTIMATE, IMPREGNABLE DEFENSE.
LET ME SHOW YOU, BOY!
DOSU
DOSU
DOSU
DOSU (PIERCE)
TCH. WHY WON'T YOU JUST DIE!!?
BENKEI!!?
GU (STRAIN)
!?

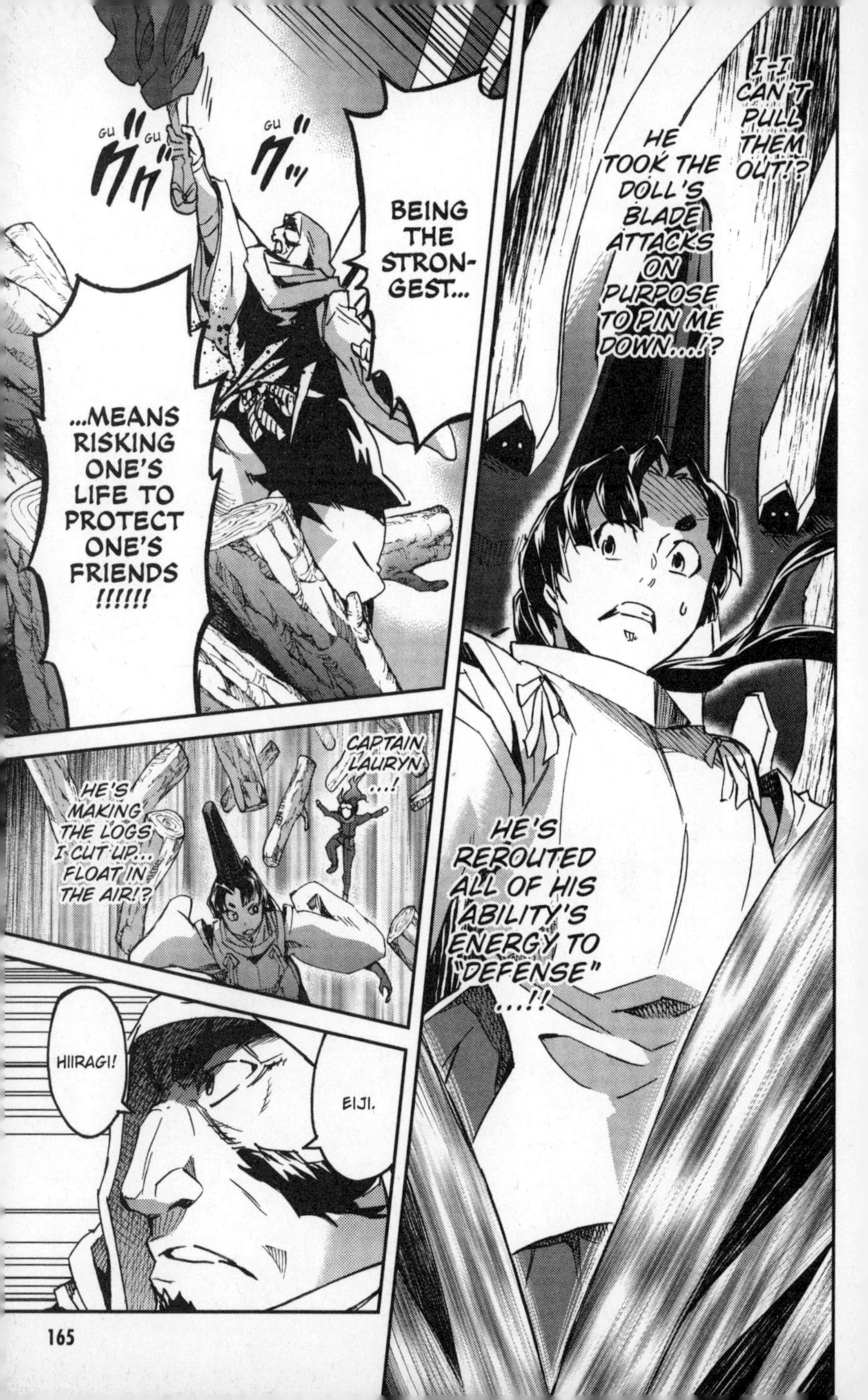
I-I CAN'T PULL THEM OUT!?
HE TOOK THE DOLL'S BLADE ATTACKS ON PURPOSE TO PIN ME DOWN...!?
HE'S REROUTED ALL OF HIS ABILITY'S ENERGY TO "DEFENSE" ...!!
GU
GU GU
BEING THE STRONGEST...
...MEANS RISKING ONE'S LIFE TO PROTECT ONE'S FRIENDS !!!!!!
CAPTAIN LAURYN ...!
HE'S MAKING THE LOGS I CUT UP... FLOAT IN THE AIR!?
EIJI.
HIIRAGI!

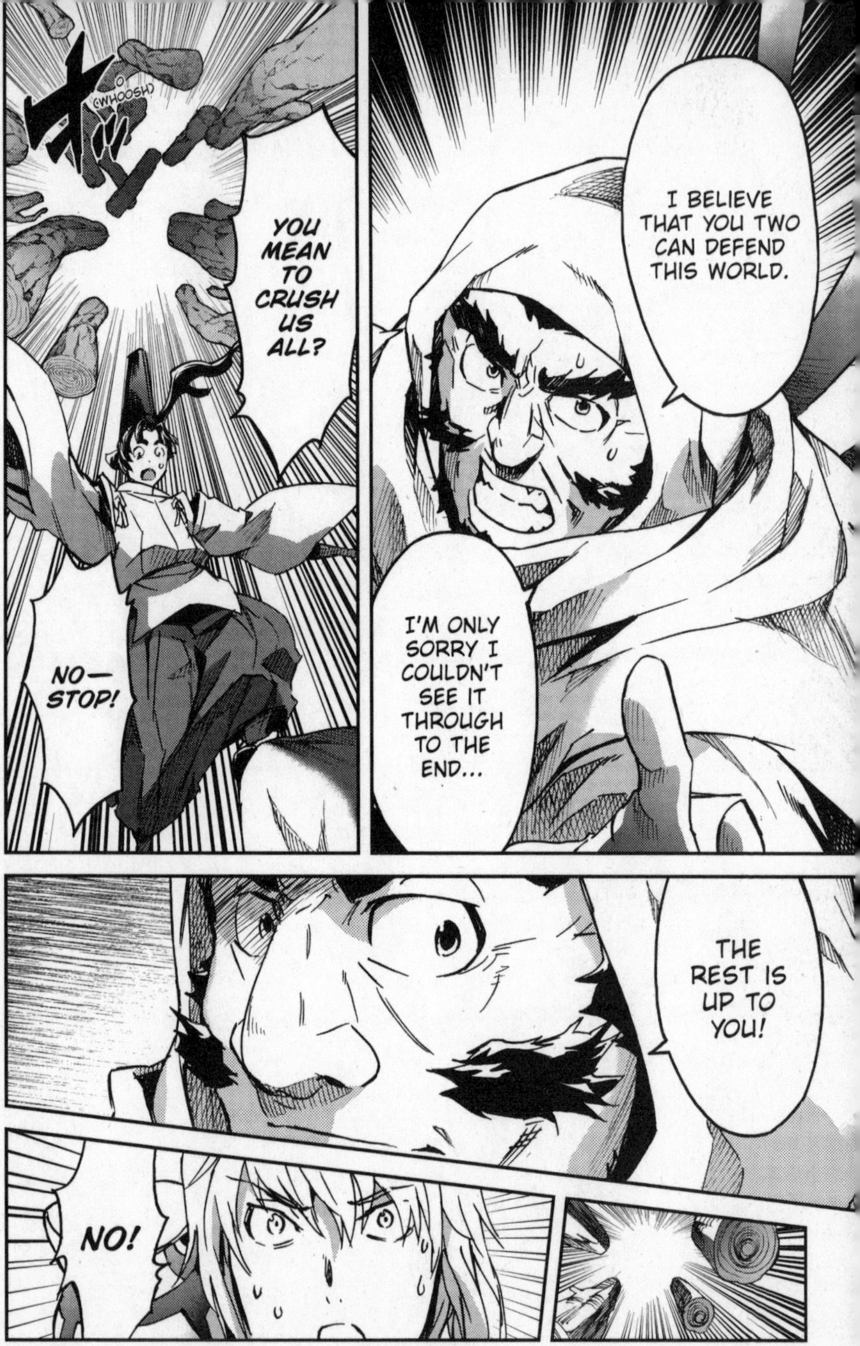
I BELIEVE THAT YOU TWO CAN DEFEND THIS WORLD.
I'M ONLY SORRY I COULDN'T SEE IT THROUGH TO THE END...
(WHOOSH)
YOU MEAN TO CRUSH US ALL?
NO—STOP!
THE REST IS UP TO YOU!
NO!

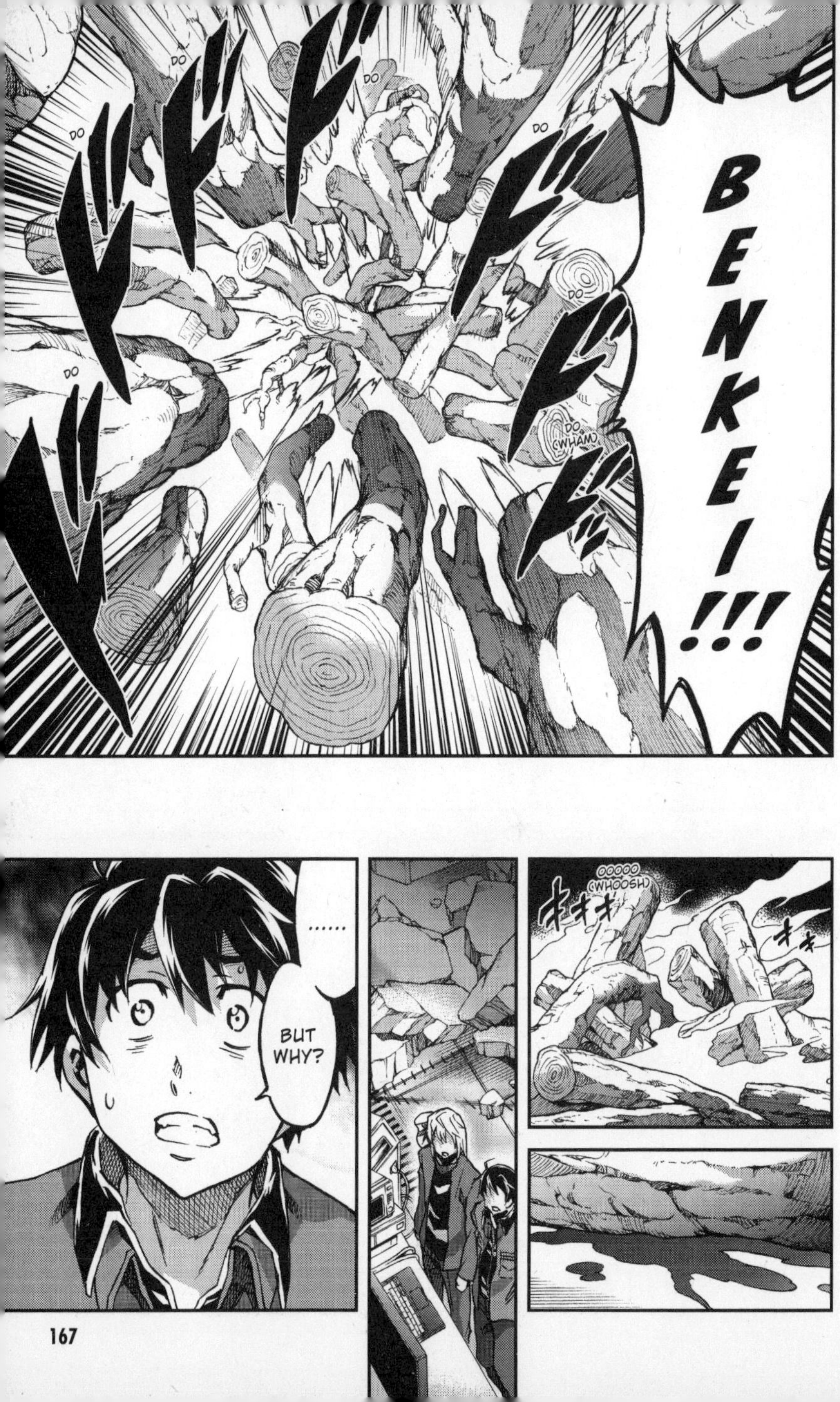
BENKEI!!!
DO (WHAM)
DO
DO
DO
DO
DO
OOOOO (WHOOSH)
......
BUT WHY?

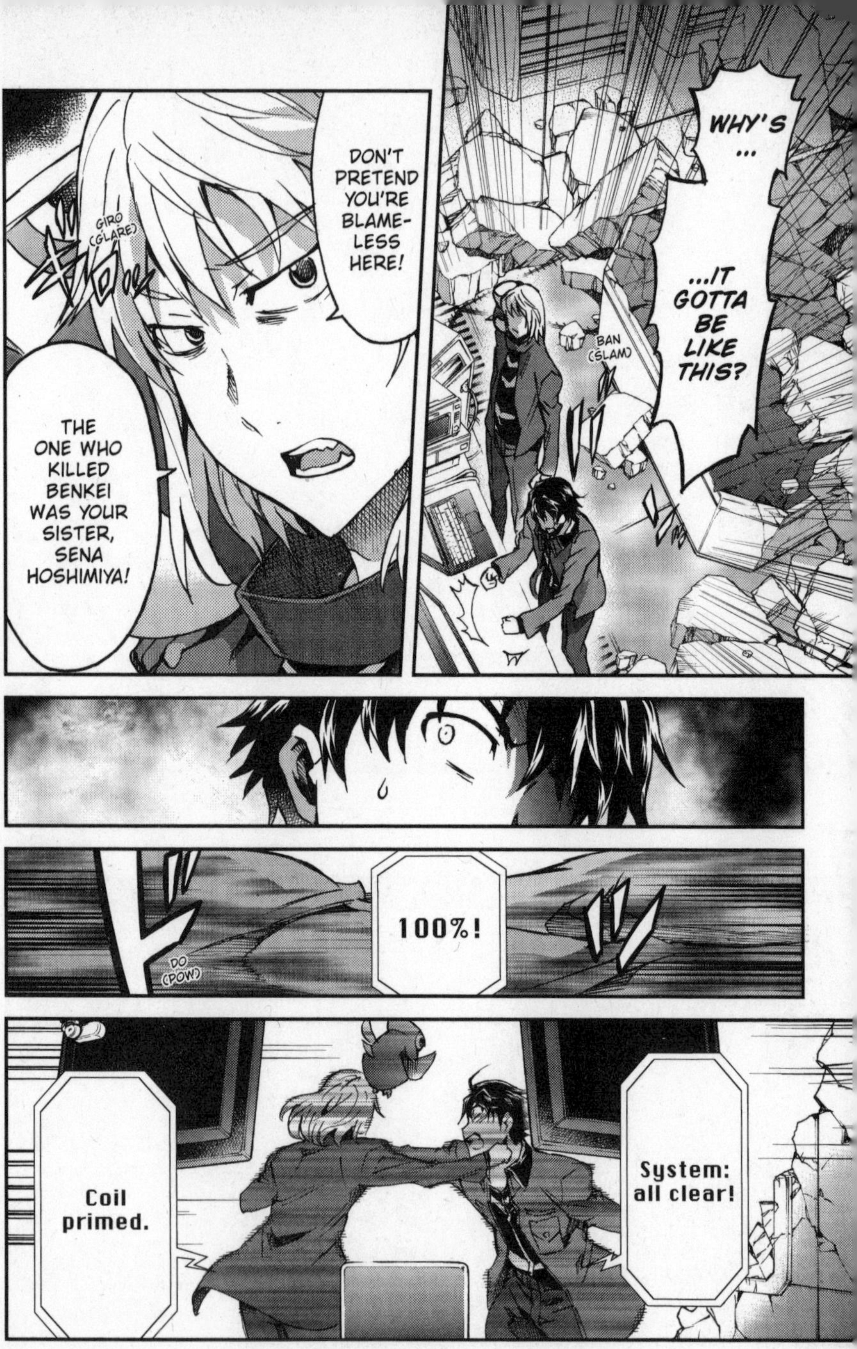
WHY'S ...
...IT GOTTA BE LIKE THIS?
BAN (SLAM)
DON'T PRETEND YOU'RE BLAME-LESS HERE!
GIRO (GLARE)
THE ONE WHO KILLED BENKEI WAS YOUR SISTER, SENA HOSHIMIYA!
100%!
DO (POW)
System: all clear!
Coil primed.

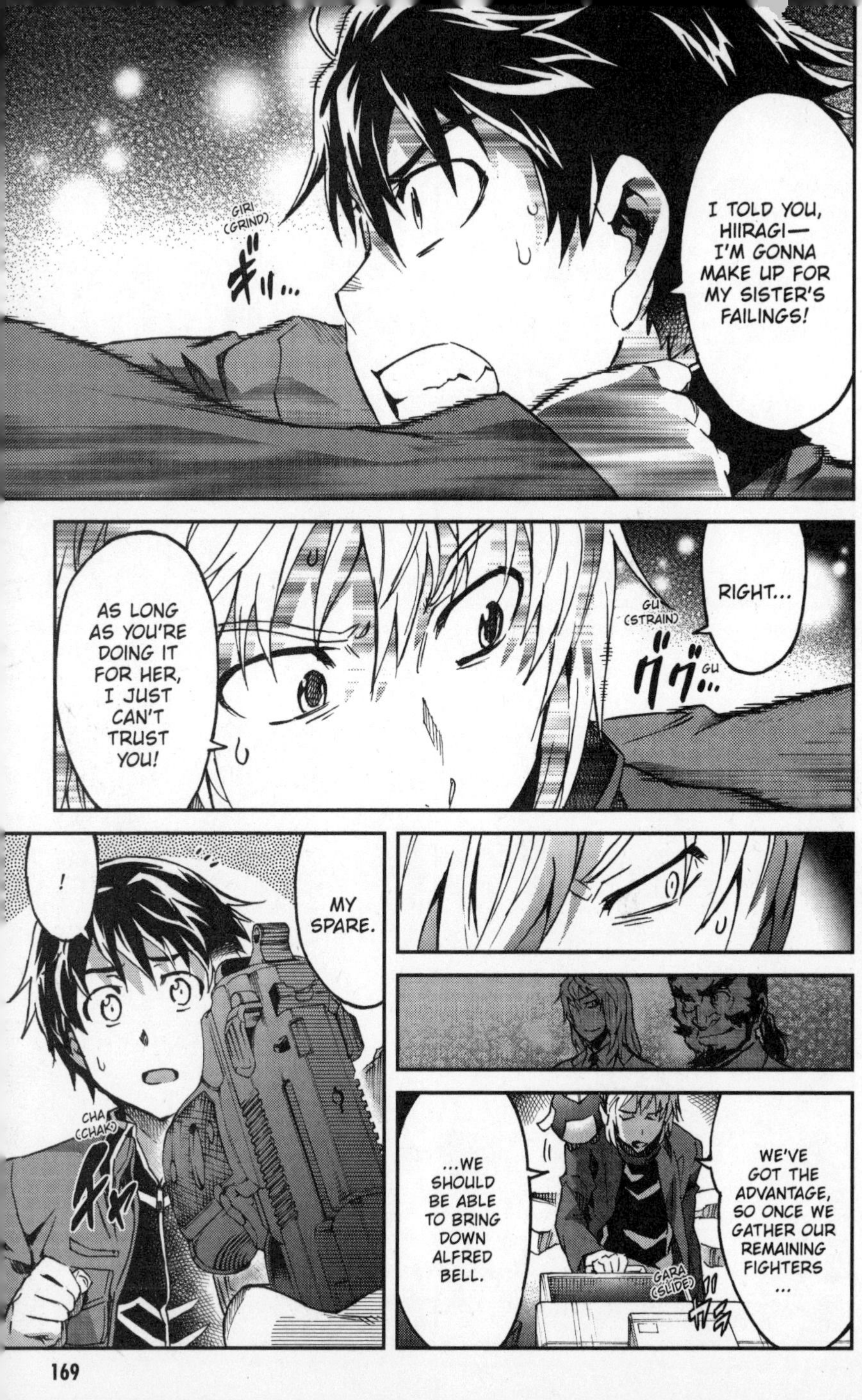
I TOLD YOU, HIIRAGI— I'M GONNA MAKE UP FOR MY SISTER'S FAILINGS!
GIRI (GRIND)
RIGHT...
GU (STRAIN) GU
AS LONG AS YOU'RE DOING IT FOR HER, I JUST CAN'T TRUST YOU!
WE'VE GOT THE ADVANTAGE, SO ONCE WE GATHER OUR REMAINING FIGHTERS...
GARA (SLIDE)
...WE SHOULD BE ABLE TO BRING DOWN ALFRED BELL.
MY SPARE.
!
CHA (CHAK)

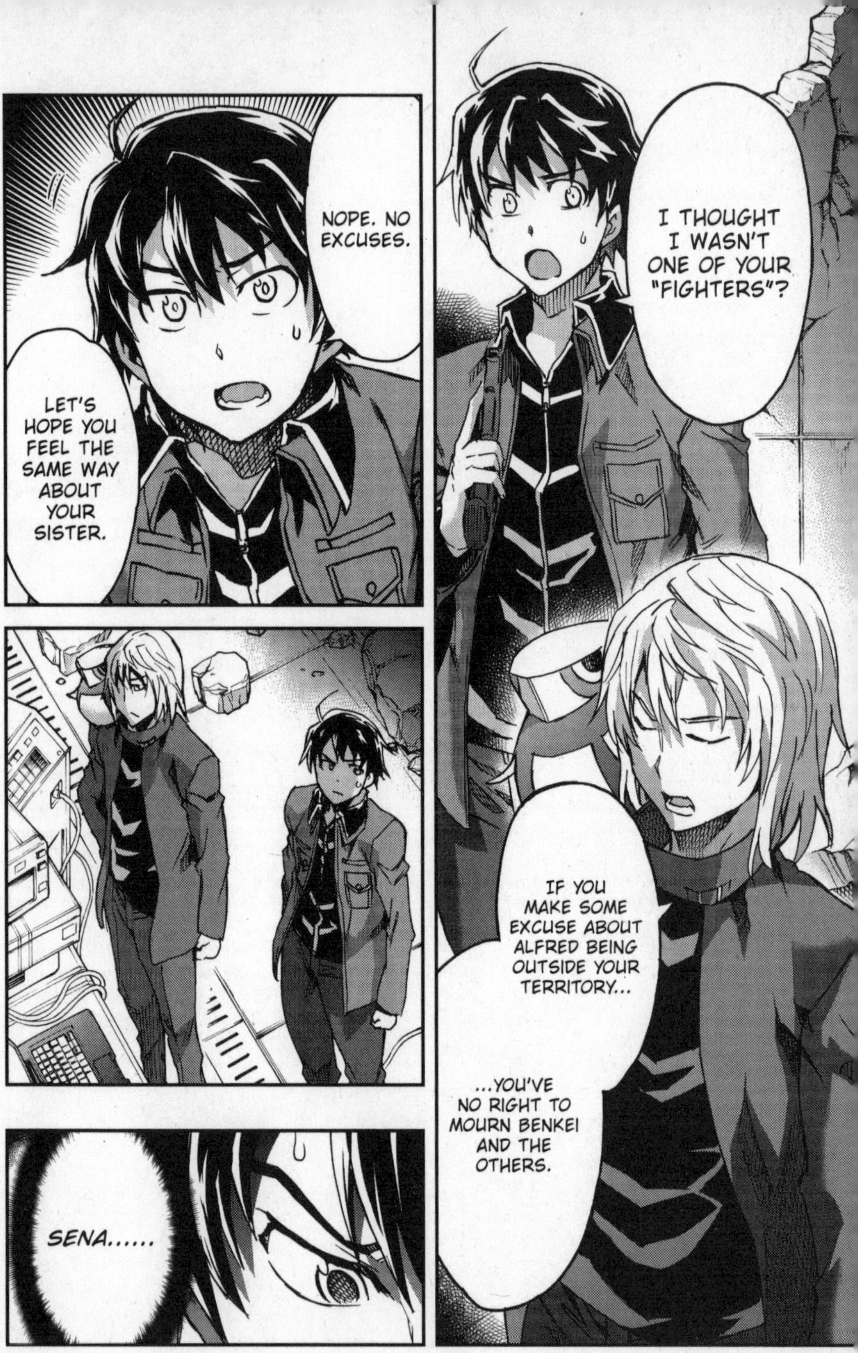
I THOUGHT I WASN'T ONE OF YOUR "FIGHTERS"?
IF YOU MAKE SOME EXCUSE ABOUT ALFRED BEING OUTSIDE YOUR TERRITORY...
...YOU'VE NO RIGHT TO MOURN BENKEI AND THE OTHERS.
NOPE. NO EXCUSES.
LET'S HOPE YOU FEEL THE SAME WAY ABOUT YOUR SISTER.
SENA......

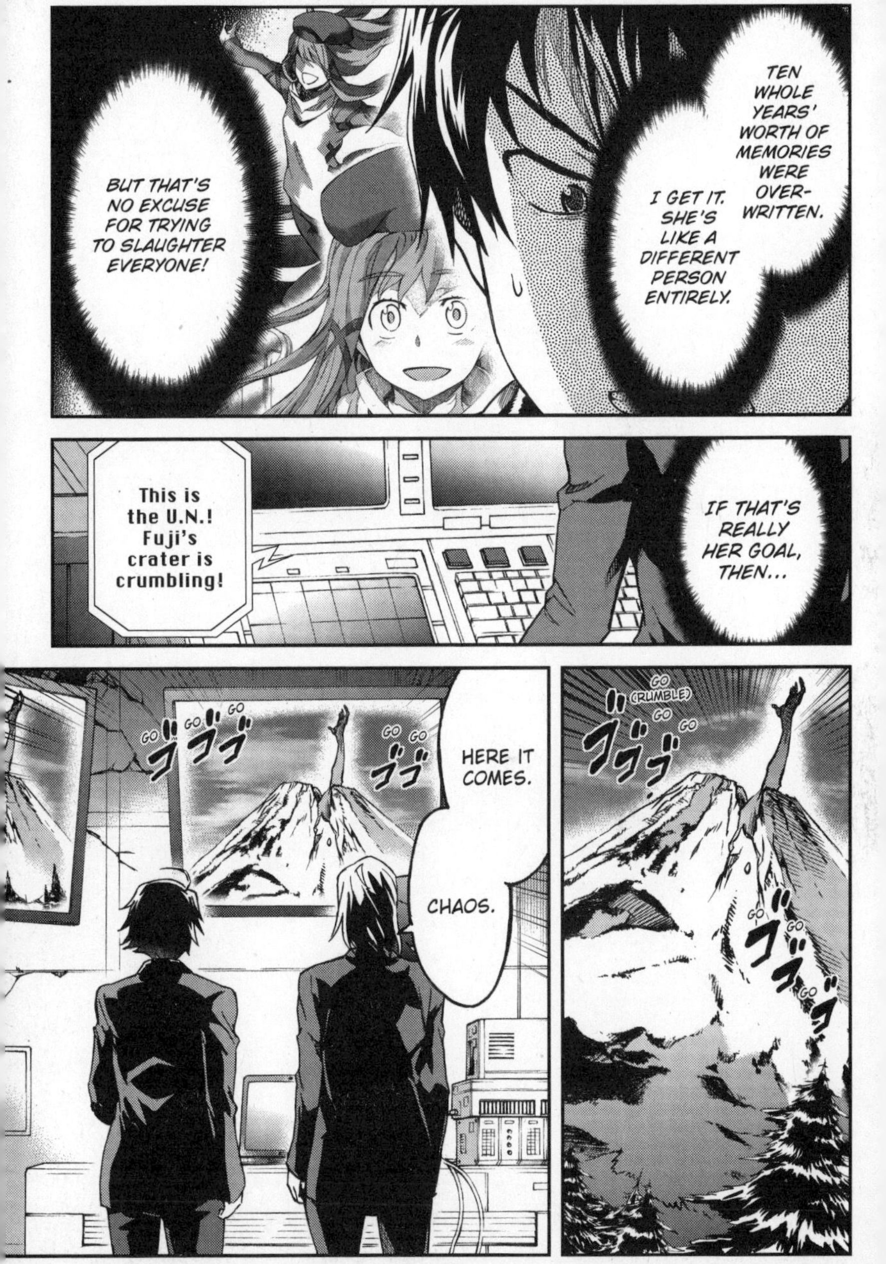
TEN WHOLE YEARS' WORTH OF MEMORIES WERE OVER-WRITTEN.
I GET IT. SHE'S LIKE A DIFFERENT PERSON ENTIRELY.
BUT THAT'S NO EXCUSE FOR TRYING TO SLAUGHTER EVERYONE!
IF THAT'S REALLY HER GOAL, THEN...
This is the U.N.! Fuji's crater is crumbling!
GO (RUMBLE) GO GO
GO GO GO
GO GO GO
GO GO
HERE IT COMES.
CHAOS.

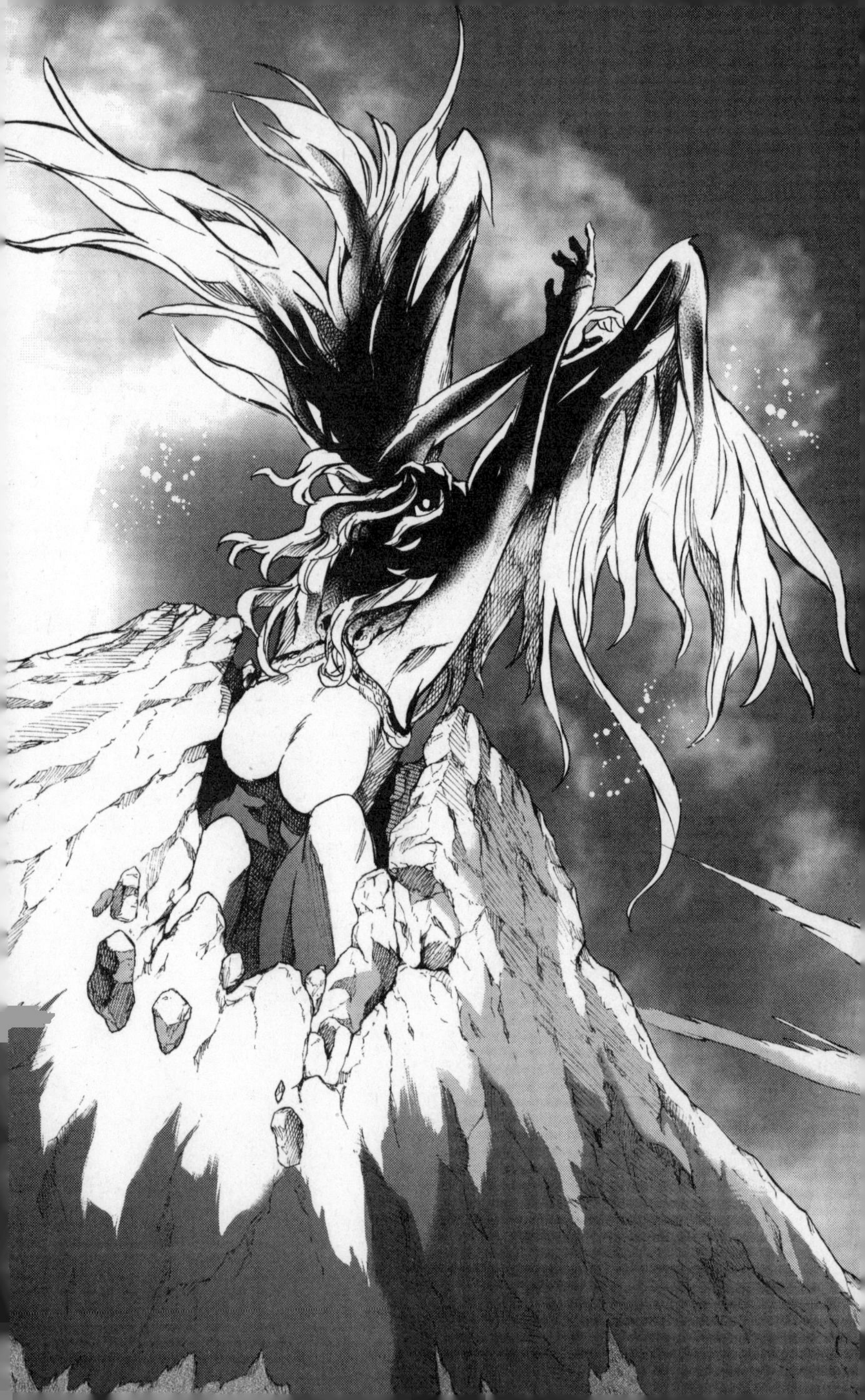

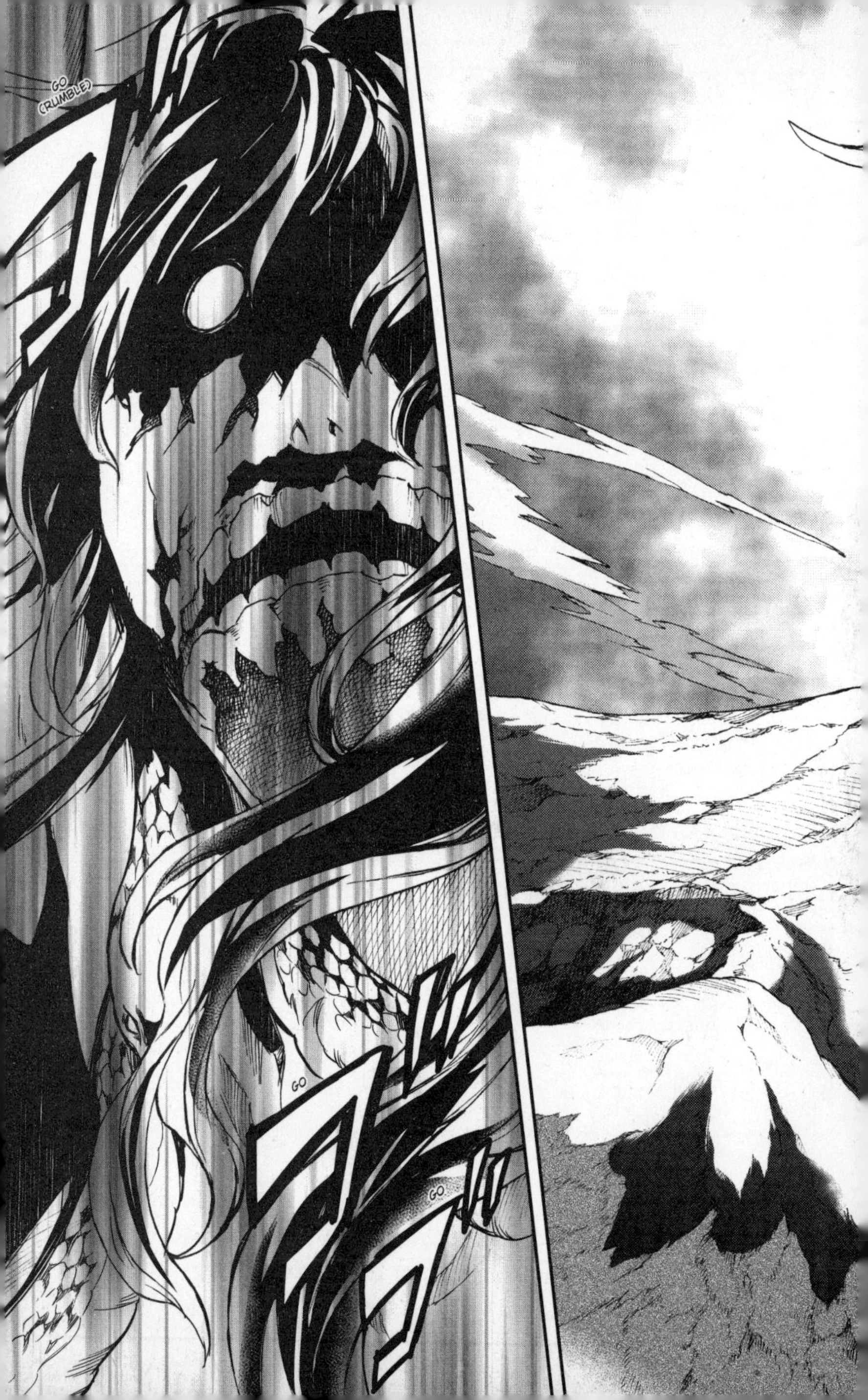
GO
(RUMBLE)
GO
GO

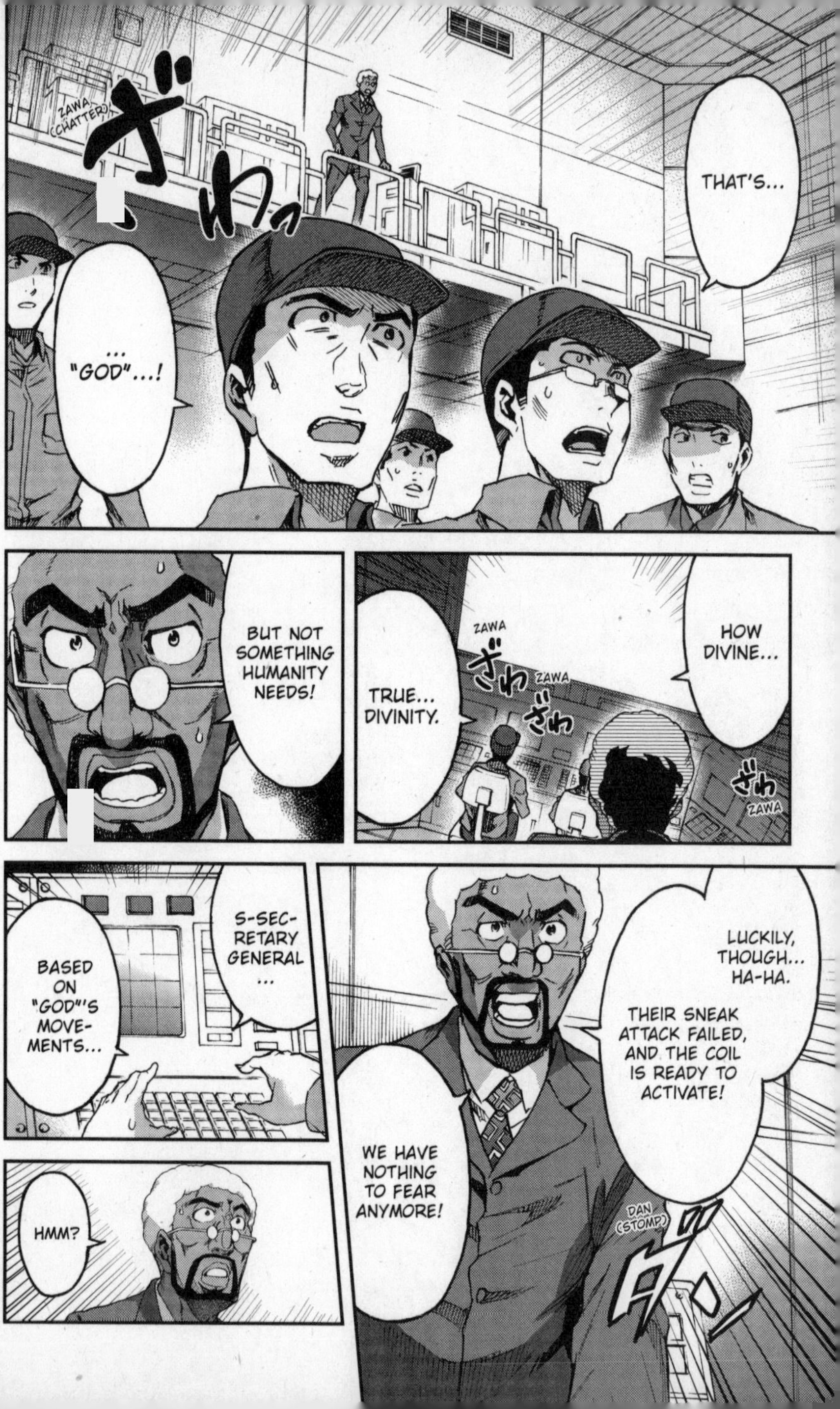

THAT'S...
ZAWA (CHATTER)
ざわっ
... "GOD"...!
HOW DIVINE...
ZAWA
ZAWA
ZAWA
TRUE... DIVINITY.
BUT NOT SOMETHING HUMANITY NEEDS!
LUCKILY, THOUGH... HA-HA.
THEIR SNEAK ATTACK FAILED, AND THE COIL IS READY TO ACTIVATE!
WE HAVE NOTHING TO FEAR ANYMORE!
DAN (STOMP)
S-SECRETARY GENERAL...
BASED ON "GOD"'S MOVEMENTS...
HMM?

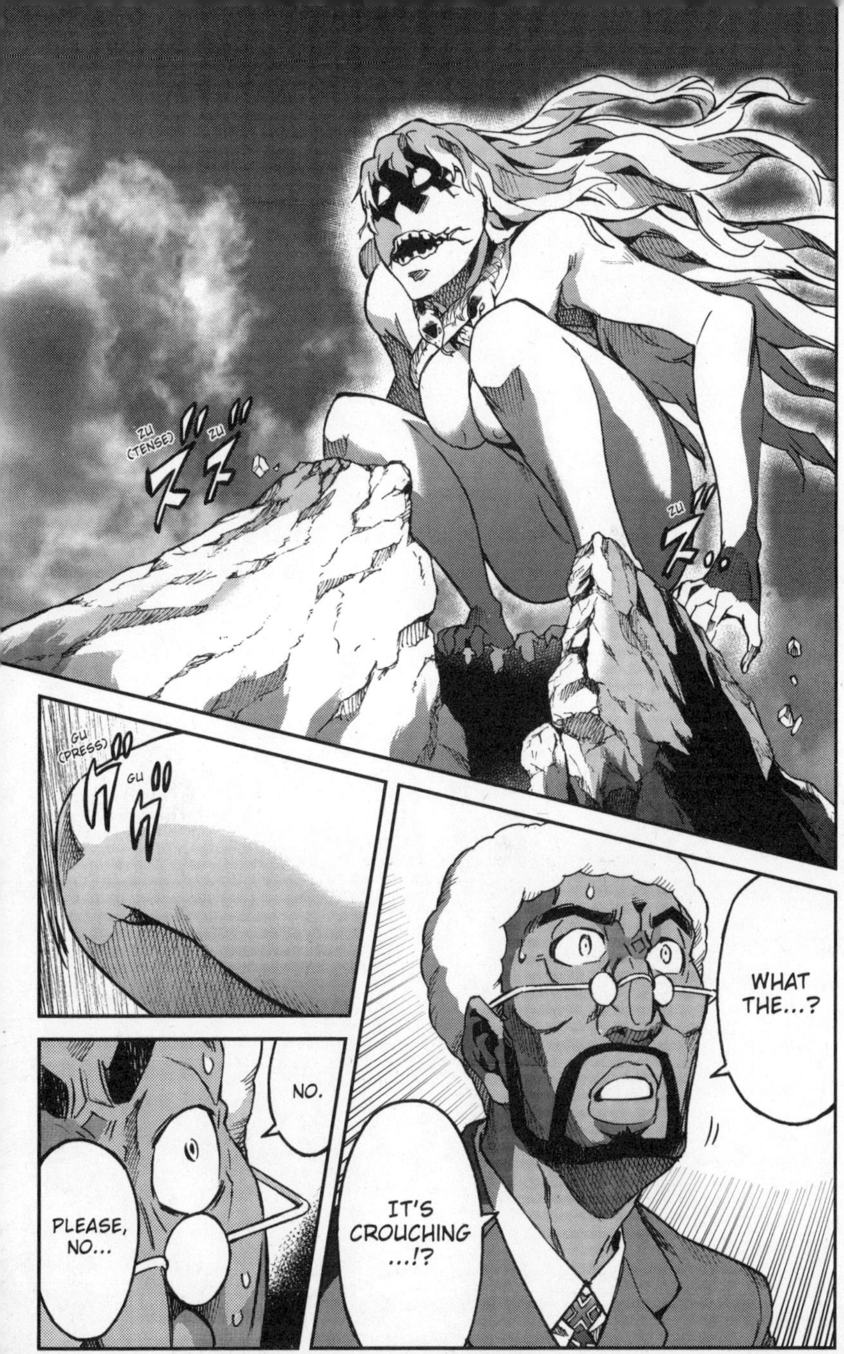
ZU (TENSE) ZU
ZU
WHAT THE...?
IT'S CROUCHING ...!?
GU (PRESS) GU
NO.
PLEASE, NO...

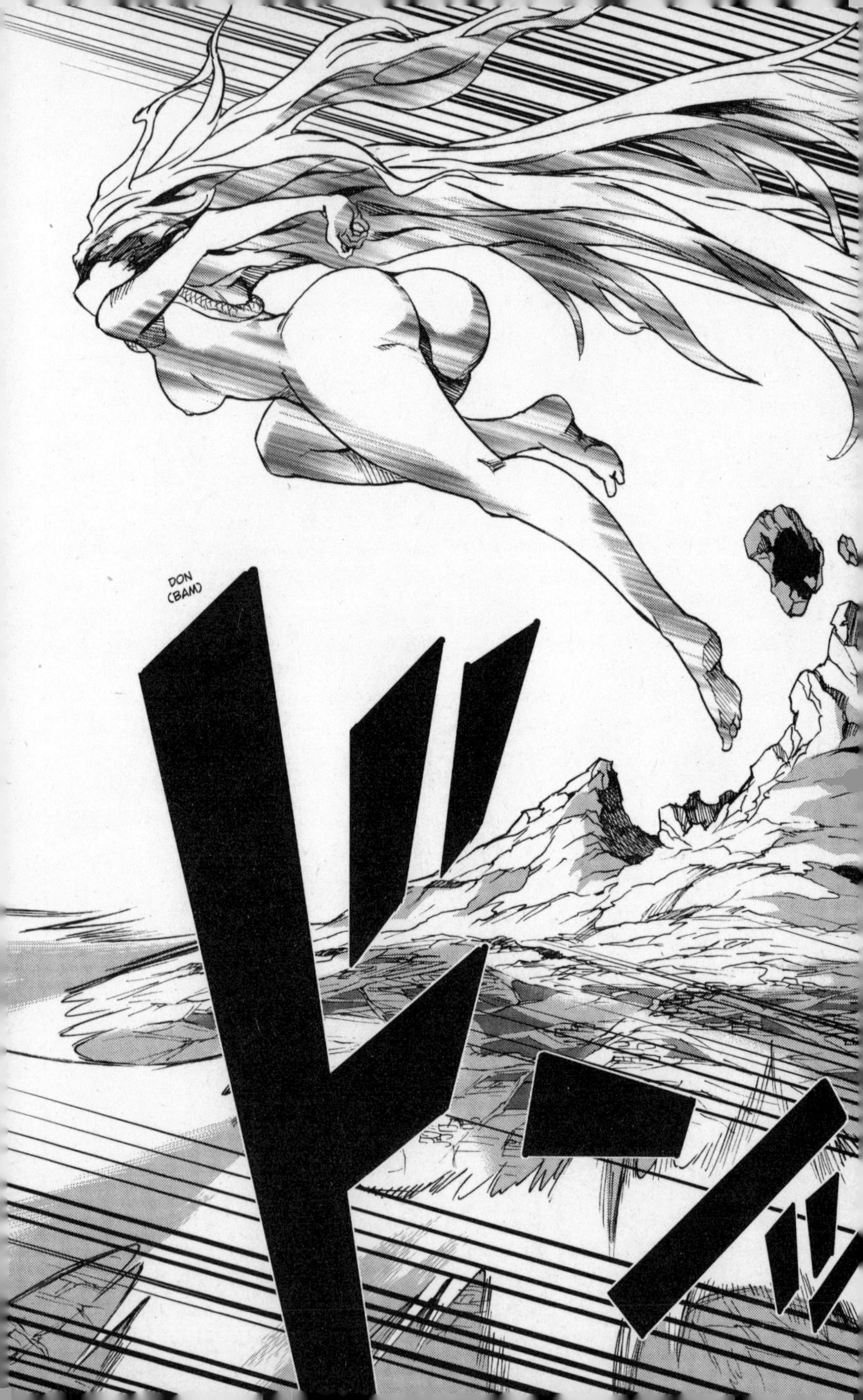
DON
(BAM)

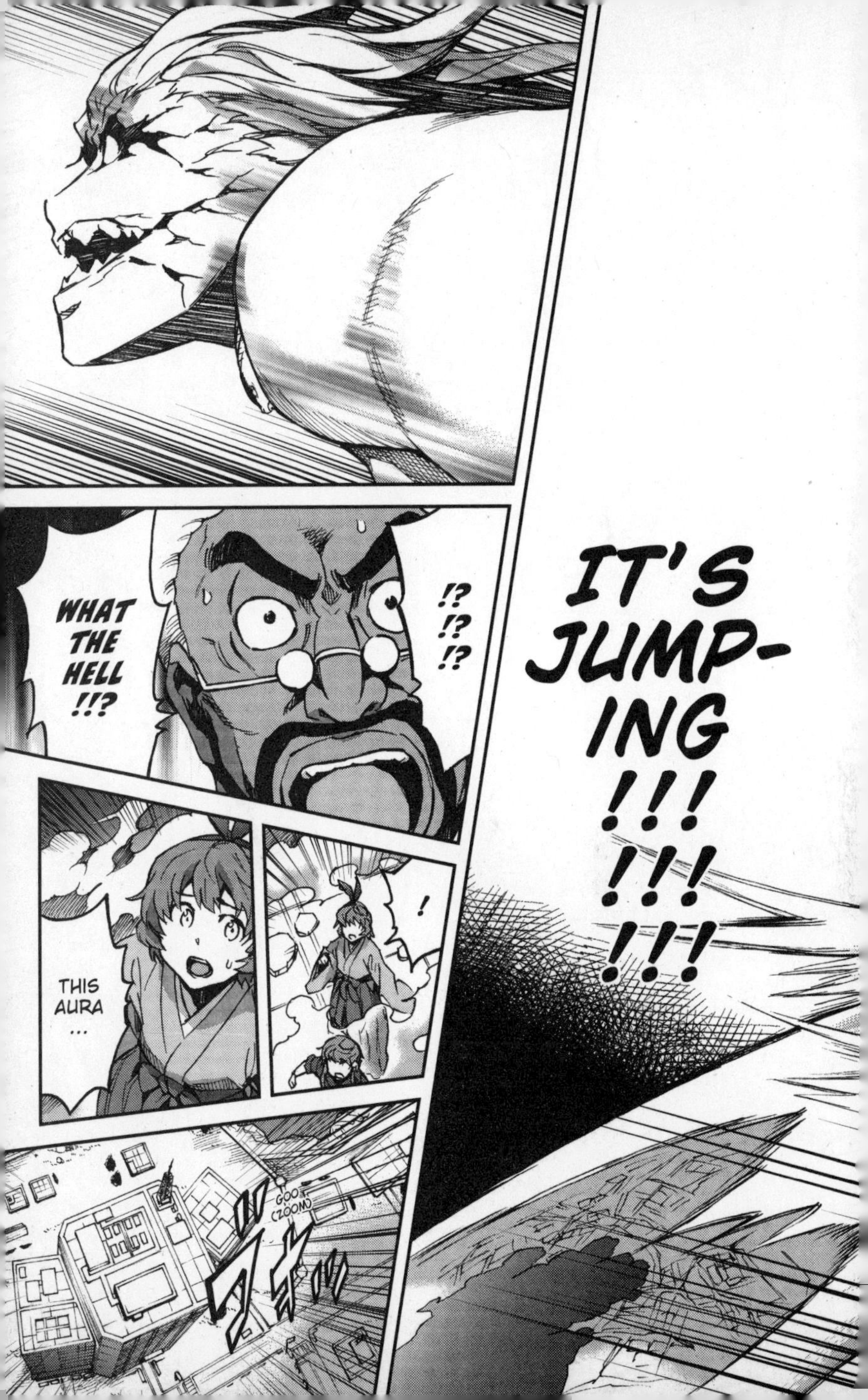
IT'S JUMP-ING!!!!!!!!!
!?!?!?
WHAT THE HELL!!?
!
THIS AURA...
GOO (ZOOM)

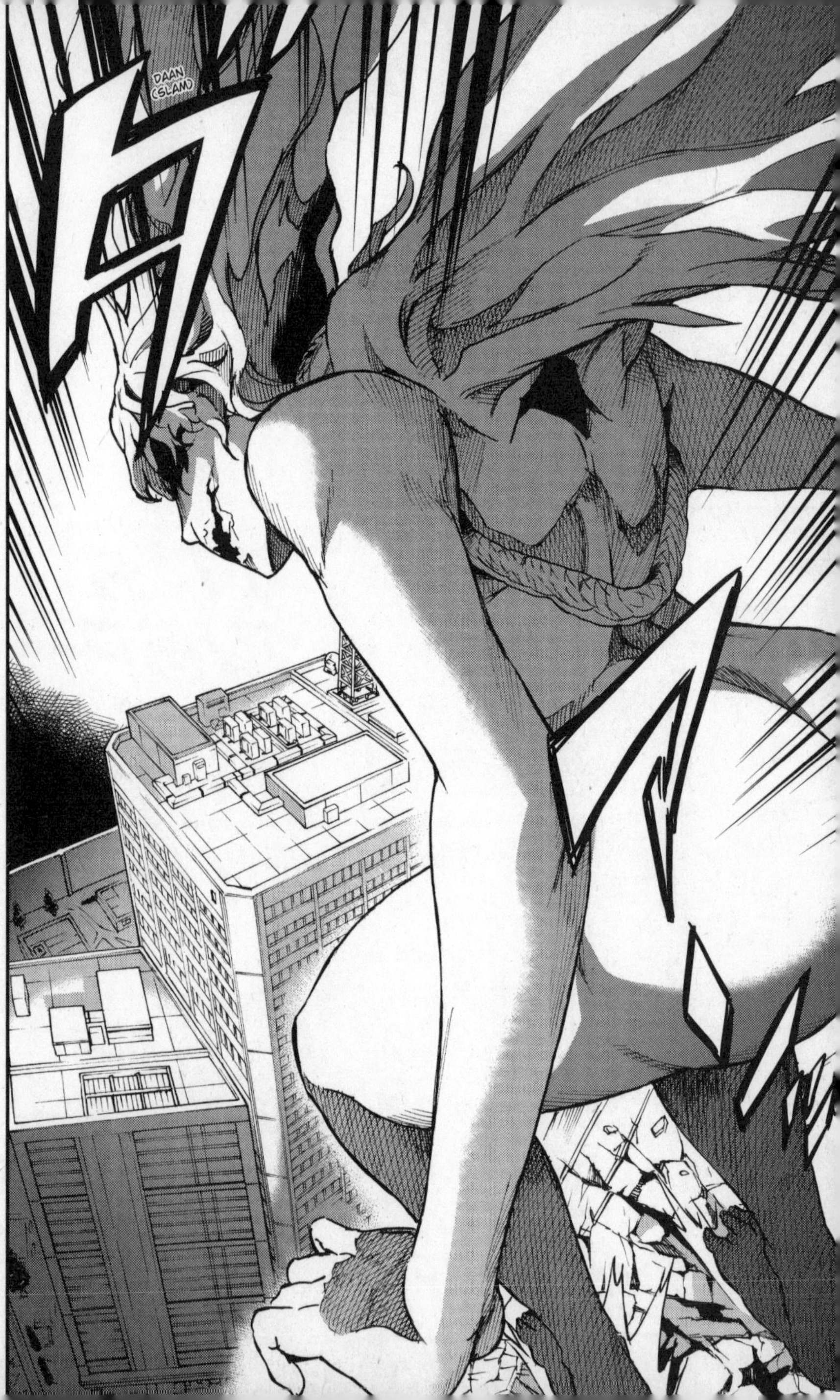
DAAN (SLAM)

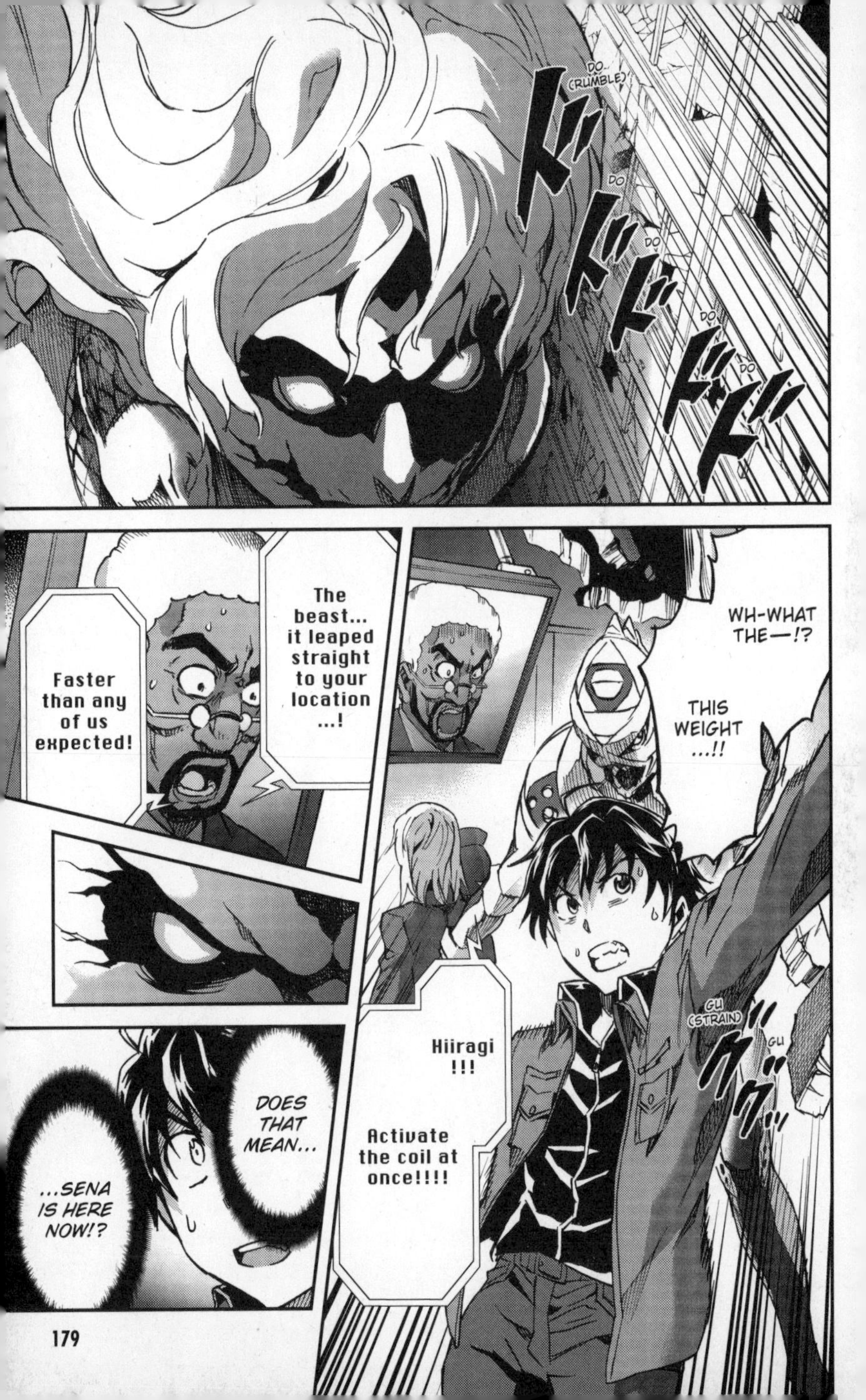
DO (RUMBLE)
DO
DO
DO
DO
WH-WHAT THE—!?
THIS WEIGHT ...!!
GU (STRAIN)
GU
Hiiragi !!!
Activate the coil at once!!!!
The beast... it leaped straight to your location ...!
Faster than any of us expected!
DOES THAT MEAN...
...SENA IS HERE NOW!?

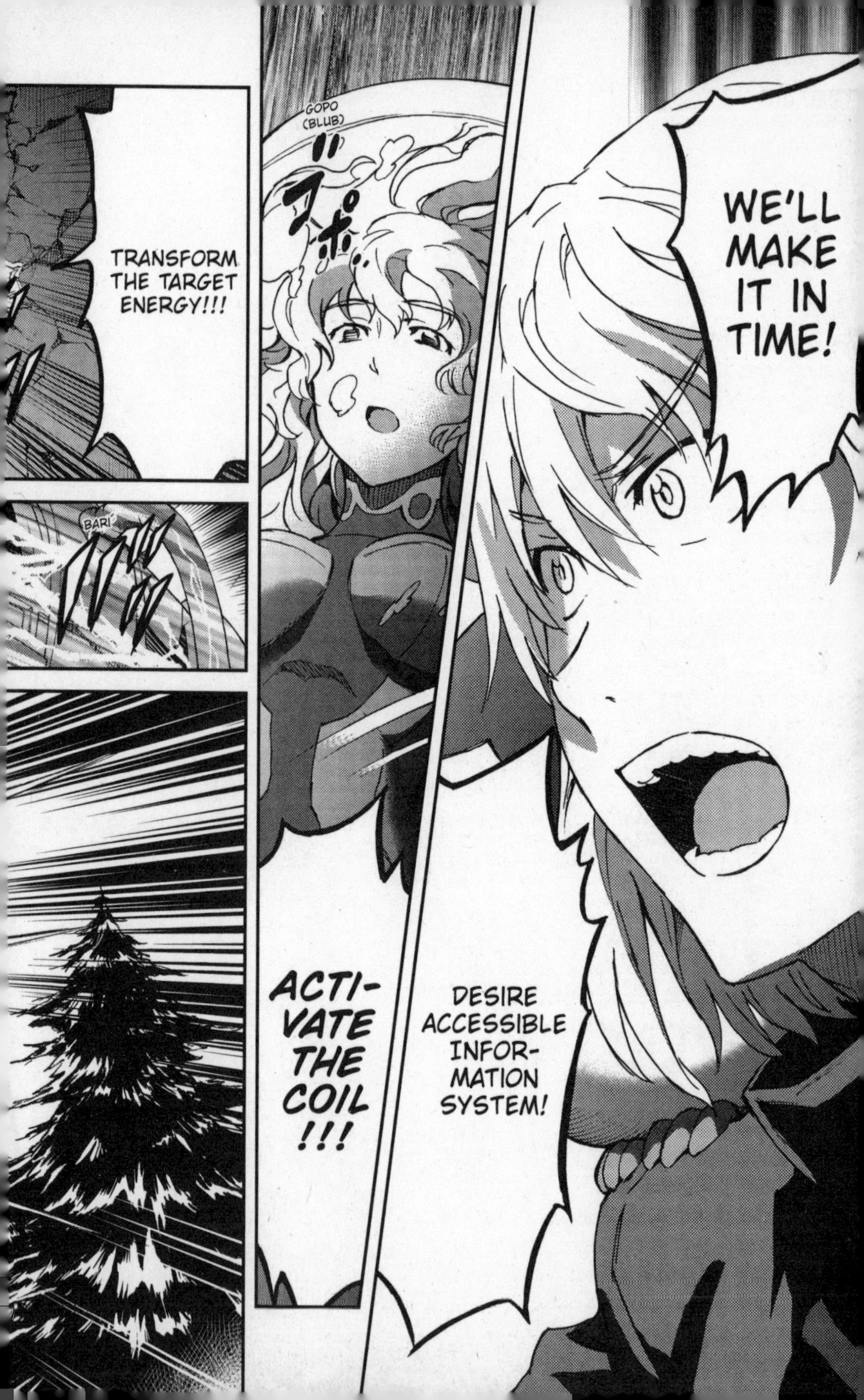

WE'LL MAKE IT IN TIME!
DESIRE ACCESSIBLE INFOR-MATION SYSTEM!
GOPO (BLUB)
ACTI-VATE THE COIL!!!
TRANSFORM THE TARGET ENERGY!!!
BARI

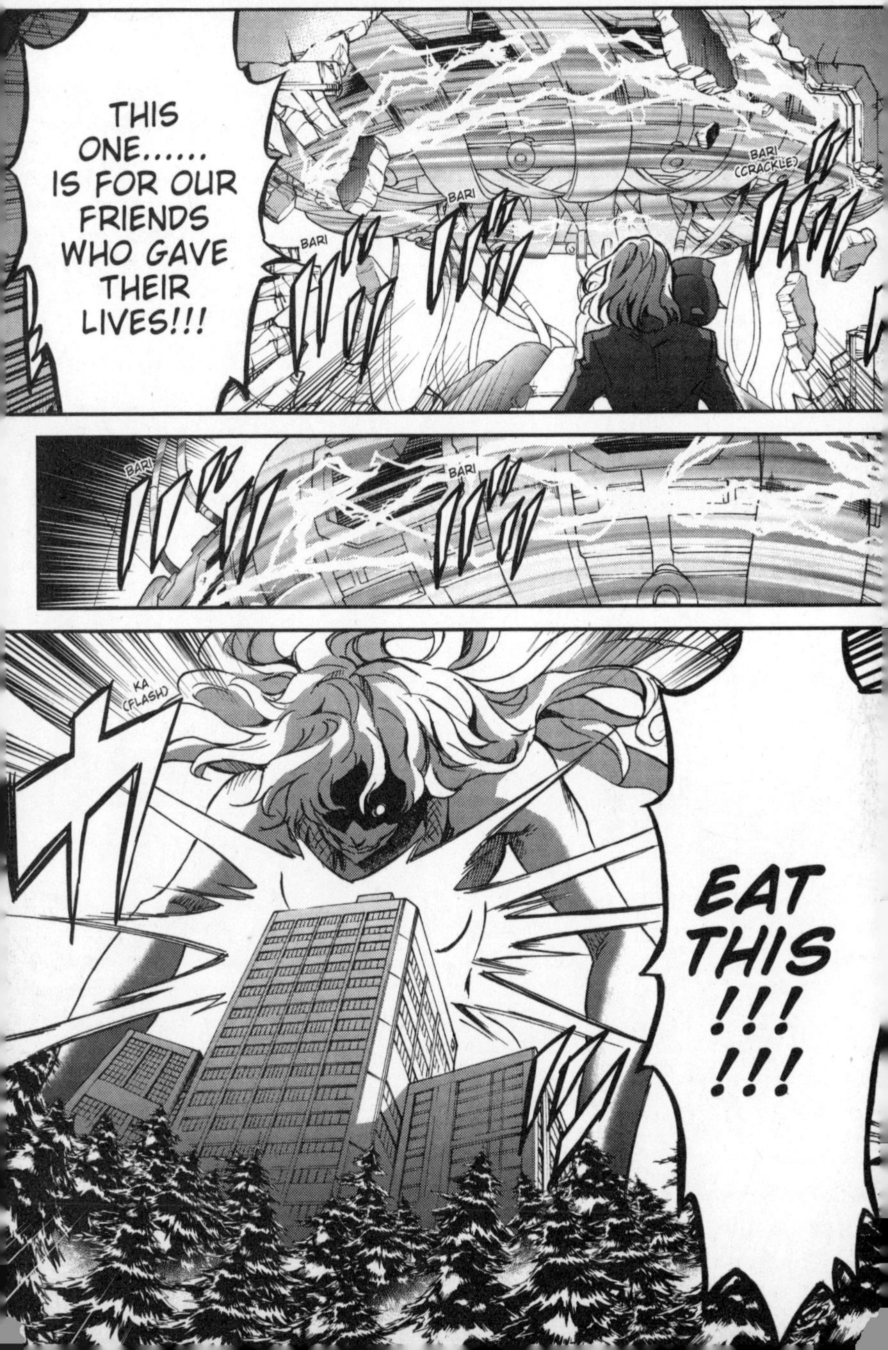
BARI (CRACKLE)
BARI
BARI
THIS ONE...... IS FOR OUR FRIENDS WHO GAVE THEIR LIVES!!!
BARI
BARI
EAT THIS!!!!!!
KA (FLASH)

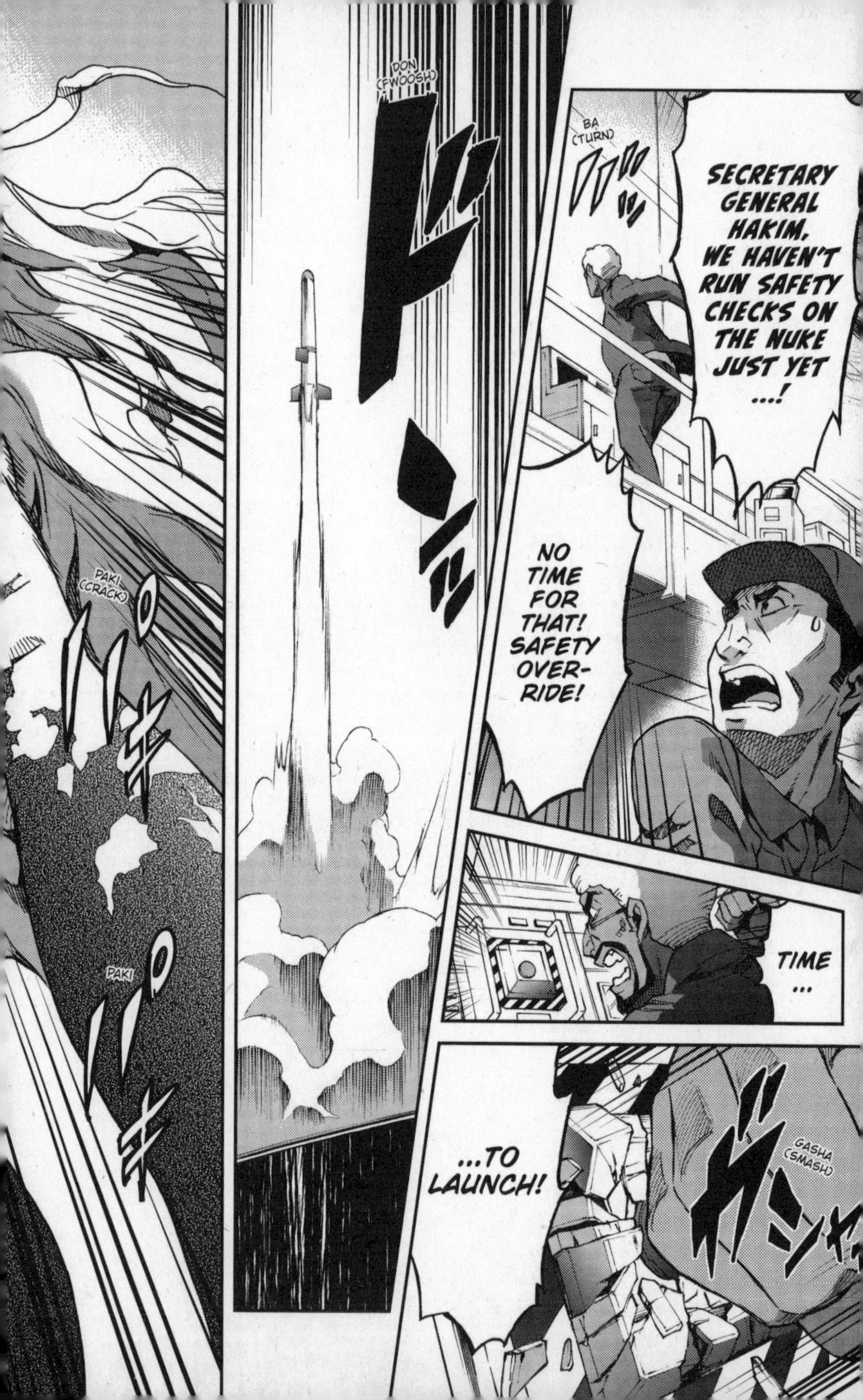
BA (TURN)
SECRETARY GENERAL HAKIM, WE HAVEN'T RUN SAFETY CHECKS ON THE NUKE JUST YET ...!
NO TIME FOR THAT! SAFETY OVER-RIDE!
TIME ...
...TO LAUNCH!
GASHA (SMASH)
DON (FWOOSH)
PAKI (CRACK)
PAKI

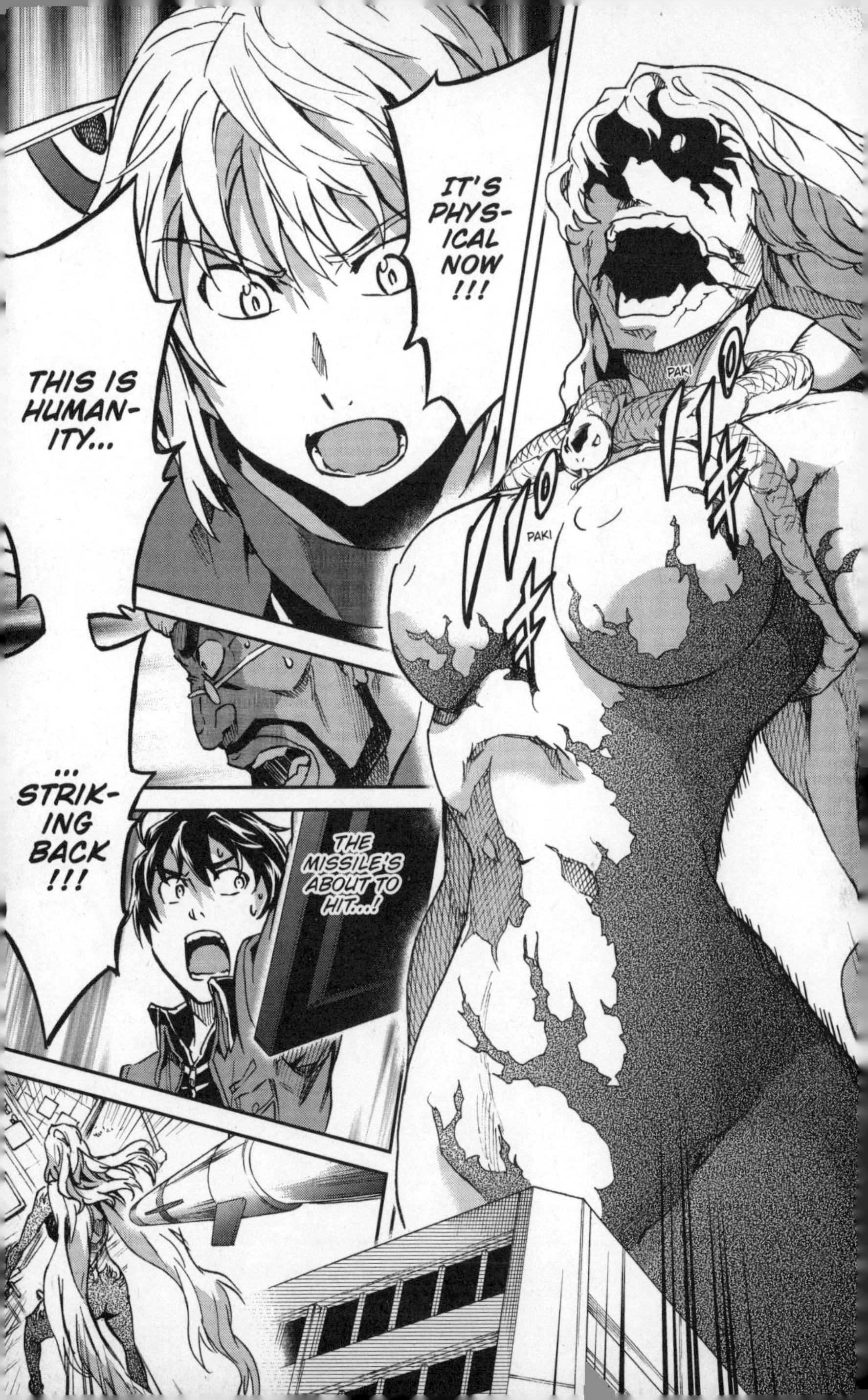
PAKI
PAKI
IT'S PHYS-ICAL NOW!!!
THIS IS HUMAN-ITY...
...STRIK-ING BACK!!!
THE MISSILE'S ABOUT TO HIT...!

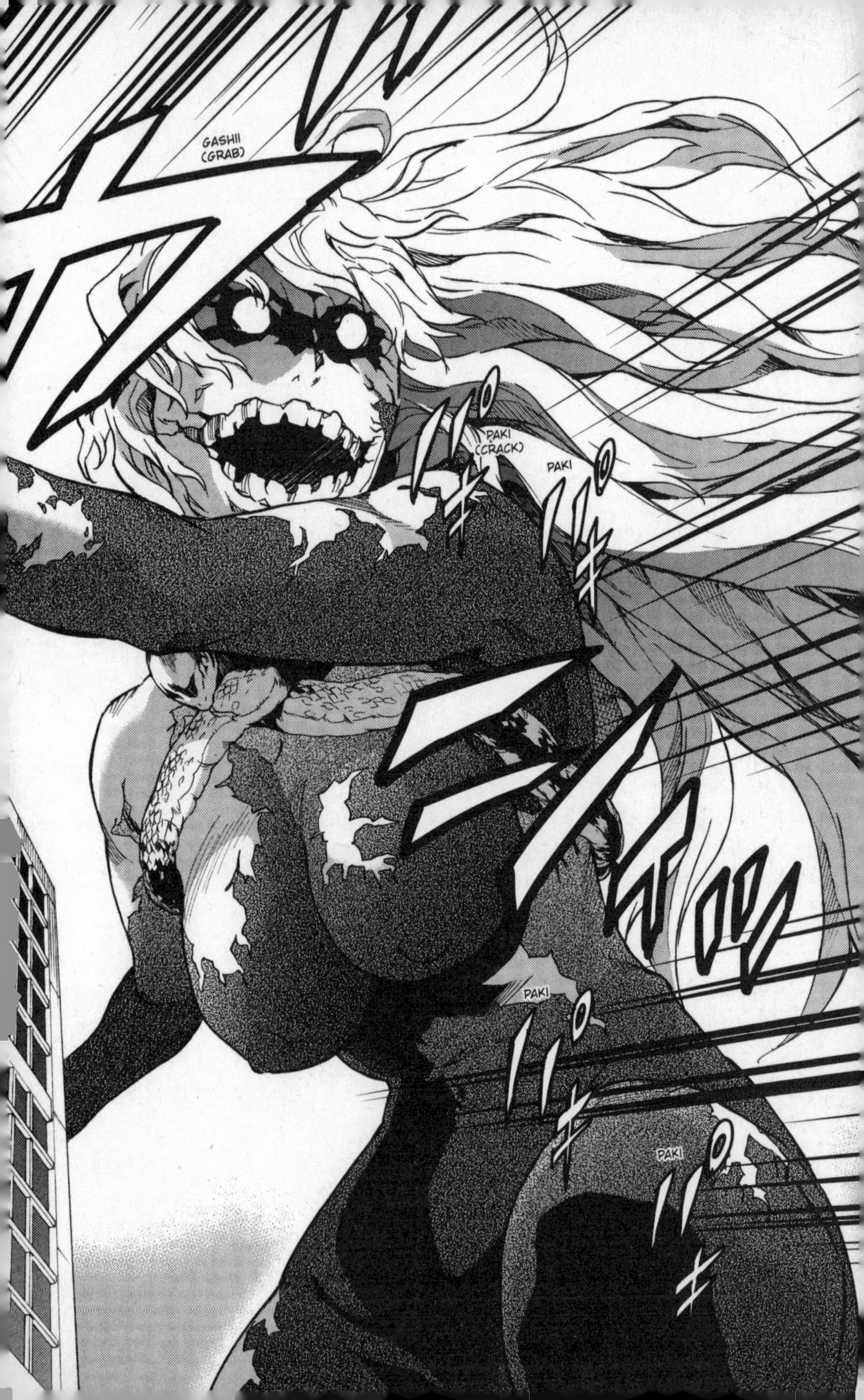
GASHII (GRAB)
PAKI (CRACK)
PAKI
PAKI
PAKI

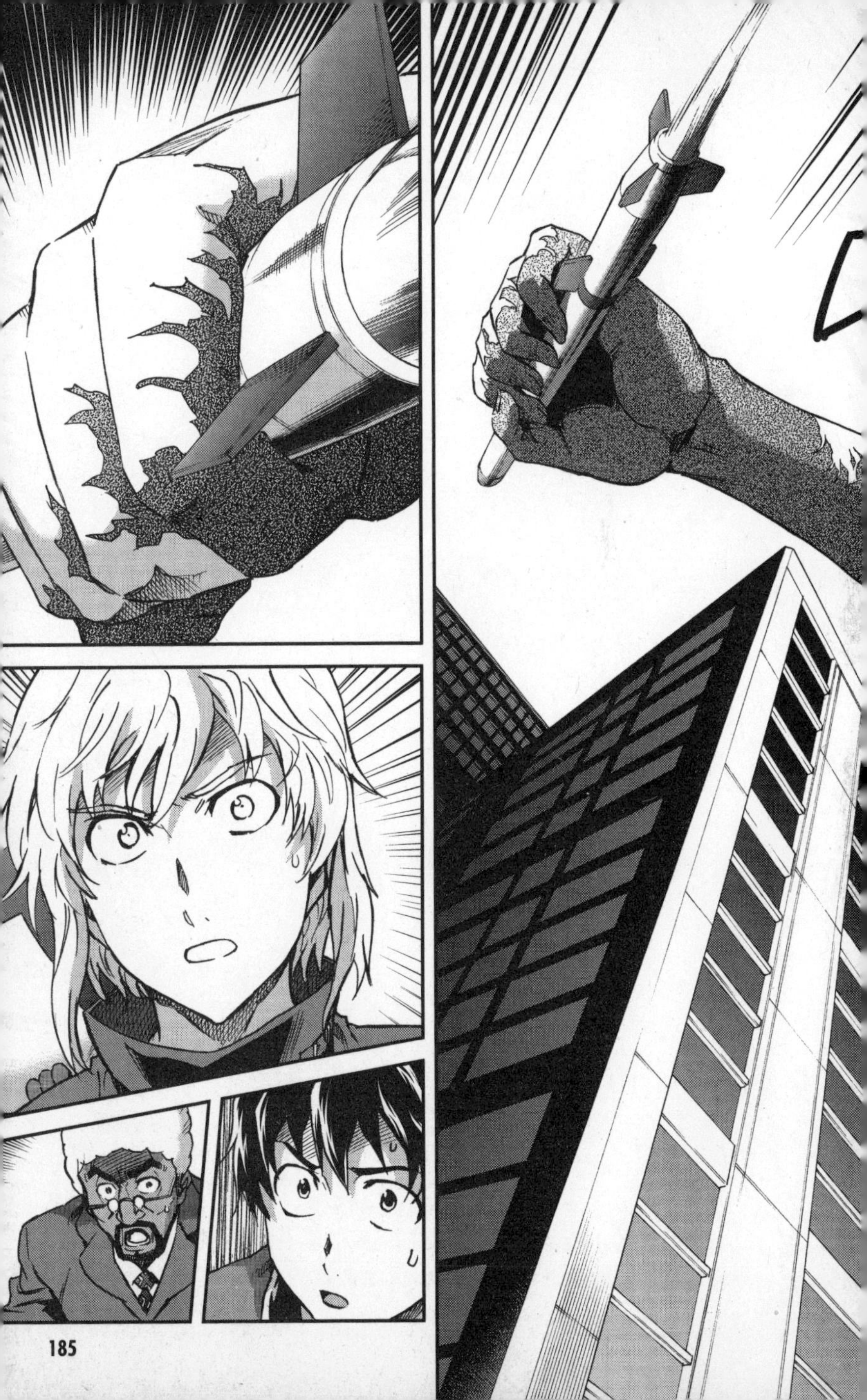

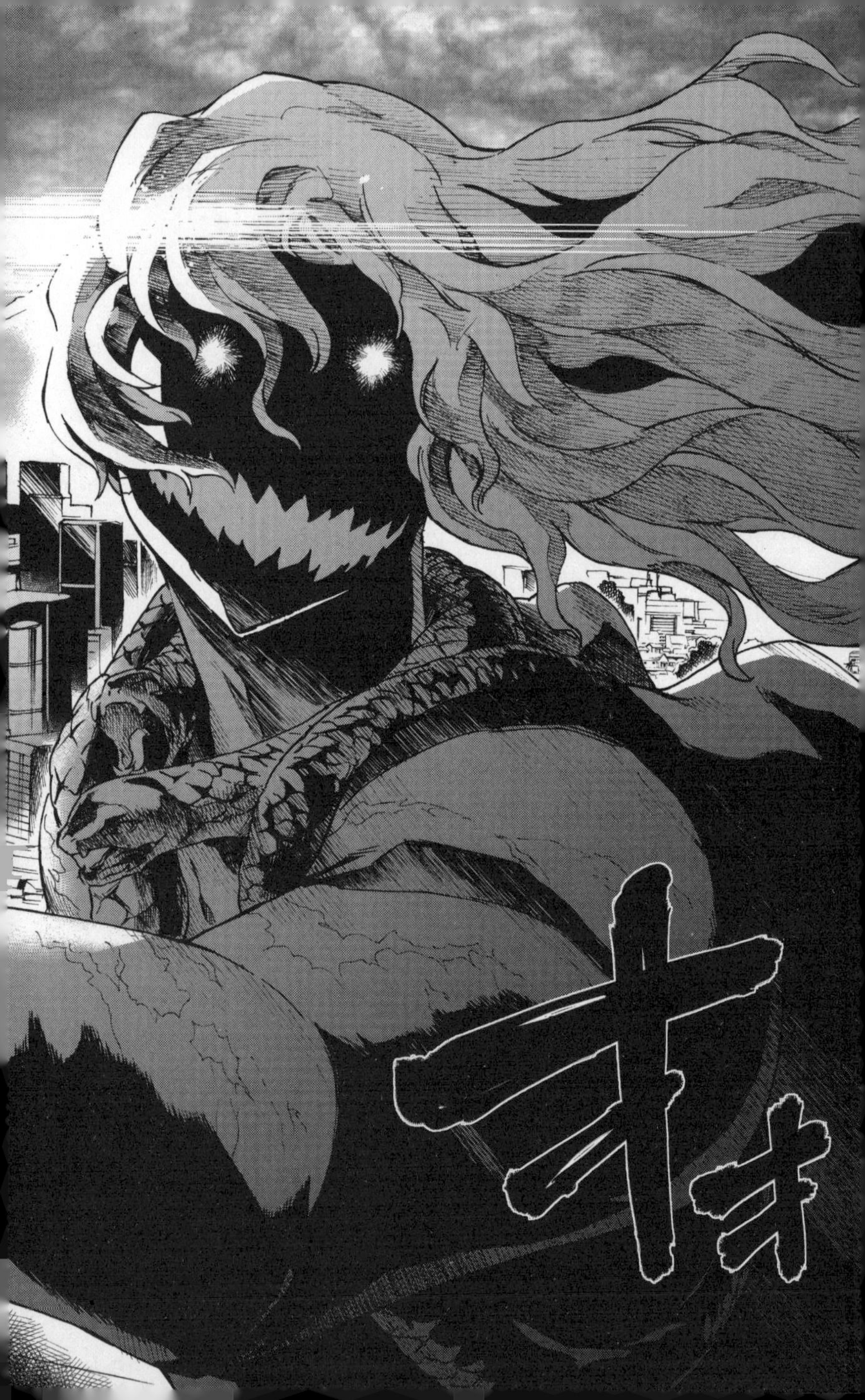
オォ

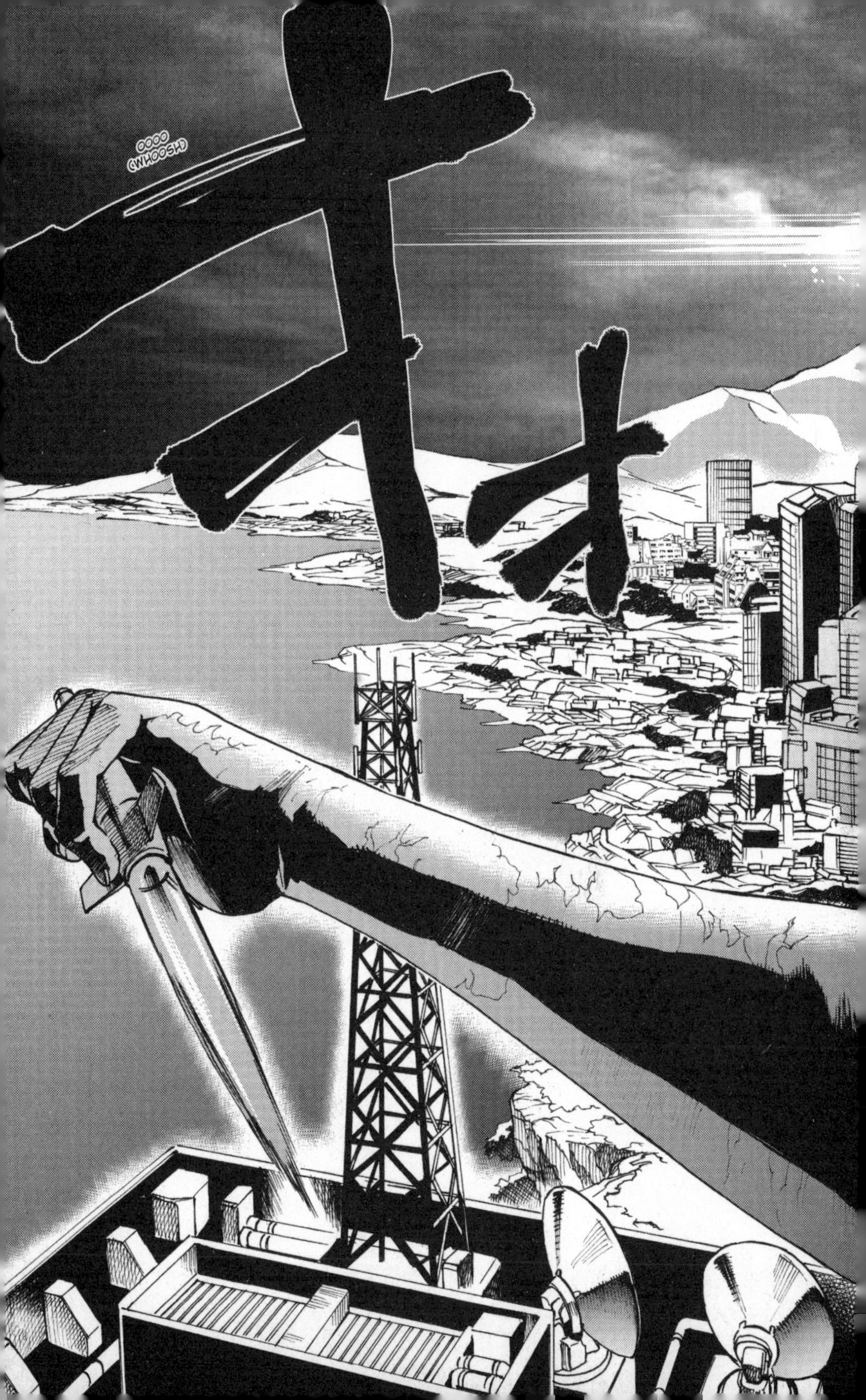
OOOO
(WHOOSH)

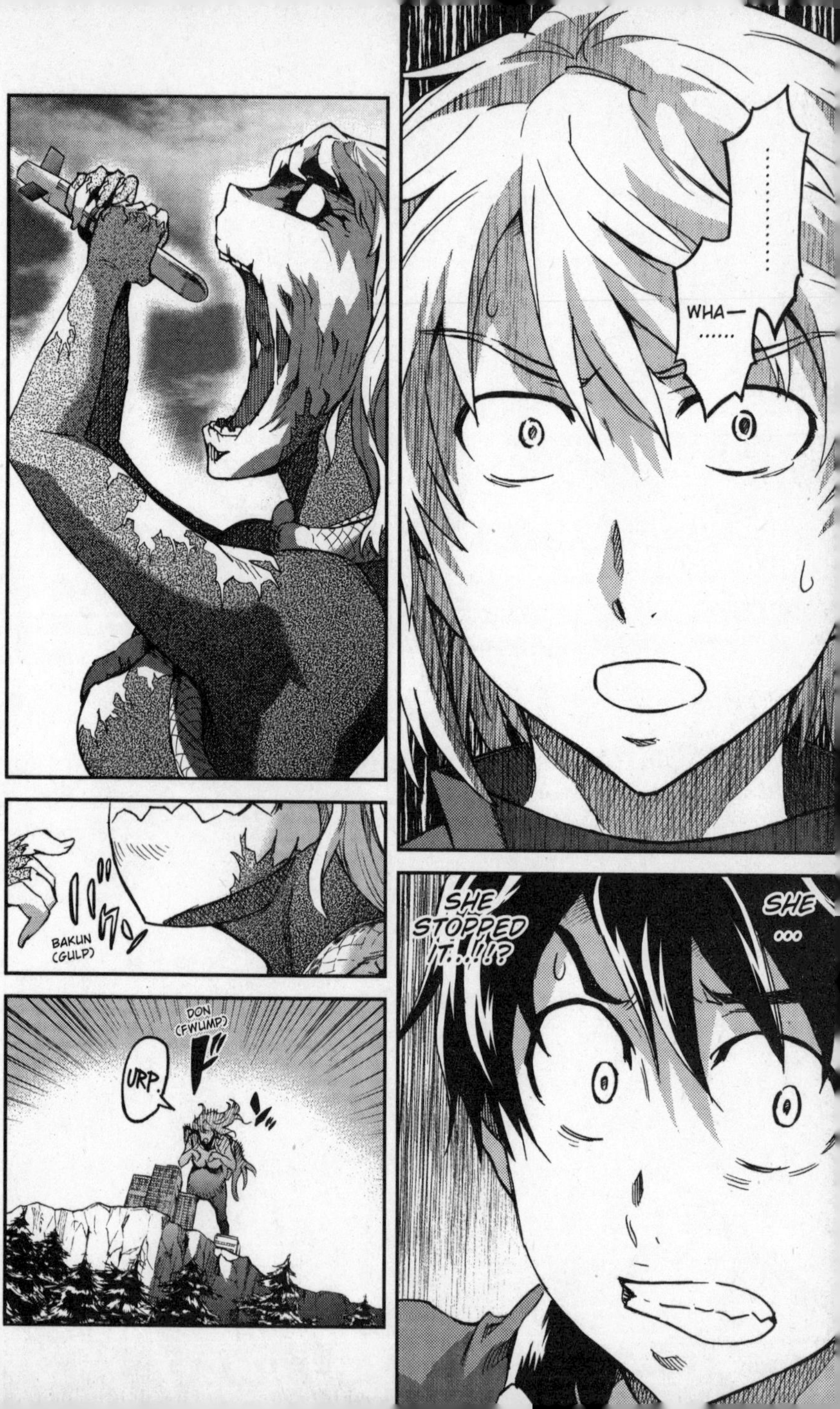
……!
WHA—
……
BAKUN (GULP)
SHE …
SHE STOPPED IT…!!?
URP.
DON (FWUMP)

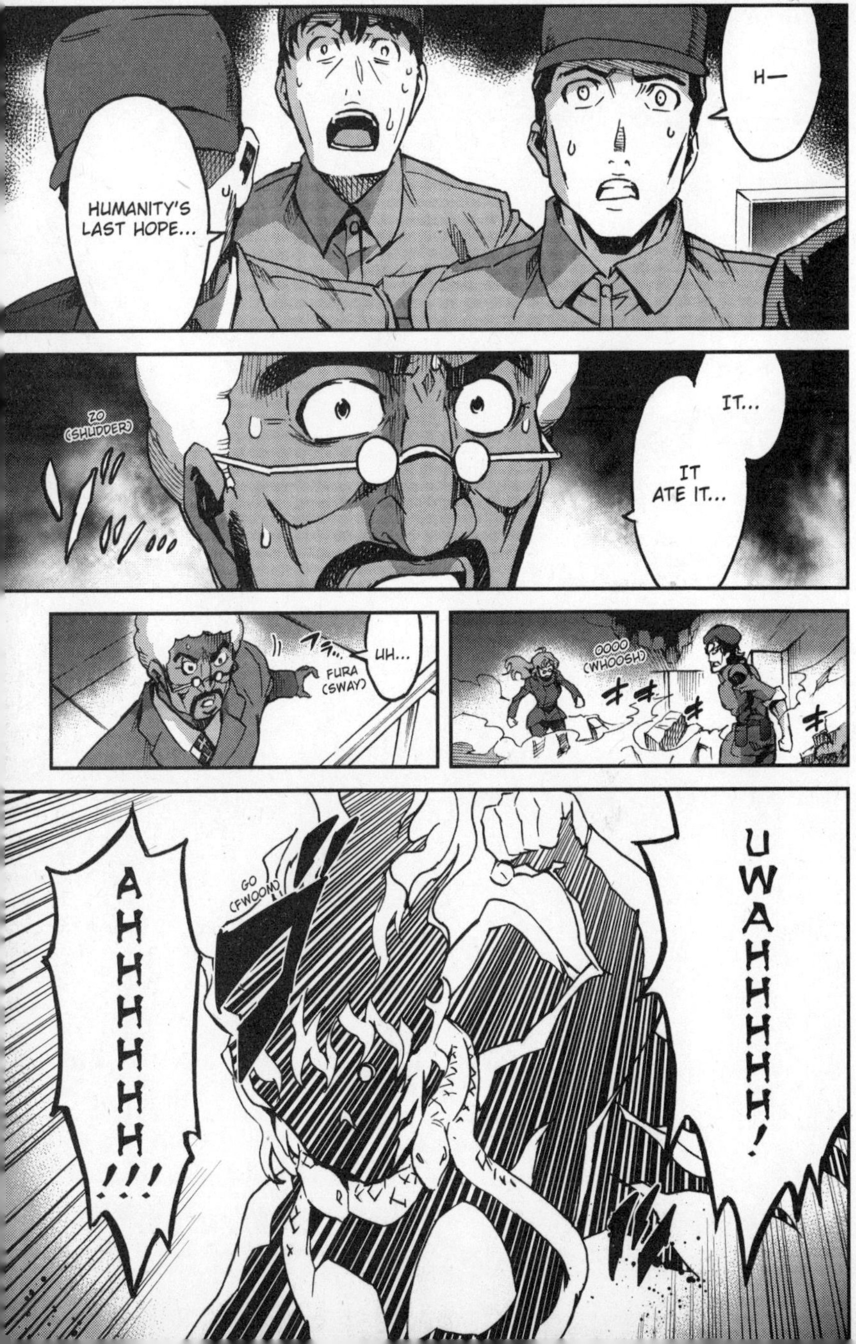
H—
HUMANITY'S LAST HOPE...
IT...
IT ATE IT...
ZO (SHUDDER)
OOOO (WHOOSH)
UH...
FURA (SWAY)
UWAHHHHHH!
GO (FWOOM)
AHHHHHHH!!!

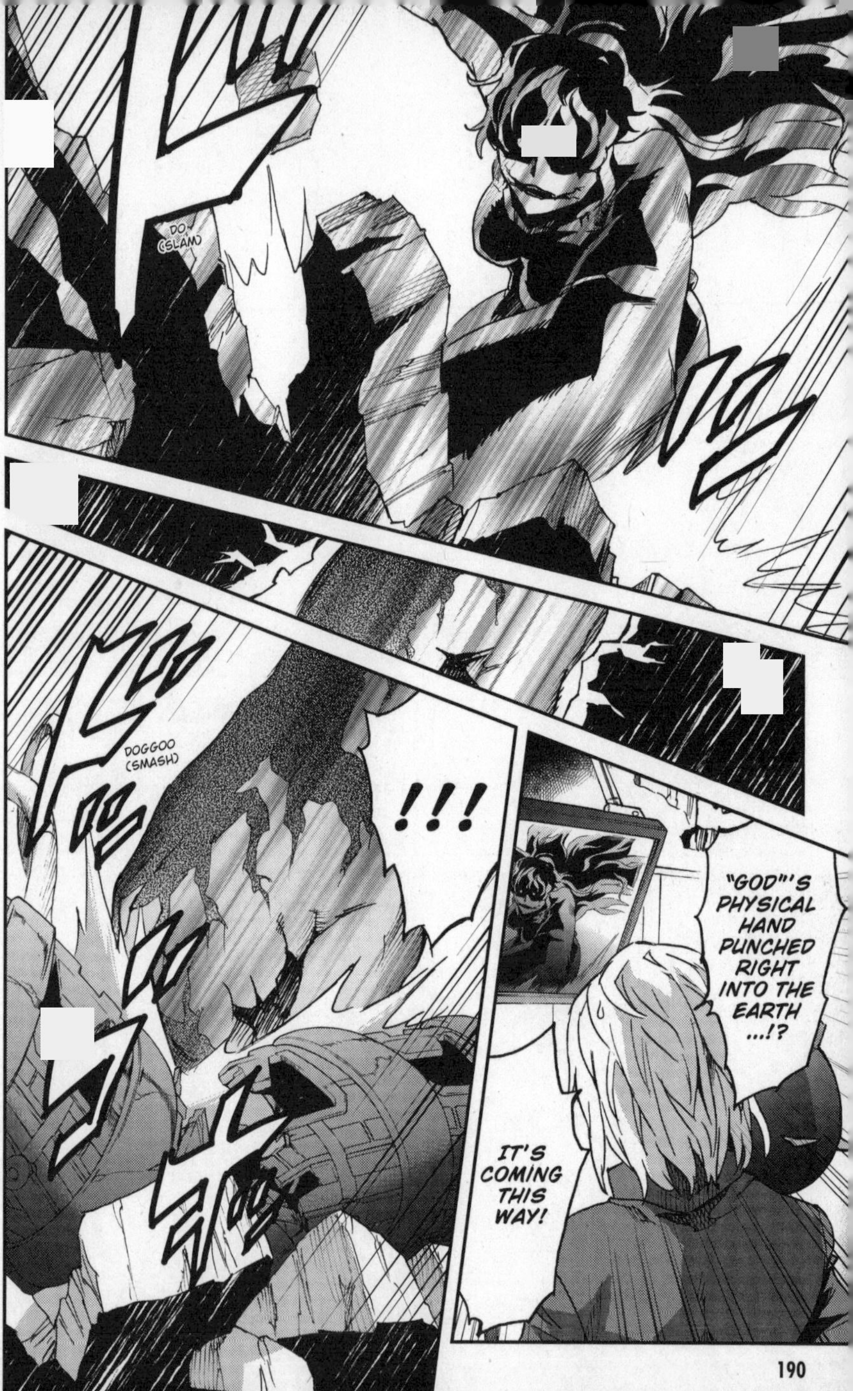
DO
(SLAM)
"GOD"'S PHYSICAL HAND PUNCHED RIGHT INTO THE EARTH ...!?
IT'S COMING THIS WAY!
DOGGOO
(SMASH)
!!!

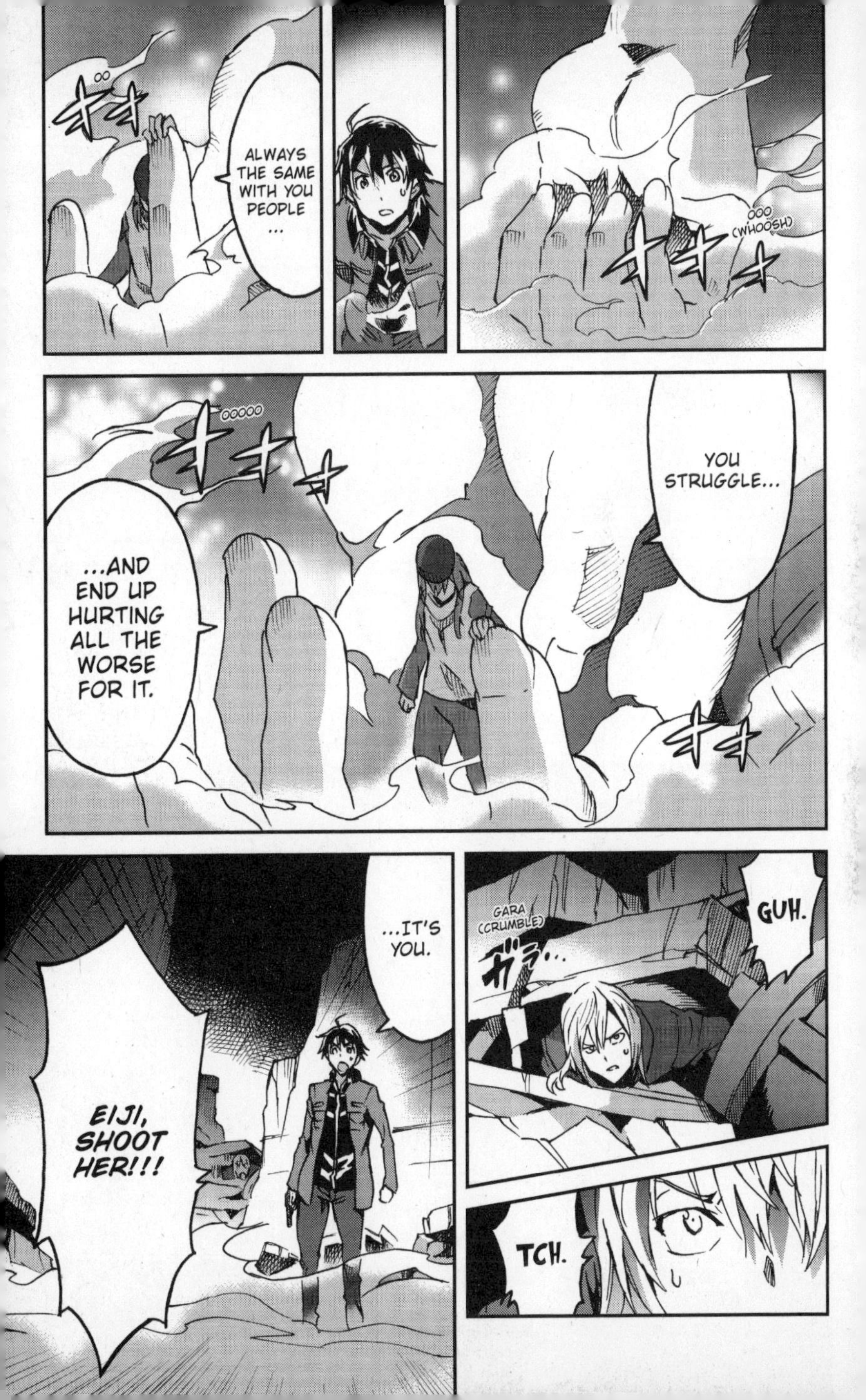
OOO (WHOOSH)
ALWAYS THE SAME WITH YOU PEOPLE ...
OO
YOU STRUGGLE...
OOOOO
...AND END UP HURTING ALL THE WORSE FOR IT.
GUH.
GARA (CRUMBLE)
TCH.
...IT'S YOU.
EIJI, SHOOT HER!!!

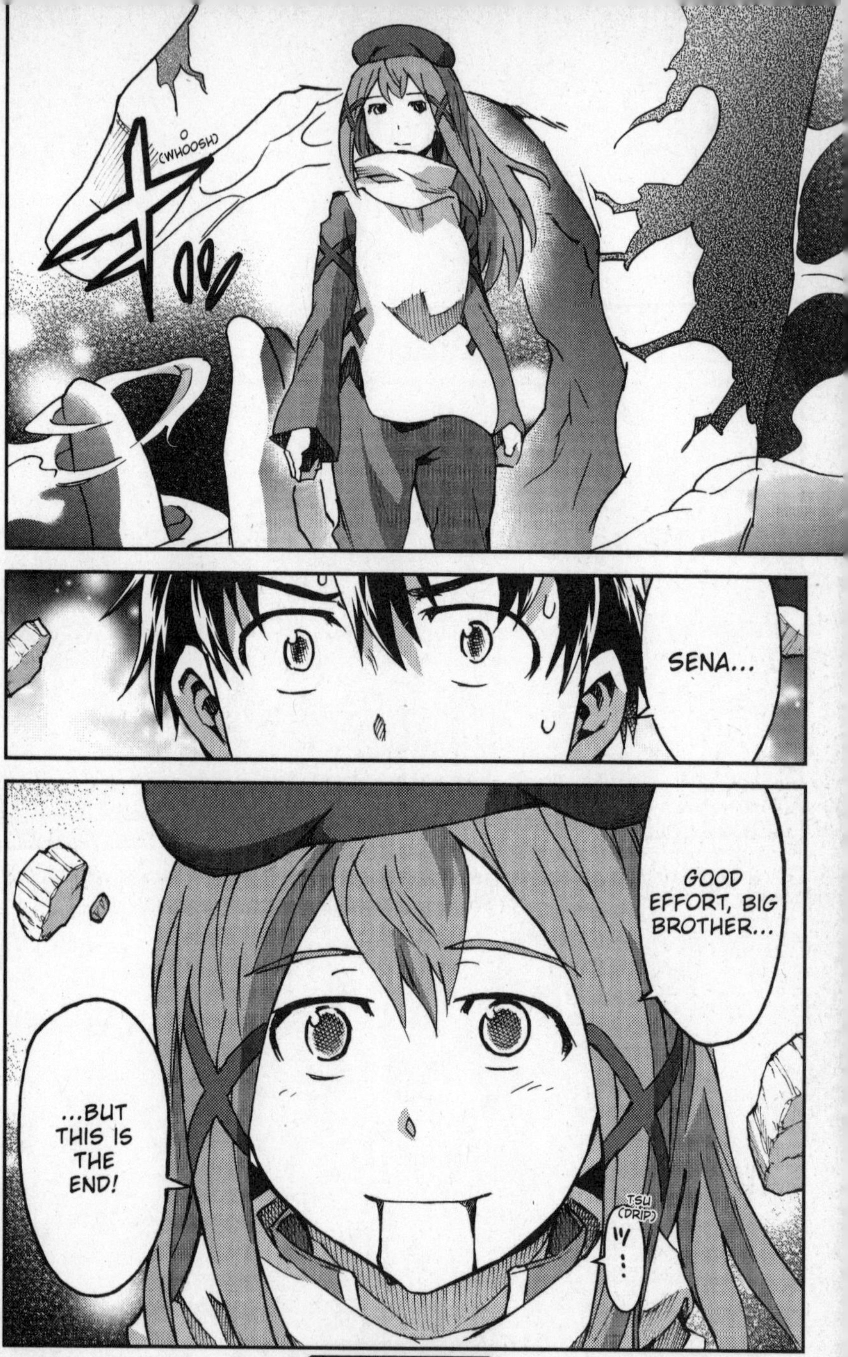
O (WHOOSH)
SENA...
GOOD EFFORT, BIG BROTHER...
...BUT THIS IS THE END!
TSU (DRIP)

Subject 48: END

BIG
ORDER

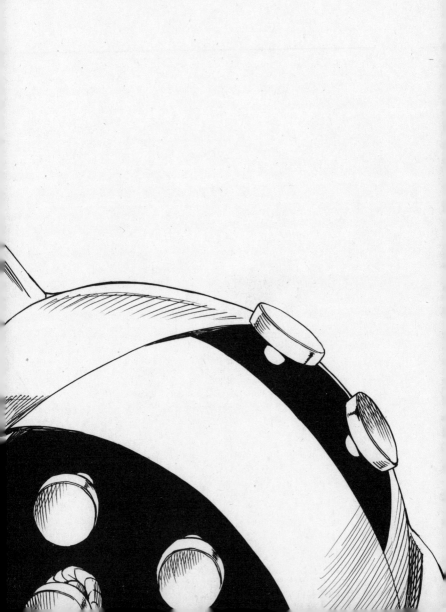

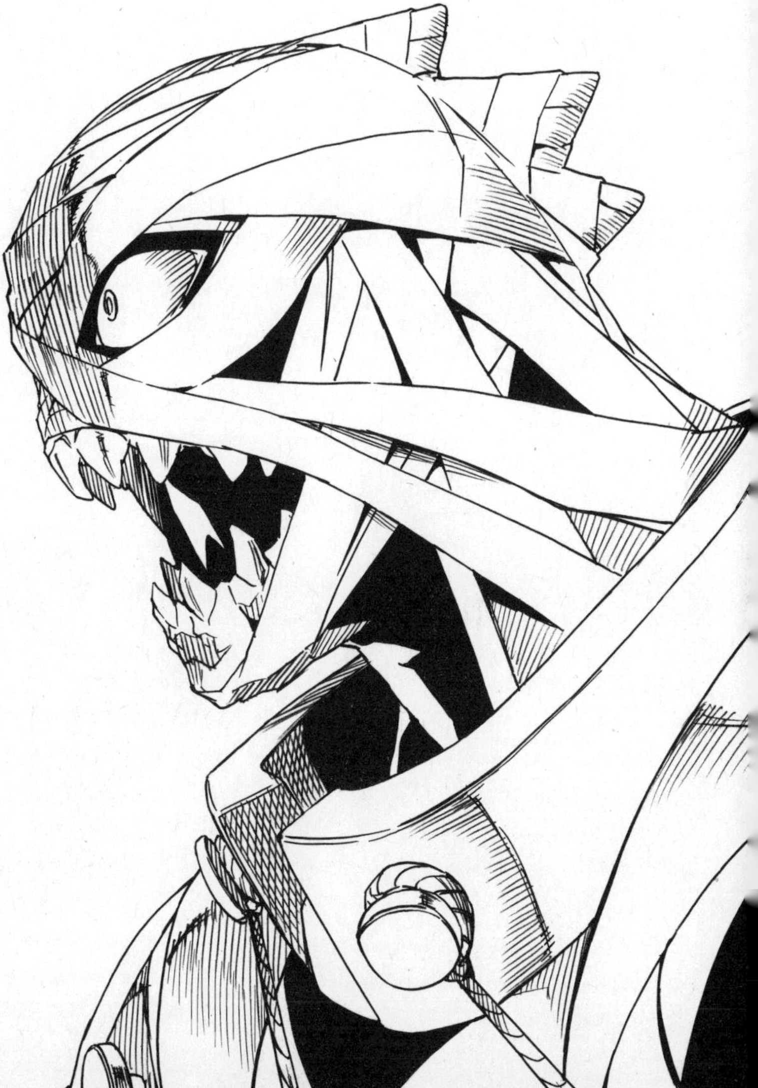

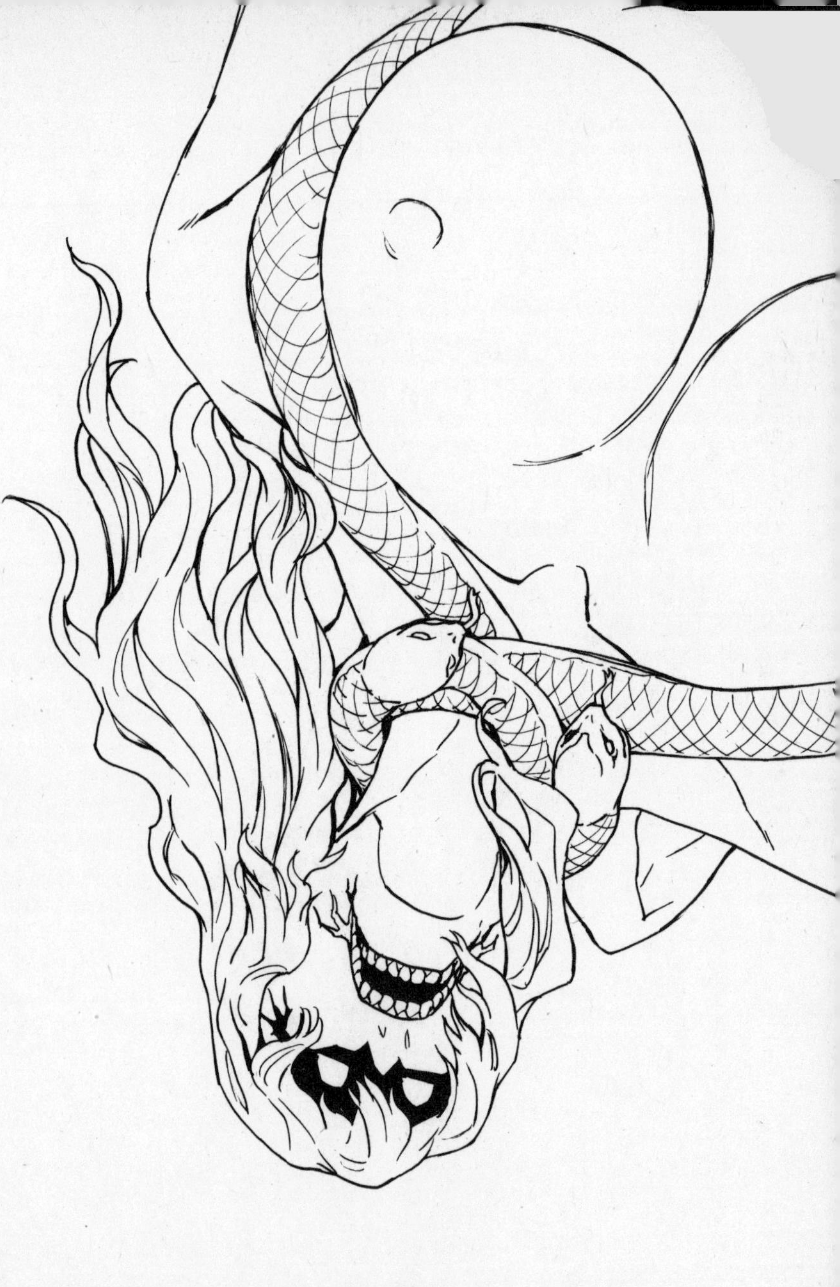

Subject 49

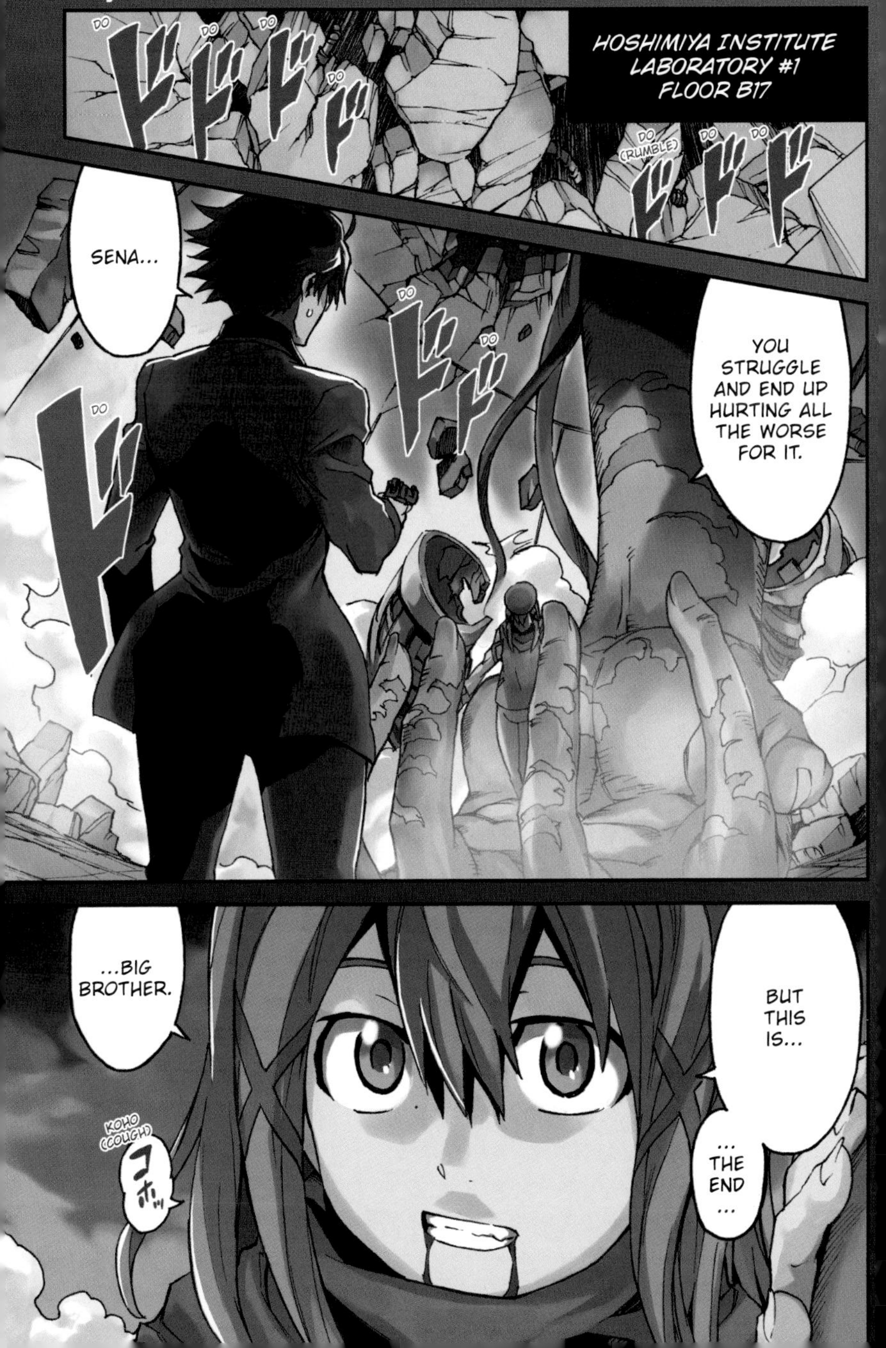
HOSHIMIYA INSTITUTE LABORATORY #1 FLOOR B17
DO (RUMBLE) DO DO
DO DO DO DO
SENA...
YOU STRUGGLE AND END UP HURTING ALL THE WORSE FOR IT.
DO DO
DO
BUT THIS IS...
...THE END...
...BIG BROTHER.
KOHO (COUGH)

Subject 49: "Beyond the End"
Place: Tokyo

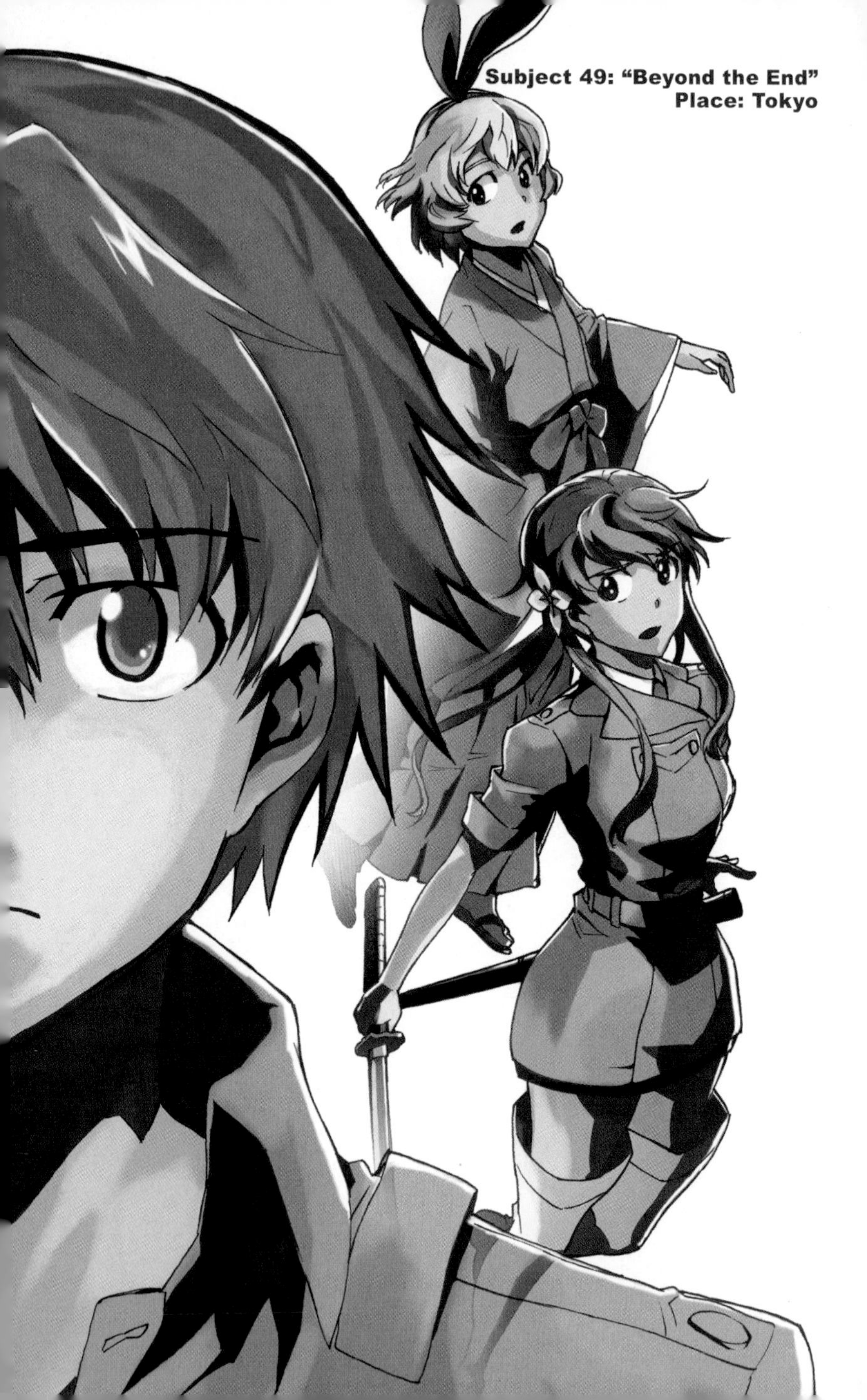

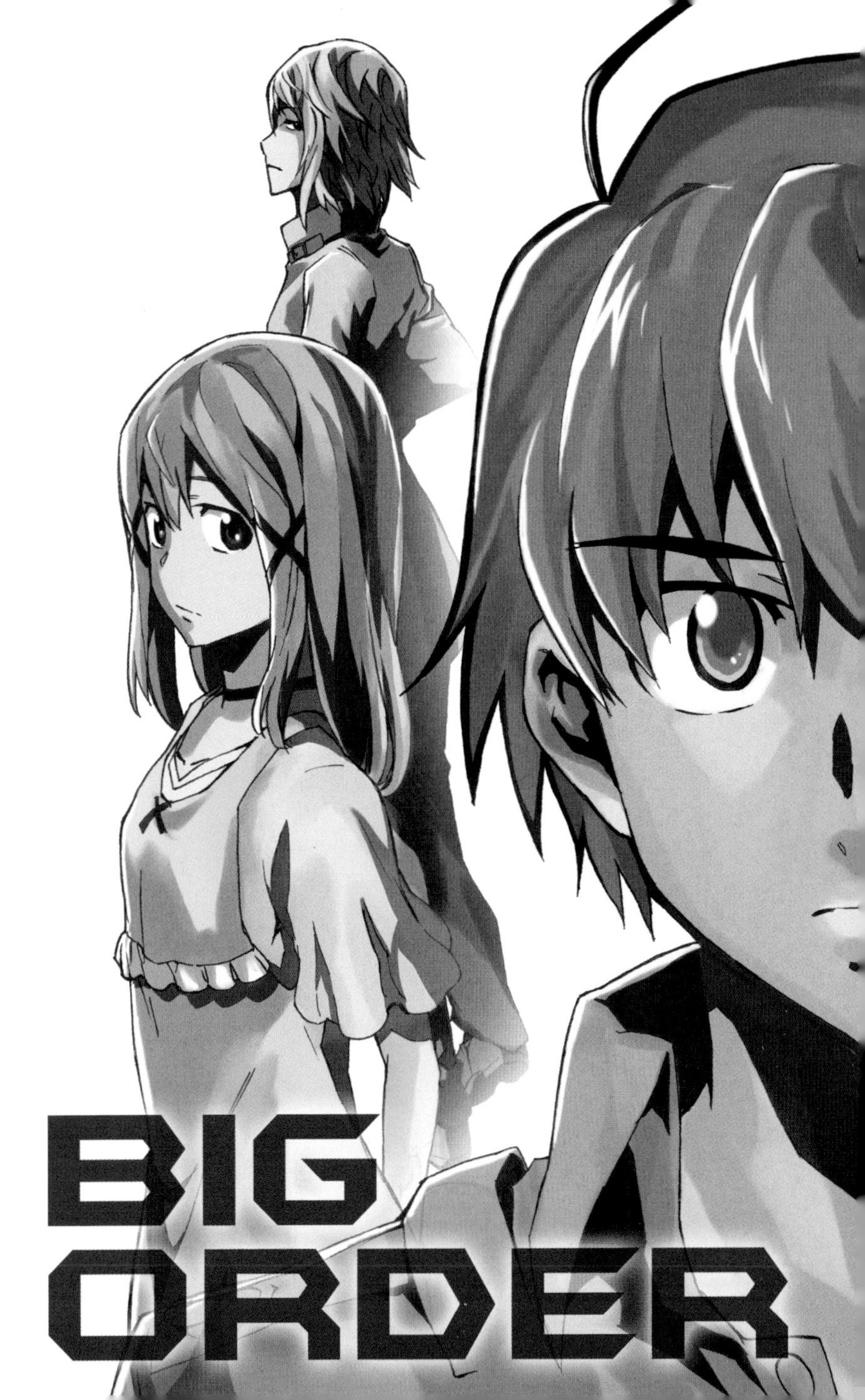
BIG
ORDER

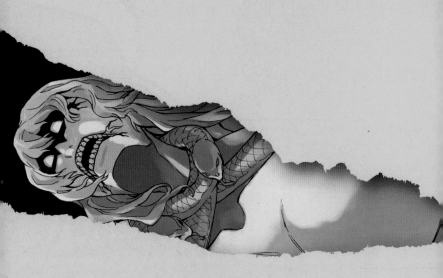

**BIG
ORDER**

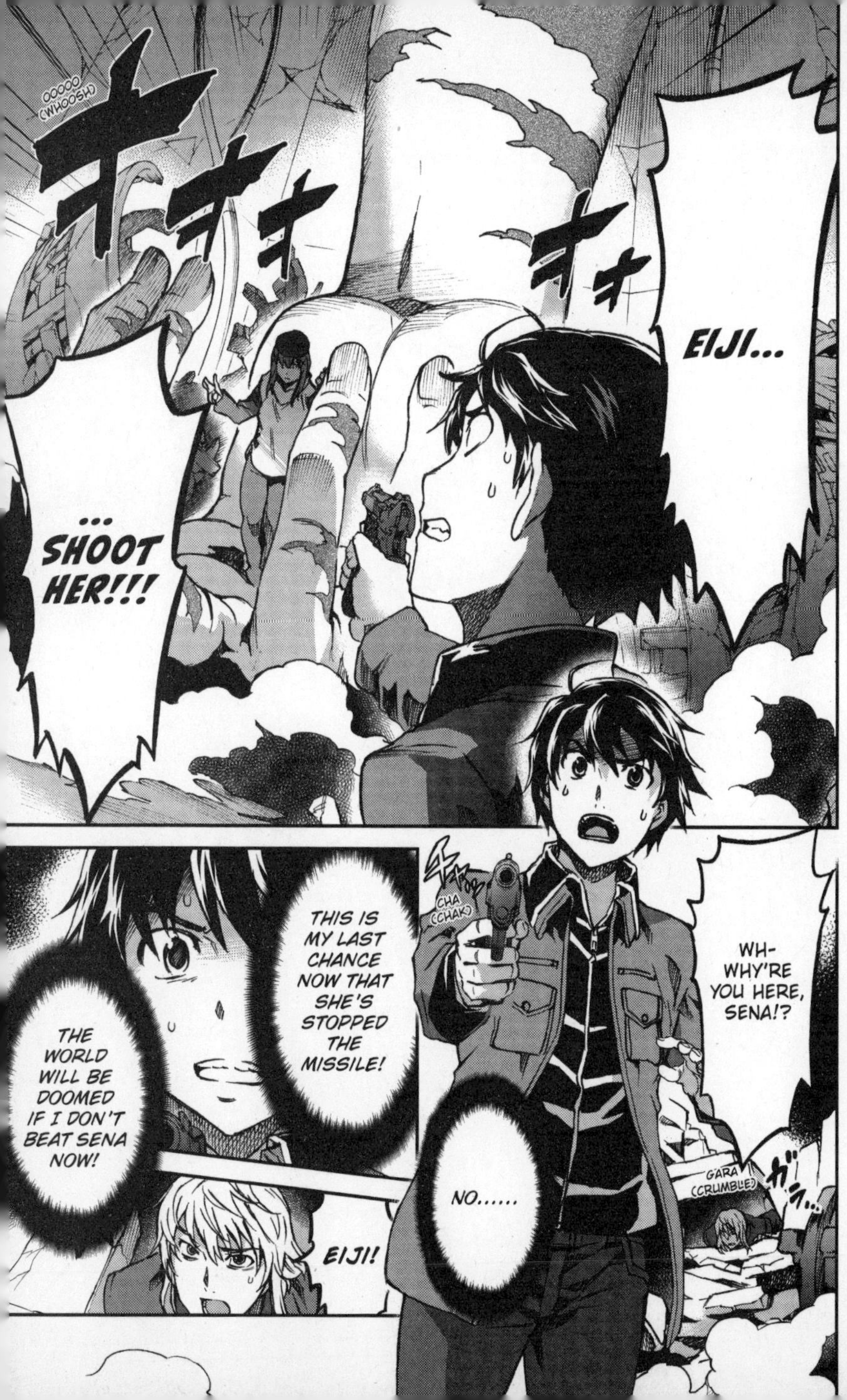

EIJI...
...SHOOT HER!!!
OOOOO (WHOOSH)
CHA (CHAK)
WH- WHY'RE YOU HERE, SENA!?
GARA (CRUMBLE)
NO......
THIS IS MY LAST CHANCE NOW THAT SHE'S STOPPED THE MISSILE!
THE WORLD WILL BE DOOMED IF I DON'T BEAT SENA NOW!
EIJI!

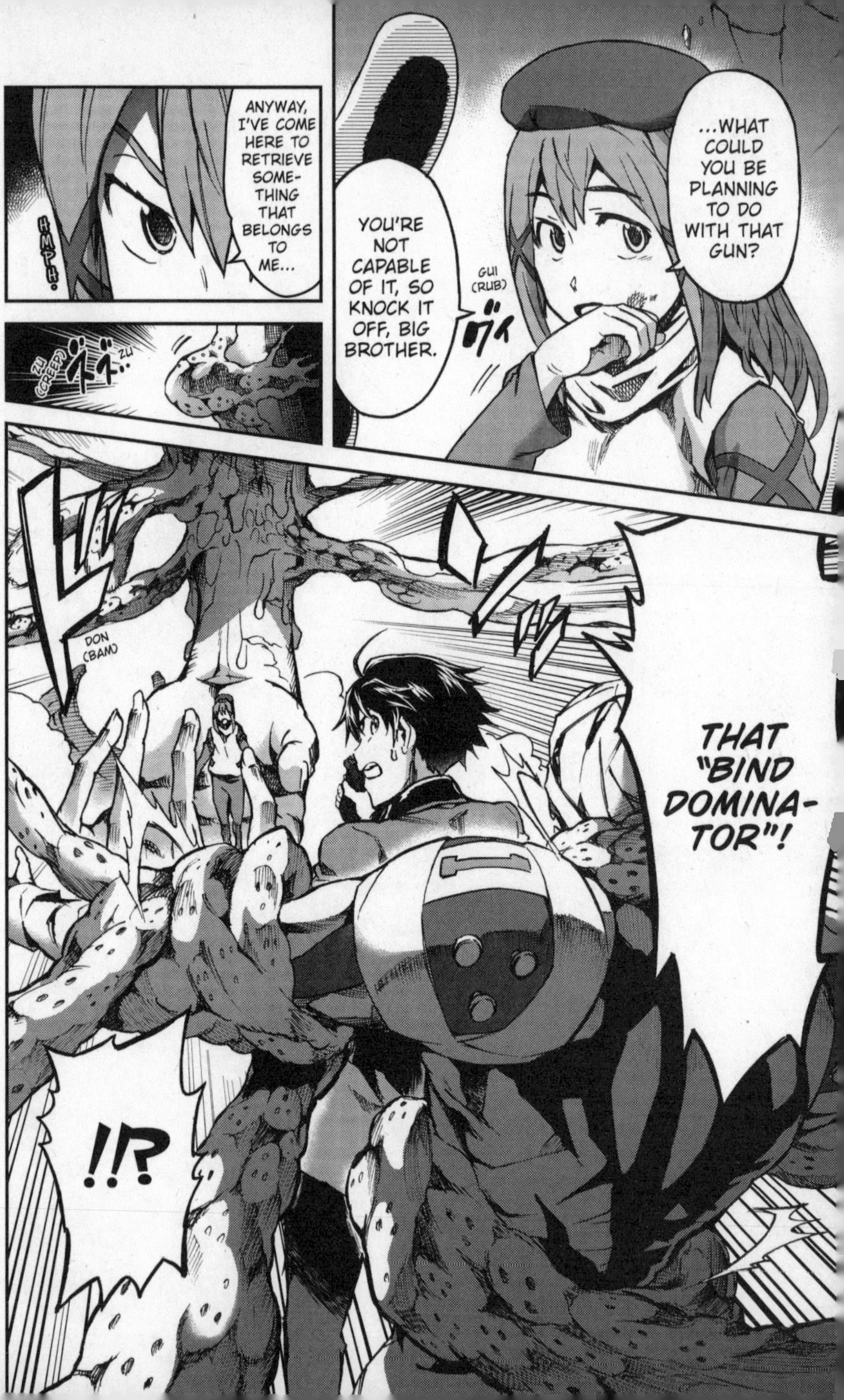
...WHAT COULD YOU BE PLANNING TO DO WITH THAT GUN?
GUI (RUB)
YOU'RE NOT CAPABLE OF IT, SO KNOCK IT OFF, BIG BROTHER.
ANYWAY, I'VE COME HERE TO RETRIEVE SOME-THING THAT BELONGS TO ME...
HMPH.
ZU ZU (CREEP)
THAT "BIND DOMINA-TOR"!
DON (BAM)
!!?

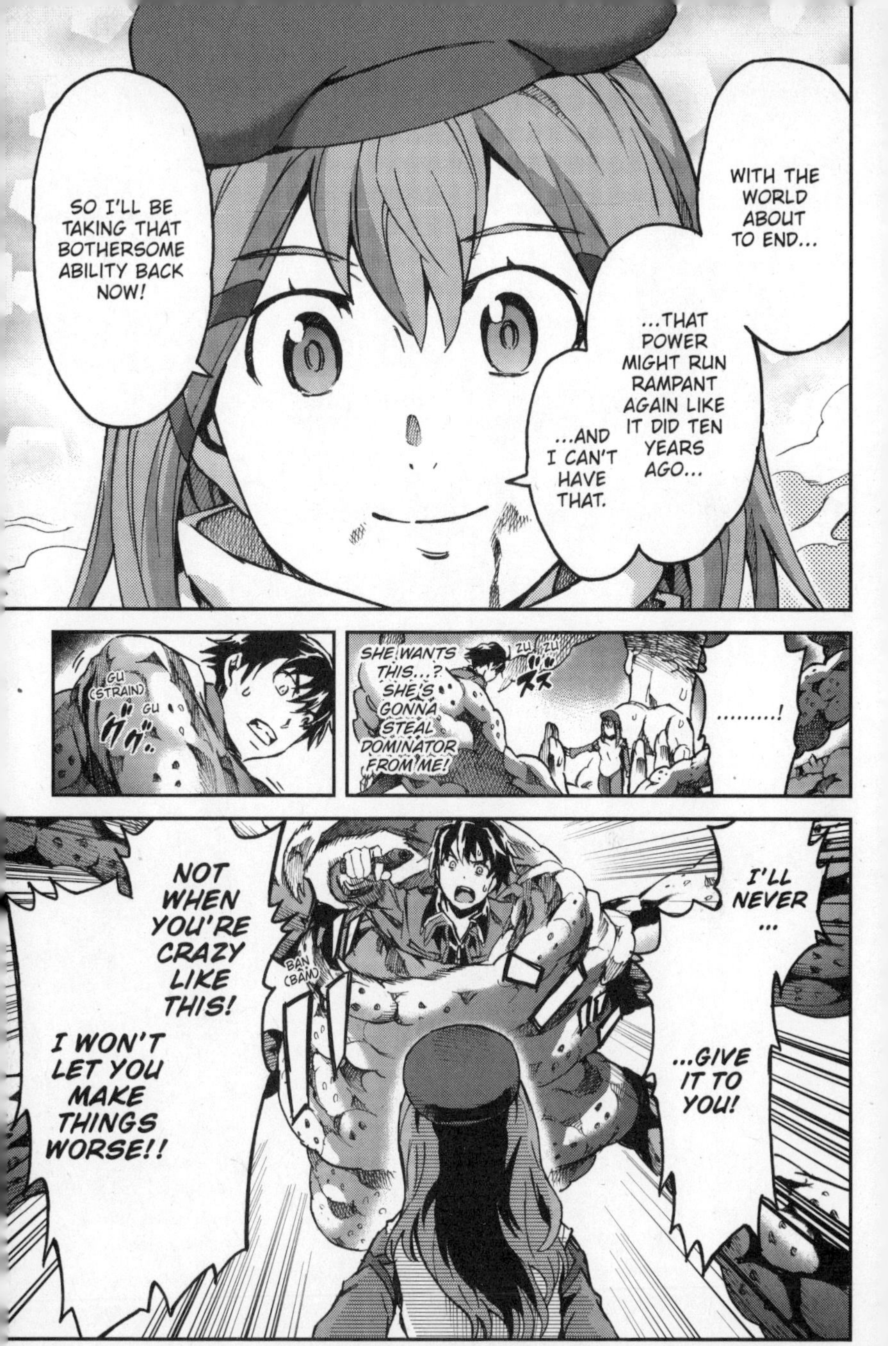
WITH THE WORLD ABOUT TO END...
...THAT POWER MIGHT RUN RAMPANT AGAIN LIKE IT DID TEN YEARS AGO...
...AND I CAN'T HAVE THAT.
SO I'LL BE TAKING THAT BOTHERSOME ABILITY BACK NOW!
.........!
ZU ZU
SHE WANTS THIS...? SHE'S GONNA STEAL DOMINATOR FROM ME!
GU (STRAIN) GU
I'LL NEVER...
...GIVE IT TO YOU!
BAN (BAM)
NOT WHEN YOU'RE CRAZY LIKE THIS!
I WON'T LET YOU MAKE THINGS WORSE!!

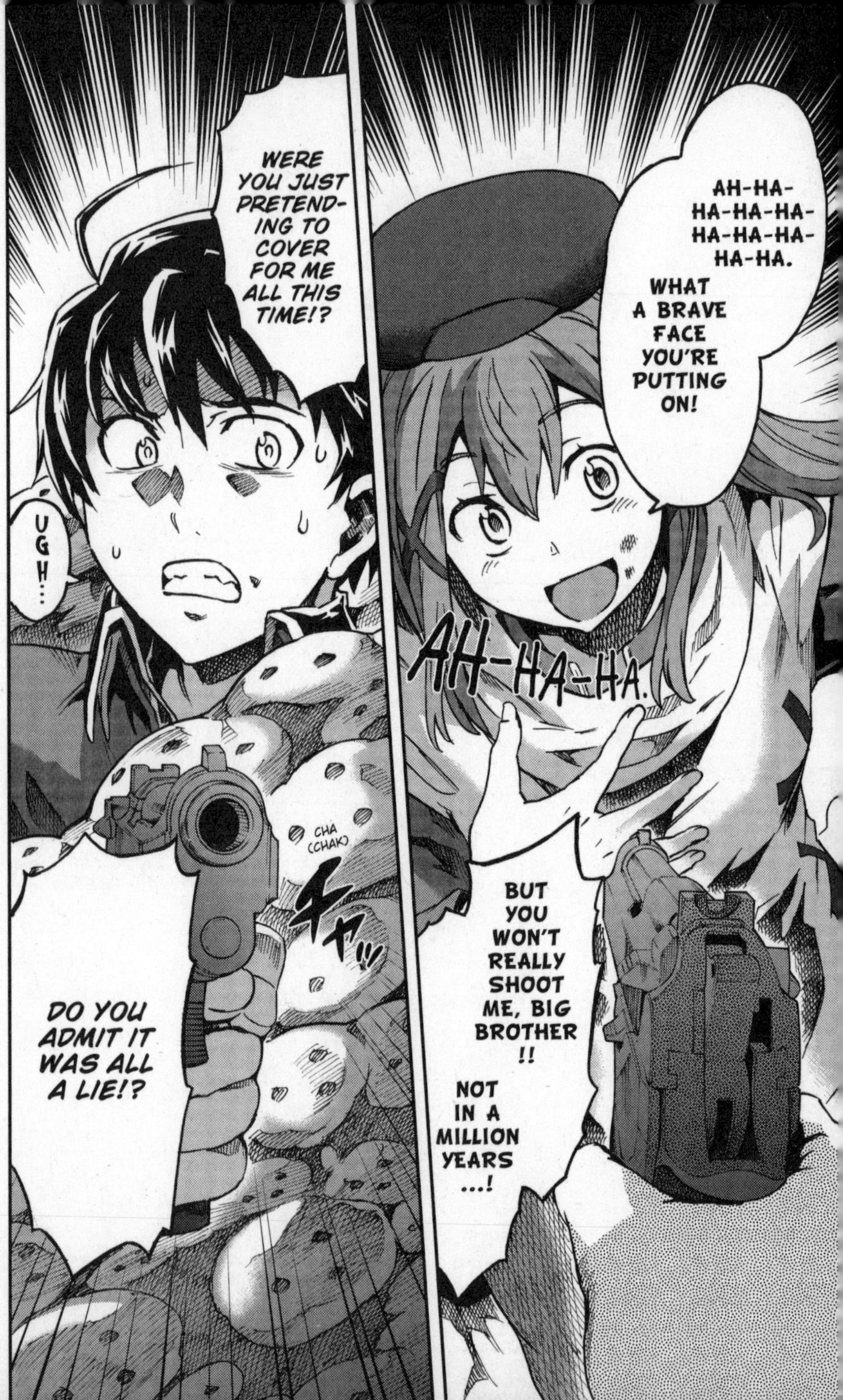
AH-HA-HA-HA-HA-HA-HA-HA-HA-HA.
WHAT A BRAVE FACE YOU'RE PUTTING ON!
AH-HA-HA.
BUT YOU WON'T REALLY SHOOT ME, BIG BROTHER!!
NOT IN A MILLION YEARS...!
WERE YOU JUST PRETENDING TO COVER FOR ME ALL THIS TIME!?
UGH...
CHA (CHAK)
DO YOU ADMIT IT WAS ALL A LIE!?

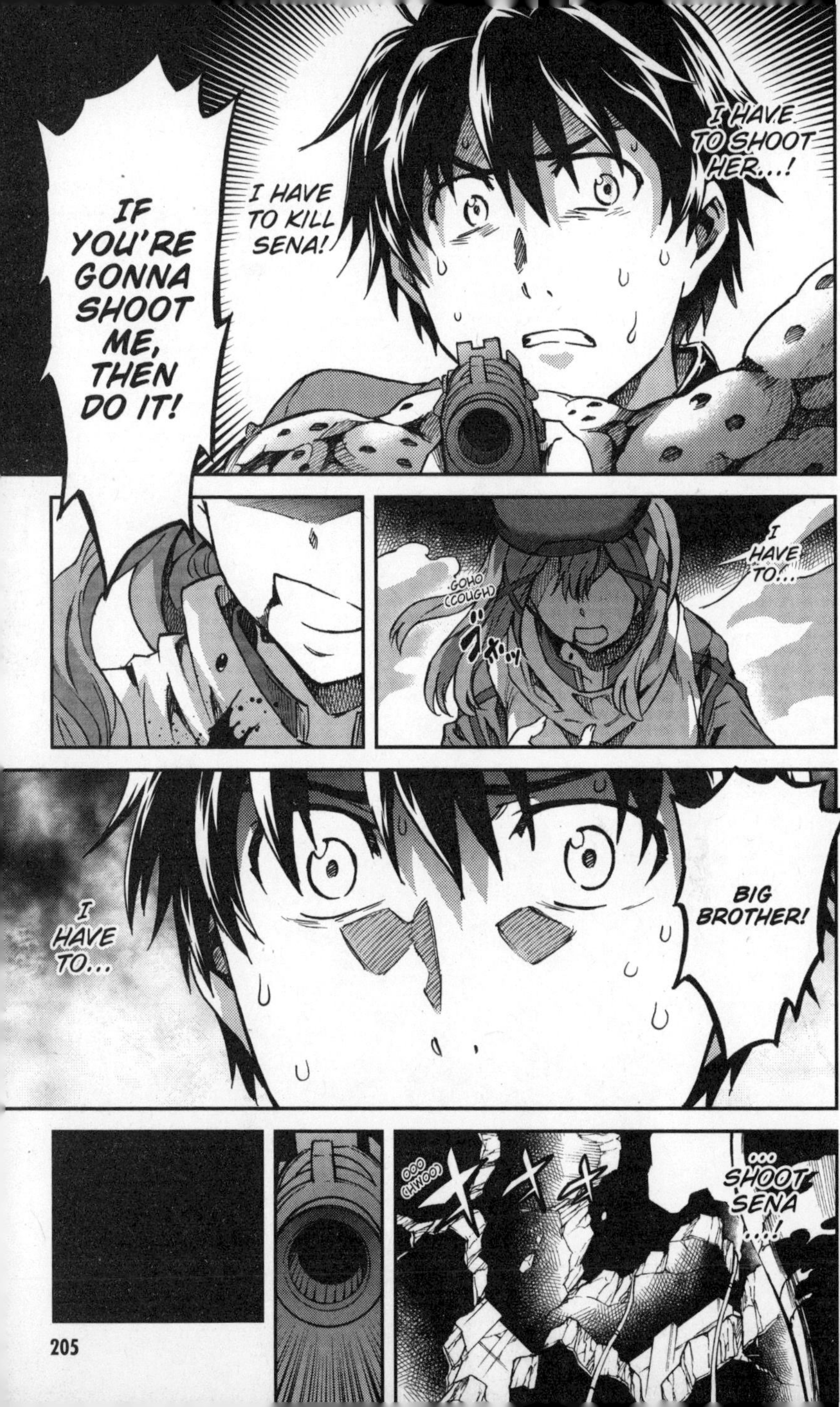
I HAVE TO SHOOT HER...!
I HAVE TO KILL SENA!
IF YOU'RE GONNA SHOOT ME, THEN DO IT!
I HAVE TO...
GOHO (COUGH)
BIG BROTHER!
I HAVE TO...
...SHOOT SENA...!
OOO (HWOO)

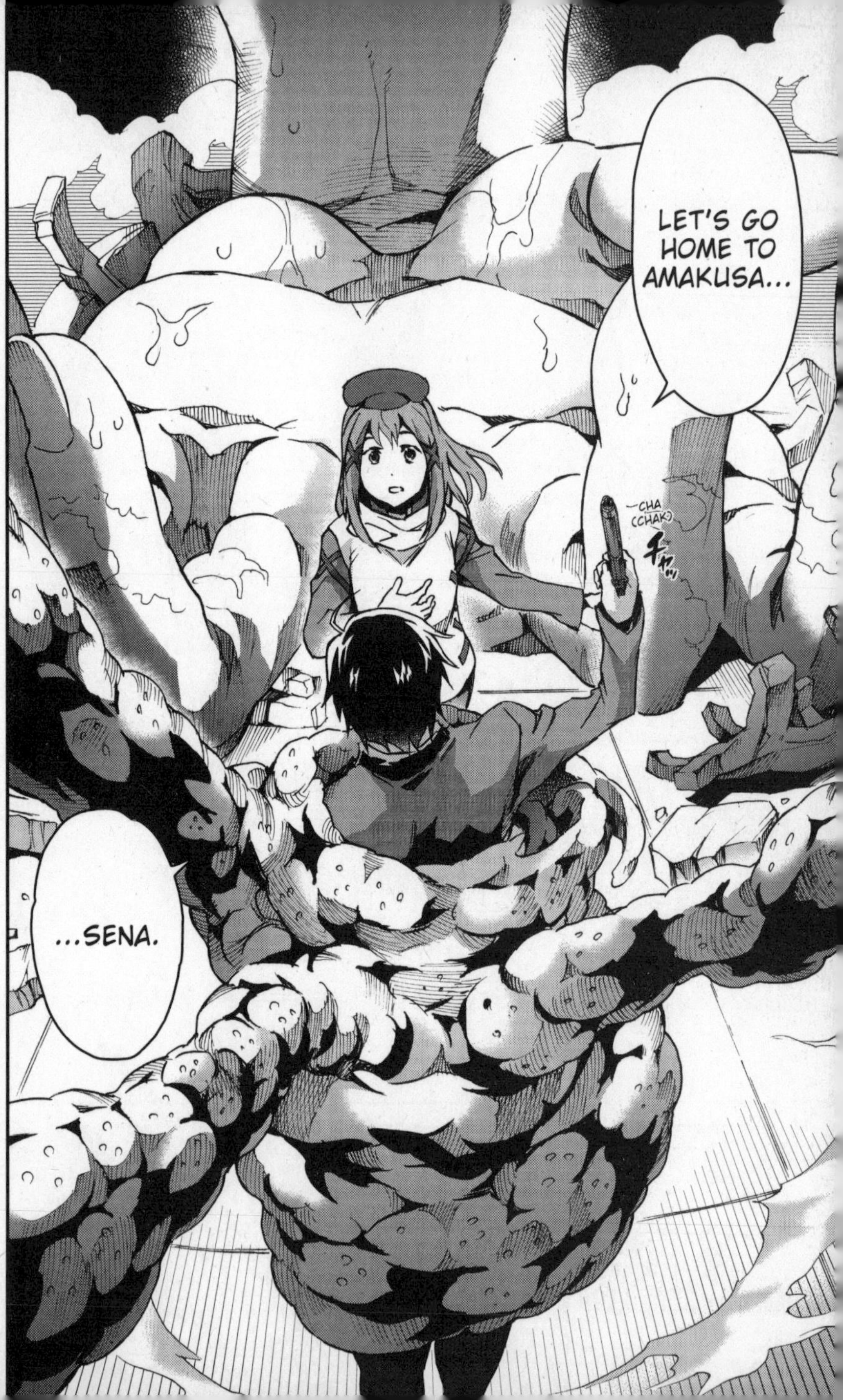
LET'S GO HOME TO AMAKUSA...
CHA (CHAK)
チャッ
...SENA.

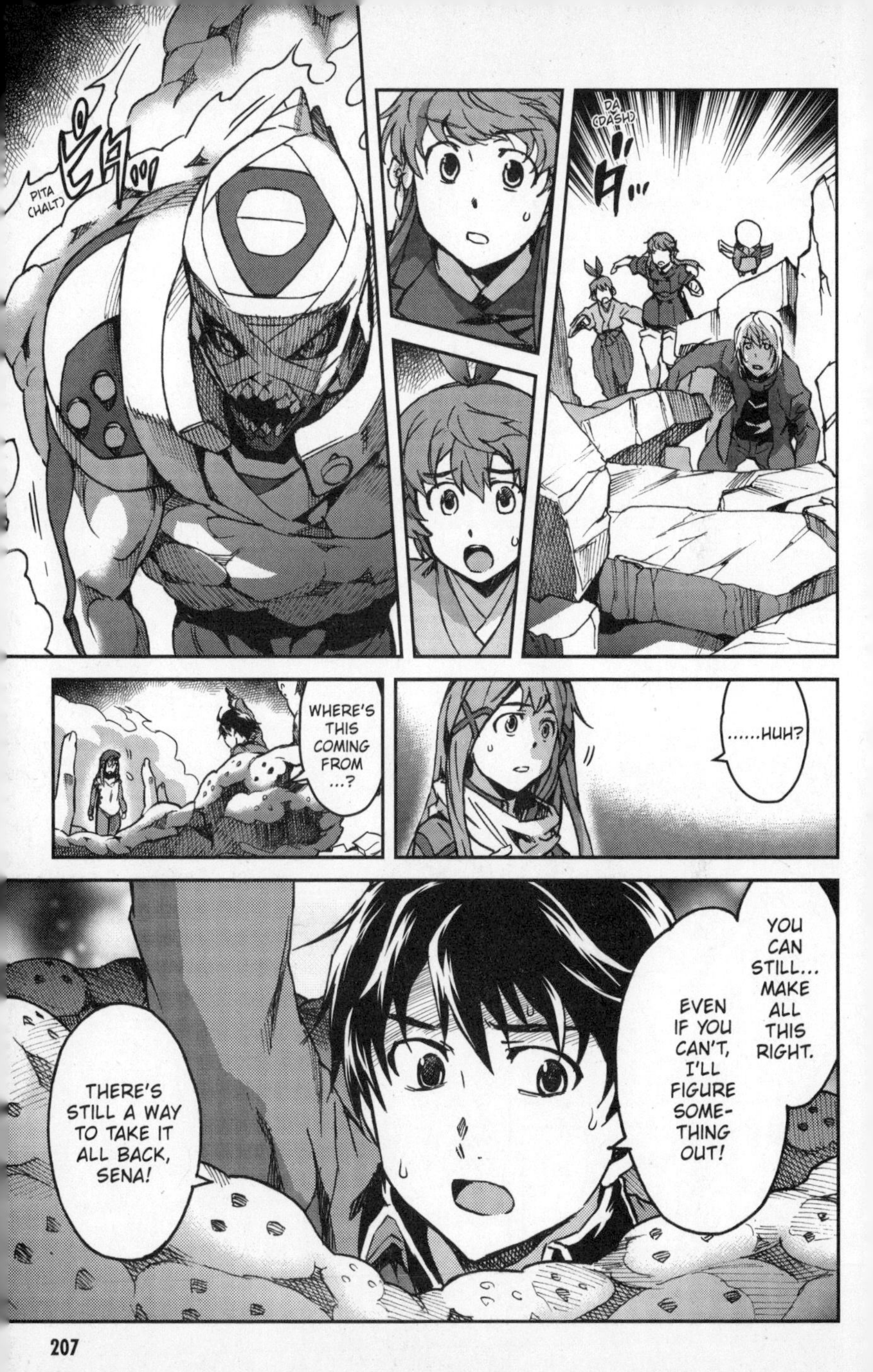
DA (DASH)
PITA (HALT)
......HUH?
WHERE'S THIS COMING FROM ...?
YOU CAN STILL... MAKE ALL THIS RIGHT.
EVEN IF YOU CAN'T, I'LL FIGURE SOME-THING OUT!
THERE'S STILL A WAY TO TAKE IT ALL BACK, SENA!

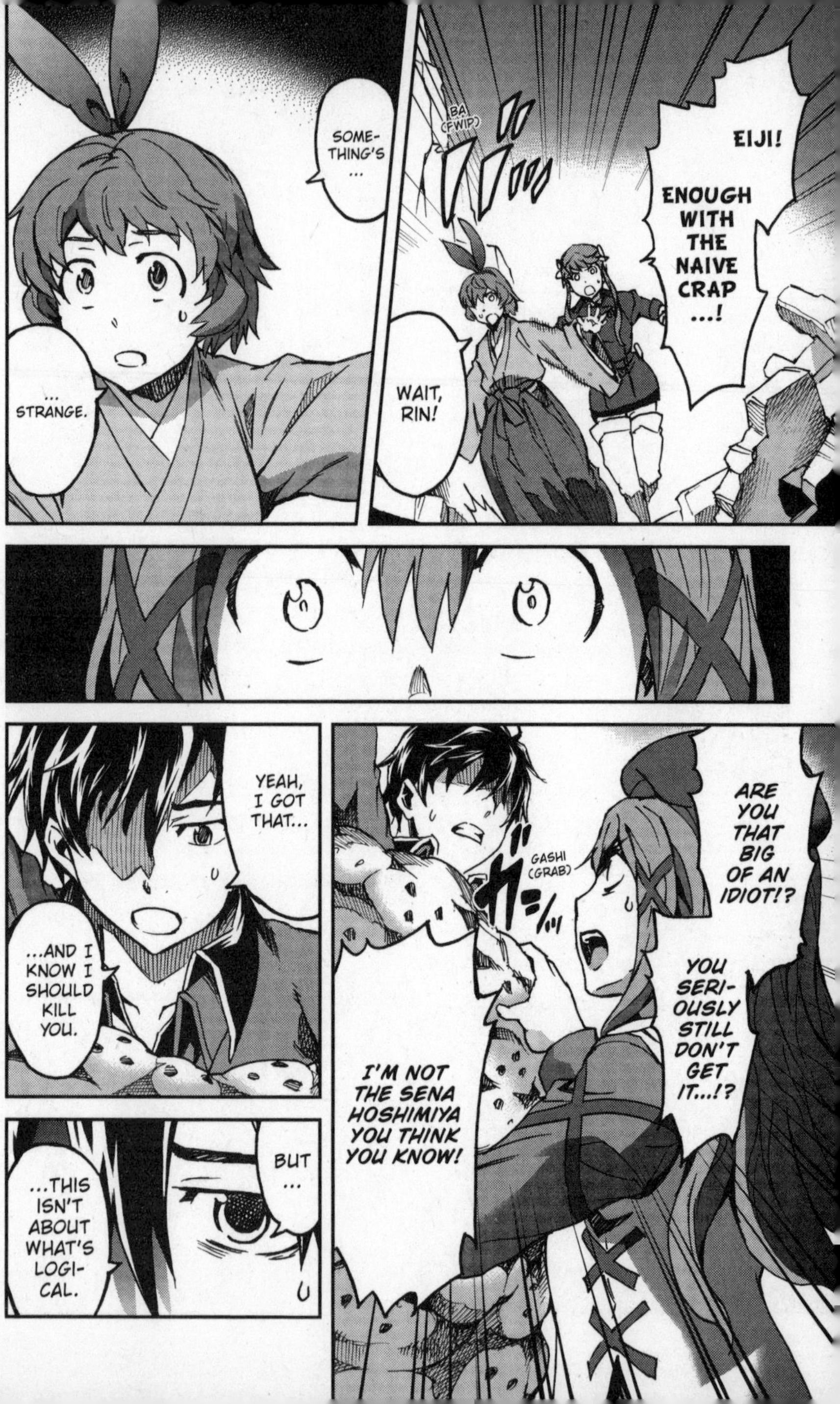
EIJI!
ENOUGH WITH THE NAIVE CRAP ...!
BA (FWIP)
WAIT, RIN!
SOME-THING'S ...
... STRANGE.
ARE YOU THAT BIG OF AN IDIOT!?
GASHI (GRAB)
YOU SERI-OUSLY STILL DON'T GET IT...!?
I'M NOT THE SENA HOSHIMIYA YOU THINK YOU KNOW!
YEAH, I GOT THAT...
...AND I KNOW I SHOULD KILL YOU.
BUT ...
...THIS ISN'T ABOUT WHAT'S LOGI-CAL.

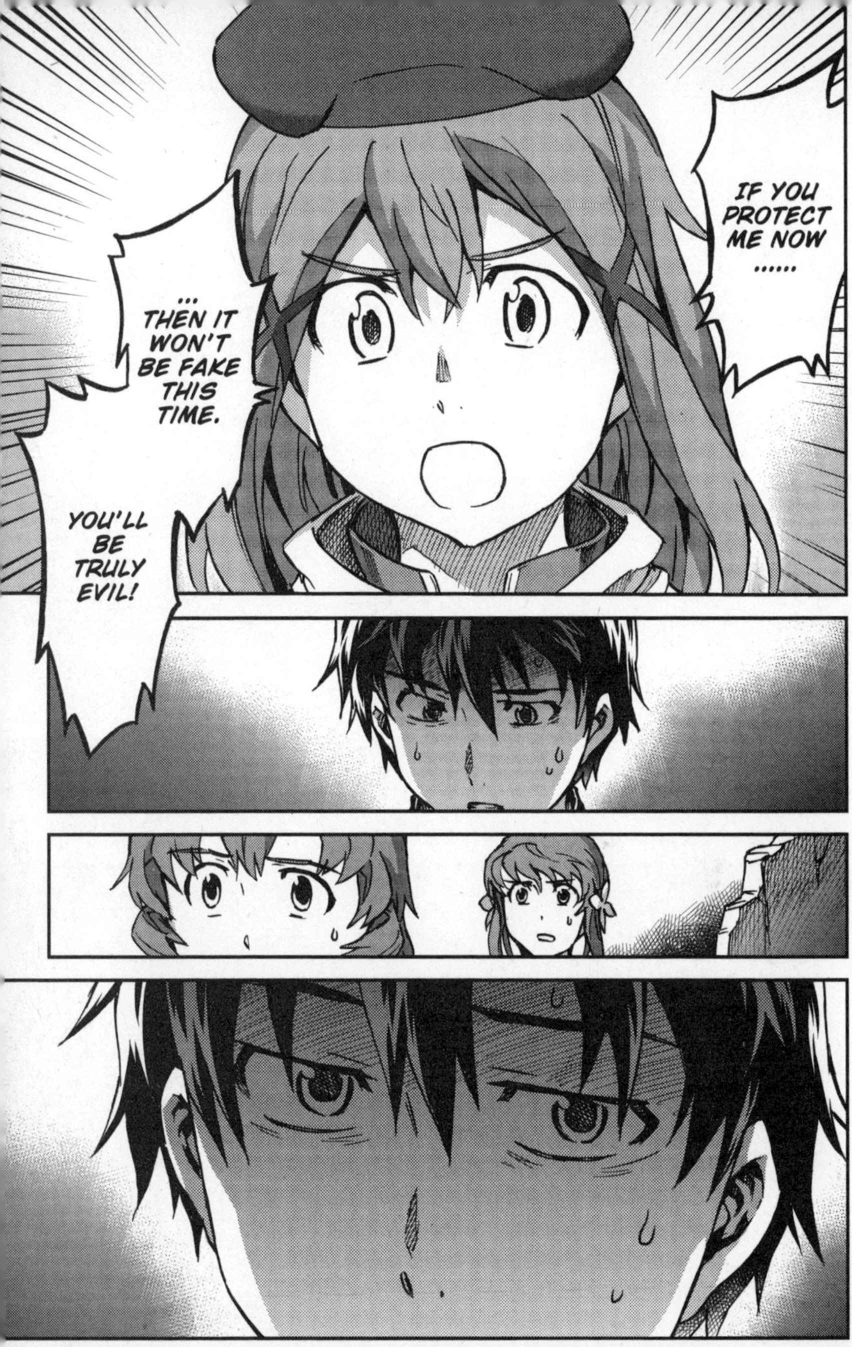
IF YOU PROTECT ME NOW ......
... THEN IT WON'T BE FAKE THIS TIME.
YOU'LL BE TRULY EVIL!

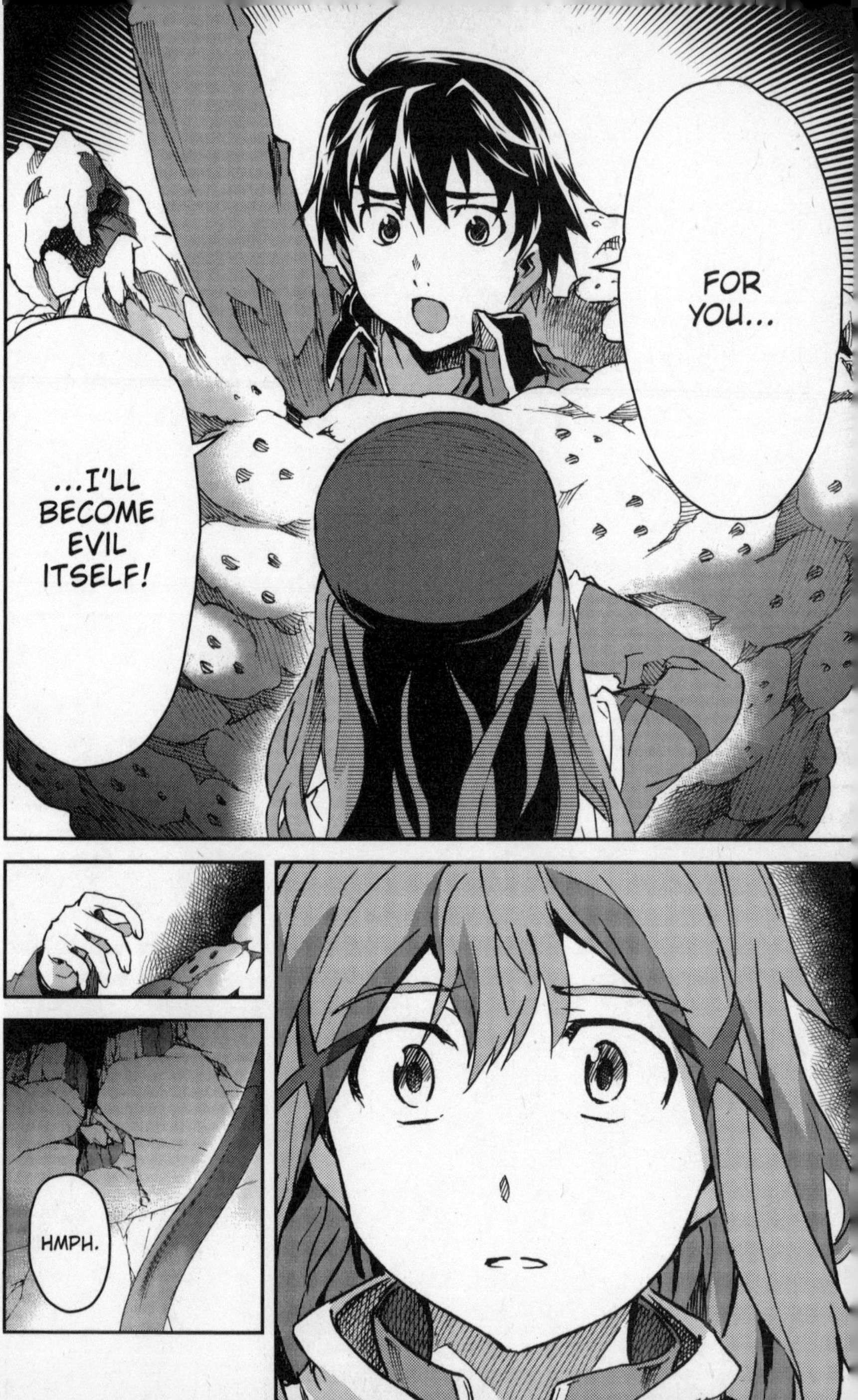
FOR YOU...
...I'LL BECOME EVIL ITSELF!
HMPH.

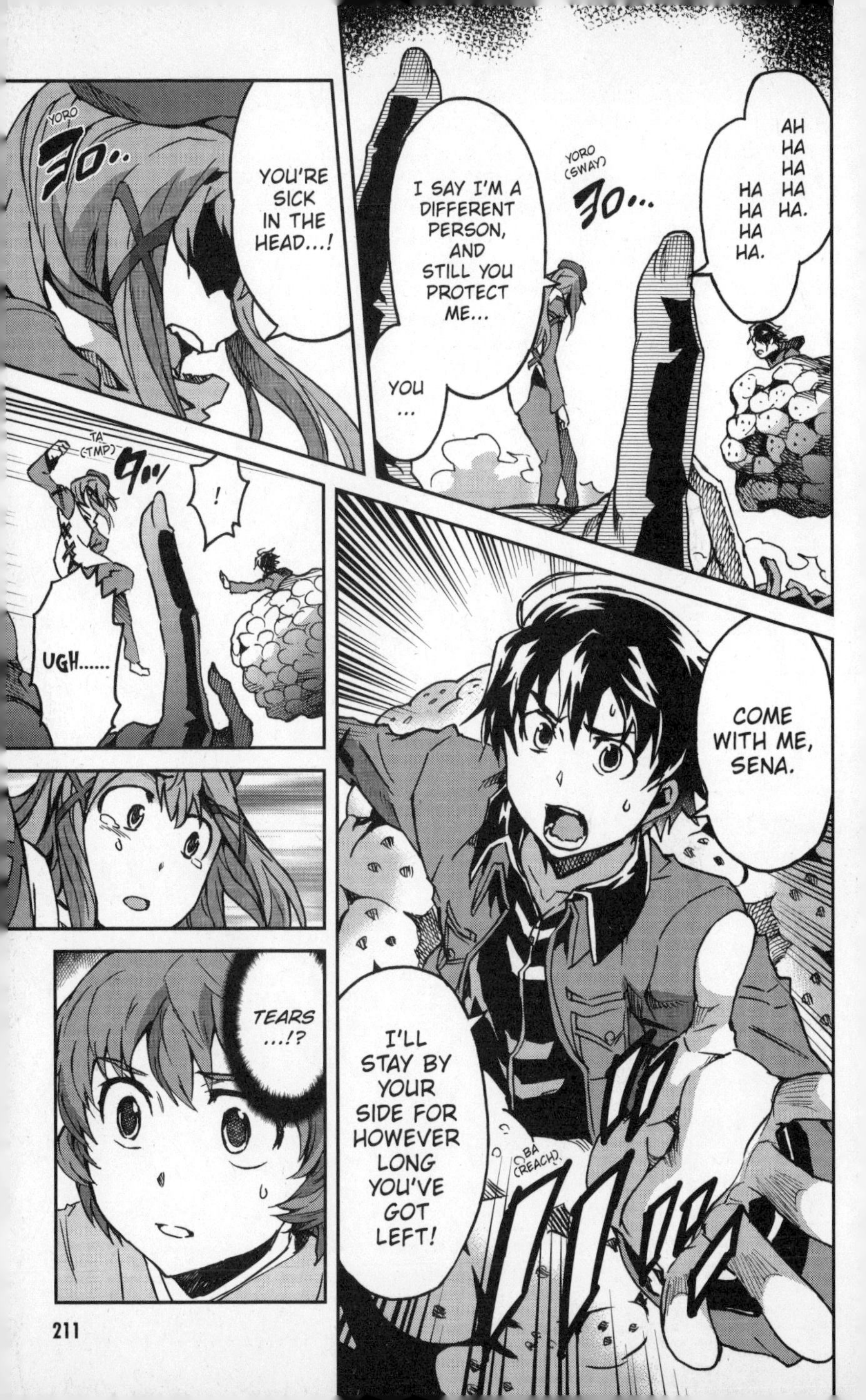
AH HA HA HA HA HA. HA HA HA HA.
YORO (SWAY)
I SAY I'M A DIFFERENT PERSON, AND STILL YOU PROTECT ME...
YOU...
YORO
YOU'RE SICK IN THE HEAD...!
COME WITH ME, SENA.
I'LL STAY BY YOUR SIDE FOR HOWEVER LONG YOU'VE GOT LEFT!
BA (REACH)
TA (TMP)
!
UGH......
TEARS ...!?

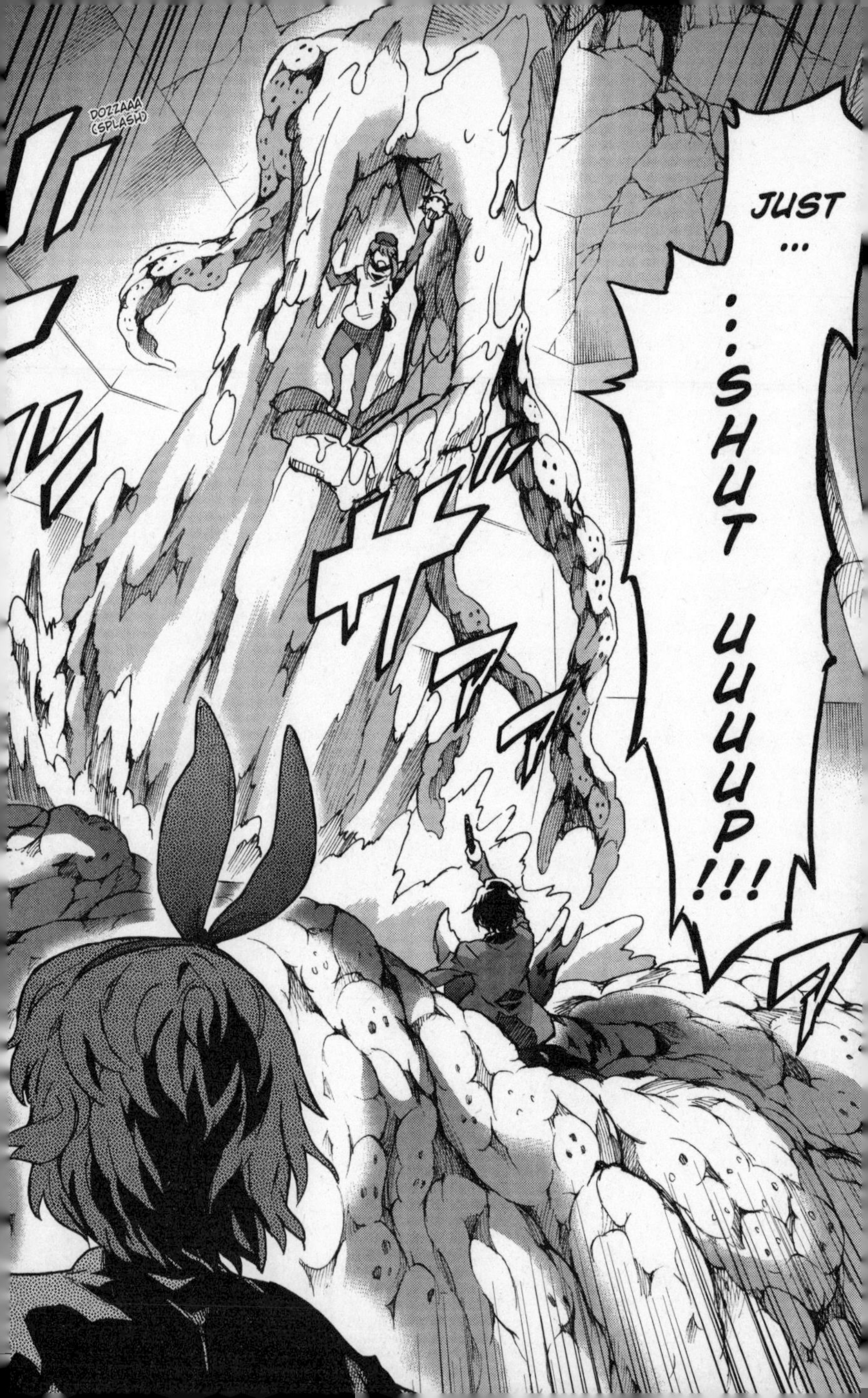
JUST ... ...SHUT UUUUUP!!!
DOZZAAA (SPLASH)

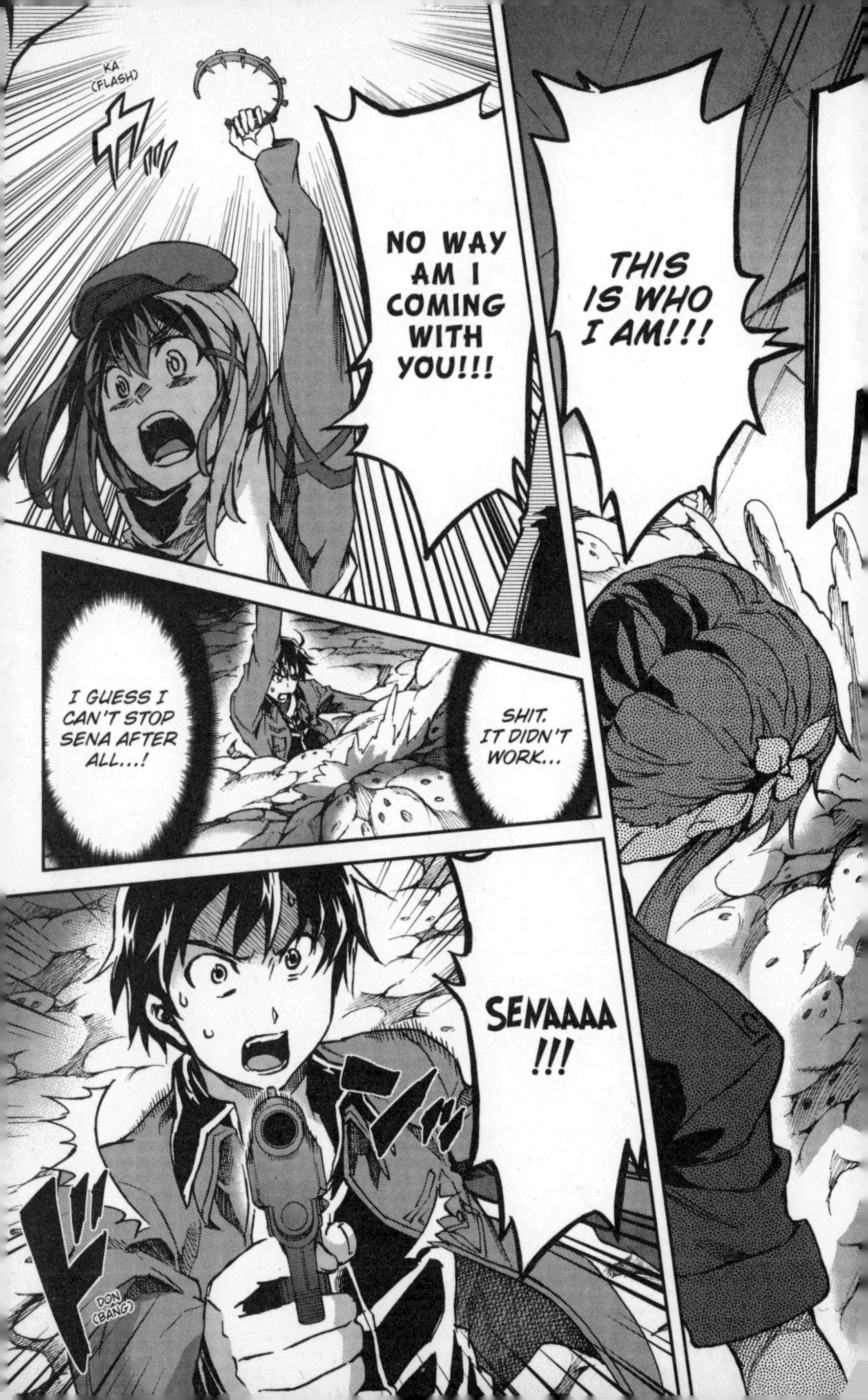
THIS IS WHO I AM!!!
KA (FLASH)
NO WAY AM I COMING WITH YOU!!!
SHIT. IT DIDN'T WORK...
I GUESS I CAN'T STOP SENA AFTER ALL...!
SENAAAA !!!
DON (BANG)

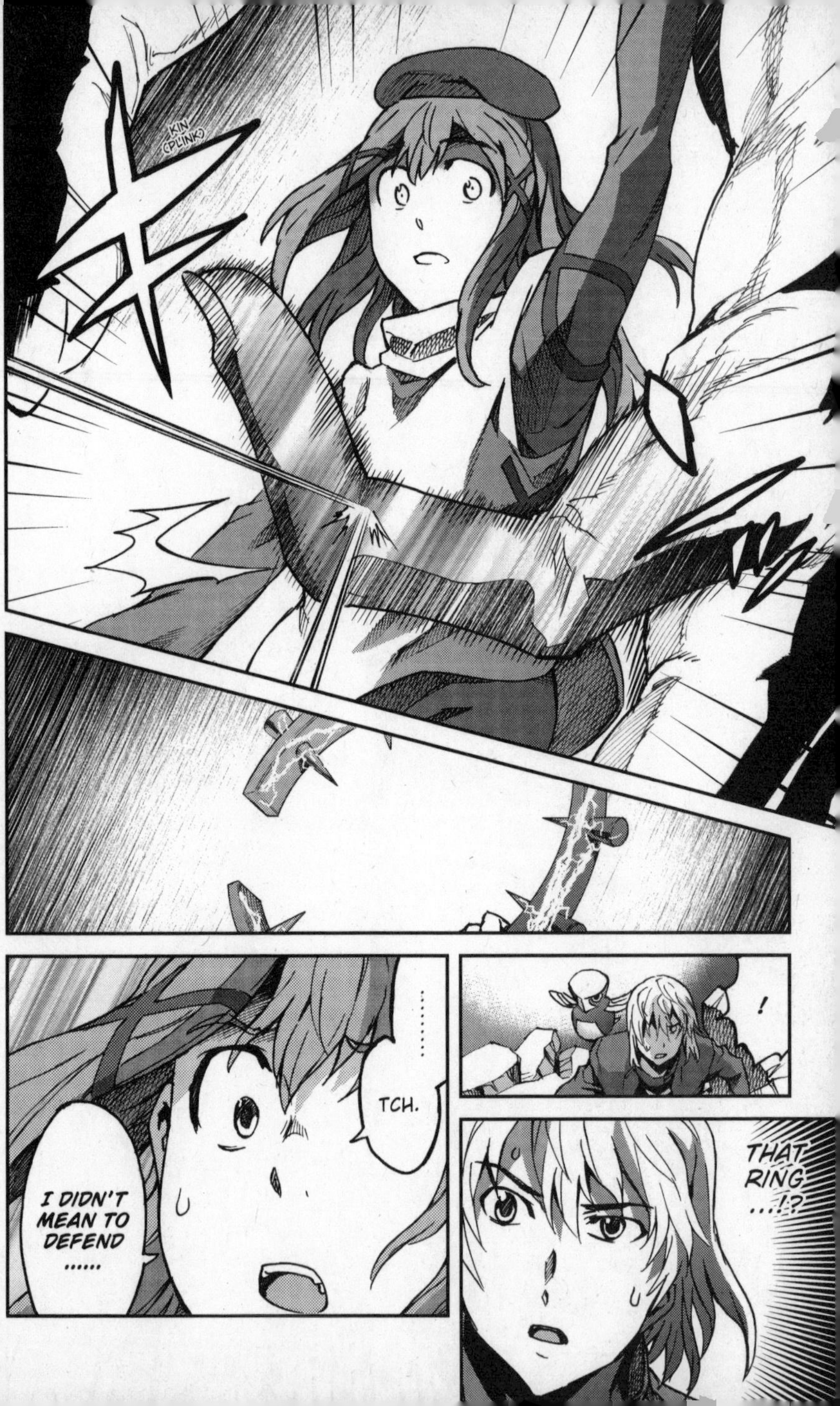
KIN
(PLINK)
!
THAT RING ....!?
......
TCH.
I DIDN'T MEAN TO DEFEND ......

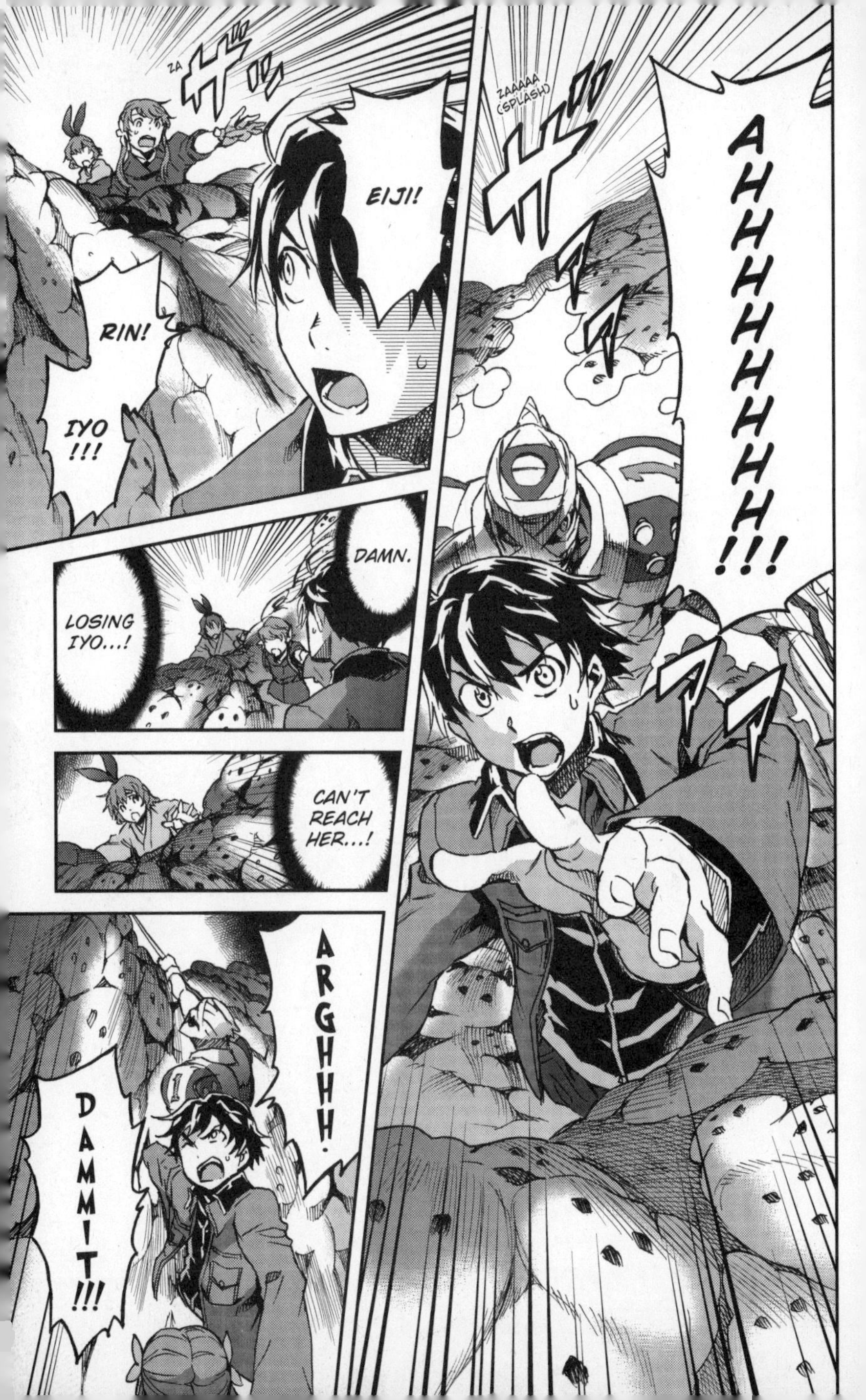

ZAAAAA (SPLASH)
AHHHHHHHHH!!!
ZA
EIJI!
RIN!
IYO!!!
DAMN.
LOSING IYO...!
CAN'T REACH HER...!
ARGHHH.
DAMMIT!!!

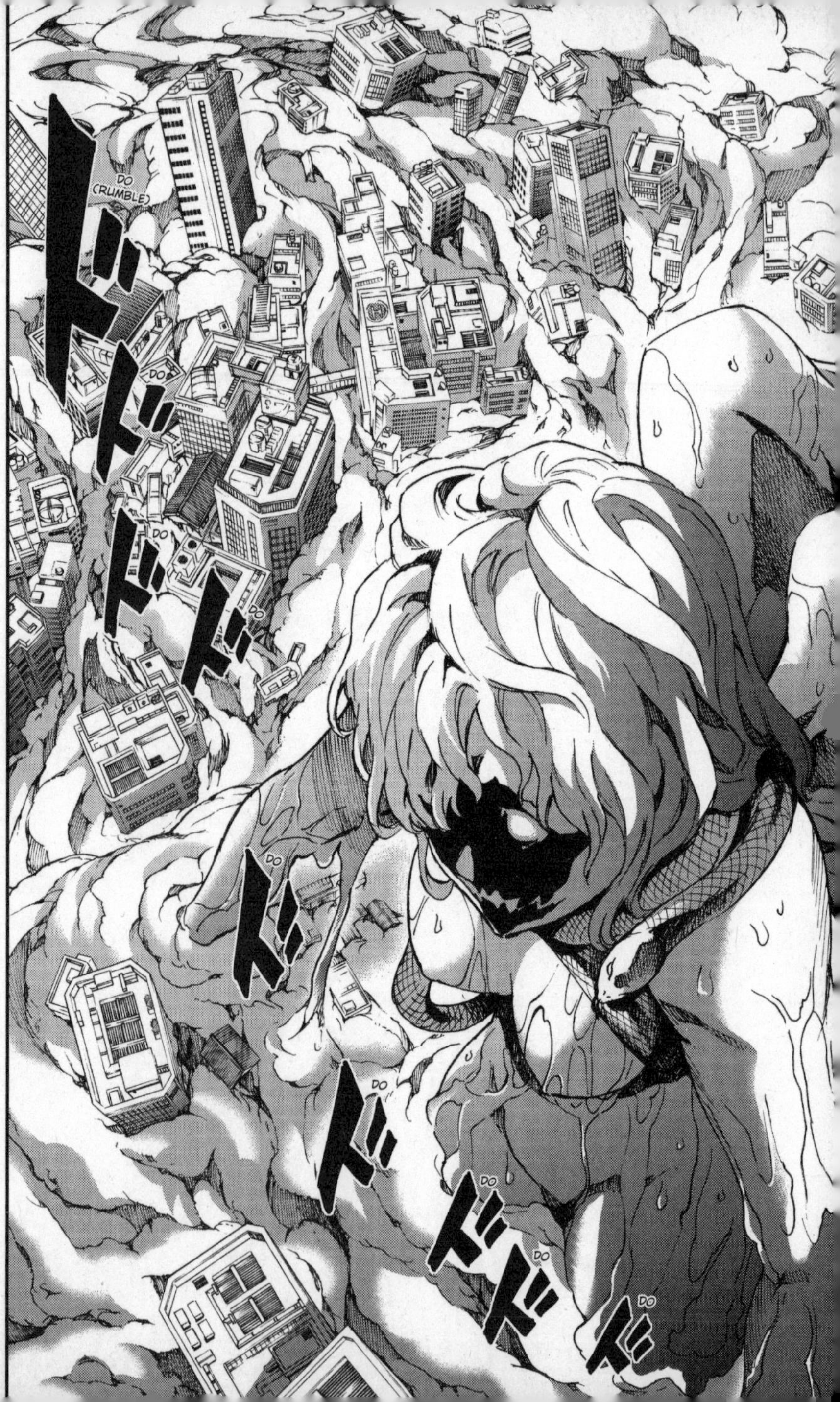

ド
DO
(CRUMBLE)
ドドドドド
DO
DO
DO
ドドドドド
DO
DO
DO
DO
DO

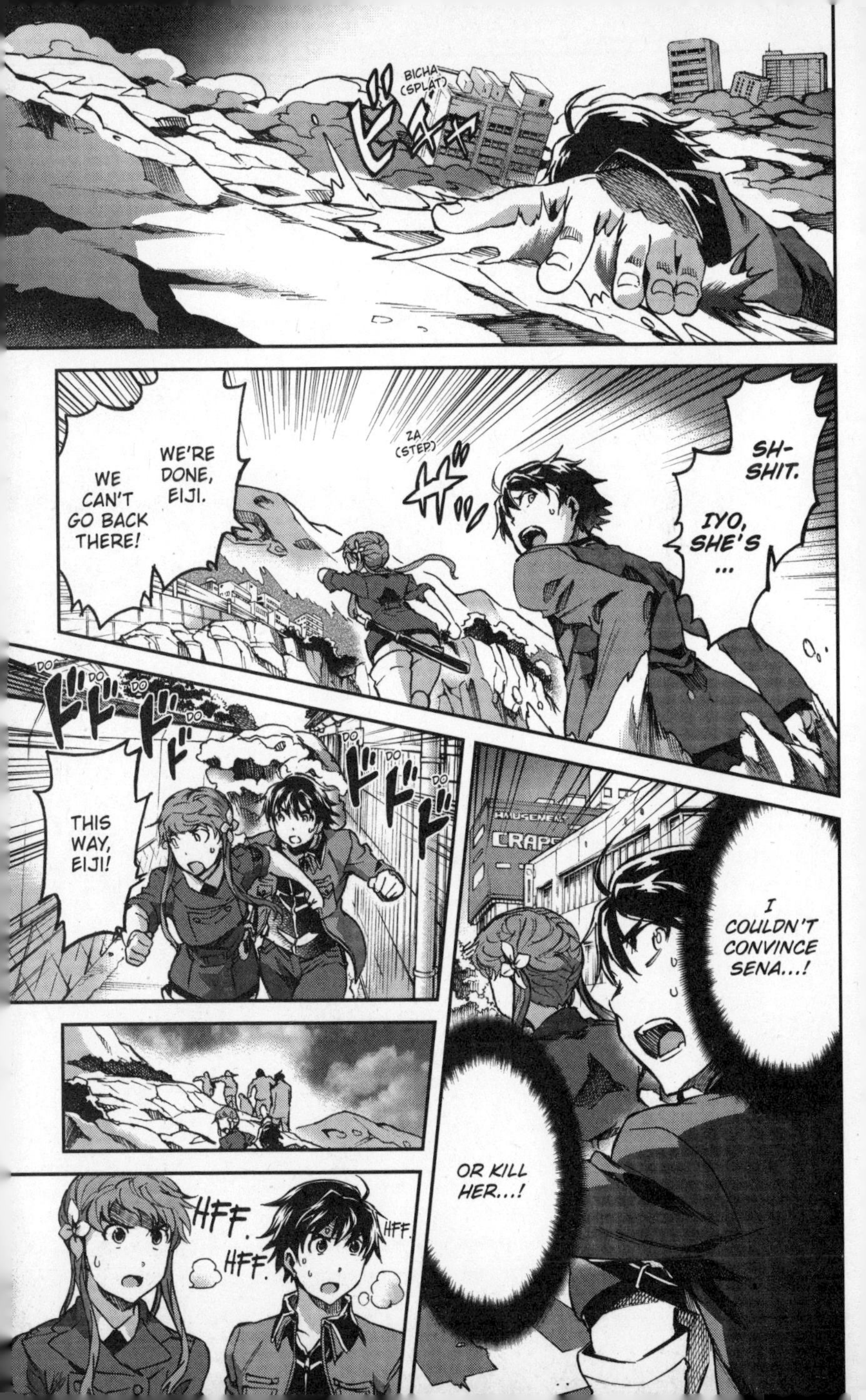
BICHA (SPLAT)
SH-SHIT.
IYO, SHE'S ...
ZA (STEP)
WE'RE DONE, EIJI.
WE CAN'T GO BACK THERE!
I COULDN'T CONVINCE SENA...!
OR KILL HER...!
DO DO DO DO
DO DO DO
THIS WAY, EIJI!
HFF.
HFF.
HFF.

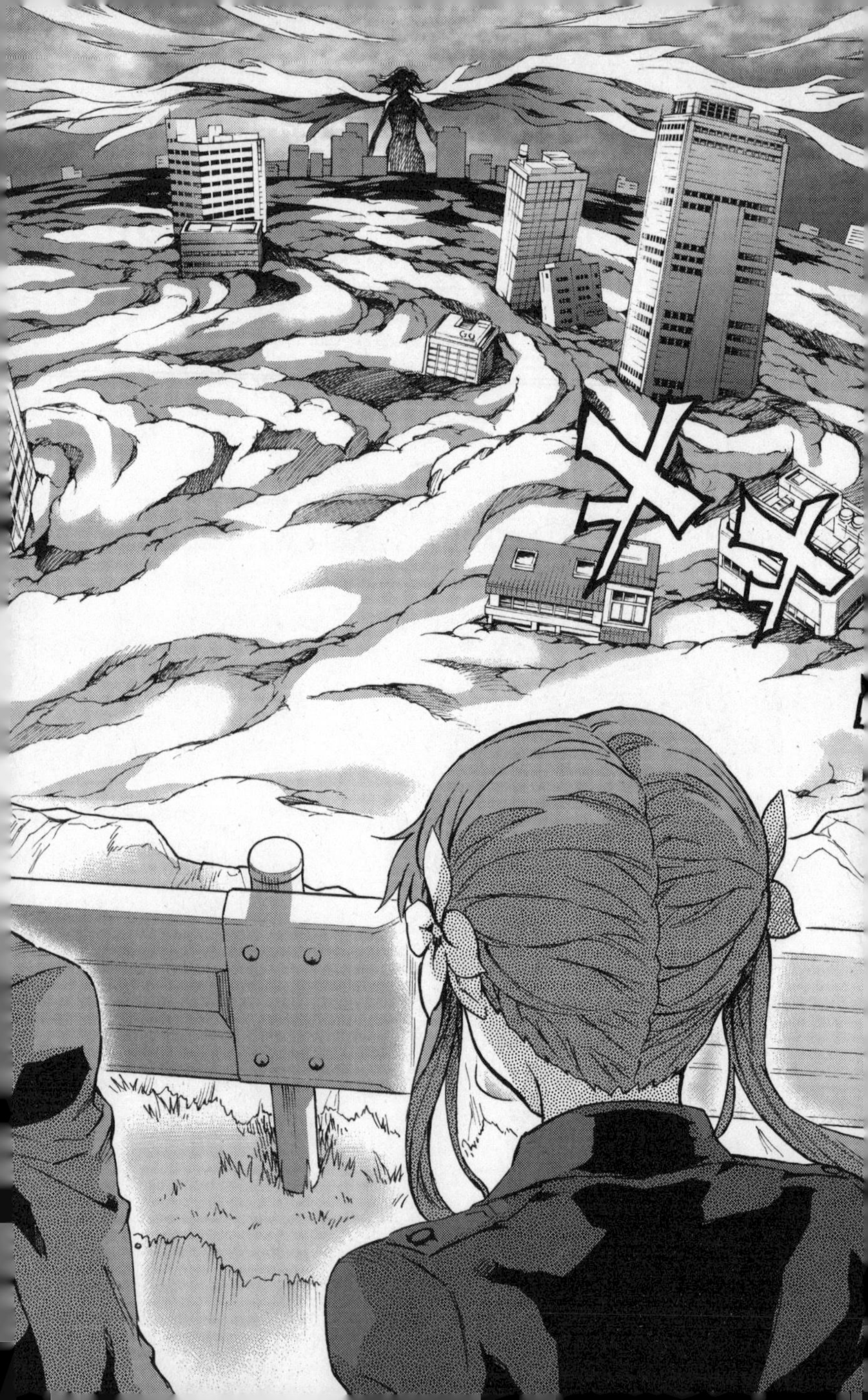

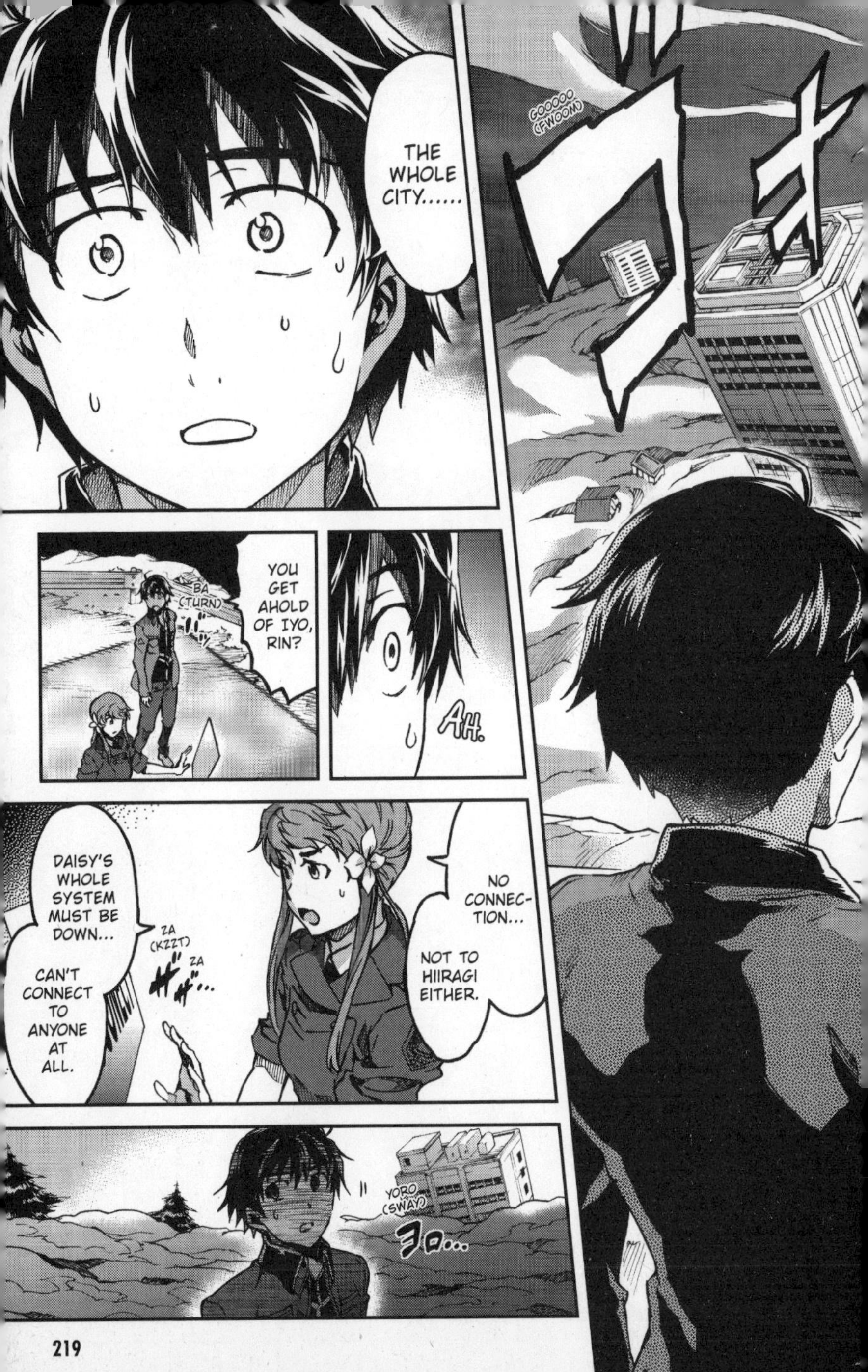
GOOOOO (FWOOM)
THE WHOLE CITY......
AH.
YOU GET AHOLD OF IYO, RIN?
BA (TURN)
NO CONNECTION...
NOT TO HIIRAGI EITHER.
ZA (KZZT) ZA
DAISY'S WHOLE SYSTEM MUST BE DOWN...
CAN'T CONNECT TO ANYONE AT ALL.
YORO (SWAY)

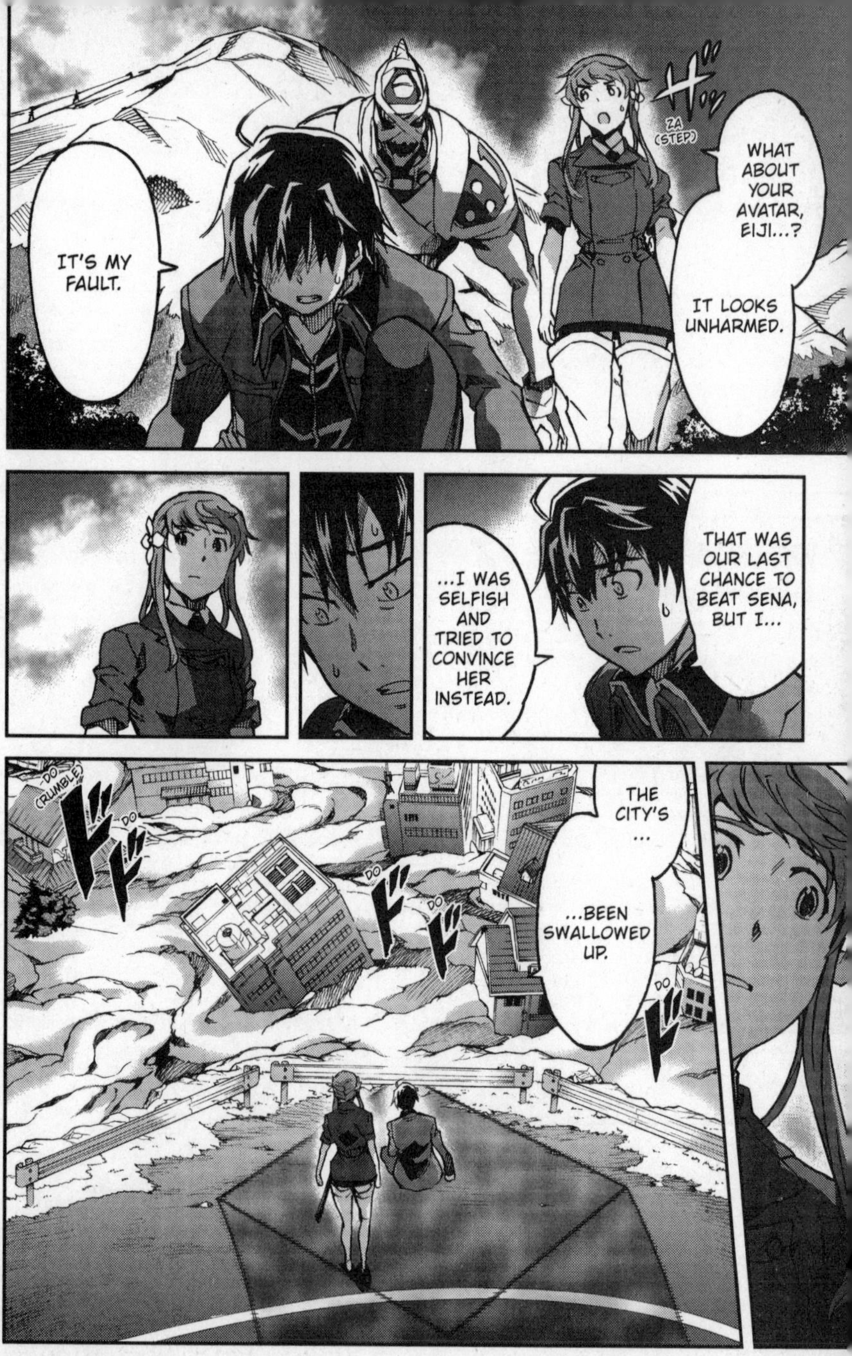
ZA (STEP)
WHAT ABOUT YOUR AVATAR, EIJI...?
IT LOOKS UNHARMED.
IT'S MY FAULT.
THAT WAS OUR LAST CHANCE TO BEAT SENA, BUT I...
...I WAS SELFISH AND TRIED TO CONVINCE HER INSTEAD.
THE CITY'S ...
...BEEN SWALLOWED UP.
DO
DO (RUMBLE)
DO
DO
DO

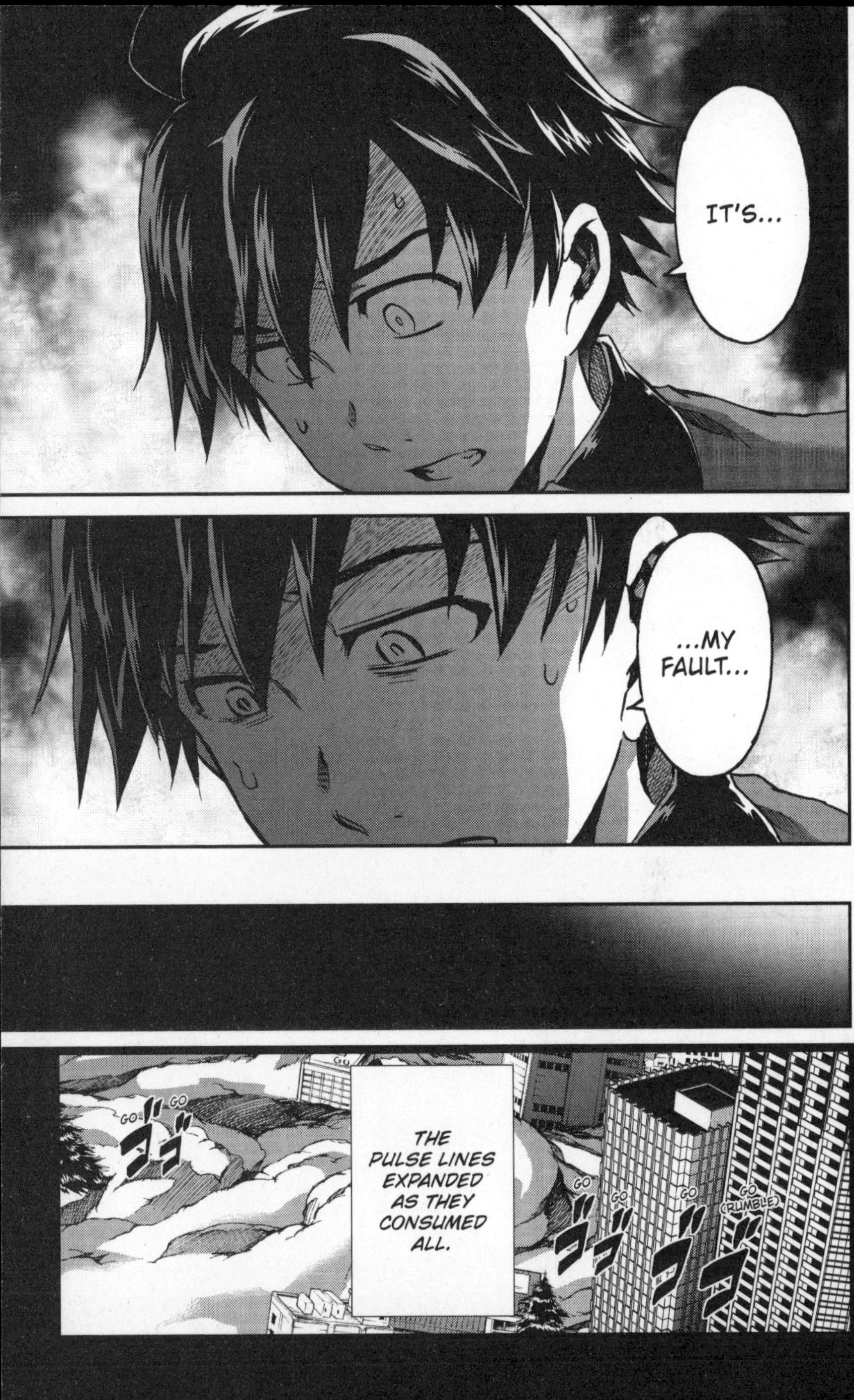
IT'S...
...MY FAULT...
GO GO GO GO (RUMBLE)
THE PULSE LINES EXPANDED AS THEY CONSUMED ALL.
GO GO

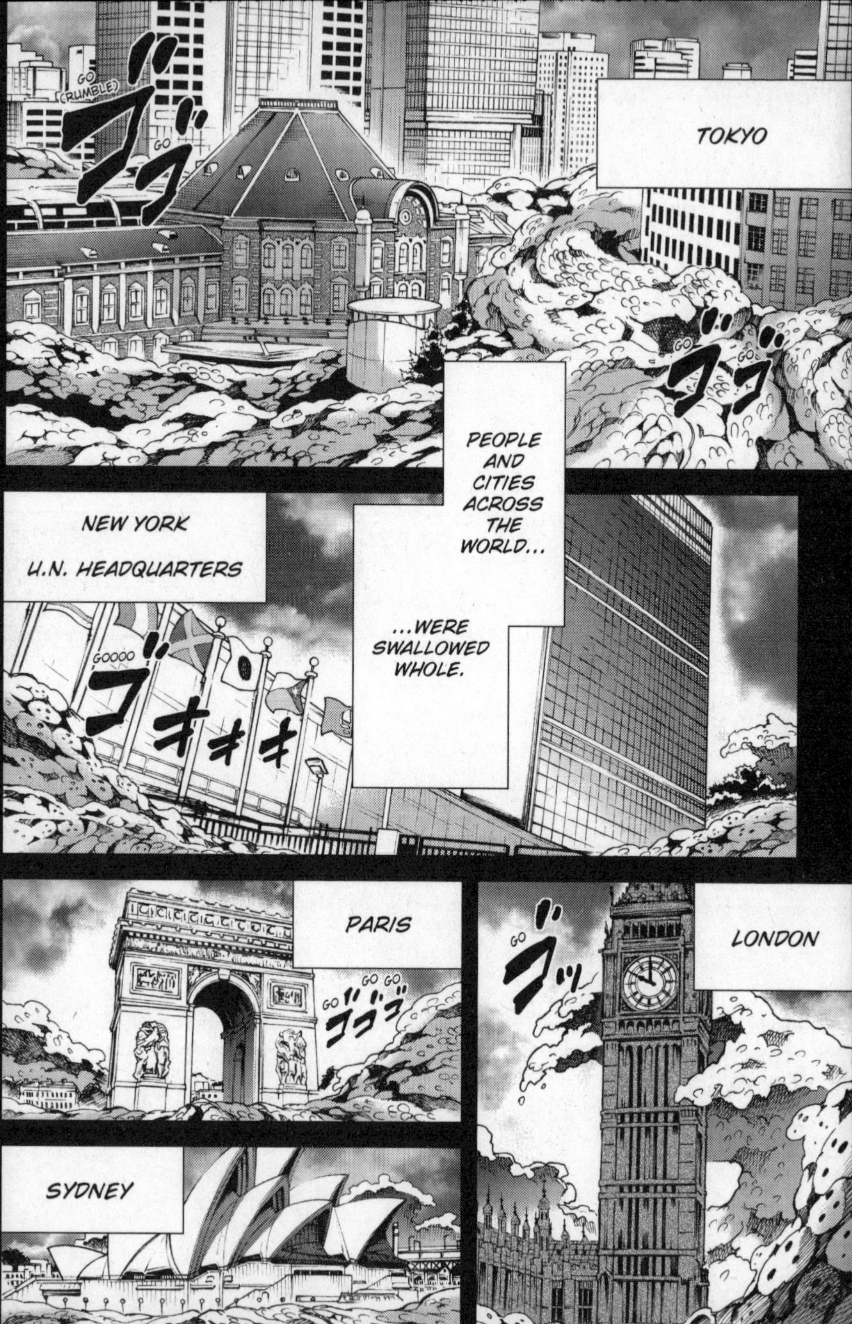
TOKYO
GO
(RUMBLE)
GO
GO
GO
PEOPLE AND CITIES ACROSS THE WORLD...
...WERE SWALLOWED WHOLE.
NEW YORK
U.N. HEADQUARTERS
GOOOO
LONDON
GO
PARIS
GO GO
GO
SYDNEY

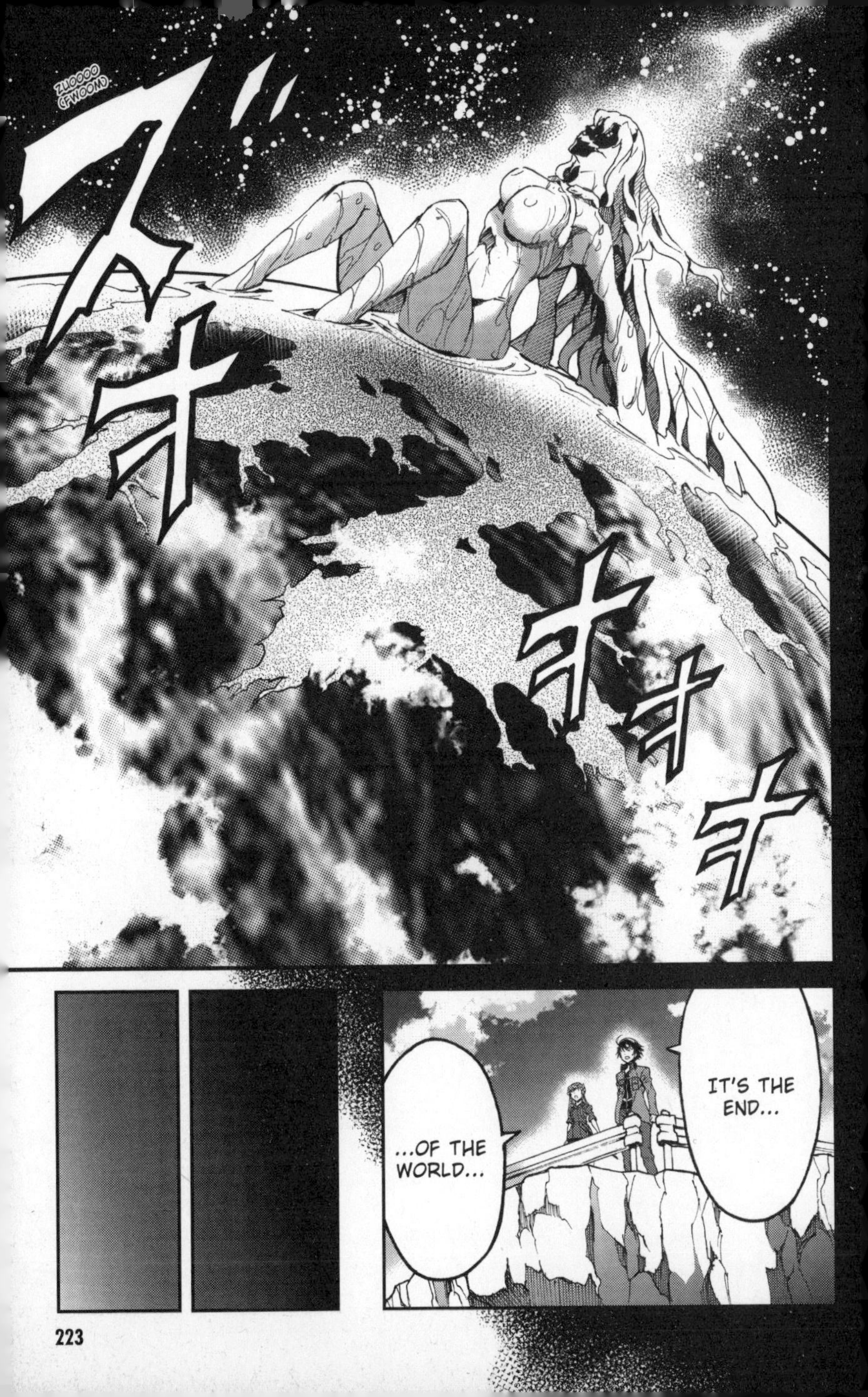
ZUOOOO (FWOOM)
IT'S THE END...
...OF THE WORLD...

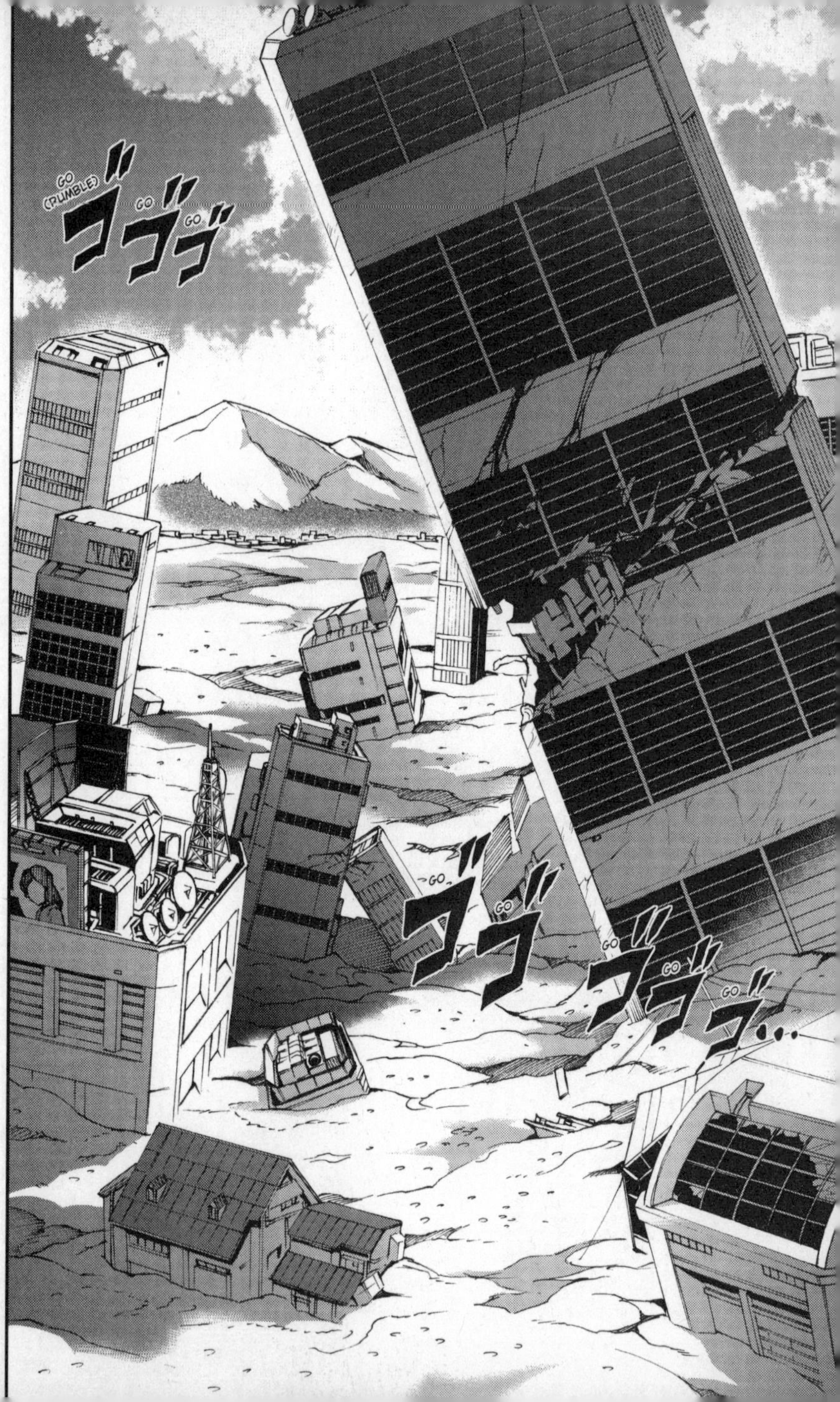
ゴゴゴ
GO (RUMBLE) GO GO
ゴゴゴゴゴ…
GO GO GO GO GO

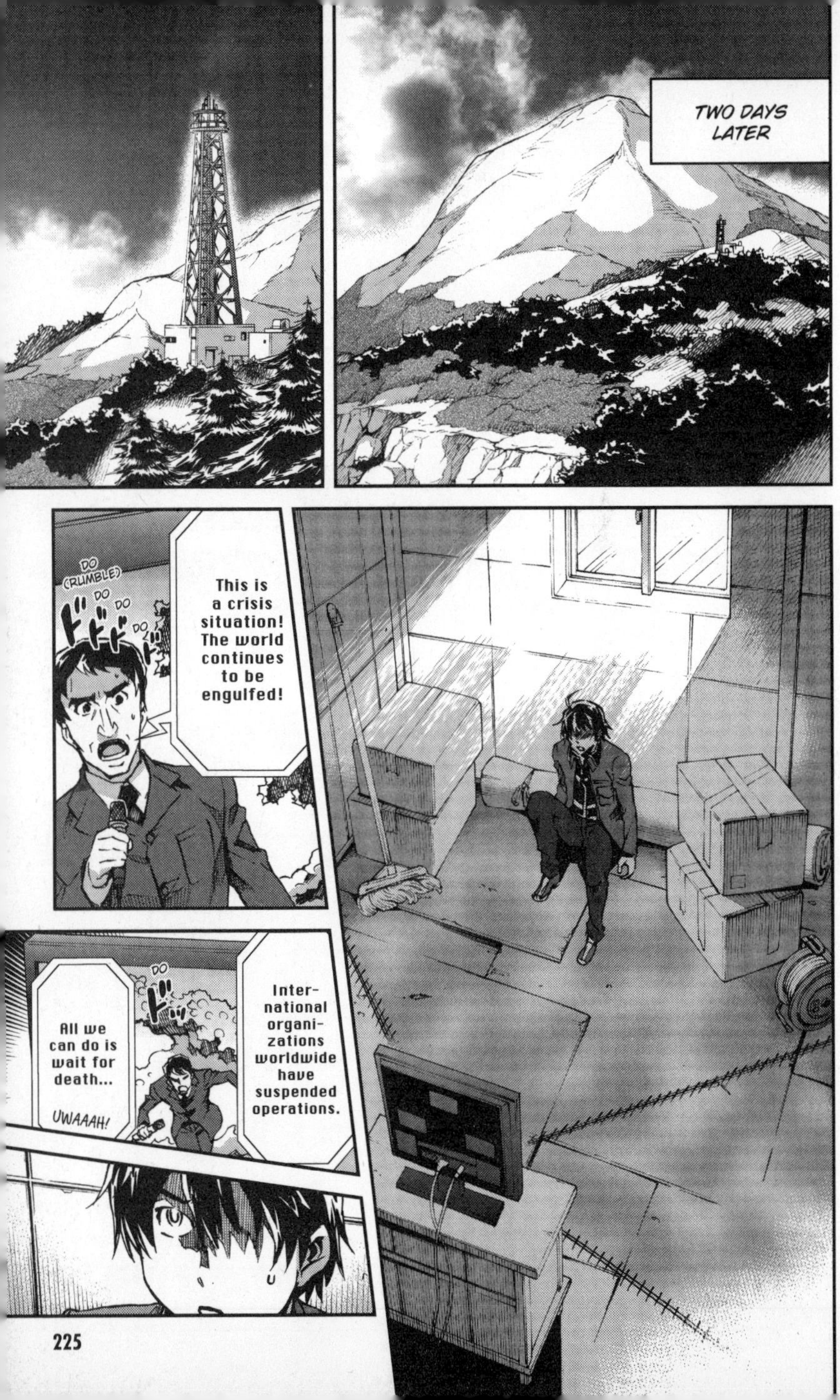
TWO DAYS LATER
DO (RUMBLE) DO DO DO
This is a crisis situation! The world continues to be engulfed!
DO
International organizations worldwide have suspended operations.
All we can do is wait for death...
UWAAAH!

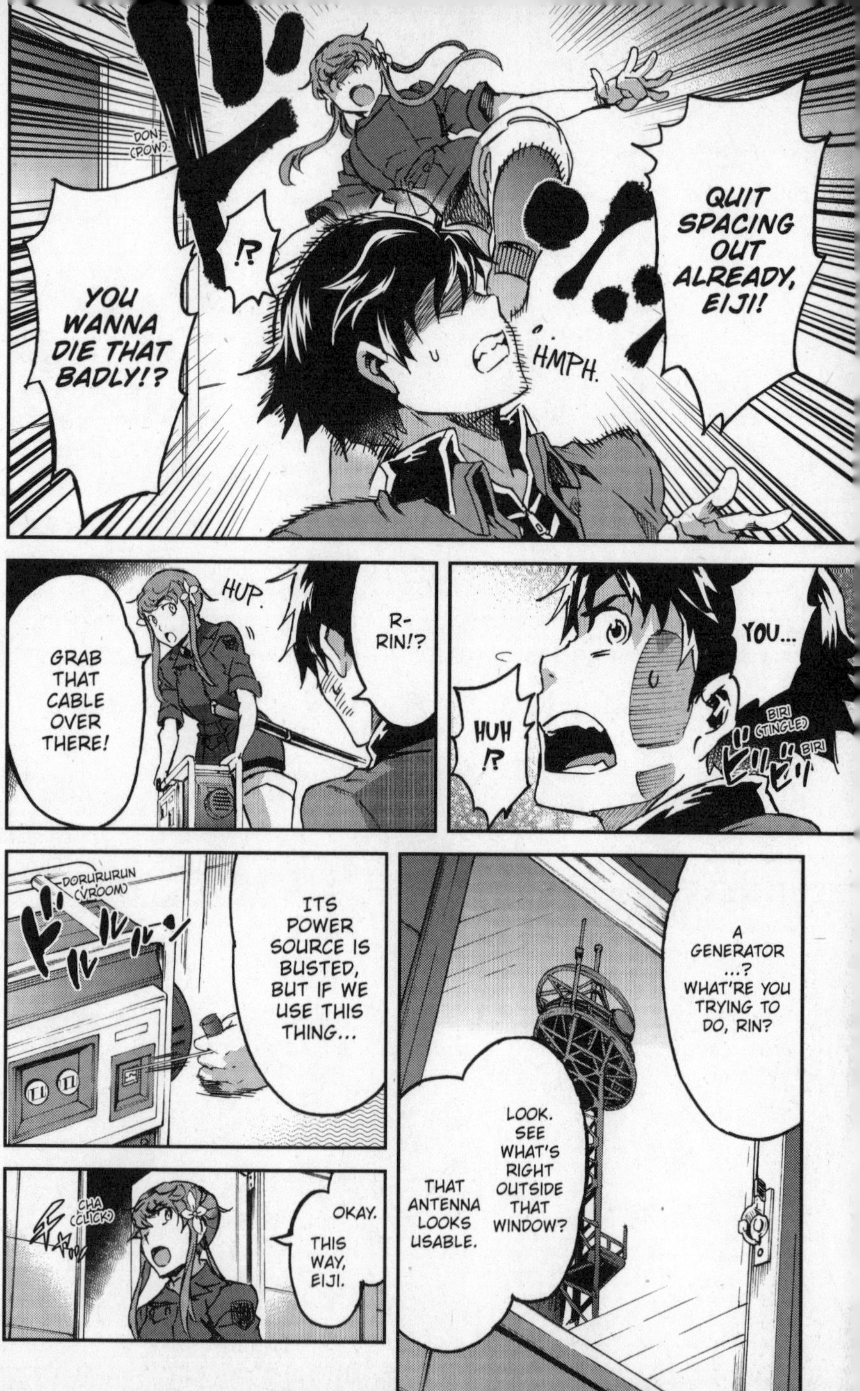
QUIT SPACING OUT ALREADY, EIJI!
DON (POW)
HMPH.
!?
YOU WANNA DIE THAT BADLY!?
YOU...
BIRI (TINGLE) BIRI
HUH !?
R-RIN!?
HUP.
GRAB THAT CABLE OVER THERE!
A GENERATOR ...? WHAT'RE YOU TRYING TO DO, RIN?
LOOK. SEE WHAT'S RIGHT OUTSIDE THAT WINDOW?
THAT ANTENNA LOOKS USABLE.
ITS POWER SOURCE IS BUSTED, BUT IF WE USE THIS THING...
DORURURUN (VROOM)
OKAY.
THIS WAY, EIJI.
CHA (CLICK)

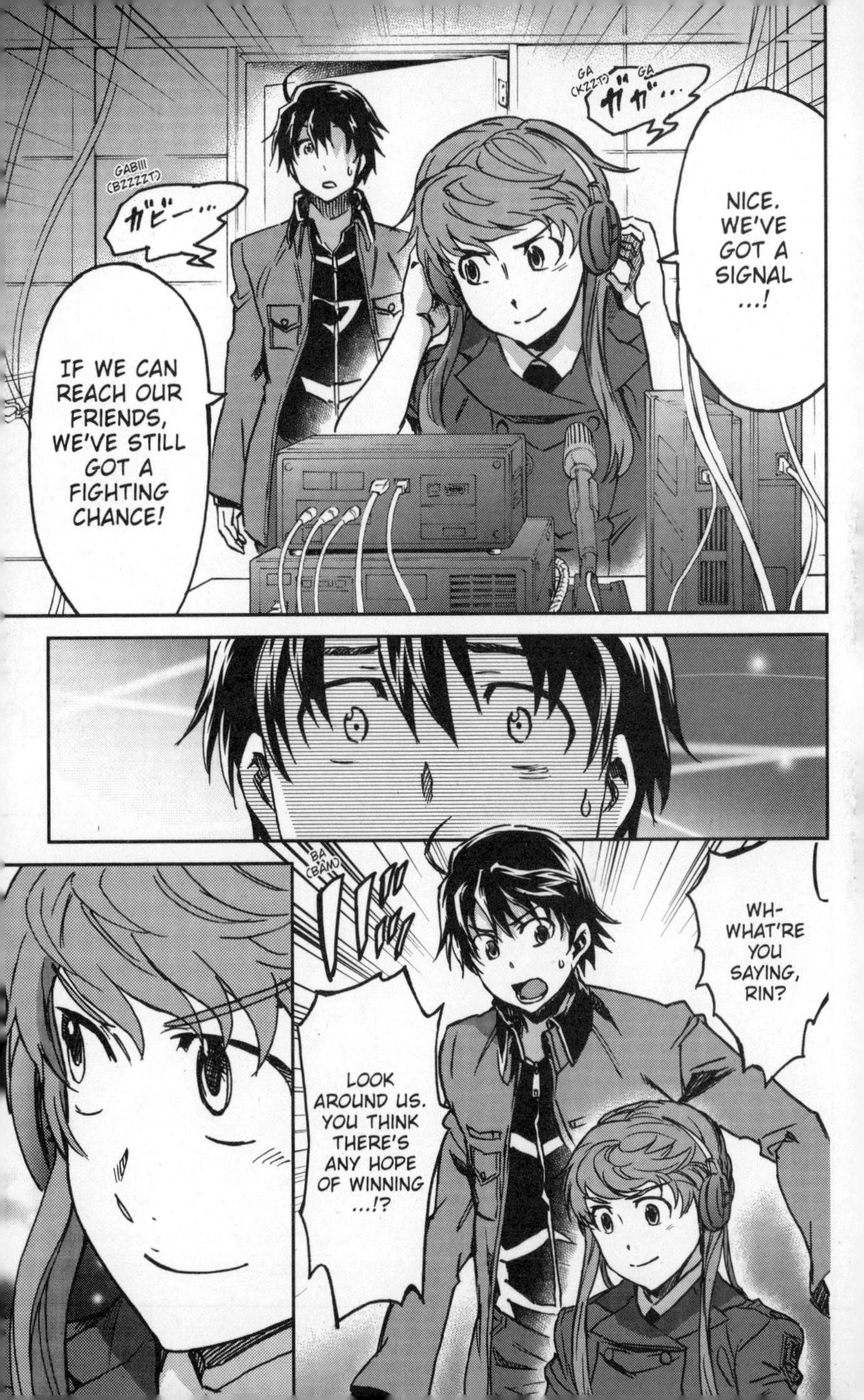
GA (KZZZT) GA
ガガ…
NICE. WE'VE GOT A SIGNAL ...!
GABIII (BZZZZT)
ガビー…
IF WE CAN REACH OUR FRIENDS, WE'VE STILL GOT A FIGHTING CHANCE!
BA (BAM)
WH- WHAT'RE YOU SAYING, RIN?
LOOK AROUND US. YOU THINK THERE'S ANY HOPE OF WINNING ...!?

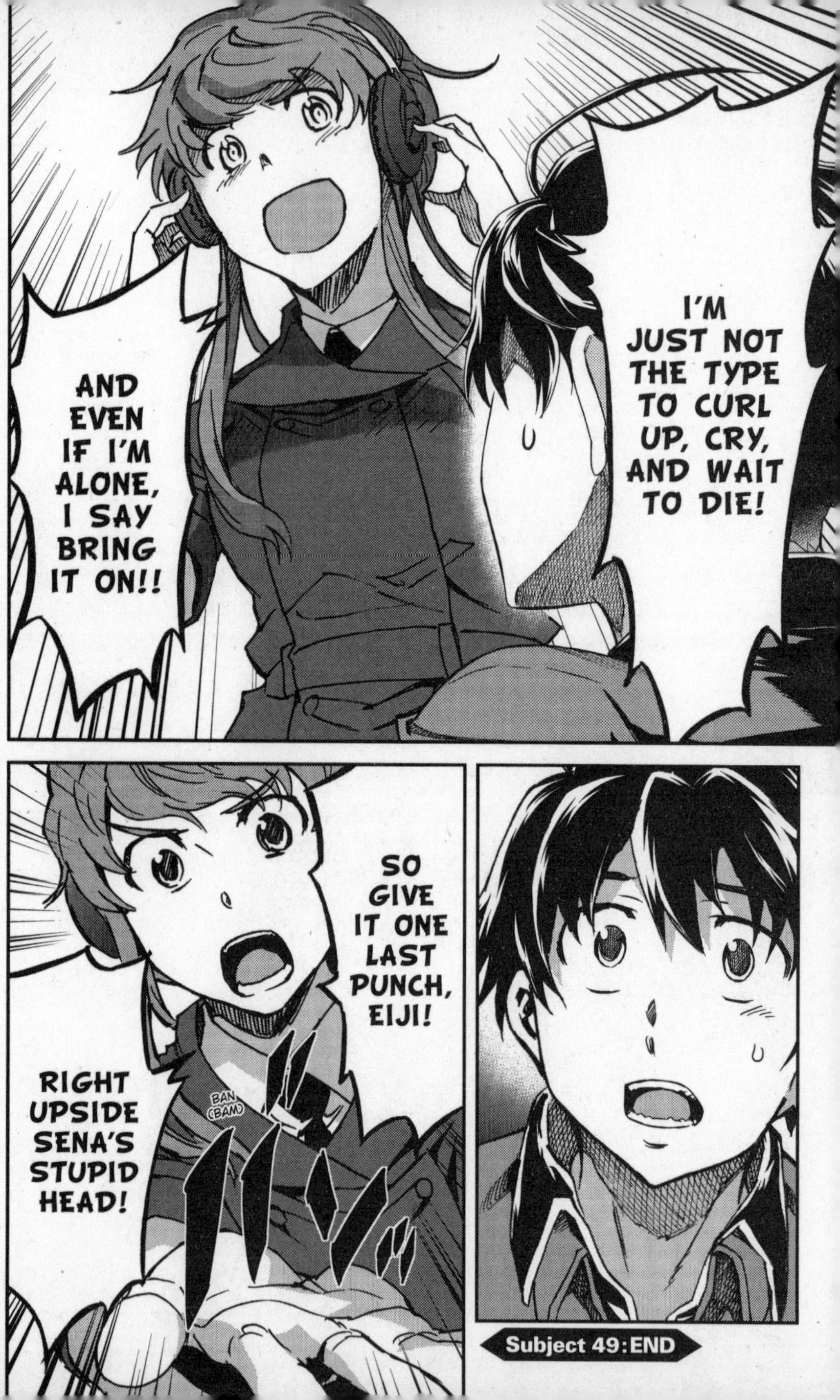

I'M JUST NOT THE TYPE TO CURL UP, CRY, AND WAIT TO DIE!
AND EVEN IF I'M ALONE, I SAY BRING IT ON!!
SO GIVE IT ONE LAST PUNCH, EIJI!
RIGHT UPSIDE SENA'S STUPID HEAD!
BAN (BAM)
Subject 49: END

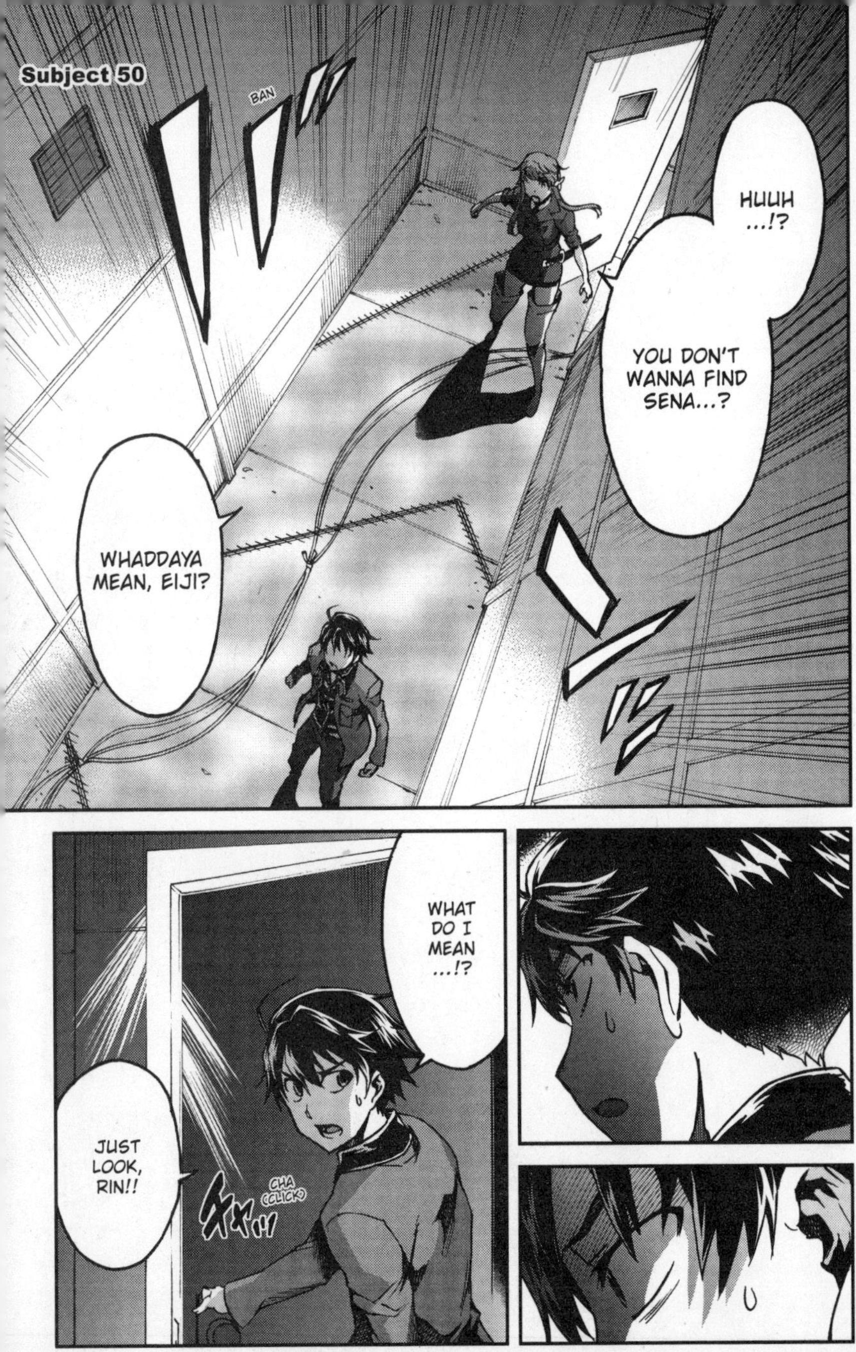
Subject 50
BAN
HUUH ...!?
YOU DON'T WANNA FIND SENA...?
WHADDAYA MEAN, EIJI?
WHAT DO I MEAN ...!?
JUST LOOK, RIN!!
CHA (CLICK)

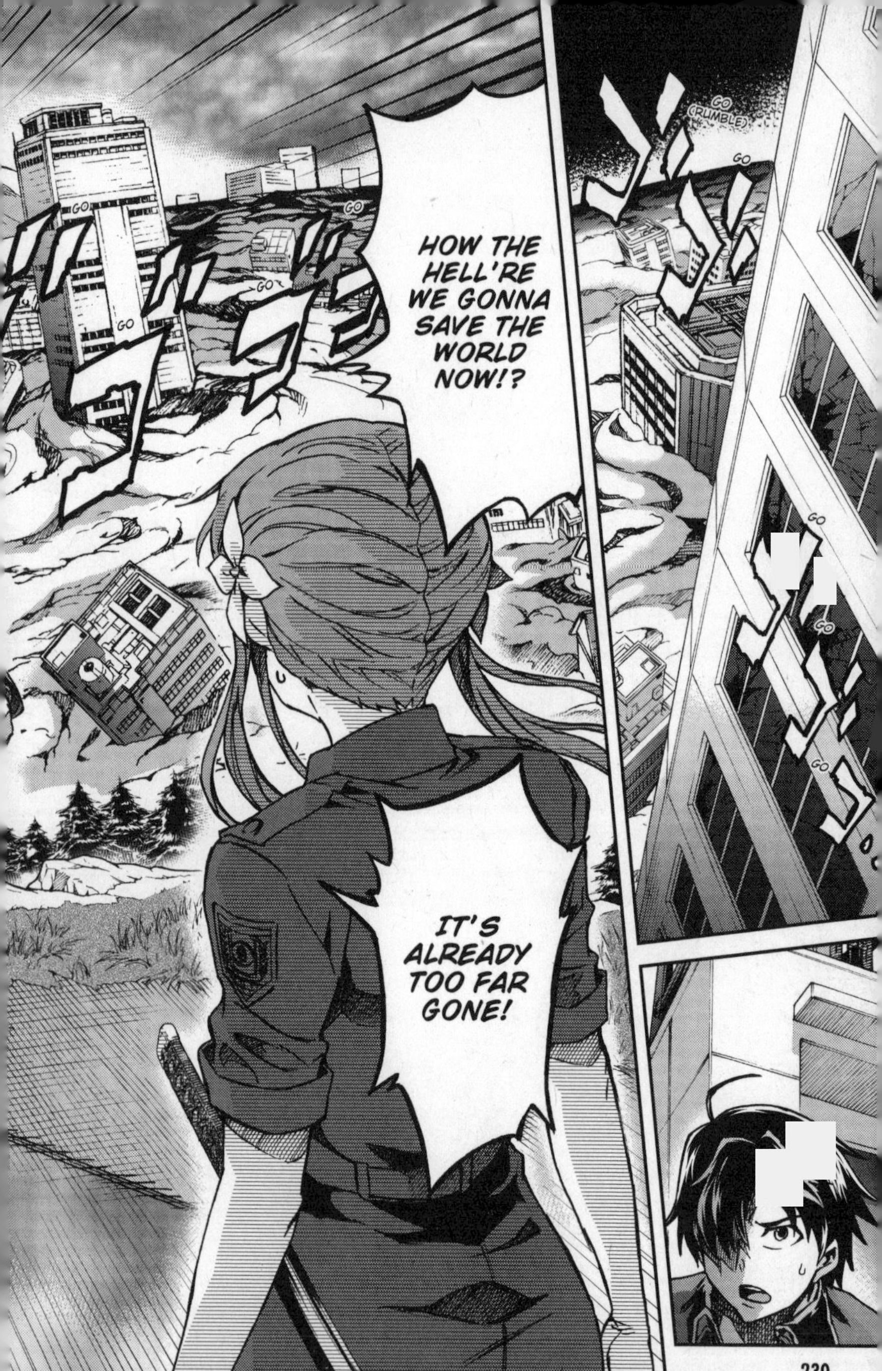
GO
(RUMBLE)
GO
GO
GO
GO
GO
GO
GO
GO
HOW THE HELL'RE WE GONNA SAVE THE WORLD NOW!?
IT'S ALREADY TOO FAR GONE!

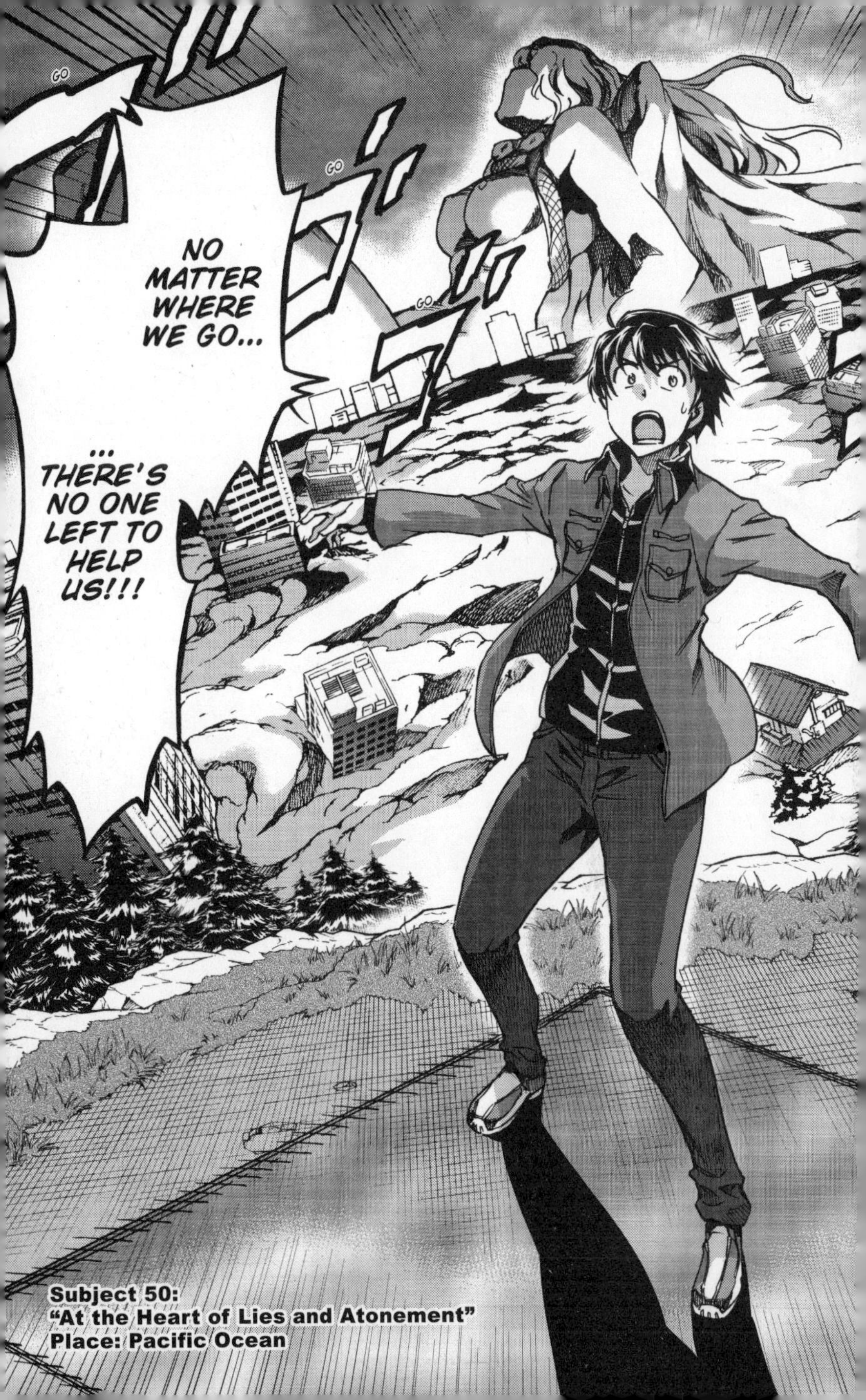
NO MATTER WHERE WE GO...
... THERE'S NO ONE LEFT TO HELP US!!!
GO
GO
GO...

Subject 50:
"At the Heart of Lies and Atonement"
Place: Pacific Ocean

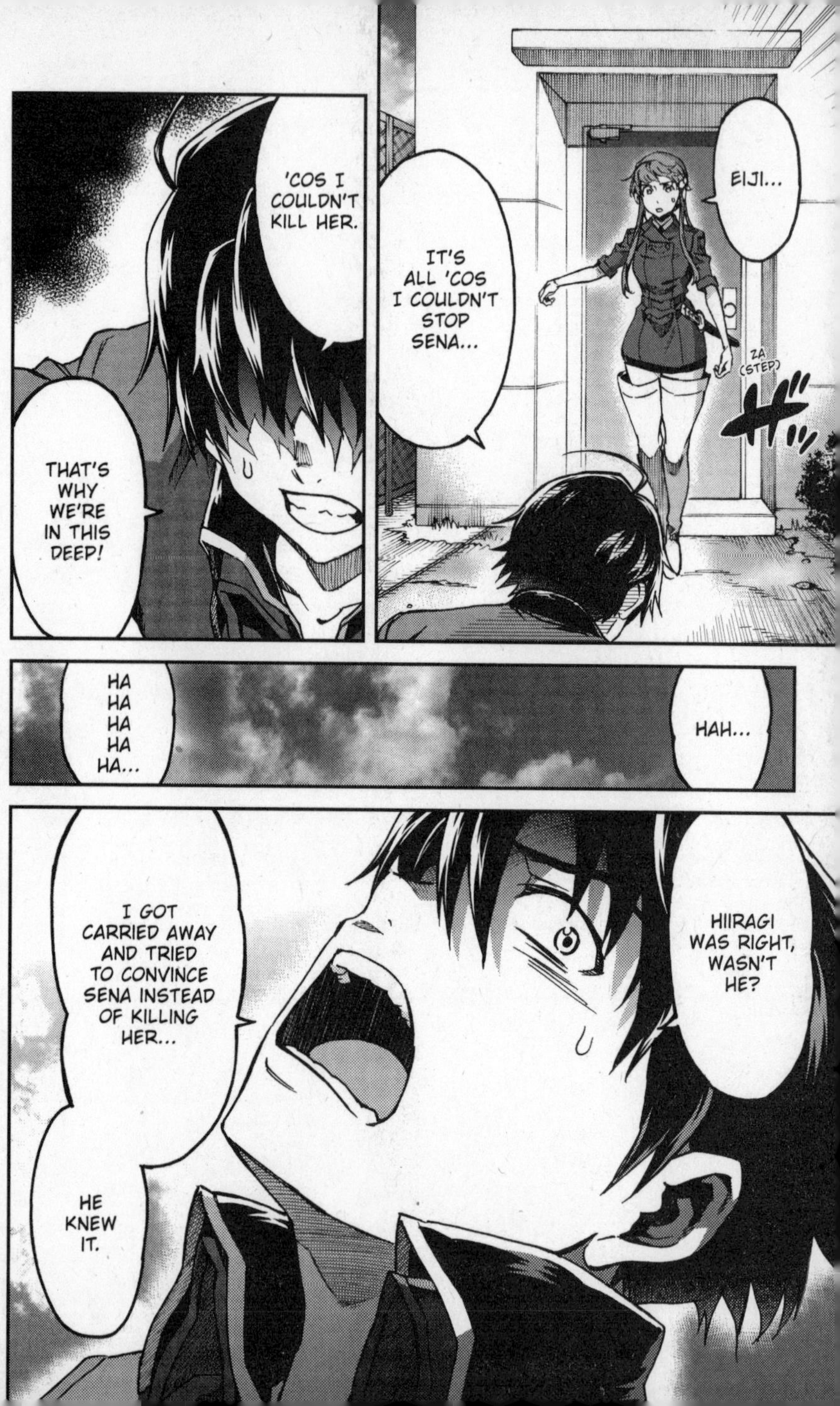
EIJI...
IT'S ALL 'COS I COULDN'T STOP SENA...
ZA (STEP)
'COS I COULDN'T KILL HER.
THAT'S WHY WE'RE IN THIS DEEP!
HAH...
HA HA HA HA HA...
HIIRAGI WAS RIGHT, WASN'T HE?
I GOT CARRIED AWAY AND TRIED TO CONVINCE SENA INSTEAD OF KILLING HER...
HE KNEW IT.

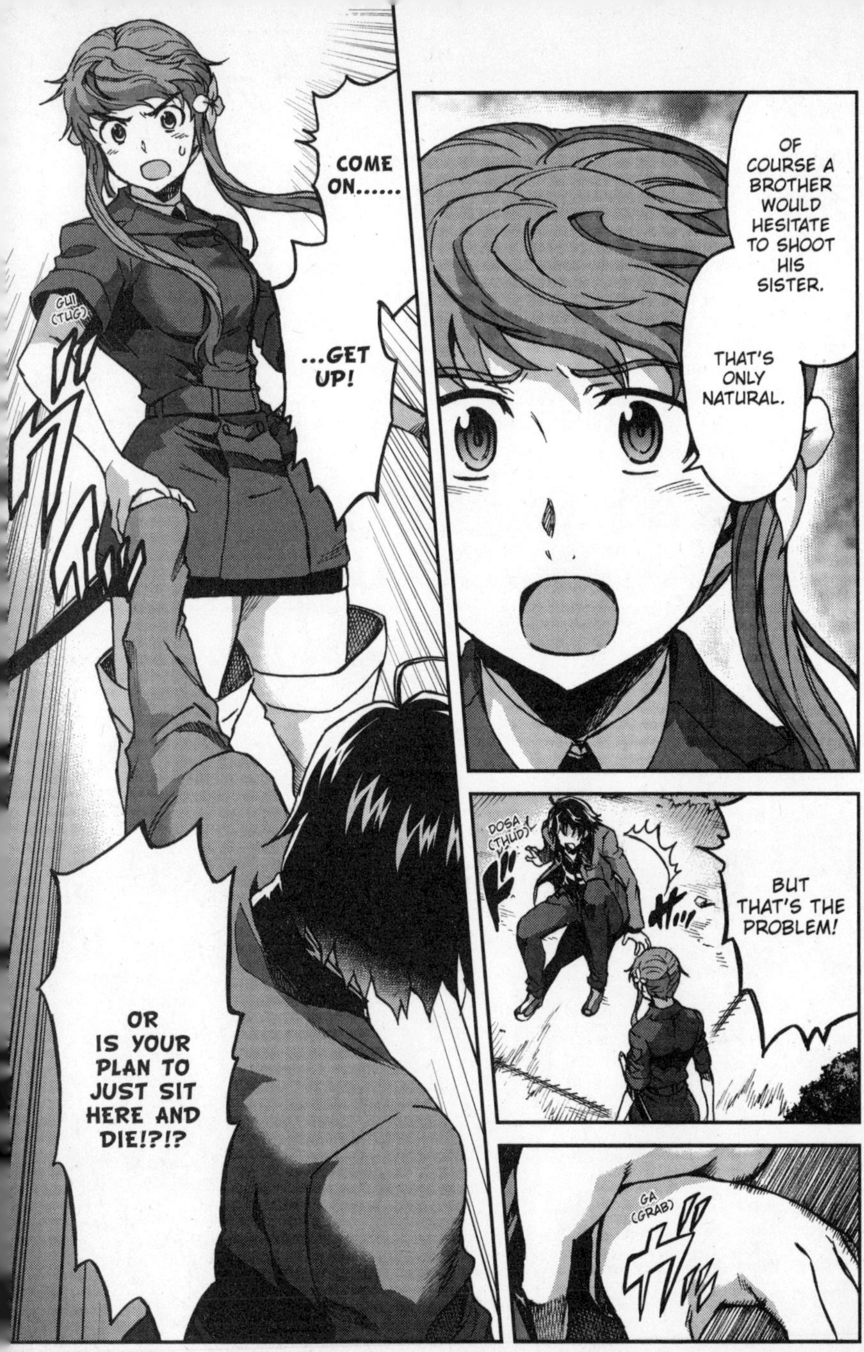
OF COURSE A BROTHER WOULD HESITATE TO SHOOT HIS SISTER.
THAT'S ONLY NATURAL.
DOSA (THUD)
BUT THAT'S THE PROBLEM!
GA (GRAB)
COME ON......
GUI (TUG)
...GET UP!
OR IS YOUR PLAN TO JUST SIT HERE AND DIE!?!?

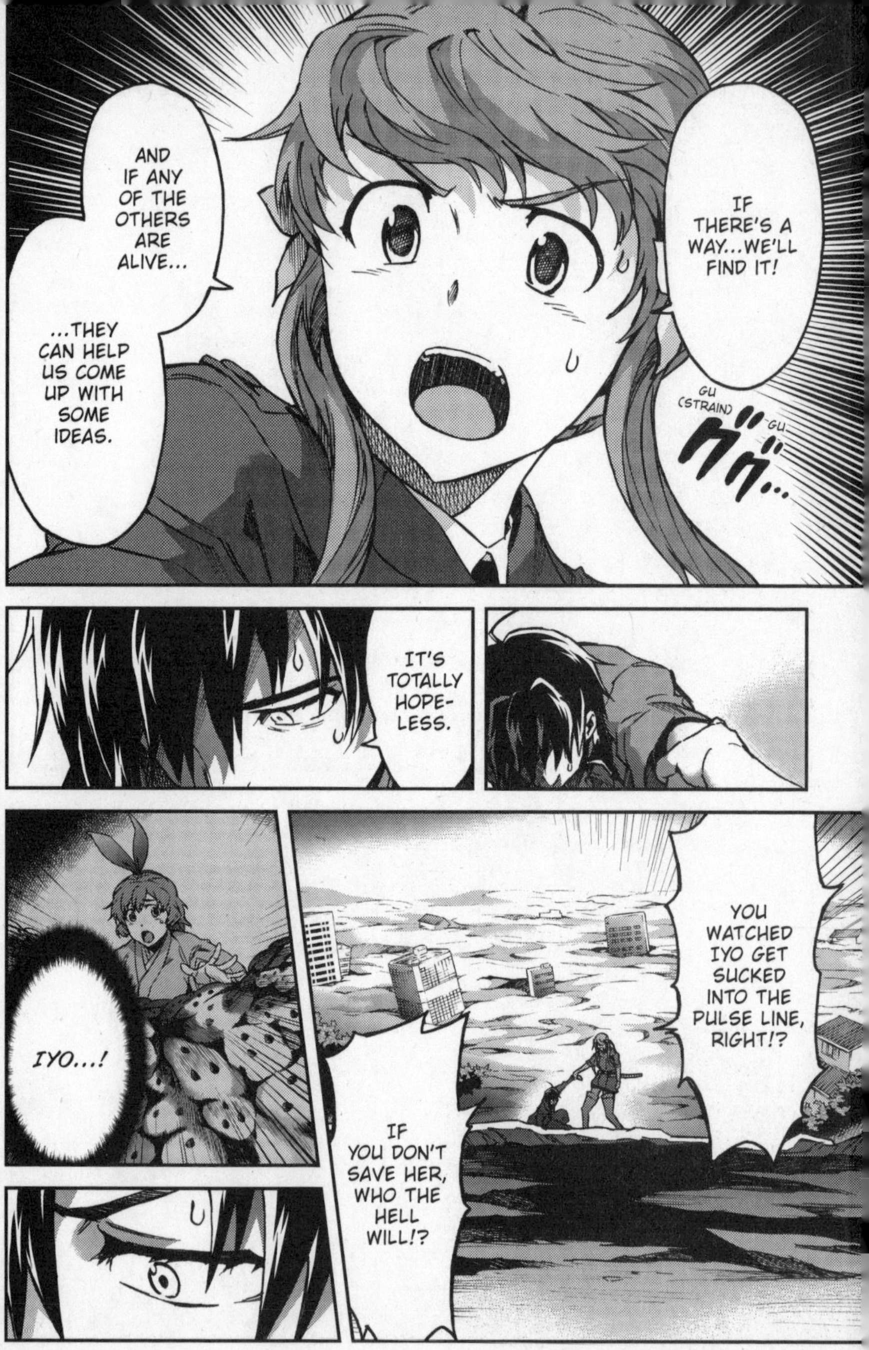
IF THERE'S A WAY...WE'LL FIND IT!
GU (STRAIN) GU
ググ...
AND IF ANY OF THE OTHERS ARE ALIVE...
...THEY CAN HELP US COME UP WITH SOME IDEAS.
IT'S TOTALLY HOPE-LESS.
YOU WATCHED IYO GET SUCKED INTO THE PULSE LINE, RIGHT!?
IF YOU DON'T SAVE HER, WHO THE HELL WILL!?
IYO...!

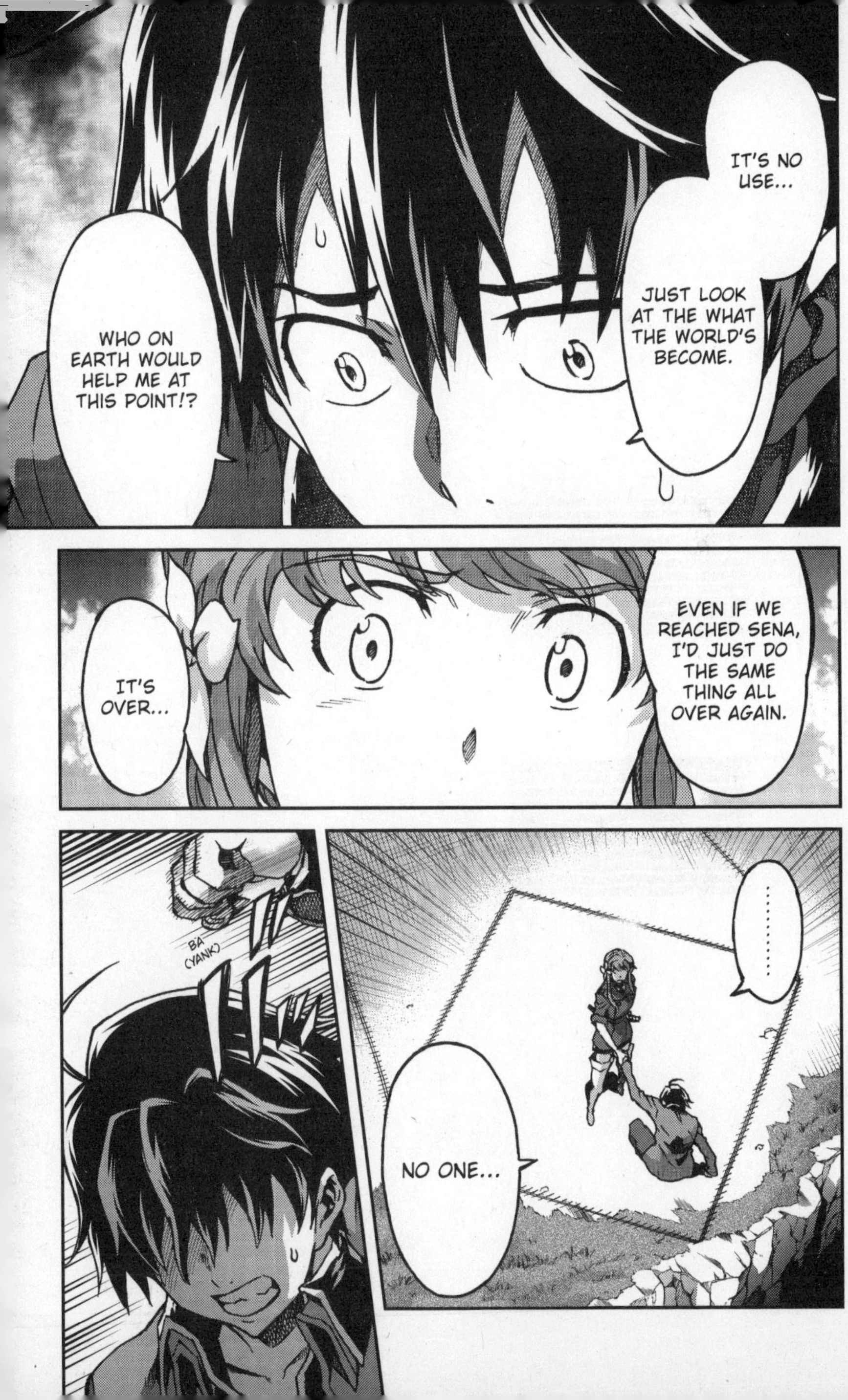
IT'S NO USE...
JUST LOOK AT THE WHAT THE WORLD'S BECOME.
WHO ON EARTH WOULD HELP ME AT THIS POINT!?
EVEN IF WE REACHED SENA, I'D JUST DO THE SAME THING ALL OVER AGAIN.
IT'S OVER...
......
NO ONE...
BA (YANK)

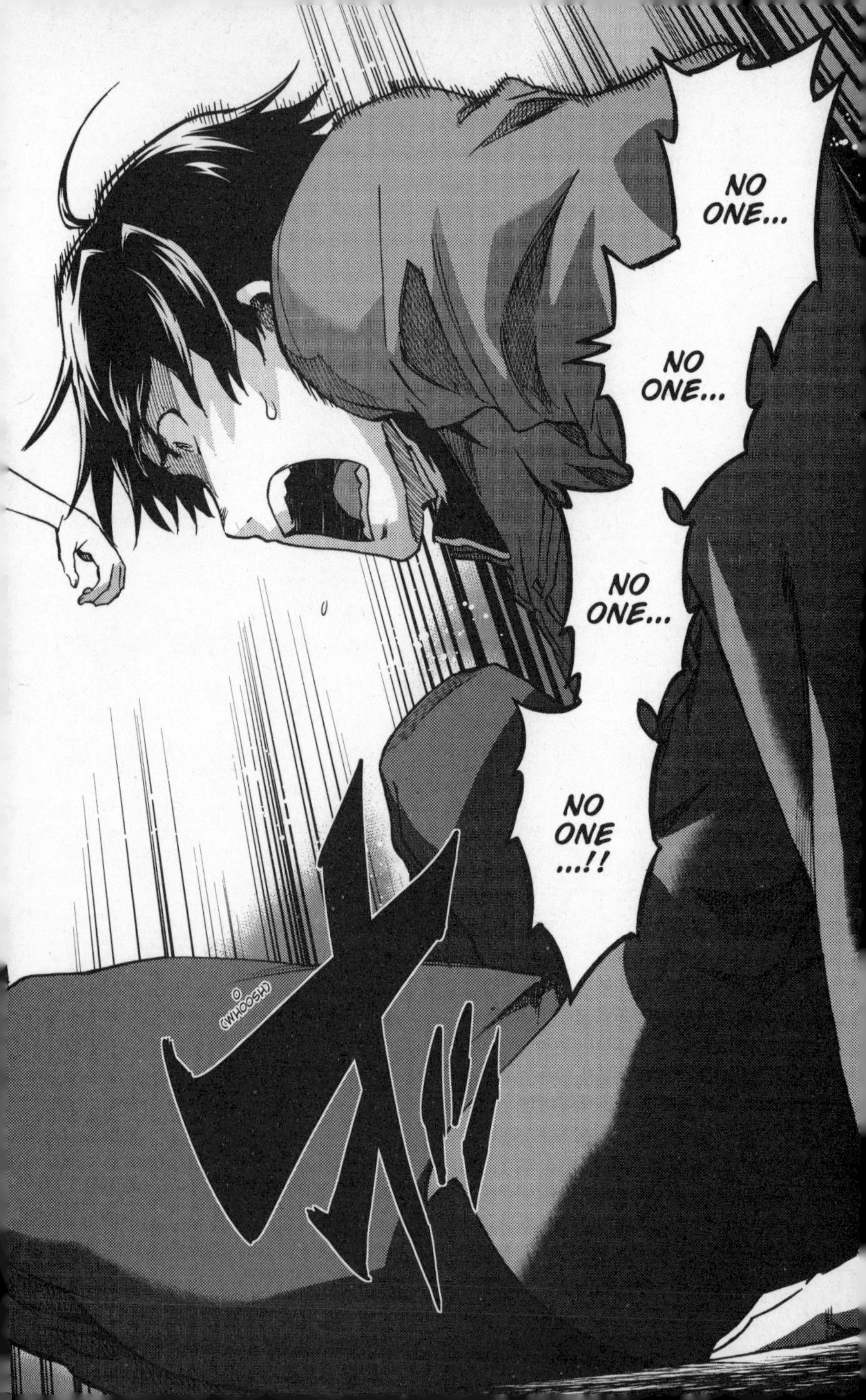
NO ONE...
NO ONE...
NO ONE...
NO ONE ...!!
(WHOOSH)

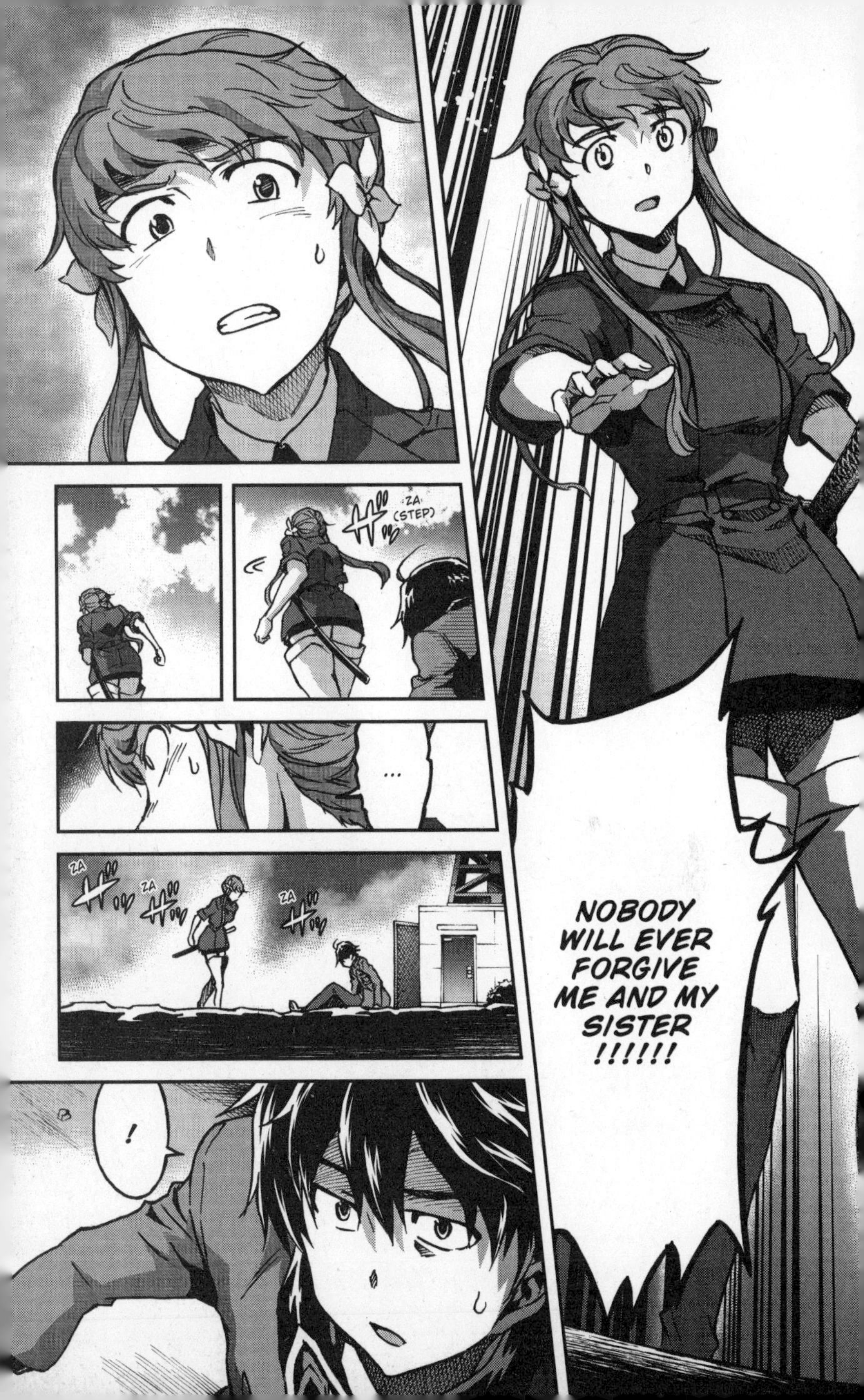
NOBODY WILL EVER FORGIVE ME AND MY SISTER !!!!!!
ZA (STEP)
...
ZA
ZA
ZA
!

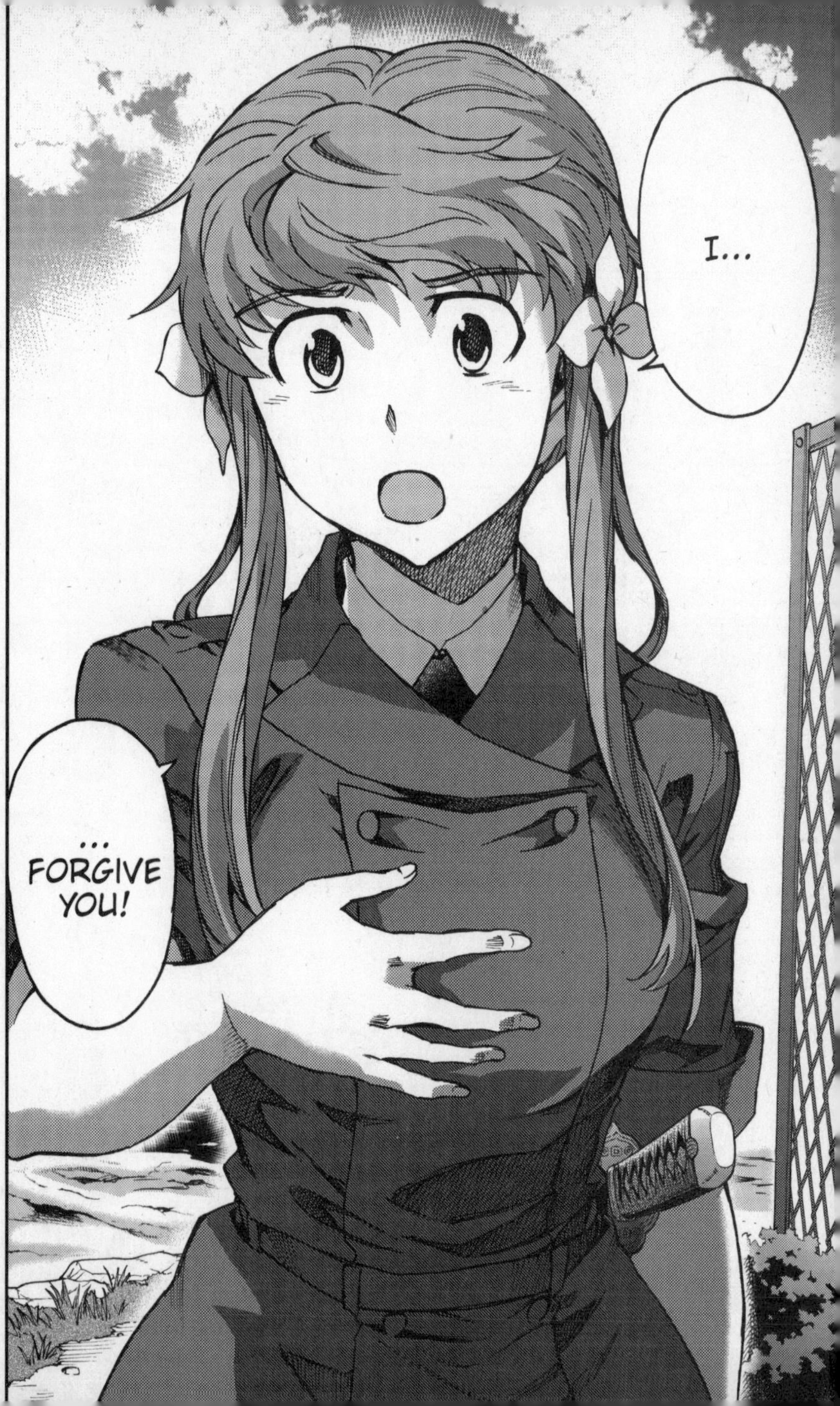
I...
...FORGIVE YOU!

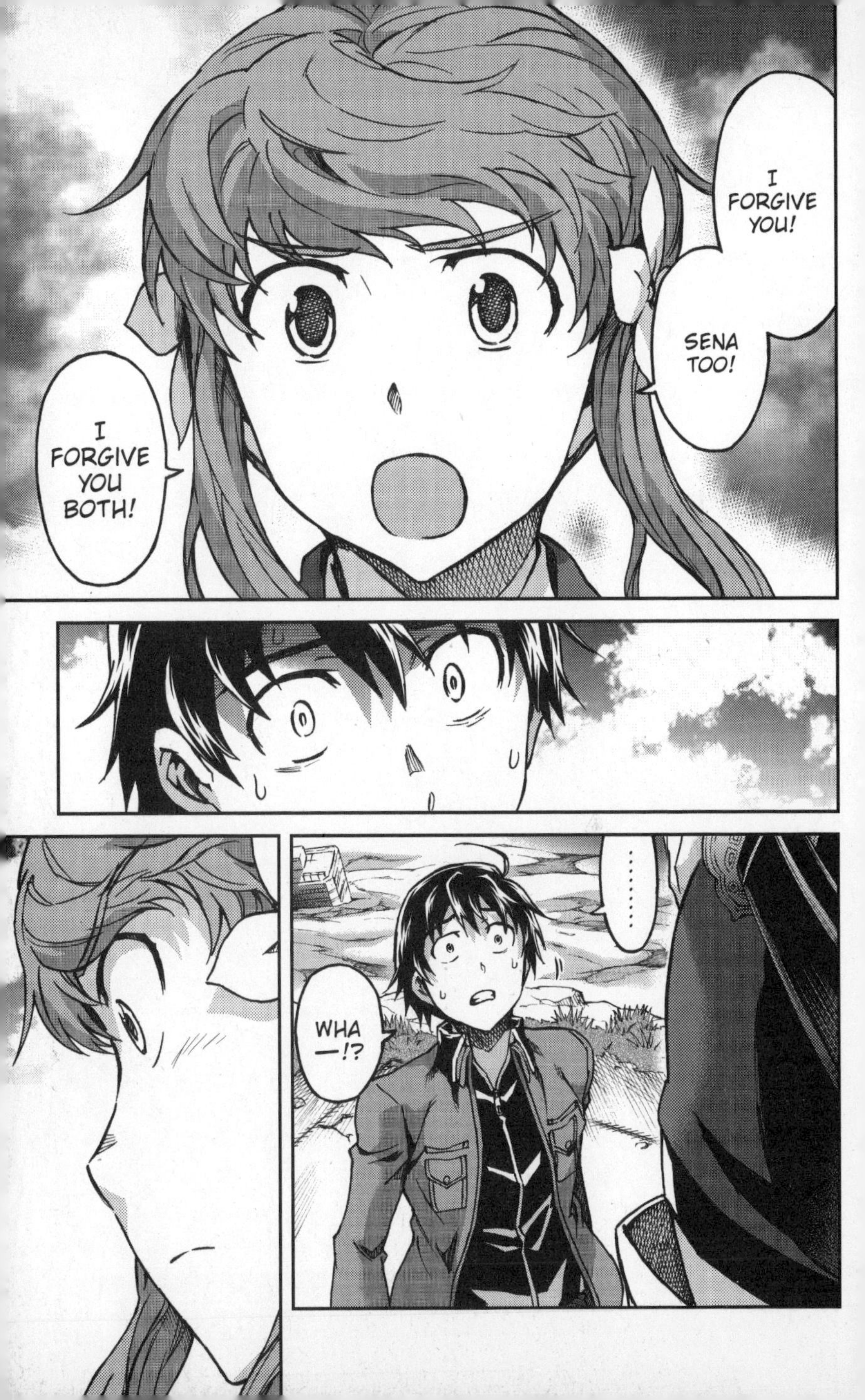
I FORGIVE YOU!
SENA TOO!
I FORGIVE YOU BOTH!
......
WHA—!?

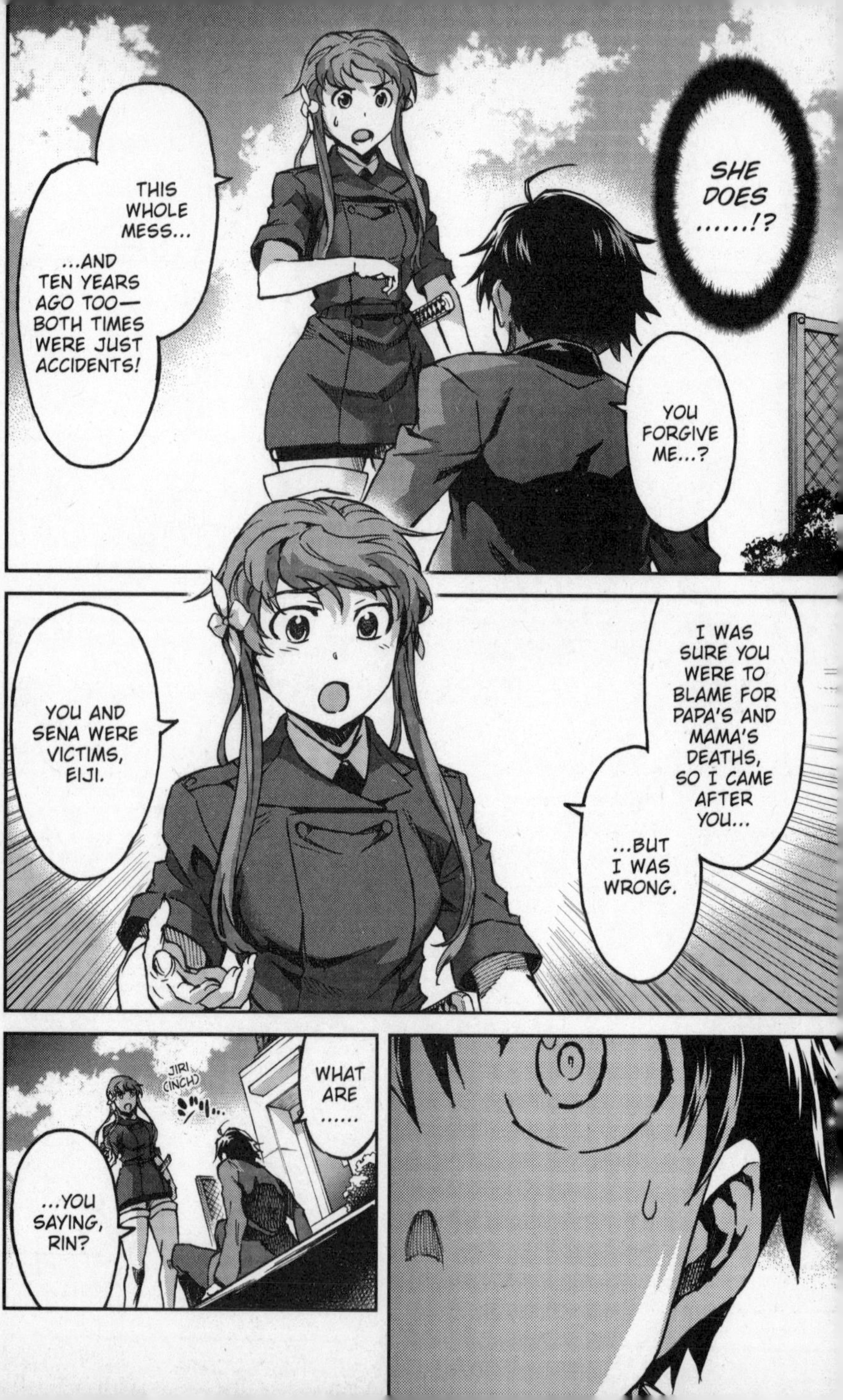
SHE DOES ......!?
THIS WHOLE MESS...
...AND TEN YEARS AGO TOO—BOTH TIMES WERE JUST ACCIDENTS!
YOU FORGIVE ME...?
I WAS SURE YOU WERE TO BLAME FOR PAPA'S AND MAMA'S DEATHS, SO I CAME AFTER YOU...
...BUT I WAS WRONG.
YOU AND SENA WERE VICTIMS, EIJI.
WHAT ARE ......
JIRI (INCH)
...YOU SAYING, RIN?

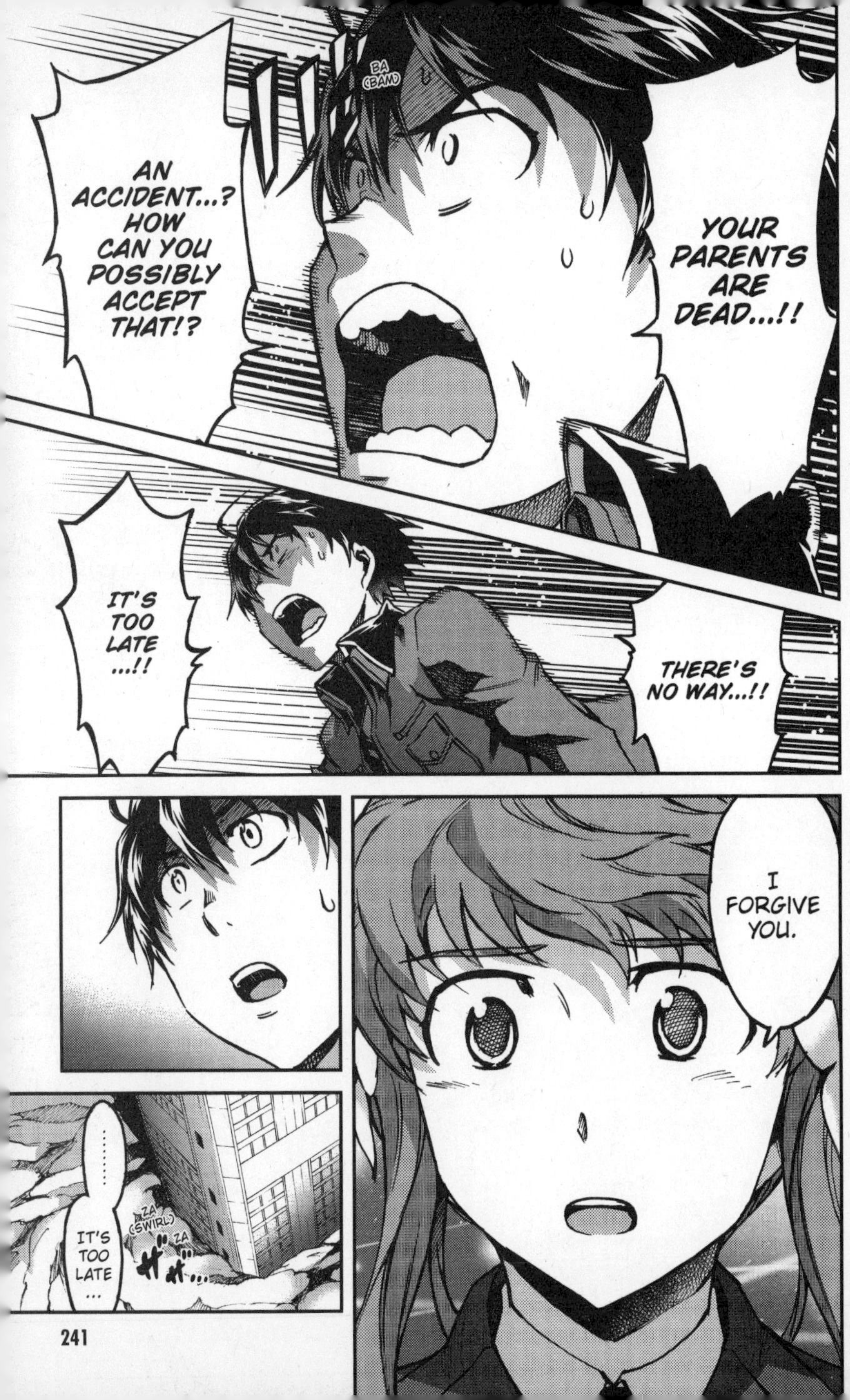
BA (BAM)
YOUR PARENTS ARE DEAD...!!
AN ACCIDENT...? HOW CAN YOU POSSIBLY ACCEPT THAT!?
THERE'S NO WAY...!!
IT'S TOO LATE...!!
I FORGIVE YOU.
......
ZA (SWIRL) ZA
IT'S TOO LATE...

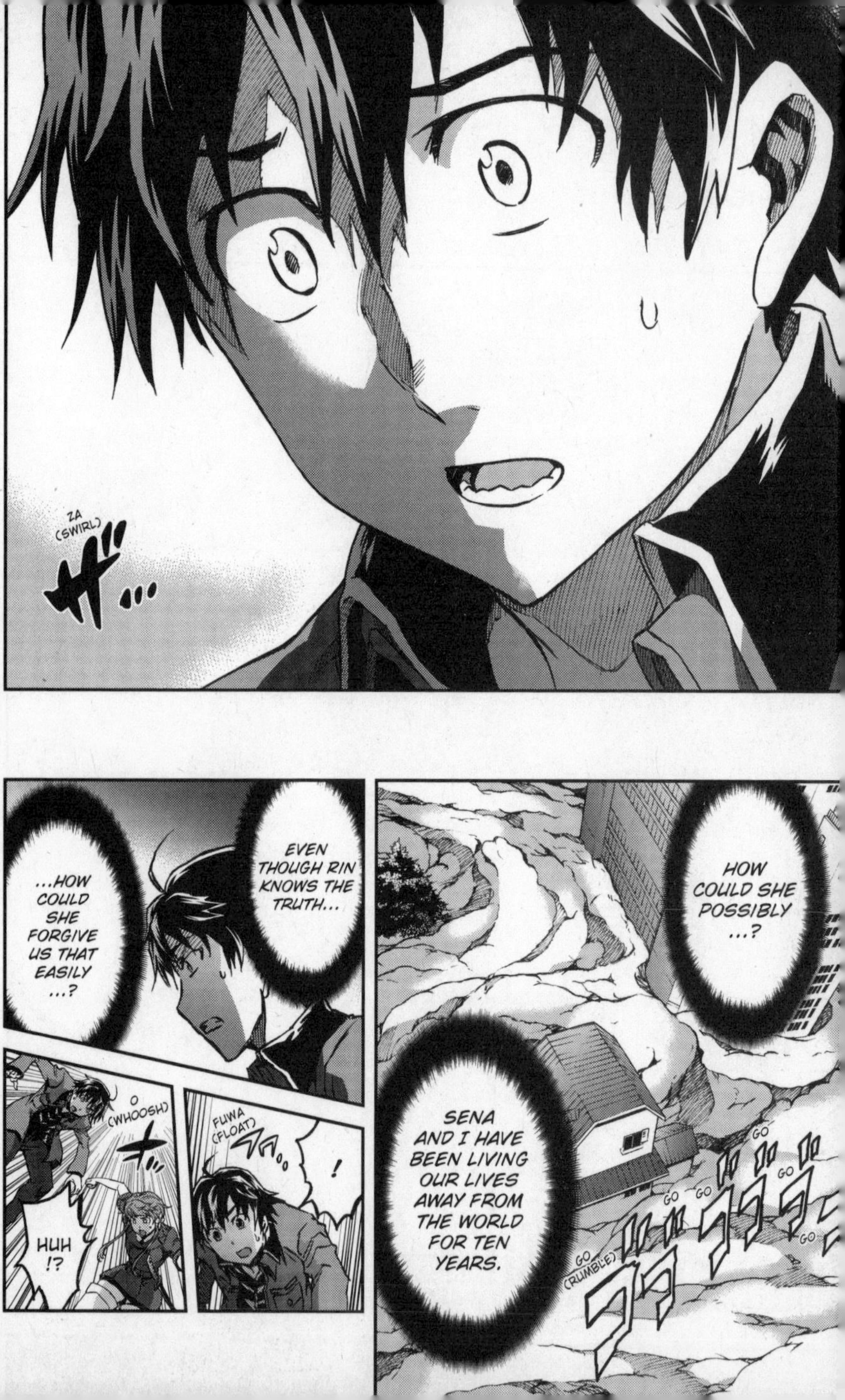
ZA (SWIRL)
HOW COULD SHE POSSIBLY ...?
SENA AND I HAVE BEEN LIVING OUR LIVES AWAY FROM THE WORLD FOR TEN YEARS.
GO (RUMBLE)
GO
GO
GO
GO
GO
EVEN THOUGH RIN KNOWS THE TRUTH...
...HOW COULD SHE FORGIVE US THAT EASILY ...?
FUWA (FLOAT)
!
O (WHOOSH)
HUH !?

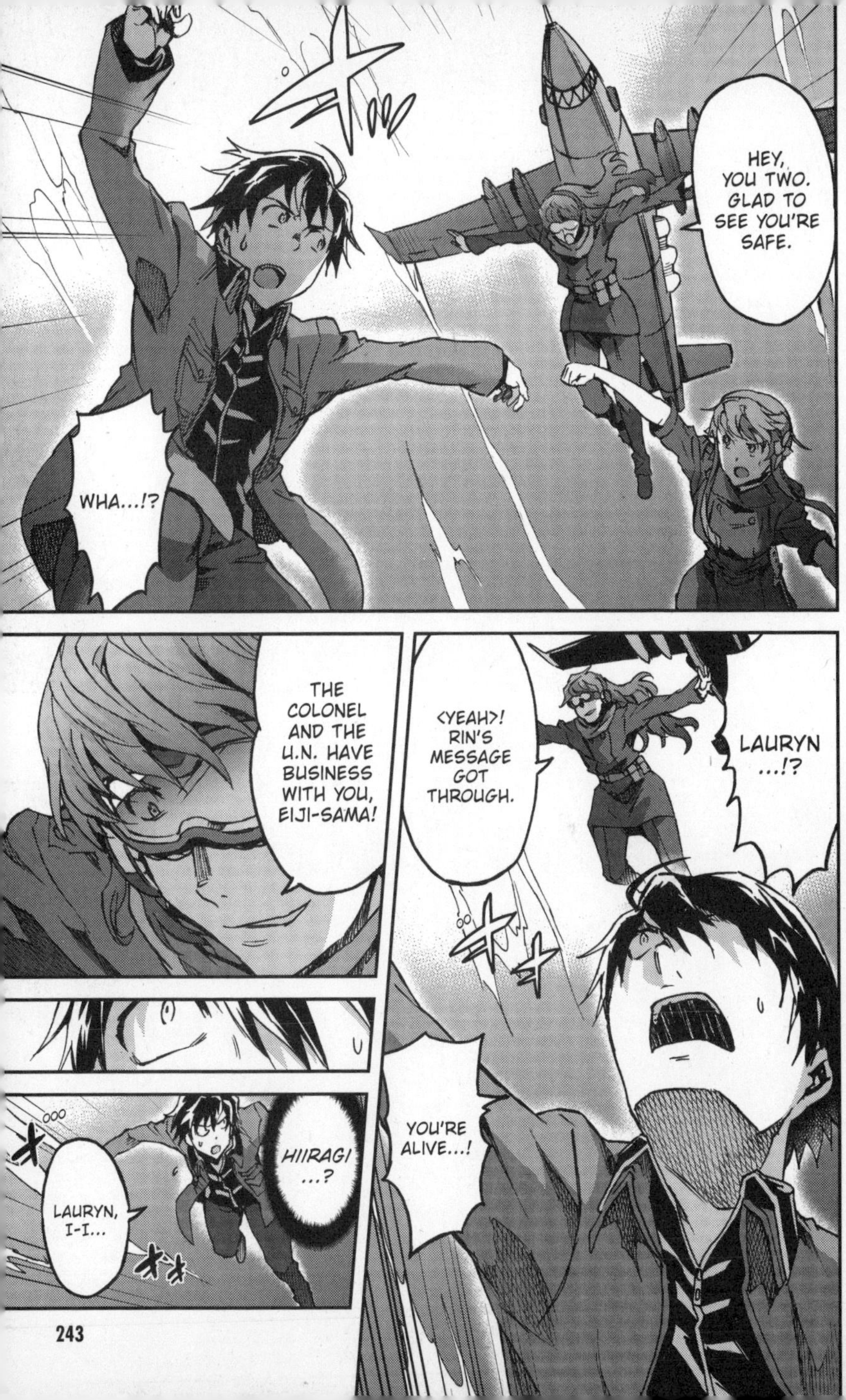
HEY, YOU TWO. GLAD TO SEE YOU'RE SAFE.
WHA...!?
LAURYN ...!?
<YEAH>! RIN'S MESSAGE GOT THROUGH.
YOU'RE ALIVE...!
THE COLONEL AND THE U.N. HAVE BUSINESS WITH YOU, EIJI-SAMA!
HIIRAGI ...?
LAURYN, I-I...

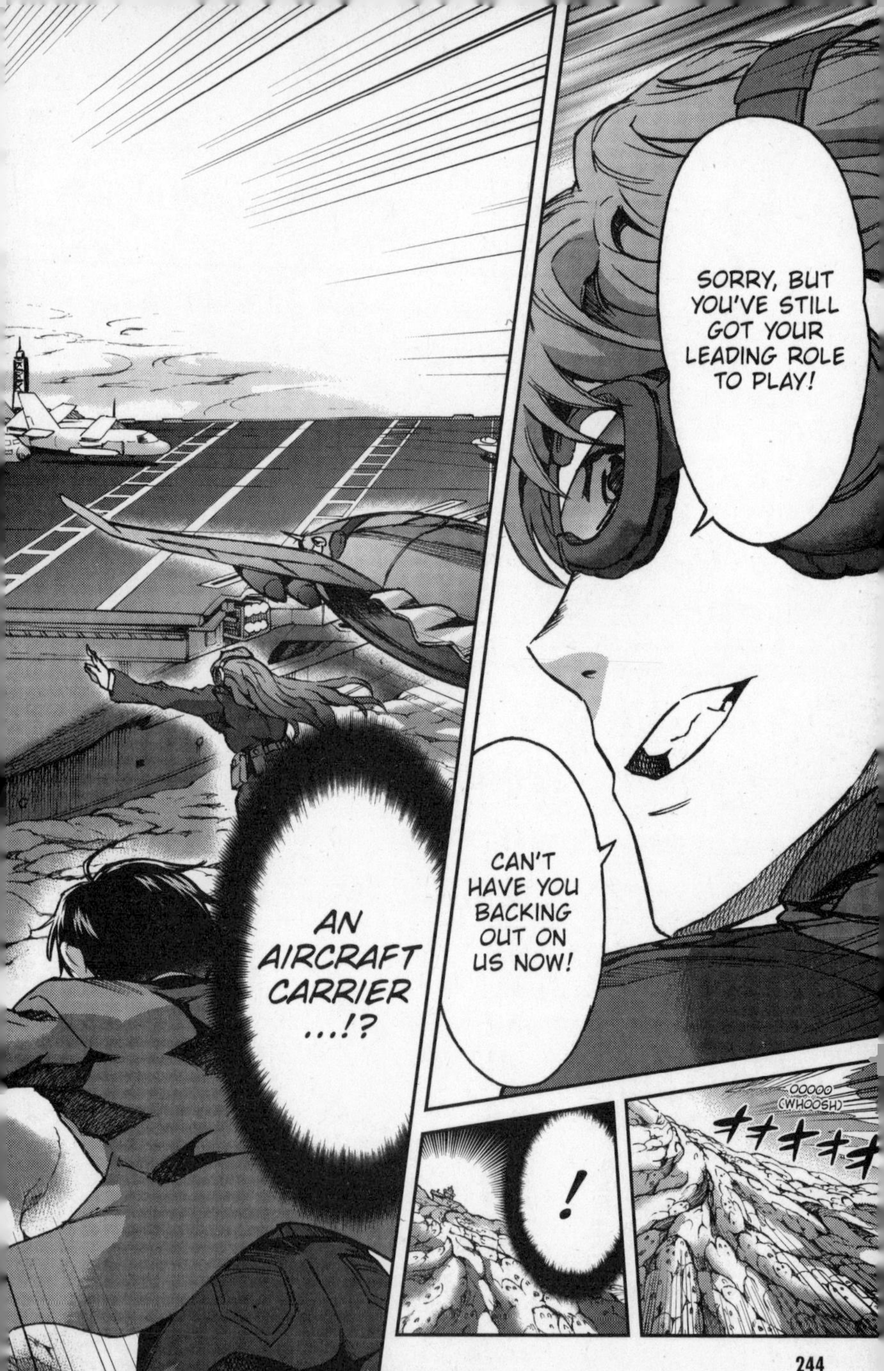
SORRY, BUT YOU'VE STILL GOT YOUR LEADING ROLE TO PLAY!
CAN'T HAVE YOU BACKING OUT ON US NOW!
OOOOO (WHOOSH)
!
AN AIRCRAFT CARRIER ...!?

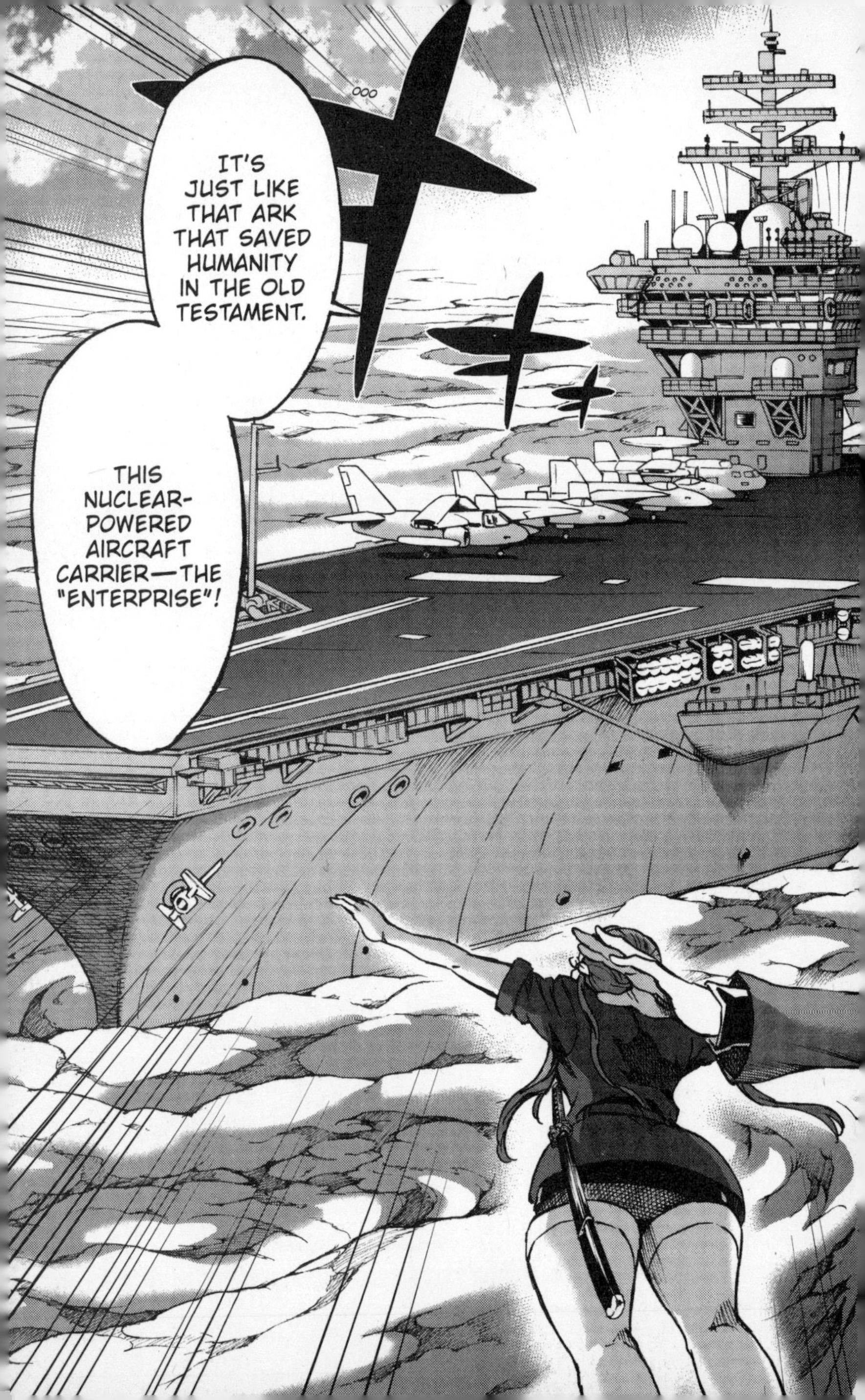
IT'S JUST LIKE THAT ARK THAT SAVED HUMANITY IN THE OLD TESTAMENT.
THIS NUCLEAR-POWERED AIRCRAFT CARRIER—THE "ENTERPRISE"!

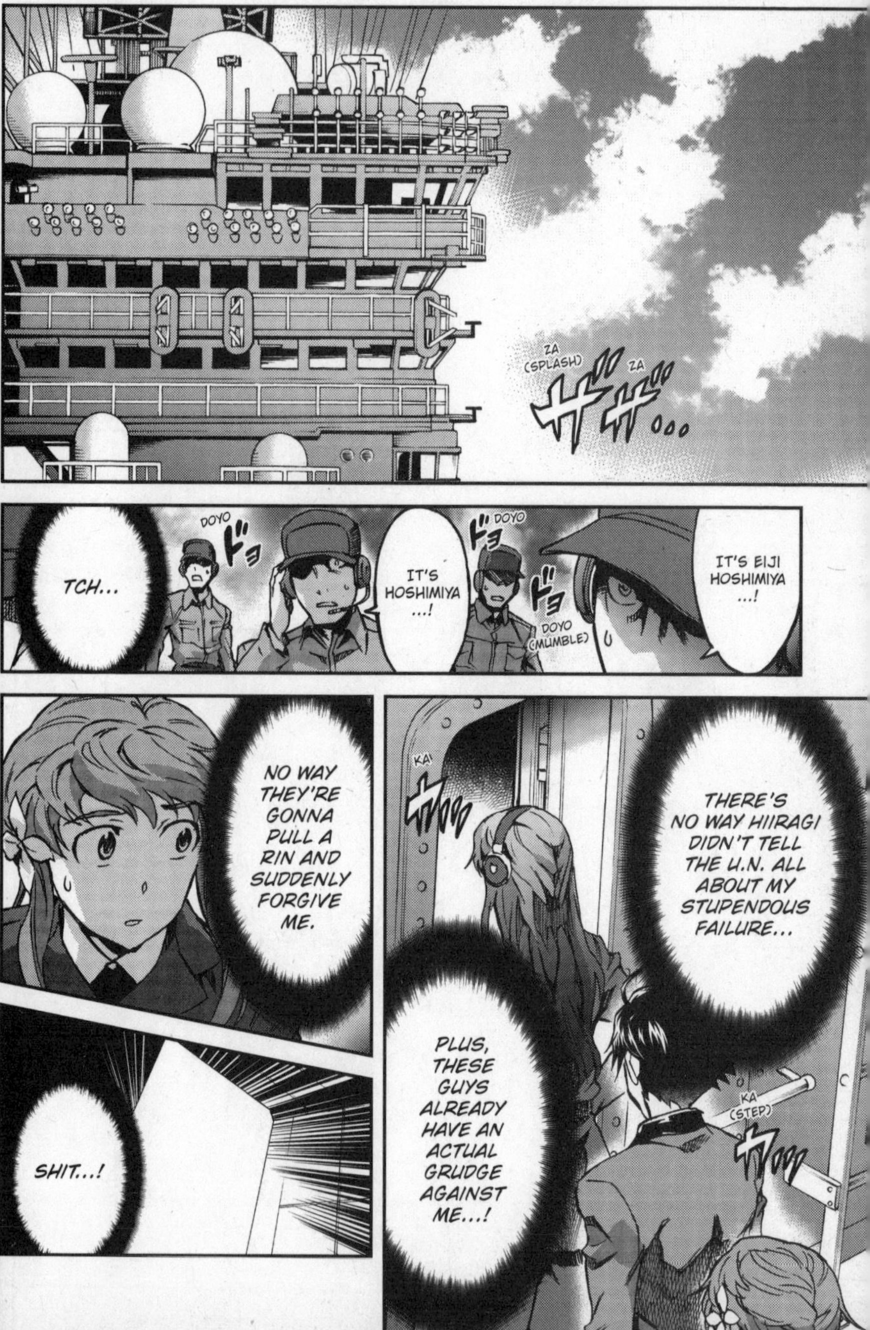
ZA (SPLASH) ZA
IT'S EIJI HOSHIMIYA ...!
DOYO
DOYO (MUMBLE)
IT'S HOSHIMIYA ...!
DOYO
TCH...
KA
THERE'S NO WAY HIIRAGI DIDN'T TELL THE U.N. ALL ABOUT MY STUPENDOUS FAILURE...
PLUS, THESE GUYS ALREADY HAVE AN ACTUAL GRUDGE AGAINST ME...!
KA (STEP)
NO WAY THEY'RE GONNA PULL A RIN AND SUDDENLY FORGIVE ME.
SHIT...!

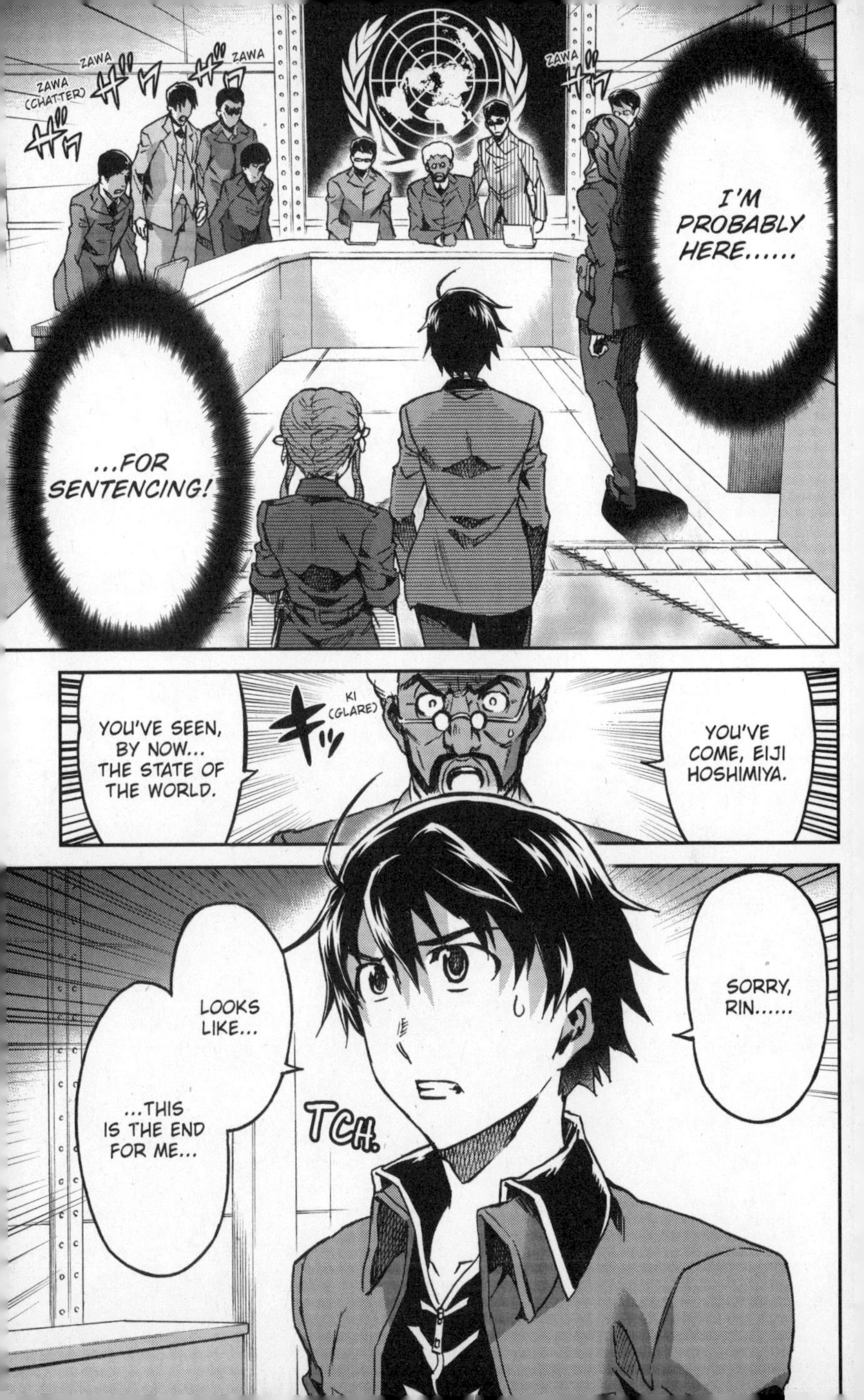
ZAWA
I'M PROBABLY HERE......
ZAWA
ZAWA
ZAWA (CHATTER)
...FOR SENTENCING!
YOU'VE COME, EIJI HOSHIMIYA.
KI (GLARE)
YOU'VE SEEN, BY NOW... THE STATE OF THE WORLD.
SORRY, RIN......
TCH.
LOOKS LIKE...
...THIS IS THE END FOR ME...

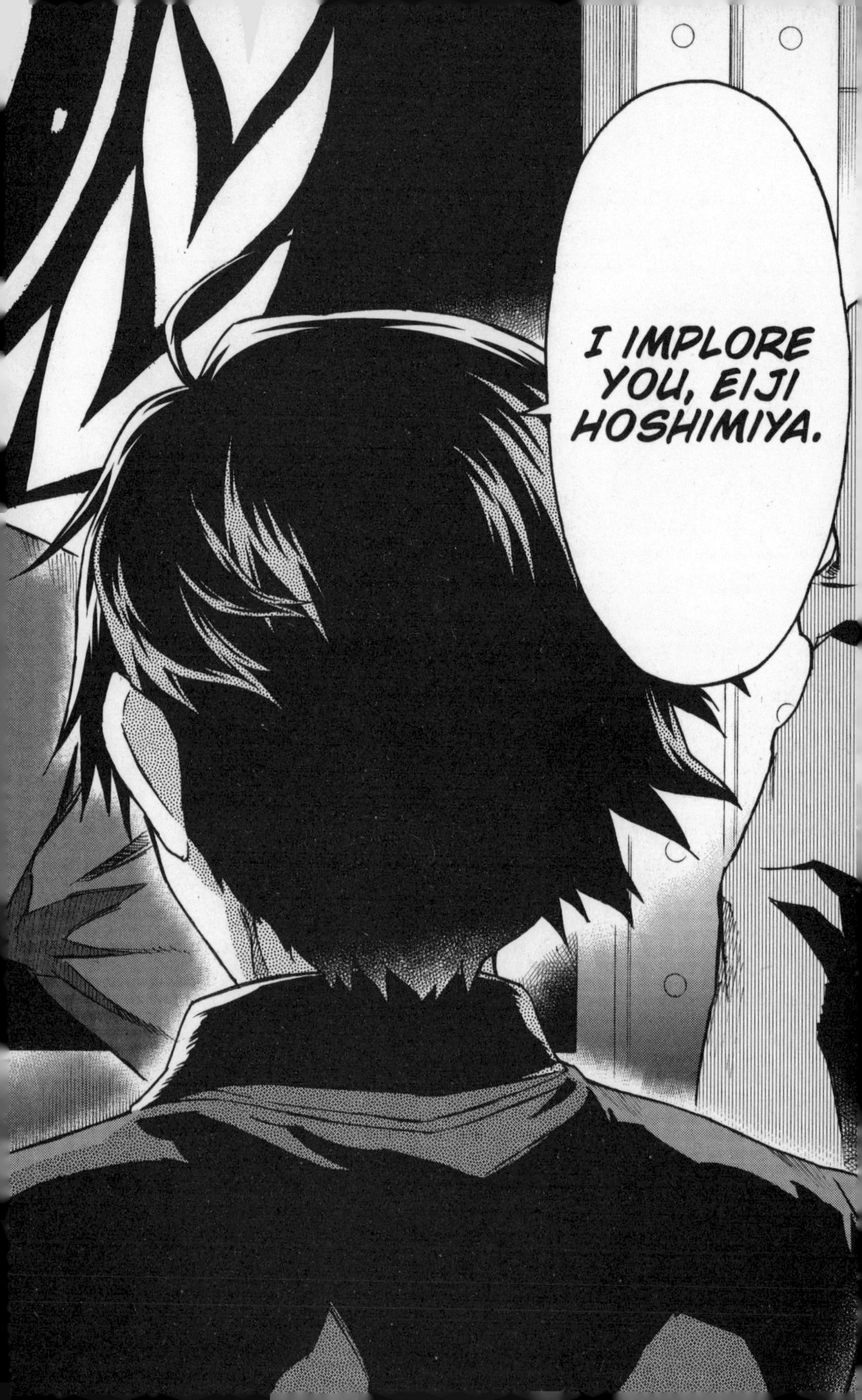
I IMPLORE YOU, EIJI HOSHIMIYA.

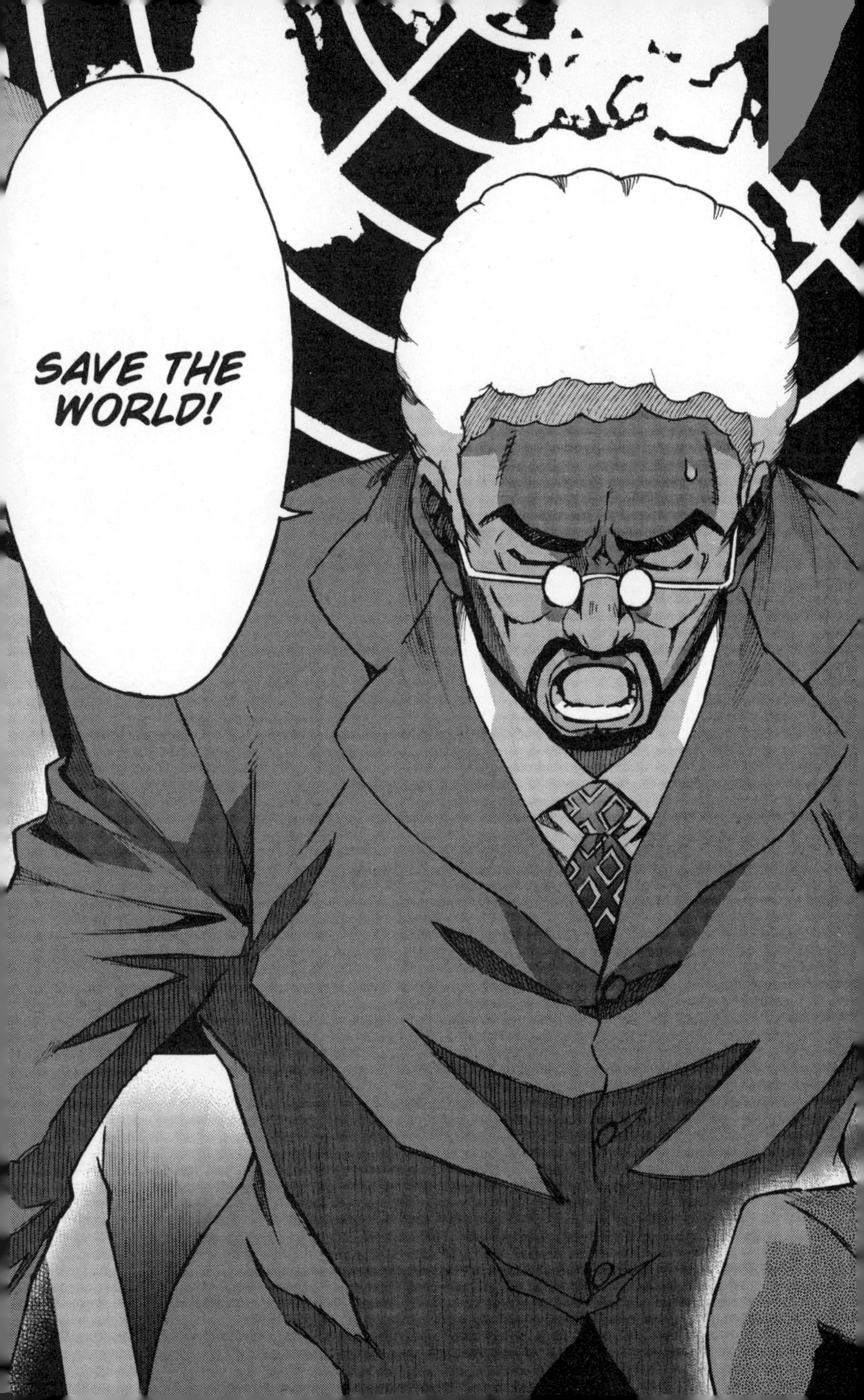
SAVE THE WORLD!

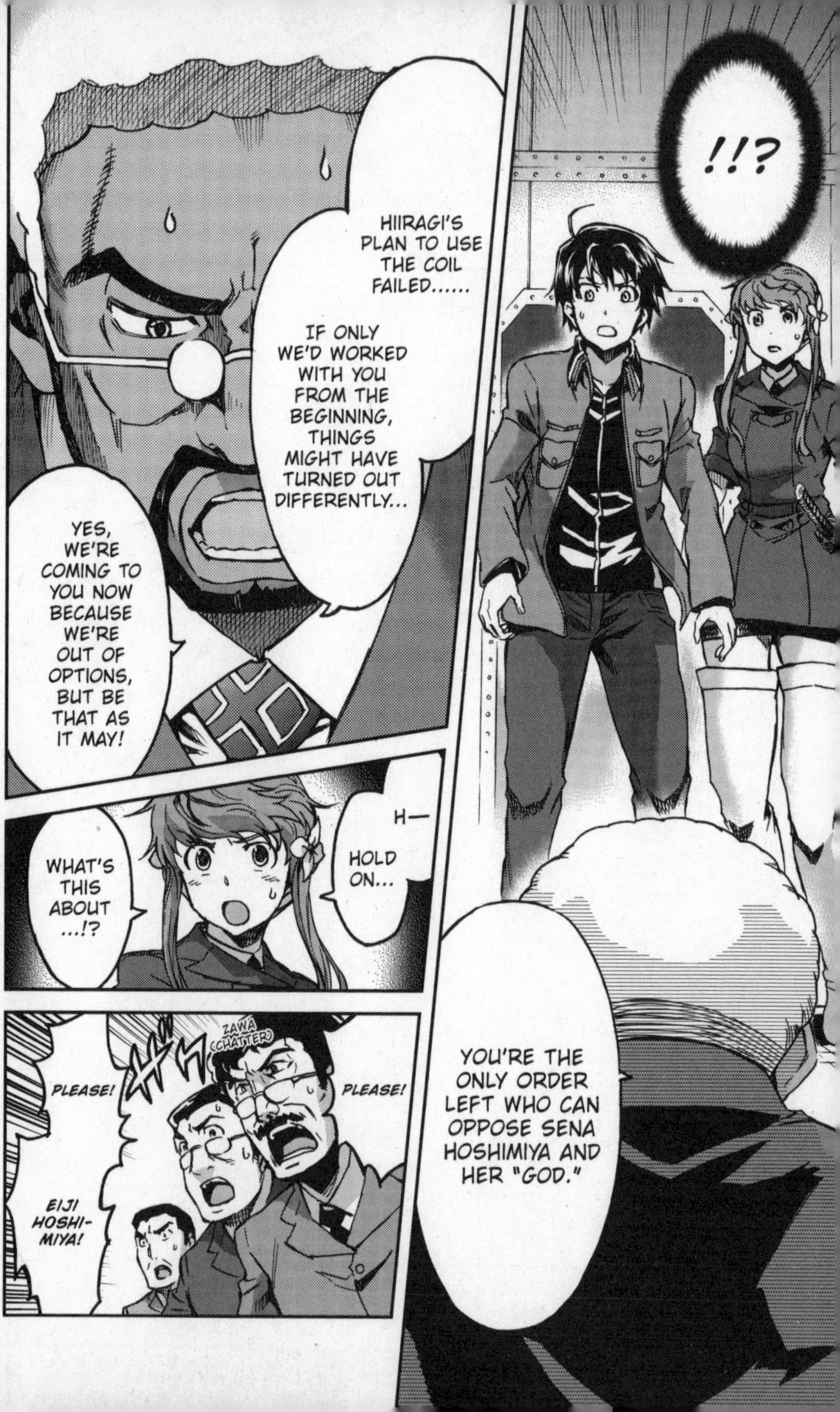
!!?
YOU'RE THE ONLY ORDER LEFT WHO CAN OPPOSE SENA HOSHIMIYA AND HER "GOD."
HIIRAGI'S PLAN TO USE THE COIL FAILED......
IF ONLY WE'D WORKED WITH YOU FROM THE BEGINNING, THINGS MIGHT HAVE TURNED OUT DIFFERENTLY...
YES, WE'RE COMING TO YOU NOW BECAUSE WE'RE OUT OF OPTIONS, BUT BE THAT AS IT MAY!
H— HOLD ON...
WHAT'S THIS ABOUT ...!?
ZAWA (CHATTER)
PLEASE!
PLEASE!
EIJI HOSHIMIYA!

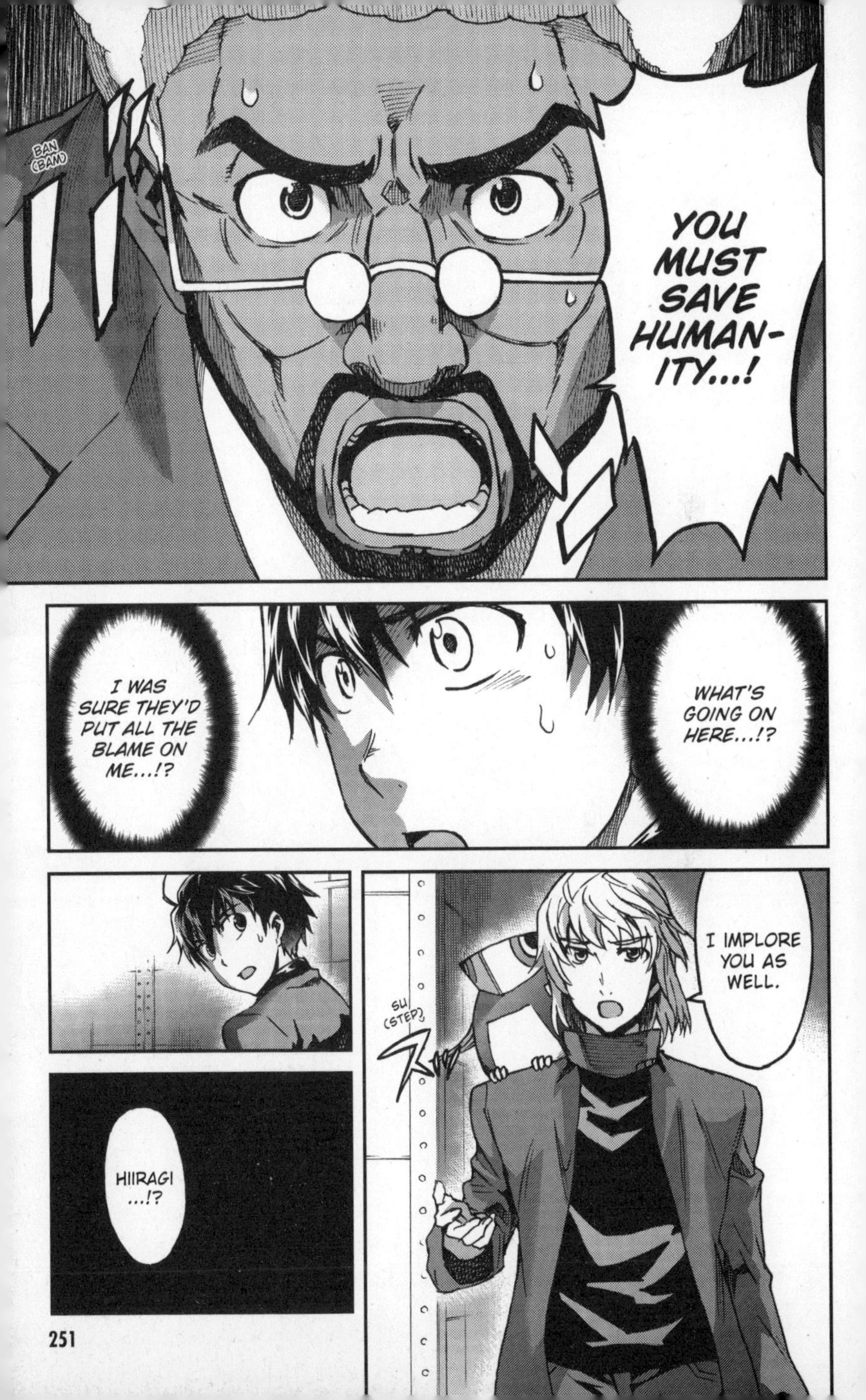
YOU MUST SAVE HUMAN-ITY...!
BAN (BAM)
WHAT'S GOING ON HERE...!?
I WAS SURE THEY'D PUT ALL THE BLAME ON ME...!?
I IMPLORE YOU AS WELL.
SU (STEP)
HIIRAGI ...!?

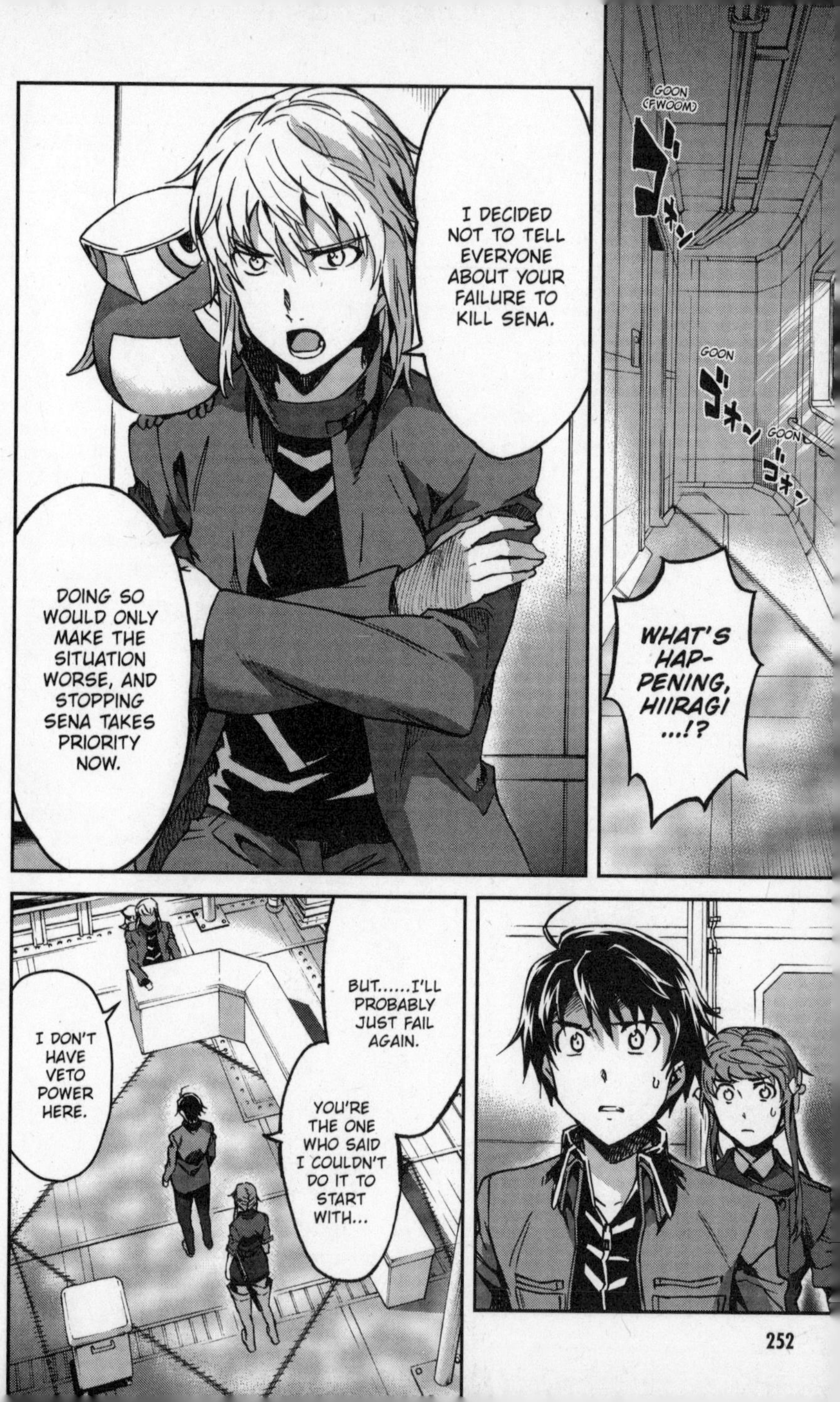
GOON (FWOOM)
ゴォン
GOON
ゴォン
GOON
ゴォン
WHAT'S HAP-PENING, HIIRAGI...!?
I DECIDED NOT TO TELL EVERYONE ABOUT YOUR FAILURE TO KILL SENA.
DOING SO WOULD ONLY MAKE THE SITUATION WORSE, AND STOPPING SENA TAKES PRIORITY NOW.
BUT......I'LL PROBABLY JUST FAIL AGAIN.
YOU'RE THE ONE WHO SAID I COULDN'T DO IT TO START WITH...
I DON'T HAVE VETO POWER HERE.

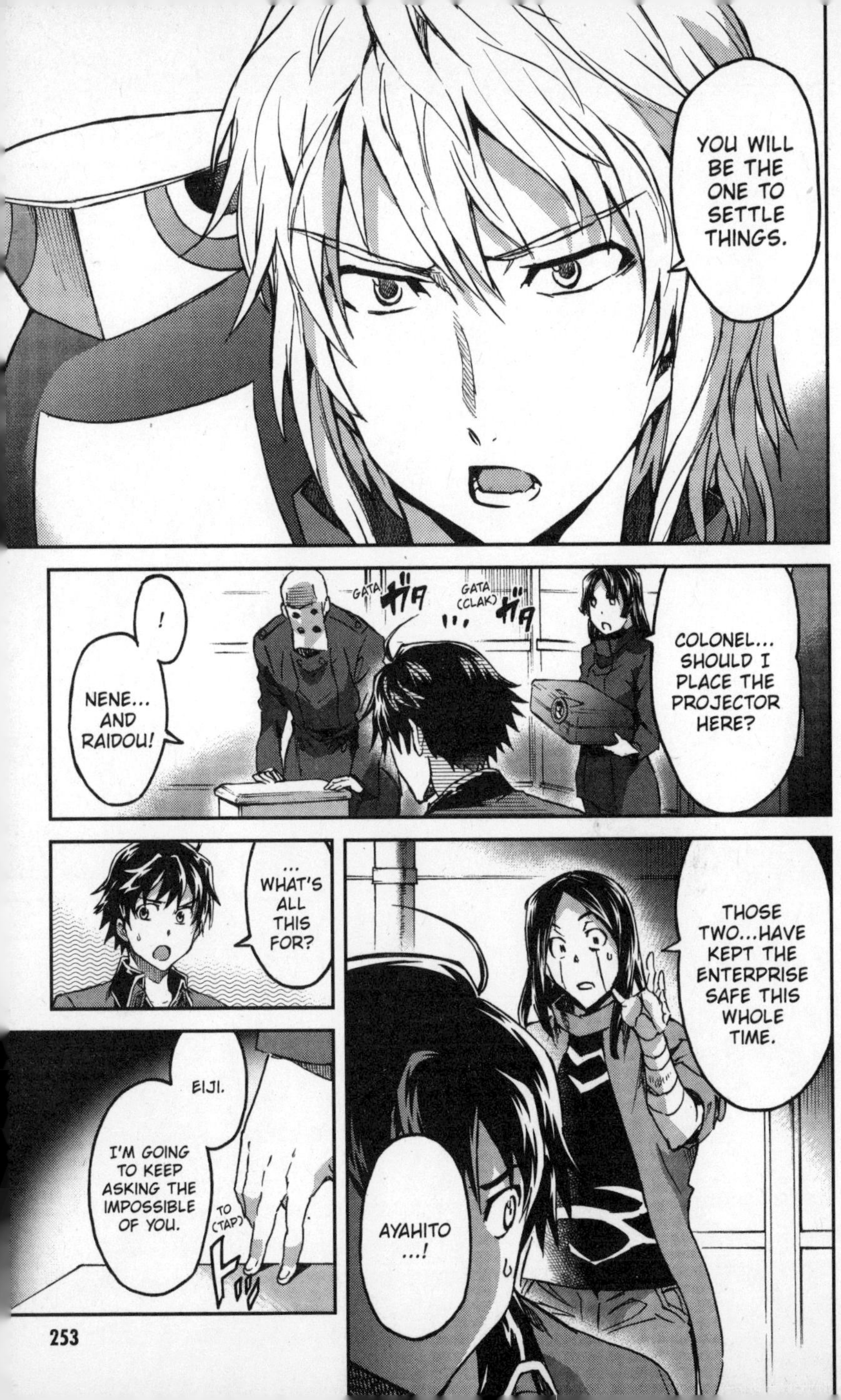
YOU WILL BE THE ONE TO SETTLE THINGS.
COLONEL... SHOULD I PLACE THE PROJECTOR HERE?
GATA (CLAK)
GATA
!
NENE... AND RAIDOU!
THOSE TWO...HAVE KEPT THE ENTERPRISE SAFE THIS WHOLE TIME.
AYAHITO ...!
... WHAT'S ALL THIS FOR?
EIJI.
I'M GOING TO KEEP ASKING THE IMPOSSIBLE OF YOU.
TO (TAP)

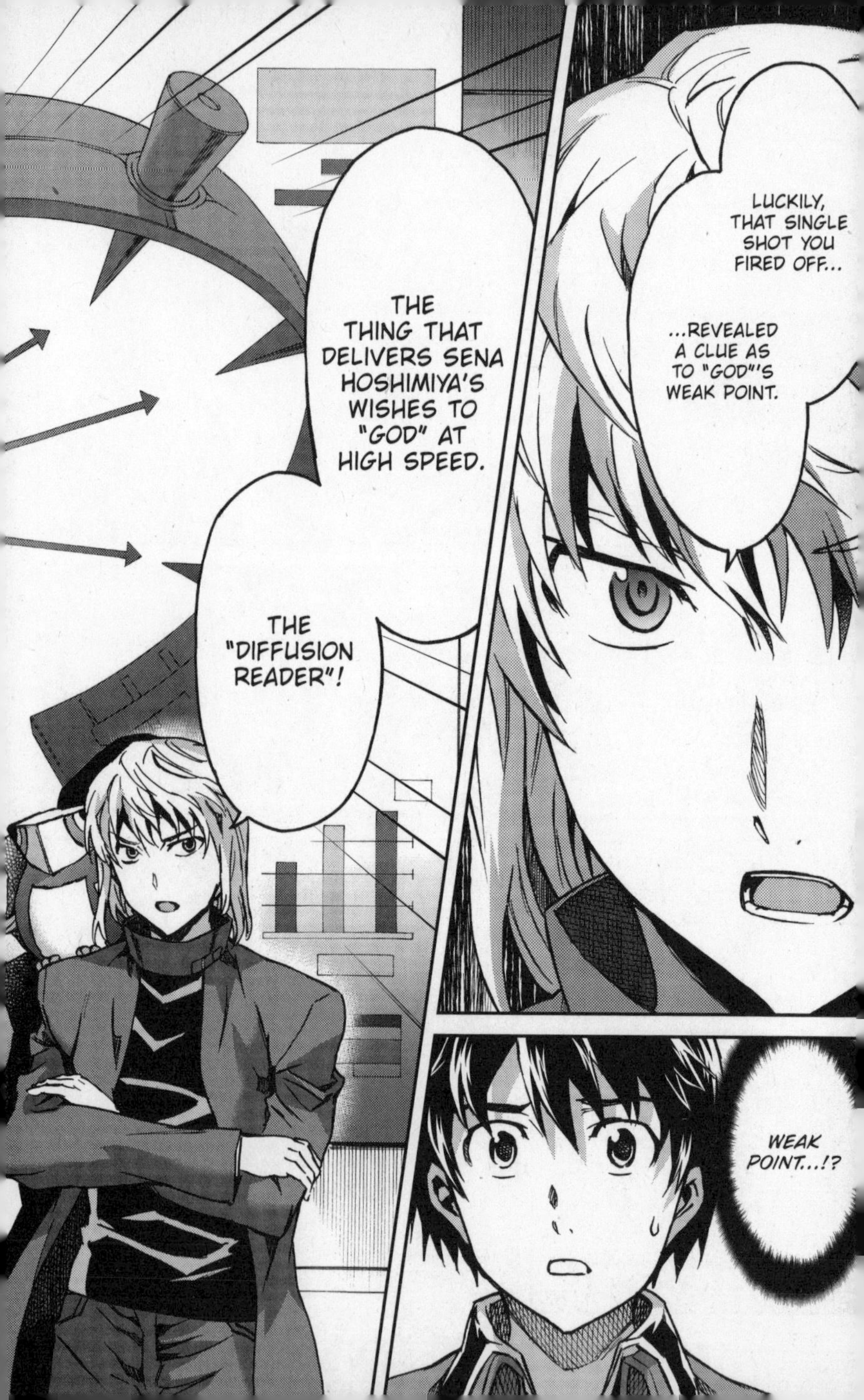
LUCKILY, THAT SINGLE SHOT YOU FIRED OFF...
...REVEALED A CLUE AS TO "GOD"'S WEAK POINT.
WEAK POINT...!?
THE THING THAT DELIVERS SENA HOSHIMIYA'S WISHES TO "GOD" AT HIGH SPEED.
THE "DIFFUSION READER"!

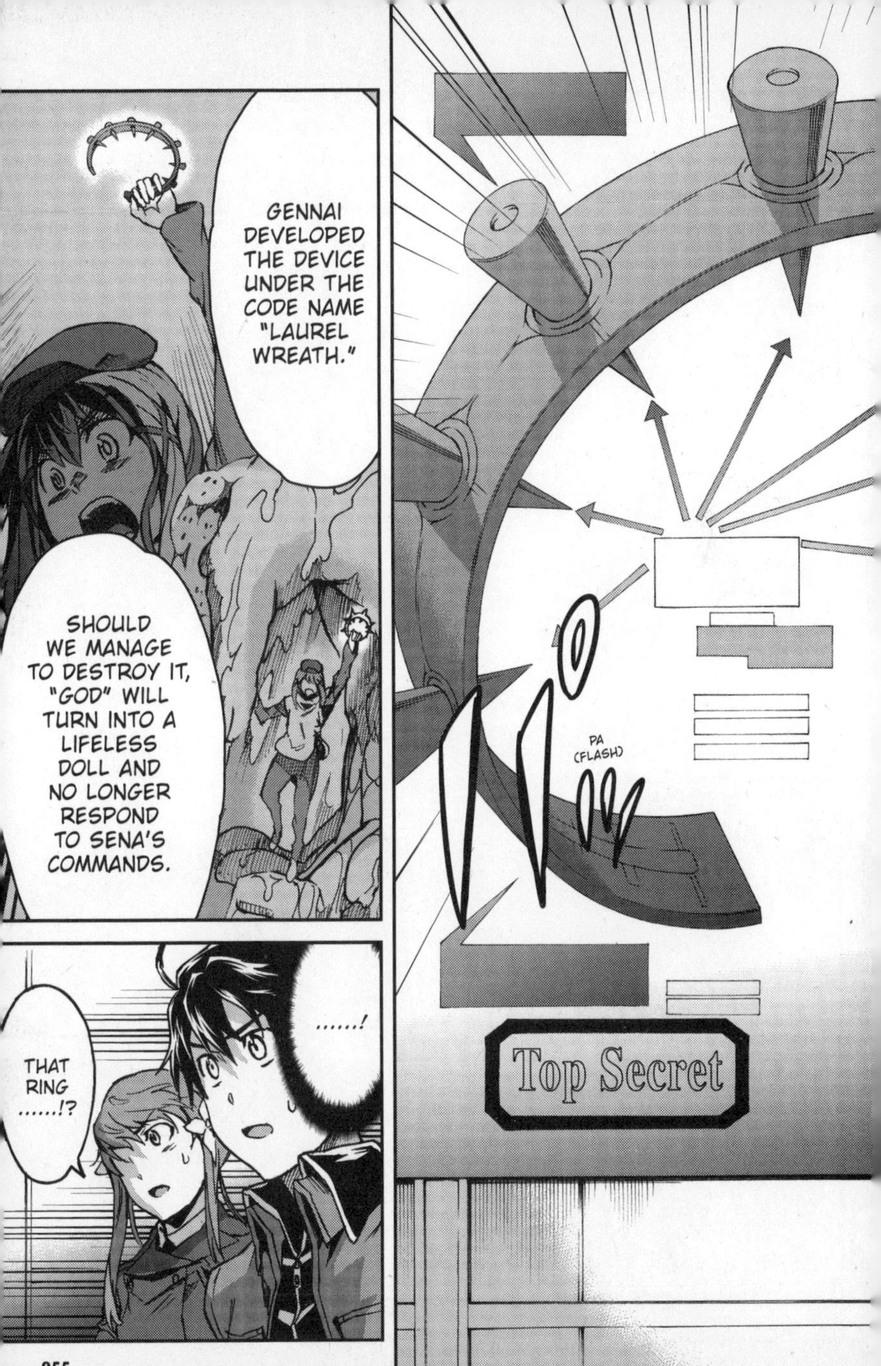
PA (FLASH)
Top Secret
GENNAI DEVELOPED THE DEVICE UNDER THE CODE NAME "LAUREL WREATH."
SHOULD WE MANAGE TO DESTROY IT, "GOD" WILL TURN INTO A LIFELESS DOLL AND NO LONGER RESPOND TO SENA'S COMMANDS.
......!
THAT RING ......!?

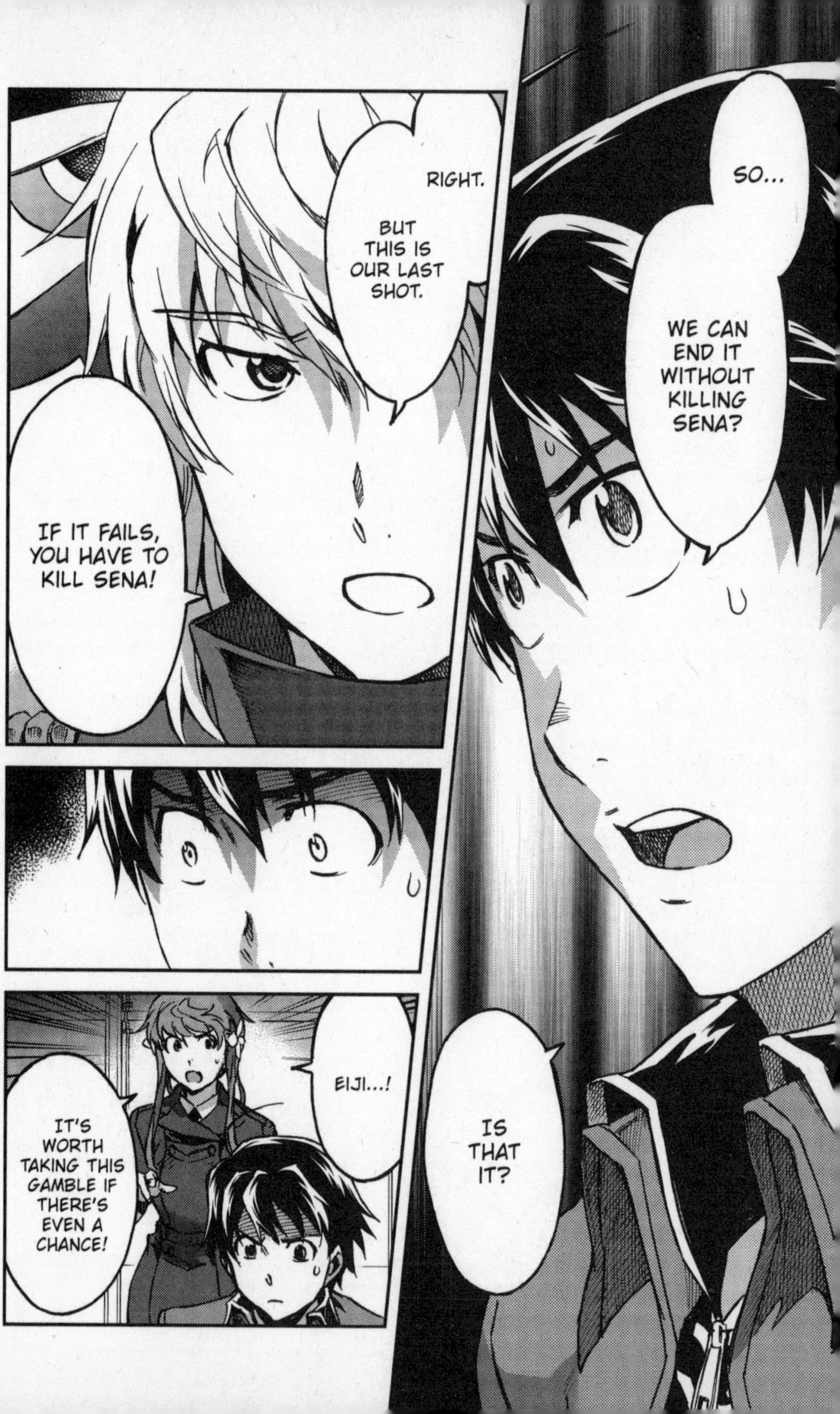
SO...
WE CAN END IT WITHOUT KILLING SENA?
IS THAT IT?
RIGHT.
BUT THIS IS OUR LAST SHOT.
IF IT FAILS, YOU HAVE TO KILL SENA!
EIJI...!
IT'S WORTH TAKING THIS GAMBLE IF THERE'S EVEN A CHANCE!

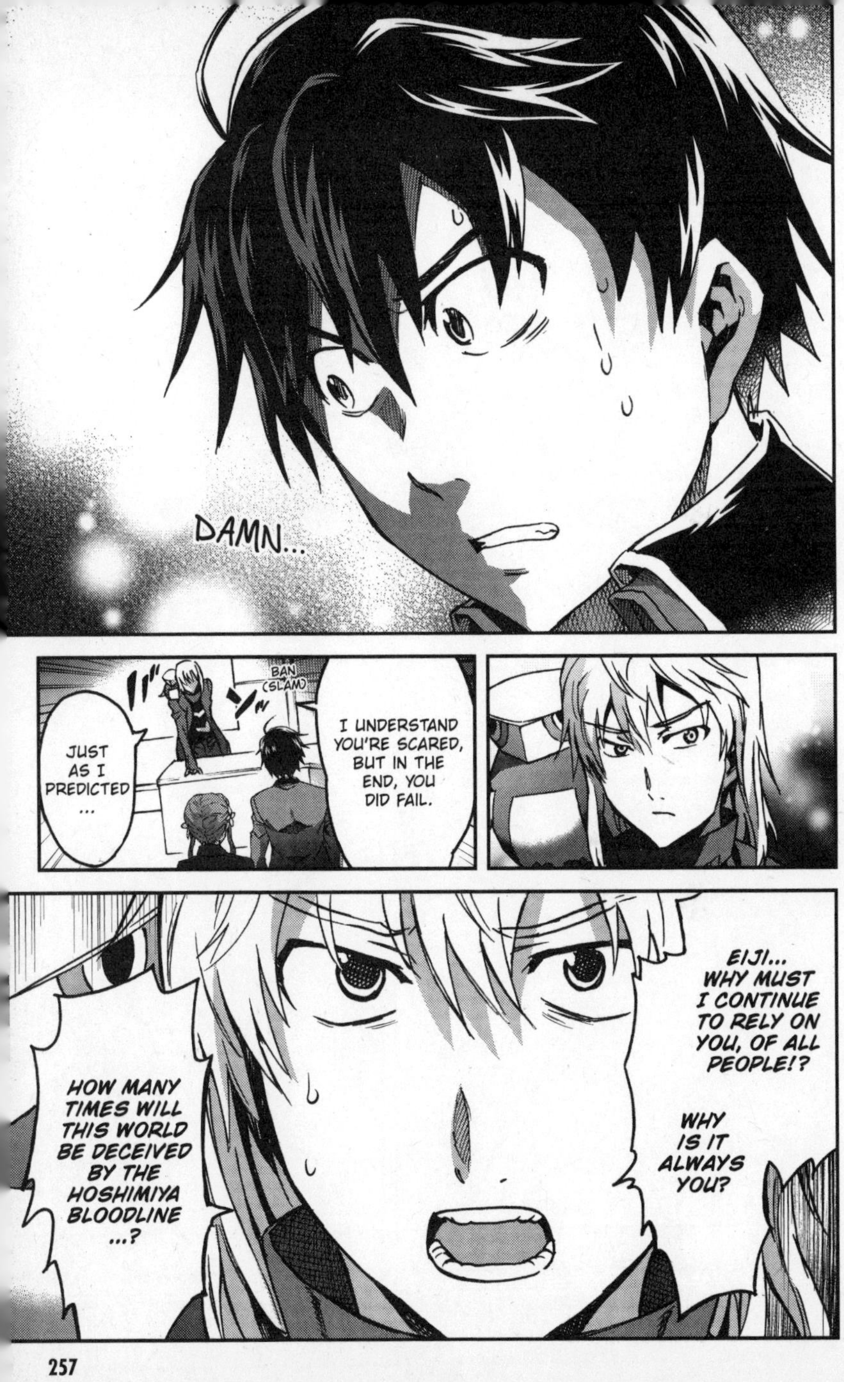
DAMN...
BAN (SLAM)
I UNDERSTAND YOU'RE SCARED, BUT IN THE END, YOU DID FAIL.
JUST AS I PREDICTED ...
EIJI... WHY MUST I CONTINUE TO RELY ON YOU, OF ALL PEOPLE!?
WHY IS IT ALWAYS YOU?
HOW MANY TIMES WILL THIS WORLD BE DECEIVED BY THE HOSHIMIYA BLOODLINE ...?

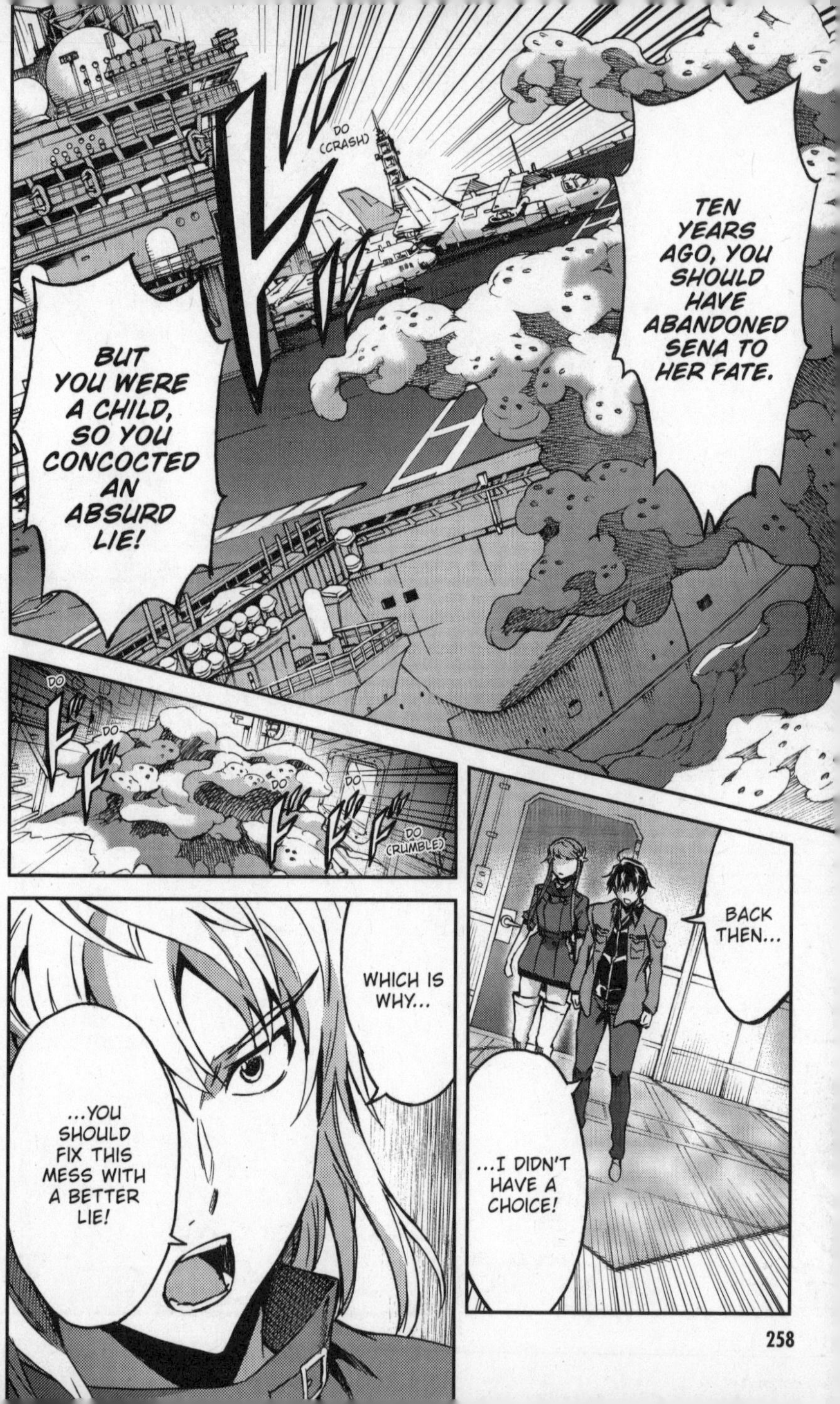
TEN YEARS AGO, YOU SHOULD HAVE ABANDONED SENA TO HER FATE.
DO (CRASH)
BUT YOU WERE A CHILD, SO YOU CONCOCTED AN ABSURD LIE!
BACK THEN...
...I DIDN'T HAVE A CHOICE!
DO
DO
DO
DO
DO (RUMBLE)
WHICH IS WHY...
...YOU SHOULD FIX THIS MESS WITH A BETTER LIE!

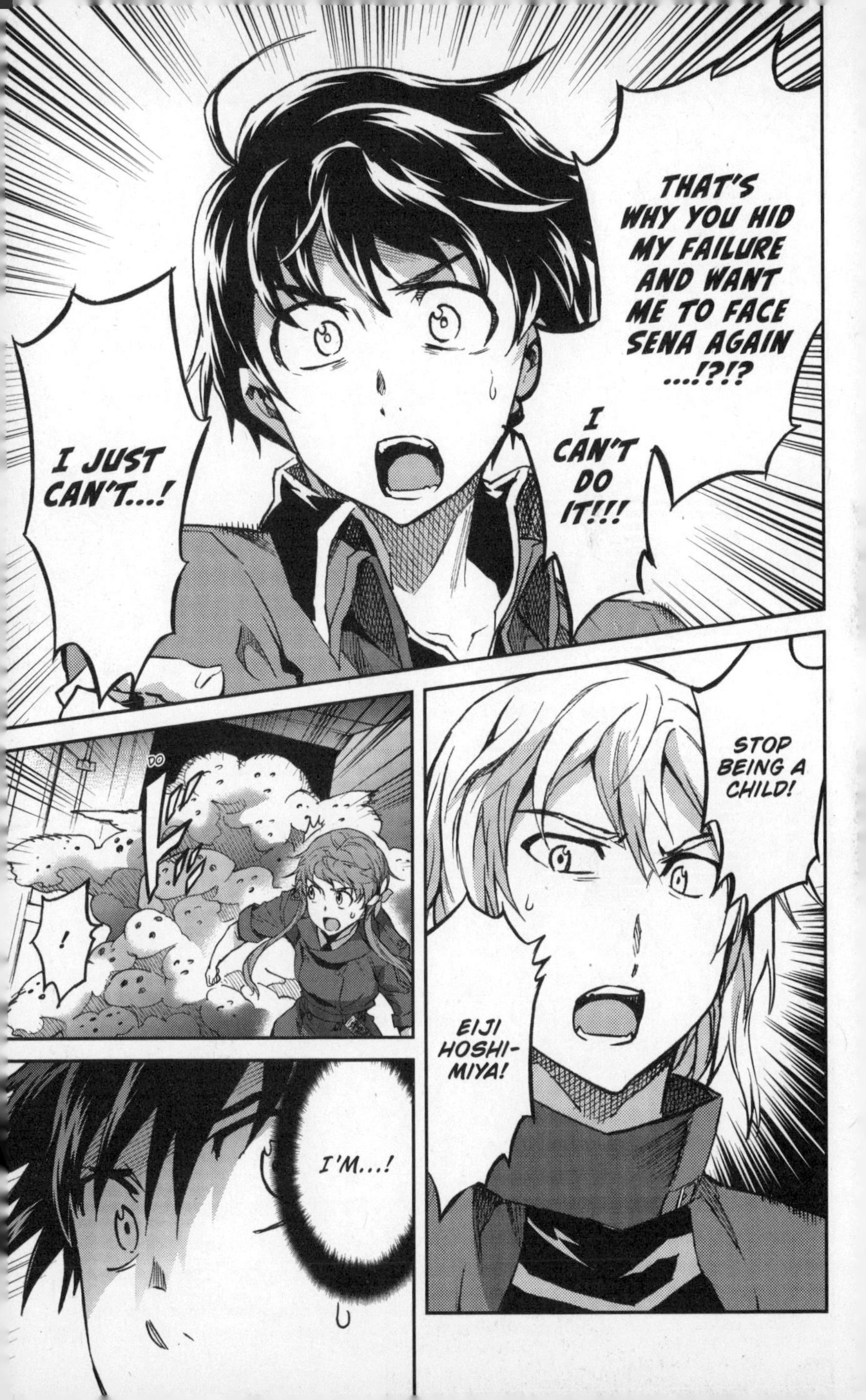
THAT'S WHY YOU HID MY FAILURE AND WANT ME TO FACE SENA AGAIN ...!?!?
I CAN'T DO IT!!!
I JUST CAN'T...!
STOP BEING A CHILD!
EIJI HOSHI-MIYA!
DO
!
I'M...!

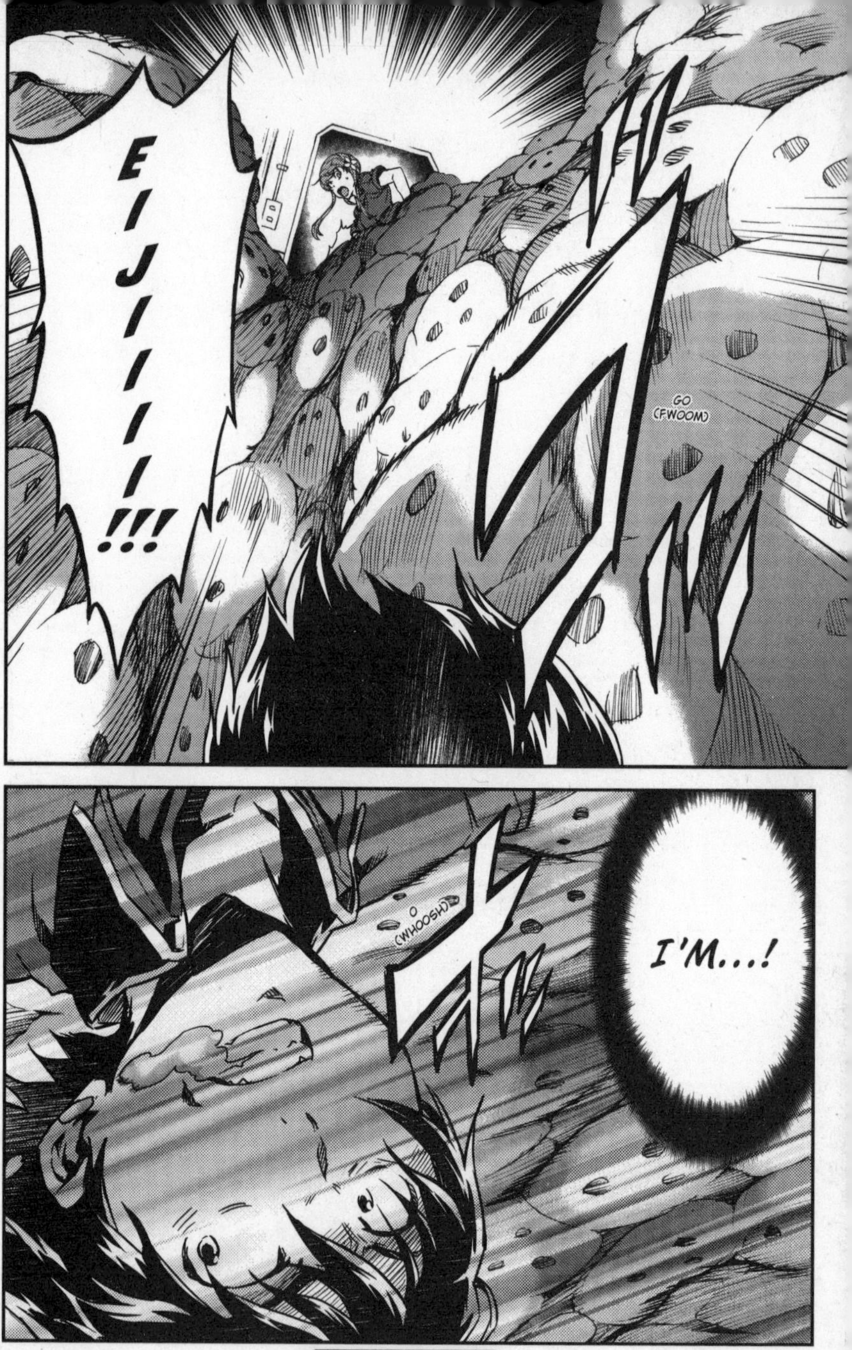
EIJIIII!!!
GO
(FWOOM)
I'M...!
O
(WHOOSH)

Subject 50: END

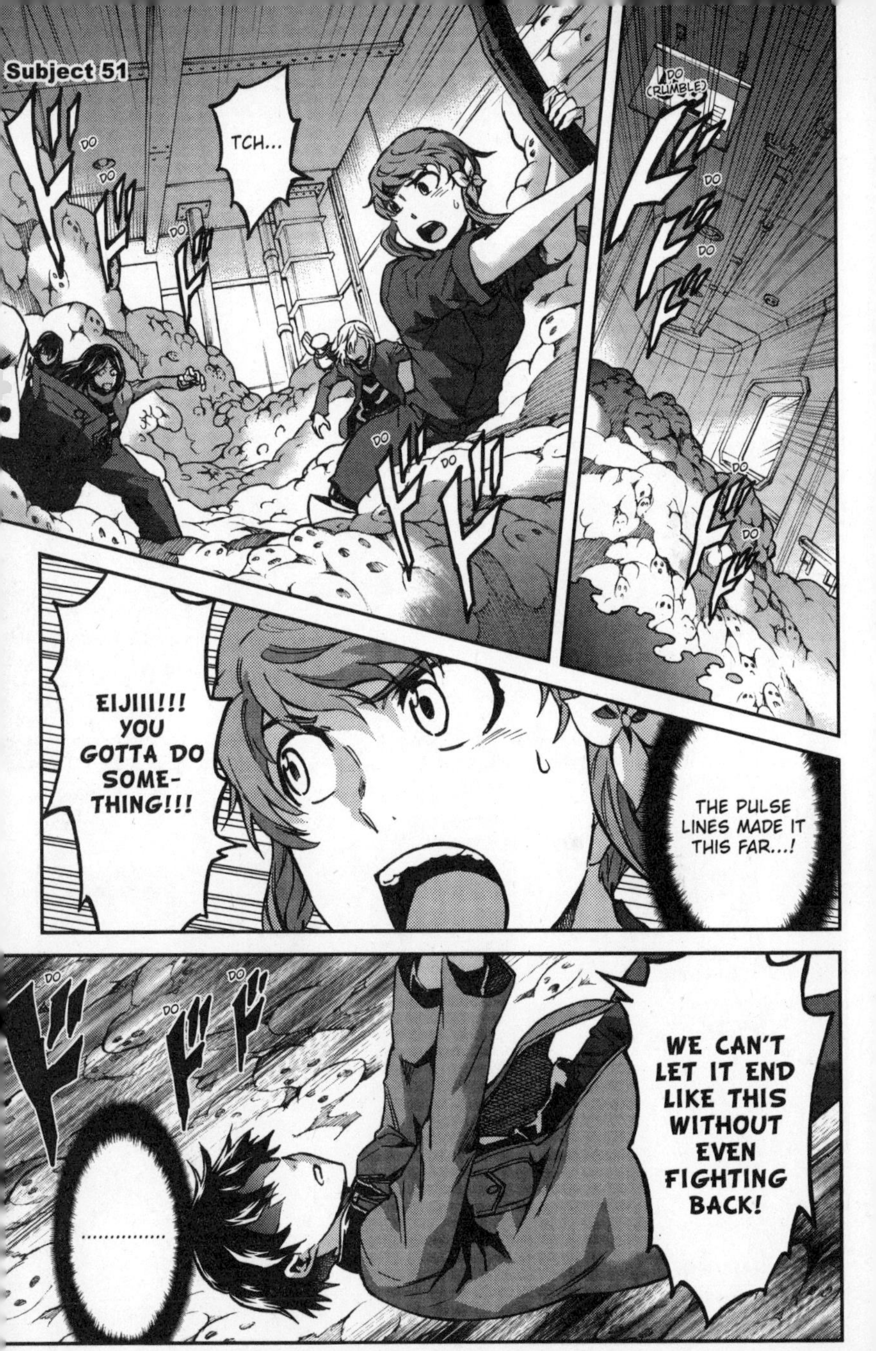
DO (RUMBLE)
DO
DO
DO
DO
TCH...
DO
DO
DO
DO
DO
THE PULSE LINES MADE IT THIS FAR...!
EIJIII!!! YOU GOTTA DO SOME-THING!!!
WE CAN'T LET IT END LIKE THIS WITHOUT EVEN FIGHTING BACK!
DO
DO
DO
....

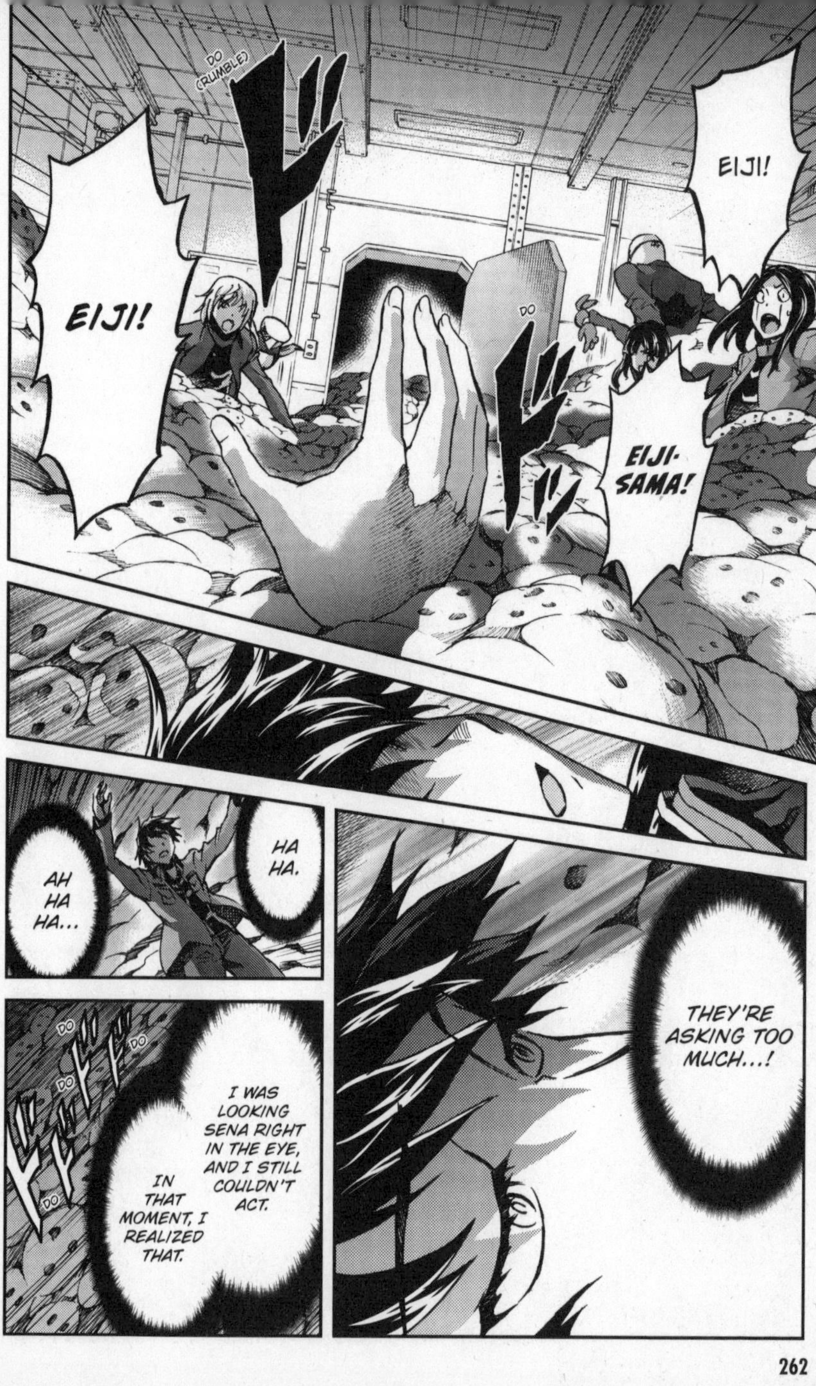
EIJI!
DO (RUMBLE)
DO
EIJI-SAMA!
EIJI!
THEY'RE ASKING TOO MUCH...!
HA HA.
AH HA HA...
I WAS LOOKING SENA RIGHT IN THE EYE, AND I STILL COULDN'T ACT.
IN THAT MOMENT, I REALIZED THAT.
DO
DO
DO
DO

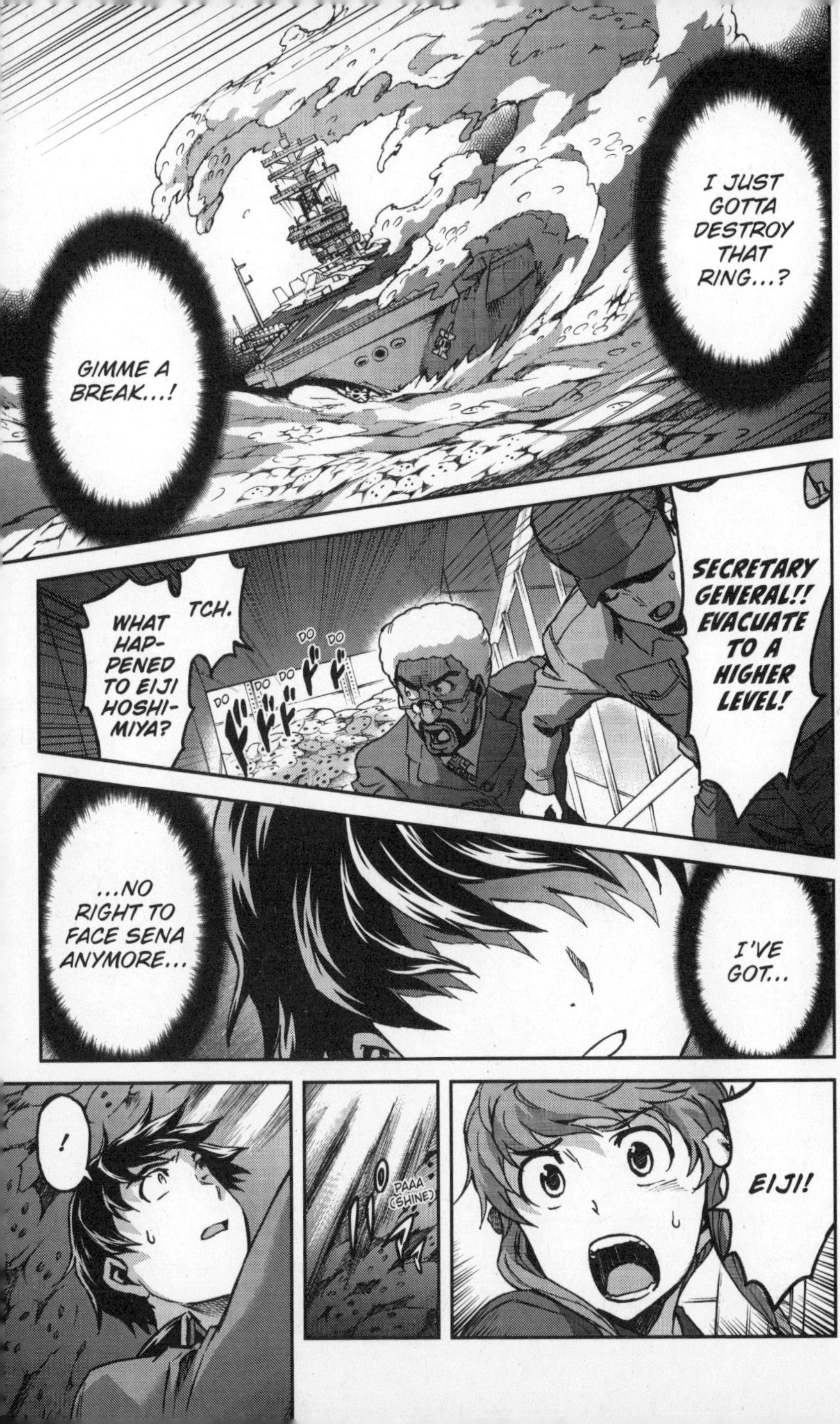
I JUST GOTTA DESTROY THAT RING...?
GIMME A BREAK...!
SECRETARY GENERAL!! EVACUATE TO A HIGHER LEVEL!
TCH.
DO DO
WHAT HAP-PENED TO EIJI HOSHI-MIYA?
DO DO DO
I'VE GOT...
...NO RIGHT TO FACE SENA ANYMORE...
EIJI!
PAAA (SHINE)
!

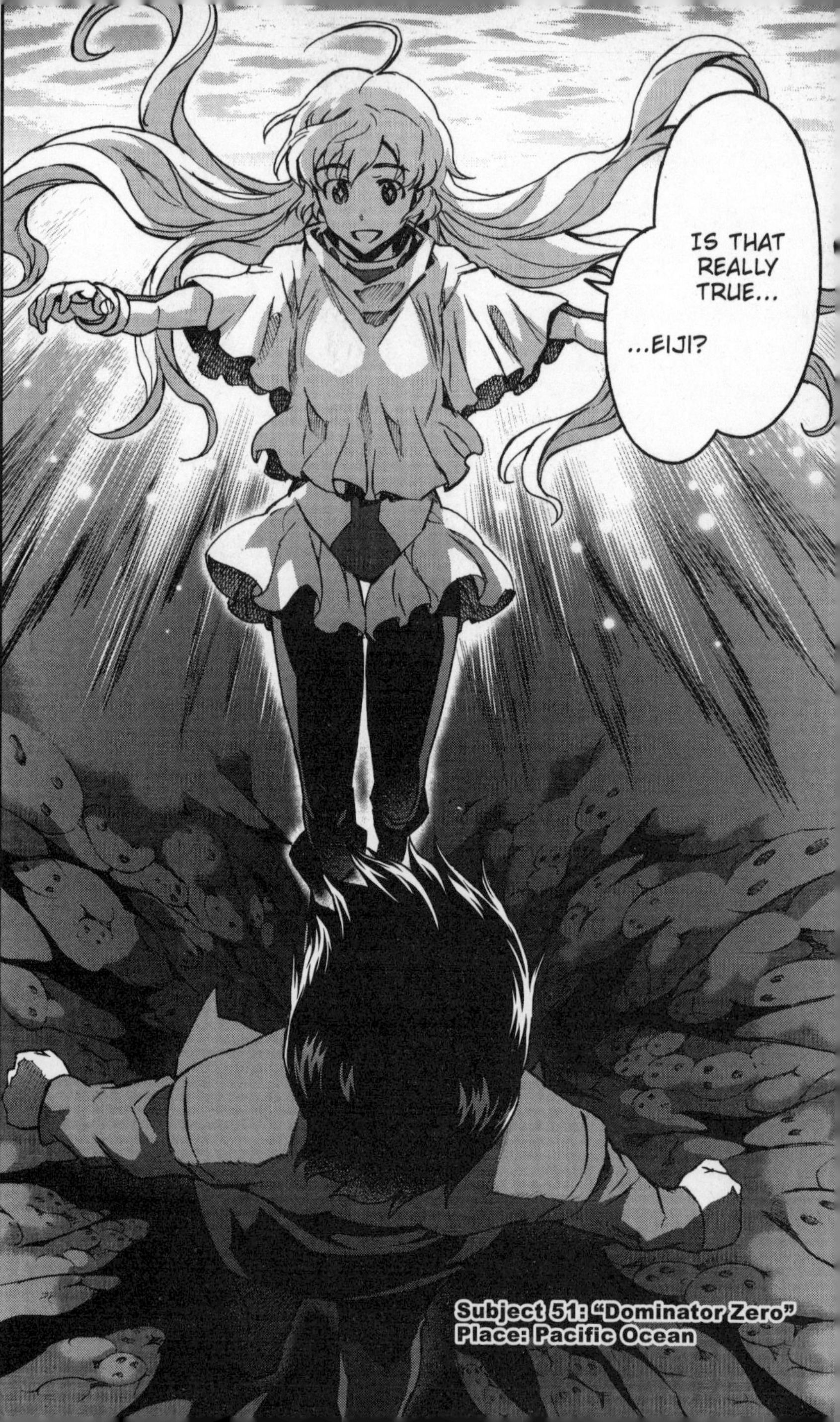
IS THAT REALLY TRUE...
...EIJI?
Subject 51: "Dominator Zero"
Place: Pacific Ocean

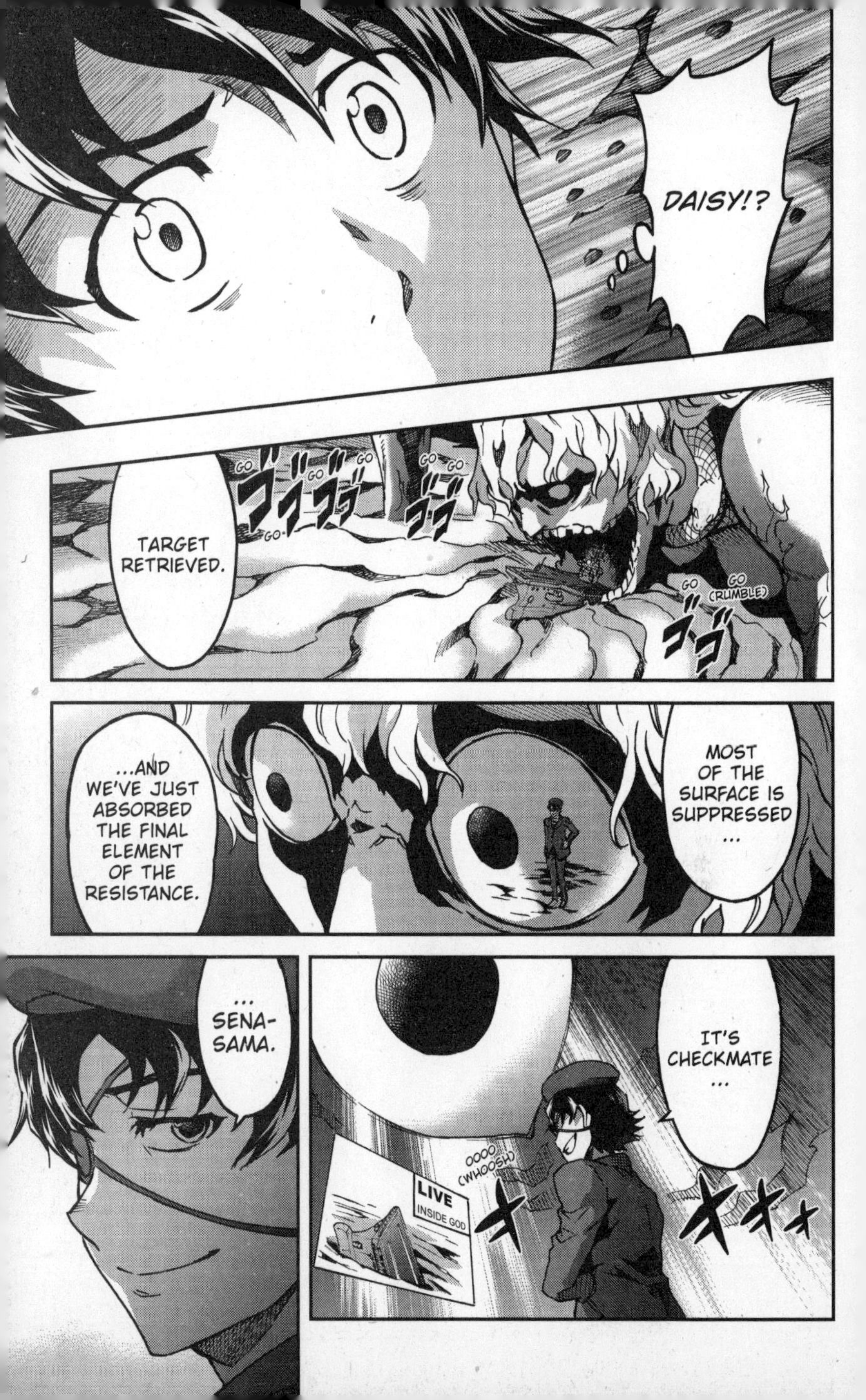
DAISY!?
GO GO (RUMBLE)
GO GO
GO GO GO GO
TARGET RETRIEVED.
MOST OF THE SURFACE IS SUPPRESSED ...
...AND WE'VE JUST ABSORBED THE FINAL ELEMENT OF THE RESISTANCE.
IT'S CHECKMATE ...
OOOO (WHOOSH)
LIVE
INSIDE GOD
... SENA-SAMA.

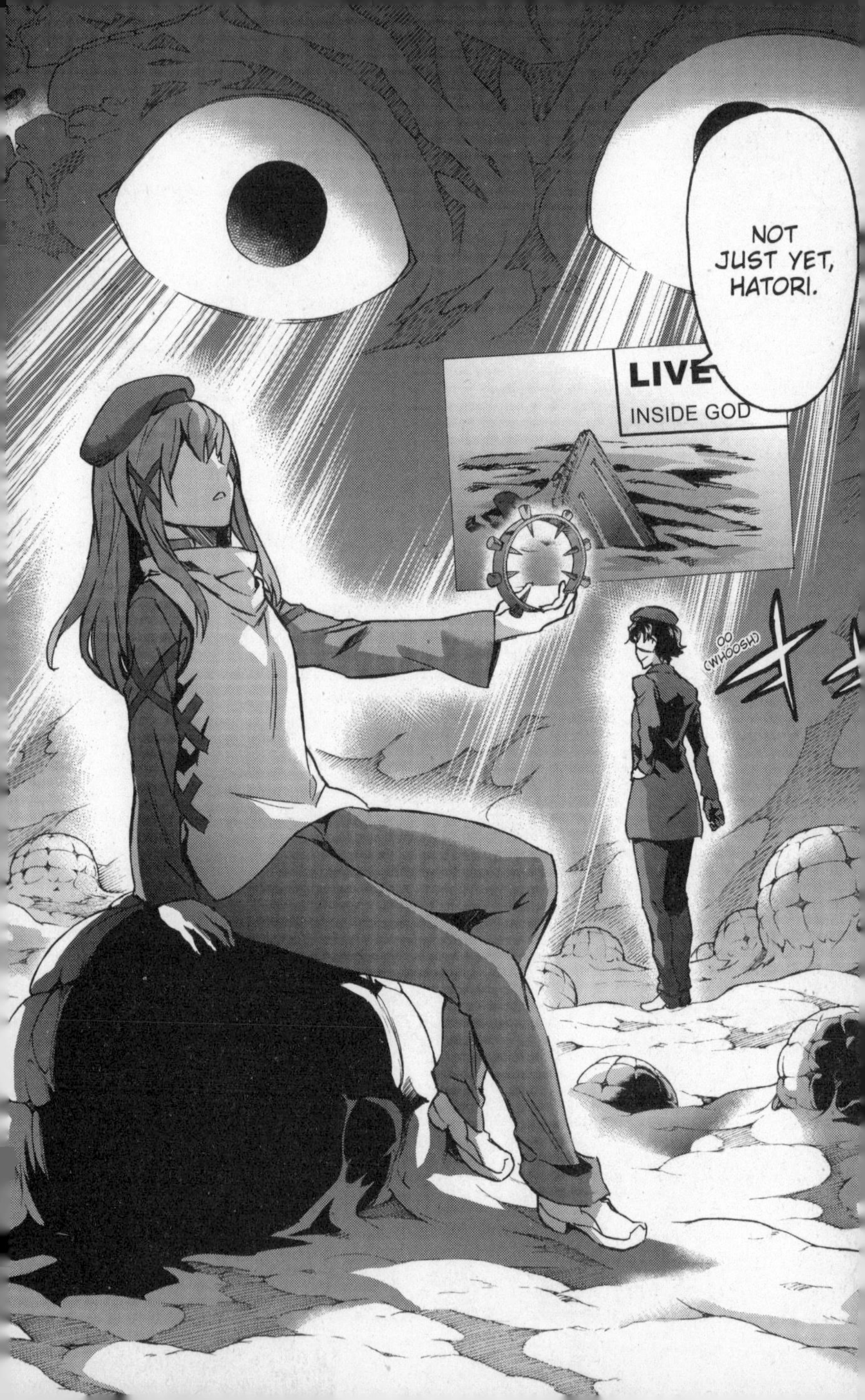
NOT JUST YET, HATORI.
LIVE
INSIDE GOD
OO (WHOOSH)

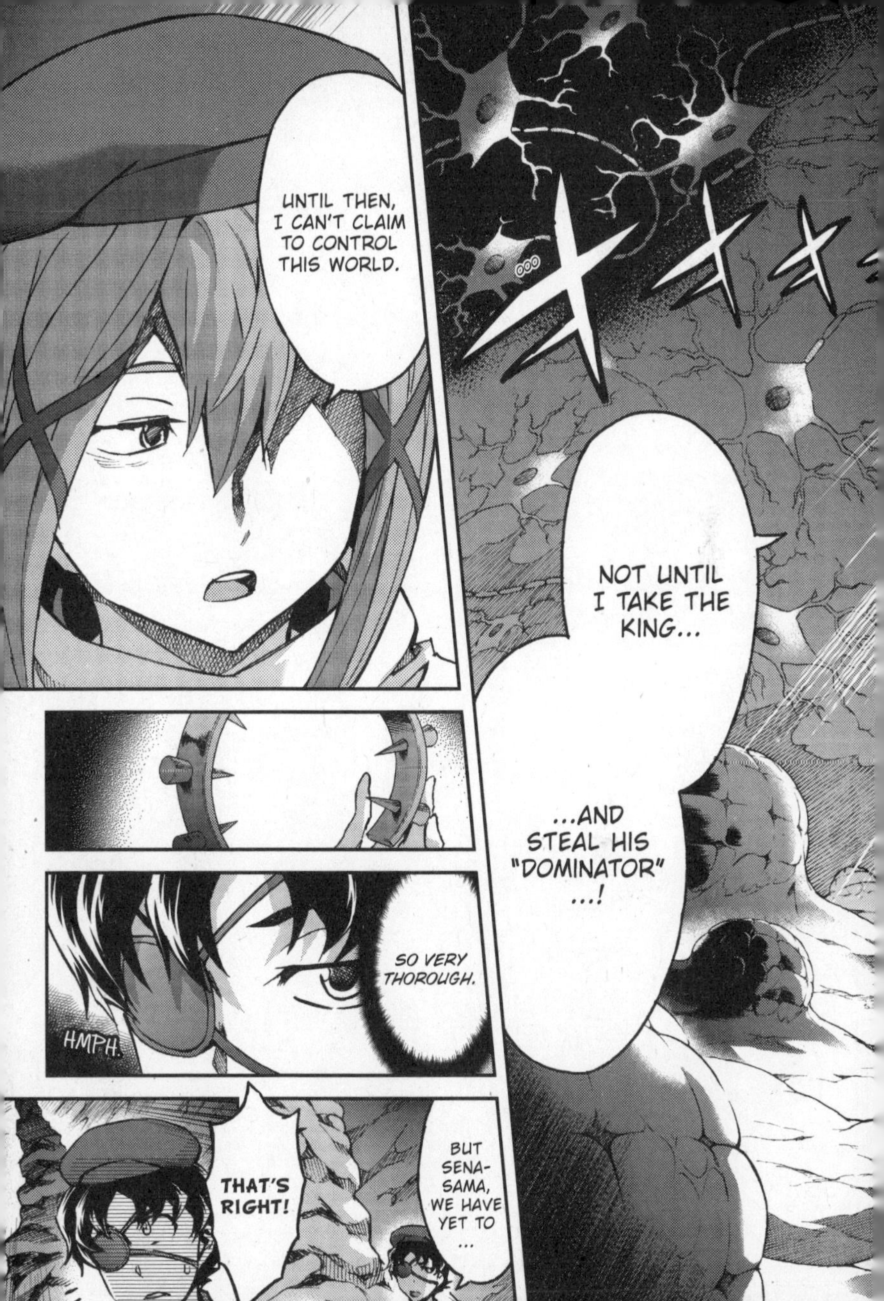
NOT UNTIL I TAKE THE KING...
...AND STEAL HIS "DOMINATOR" ...!
UNTIL THEN, I CAN'T CLAIM TO CONTROL THIS WORLD.
SO VERY THOROUGH.
HMPH.
BUT SENA-SAMA, WE HAVE YET TO ...
THAT'S RIGHT!

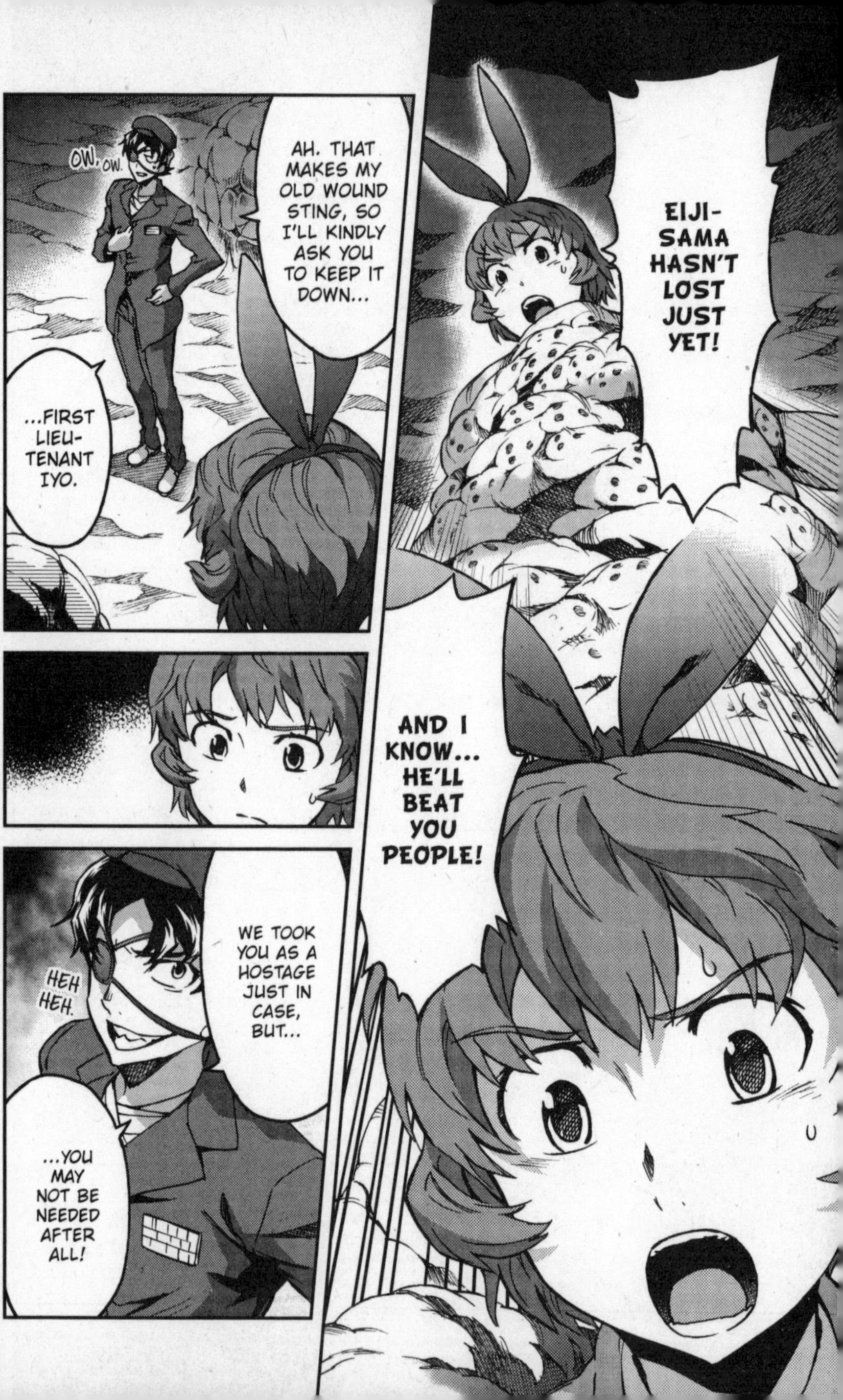
EIJI-SAMA HASN'T LOST JUST YET!
AND I KNOW... HE'LL BEAT YOU PEOPLE!
OW. OW.
AH. THAT MAKES MY OLD WOUND STING, SO I'LL KINDLY ASK YOU TO KEEP IT DOWN...
...FIRST LIEU-TENANT IYO.
WE TOOK YOU AS A HOSTAGE JUST IN CASE, BUT...
HEH HEH.
...YOU MAY NOT BE NEEDED AFTER ALL!

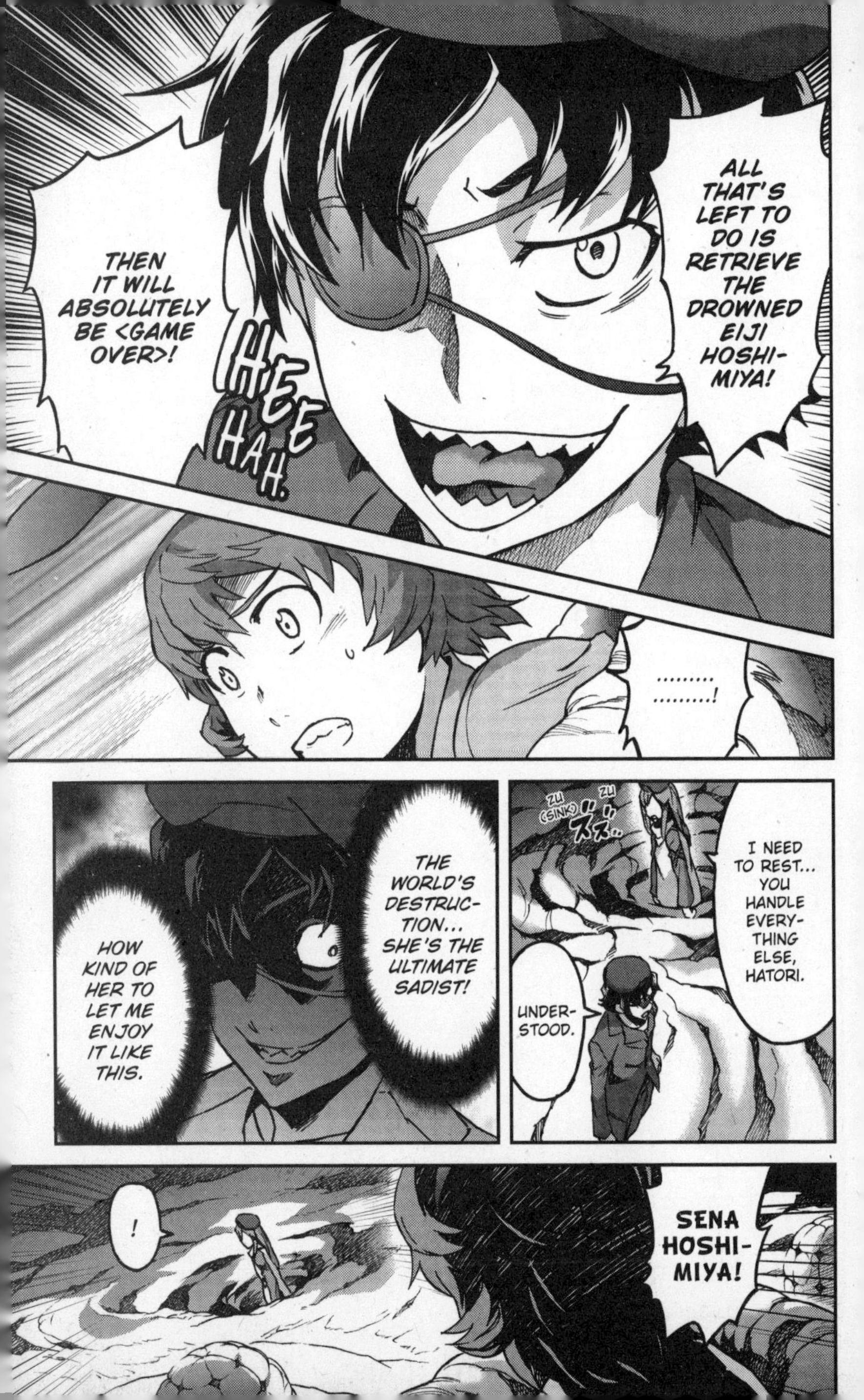
ALL THAT'S LEFT TO DO IS RETRIEVE THE DROWNED EIJI HOSHI-MIYA!
THEN IT WILL ABSOLUTELY BE <GAME OVER>!
HEE HAH.
....
.........!
ZU (SINK) ZU
I NEED TO REST... YOU HANDLE EVERY-THING ELSE, HATORI.
UNDER-STOOD.
THE WORLD'S DESTRUC-TION... SHE'S THE ULTIMATE SADIST!
HOW KIND OF HER TO LET ME ENJOY IT LIKE THIS.
SENA HOSHI-MIYA!
!

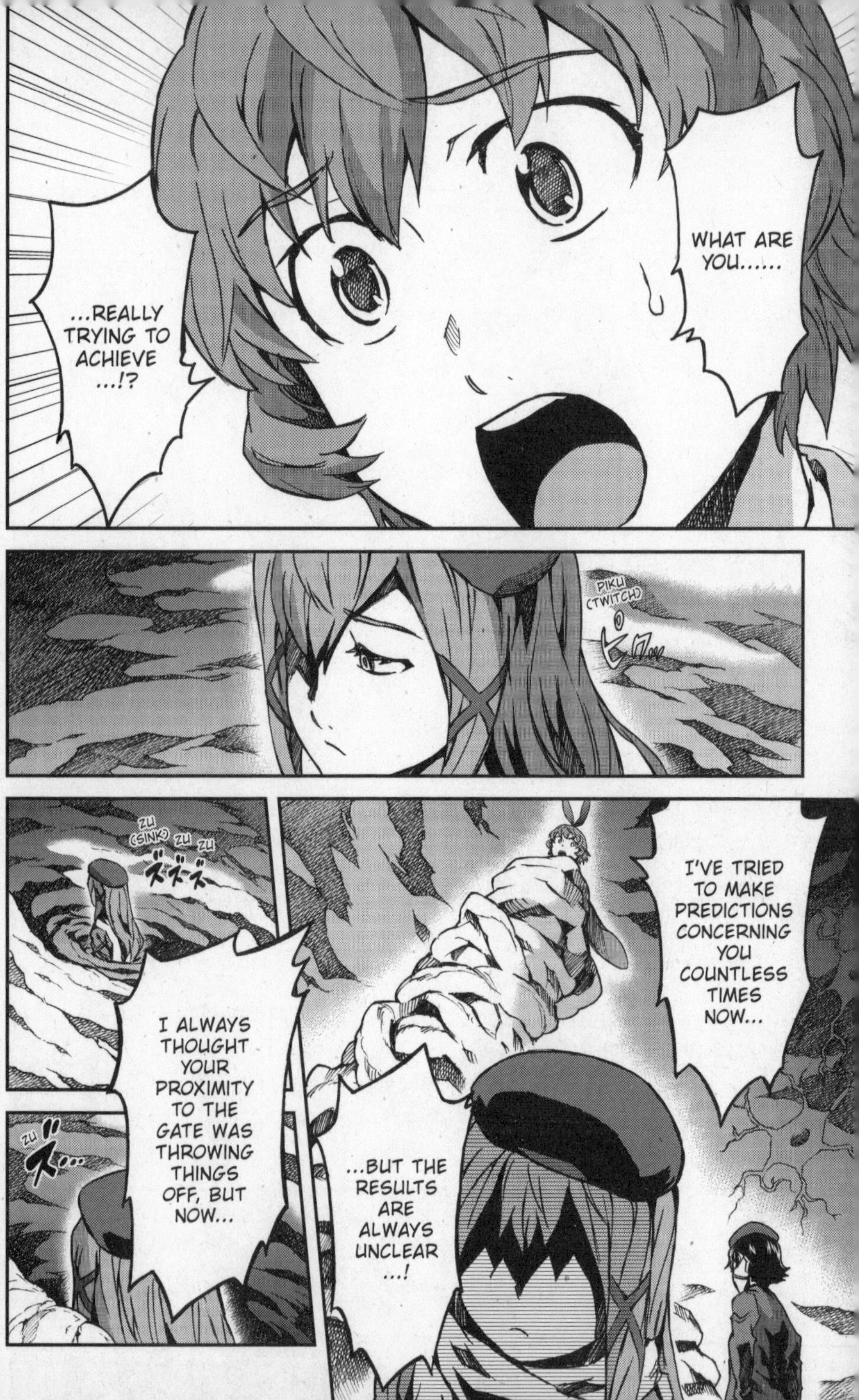
WHAT ARE YOU......
...REALLY TRYING TO ACHIEVE ...!?
PIKU (TWITCH)
I'VE TRIED TO MAKE PREDICTIONS CONCERNING YOU COUNTLESS TIMES NOW...
...BUT THE RESULTS ARE ALWAYS UNCLEAR ...!
I ALWAYS THOUGHT YOUR PROXIMITY TO THE GATE WAS THROWING THINGS OFF, BUT NOW...
ZU (SINK) ZU ZU
ZU

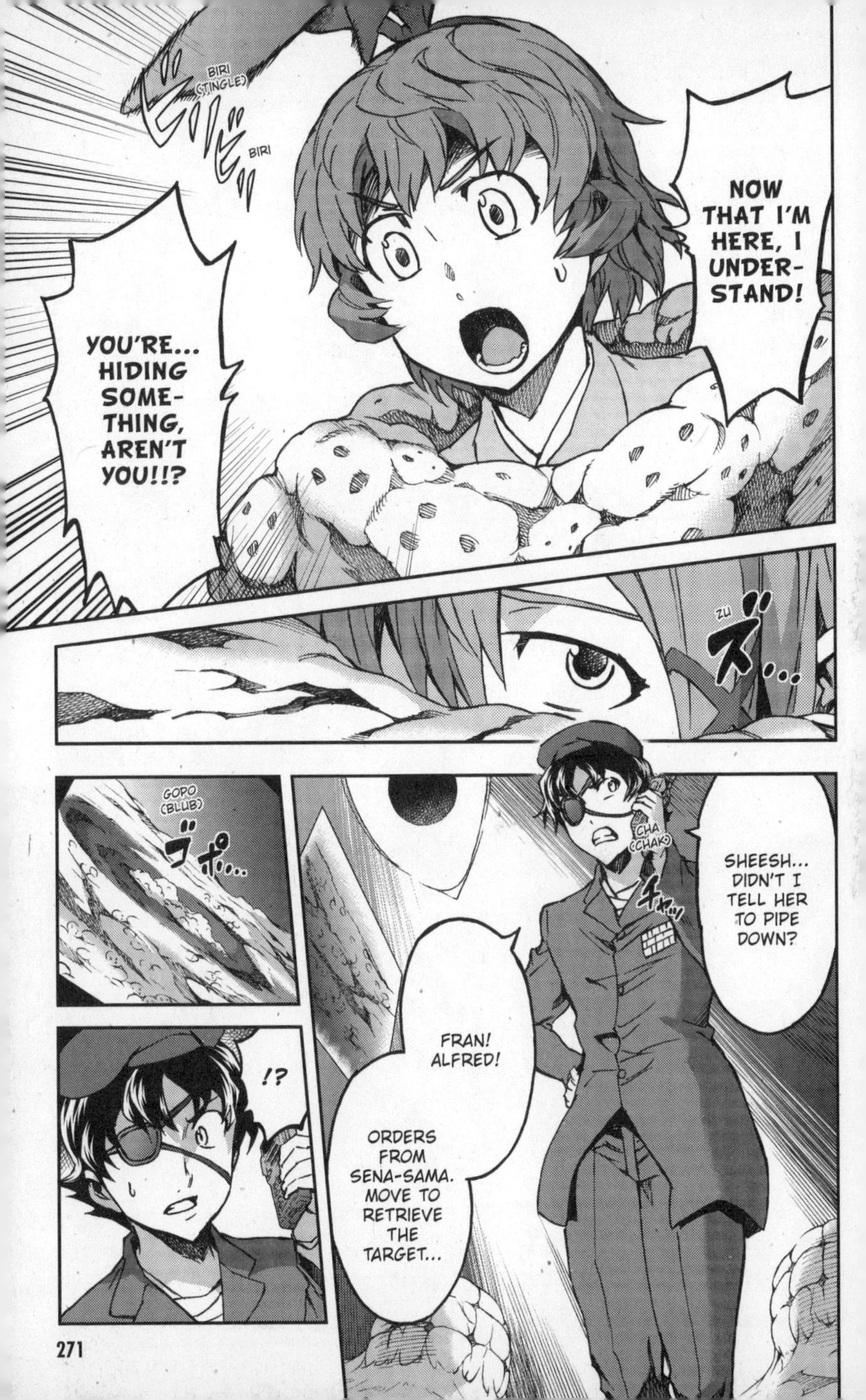
NOW THAT I'M HERE, I UNDERSTAND!
BIRI (TINGLE)
BIRI
YOU'RE... HIDING SOMETHING, AREN'T YOU!!?
ZU
CHA (CHAK)
SHEESH... DIDN'T I TELL HER TO PIPE DOWN?
FRAN! ALFRED!
ORDERS FROM SENA-SAMA. MOVE TO RETRIEVE THE TARGET...
GOPO (BLUB)
!?

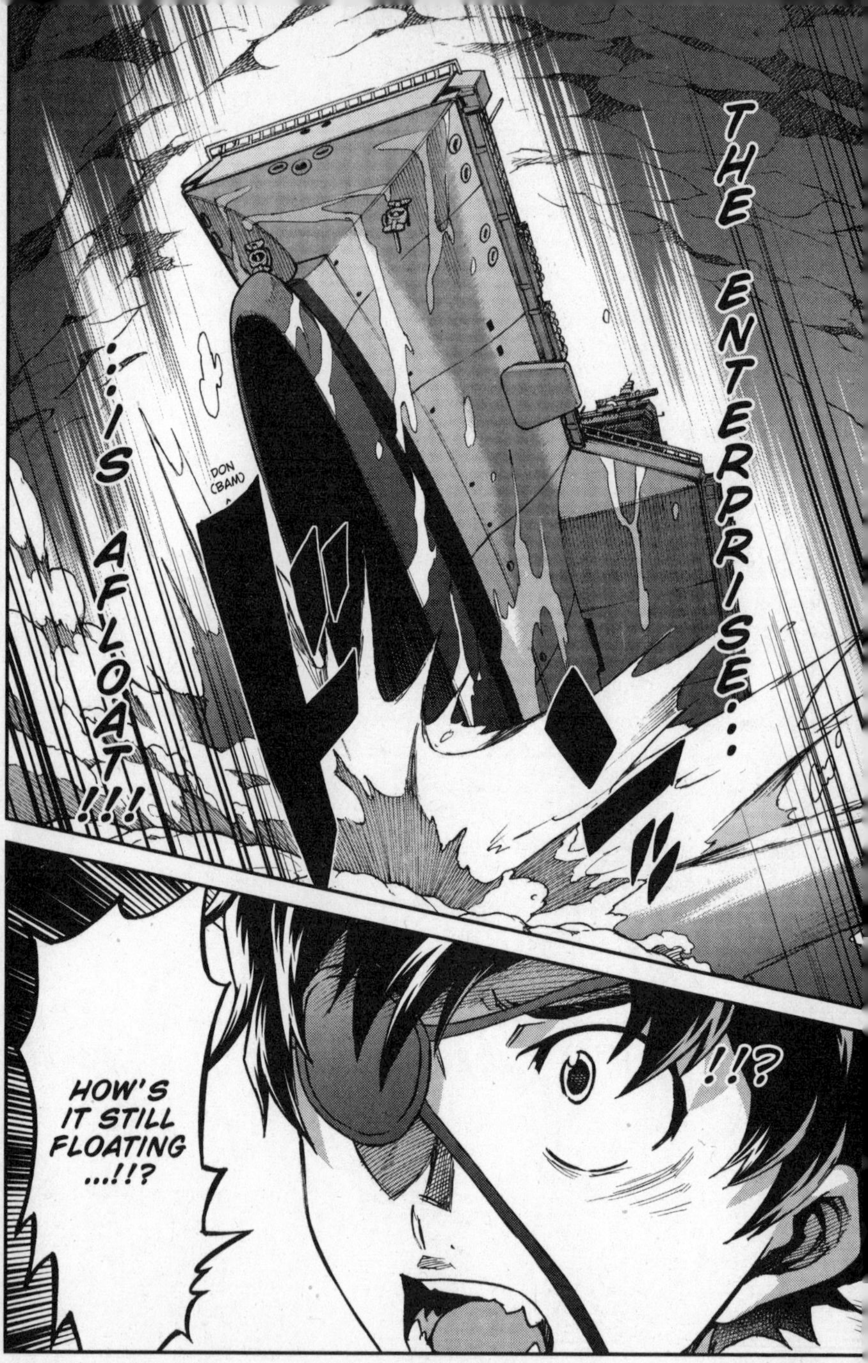
THE ENTERPRISE...
...IS AFLOAT!!!
DON (BAM)
!!?
HOW'S IT STILL FLOATING ...!!?

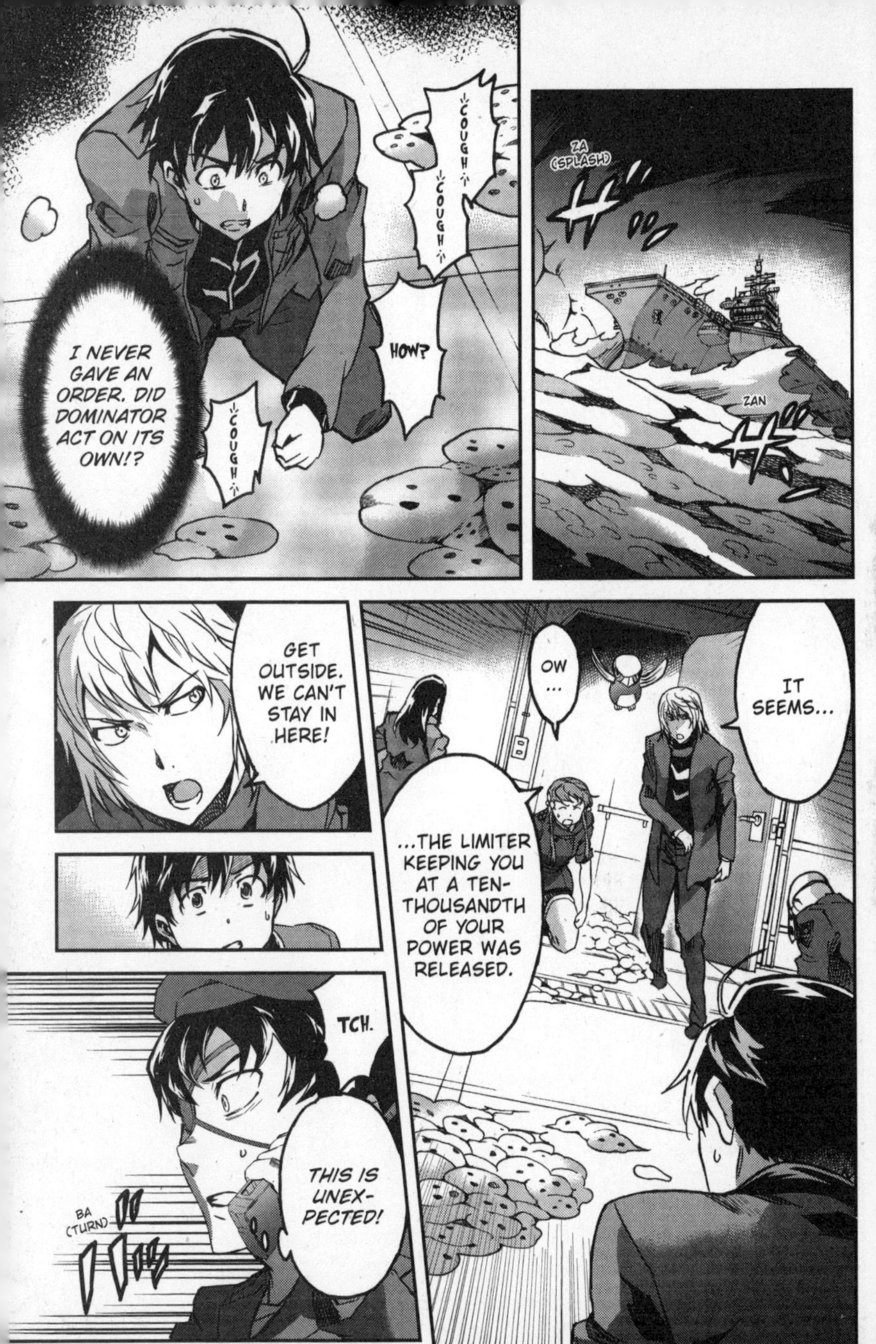
ZA (SPLASH)
ZAN
COUGH COUGH
COUGH
HOW?
COUGH
I NEVER GAVE AN ORDER. DID DOMINATOR ACT ON ITS OWN!?
IT SEEMS...
OW...
...THE LIMITER KEEPING YOU AT A TEN-THOUSANDTH OF YOUR POWER WAS RELEASED.
GET OUTSIDE. WE CAN'T STAY IN HERE!
TCH.
THIS IS UNEXPECTED!
BA (TURN)

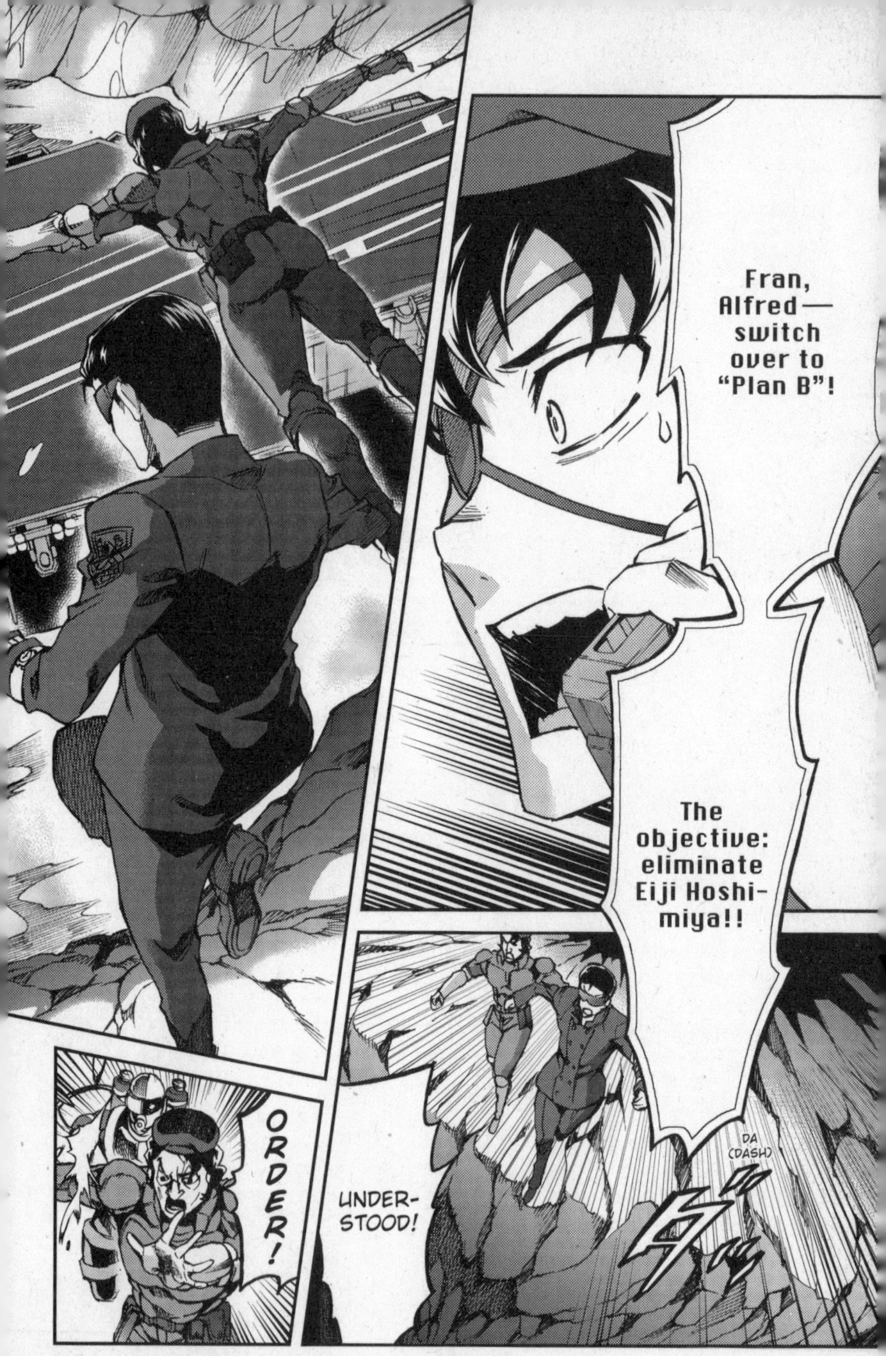
Fran, Alfred—switch over to "Plan B"!
The objective: eliminate Eiji Hoshi-miya!!
DA (DASH)
UNDER-STOOD!
ORDER!

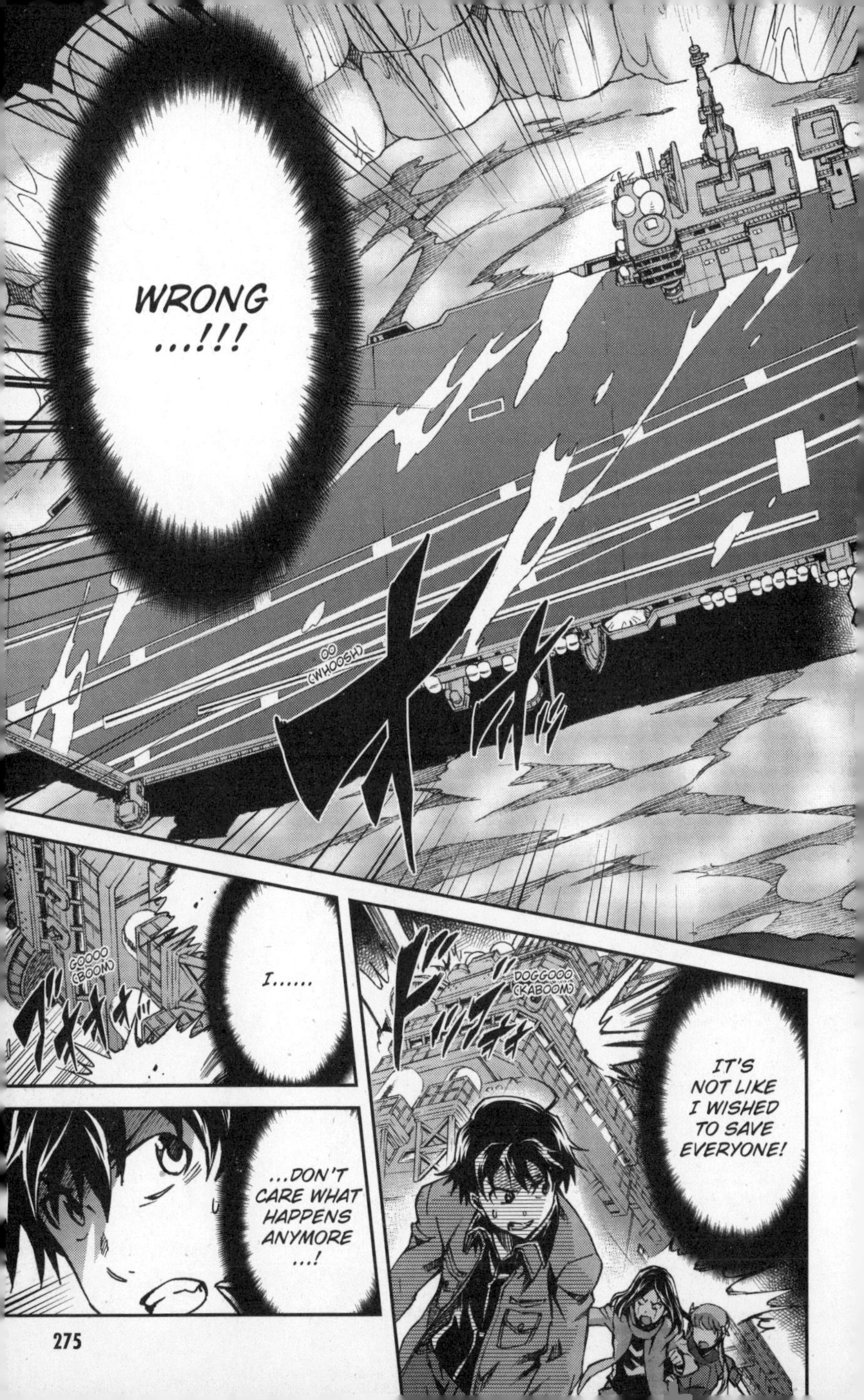
WRONG ...!!!
OO (WHOOSH)
DOGGOOO (KABOOM)
IT'S NOT LIKE I WISHED TO SAVE EVERYONE!
GOOOO (BOOM)
I......
...DON'T CARE WHAT HAPPENS ANYMORE ...!

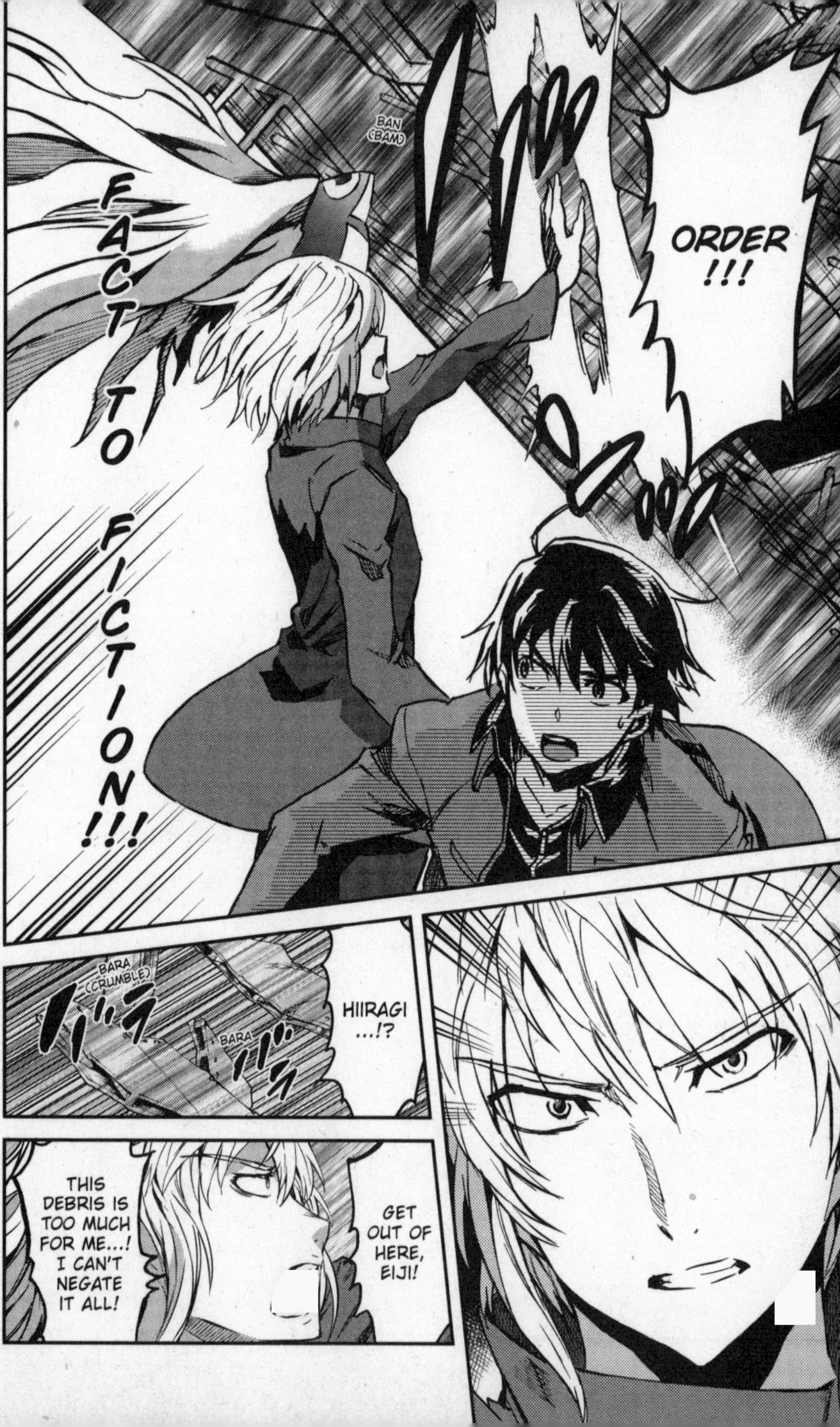
ORDER!!!
BAN (BAM)
FACT TO FICTION!!!
HIIRAGI ...!?
BARA (CRUMBLE)
BARA
GET OUT OF HERE, EIJI!
THIS DEBRIS IS TOO MUCH FOR ME...! I CAN'T NEGATE IT ALL!

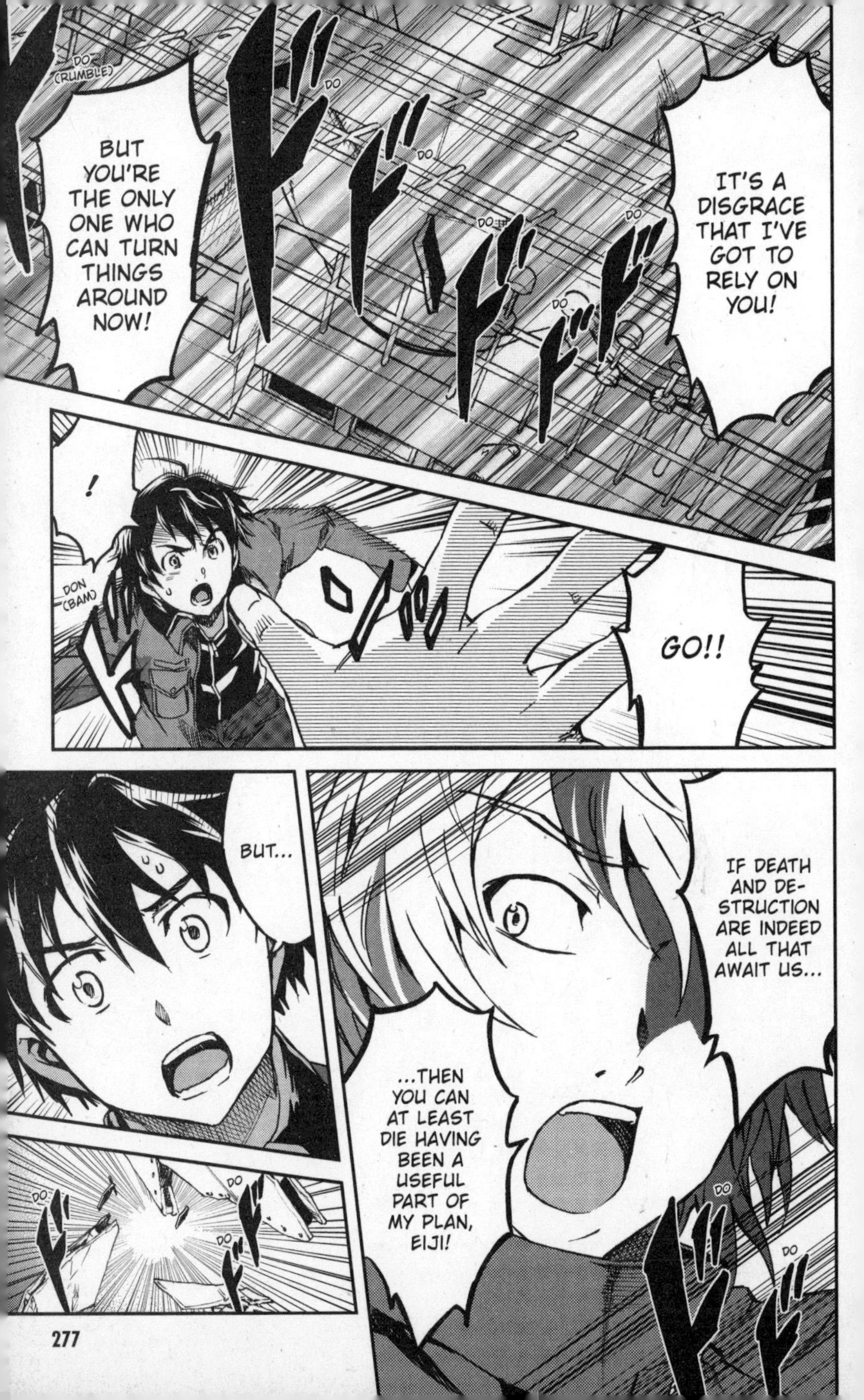
DO (RUMBLE)
DO
DO
DO
DO
DO
IT'S A DISGRACE THAT I'VE GOT TO RELY ON YOU!
BUT YOU'RE THE ONLY ONE WHO CAN TURN THINGS AROUND NOW!
GO!!
DON (BAM)
!
BUT...
IF DEATH AND DE-STRUCTION ARE INDEED ALL THAT AWAIT US...
...THEN YOU CAN AT LEAST DIE HAVING BEEN A USEFUL PART OF MY PLAN, EIJI!
DO
DO
DO
DO
DO

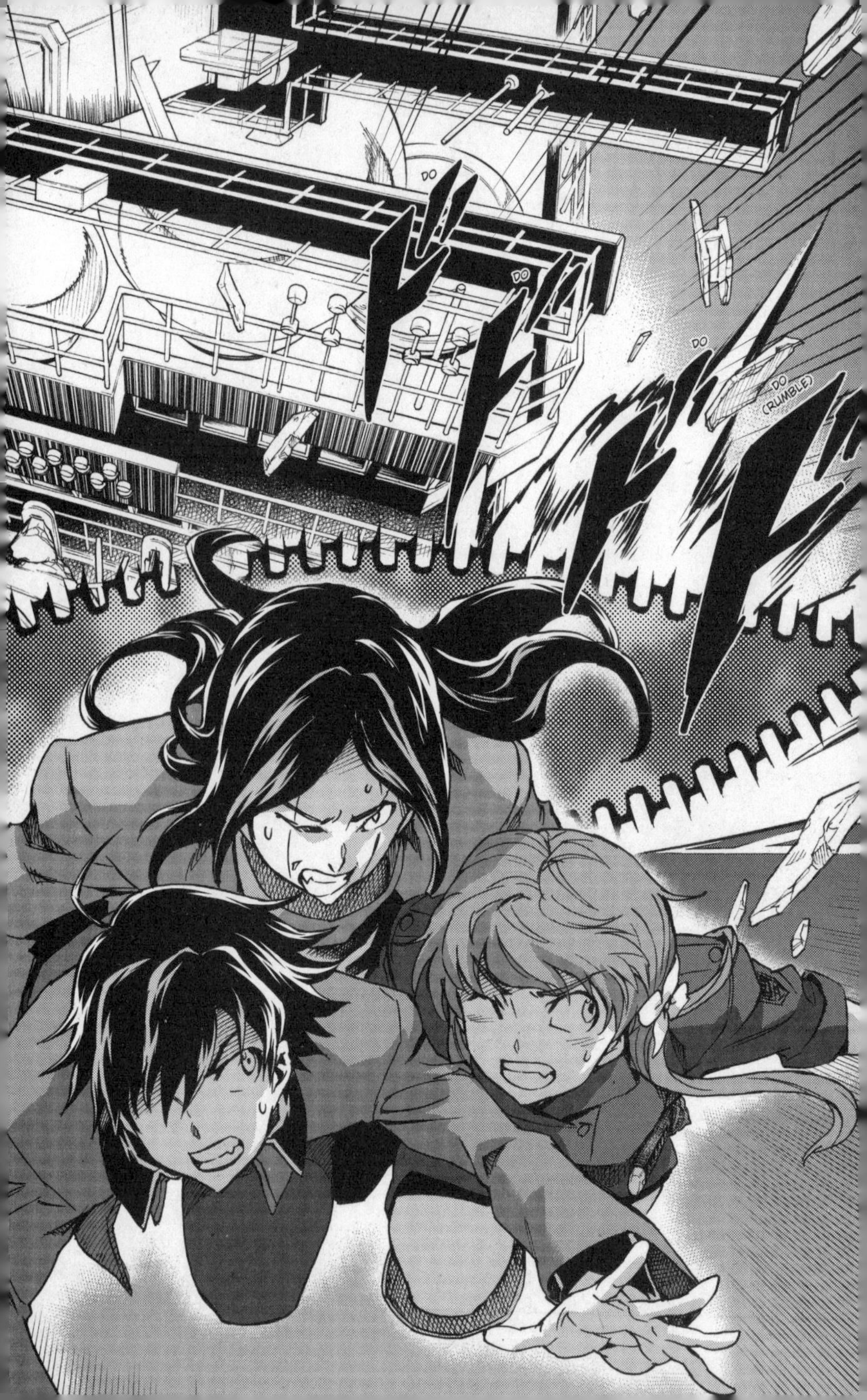
DO
DO
DO
DO
(RUMBLE)

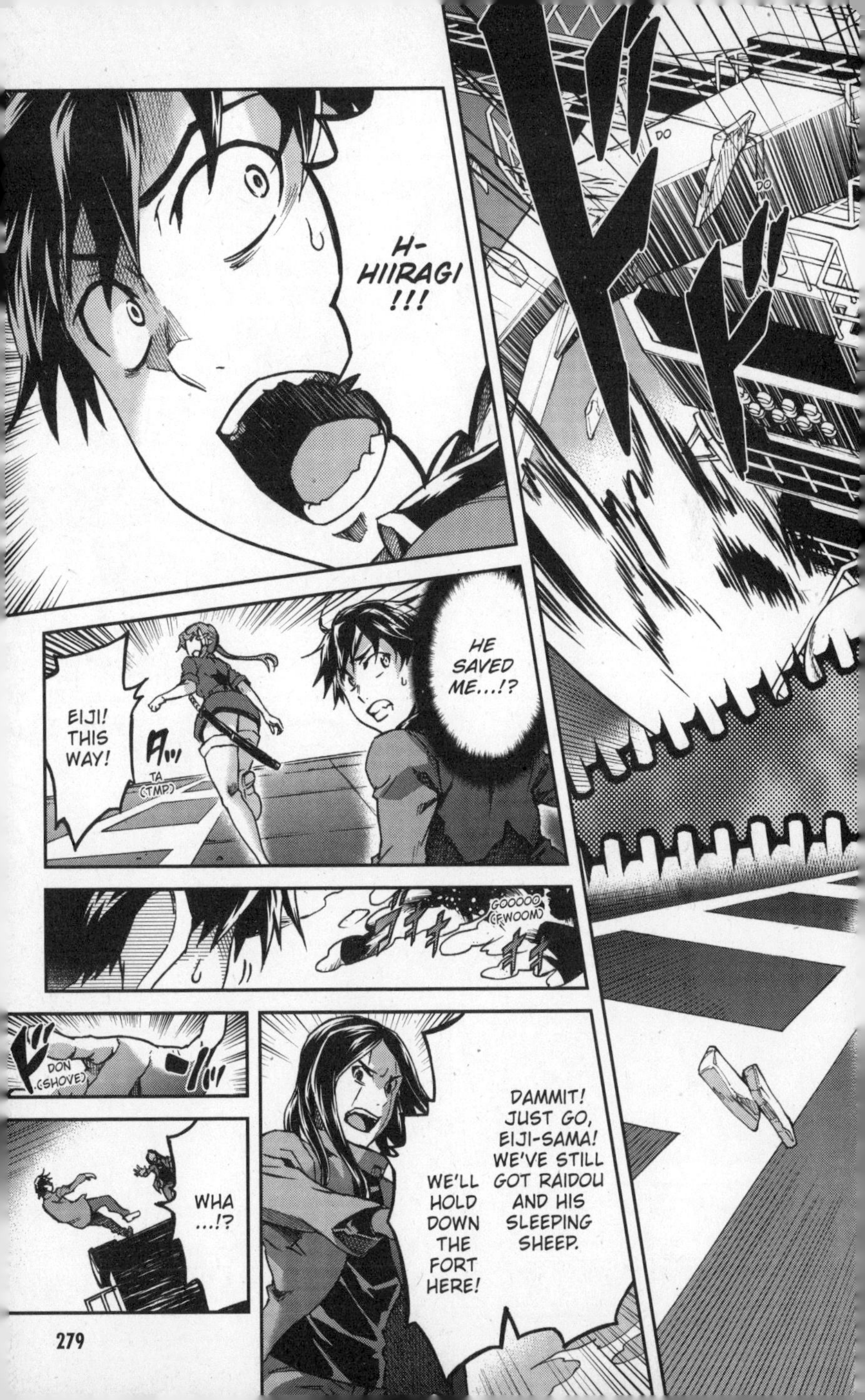
DO
DO
H-HIIRAGI!!!
HE SAVED ME...!?
EIJI! THIS WAY!
TA (TMP)
GOOOOO (FWOOM)
DAMMIT! JUST GO, EIJI-SAMA! WE'VE STILL GOT RAIDOU AND HIS SLEEPING SHEEP.
WE'LL HOLD DOWN THE FORT HERE!
DON (SHOVE)
WHA...!?

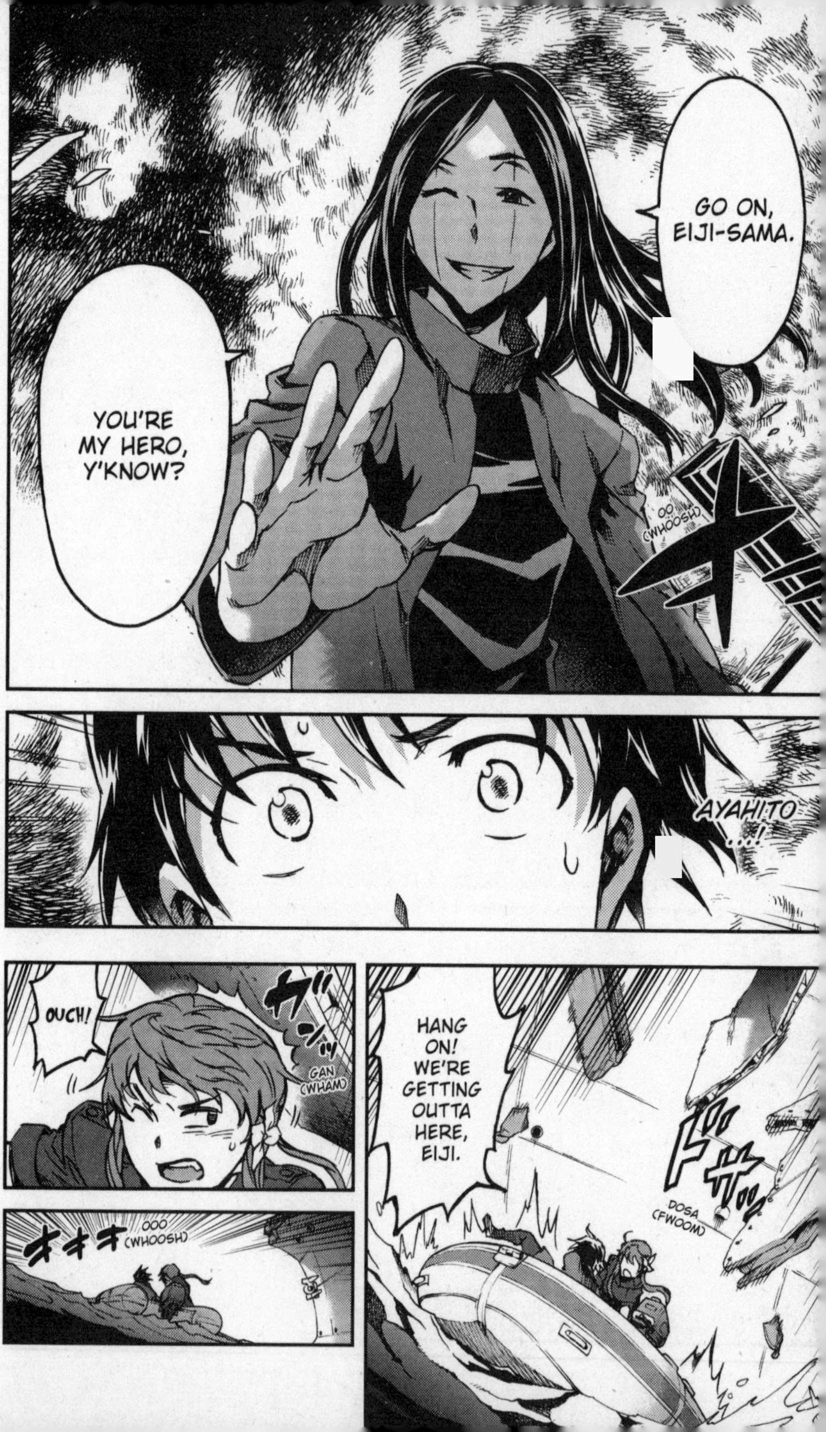
GO ON, EIJI-SAMA.
YOU'RE MY HERO, Y'KNOW?
OO (WHOOSH)
AYAHITO ...!
HANG ON! WE'RE GETTING OUTTA HERE, EIJI.
DOSA (FWOOM)
OUCH!
GAN (WHAM)
OOO (WHOOSH)

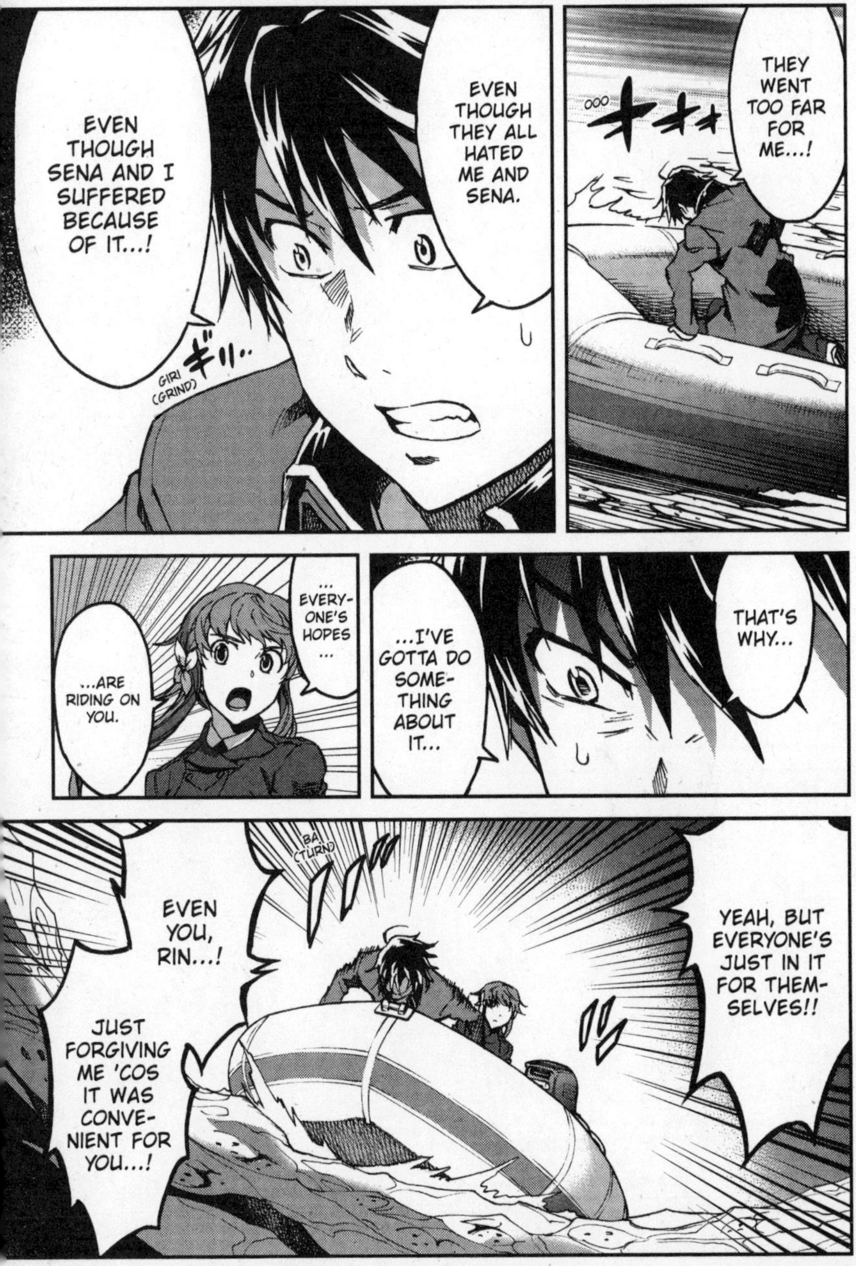
OOO
THEY WENT TOO FAR FOR ME...!
EVEN THOUGH THEY ALL HATED ME AND SENA.
EVEN THOUGH SENA AND I SUFFERED BECAUSE OF IT...!
GIRI (GRIND)
THAT'S WHY...
...I'VE GOTTA DO SOME-THING ABOUT IT...
...EVERY-ONE'S HOPES...
...ARE RIDING ON YOU.
YEAH, BUT EVERYONE'S JUST IN IT FOR THEM-SELVES!!
BA (TURN)
EVEN YOU, RIN...!
JUST FORGIVING ME 'COS IT WAS CONVE-NIENT FOR YOU...!

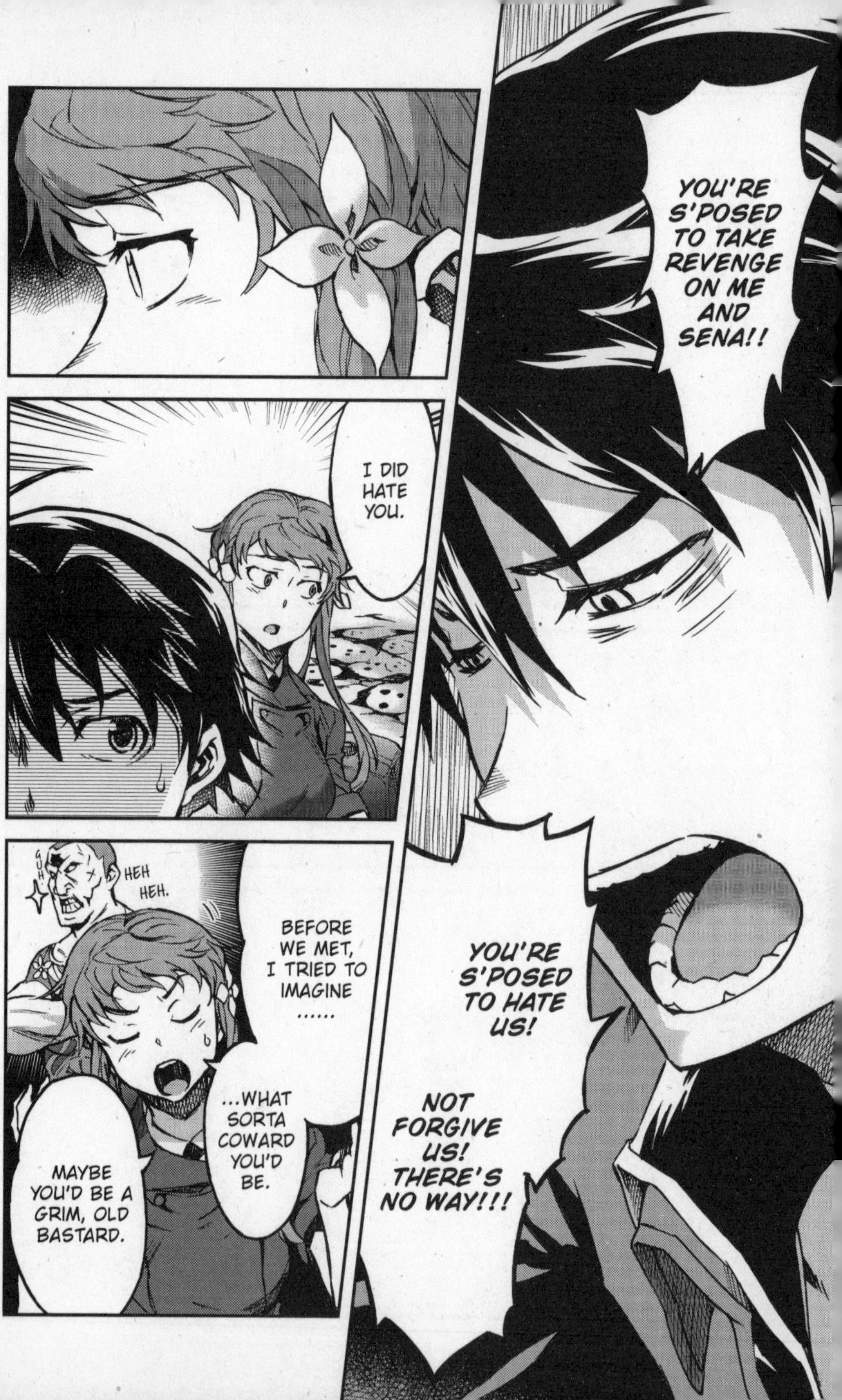
YOU'RE S'POSED TO TAKE REVENGE ON ME AND SENA!!
YOU'RE S'POSED TO HATE US!
NOT FORGIVE US! THERE'S NO WAY!!!
I DID HATE YOU.
BEFORE WE MET, I TRIED TO IMAGINE ......
HEH HEH.
GUH
...WHAT SORTA COWARD YOU'D BE.
MAYBE YOU'D BE A GRIM, OLD BASTARD.

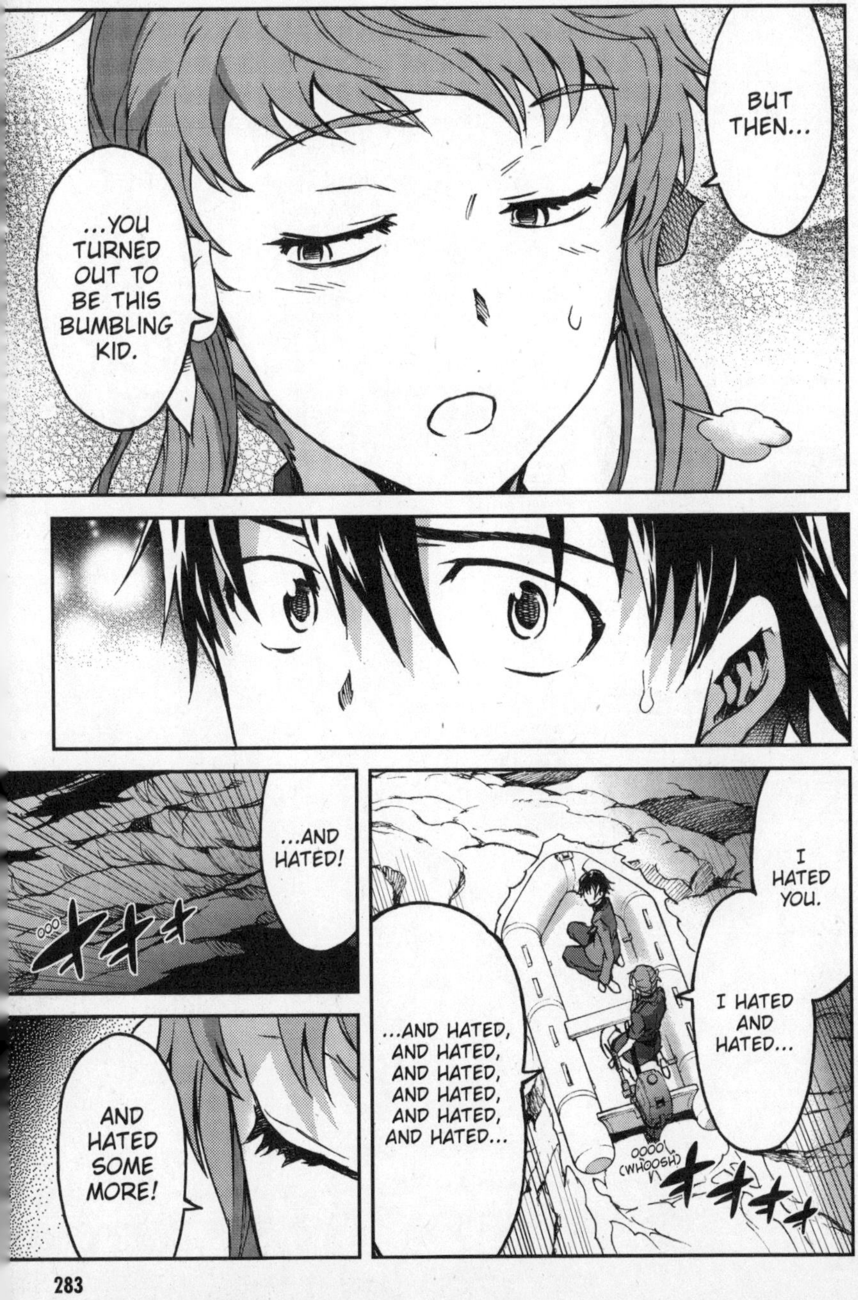
BUT THEN...
...YOU TURNED OUT TO BE THIS BUMBLING KID.
I HATED YOU.
I HATED AND HATED...
...AND HATED, AND HATED, AND HATED, AND HATED, AND HATED, AND HATED...
OOOO
(WHOOSH)
...AND HATED!
OOO
AND HATED SOME MORE!

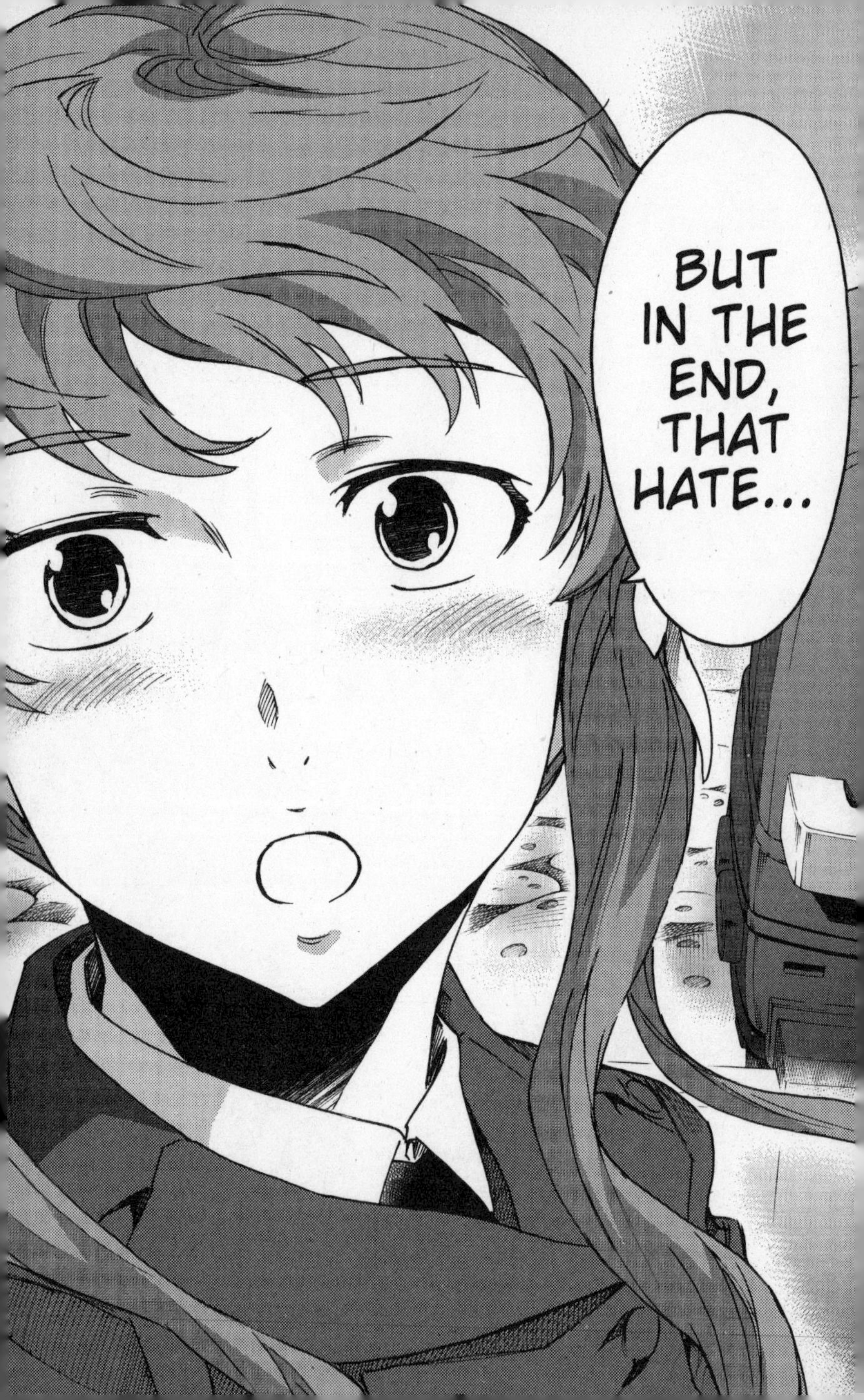
BUT IN THE END, THAT HATE...

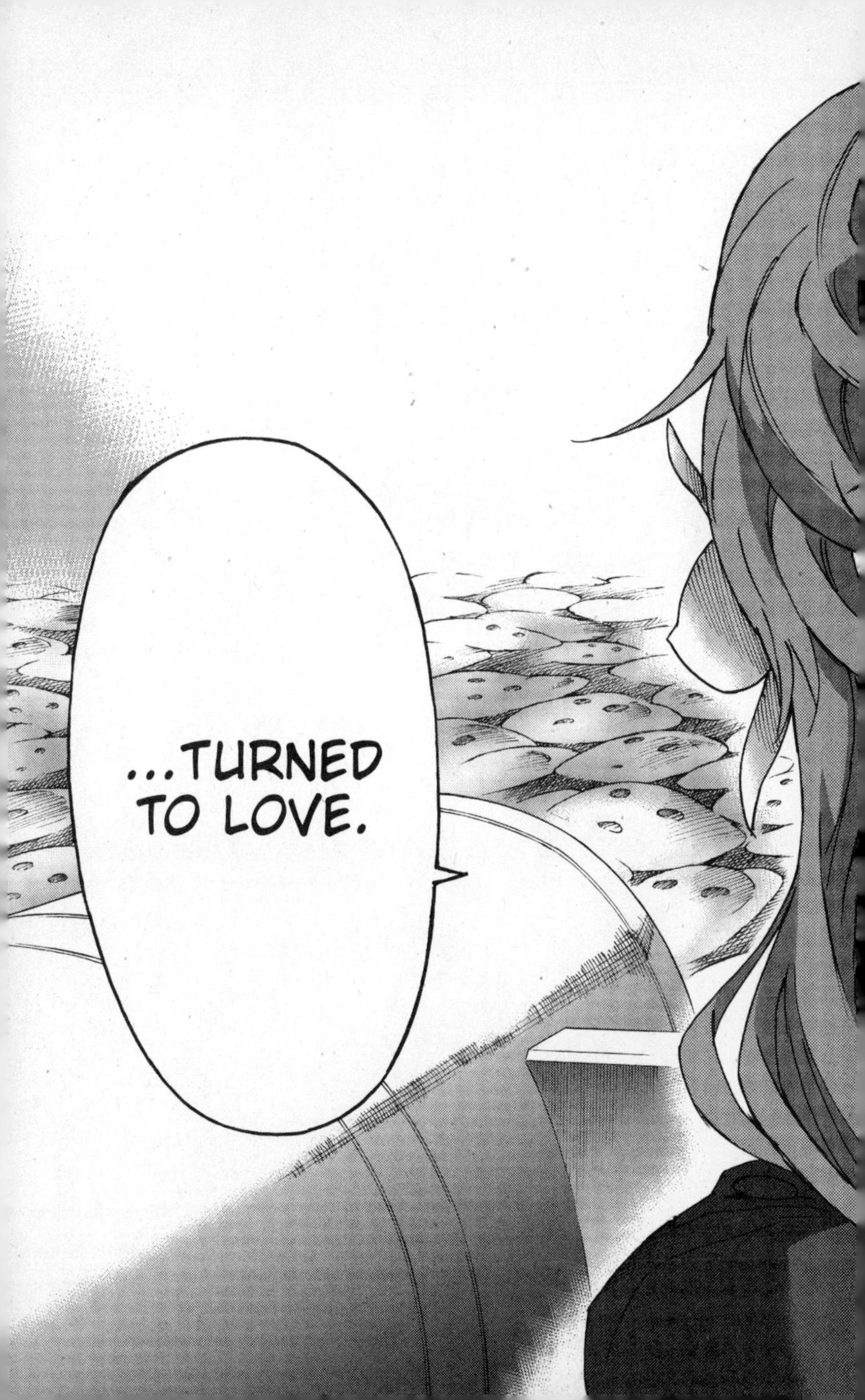
...TURNED TO LOVE.

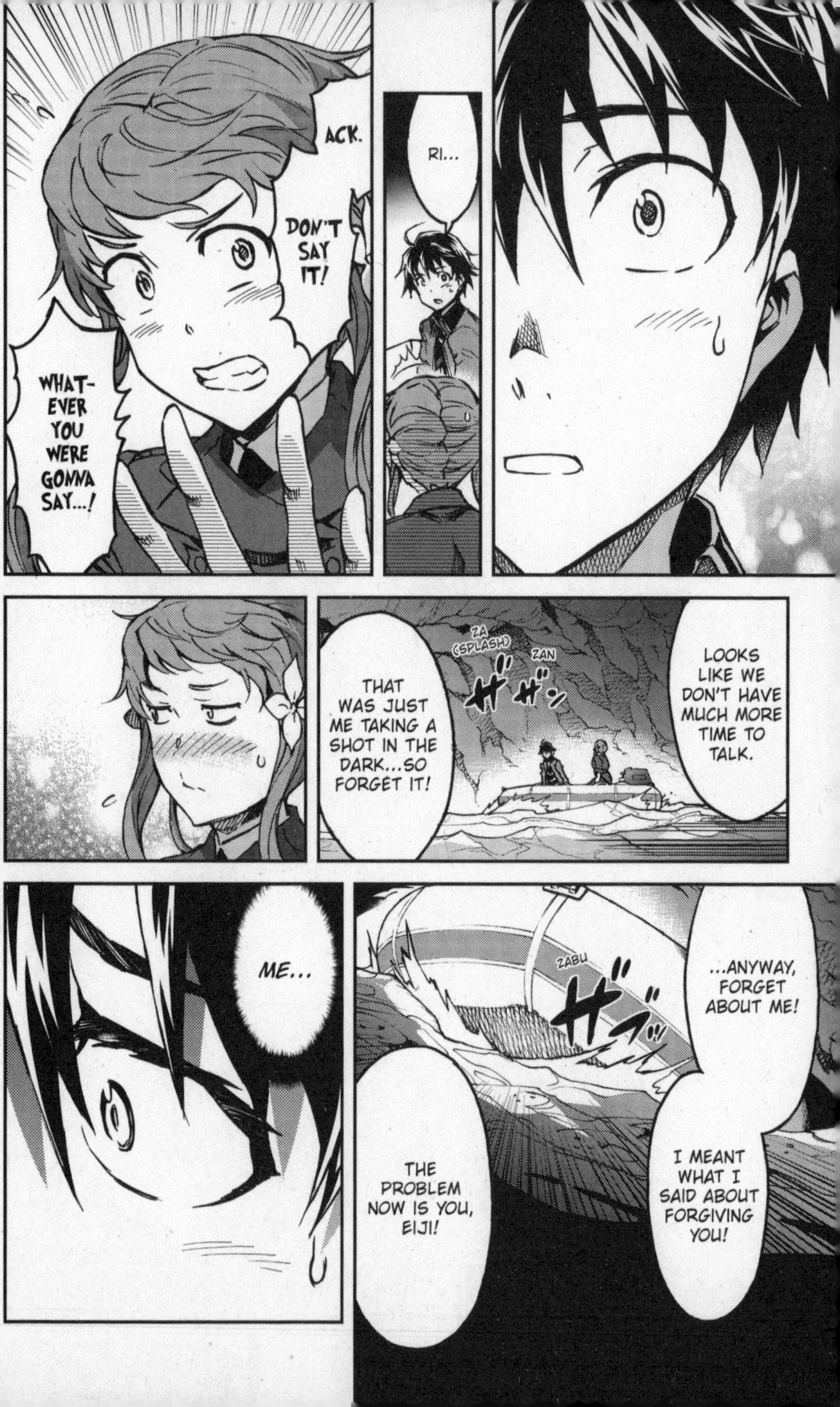
RI...
ACK.
DON'T SAY IT!
WHAT-EVER YOU WERE GONNA SAY...!
LOOKS LIKE WE DON'T HAVE MUCH MORE TIME TO TALK.
ZA (SPLASH)
ZAN
THAT WAS JUST ME TAKING A SHOT IN THE DARK...SO FORGET IT!
...ANYWAY, FORGET ABOUT ME!
ZABU
I MEANT WHAT I SAID ABOUT FORGIVING YOU!
THE PROBLEM NOW IS YOU, EIJI!
ME...

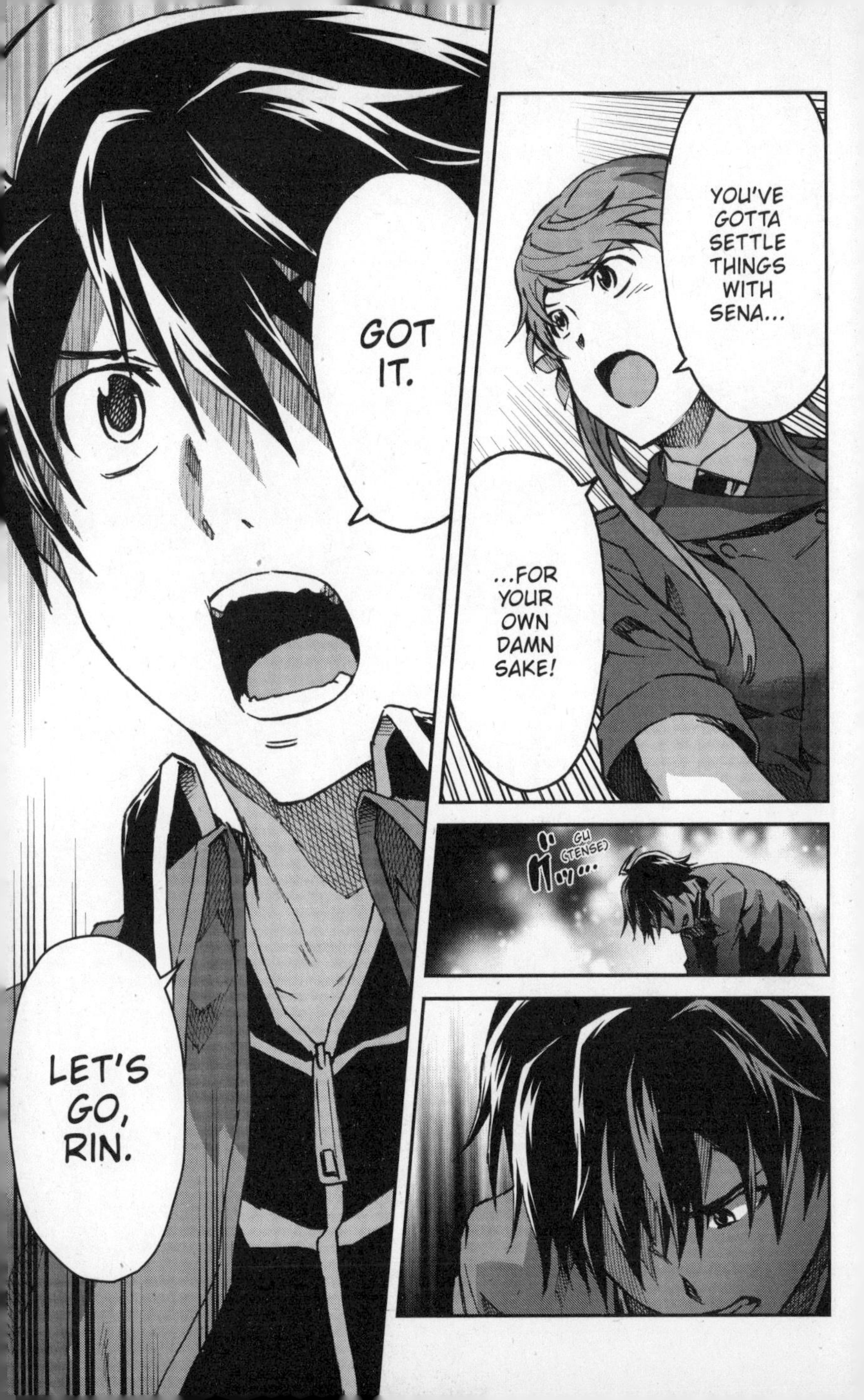
YOU'VE GOTTA SETTLE THINGS WITH SENA...
...FOR YOUR OWN DAMN SAKE!
GU (TENSE)
GOT IT.
LET'S GO, RIN.

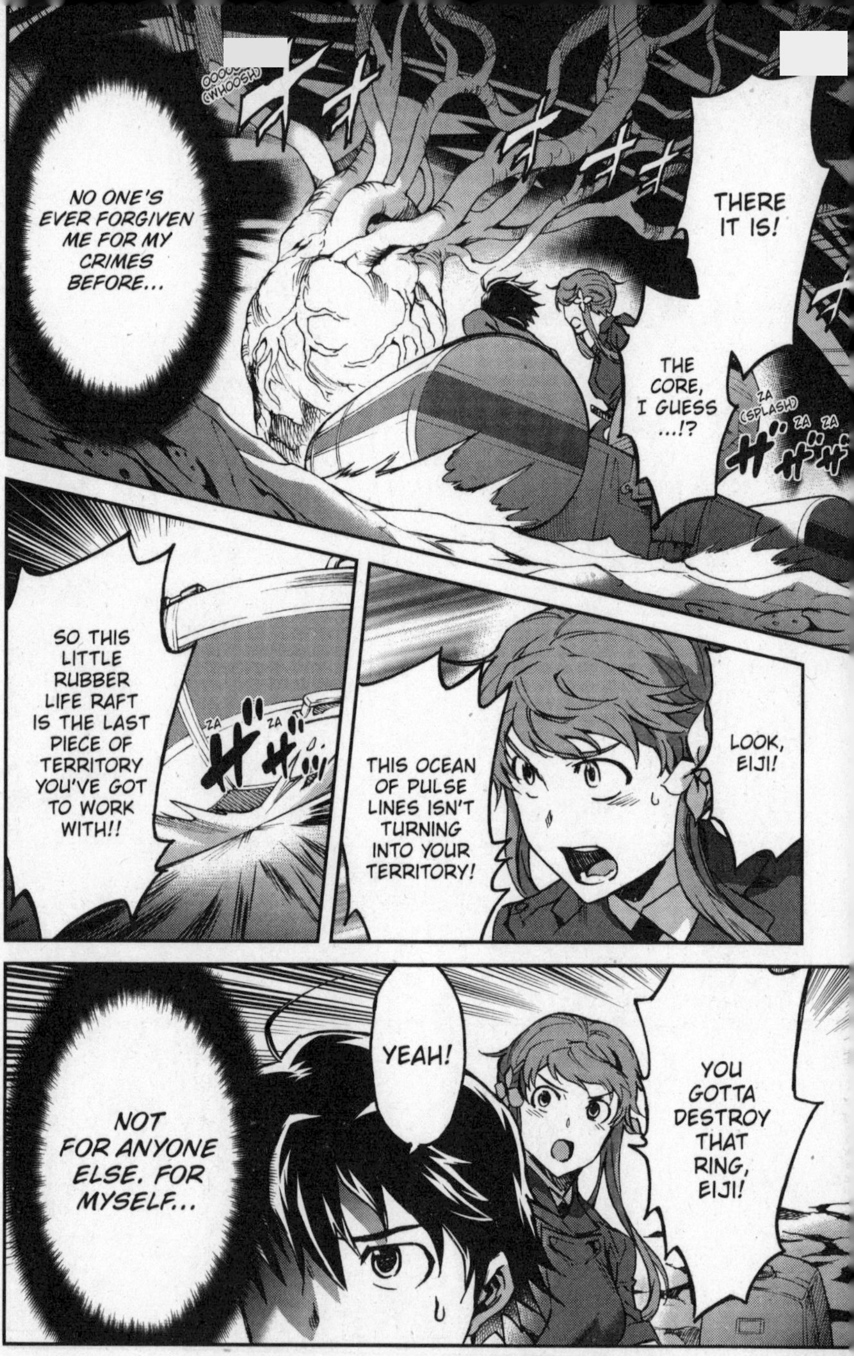
THERE IT IS!
ZA (SPLASH) ZA ZA
THE CORE, I GUESS ...!?
(WHOOSH)
NO ONE'S EVER FORGIVEN ME FOR MY CRIMES BEFORE...
LOOK, EIJI!
THIS OCEAN OF PULSE LINES ISN'T TURNING INTO YOUR TERRITORY!
SO THIS LITTLE RUBBER LIFE RAFT IS THE LAST PIECE OF TERRITORY YOU'VE GOT TO WORK WITH!!
ZA ZA
YOU GOTTA DESTROY THAT RING, EIJI!
YEAH!
NOT FOR ANYONE ELSE. FOR MYSELF...

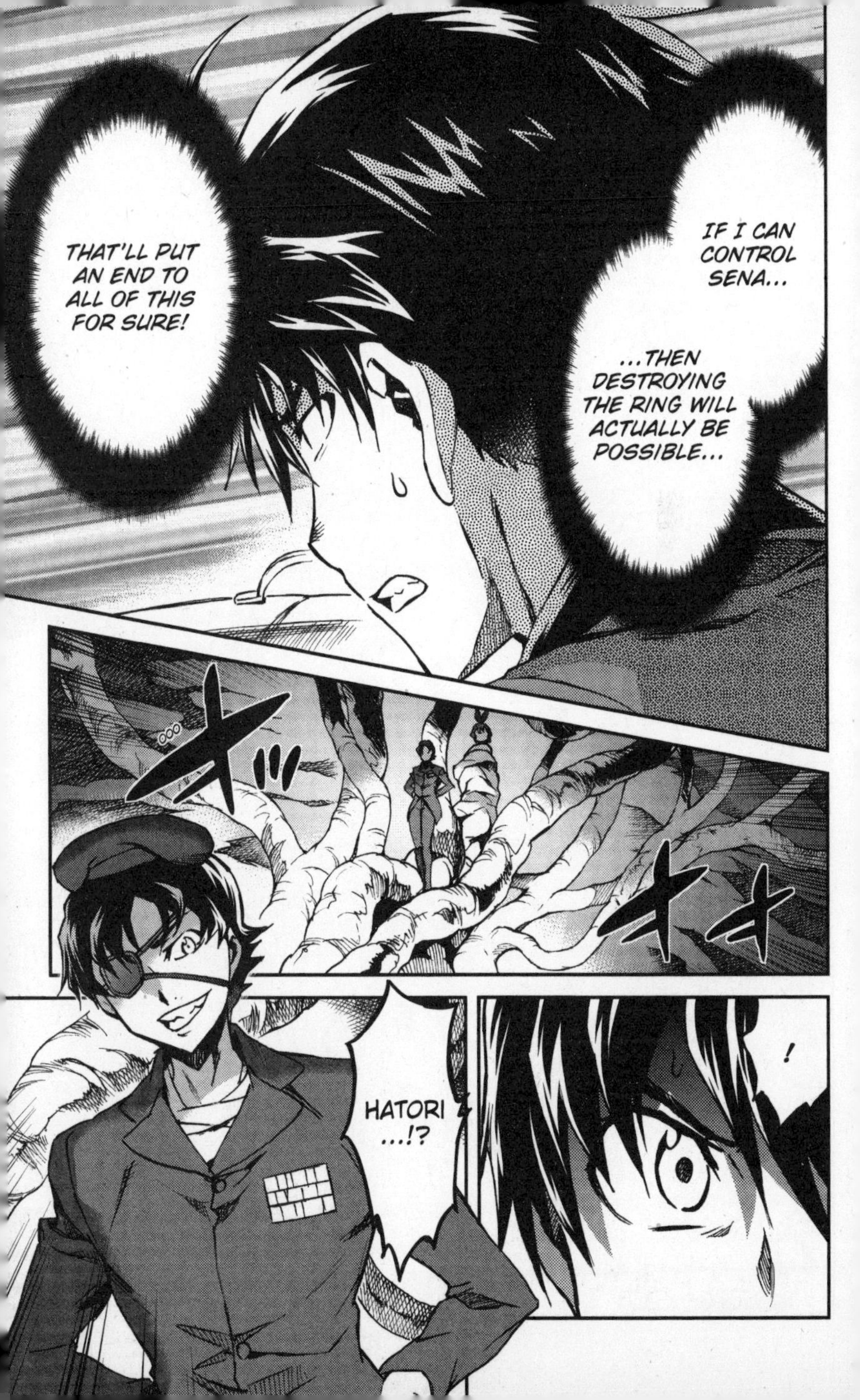
IF I CAN CONTROL SENA...
...THEN DESTROYING THE RING WILL ACTUALLY BE POSSIBLE...
THAT'LL PUT AN END TO ALL OF THIS FOR SURE!
!
HATORI ...!?

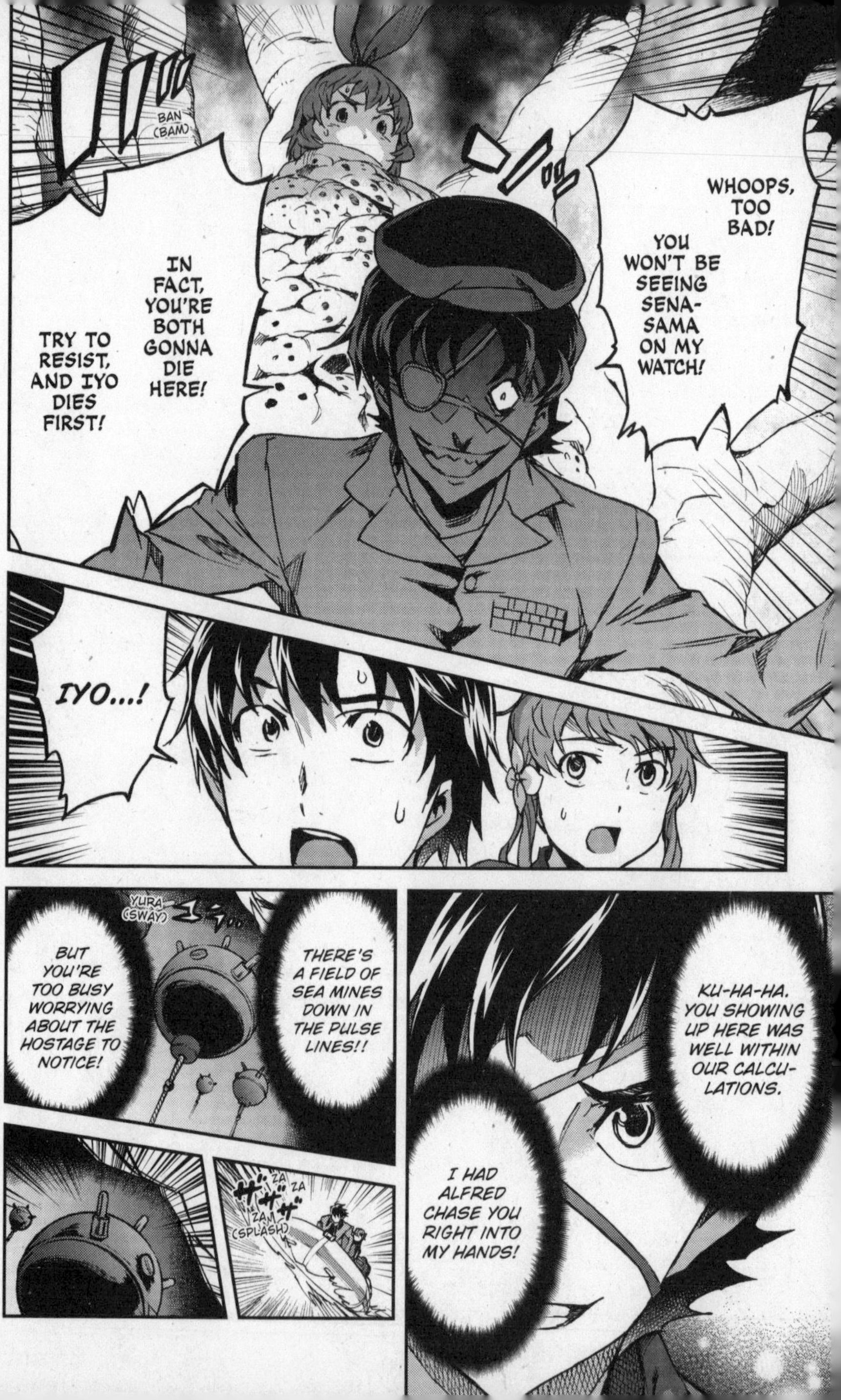
WHOOPS, TOO BAD!
YOU WON'T BE SEEING SENA-SAMA ON MY WATCH!
IN FACT, YOU'RE BOTH GONNA DIE HERE!
TRY TO RESIST, AND IYO DIES FIRST!
BAN (BAM)
IYO...!
KU-HA-HA. YOU SHOWING UP HERE WAS WELL WITHIN OUR CALCULATIONS.
I HAD ALFRED CHASE YOU RIGHT INTO MY HANDS!
YURA (SWAY)
THERE'S A FIELD OF SEA MINES DOWN IN THE PULSE LINES!!
BUT YOU'RE TOO BUSY WORRYING ABOUT THE HOSTAGE TO NOTICE!
ZA ZA ZAH (SPLASH)

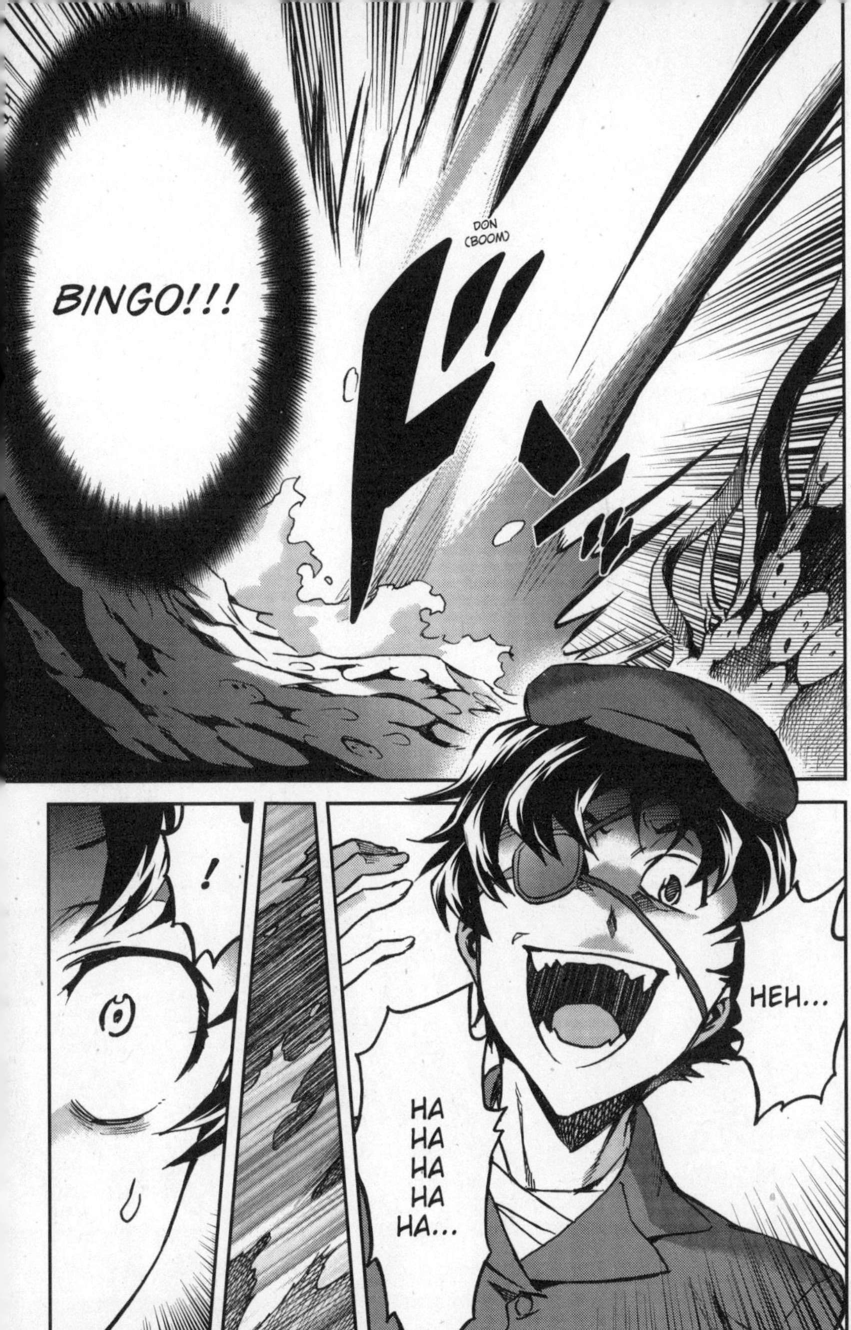
DON
(BOOM)
BINGO!!!
HEH...
HA
HA
HA
HA
HA...
!

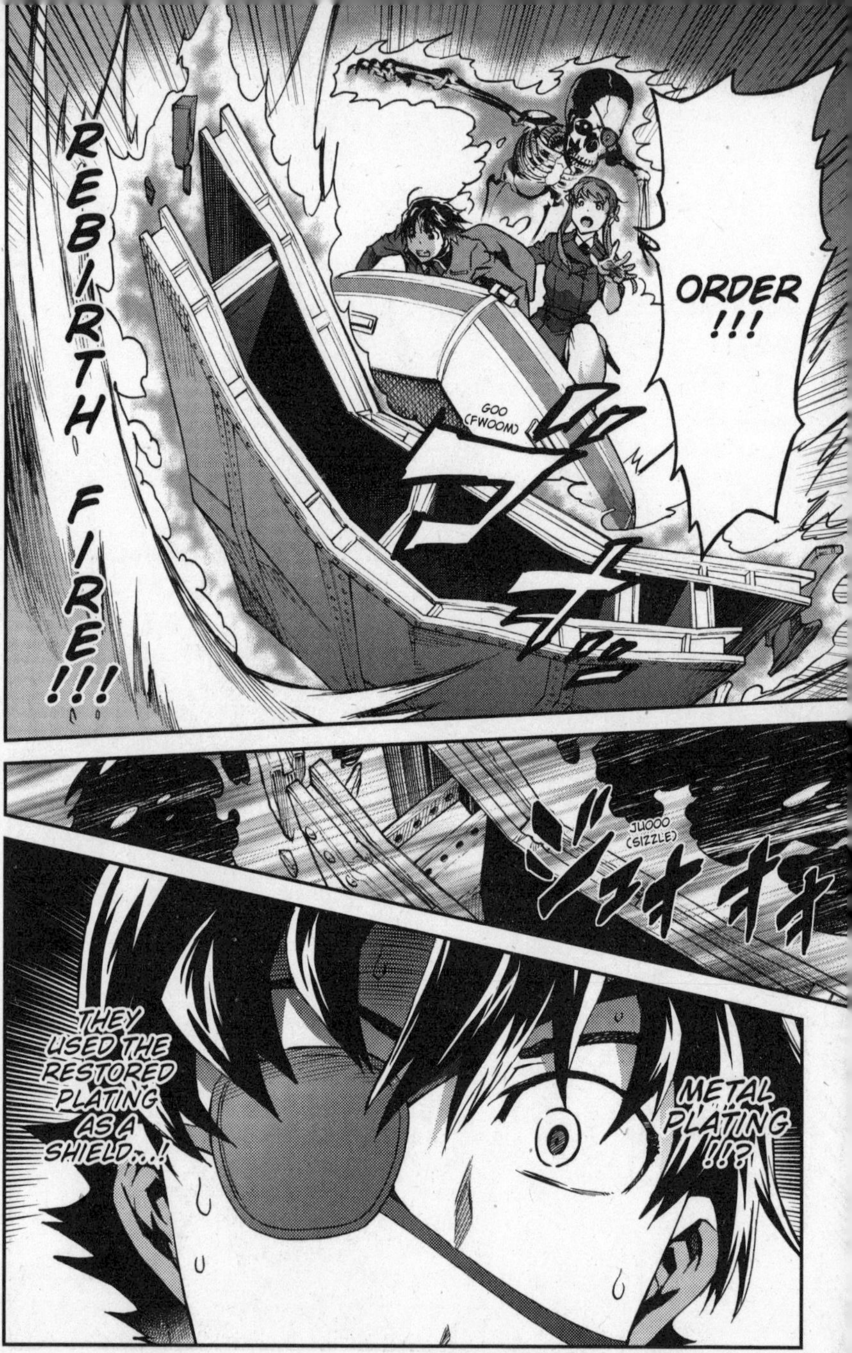
ORDER!!!
GOO (FWOOM)
REBIRTH FIRE!!!
JUOOO (SIZZLE)
METAL PLATING!!?
THEY USED THE RESTORED PLATING AS A SHIELD...!

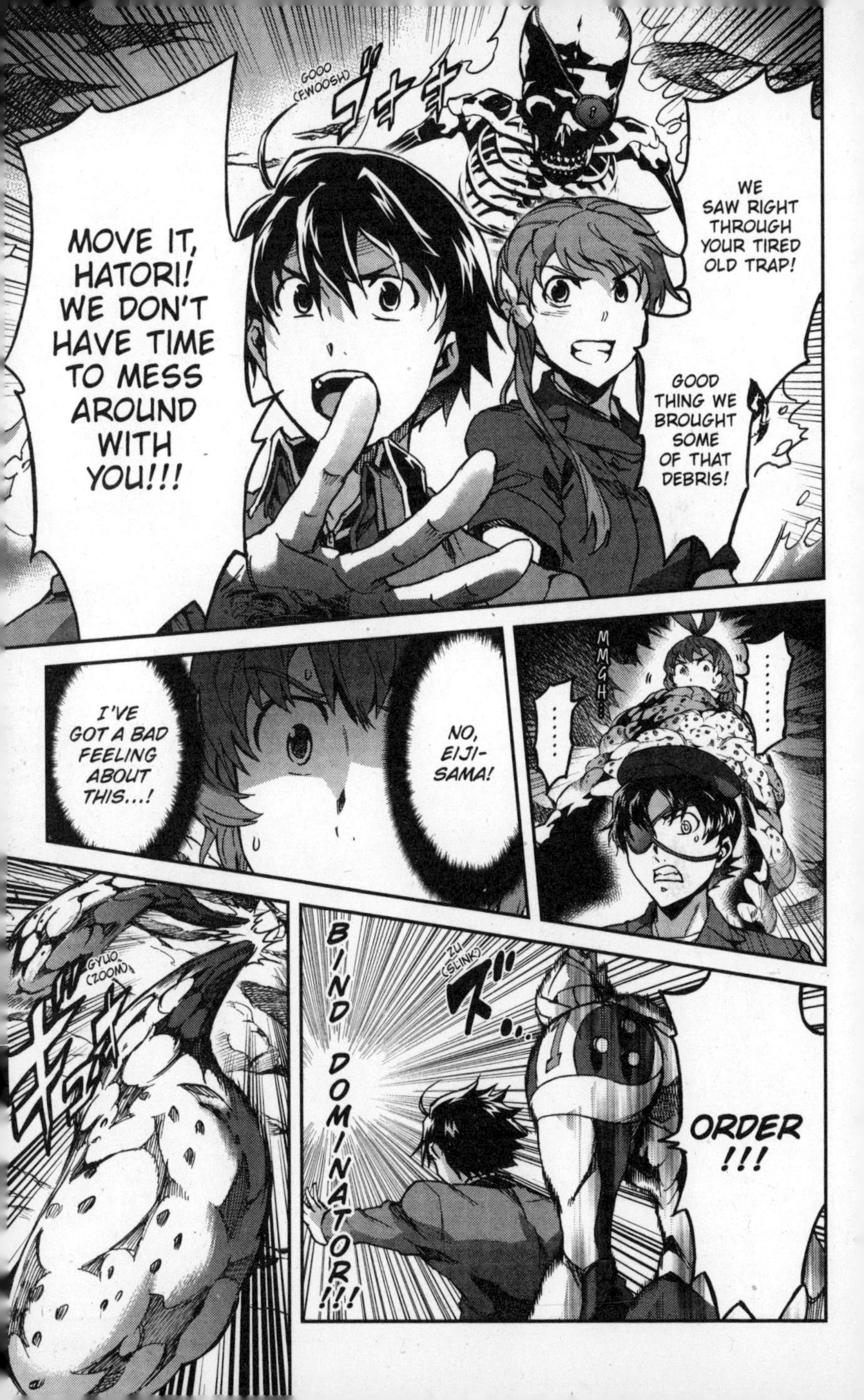
GOOO (FWOOSH)
WE SAW RIGHT THROUGH YOUR TIRED OLD TRAP!
GOOD THING WE BROUGHT SOME OF THAT DEBRIS!
MOVE IT, HATORI! WE DON'T HAVE TIME TO MESS AROUND WITH YOU!!!
MMGH...
NO, EIJI-SAMA!
I'VE GOT A BAD FEELING ABOUT THIS...!
ZU (SLINK)
BIND DOMINATOR!!!
ORDER!!!
GYUO (ZOOM)

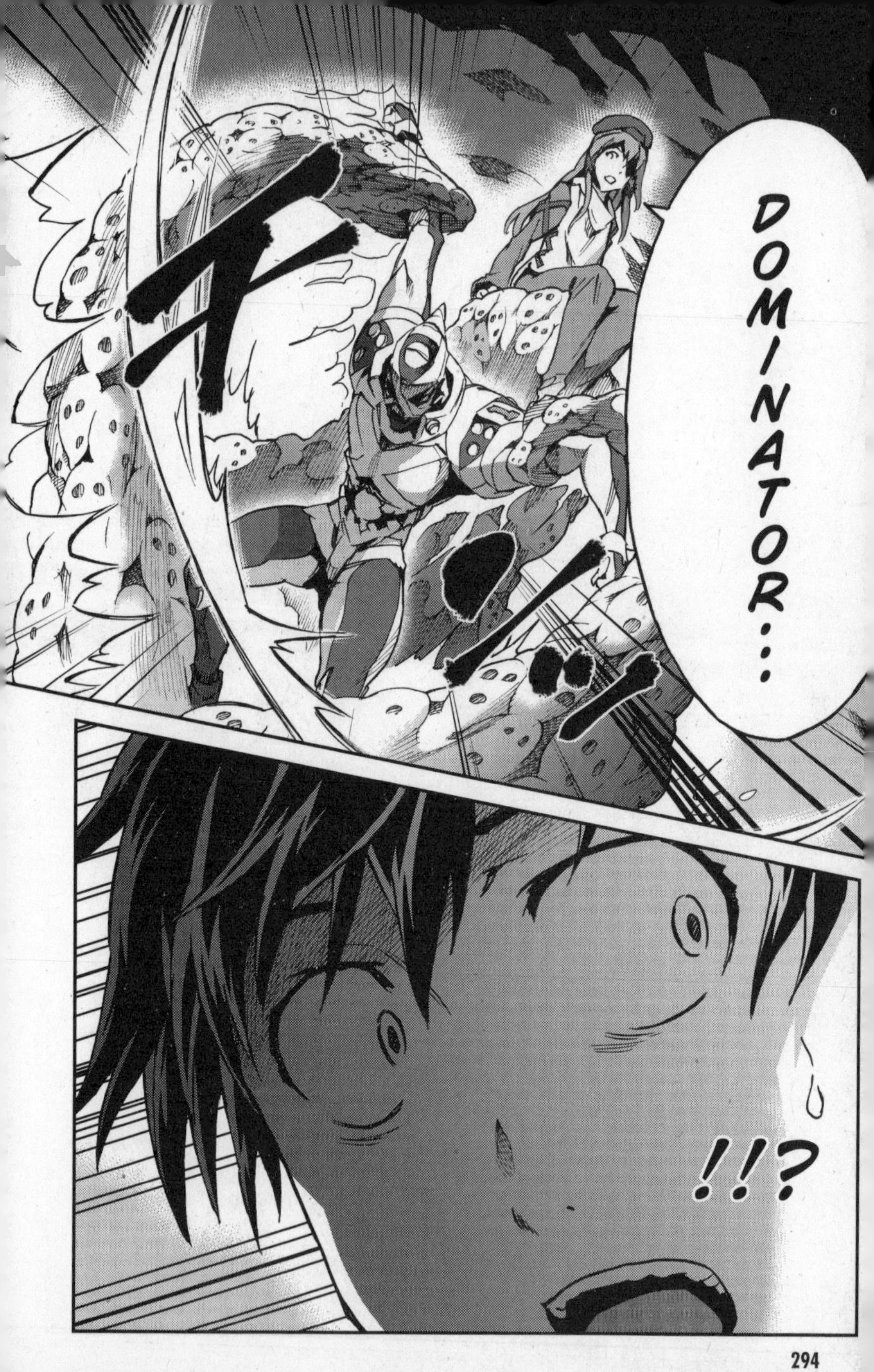
DOMINATOR...
!!?

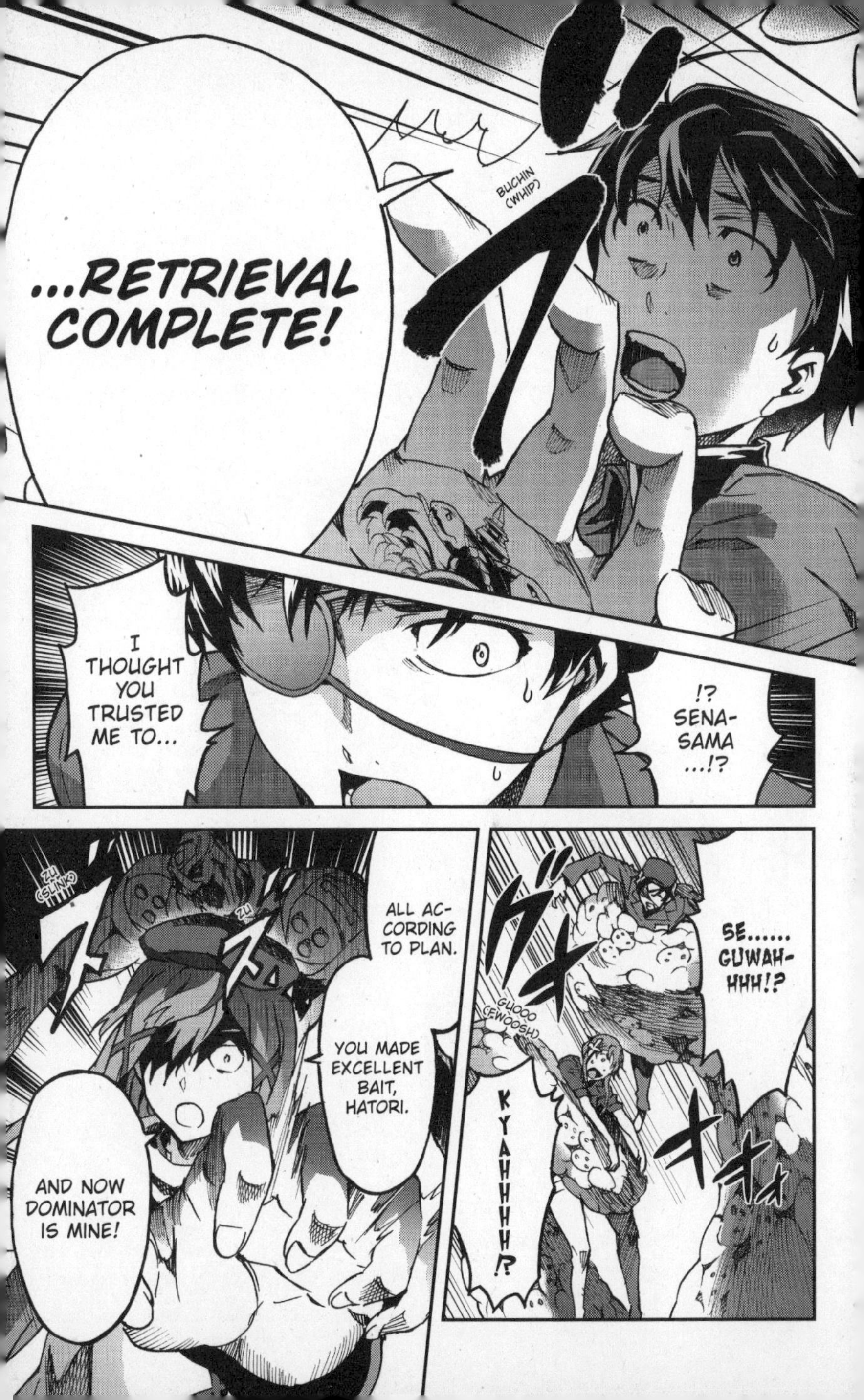
BUCHIN (WHIP)
...RETRIEVAL COMPLETE!
!? SENA-SAMA ...!?
I THOUGHT YOU TRUSTED ME TO...
SE...... GUWAH-HHH!?
GUOOO (FWOOSH)
KYAHHHHH!?
ZU
ZU (SLINK)
ALL AC-CORDING TO PLAN.
YOU MADE EXCELLENT BAIT, HATORI.
AND NOW DOMINATOR IS MINE!

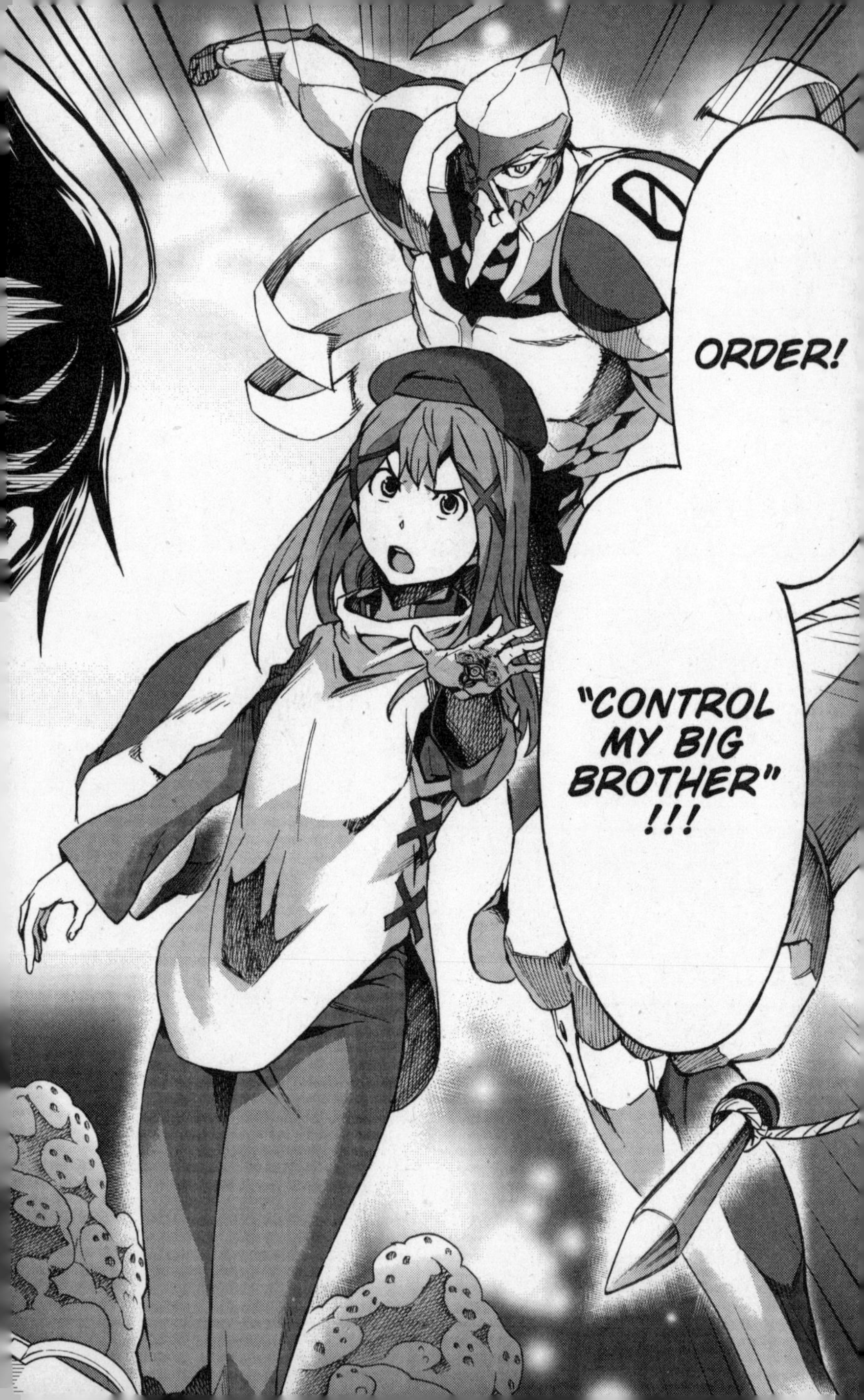
ORDER!
"CONTROL MY BIG BROTHER" !!!

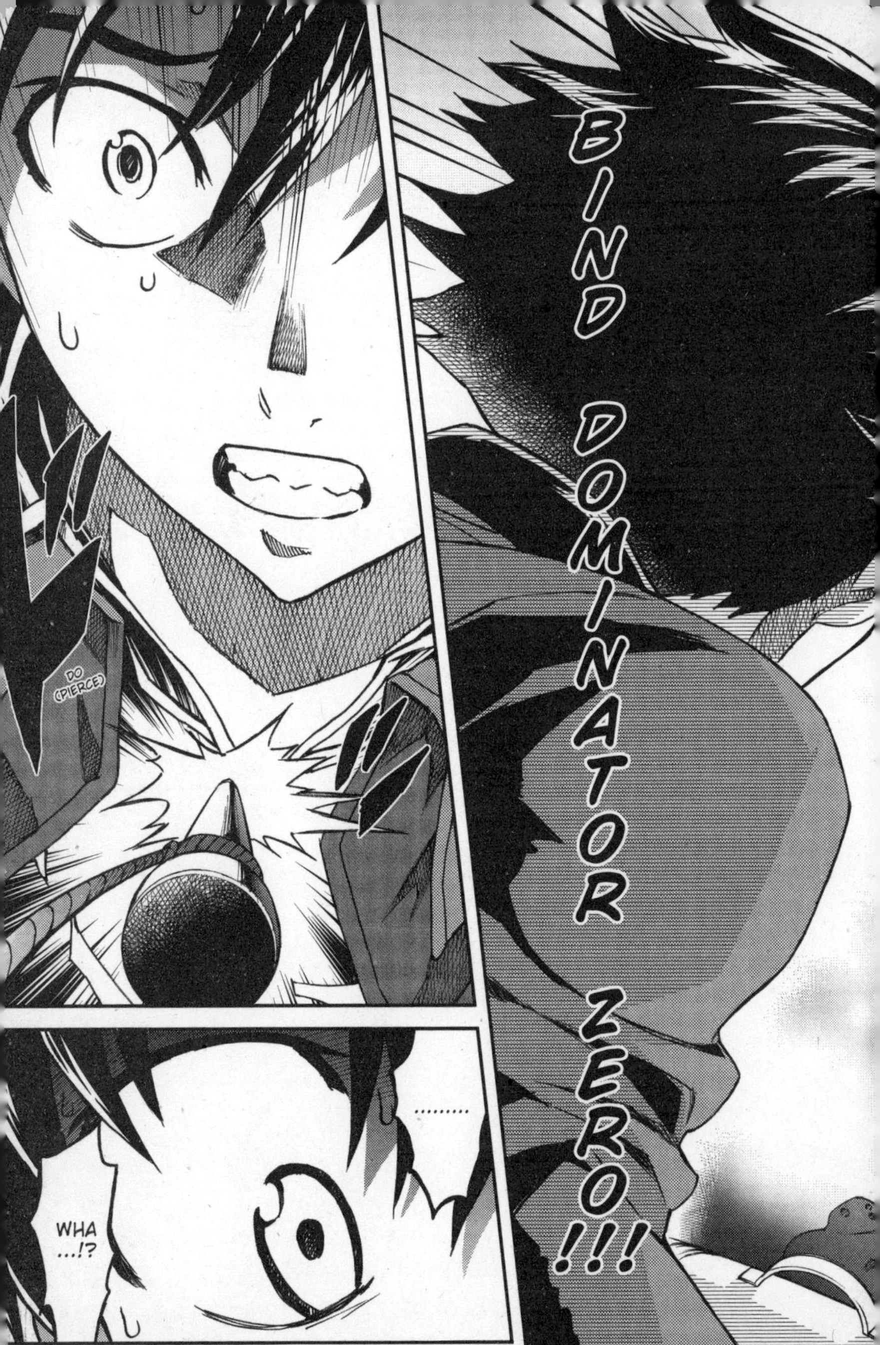
BIND DOMINATOR ZERO!!!
DO (PIERCE)
....
WHA ...!?

Subject 51: END

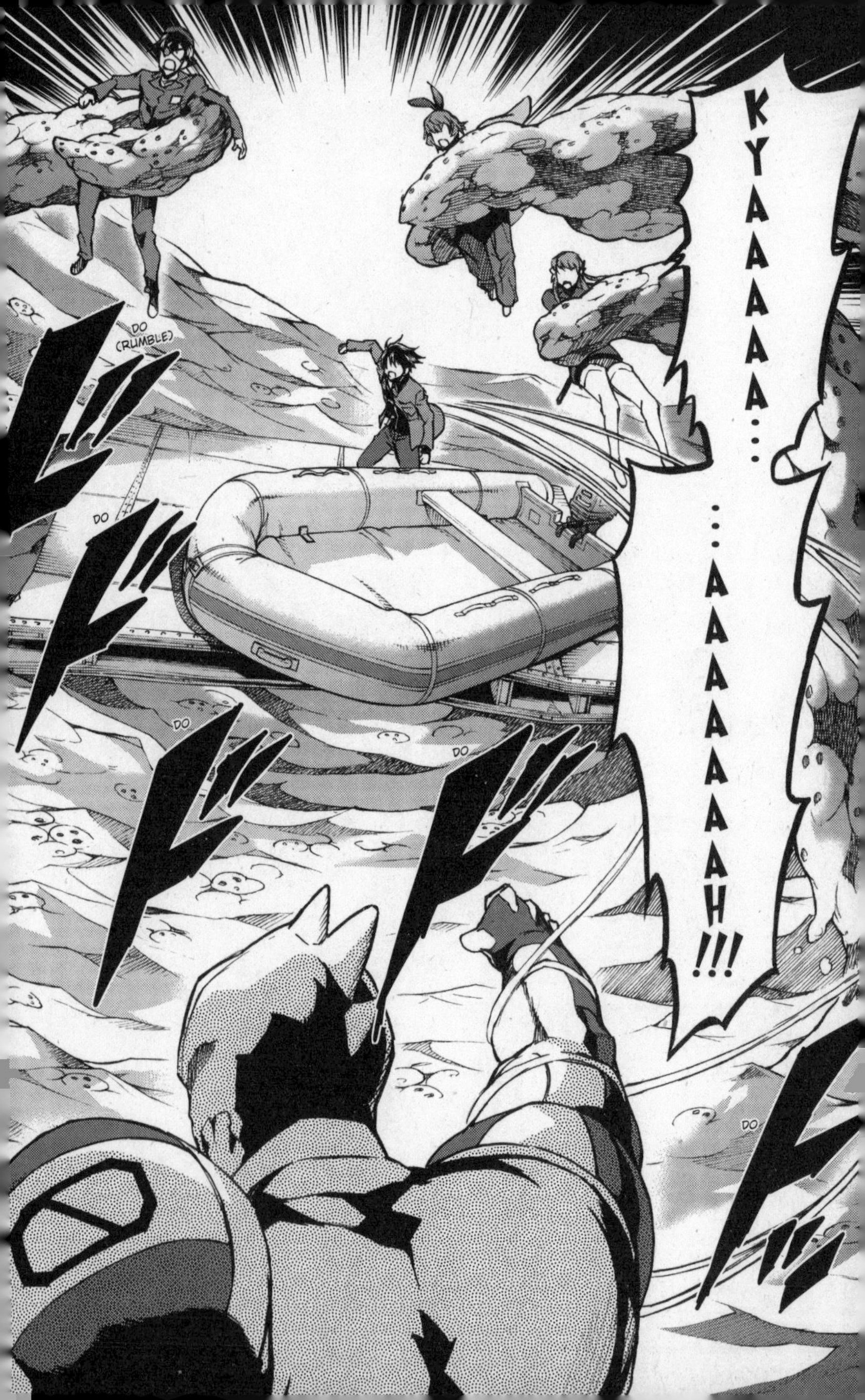
KYAAAAA... ...AAAAAAAAAH!!!
DO (RUMBLE)
DO
DO
DO
DO

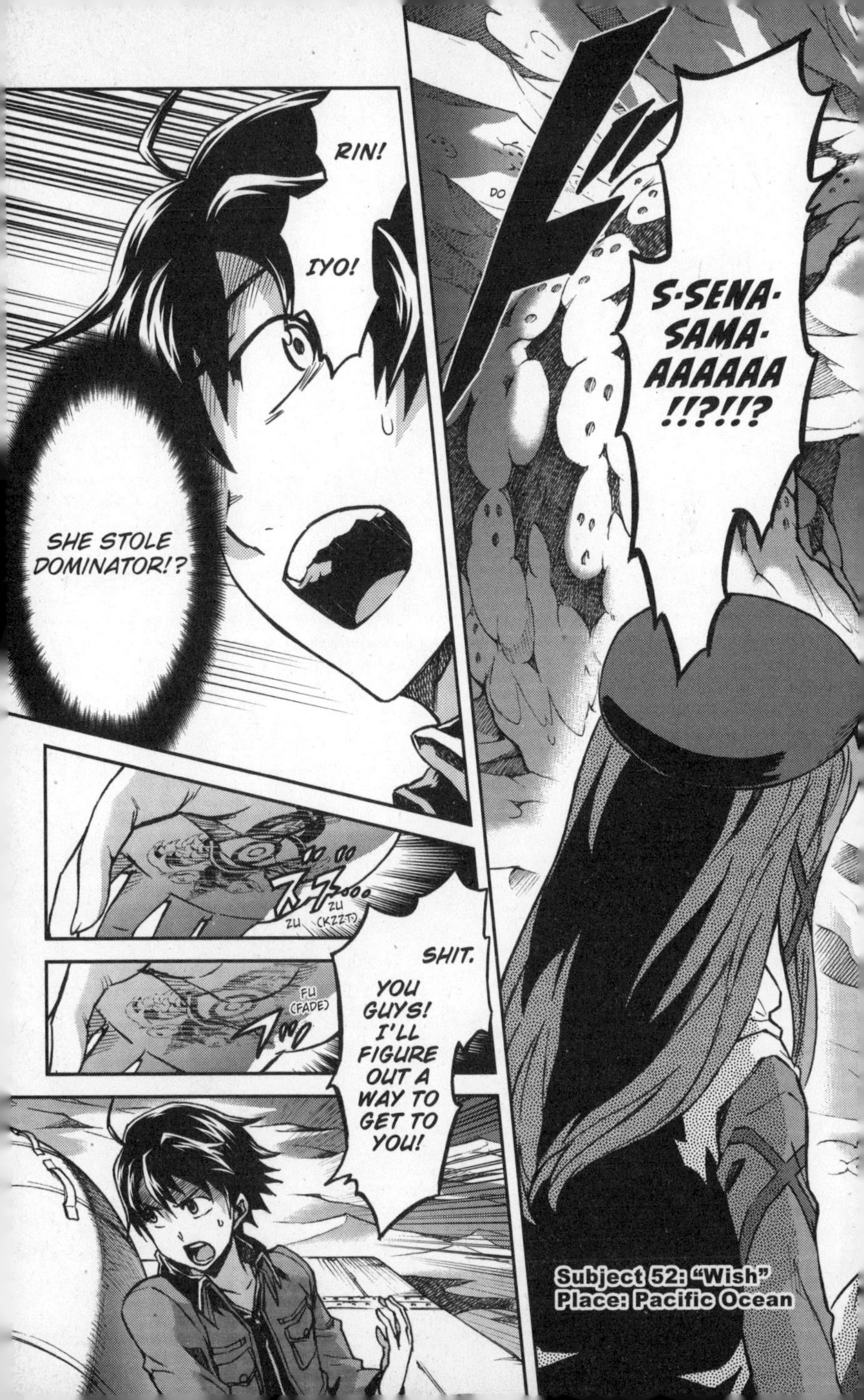
DO
S-SENA-SAMA-AAAAAA!!?!!?
Subject 52: "Wish"
Place: Pacific Ocean
RIN!
IYO!
SHE STOLE DOMINATOR!?
ZU ZU (KZZT)
FU (FADE)
SHIT.
YOU GUYS! I'LL FIGURE OUT A WAY TO GET TO YOU!

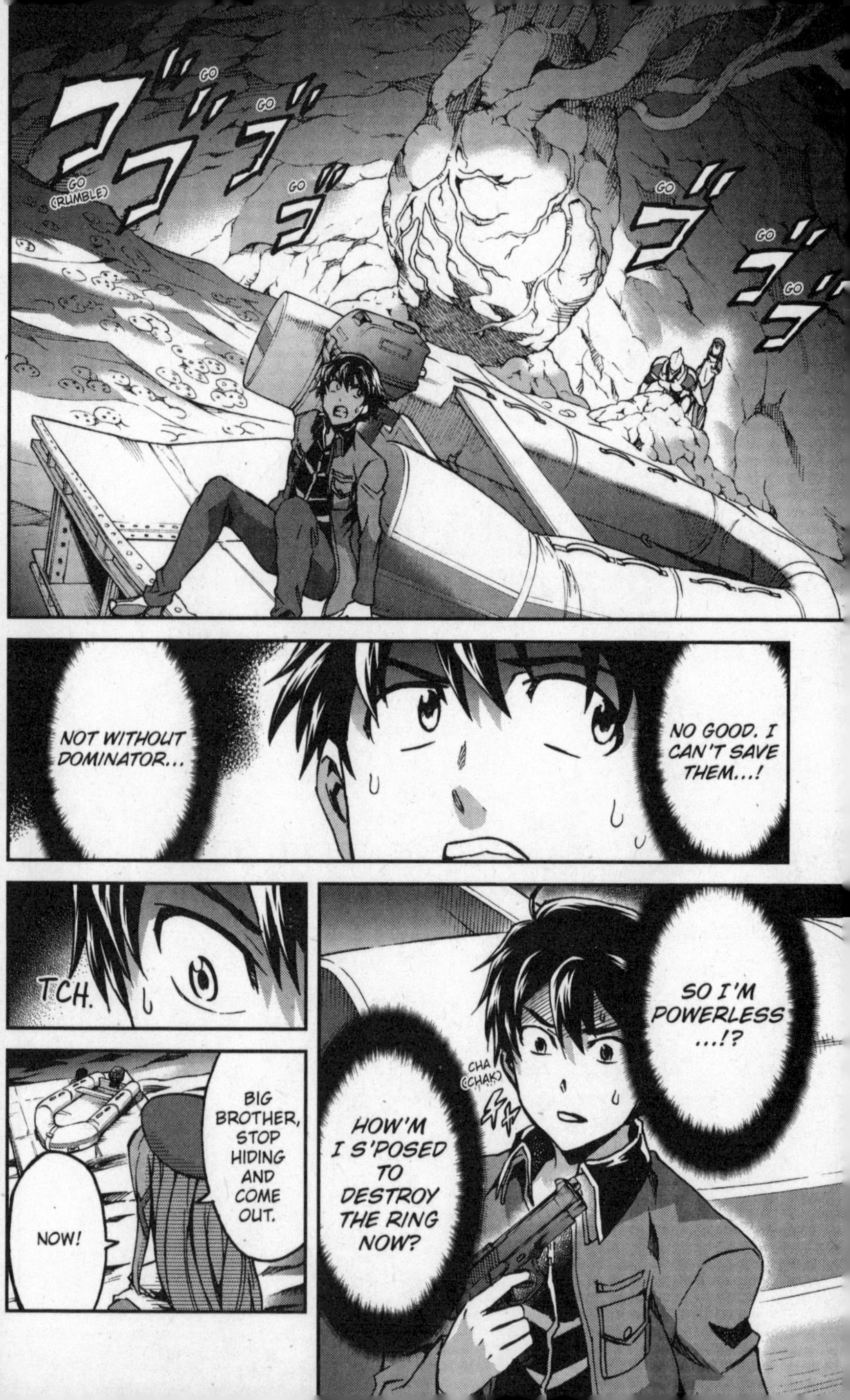
GO
GO
GO
GO
GO
GO
GO
(RUMBLE)
GO
NO GOOD. I CAN'T SAVE THEM...!
NOT WITHOUT DOMINATOR...
SO I'M POWERLESS ...!?
CHA (CHAK)
HOW'M I S'POSED TO DESTROY THE RING NOW?
TCH.
BIG BROTHER, STOP HIDING AND COME OUT.
NOW!

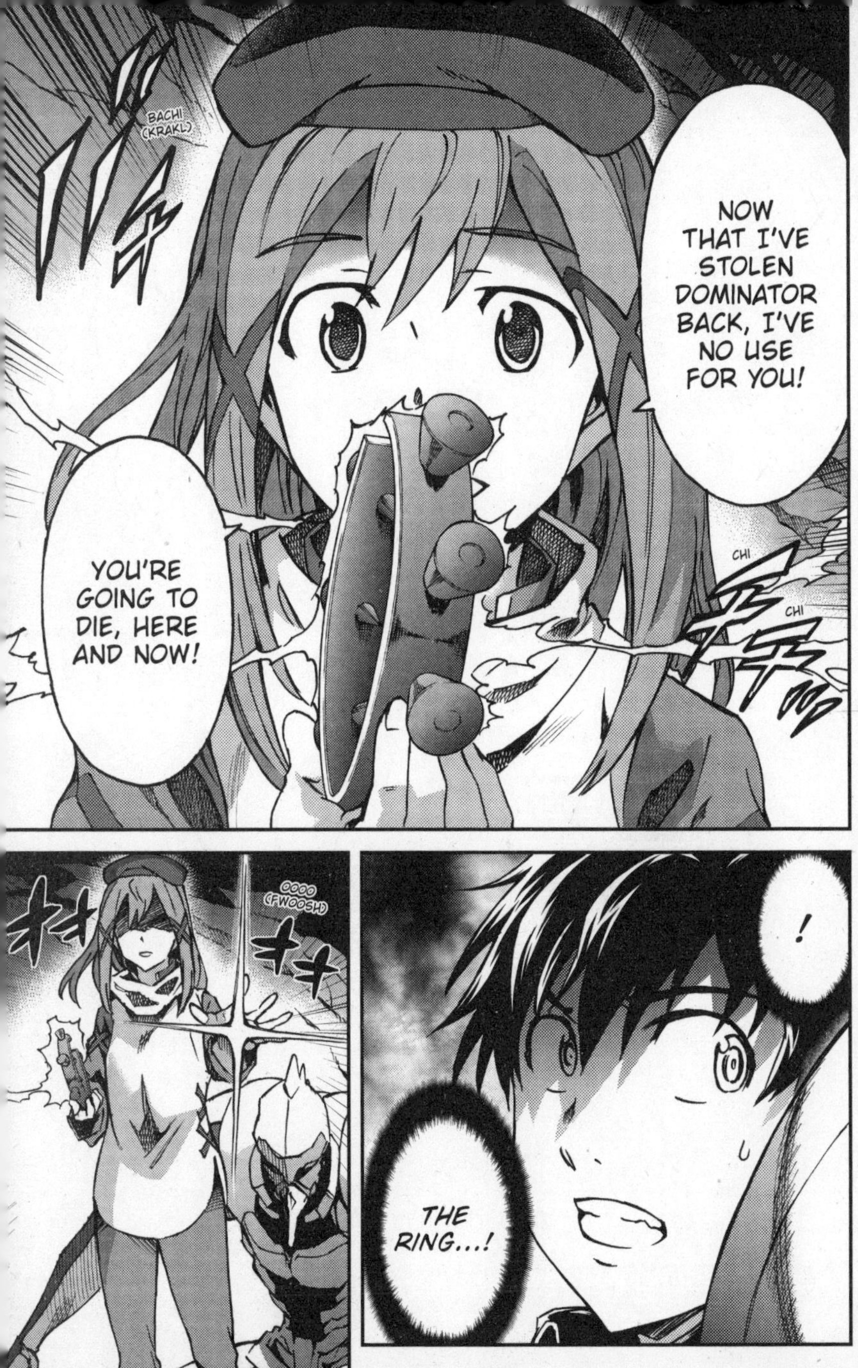
BACHI (KRAKL)
NOW THAT I'VE STOLEN DOMINATOR BACK, I'VE NO USE FOR YOU!
YOU'RE GOING TO DIE, HERE AND NOW!
CHI
CHI
OOOO (FWOOSH)
!
THE RING...!

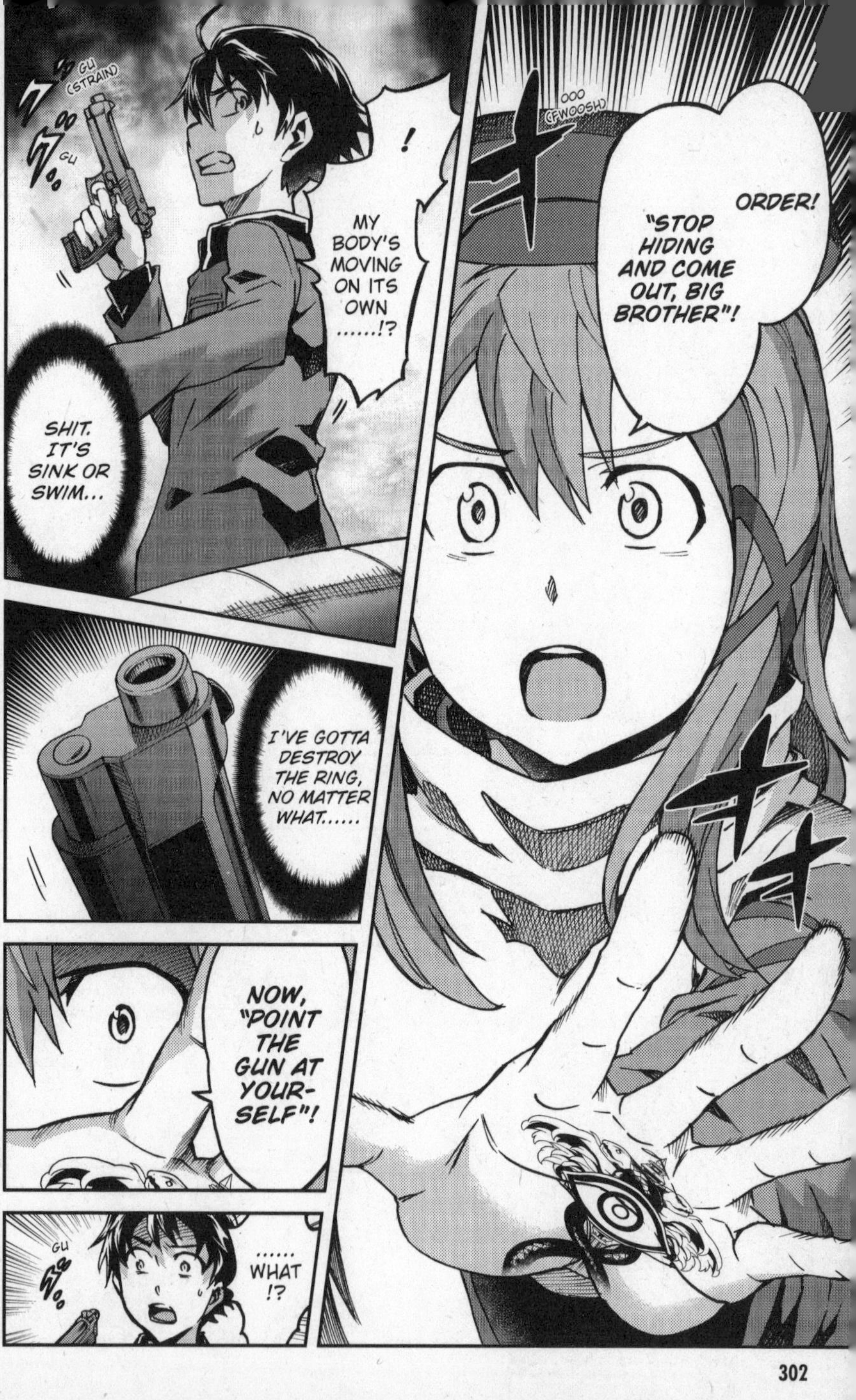
OOO (FWOOSH)
ORDER! "STOP HIDING AND COME OUT, BIG BROTHER"!
GU (STRAIN)
GU
!
MY BODY'S MOVING ON ITS OWN ......!?
SHIT. IT'S SINK OR SWIM...
I'VE GOTTA DESTROY THE RING, NO MATTER WHAT......
NOW, "POINT THE GUN AT YOUR-SELF"!
GU
...... WHAT !?

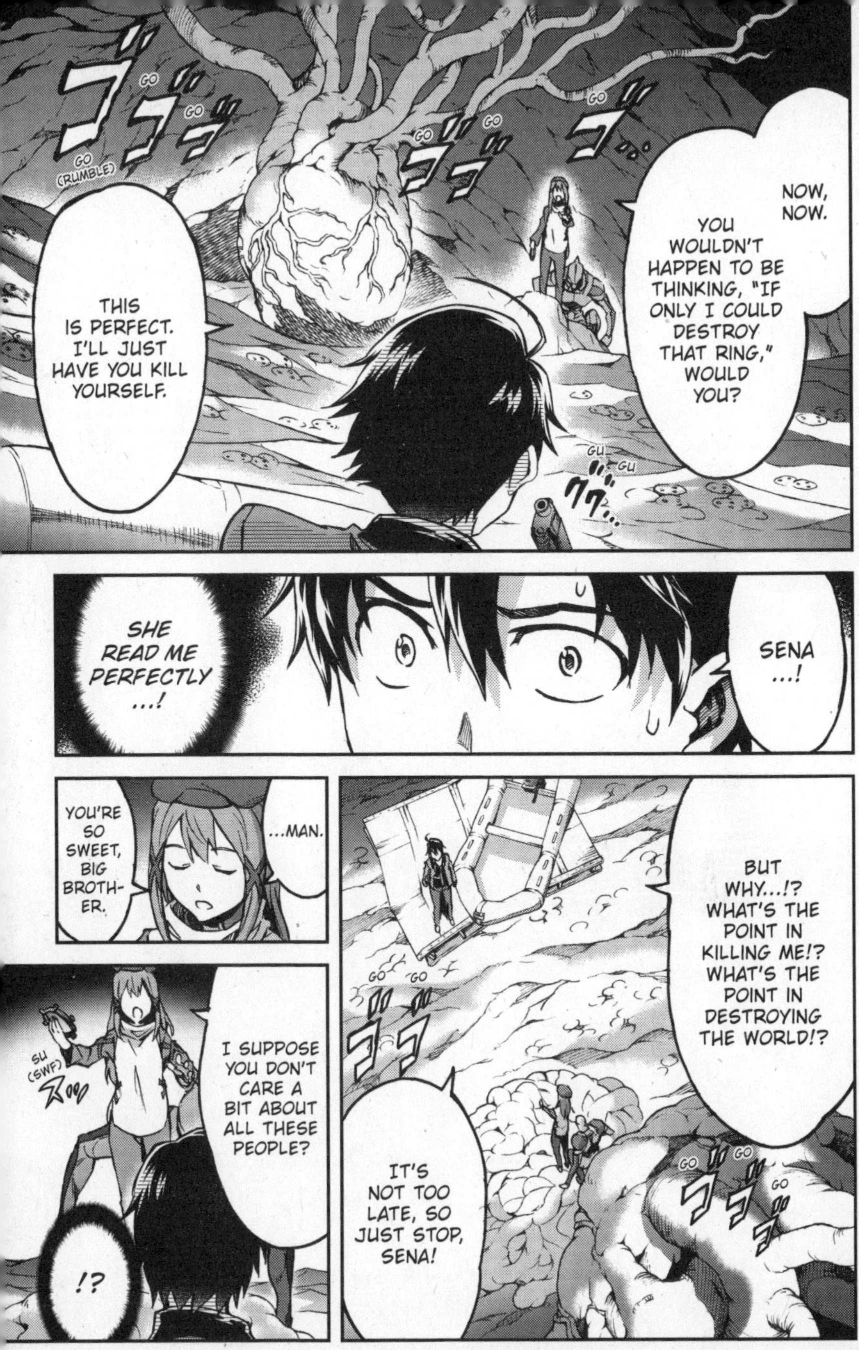
NOW, NOW.
YOU WOULDN'T HAPPEN TO BE THINKING, "IF ONLY I COULD DESTROY THAT RING," WOULD YOU?
GO
GO GO
GO GO GO (RUMBLE)
GU GU
THIS IS PERFECT. I'LL JUST HAVE YOU KILL YOURSELF.
SENA ...!
SHE READ ME PERFECTLY ...!
BUT WHY...!? WHAT'S THE POINT IN KILLING ME!? WHAT'S THE POINT IN DESTROYING THE WORLD!?
GO GO
GO GO GO
IT'S NOT TOO LATE, SO JUST STOP, SENA!
...MAN.
YOU'RE SO SWEET, BIG BROTH-ER.
I SUPPOSE YOU DON'T CARE A BIT ABOUT ALL THESE PEOPLE?
SU (SWF)
!?

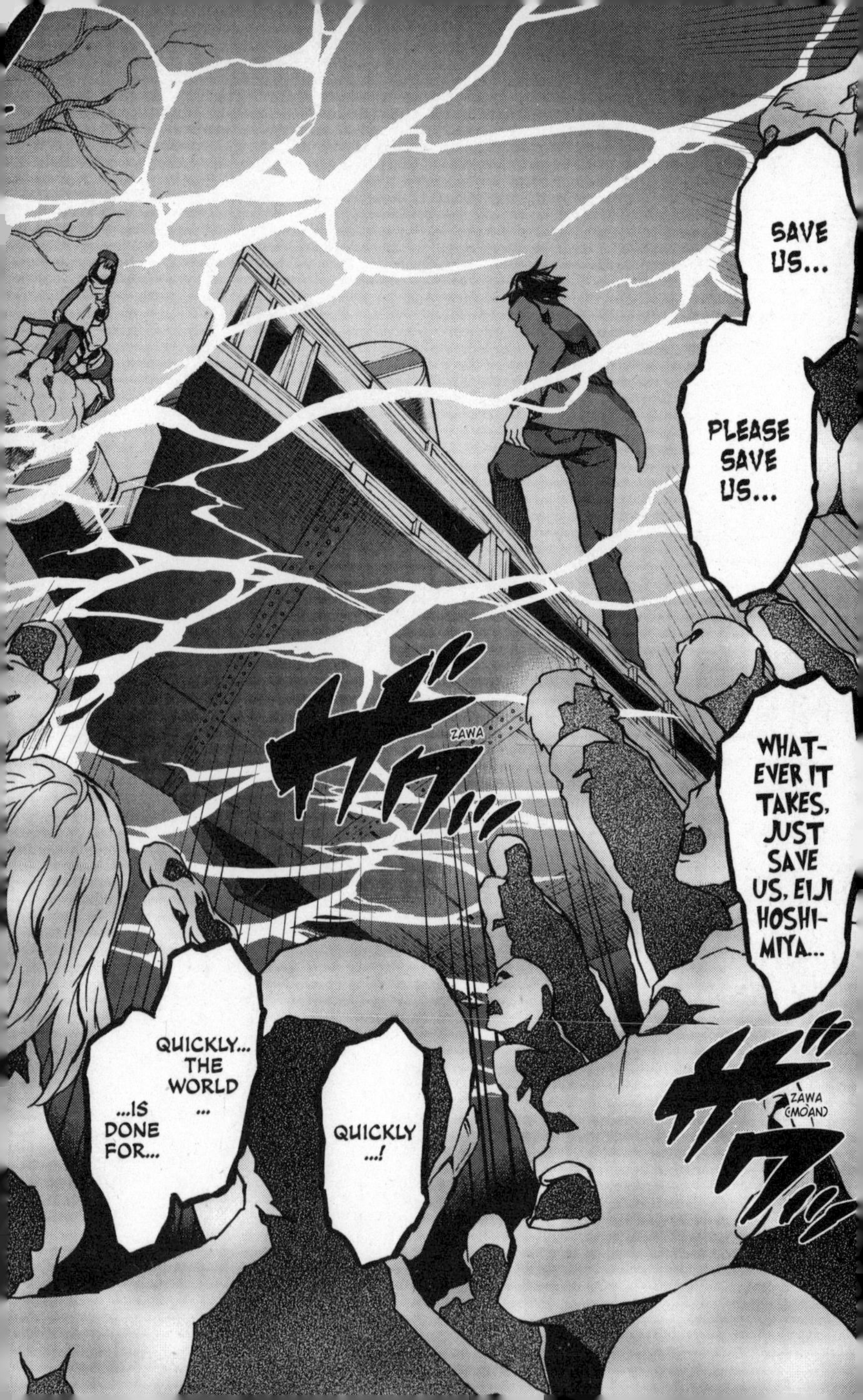
SAVE US...
PLEASE SAVE US...
WHAT-EVER IT TAKES, JUST SAVE US, EIJI HOSHI-MIYA...
ザワ
ZAWA
ザワ
ZAWA (MOAN)
QUICKLY ...!
QUICKLY... THE WORLD ... ...IS DONE FOR...

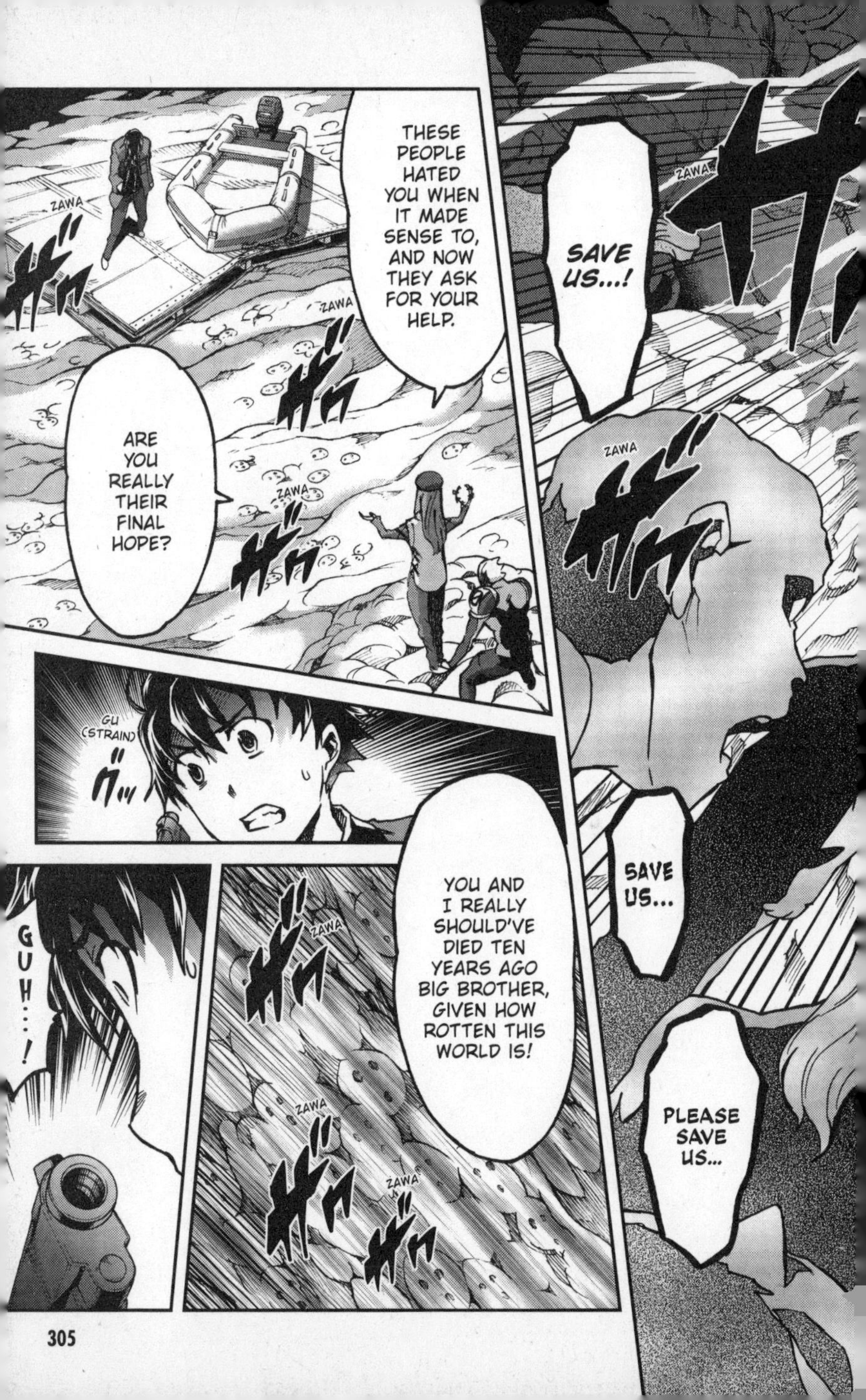
ZAWA
SAVE US...!
ZAWA
SAVE US...
PLEASE SAVE US...
THESE PEOPLE HATED YOU WHEN IT MADE SENSE TO, AND NOW THEY ASK FOR YOUR HELP.
ZAWA
ZAWA
ARE YOU REALLY THEIR FINAL HOPE?
ZAWA
GU (STRAIN)
YOU AND I REALLY SHOULD'VE DIED TEN YEARS AGO BIG BROTHER, GIVEN HOW ROTTEN THIS WORLD IS!
ZAWA
ZAWA
ZAWA
GUH...!

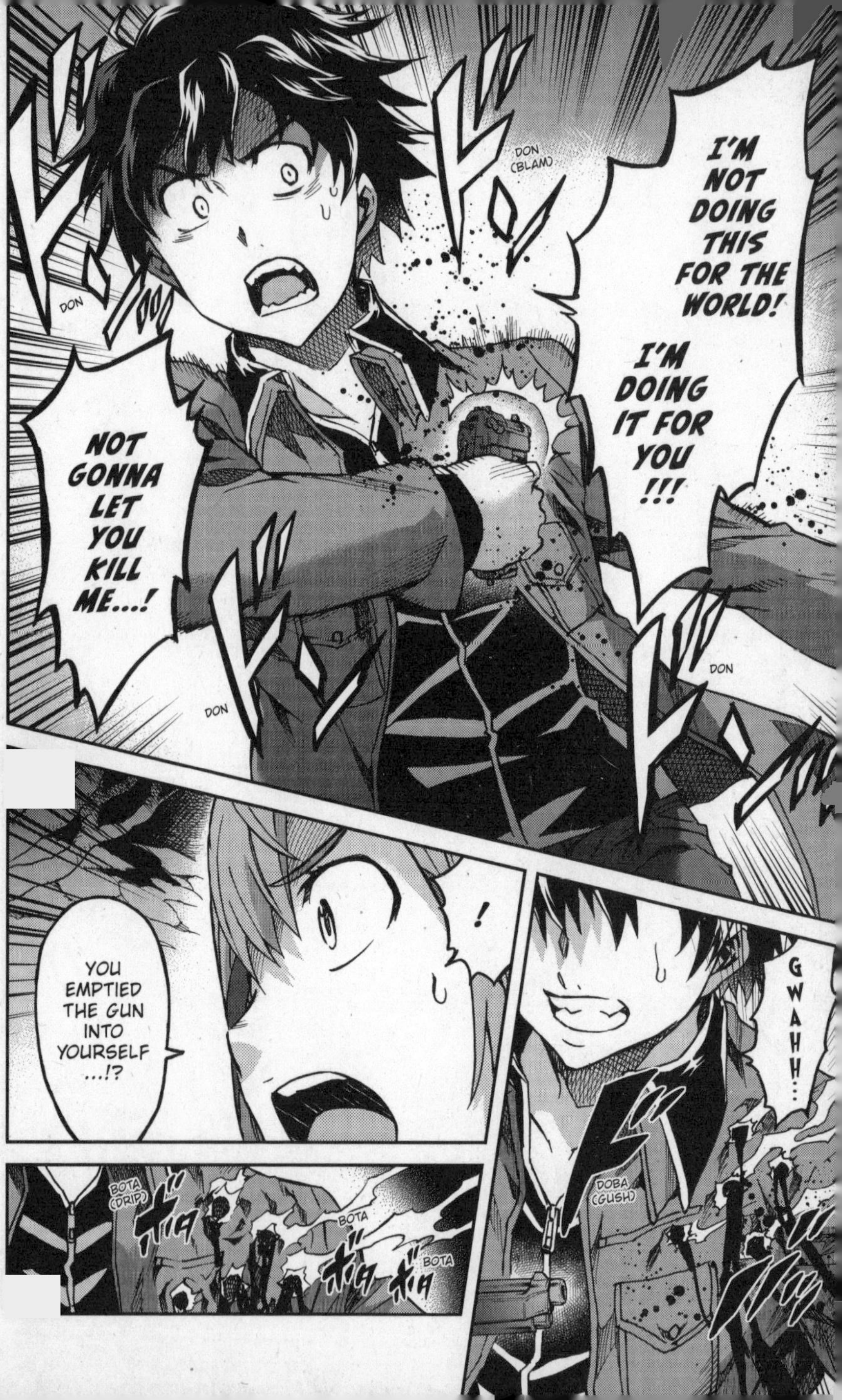
I'M NOT DOING THIS FOR THE WORLD!
I'M DOING IT FOR YOU!!!
DON (BLAM)
DON
DON
NOT GONNA LET YOU KILL ME...!
DON
GWAHH...
!
YOU EMPTIED THE GUN INTO YOURSELF...!?
DOBA (GUSH)
BOTA (DRIP)
BOTA
BOTA

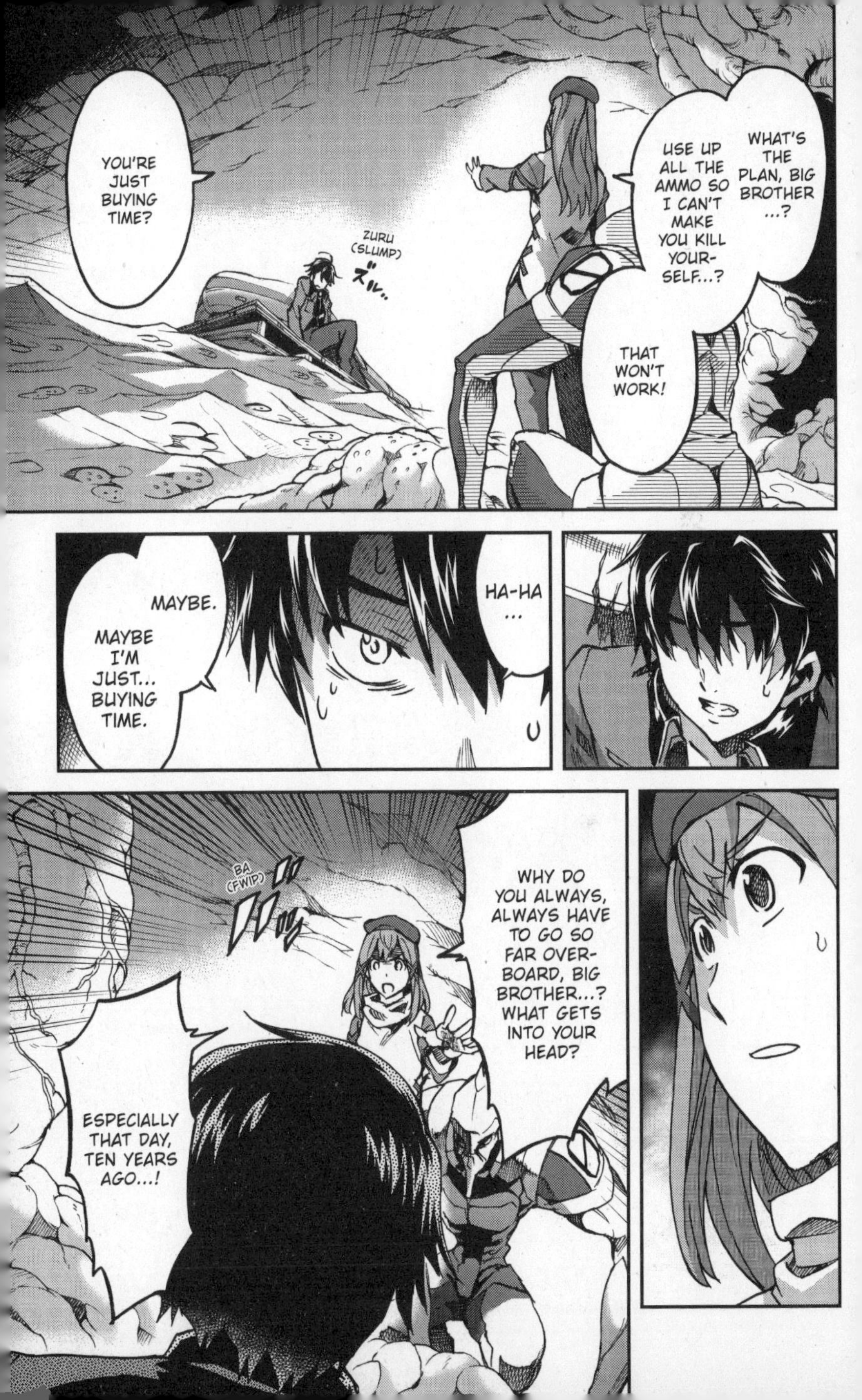
WHAT'S THE PLAN, BIG BROTHER ...?
USE UP ALL THE AMMO SO I CAN'T MAKE YOU KILL YOUR-SELF...?
THAT WON'T WORK!
ZURU (SLUMP)
ズル..
YOU'RE JUST BUYING TIME?
HA-HA ...
MAYBE.
MAYBE I'M JUST... BUYING TIME.
WHY DO YOU ALWAYS, ALWAYS HAVE TO GO SO FAR OVER-BOARD, BIG BROTHER...? WHAT GETS INTO YOUR HEAD?
BA (FWIP)
ESPECIALLY THAT DAY, TEN YEARS AGO...!

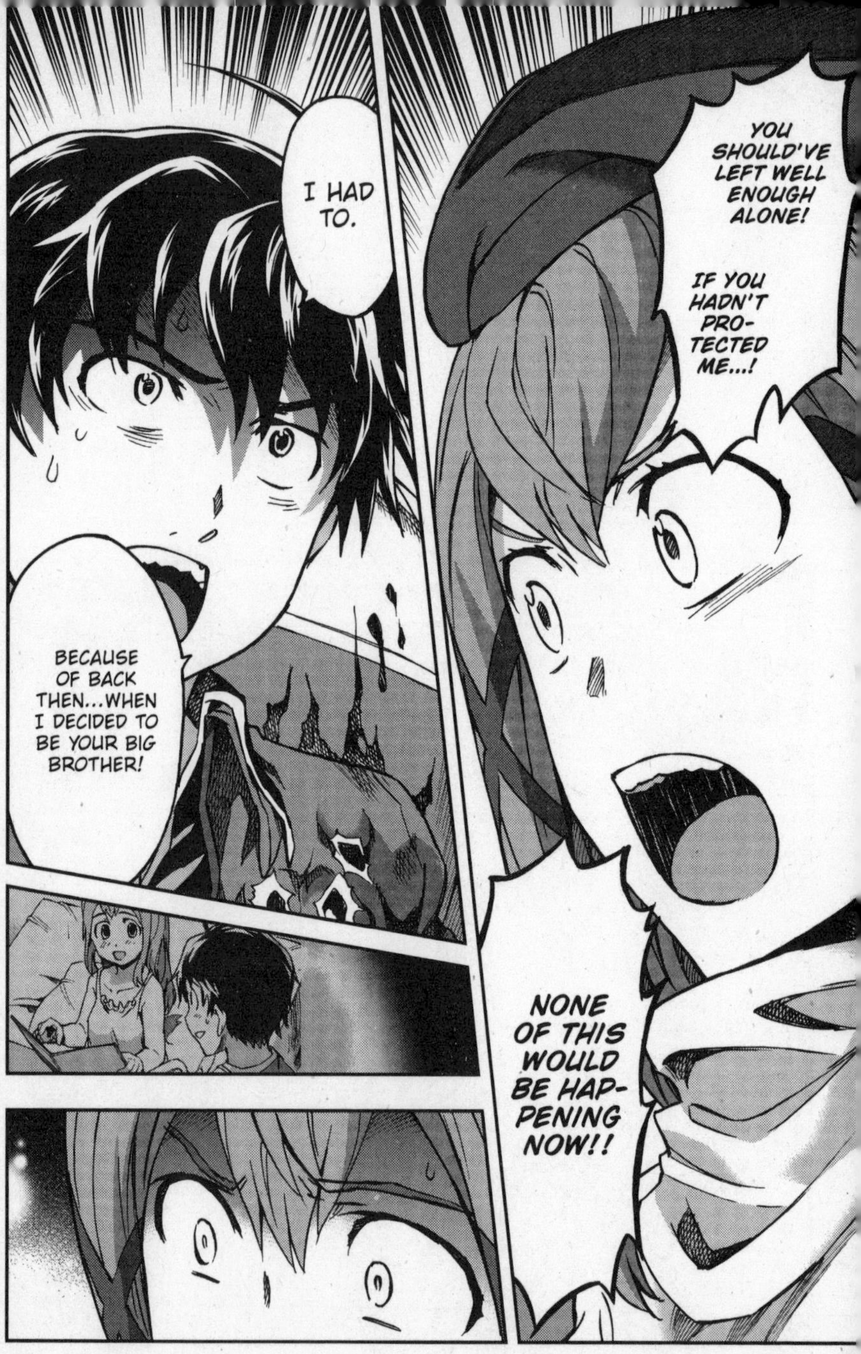
YOU SHOULD'VE LEFT WELL ENOUGH ALONE!
IF YOU HADN'T PROTECTED ME...!
NONE OF THIS WOULD BE HAPPENING NOW!!
I HAD TO.
BECAUSE OF BACK THEN...WHEN I DECIDED TO BE YOUR BIG BROTHER!

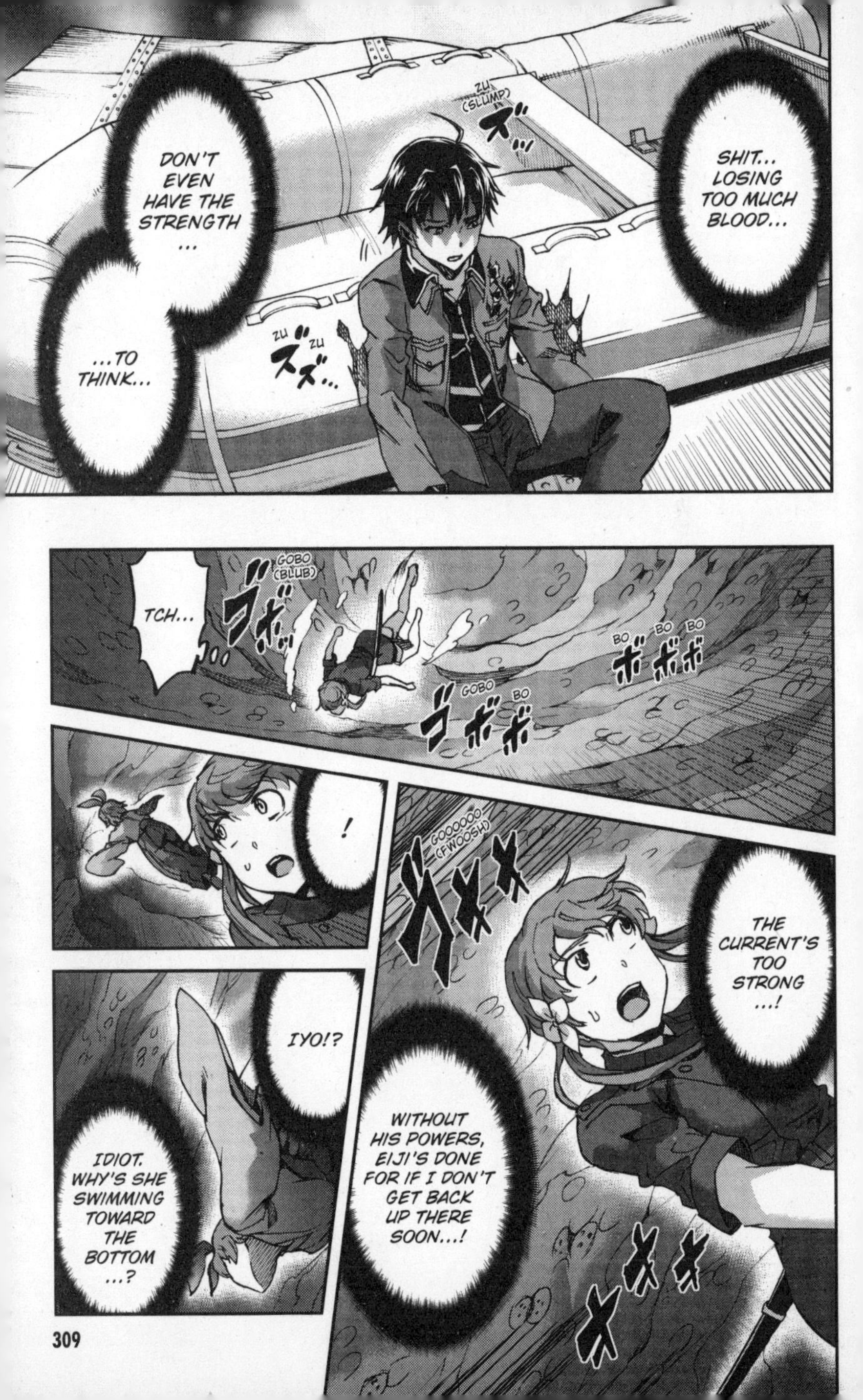
SHIT... LOSING TOO MUCH BLOOD...
ZU (SLUMP)
ZU ZU
DON'T EVEN HAVE THE STRENGTH ...
...TO THINK...
BO BO BO
GOBO BO
GOBO (BLUB)
TCH...
GOOOOOO (FWOOSH)
THE CURRENT'S TOO STRONG ...!
WITHOUT HIS POWERS, EIJI'S DONE FOR IF I DON'T GET BACK UP THERE SOON...!
!
IYO!?
IDIOT. WHY'S SHE SWIMMING TOWARD THE BOTTOM ...?

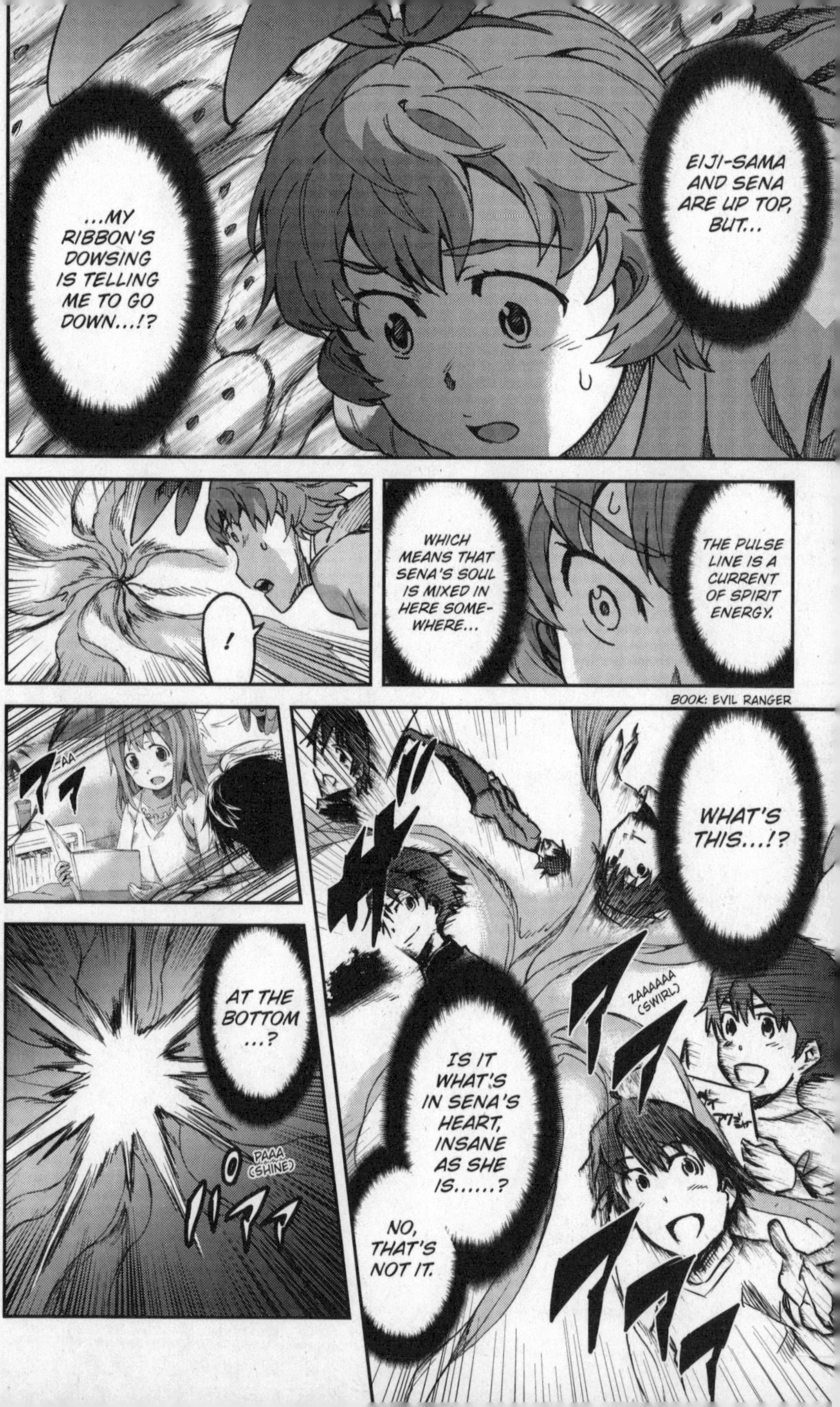
EIJI-SAMA AND SENA ARE UP TOP, BUT...
...MY RIBBON'S DOWSING IS TELLING ME TO GO DOWN...!?
THE PULSE LINE IS A CURRENT OF SPIRIT ENERGY.
WHICH MEANS THAT SENA'S SOUL IS MIXED IN HERE SOME-WHERE...
!
BOOK: EVIL RANGER
WHAT'S THIS...!?
ZAAAAAA (SWIRL)
IS IT WHAT'S IN SENA'S HEART, INSANE AS SHE IS......?
NO, THAT'S NOT IT.
AA
AT THE BOTTOM ...?
PAAA (SHINE)

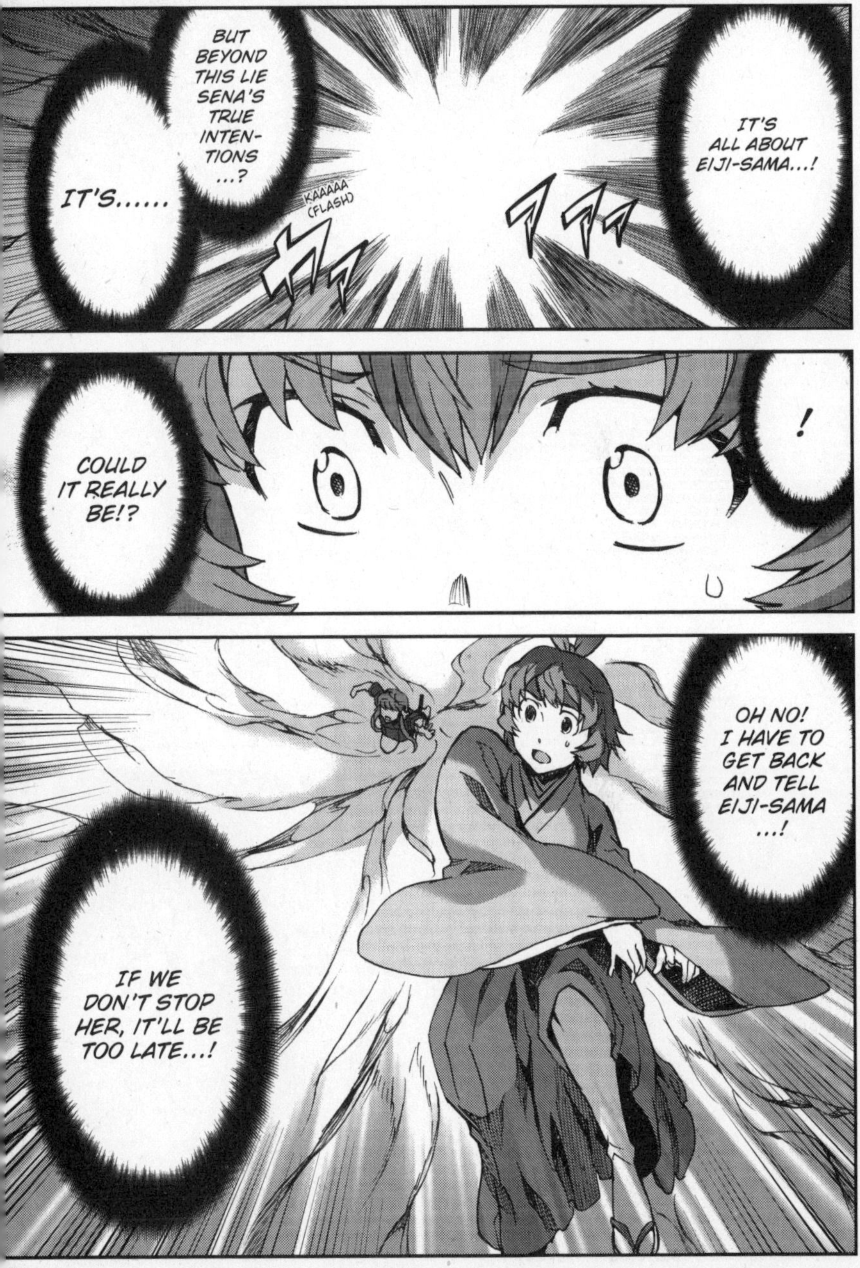
IT'S ALL ABOUT EIJI-SAMA...!
BUT BEYOND THIS LIE SENA'S TRUE INTENTIONS ...?
KAAAAA (FLASH)
IT'S......
!
COULD IT REALLY BE!?
OH NO! I HAVE TO GET BACK AND TELL EIJI-SAMA ...!
IF WE DON'T STOP HER, IT'LL BE TOO LATE...!

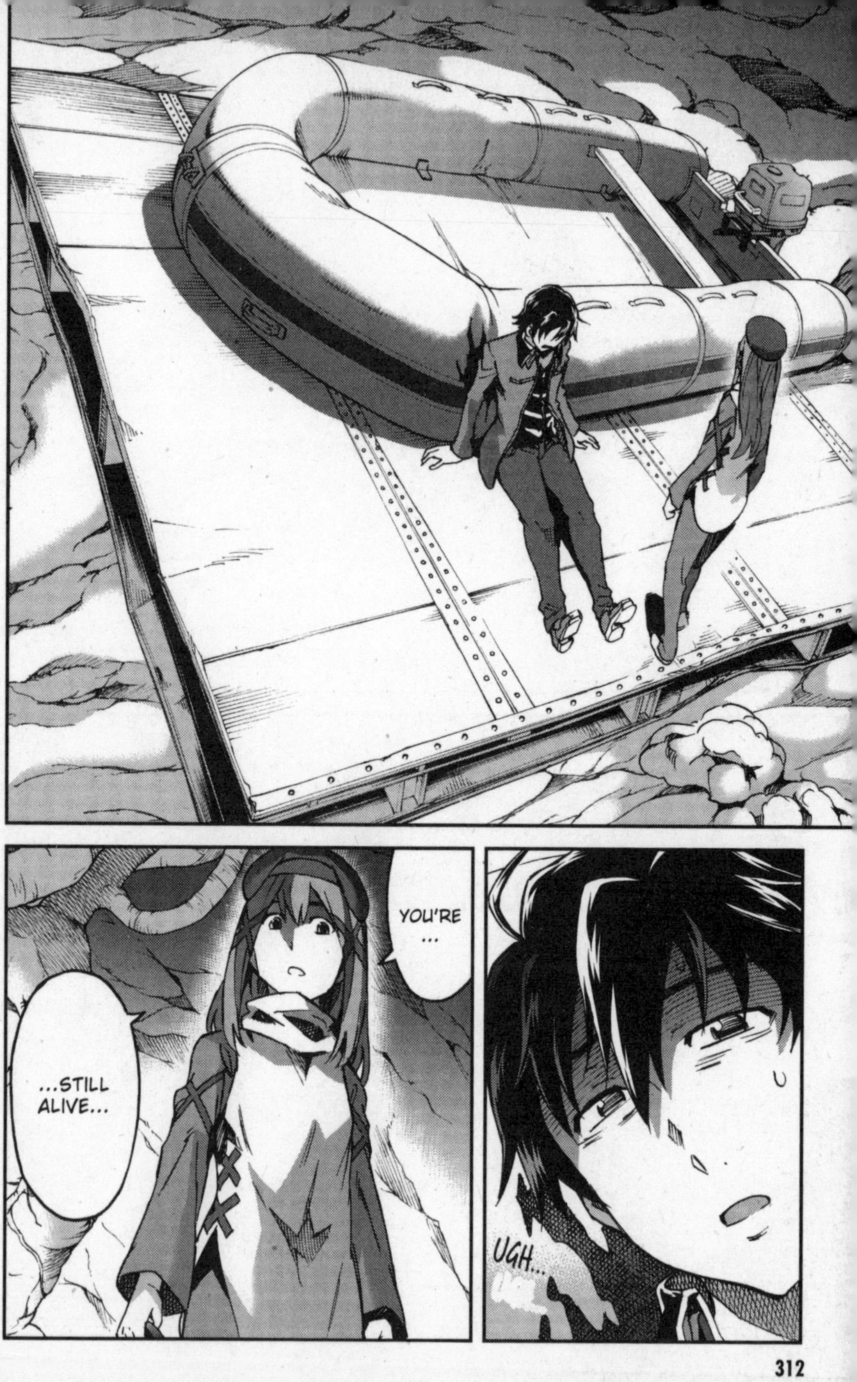
UGH...
YOU'RE ...
...STILL ALIVE...

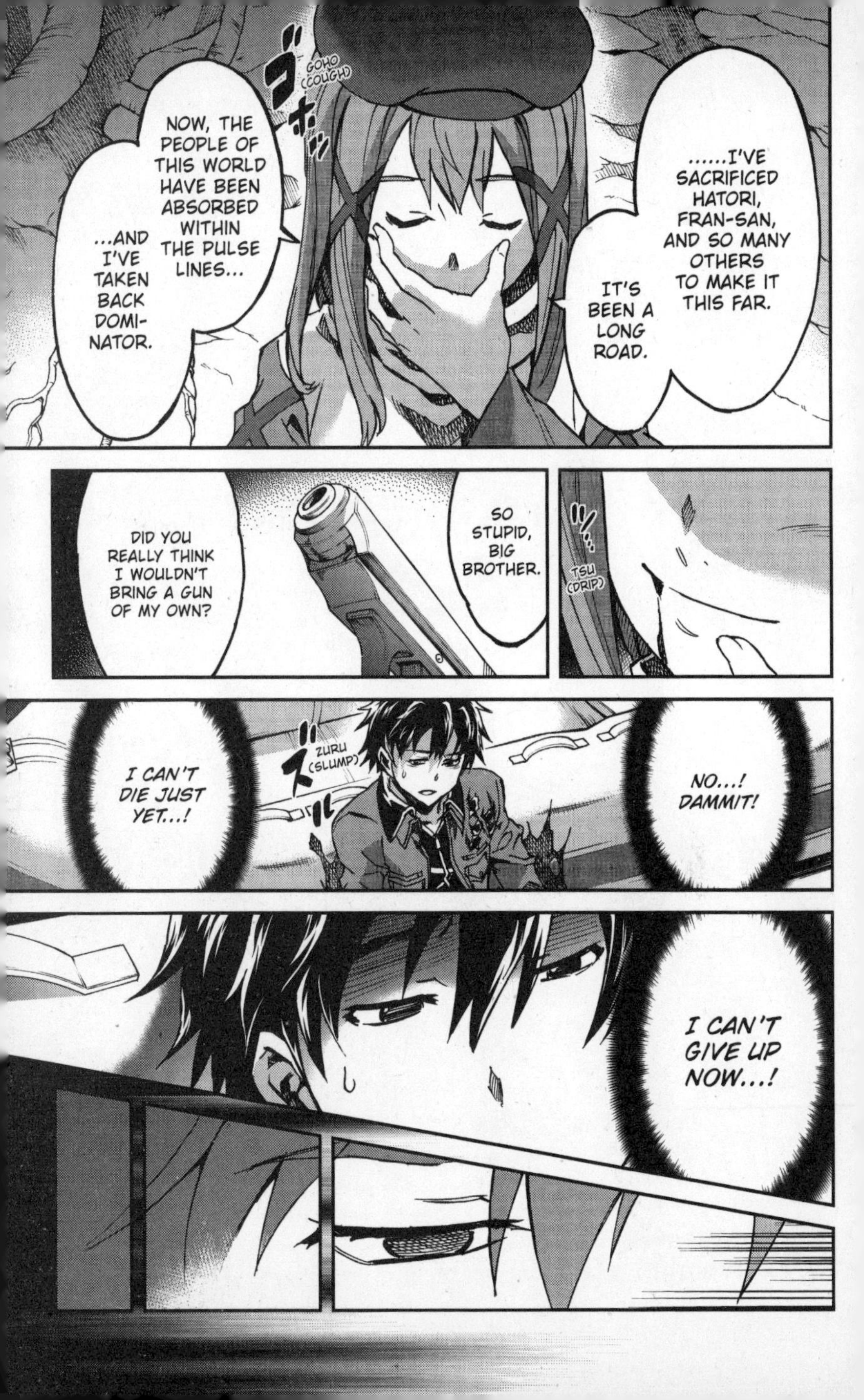
......I'VE SACRIFICED HATORI, FRAN-SAN, AND SO MANY OTHERS TO MAKE IT THIS FAR.
IT'S BEEN A LONG ROAD.
GOHO (COUGH)
NOW, THE PEOPLE OF THIS WORLD HAVE BEEN ABSORBED WITHIN THE PULSE LINES...
...AND I'VE TAKEN BACK DOMINATOR.
TSU (DRIP)
SO STUPID, BIG BROTHER.
DID YOU REALLY THINK I WOULDN'T BRING A GUN OF MY OWN?
NO...! DAMMIT!
ZURU (SLUMP)
I CAN'T DIE JUST YET...!
I CAN'T GIVE UP NOW...!

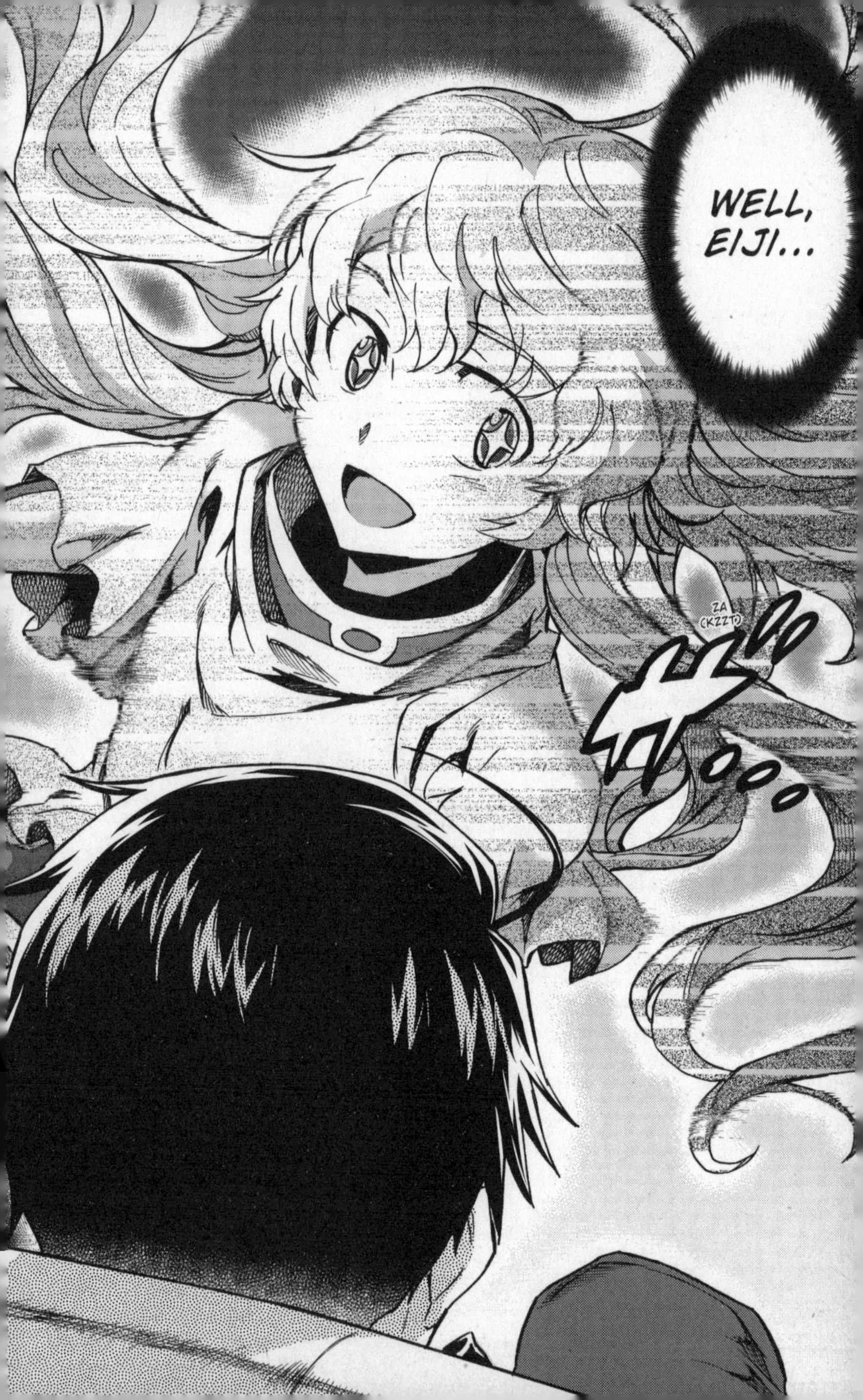
WELL,
EIJI...
ZA
(KZZT)

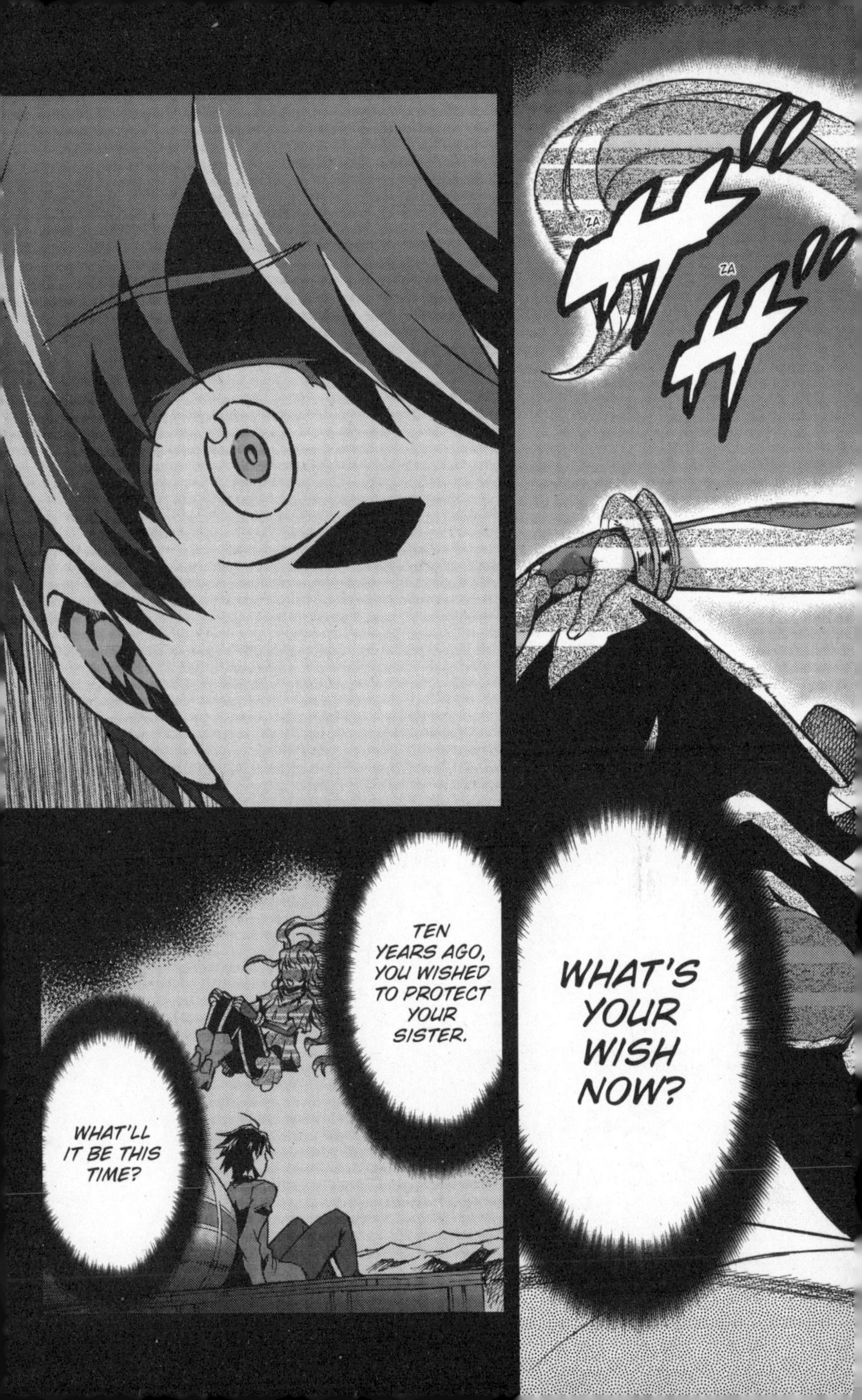
ZA
ZA
WHAT'S YOUR WISH NOW?
TEN YEARS AGO, YOU WISHED TO PROTECT YOUR SISTER.
WHAT'LL IT BE THIS TIME?

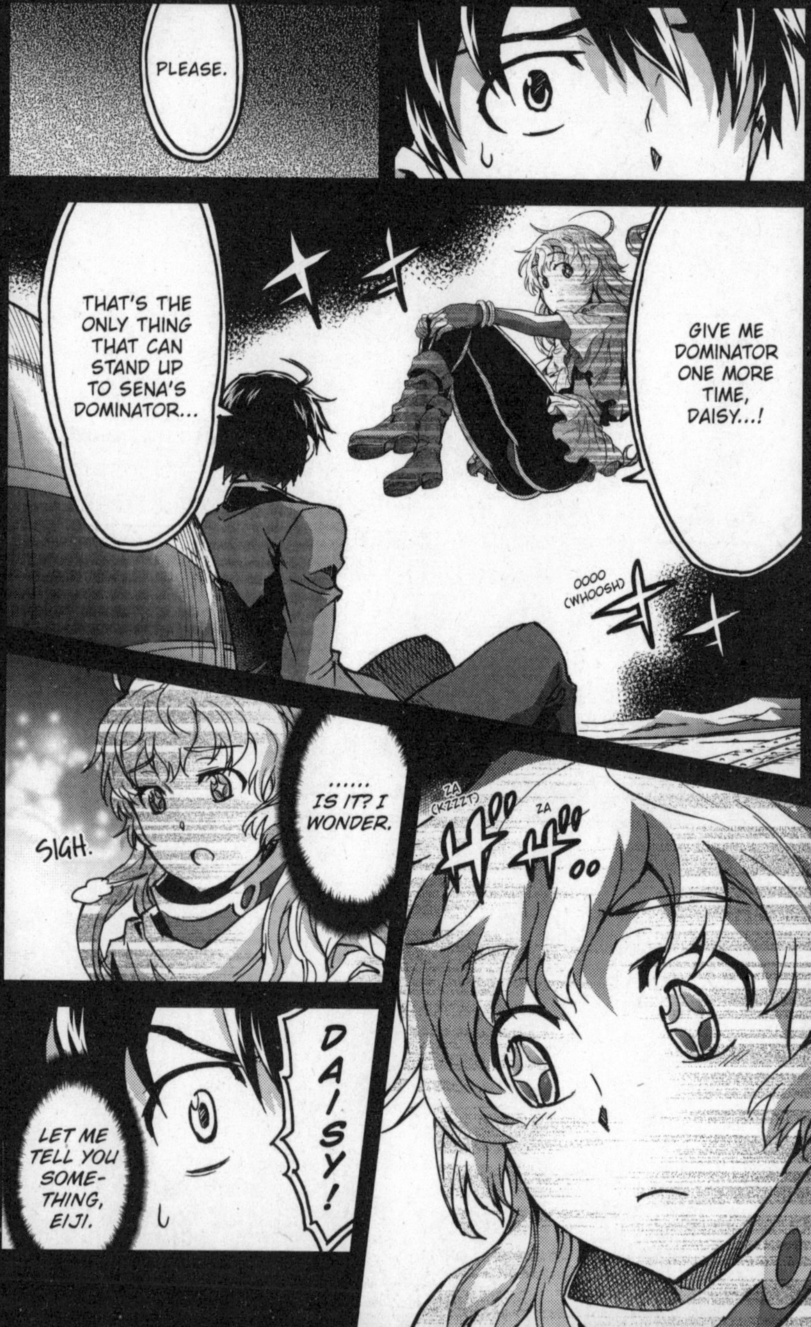
PLEASE.
GIVE ME DOMINATOR ONE MORE TIME, DAISY...!
THAT'S THE ONLY THING THAT CAN STAND UP TO SENA'S DOMINATOR...
OOOO (WHOOSH)
ZA (KZZZT)
ZA
......IS IT? I WONDER.
SIGH.
DAISY!
LET ME TELL YOU SOME-THING, EIJI.

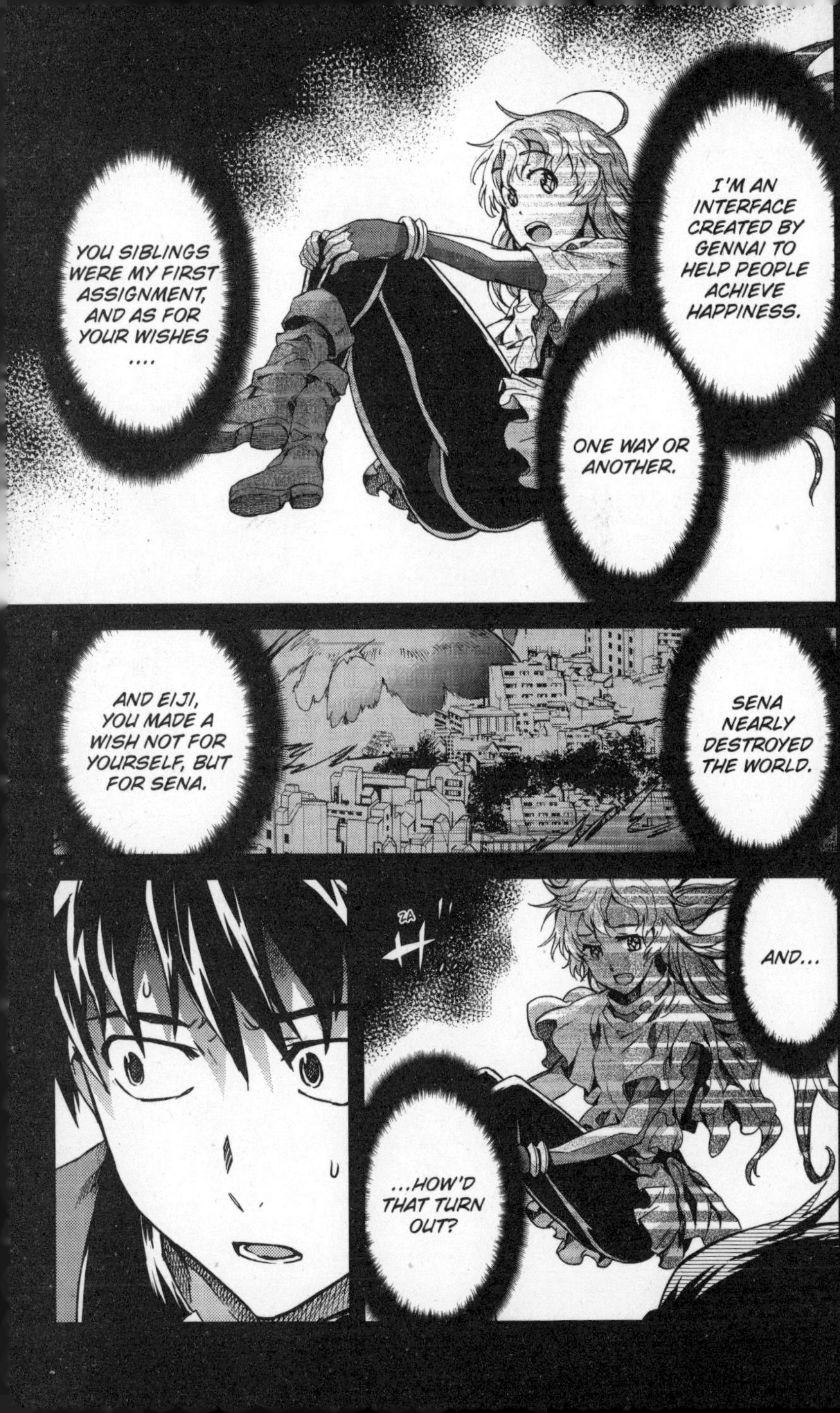
I'M AN INTERFACE CREATED BY GENNAI TO HELP PEOPLE ACHIEVE HAPPINESS.
YOU SIBLINGS WERE MY FIRST ASSIGNMENT, AND AS FOR YOUR WISHES ....
ONE WAY OR ANOTHER.
SENA NEARLY DESTROYED THE WORLD.
AND EIJI, YOU MADE A WISH NOT FOR YOURSELF, BUT FOR SENA.
ZA
AND...
...HOW'D THAT TURN OUT?

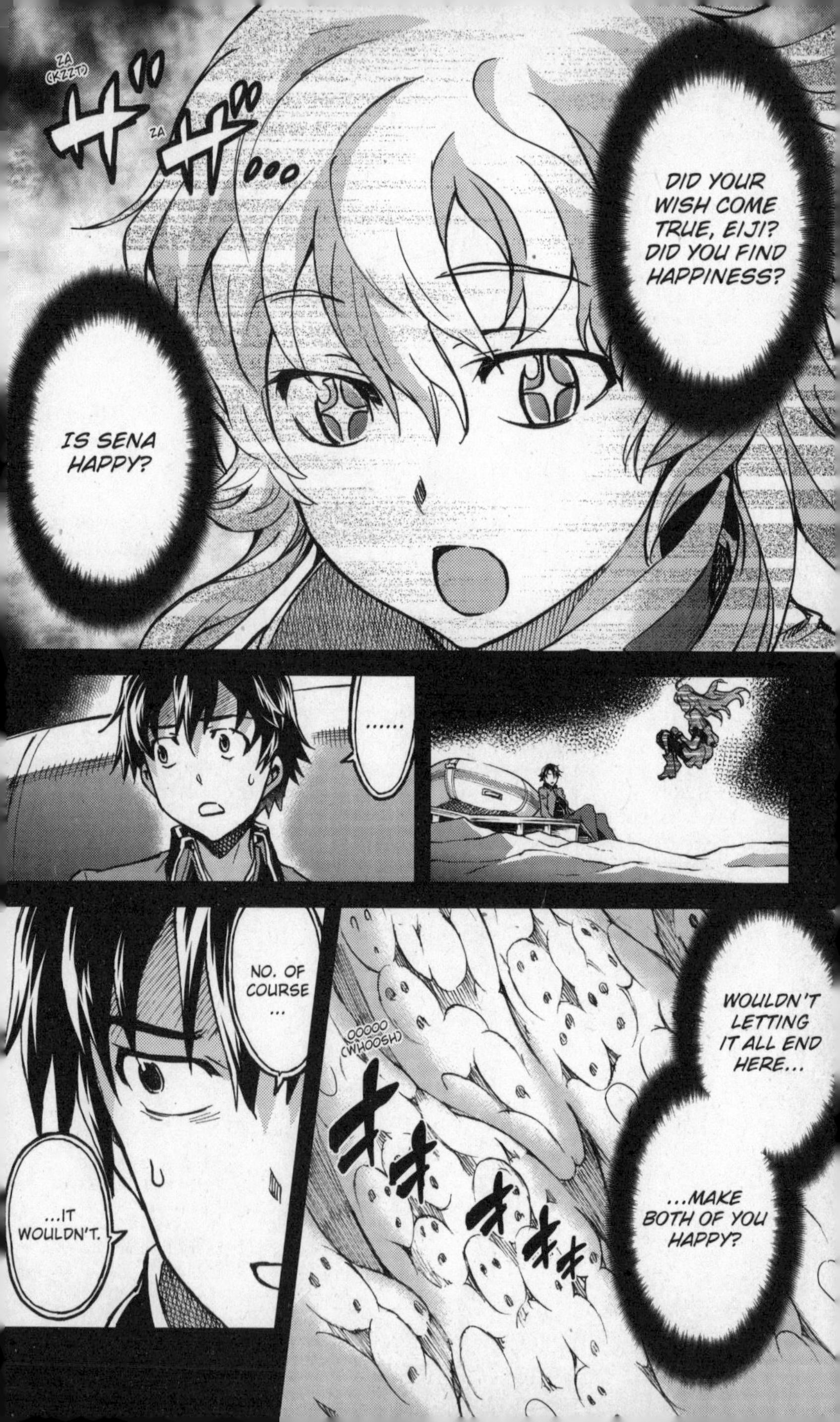
DID YOUR WISH COME TRUE, EIJI? DID YOU FIND HAPPINESS?
ZA (KZZT)
ZA
IS SENA HAPPY?
......
WOULDN'T LETTING IT ALL END HERE...
...MAKE BOTH OF YOU HAPPY?
OOOOO (WHOOSH)
NO. OF COURSE ...
...IT WOULDN'T.

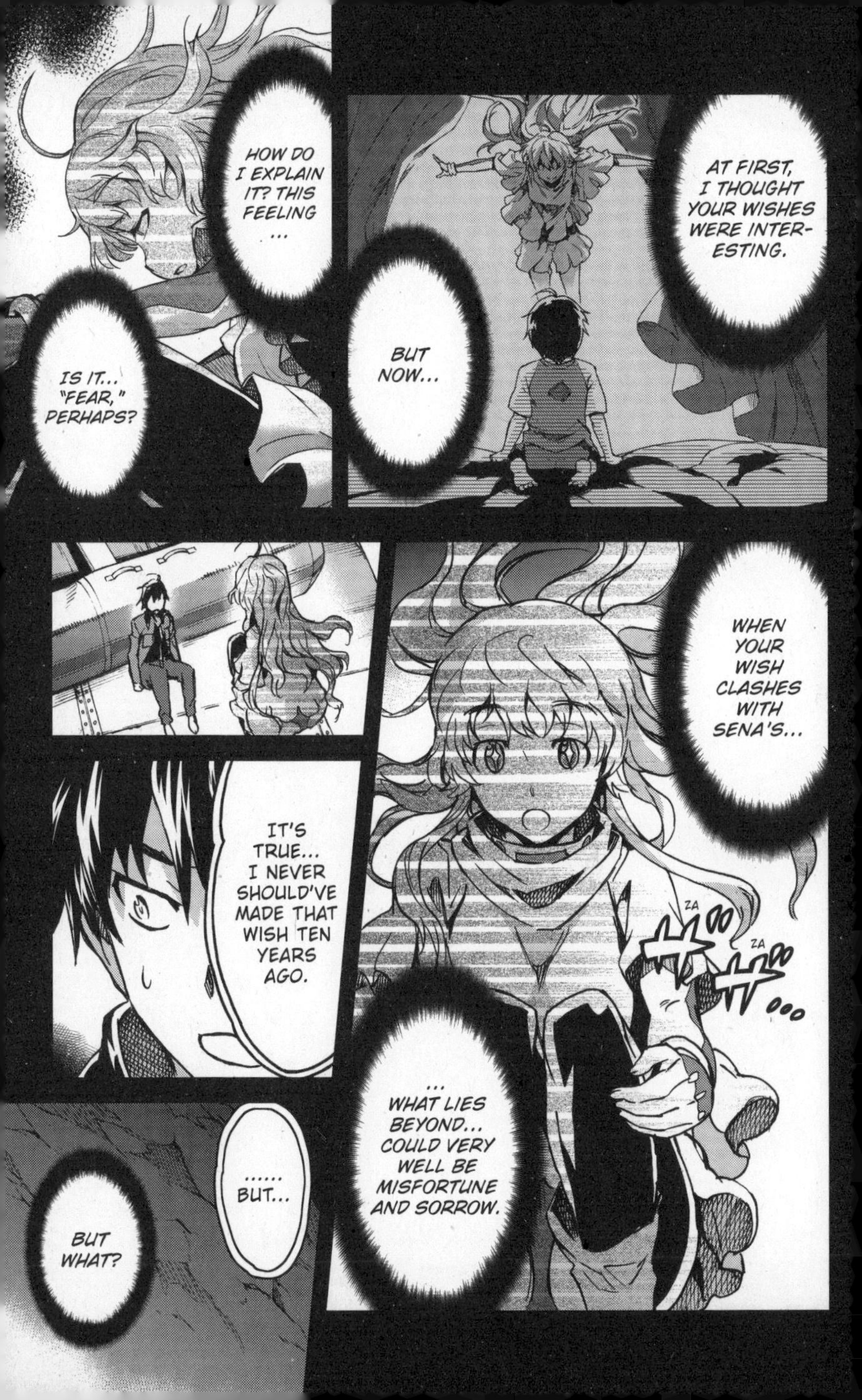
AT FIRST, I THOUGHT YOUR WISHES WERE INTER-ESTING.
BUT NOW...
HOW DO I EXPLAIN IT? THIS FEELING ...
IS IT... "FEAR," PERHAPS?
WHEN YOUR WISH CLASHES WITH SENA'S...
ZA
ZA
... WHAT LIES BEYOND... COULD VERY WELL BE MISFORTUNE AND SORROW.
IT'S TRUE... I NEVER SHOULD'VE MADE THAT WISH TEN YEARS AGO.
...... BUT...
BUT WHAT?

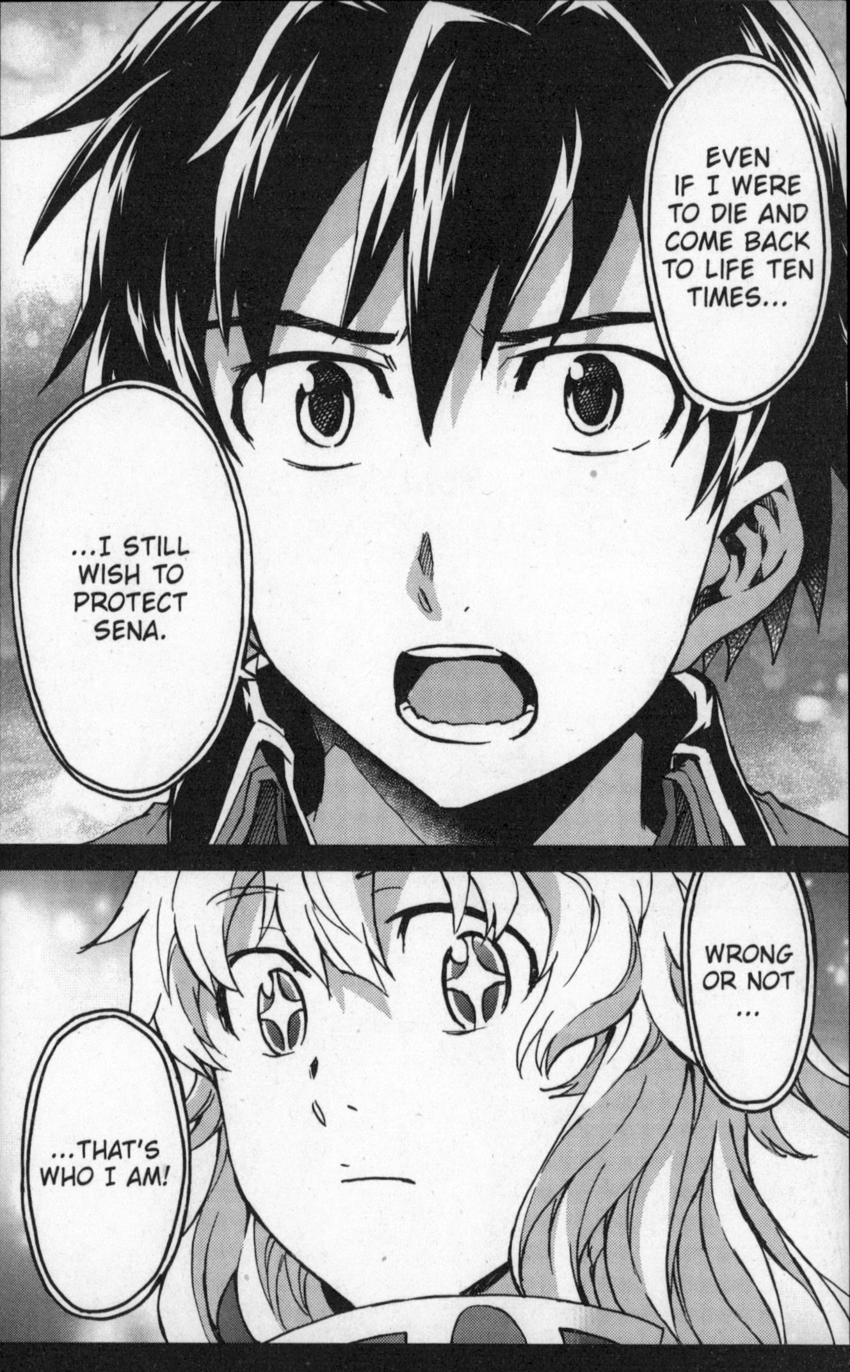
EVEN IF I WERE TO DIE AND COME BACK TO LIFE TEN TIMES...
...I STILL WISH TO PROTECT SENA.
WRONG OR NOT ...
...THAT'S WHO I AM!

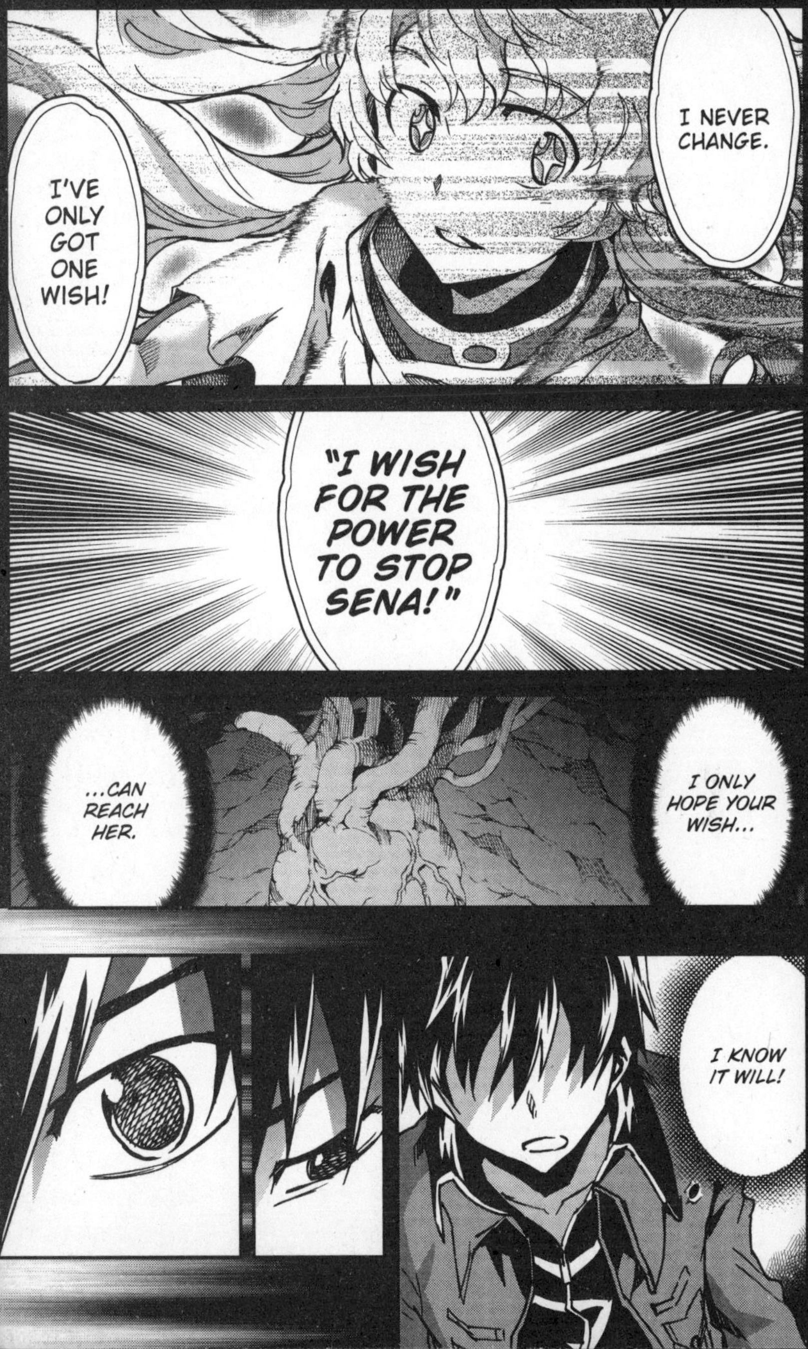
I NEVER CHANGE.
I'VE ONLY GOT ONE WISH!
"I WISH FOR THE POWER TO STOP SENA!"
I ONLY HOPE YOUR WISH...
...CAN REACH HER.
I KNOW IT WILL!

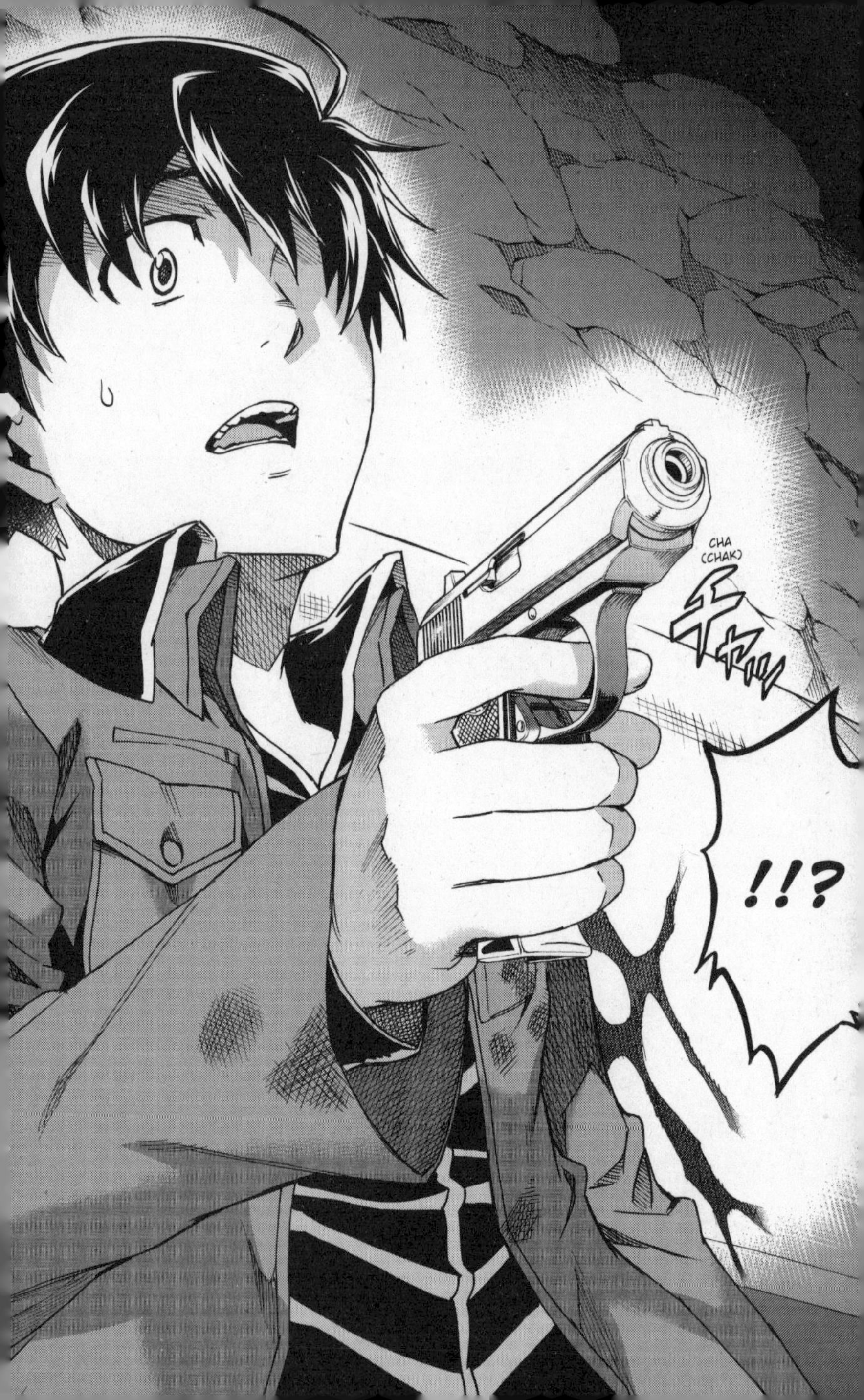
CHA (CHAK)
チャッ
!!?

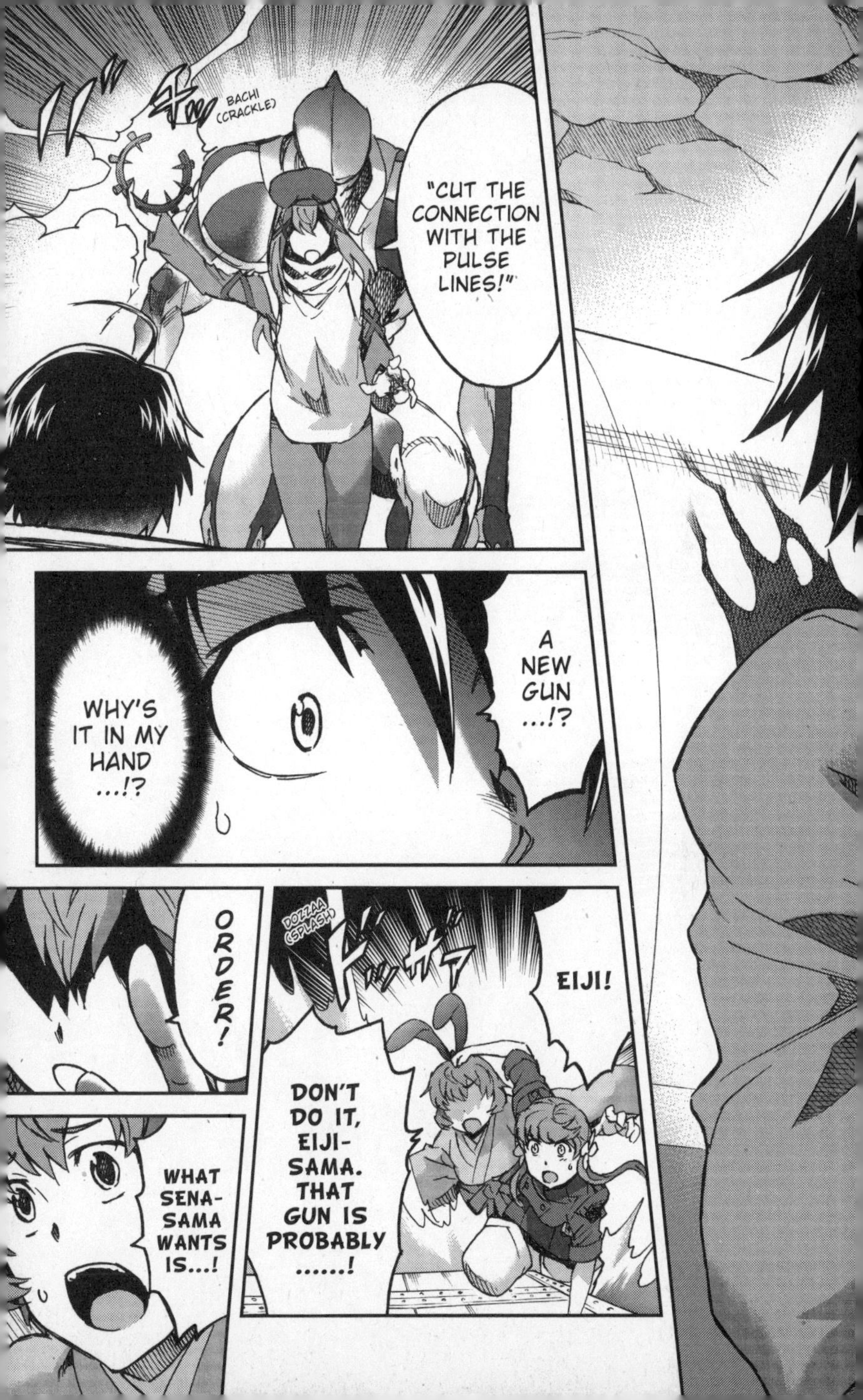
"CUT THE CONNECTION WITH THE PULSE LINES!"
BACHI (CRACKLE)
A NEW GUN ...!?
WHY'S IT IN MY HAND ...!?
DOZZAA (SPLASH)
EIJI!
DON'T DO IT, EIJI-SAMA. THAT GUN IS PROBABLY ......!
ORDER!
WHAT SENA-SAMA WANTS IS...!

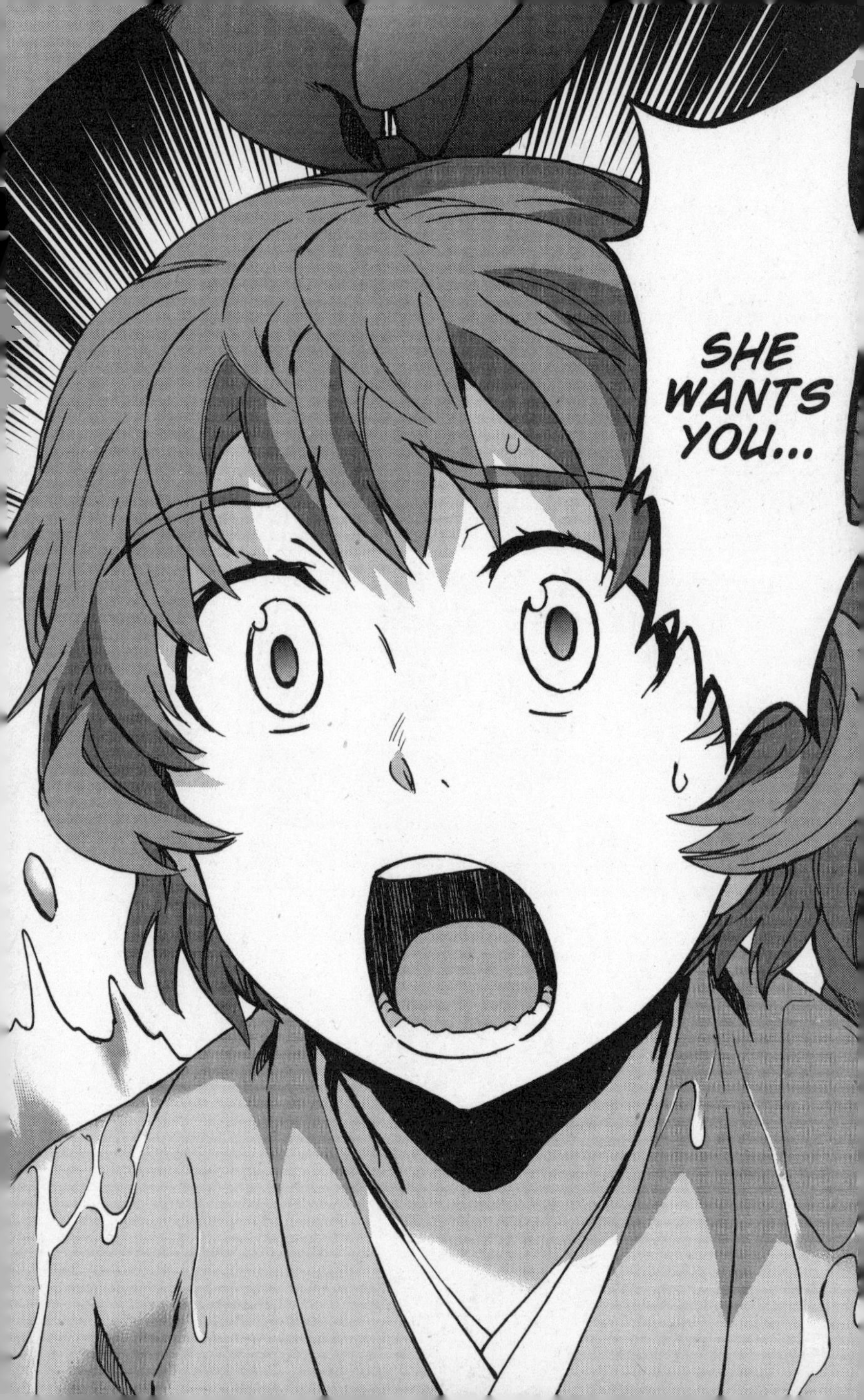
SHE WANTS YOU...

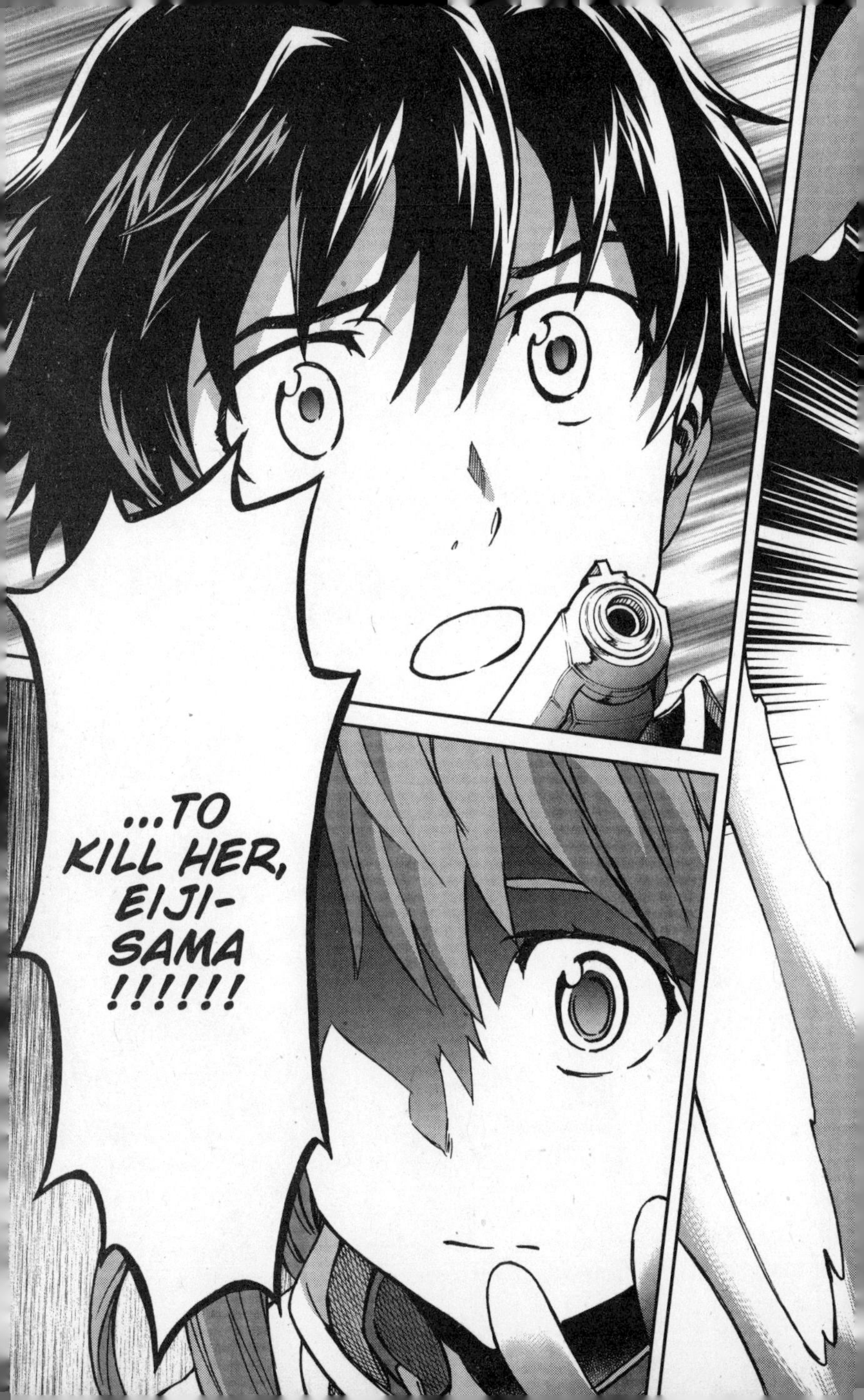
...TO KILL HER, EIJI-SAMA !!!!!!

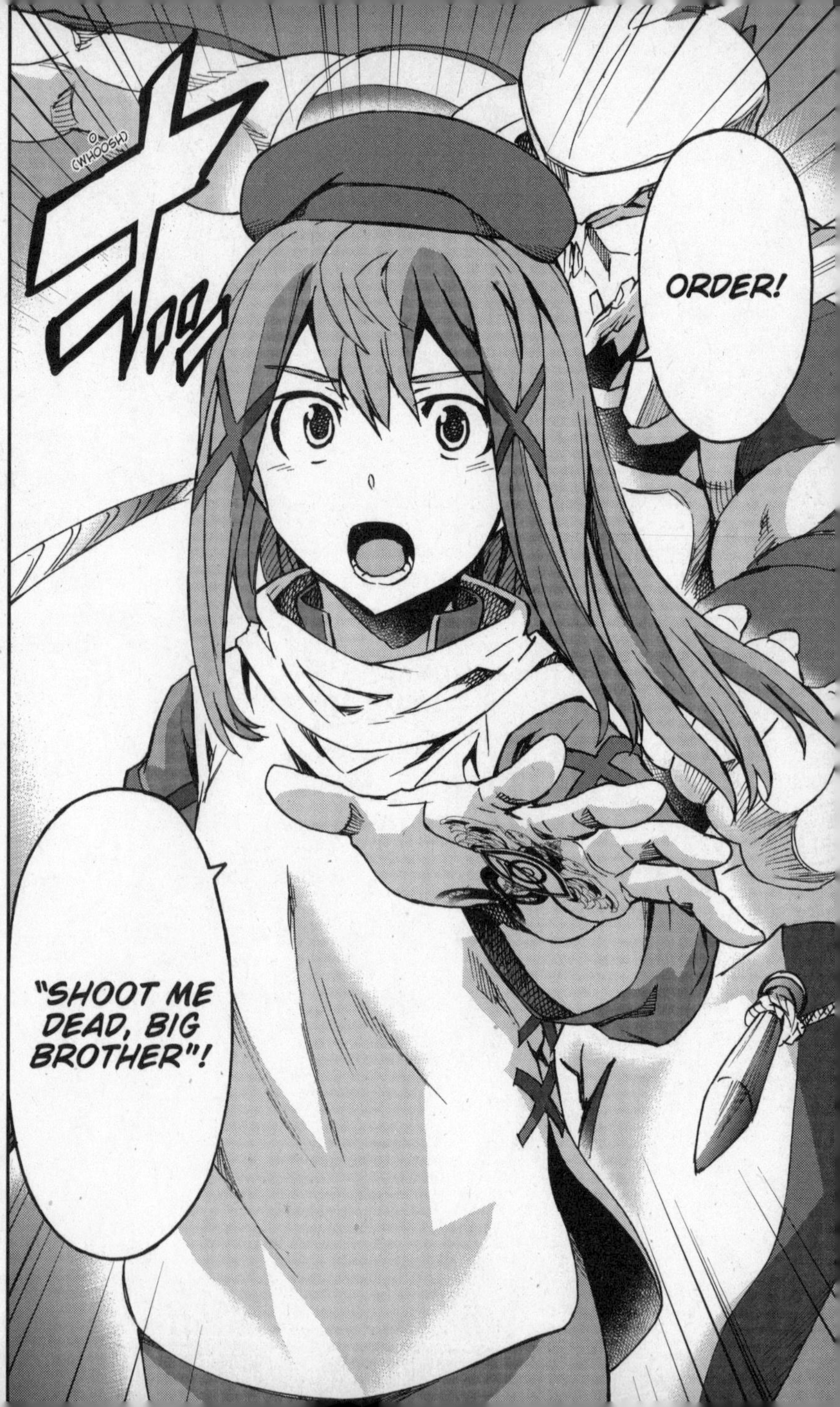
ORDER!
(WHOOSH)
"SHOOT ME DEAD, BIG BROTHER"!

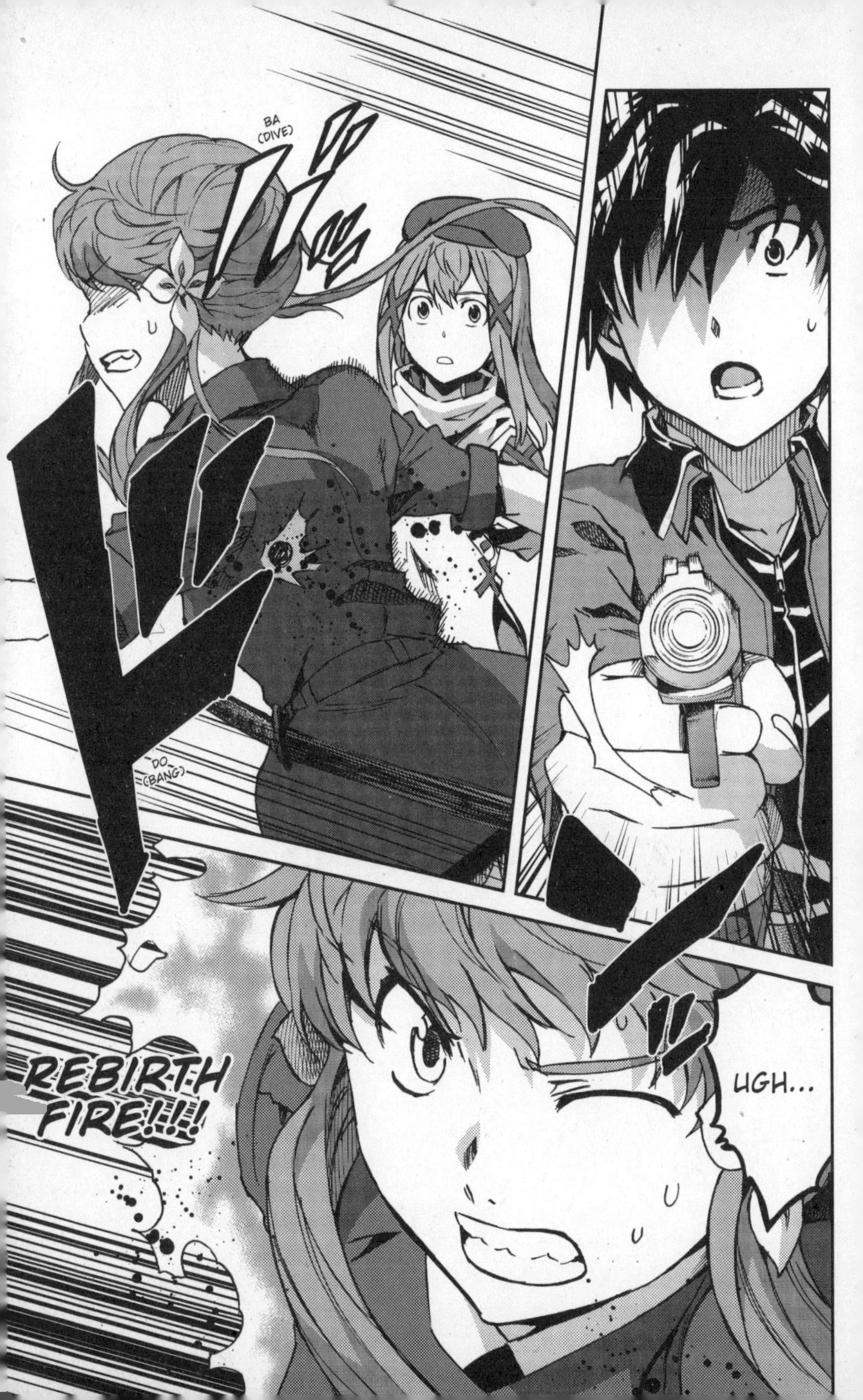
BA
(DIVE)
DO
(BANG)
UGH...
REBIRTH
FIRE!!!!

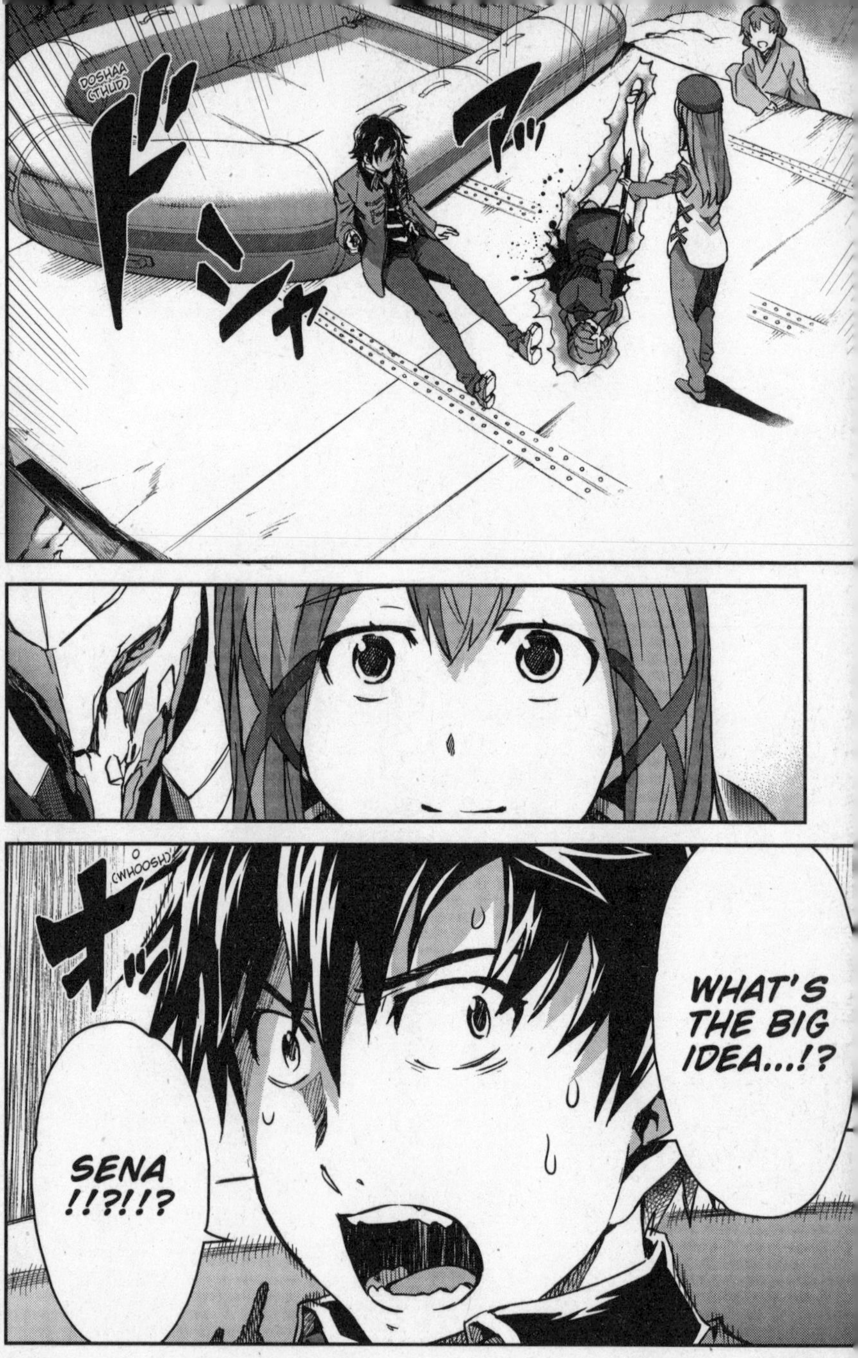
DOSHAA (THUD)
(WHOOSH)
WHAT'S THE BIG IDEA...!?
SENA !!?!!?

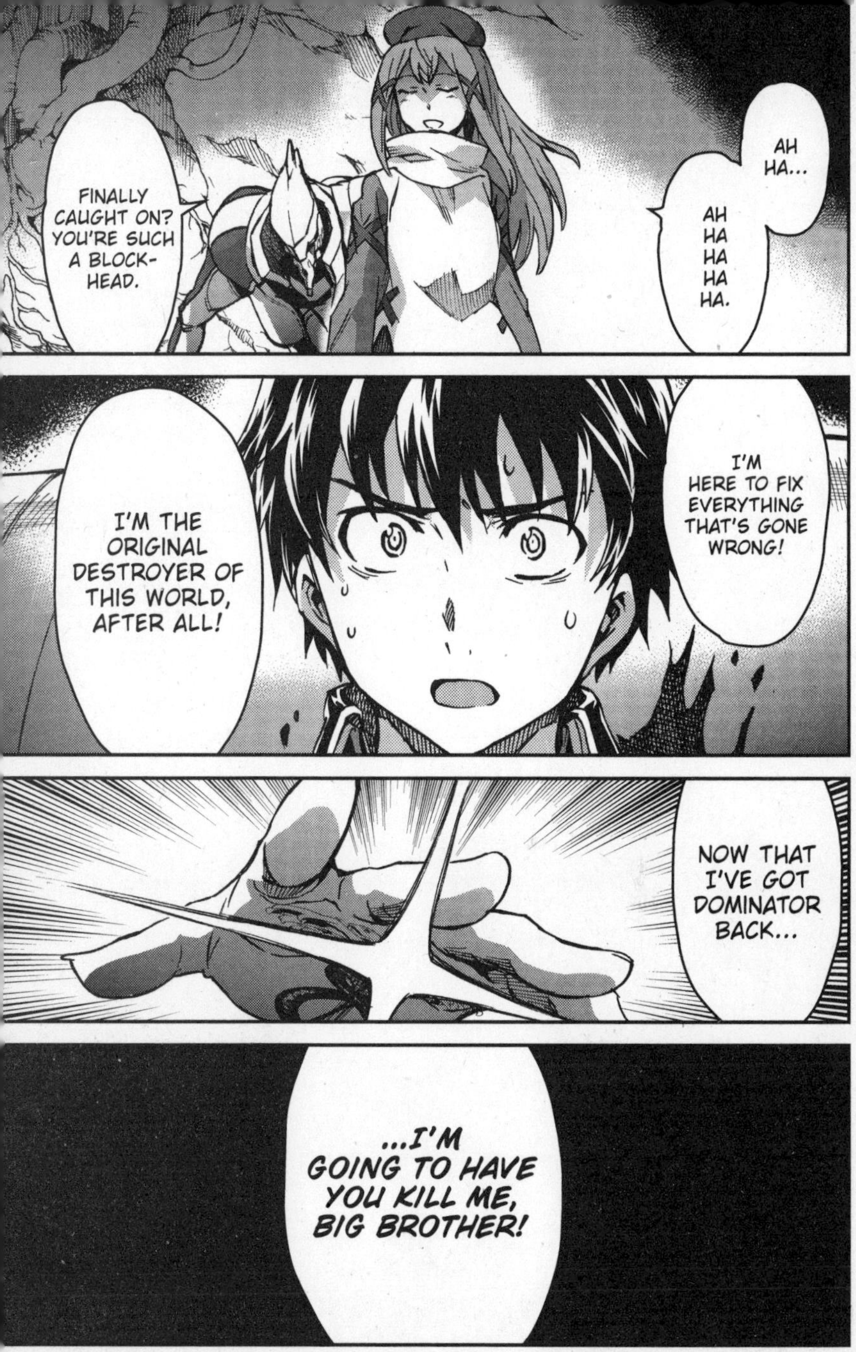
AH HA... AH HA HA HA HA.
FINALLY CAUGHT ON? YOU'RE SUCH A BLOCK-HEAD.
I'M HERE TO FIX EVERYTHING THAT'S GONE WRONG!
I'M THE ORIGINAL DESTROYER OF THIS WORLD, AFTER ALL!
NOW THAT I'VE GOT DOMINATOR BACK...
...I'M GOING TO HAVE YOU KILL ME, BIG BROTHER!

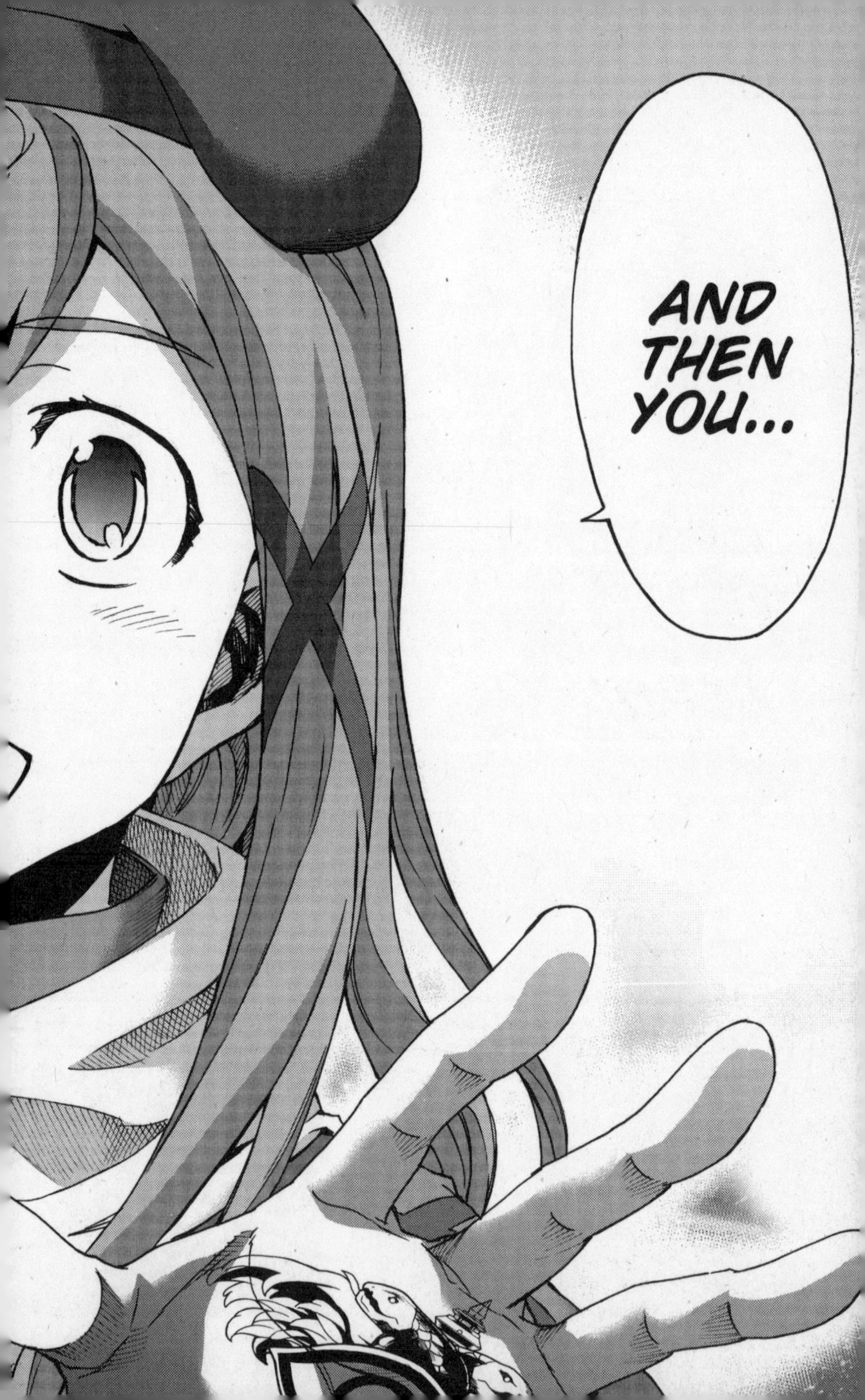
AND THEN YOU...

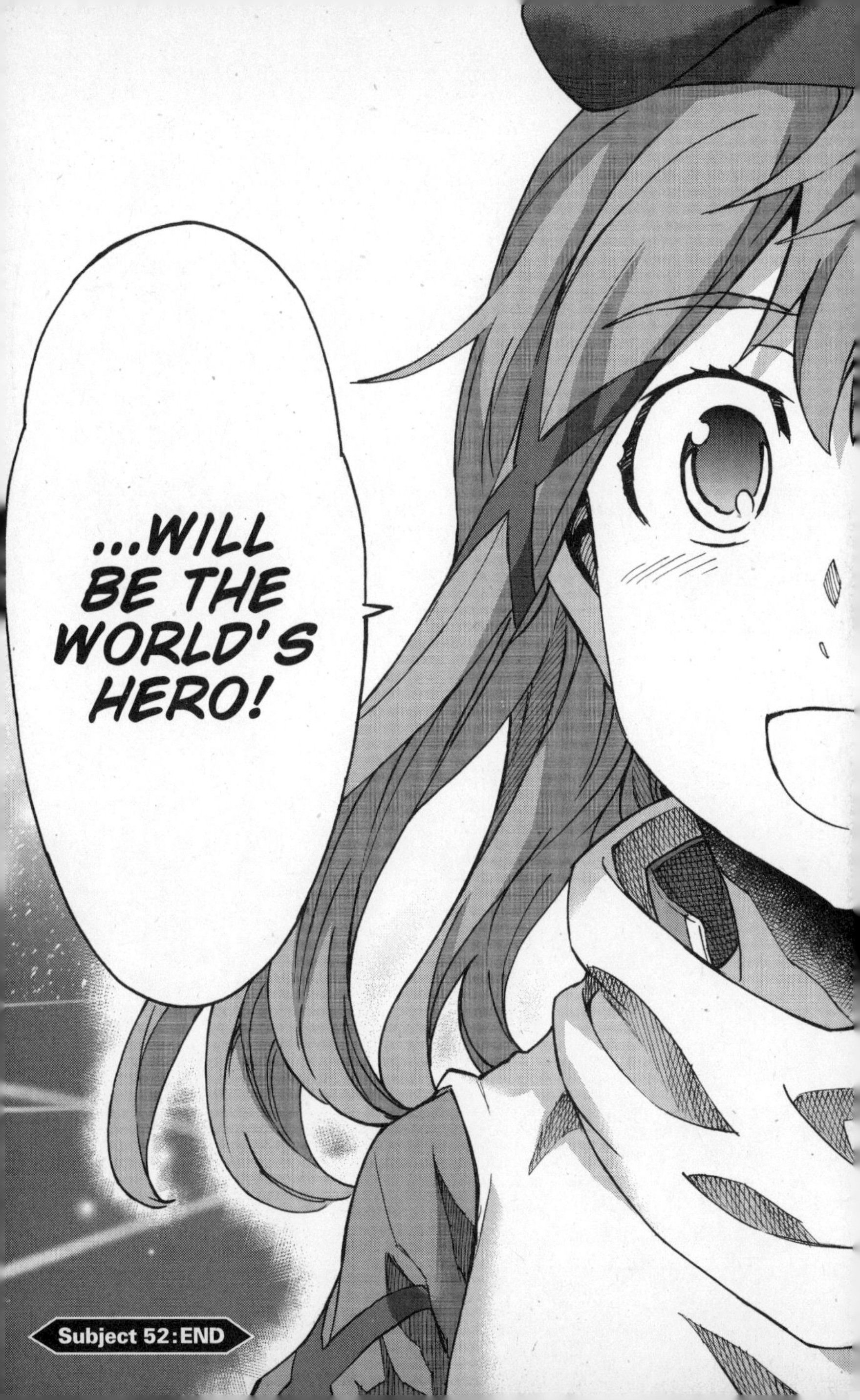
...WILL BE THE WORLD'S HERO!
Subject 52: END

BIG
ORDER

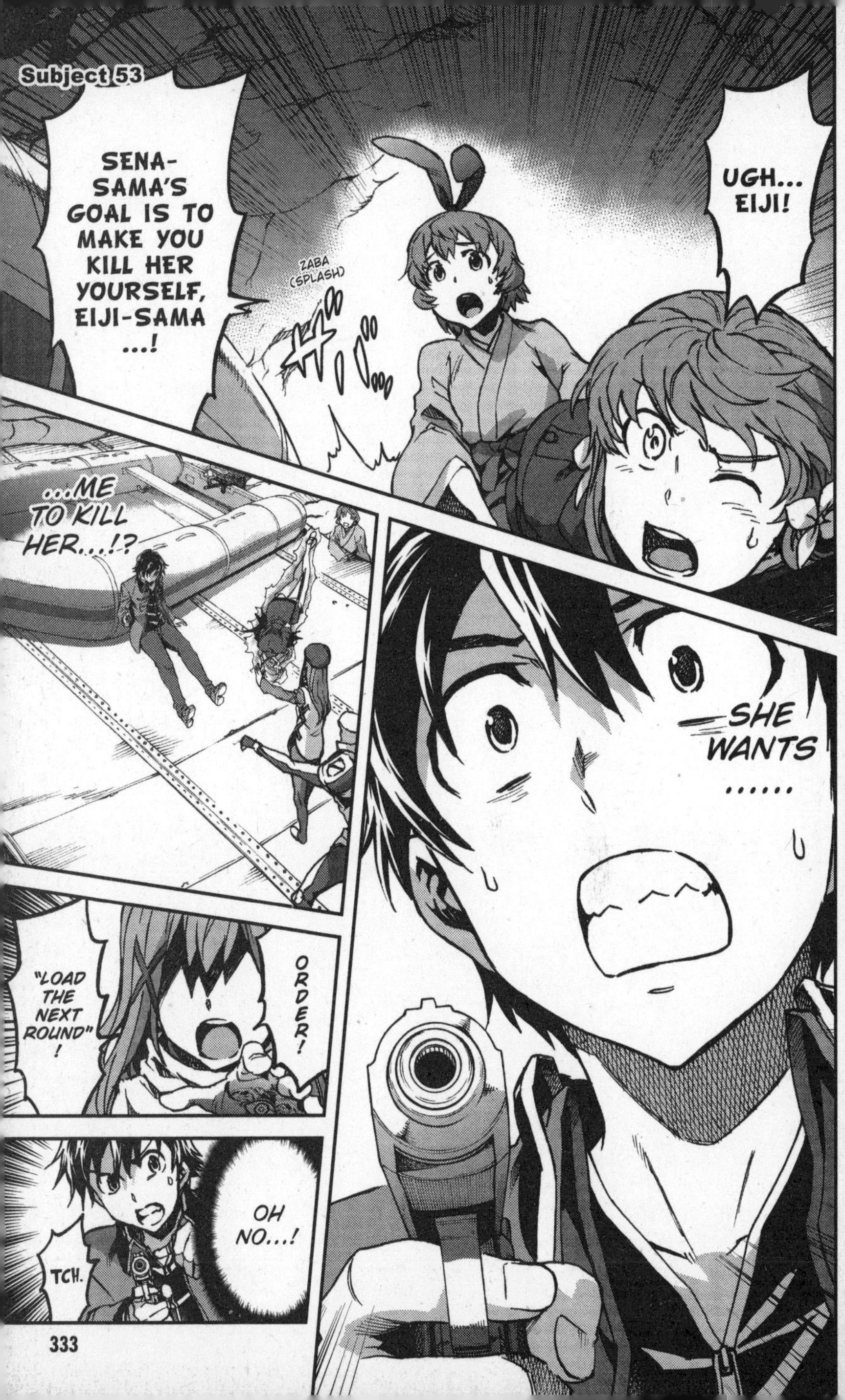
UGH... EIJI!
SENA-SAMA'S GOAL IS TO MAKE YOU KILL HER YOURSELF, EIJI-SAMA ...!
ZABA (SPLASH)
SHE WANTS ......
...ME TO KILL HER...!?
ORDER!
"LOAD THE NEXT ROUND"!
OH NO...!
TCH.

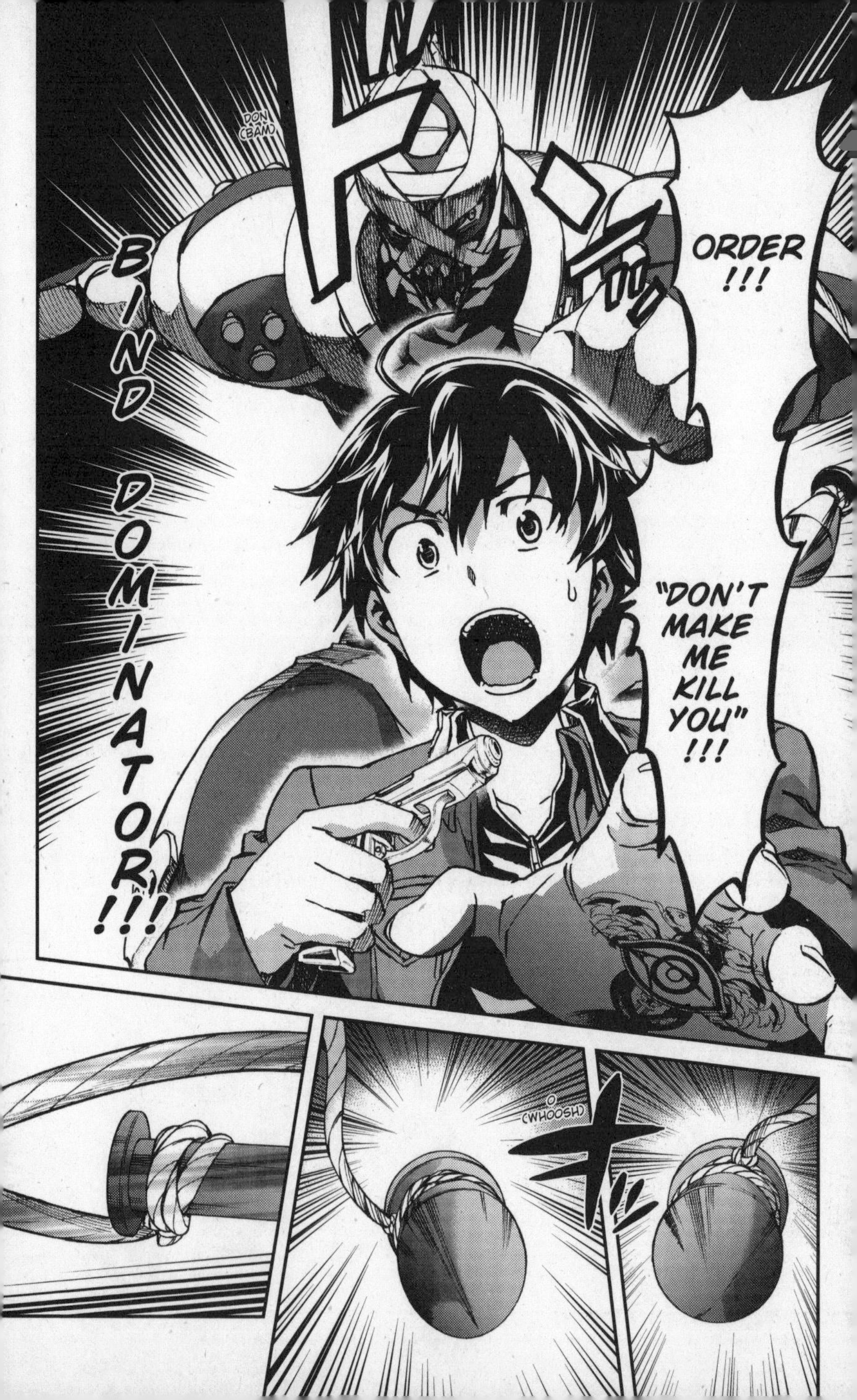
ORDER !!!
"DON'T MAKE ME KILL YOU" !!!
DON (BAM)
BIND DOMINATOR!!!
O (WHOOSH)

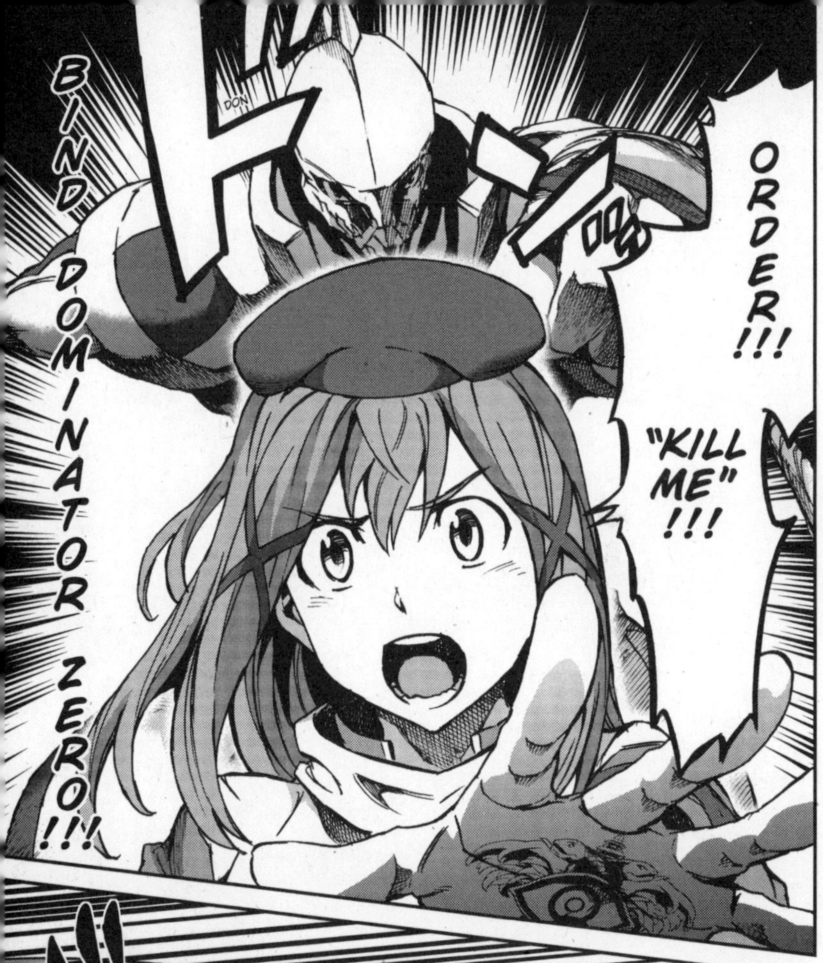
ORDER!!!
"KILL ME"!!!
DON
BIND DOMINATOR ZERO!!!
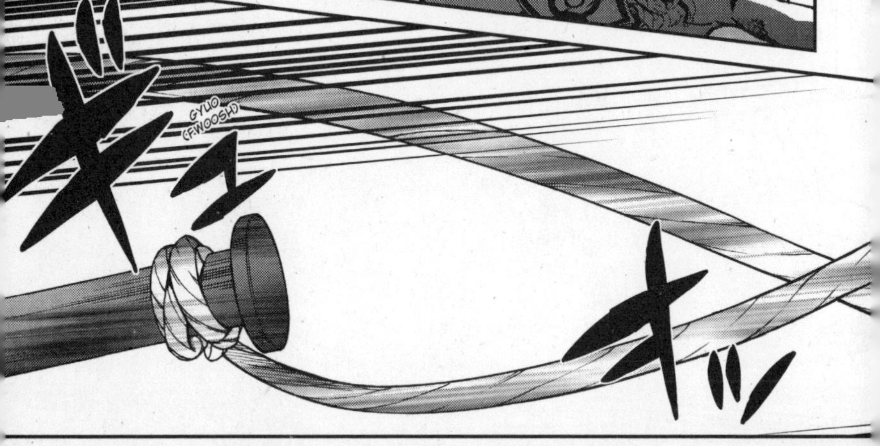
GYUO (FWOOSH)

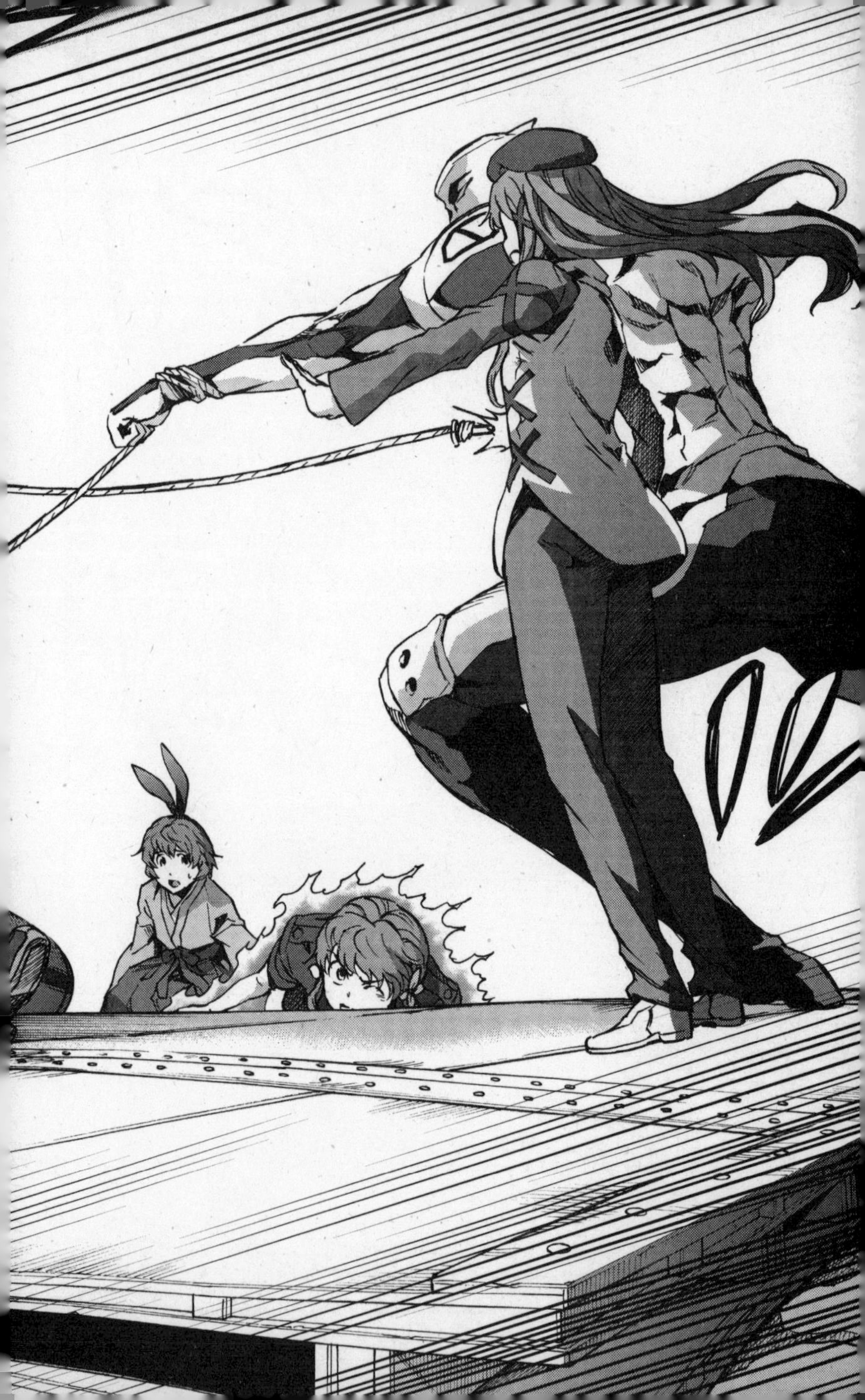

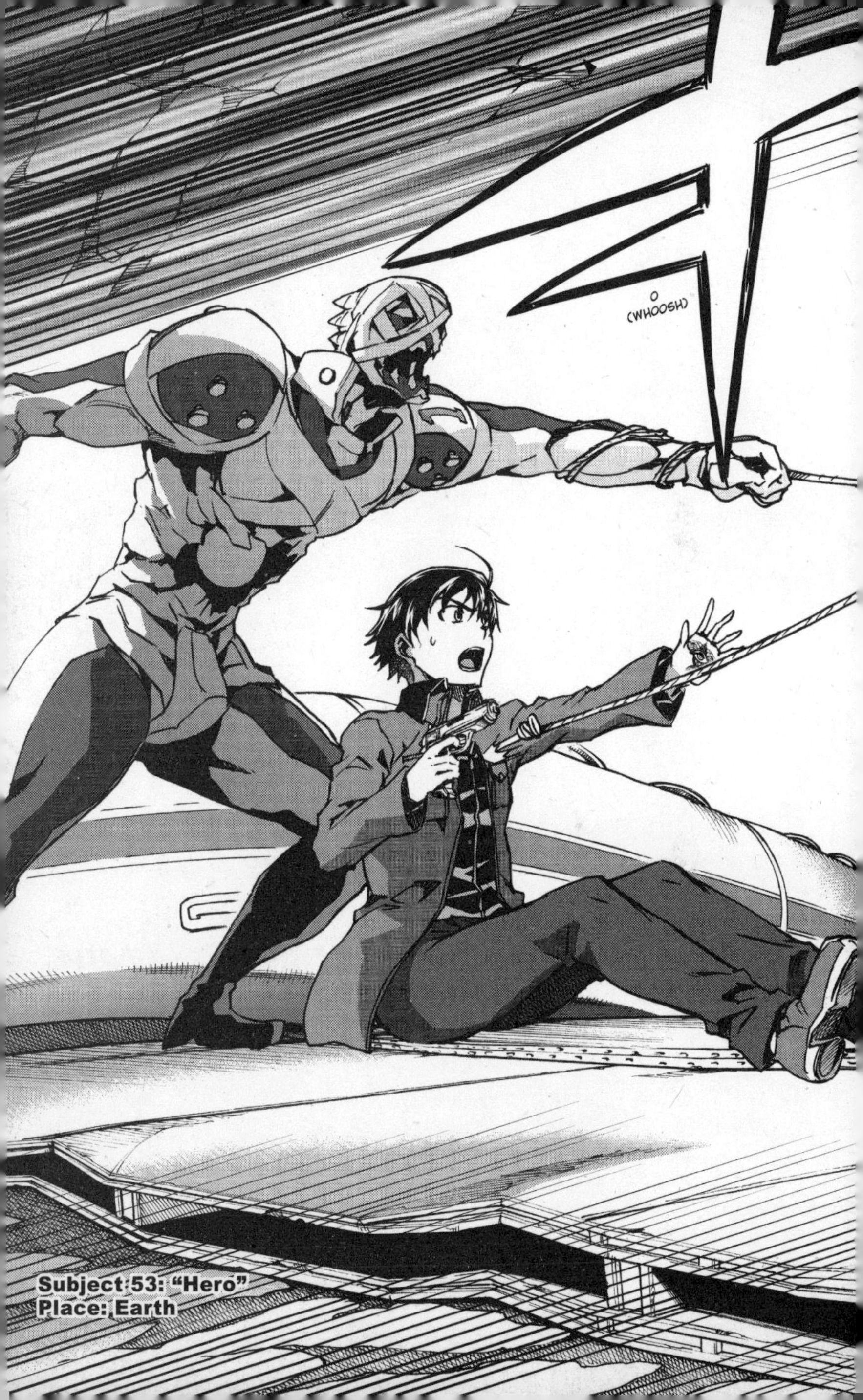
(WHOOSH)
Subject 53: “Hero”
Place: Earth

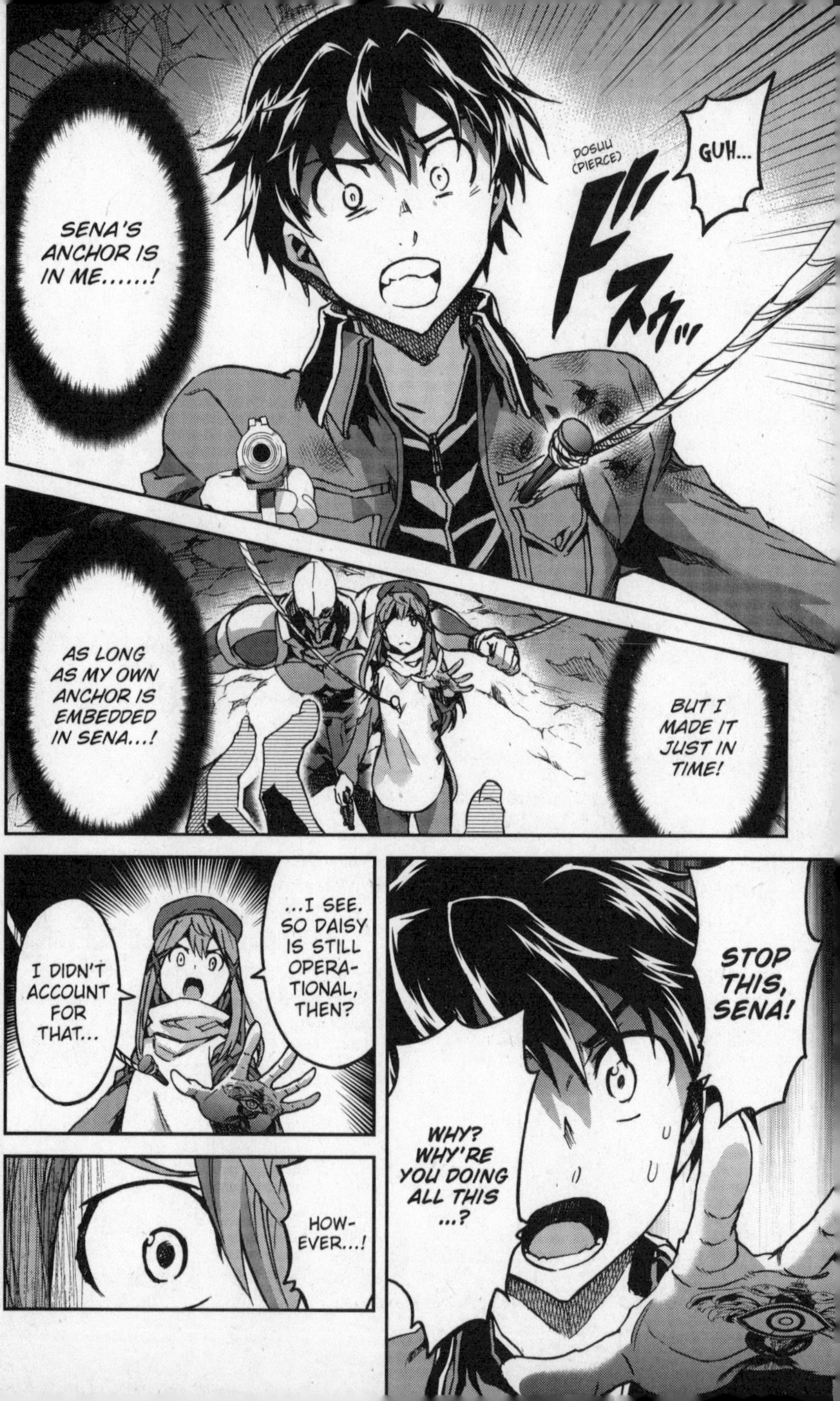
GUH...
DOSUU (PIERCE)
SENA'S ANCHOR IS IN ME......!
BUT I MADE IT JUST IN TIME!
AS LONG AS MY OWN ANCHOR IS EMBEDDED IN SENA...!
STOP THIS, SENA!
WHY? WHY'RE YOU DOING ALL THIS ...?
...I SEE. SO DAISY IS STILL OPERA-TIONAL, THEN?
I DIDN'T ACCOUNT FOR THAT...
HOW-EVER...!

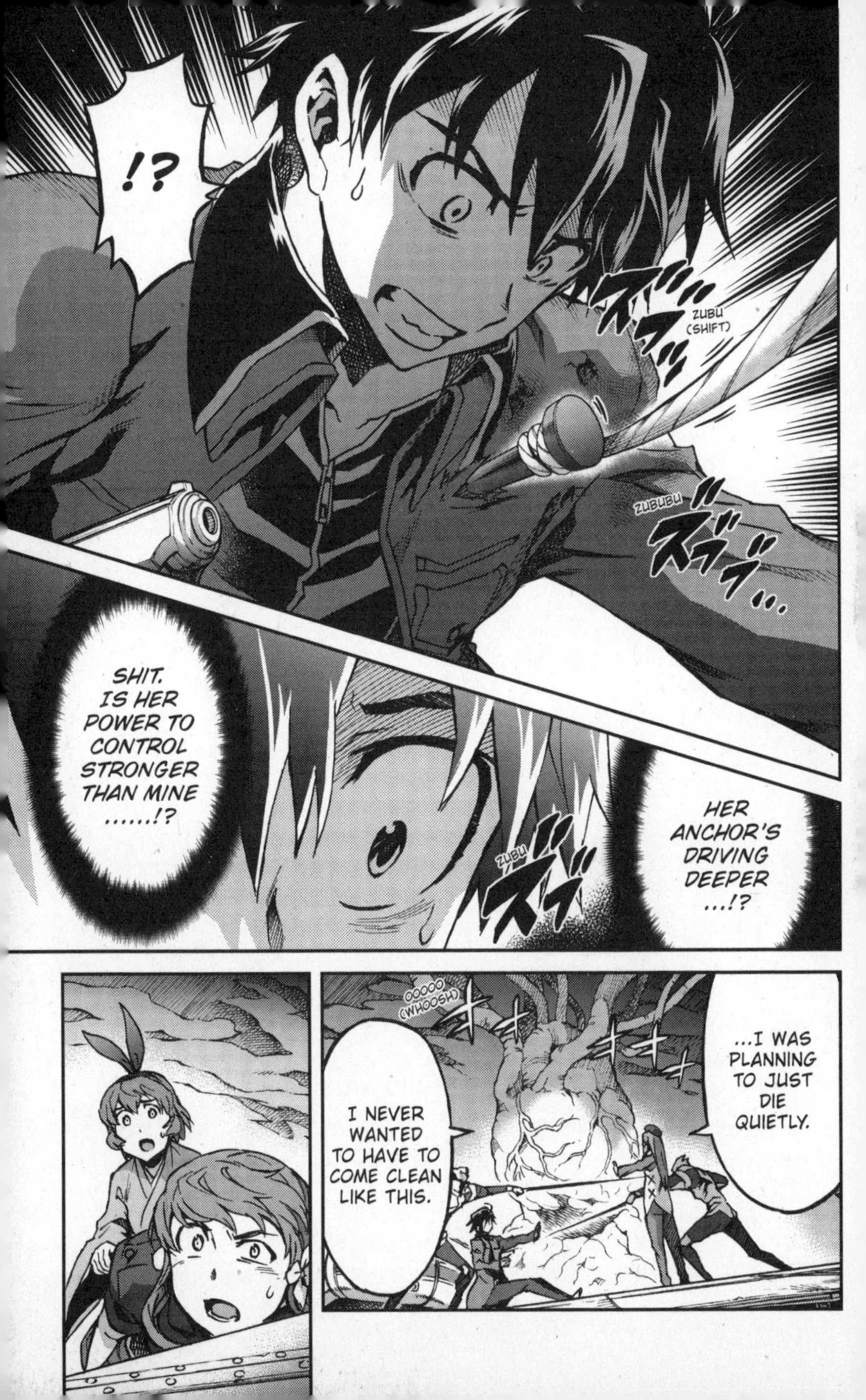
ZUBU (SHIFT)
!?
ZUBUBU
HER ANCHOR'S DRIVING DEEPER ...!?
ZUBU
SHIT. IS HER POWER TO CONTROL STRONGER THAN MINE ......!?
OOOOO (WHOOSH)
...I WAS PLANNING TO JUST DIE QUIETLY.
I NEVER WANTED TO HAVE TO COME CLEAN LIKE THIS.

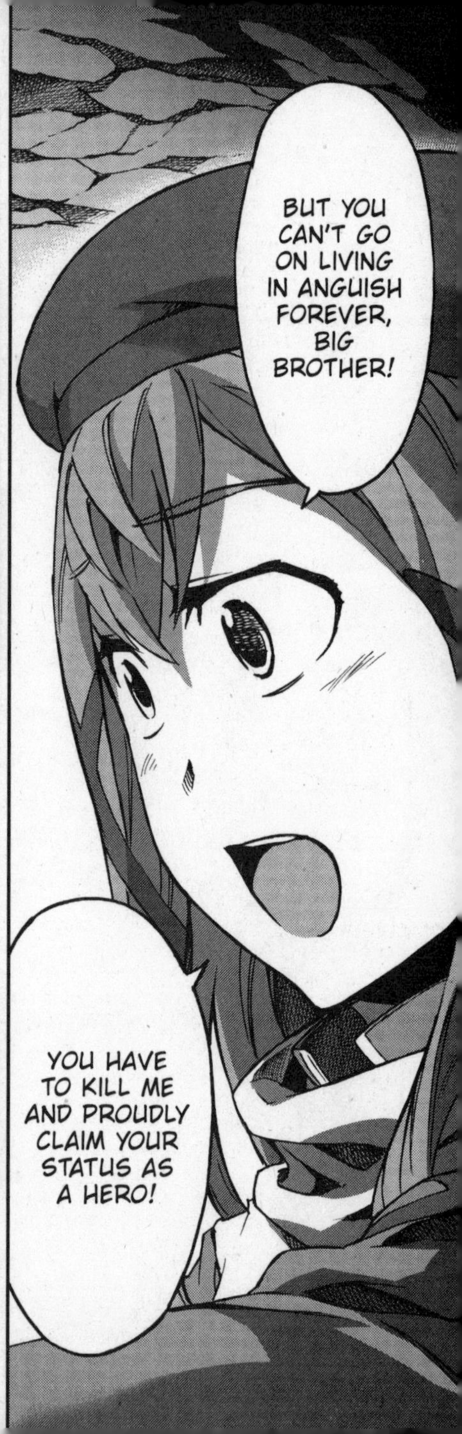
BUT YOU CAN'T GO ON LIVING IN ANGUISH FOREVER, BIG BROTHER!
YOU HAVE TO KILL ME AND PROUDLY CLAIM YOUR STATUS AS A HERO!

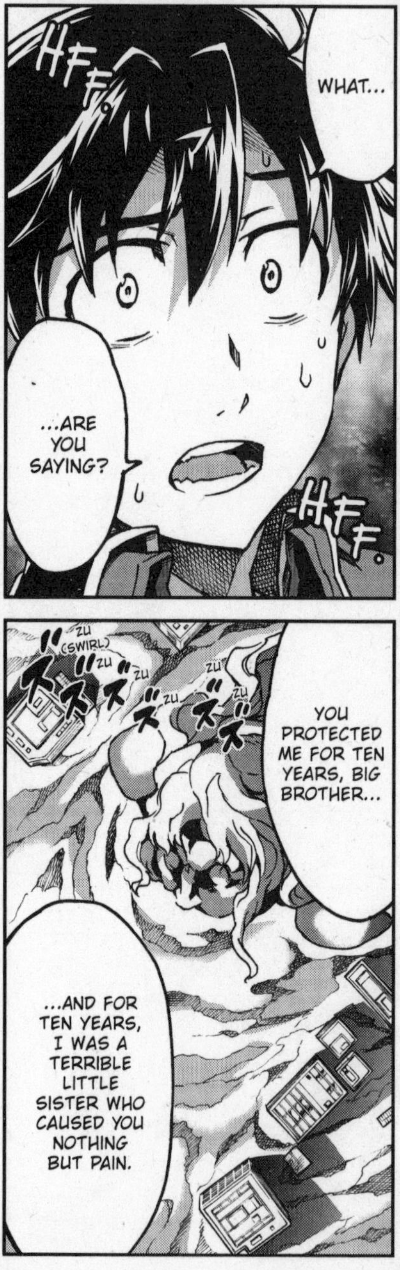
HFF.
WHAT...
...ARE YOU SAYING?
HFF.
ZU ZU ZU ZU ZU ZU ZU
(SWIRL)
YOU PROTECTED ME FOR TEN YEARS, BIG BROTHER...
...AND FOR TEN YEARS, I WAS A TERRIBLE LITTLE SISTER WHO CAUSED YOU NOTHING BUT PAIN.

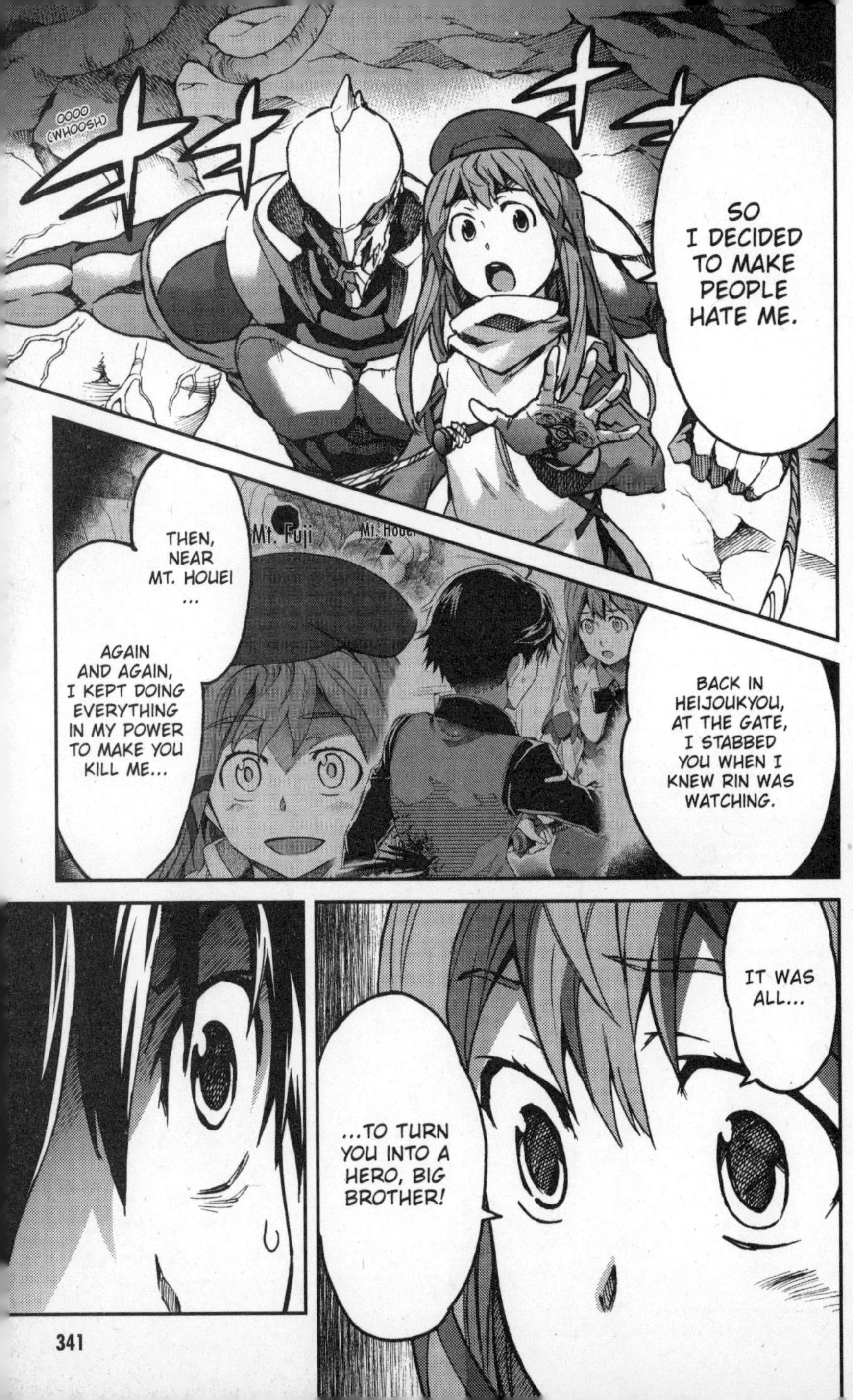
SO I DECIDED TO MAKE PEOPLE HATE ME.
OOOO (WHOOSH)
BACK IN HEIJOUKYOU, AT THE GATE, I STABBED YOU WHEN I KNEW RIN WAS WATCHING.
Mt. Fuji
THEN, NEAR MT. HOUEI ...
AGAIN AND AGAIN, I KEPT DOING EVERYTHING IN MY POWER TO MAKE YOU KILL ME...
IT WAS ALL...
...TO TURN YOU INTO A HERO, BIG BROTHER!

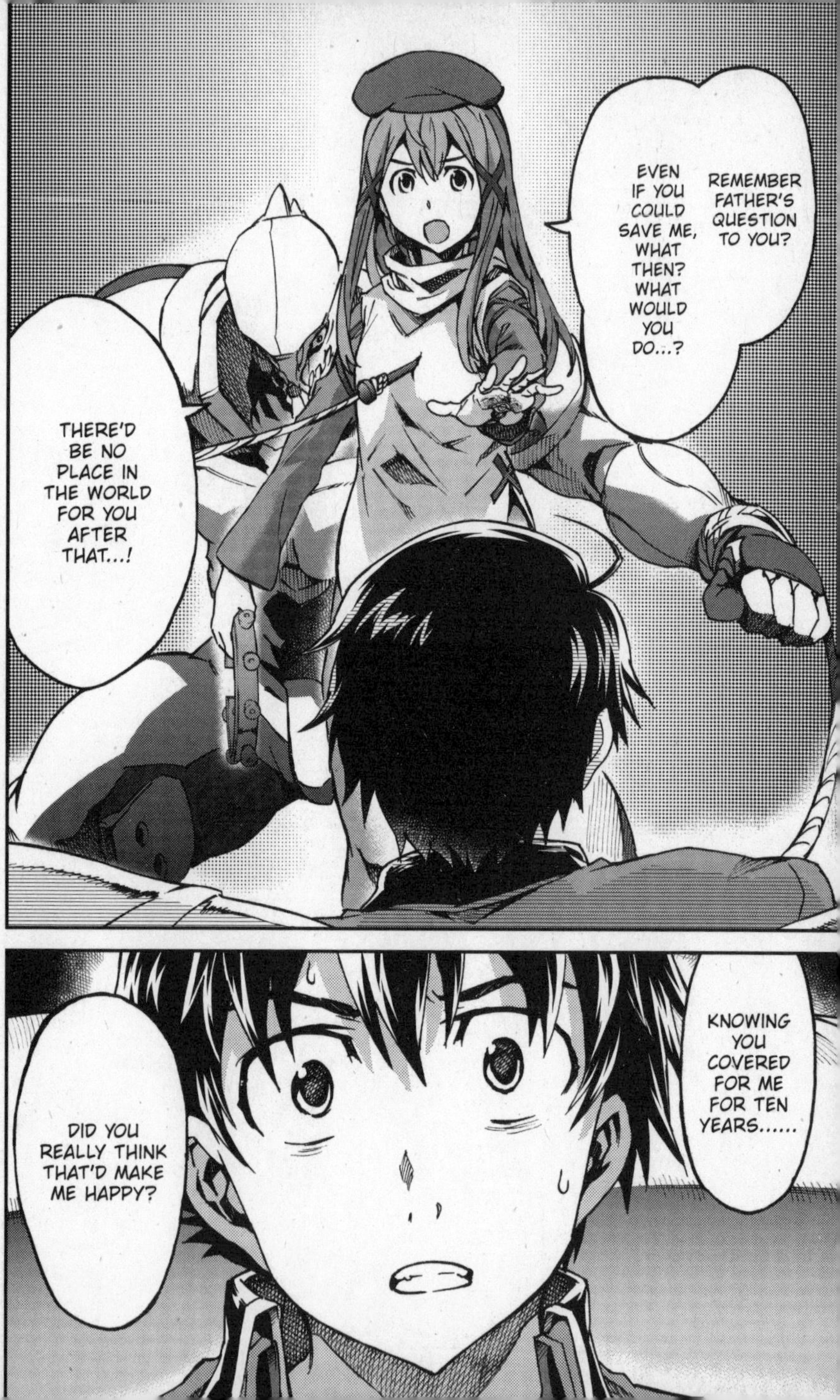
REMEMBER FATHER'S QUESTION TO YOU?
EVEN IF YOU COULD SAVE ME, WHAT THEN? WHAT WOULD YOU DO...?
THERE'D BE NO PLACE IN THE WORLD FOR YOU AFTER THAT...!
KNOWING YOU COVERED FOR ME FOR TEN YEARS......
DID YOU REALLY THINK THAT'D MAKE ME HAPPY?

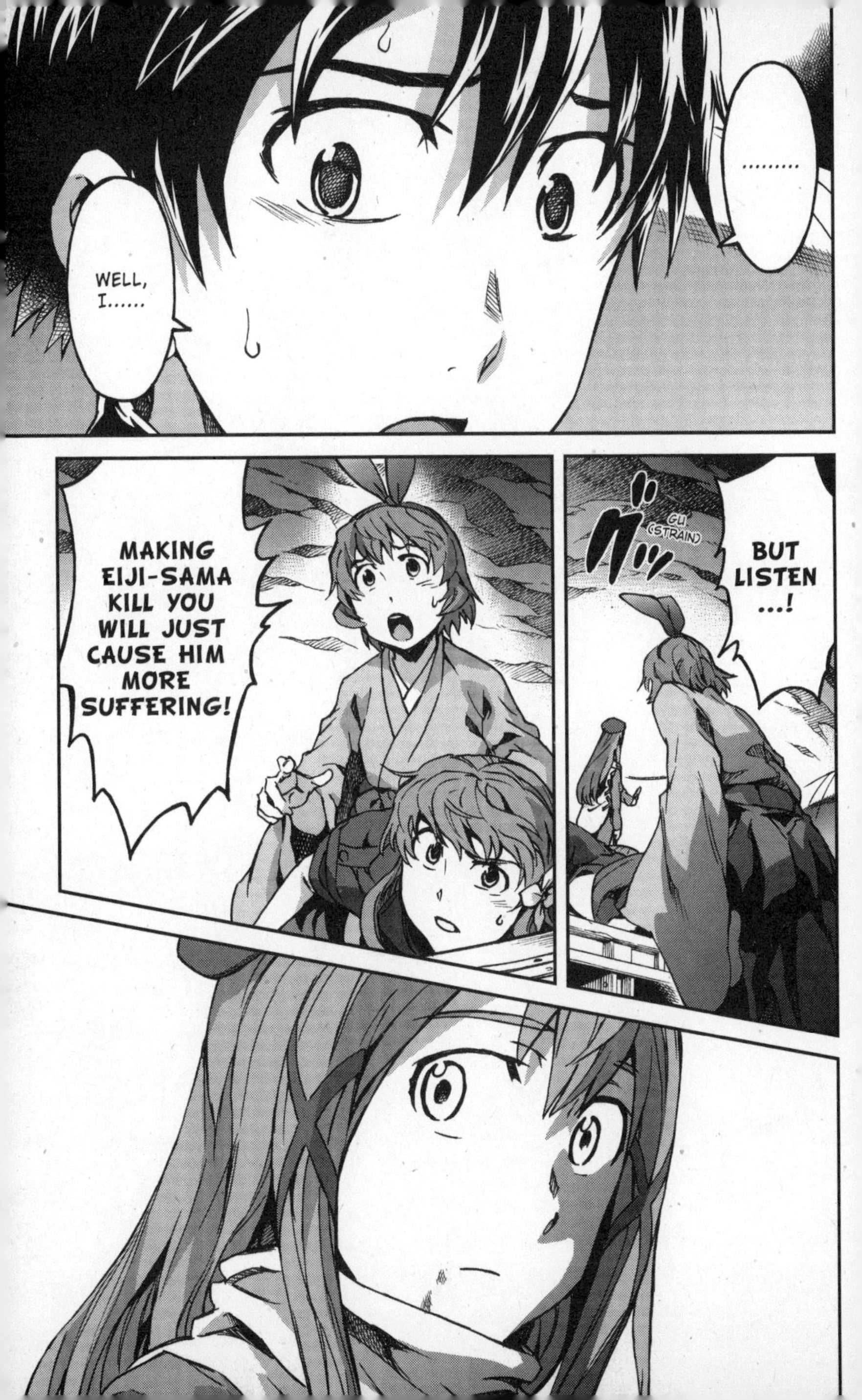
....
WELL, I......
BUT LISTEN ...!
GU (STRAIN)
MAKING EIJI-SAMA KILL YOU WILL JUST CAUSE HIM MORE SUFFERING!

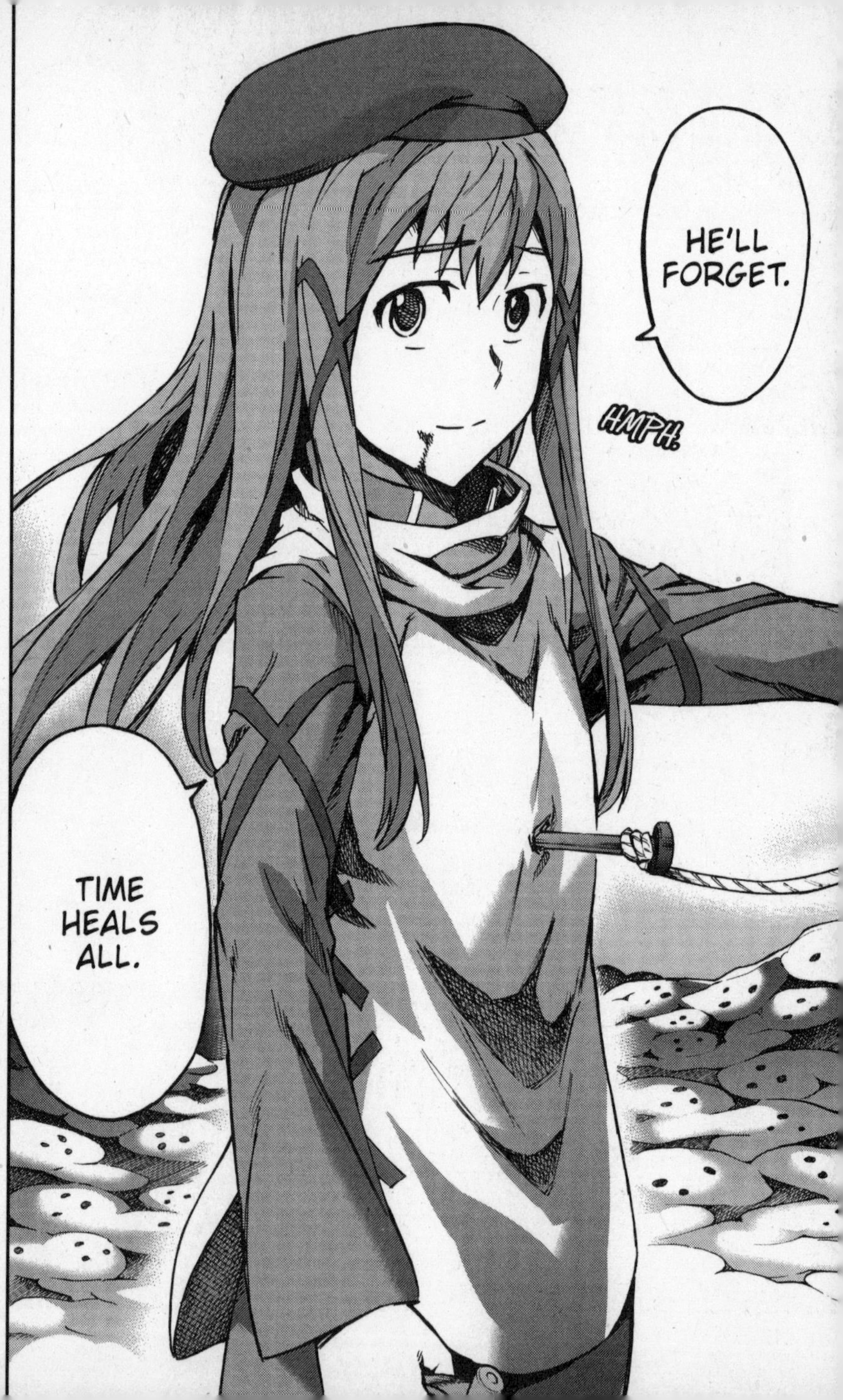
HE'LL FORGET.
HMPH.
TIME HEALS ALL.

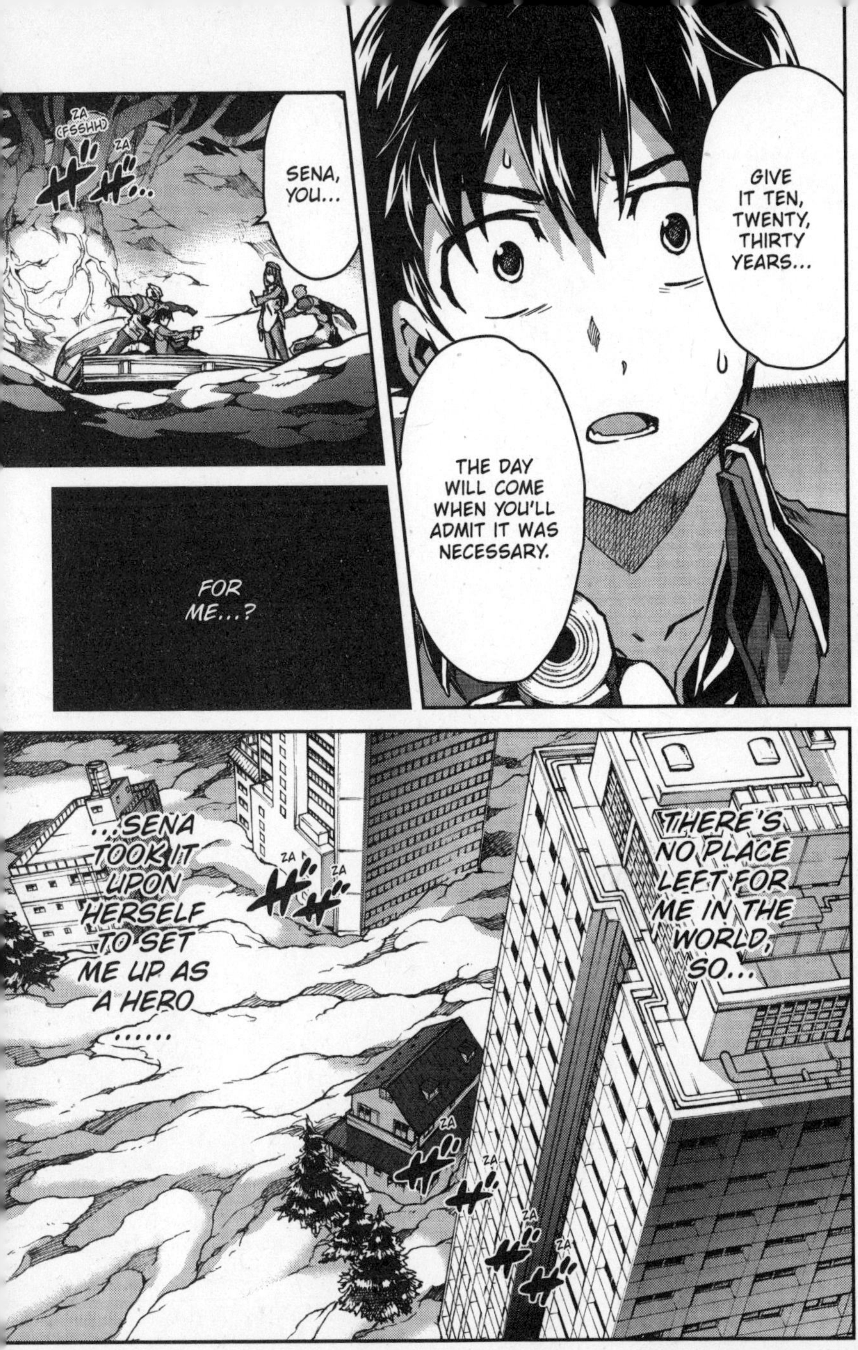
GIVE IT TEN, TWENTY, THIRTY YEARS...
THE DAY WILL COME WHEN YOU'LL ADMIT IT WAS NECESSARY.
ZA (FSSHH) ZA
SENA, YOU...
FOR ME...?
THERE'S NO PLACE LEFT FOR ME IN THE WORLD, SO...
ZA ZA
...SENA TOOK IT UPON HERSELF TO SET ME UP AS A HERO......
ZA ZA ZA ZA

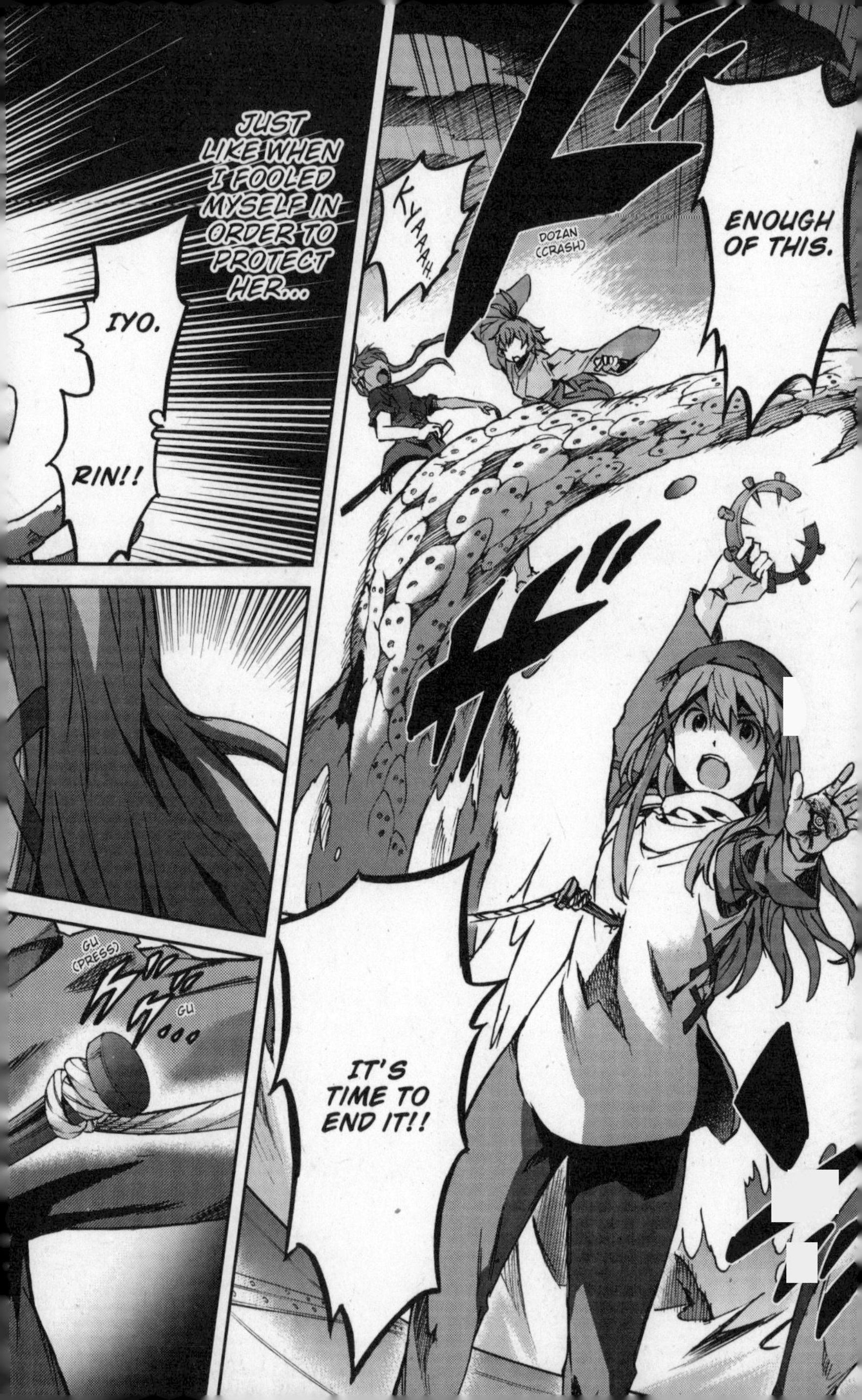
ENOUGH OF THIS.
DOZAN (CRASH)
KYAAAAH.
IT'S TIME TO END IT!!
JUST LIKE WHEN I FOOLED MYSELF IN ORDER TO PROTECT HER...
IYO.
RIN!!
GU (PRESS)
GU

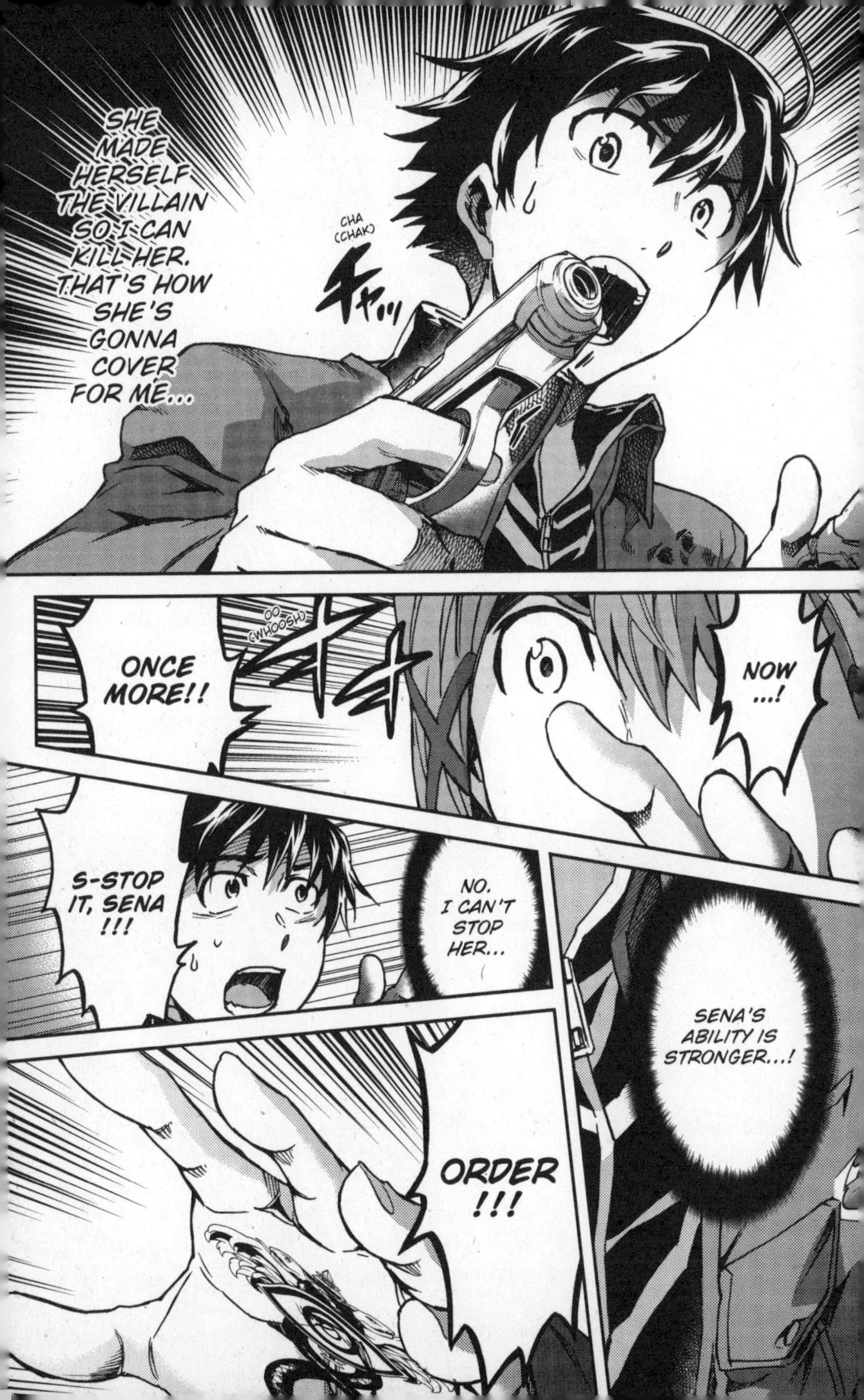
CHA (CHAK)
チャッ
SHE MADE HERSELF THE VILLAIN SO I CAN KILL HER. THAT'S HOW SHE'S GONNA COVER FOR ME...
NOW ...!
OO (WHOOSH)
ONCE MORE!!
NO. I CAN'T STOP HER...
SENA'S ABILITY IS STRONGER...!
S-STOP IT, SENA!!!
ORDER!!!

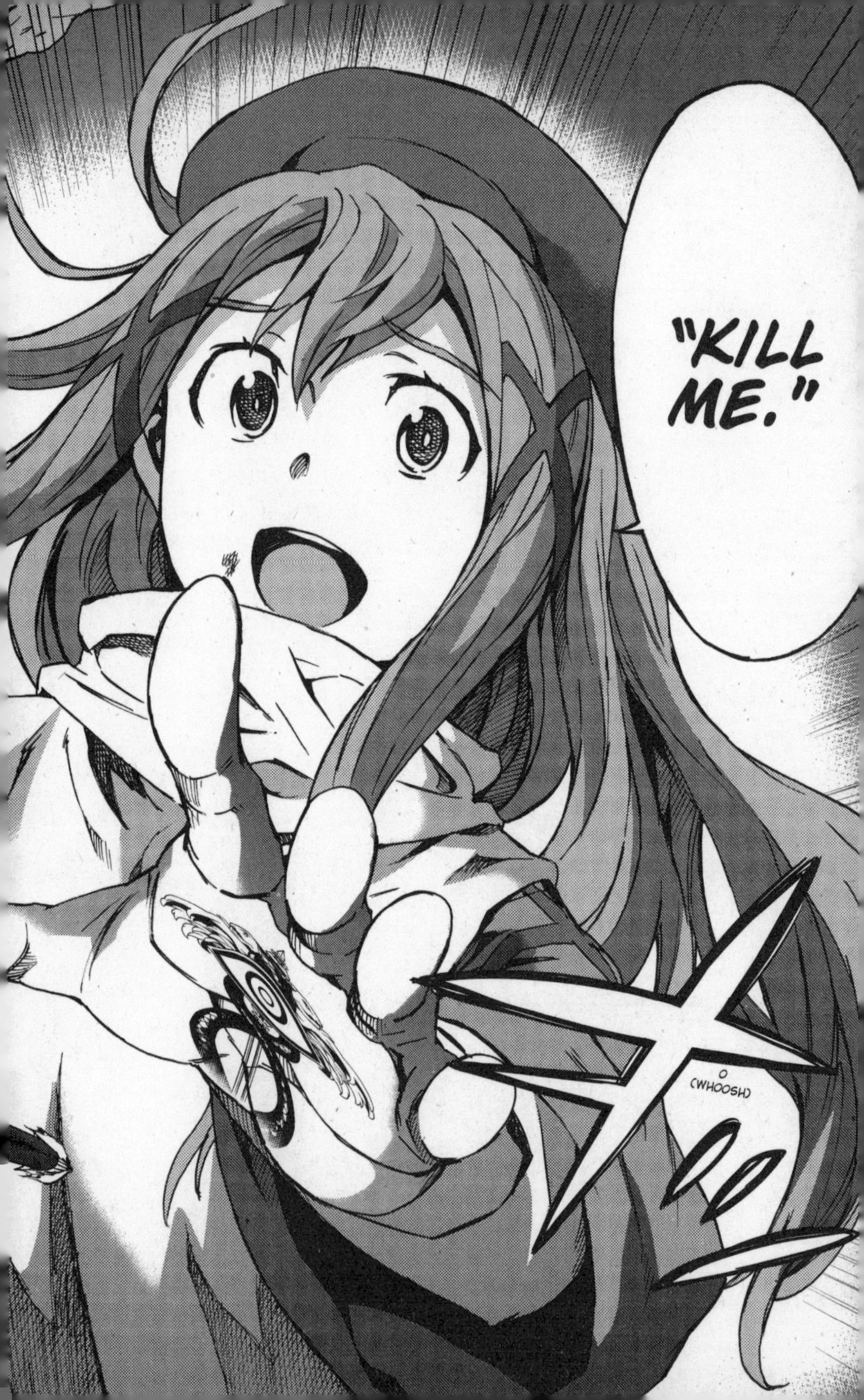
"KILL ME."
(WHOOSH)

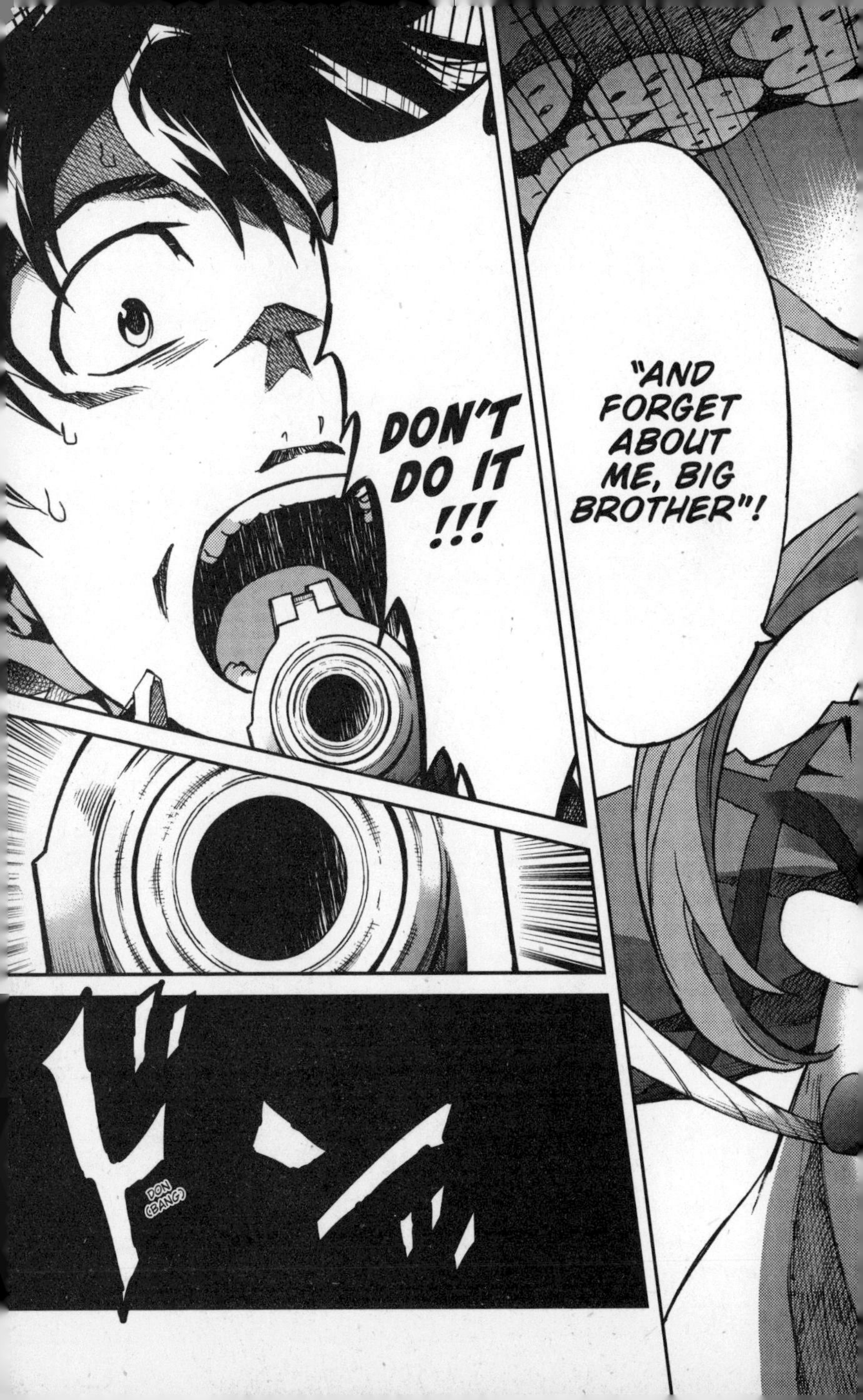
"AND FORGET ABOUT ME, BIG BROTHER"!
DON'T DO IT !!!
DON (BANG)

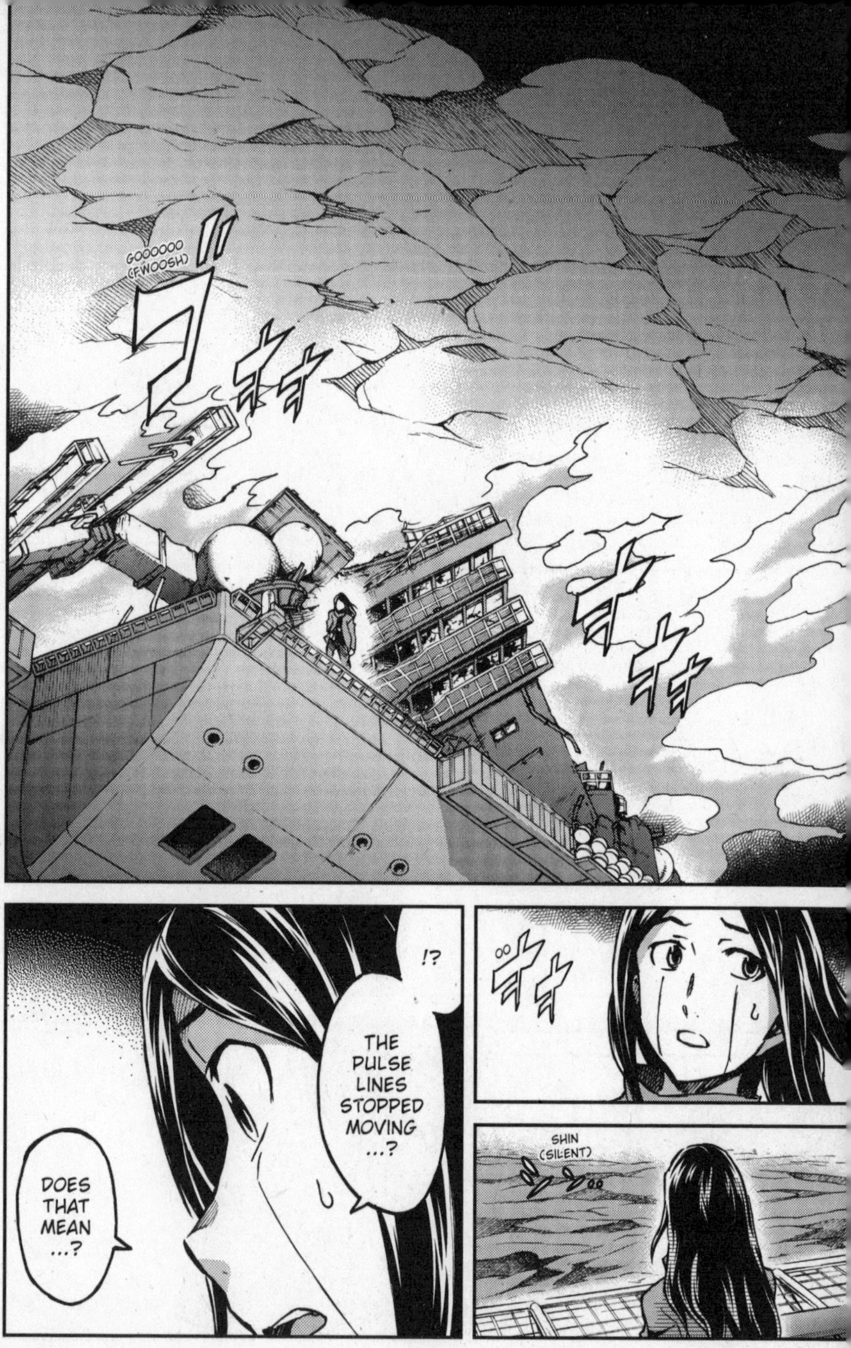
GOOOOOO (FWOOSH)
SHIN (SILENT)
!?
THE PULSE LINES STOPPED MOVING ...?
DOES THAT MEAN ...?

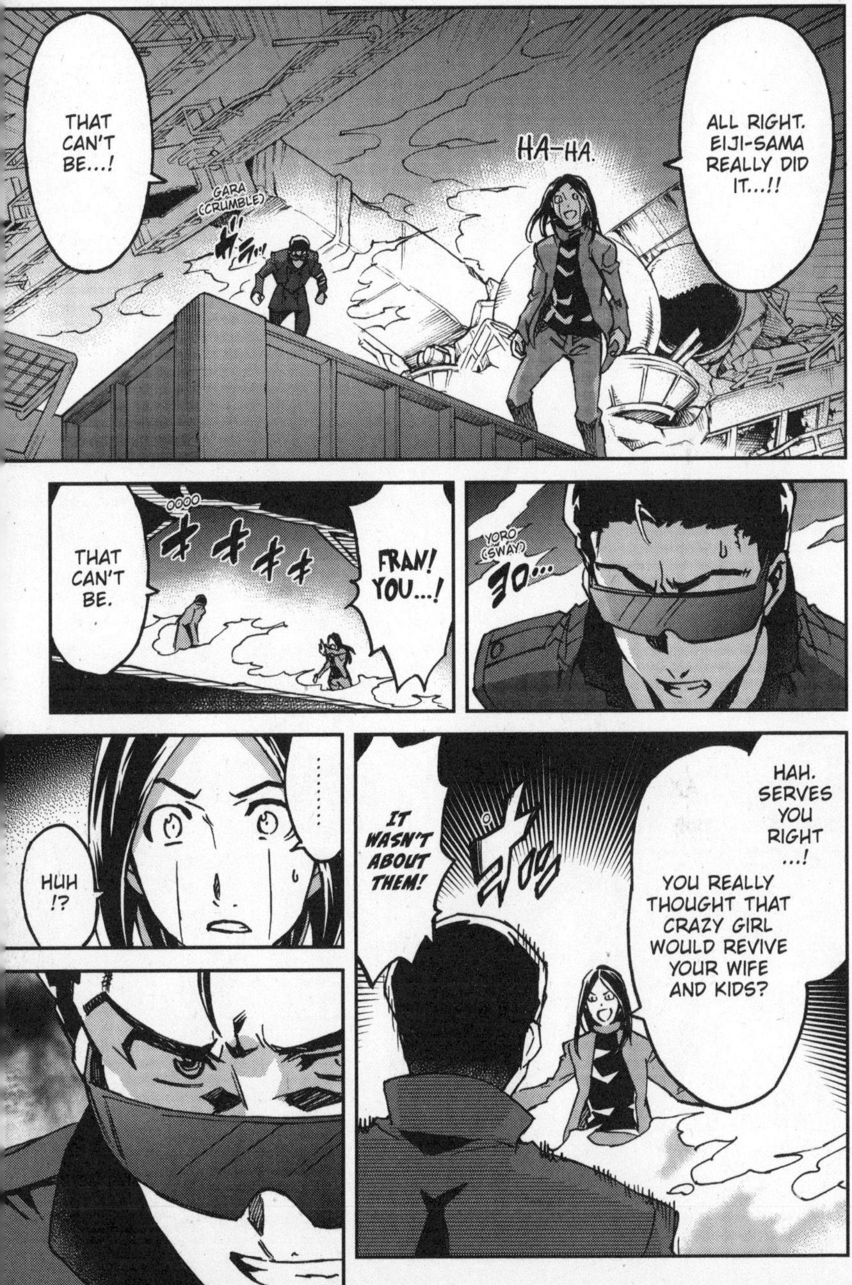
ALL RIGHT. EIJI-SAMA REALLY DID IT...!!
HA-HA.
THAT CAN'T BE...!
GARA (CRUMBLE)
YORO (SWAY)
FRAN! YOU...!
OOOO
THAT CAN'T BE.
HAH. SERVES YOU RIGHT ...!
YOU REALLY THOUGHT THAT CRAZY GIRL WOULD REVIVE YOUR WIFE AND KIDS?
IT WASN'T ABOUT THEM!
......
HUH !?

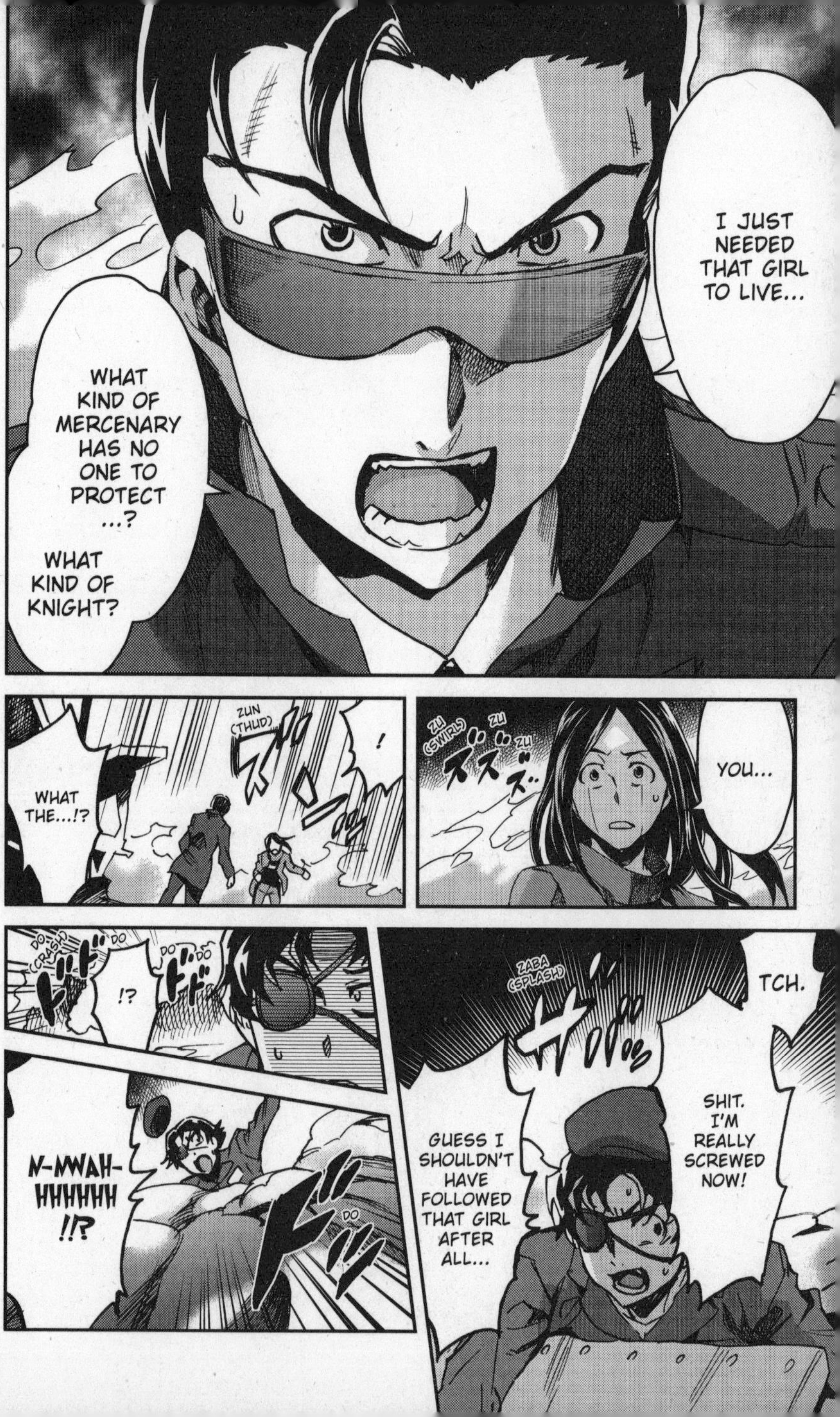
I JUST NEEDED THAT GIRL TO LIVE...
WHAT KIND OF MERCENARY HAS NO ONE TO PROTECT ...?
WHAT KIND OF KNIGHT?
YOU...
ZU (SWIRL) ZU ZU
ZUN (THUD)
!
WHAT THE...!?
TCH.
ZABA (SPLASH)
SHIT. I'M REALLY SCREWED NOW!
GUESS I SHOULDN'T HAVE FOLLOWED THAT GIRL AFTER ALL...
DO DO
DO (CRASH) DO
!?
N-NWAH-HHHHHH!!?
DO

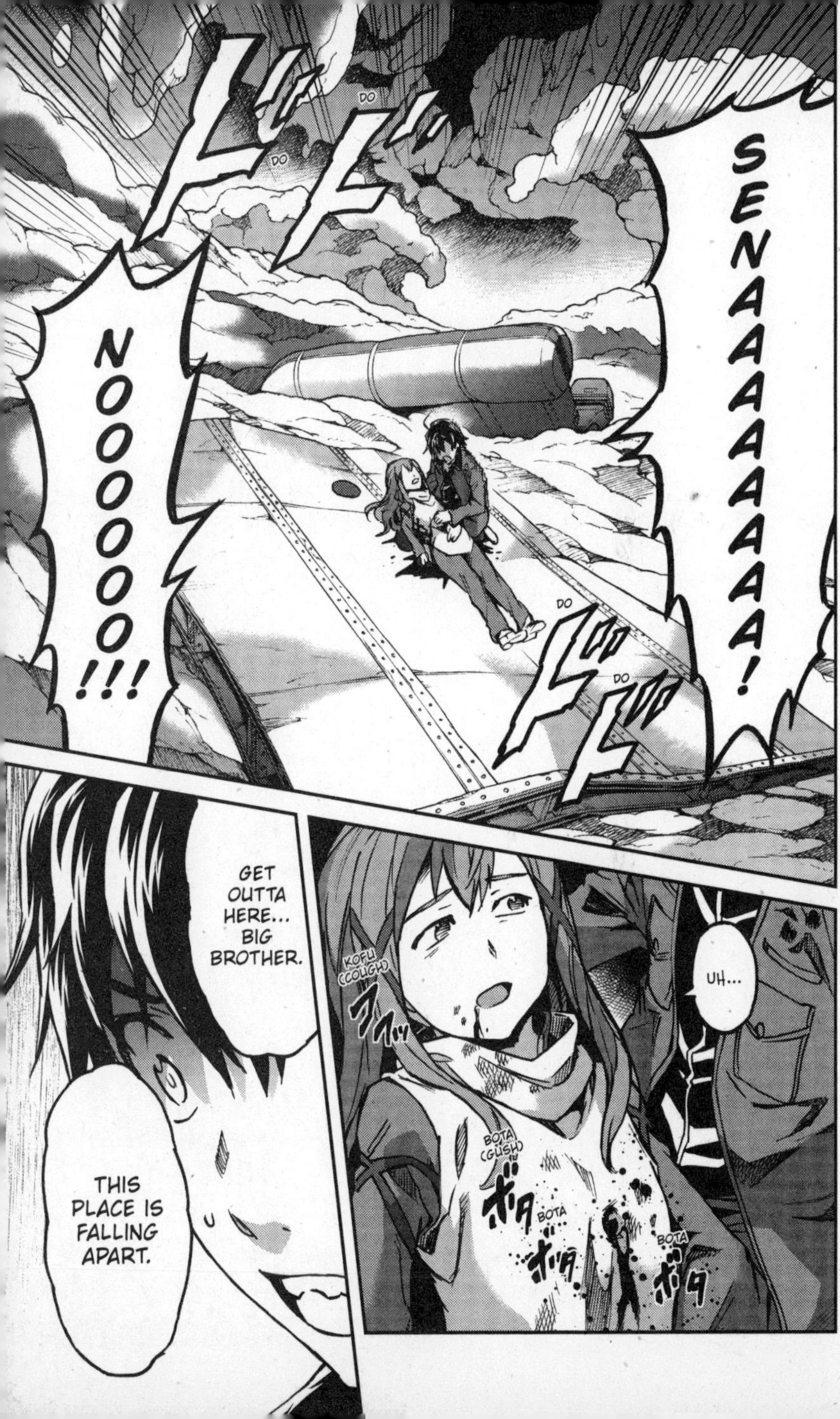
SENAAAAAAAA!
DO
DO
NOOOOOO!!!
DO
DO
UH...
KOFU (COUGH)
BOTA (GUSH)
BOTA
BOTA
GET OUTTA HERE... BIG BROTHER.
THIS PLACE IS FALLING APART.

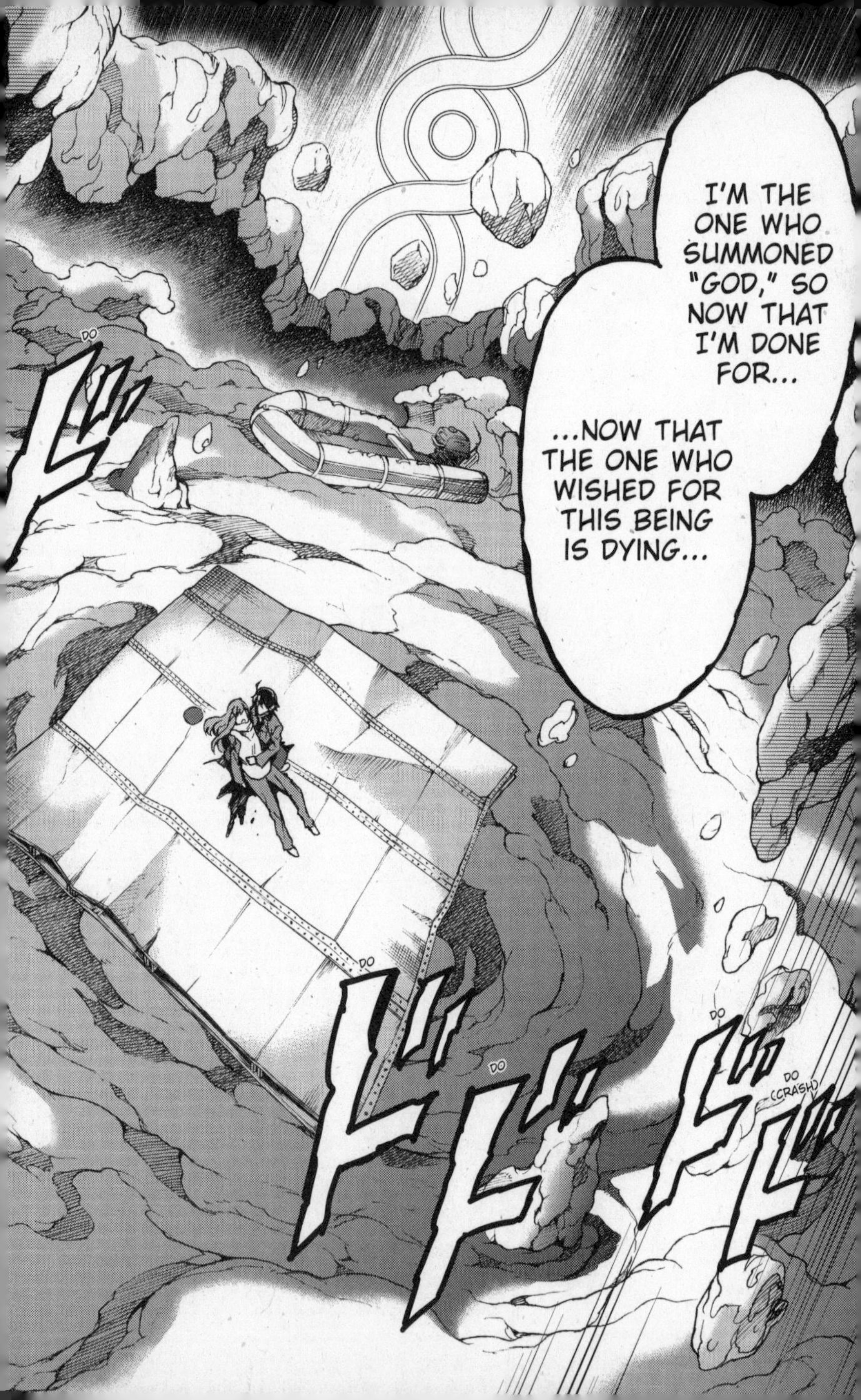
I'M THE ONE WHO SUMMONED "GOD," SO NOW THAT I'M DONE FOR...
...NOW THAT THE ONE WHO WISHED FOR THIS BEING IS DYING...
DO
DO
DO
DO
DO (CRASH)

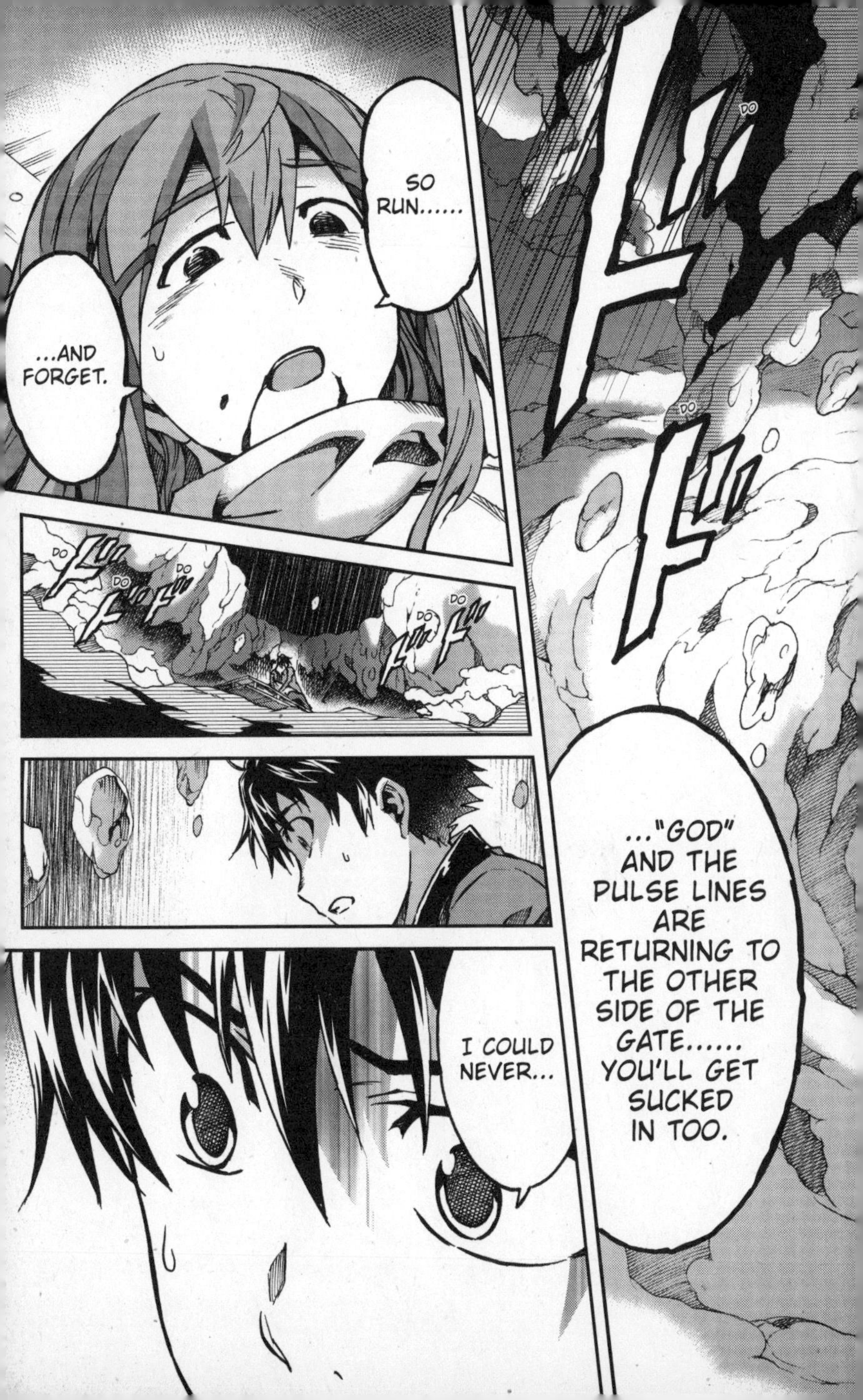
DO
DO
..."GOD" AND THE PULSE LINES ARE RETURNING TO THE OTHER SIDE OF THE GATE...... YOU'LL GET SUCKED IN TOO.
SO RUN......
...AND FORGET.
DO
DO
DO
DO
DO
I COULD NEVER...

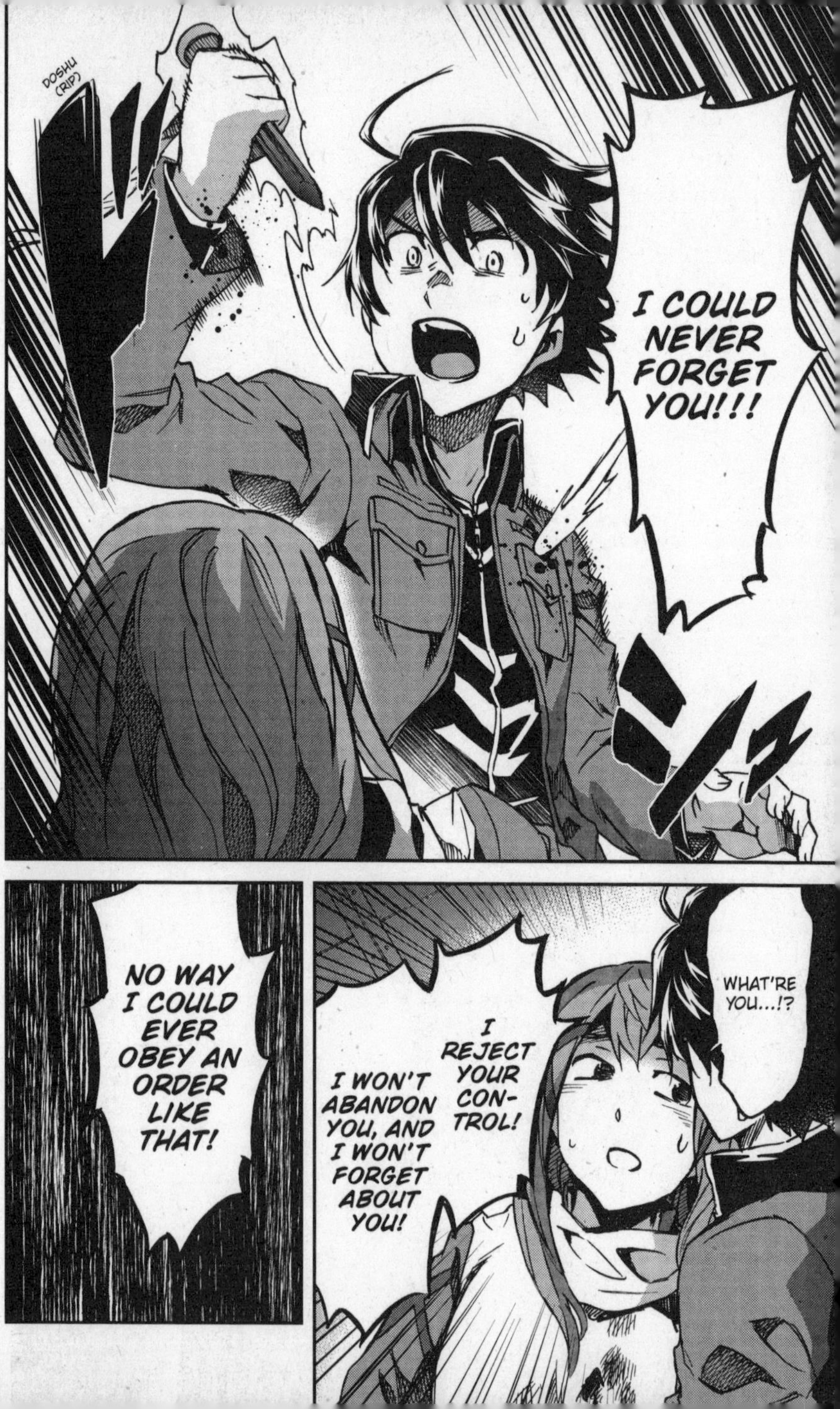
I COULD NEVER FORGET YOU!!!
DOSHU (RIP)
WHAT'RE YOU...!?
I REJECT YOUR CONTROL!
I WON'T ABANDON YOU, AND I WON'T FORGET ABOUT YOU!
NO WAY I COULD EVER OBEY AN ORDER LIKE THAT!

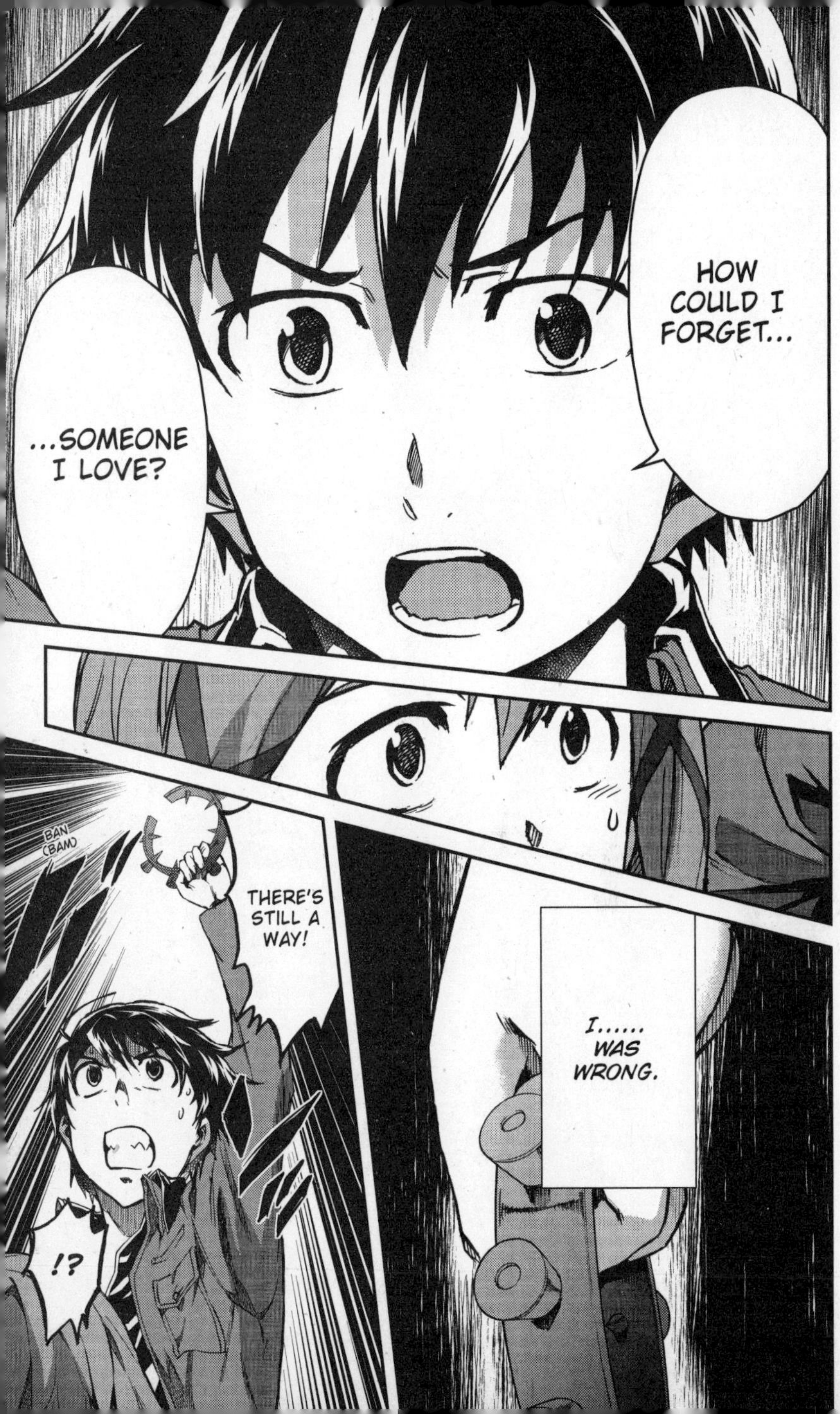
HOW COULD I FORGET...
...SOMEONE I LOVE?
I...... WAS WRONG.
BAN (BAM)
THERE'S STILL A WAY!
!?

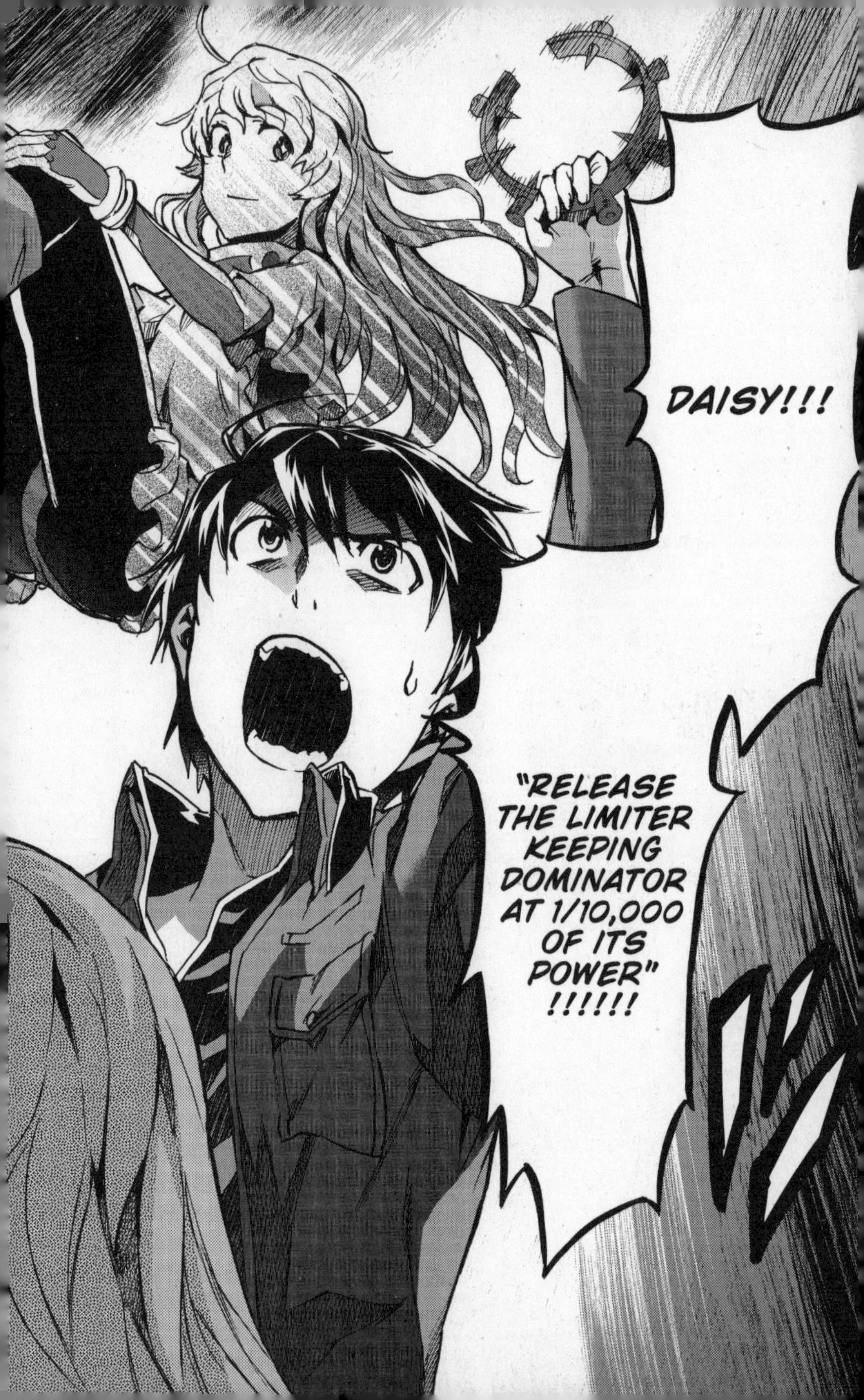
DAISY!!!
"RELEASE THE LIMITER KEEPING DOMINATOR AT 1/10,000 OF ITS POWER" !!!!!!

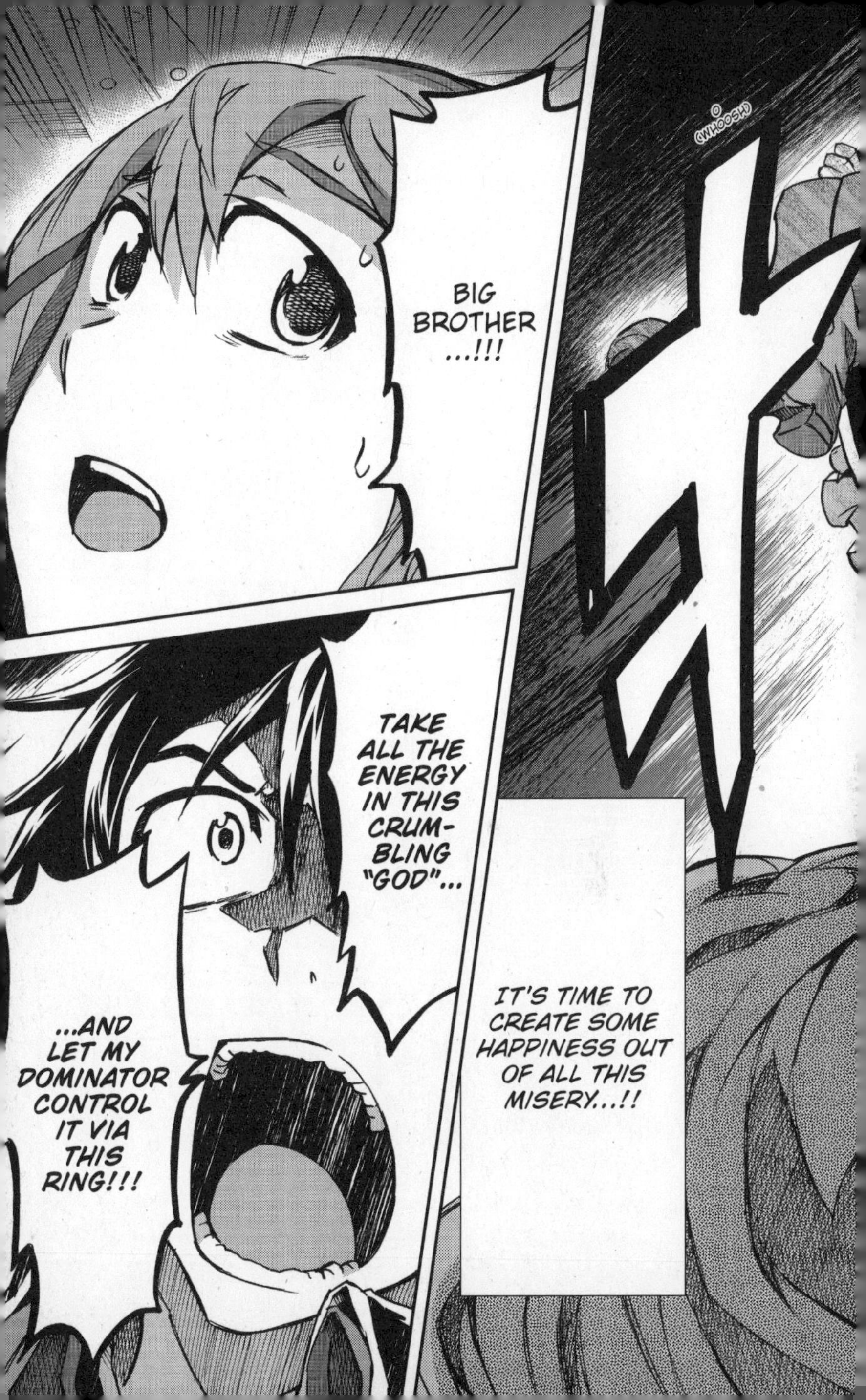
(WHOOSH)
IT'S TIME TO CREATE SOME HAPPINESS OUT OF ALL THIS MISERY...!!
BIG BROTHER ...!!!
TAKE ALL THE ENERGY IN THIS CRUM-BLING "GOD"...
...AND LET MY DOMINATOR CONTROL IT VIA THIS RING!!!

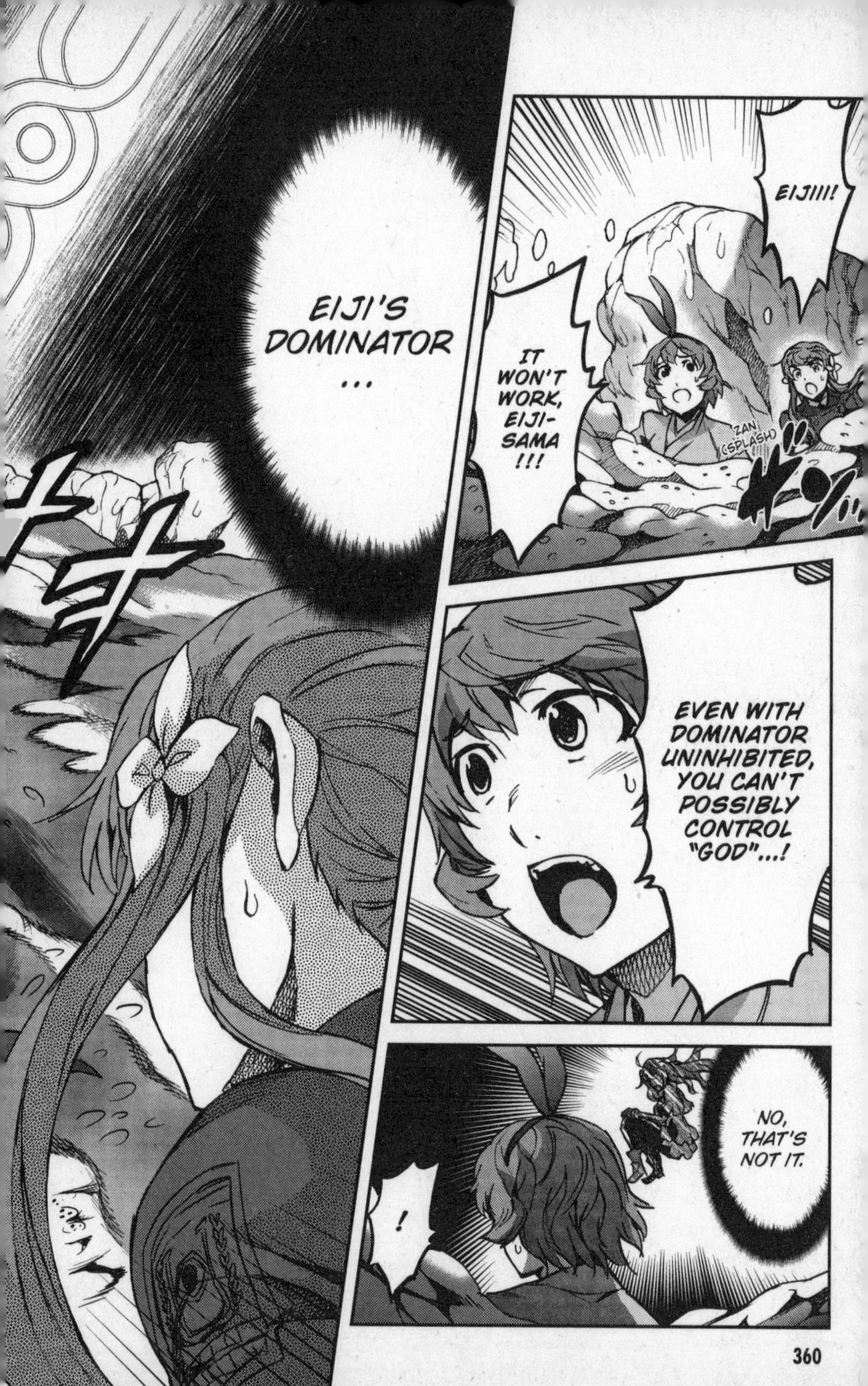
EIJIII!
IT WON'T WORK, EIJI-SAMA!!!
ZAN (SPLASH)
EVEN WITH DOMINATOR UNINHIBITED, YOU CAN'T POSSIBLY CONTROL "GOD"...!
NO, THAT'S NOT IT.
!
EIJI'S DOMINATOR...

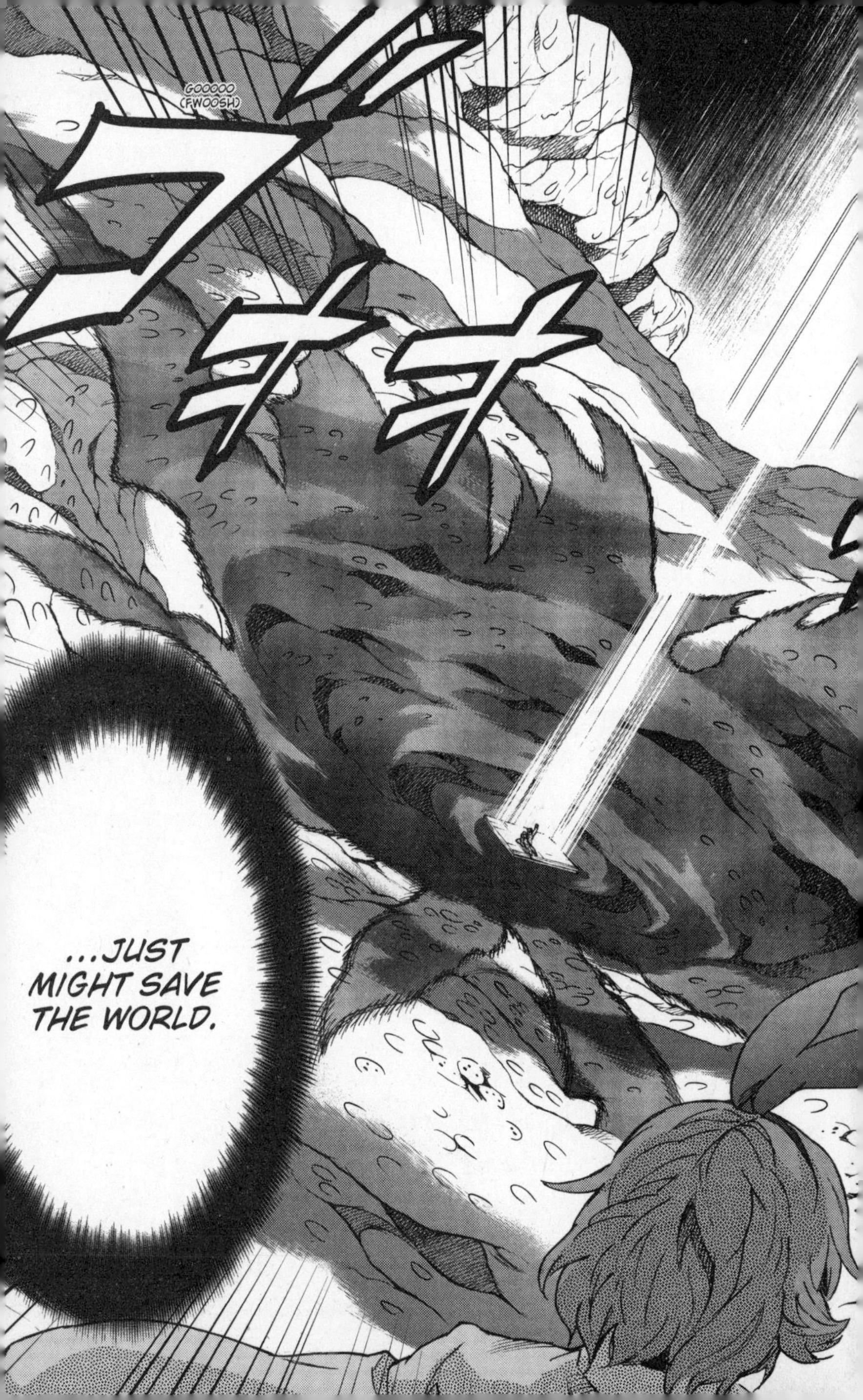
GOOOOO
(FWOOSH)
...JUST MIGHT SAVE THE WORLD.

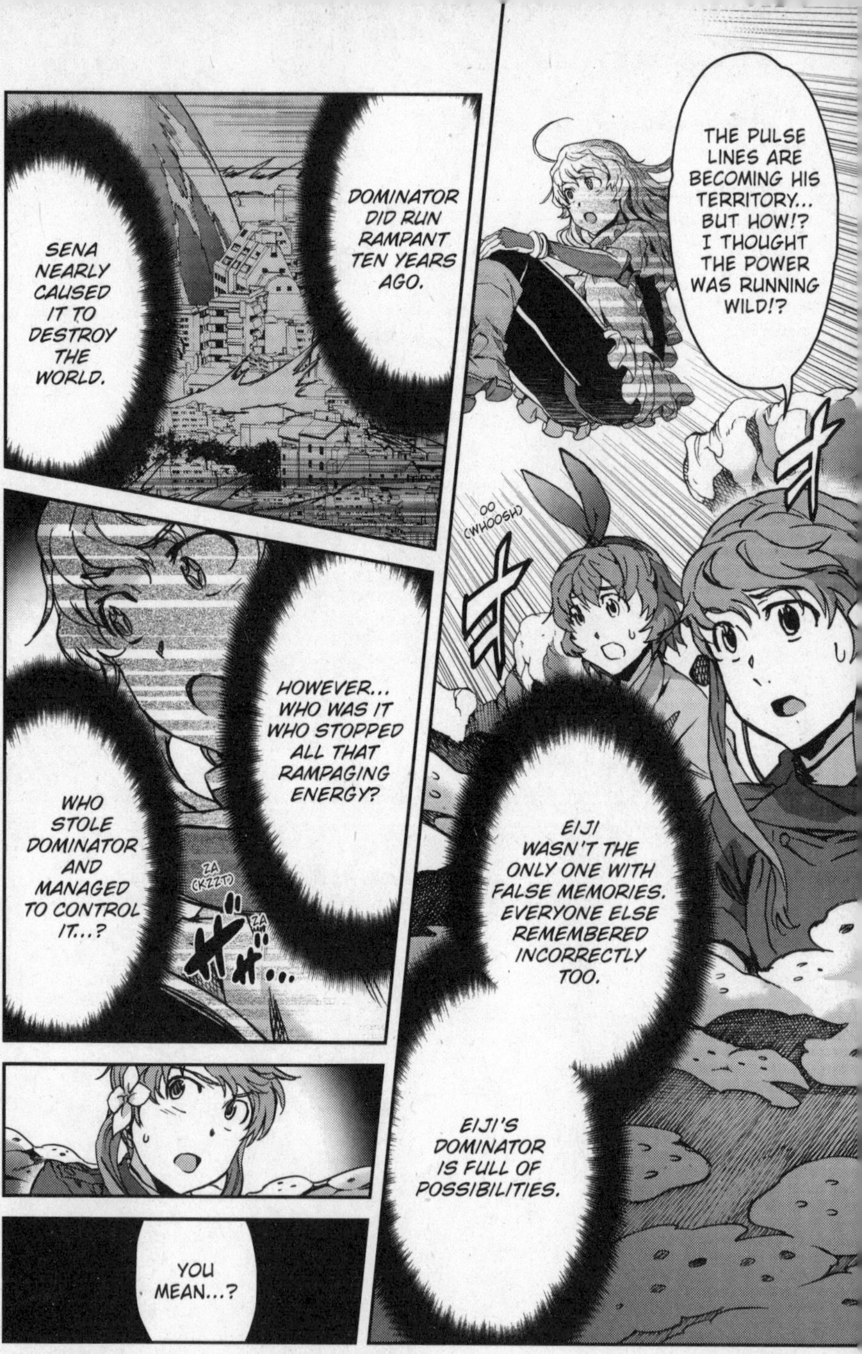
THE PULSE LINES ARE BECOMING HIS TERRITORY... BUT HOW!? I THOUGHT THE POWER WAS RUNNING WILD!?
OO (WHOOSH)
EIJI WASN'T THE ONLY ONE WITH FALSE MEMORIES. EVERYONE ELSE REMEMBERED INCORRECTLY TOO.
EIJI'S DOMINATOR IS FULL OF POSSIBILITIES.
DOMINATOR DID RUN RAMPANT TEN YEARS AGO.
SENA NEARLY CAUSED IT TO DESTROY THE WORLD.
HOWEVER... WHO WAS IT WHO STOPPED ALL THAT RAMPAGING ENERGY?
WHO STOLE DOMINATOR AND MANAGED TO CONTROL IT...?
ZA (KZZT)
ZA
YOU MEAN...?

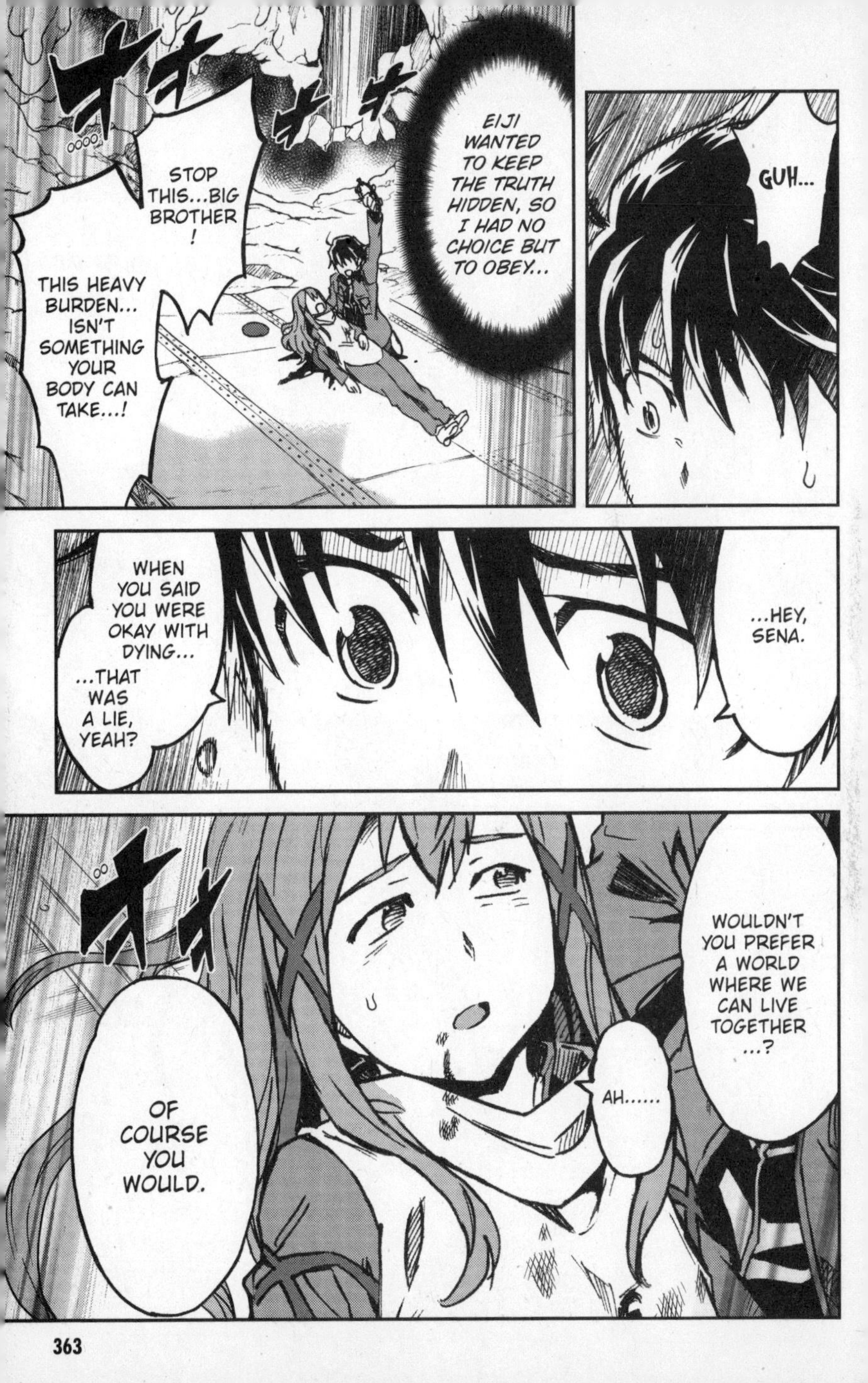
GUH...
EIJI WANTED TO KEEP THE TRUTH HIDDEN, SO I HAD NO CHOICE BUT TO OBEY...
OOOO
STOP THIS...BIG BROTHER!
THIS HEAVY BURDEN... ISN'T SOMETHING YOUR BODY CAN TAKE...!
...HEY, SENA.
WHEN YOU SAID YOU WERE OKAY WITH DYING...
...THAT WAS A LIE, YEAH?
WOULDN'T YOU PREFER A WORLD WHERE WE CAN LIVE TOGETHER...?
AH......
OO
OF COURSE YOU WOULD.

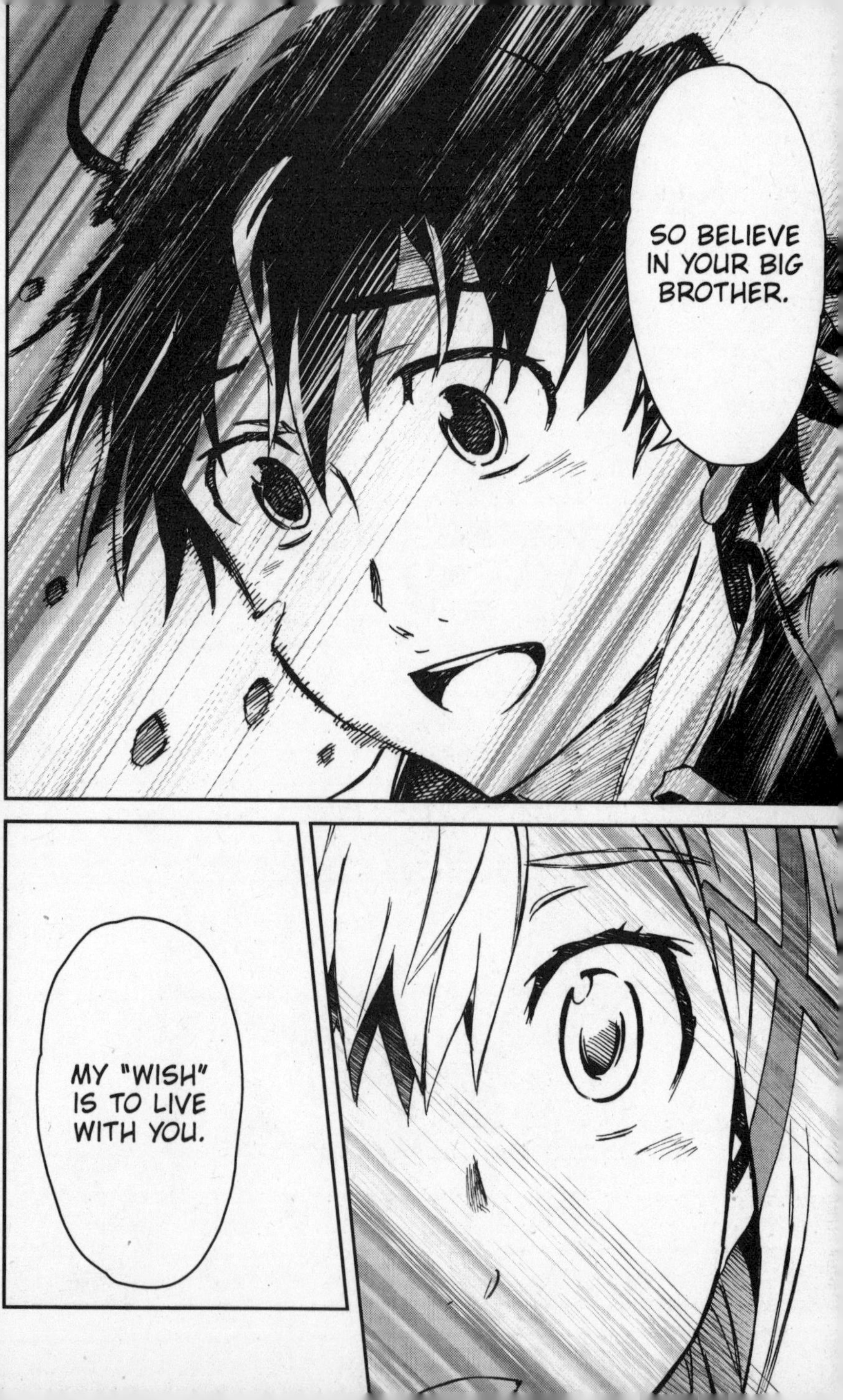
SO BELIEVE IN YOUR BIG BROTHER.
MY "WISH" IS TO LIVE WITH YOU.

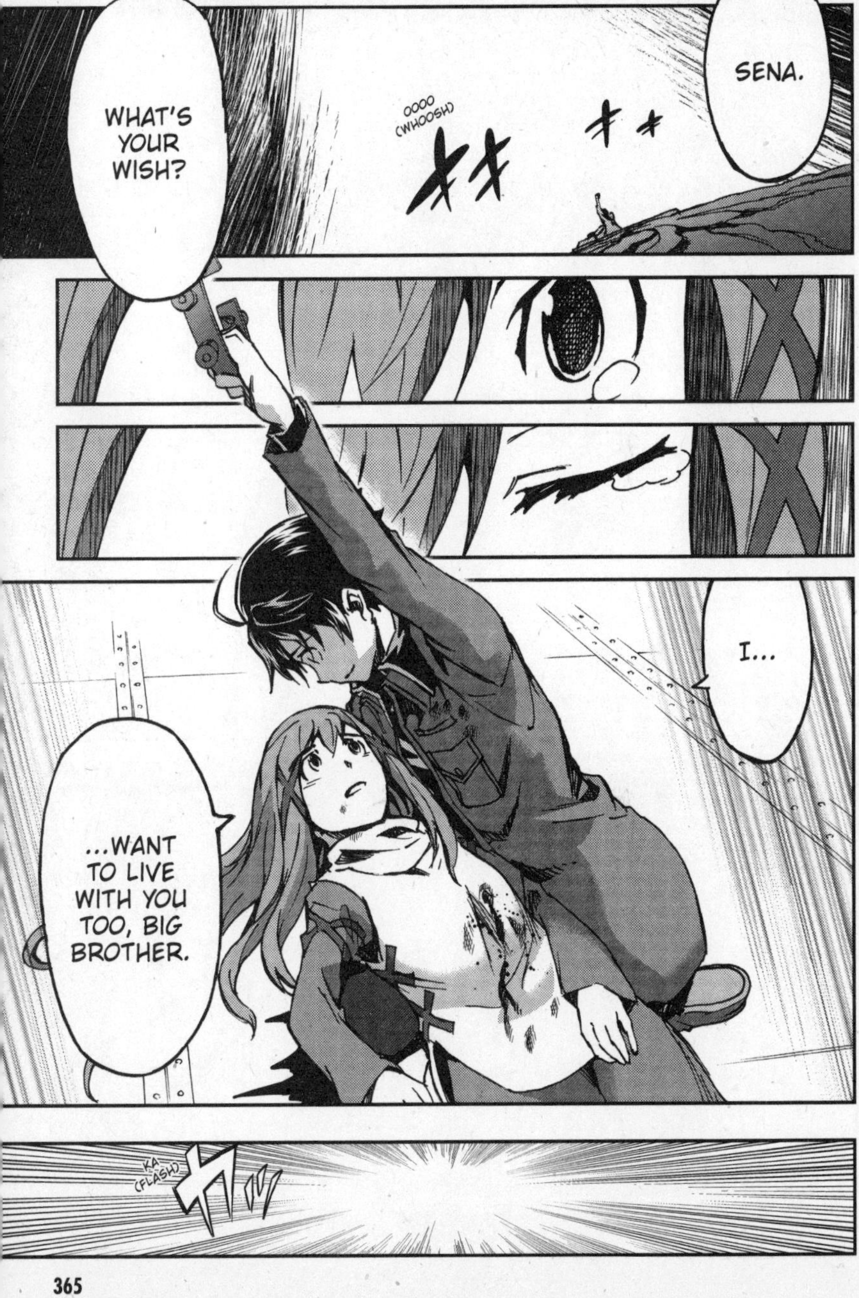
SENA.
OOOO (WHOOSH)
WHAT'S YOUR WISH?
I...
...WANT TO LIVE WITH YOU TOO, BIG BROTHER.
KA (FLASH)

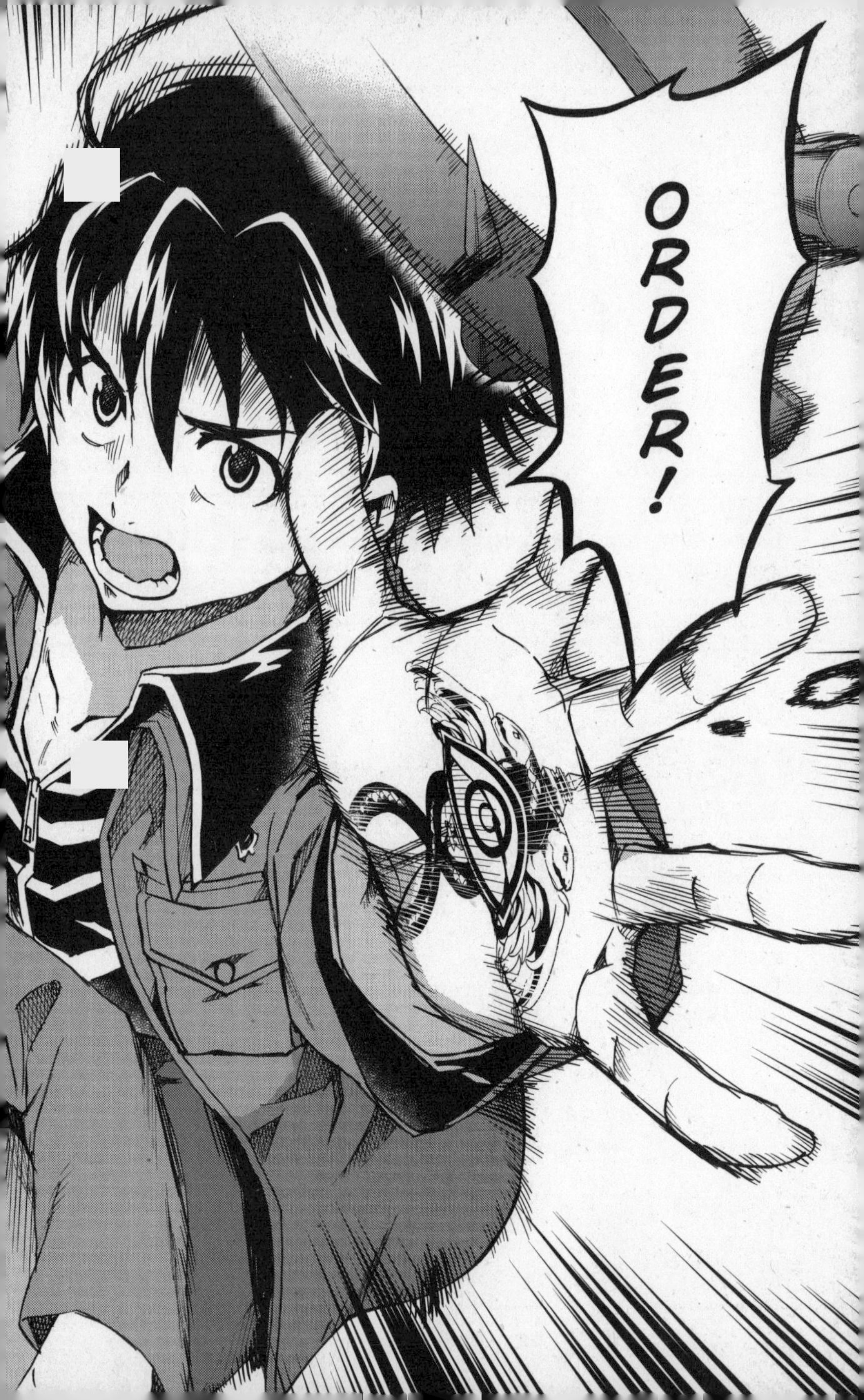
ORDER!

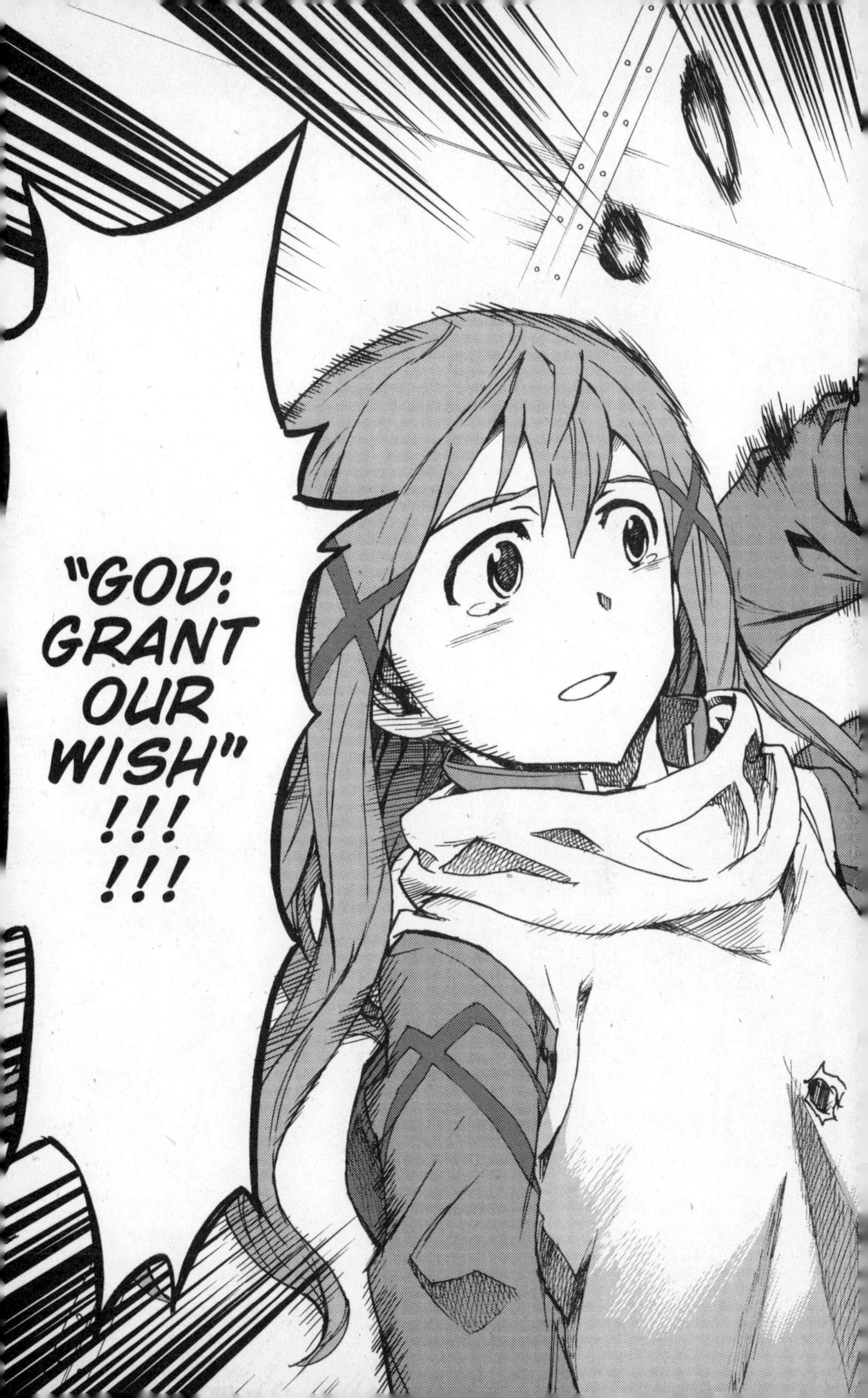
"GOD: GRANT OUR WISH" !!! !!!

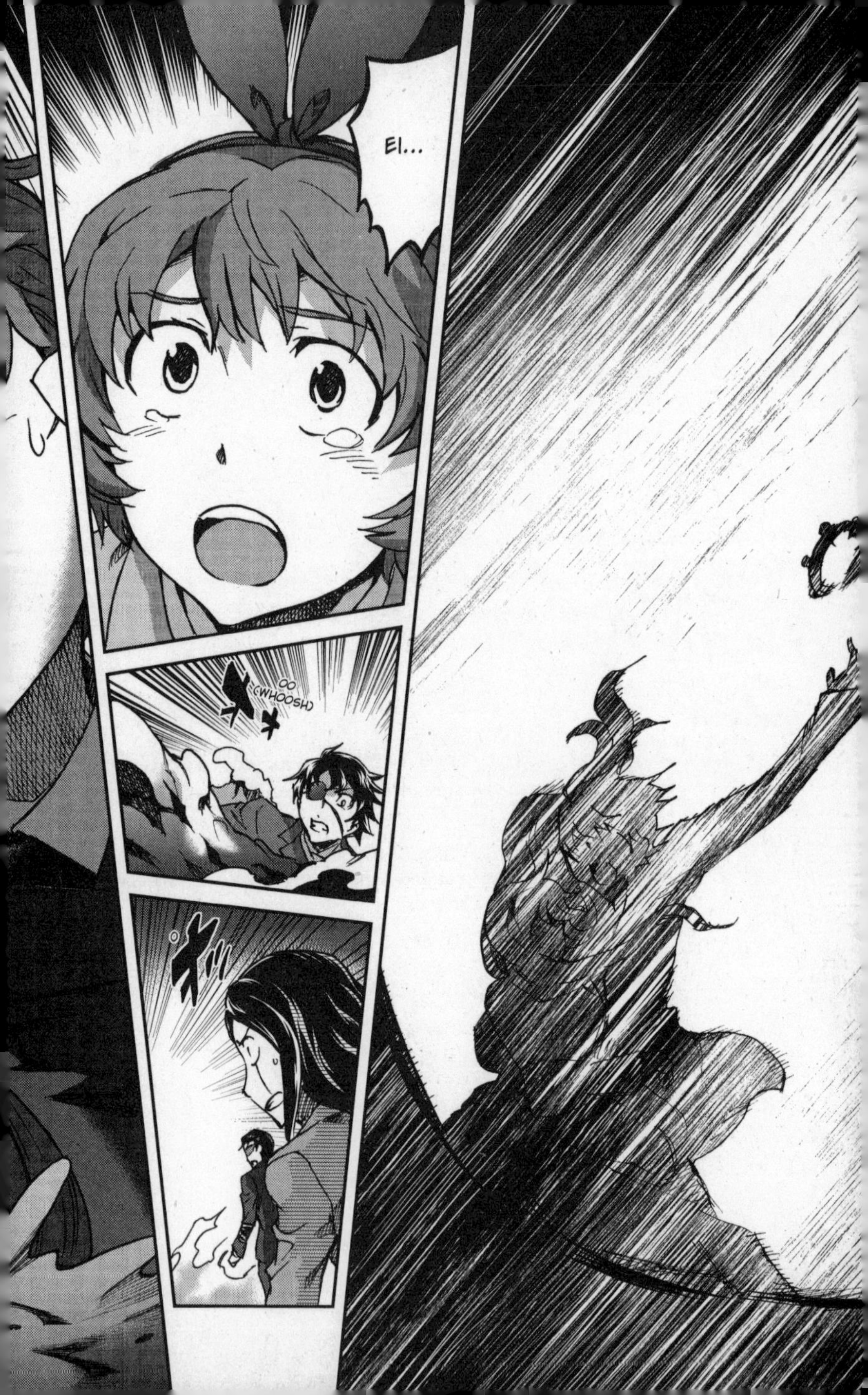
El...
(WHOOSH)

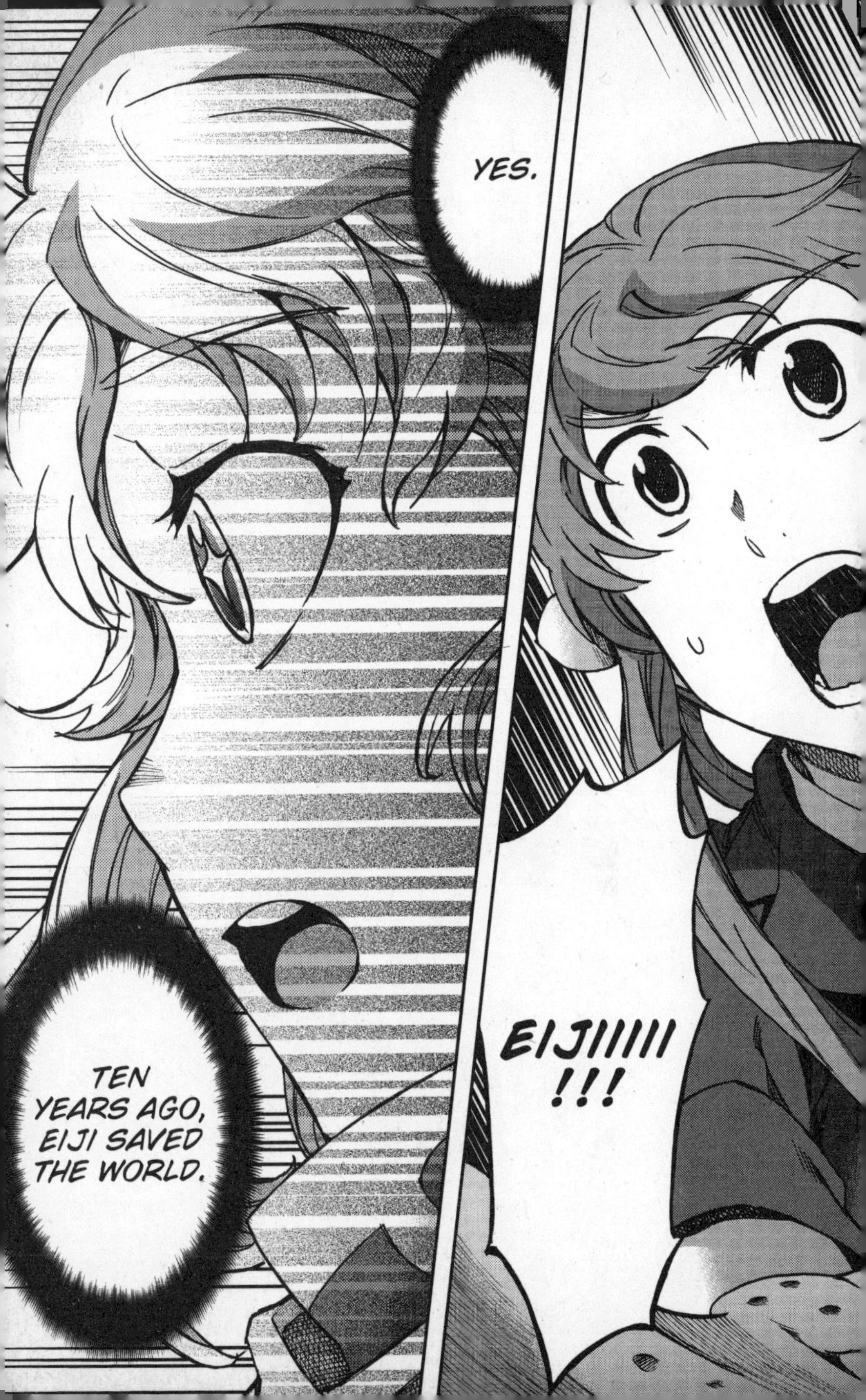
EIJIIIII
!!!
YES.
TEN YEARS AGO, EIJI SAVED THE WORLD.

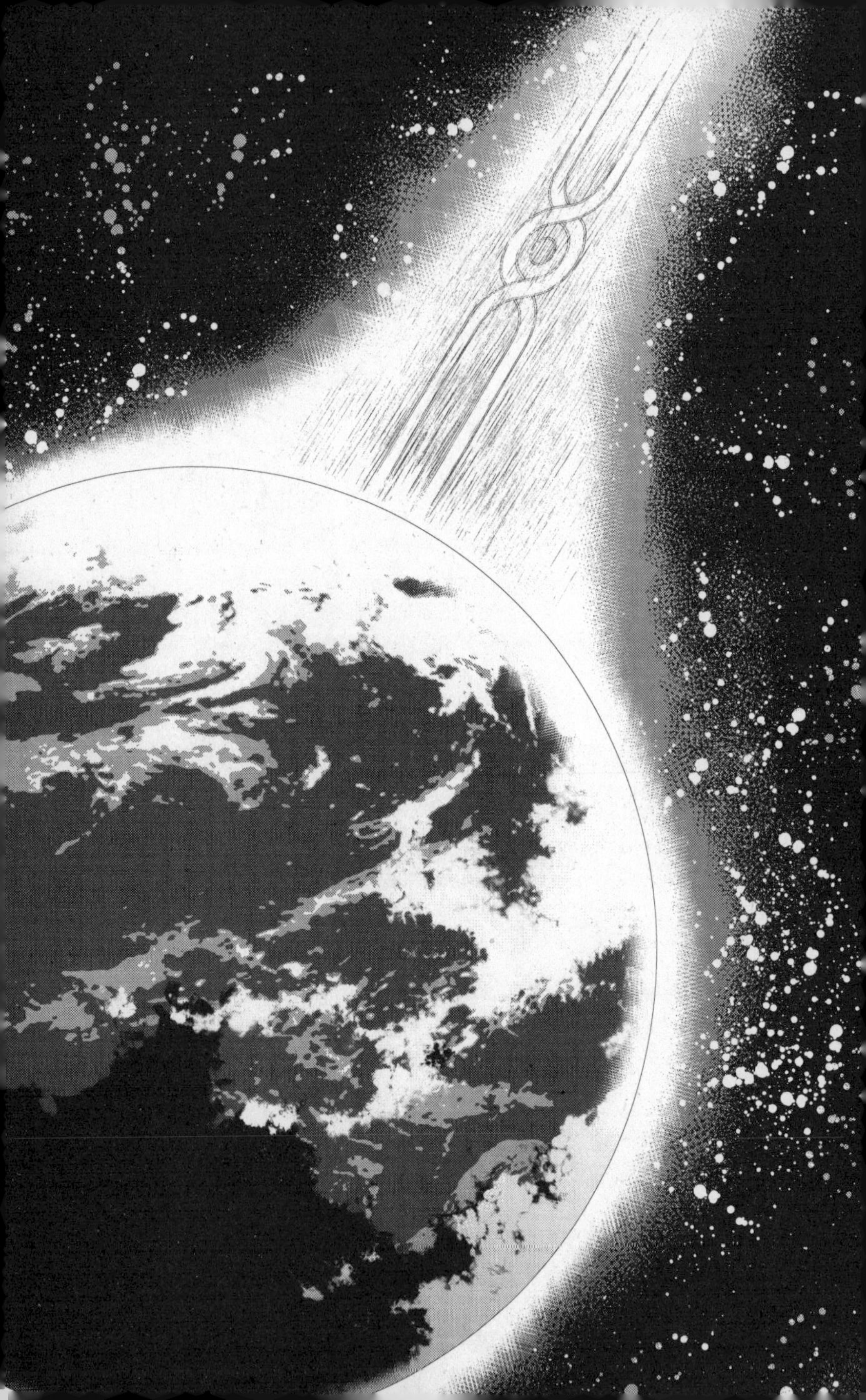

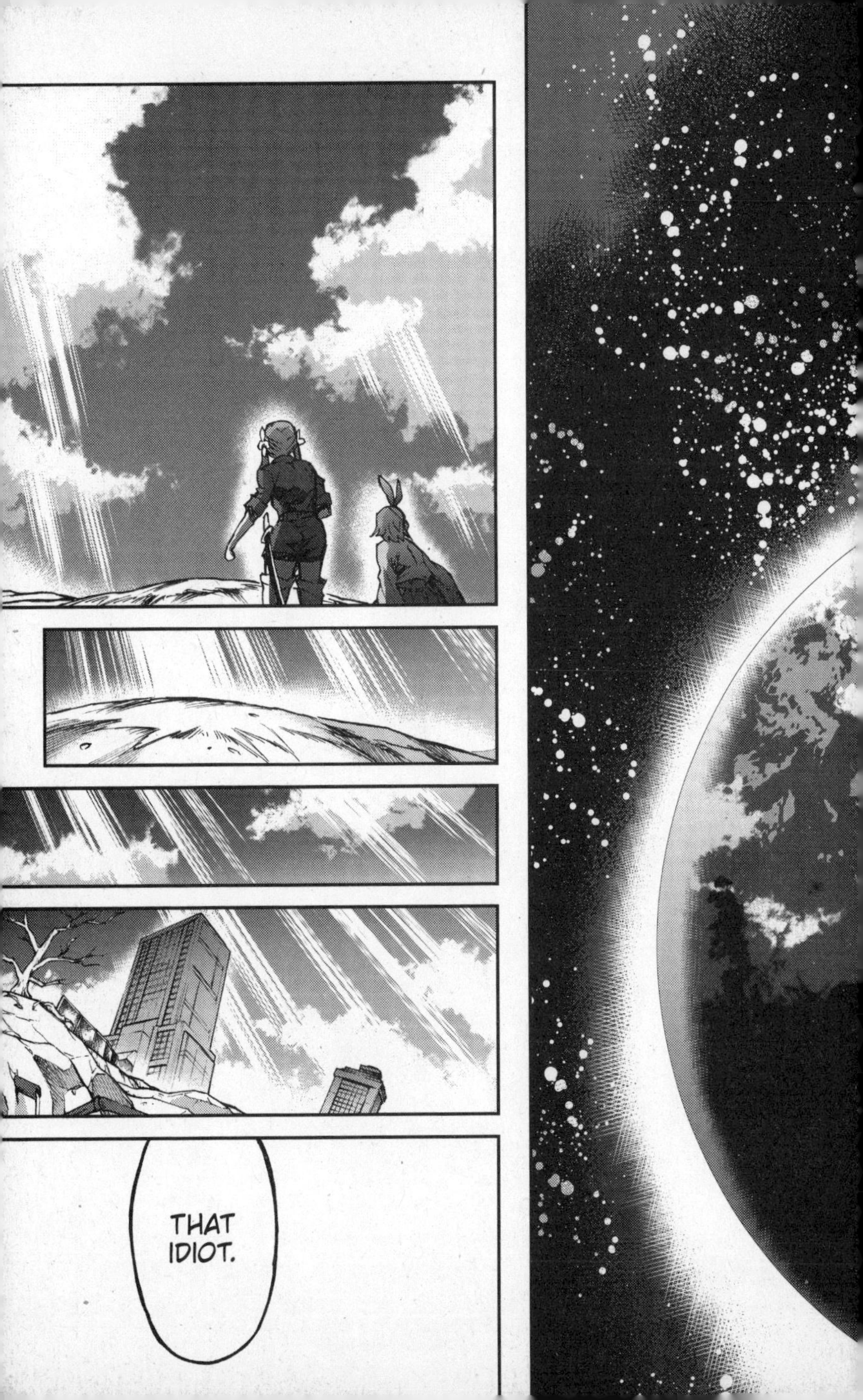
THAT IDIOT.

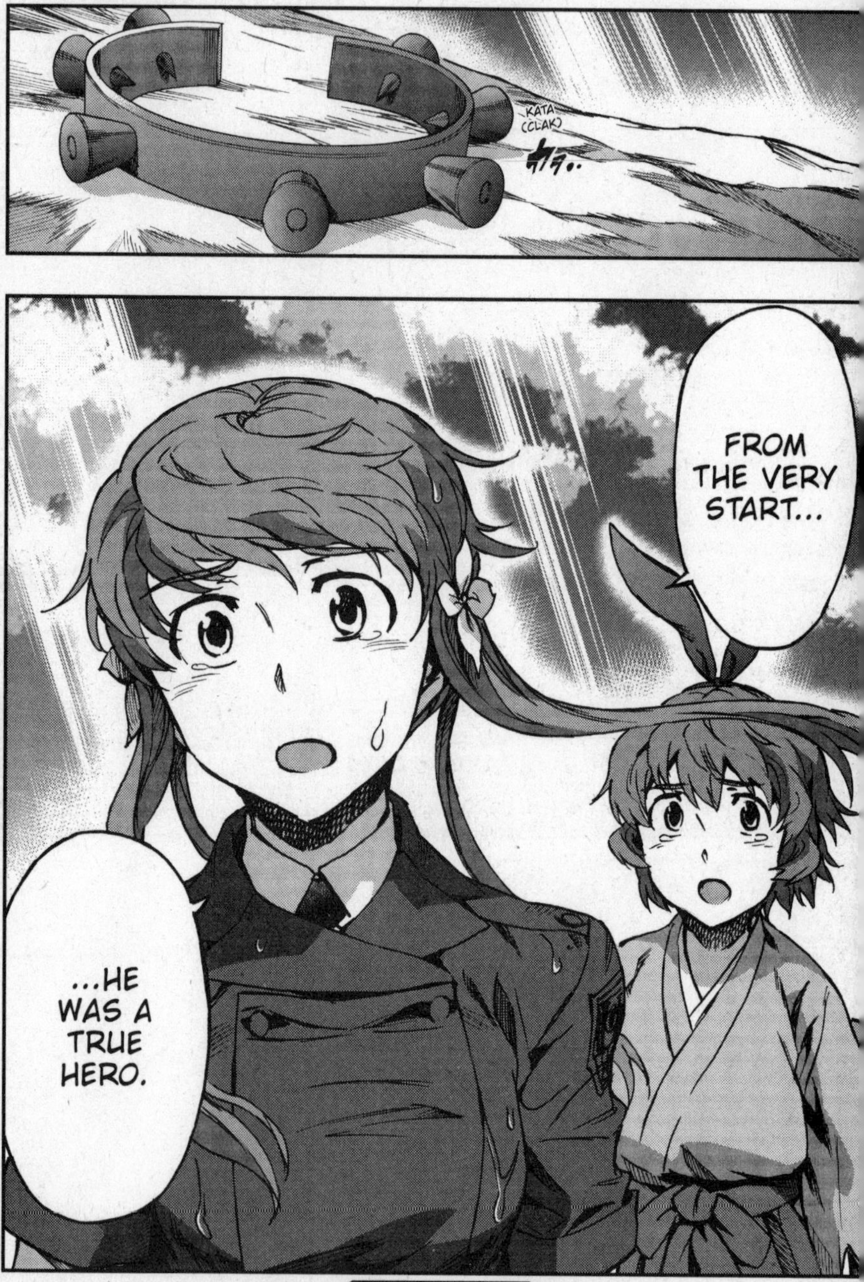
KATA (CLAK)
カタ..
FROM THE VERY START...
...HE WAS A TRUE HERO.

Subject 53: END

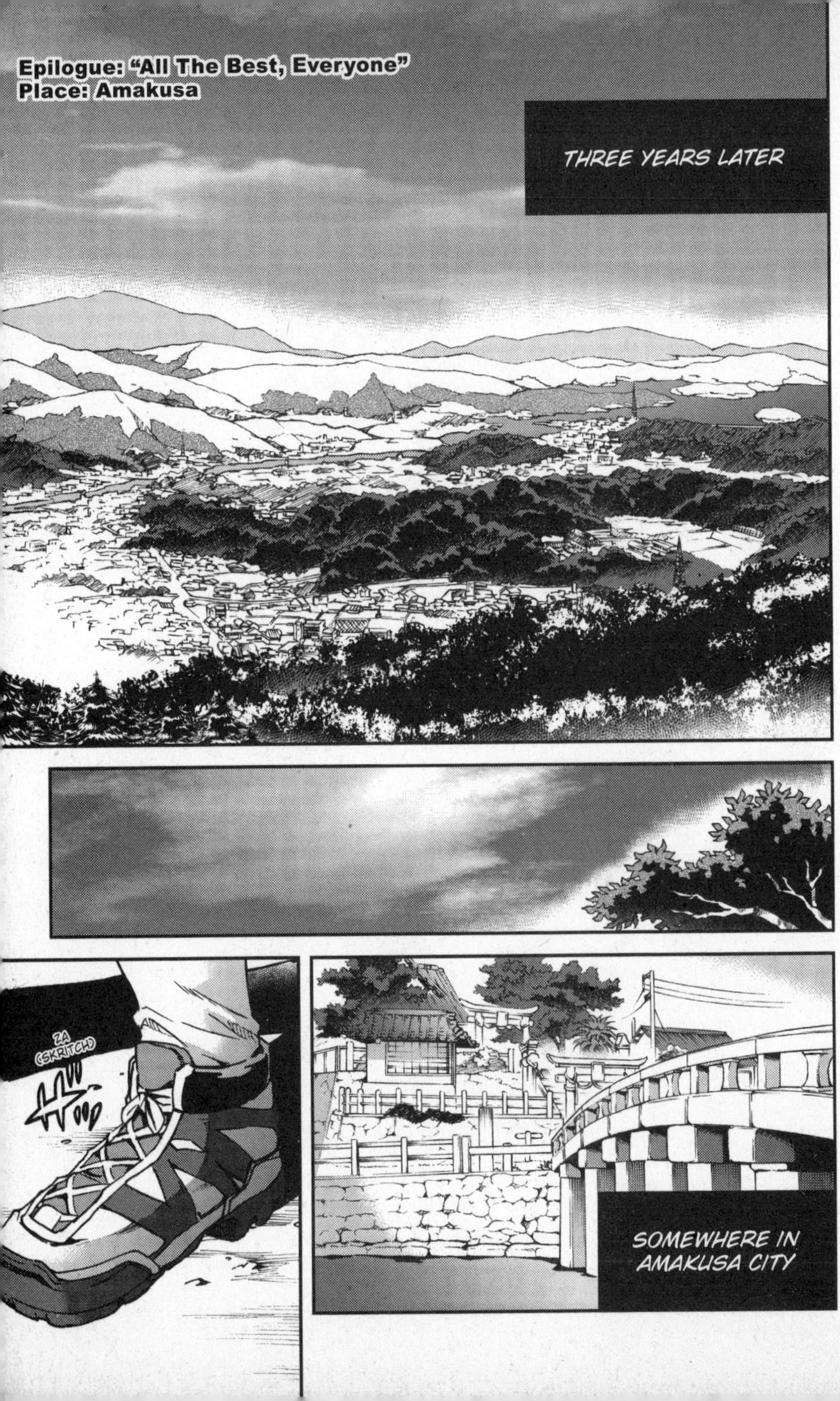
Epilogue: "All The Best, Everyone"
Place: Amakusa
THREE YEARS LATER
SOMEWHERE IN AMAKUSA CITY
ZA (SKRITCH)

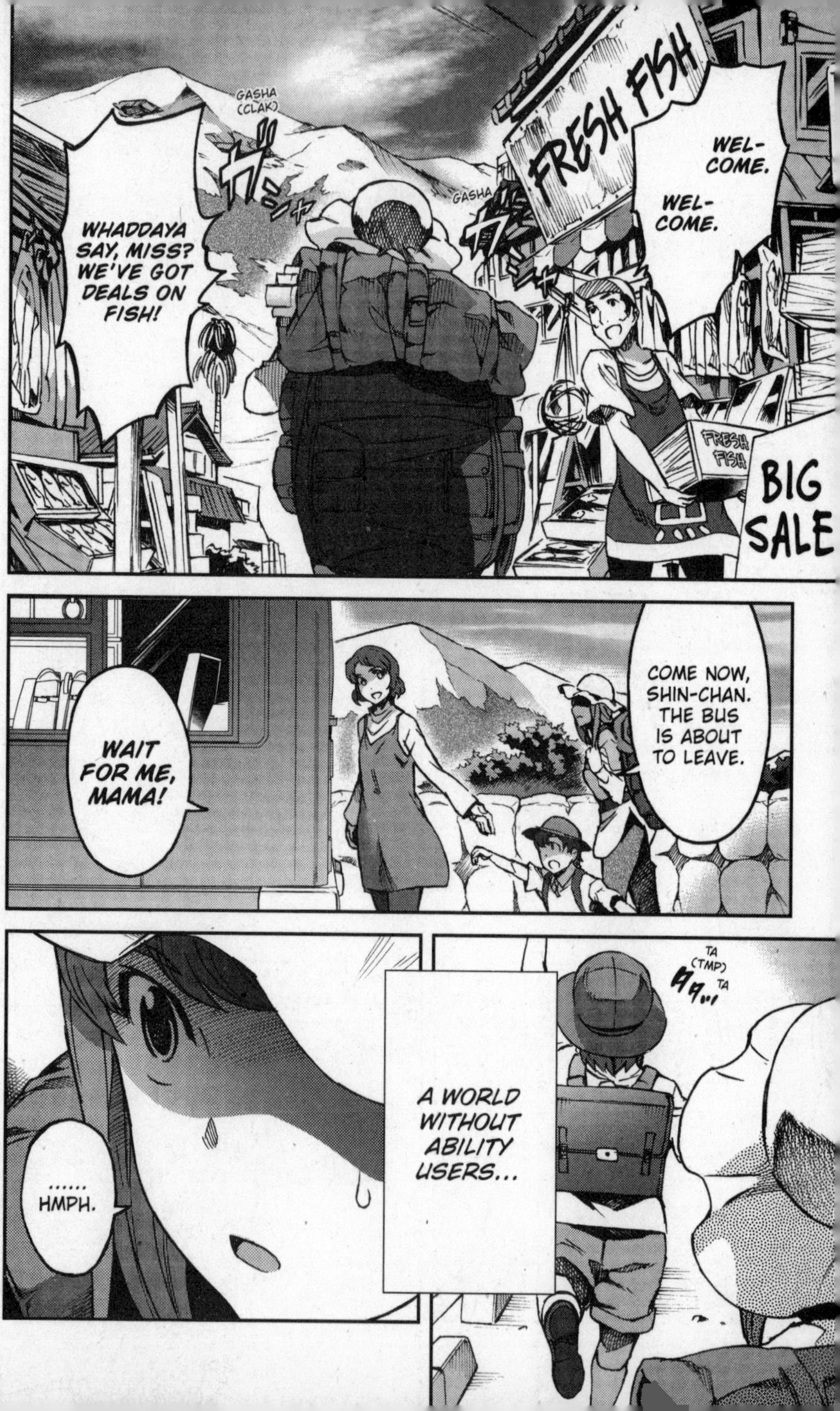
WEL-COME.
WEL-COME.
FRESH FISH
BIG SALE
FRESH FISH
GASHA
GASHA (CLAK)
WHADDAYA SAY, MISS? WE'VE GOT DEALS ON FISH!
COME NOW, SHIN-CHAN. THE BUS IS ABOUT TO LEAVE.
WAIT FOR ME, MAMA!
TA (TMP) TA
A WORLD WITHOUT ABILITY USERS...
...... HMPH.

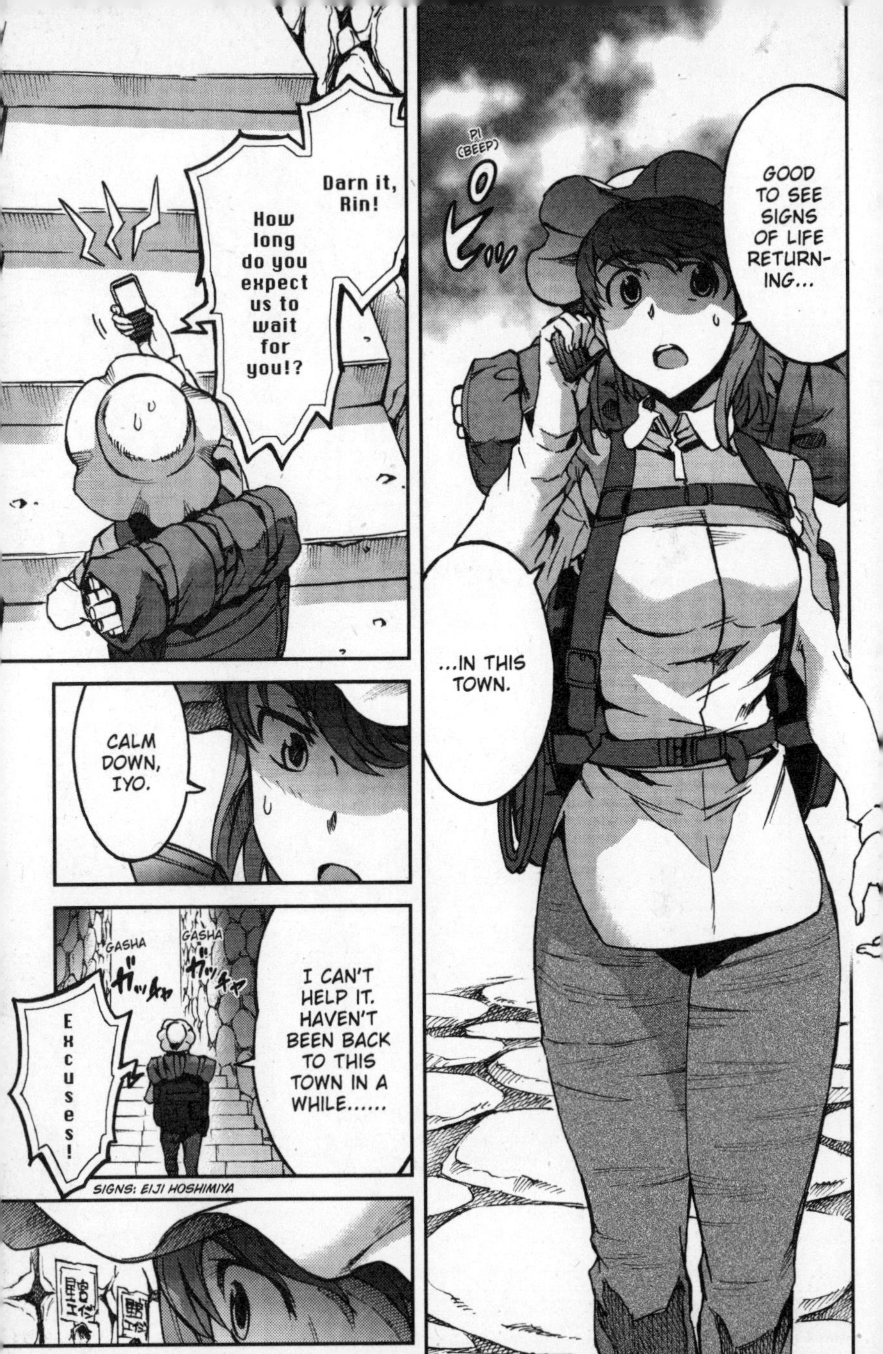
PI (BEEP)
GOOD TO SEE SIGNS OF LIFE RETURNING...
...IN THIS TOWN.
Darn it, Rin!
How long do you expect us to wait for you!?
CALM DOWN, IYO.
I CAN'T HELP IT. HAVEN'T BEEN BACK TO THIS TOWN IN A WHILE......
GASHA
GASHA
Excuses!
SIGNS: EIJI HOSHIMIYA

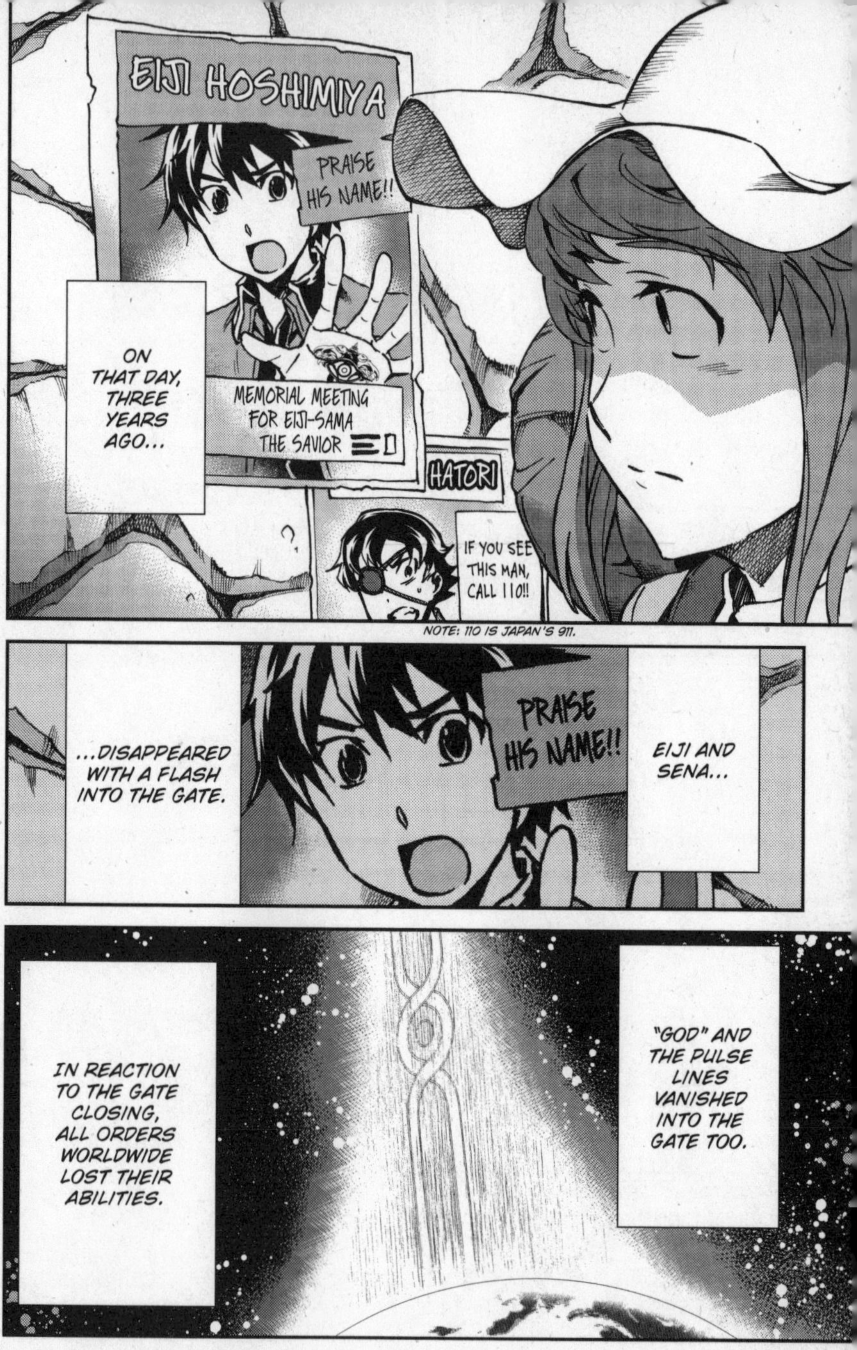
EIJI HOSHIMIYA
PRAISE HIS NAME!!
ON THAT DAY, THREE YEARS AGO...
MEMORIAL MEETING FOR EIJI-SAMA THE SAVIOR
HATORI
IF YOU SEE THIS MAN, CALL 110!!
NOTE: 110 IS JAPAN'S 911.
EIJI AND SENA...
PRAISE HIS NAME!!
...DISAPPEARED WITH A FLASH INTO THE GATE.
"GOD" AND THE PULSE LINES VANISHED INTO THE GATE TOO.
IN REACTION TO THE GATE CLOSING, ALL ORDERS WORLDWIDE LOST THEIR ABILITIES.

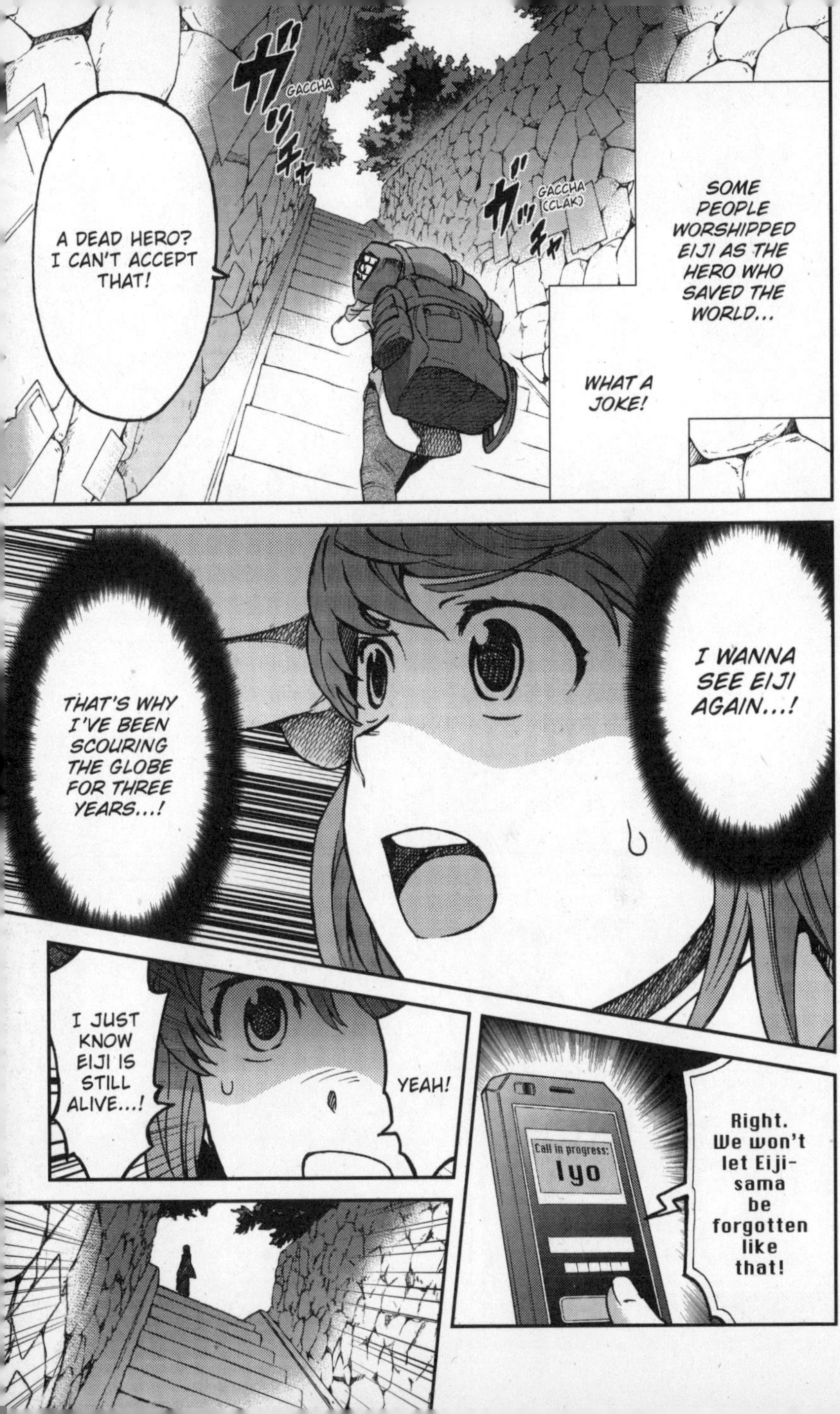
SOME PEOPLE WORSHIPPED EIJI AS THE HERO WHO SAVED THE WORLD...
WHAT A JOKE!
GACCHA (CLAK)
GACCHA
A DEAD HERO? I CAN'T ACCEPT THAT!
I WANNA SEE EIJI AGAIN...!
THAT'S WHY I'VE BEEN SCOURING THE GLOBE FOR THREE YEARS...!
Call in progress:
Iyo
Right. We won't let Eiji-sama be forgotten like that!
YEAH!
I JUST KNOW EIJI IS STILL ALIVE...!

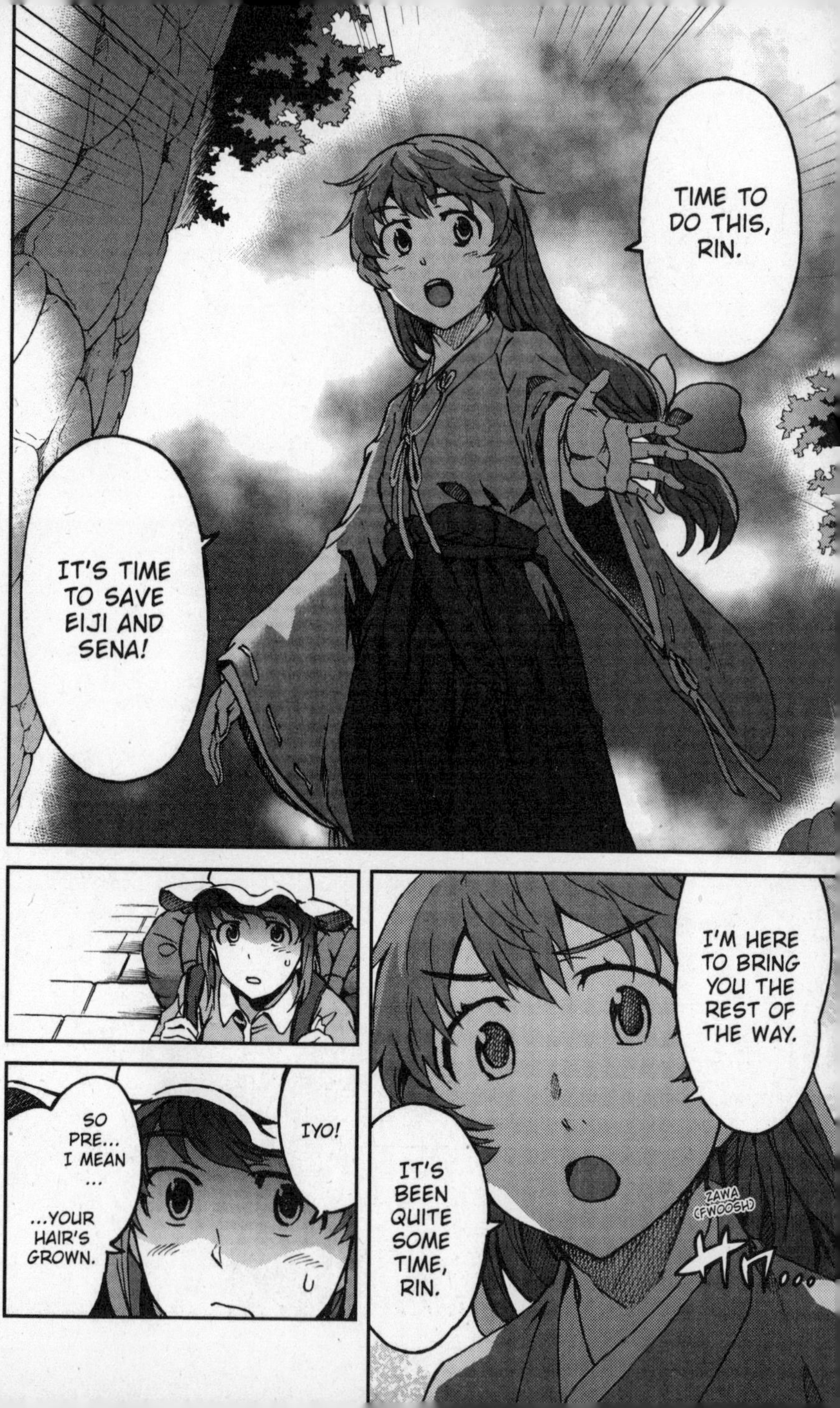
TIME TO DO THIS, RIN.
IT'S TIME TO SAVE EIJI AND SENA!
I'M HERE TO BRING YOU THE REST OF THE WAY.
IT'S BEEN QUITE SOME TIME, RIN.
ZAWA (FWOOSH)
IYO!
SO PRE... I MEAN ...
...YOUR HAIR'S GROWN.

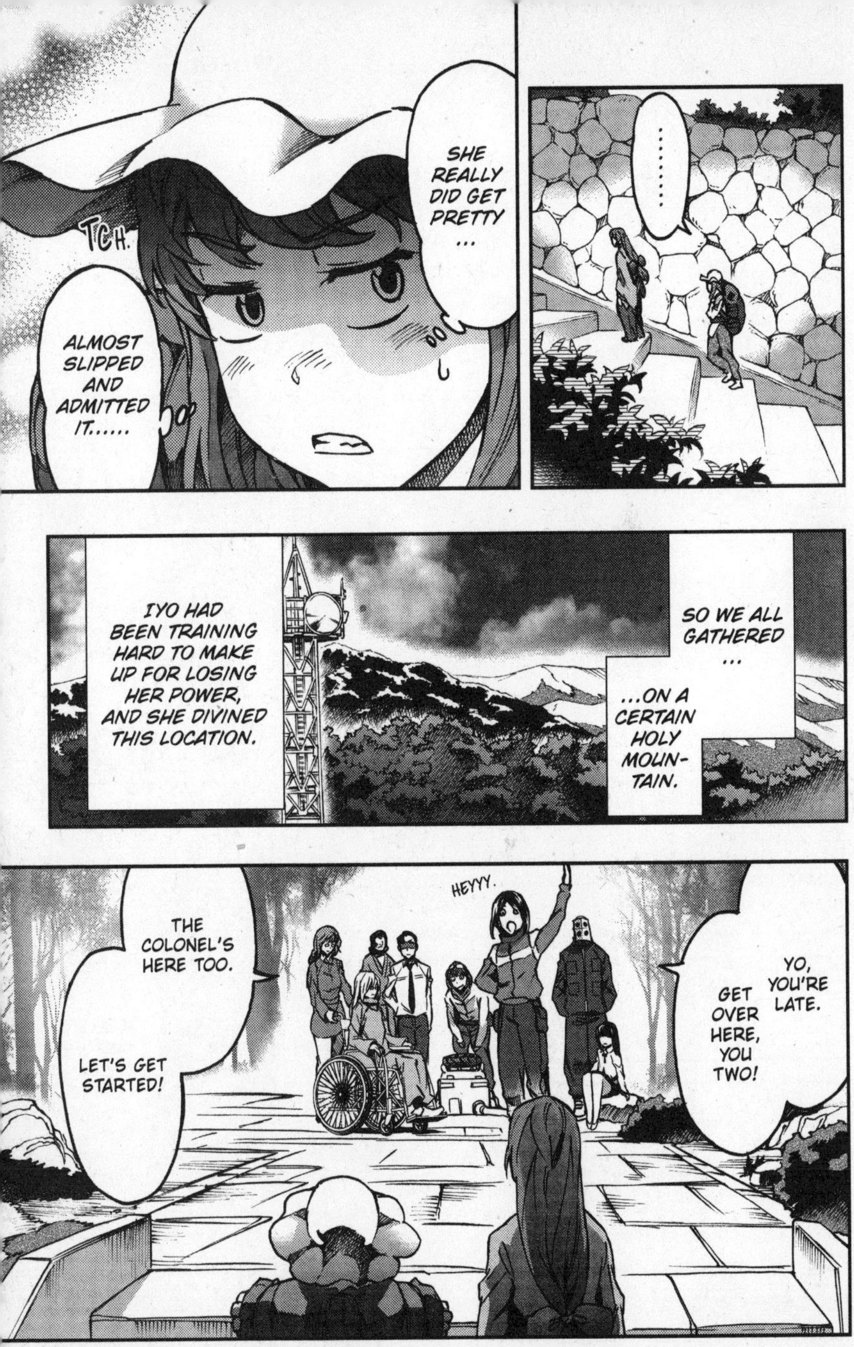
......
SHE REALLY DID GET PRETTY...
TCH.
ALMOST SLIPPED AND ADMITTED IT......
SO WE ALL GATHERED...
...ON A CERTAIN HOLY MOUNTAIN.
IYO HAD BEEN TRAINING HARD TO MAKE UP FOR LOSING HER POWER, AND SHE DIVINED THIS LOCATION.
YO, YOU'RE LATE.
GET OVER HERE, YOU TWO!
HEYYY.
THE COLONEL'S HERE TOO.
LET'S GET STARTED!

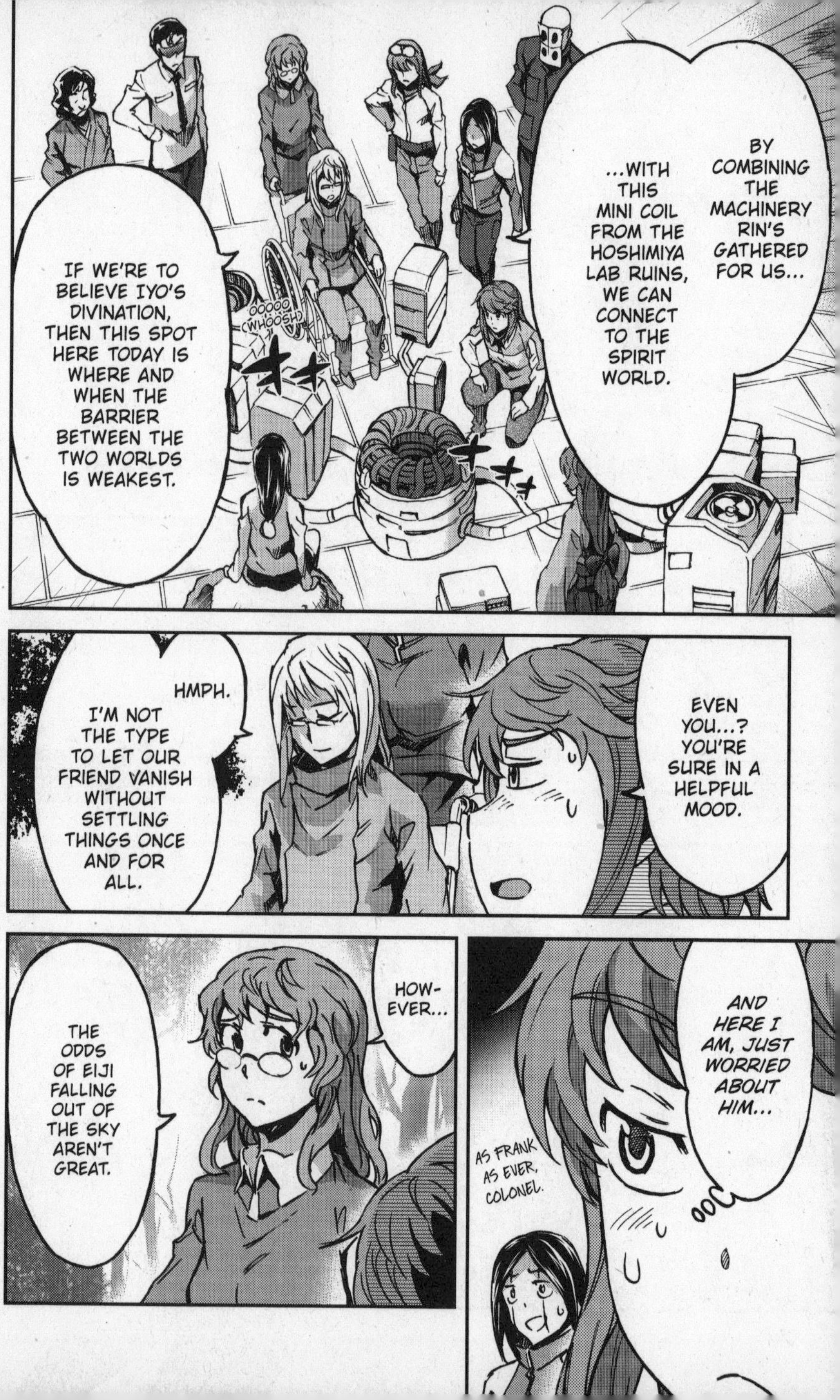
BY COMBINING THE MACHINERY RIN'S GATHERED FOR US...
...WITH THIS MINI COIL FROM THE HOSHIMIYA LAB RUINS, WE CAN CONNECT TO THE SPIRIT WORLD.
IF WE'RE TO BELIEVE IYO'S DIVINATION, THEN THIS SPOT HERE TODAY IS WHERE AND WHEN THE BARRIER BETWEEN THE TWO WORLDS IS WEAKEST.
OOOOO (WHOOSH)
EVEN YOU...? YOU'RE SURE IN A HELPFUL MOOD.
HMPH. I'M NOT THE TYPE TO LET OUR FRIEND VANISH WITHOUT SETTLING THINGS ONCE AND FOR ALL.
AND HERE I AM, JUST WORRIED ABOUT HIM...
AS FRANK AS EVER, COLONEL.
HOW-EVER...
THE ODDS OF EIJI FALLING OUT OF THE SKY AREN'T GREAT.

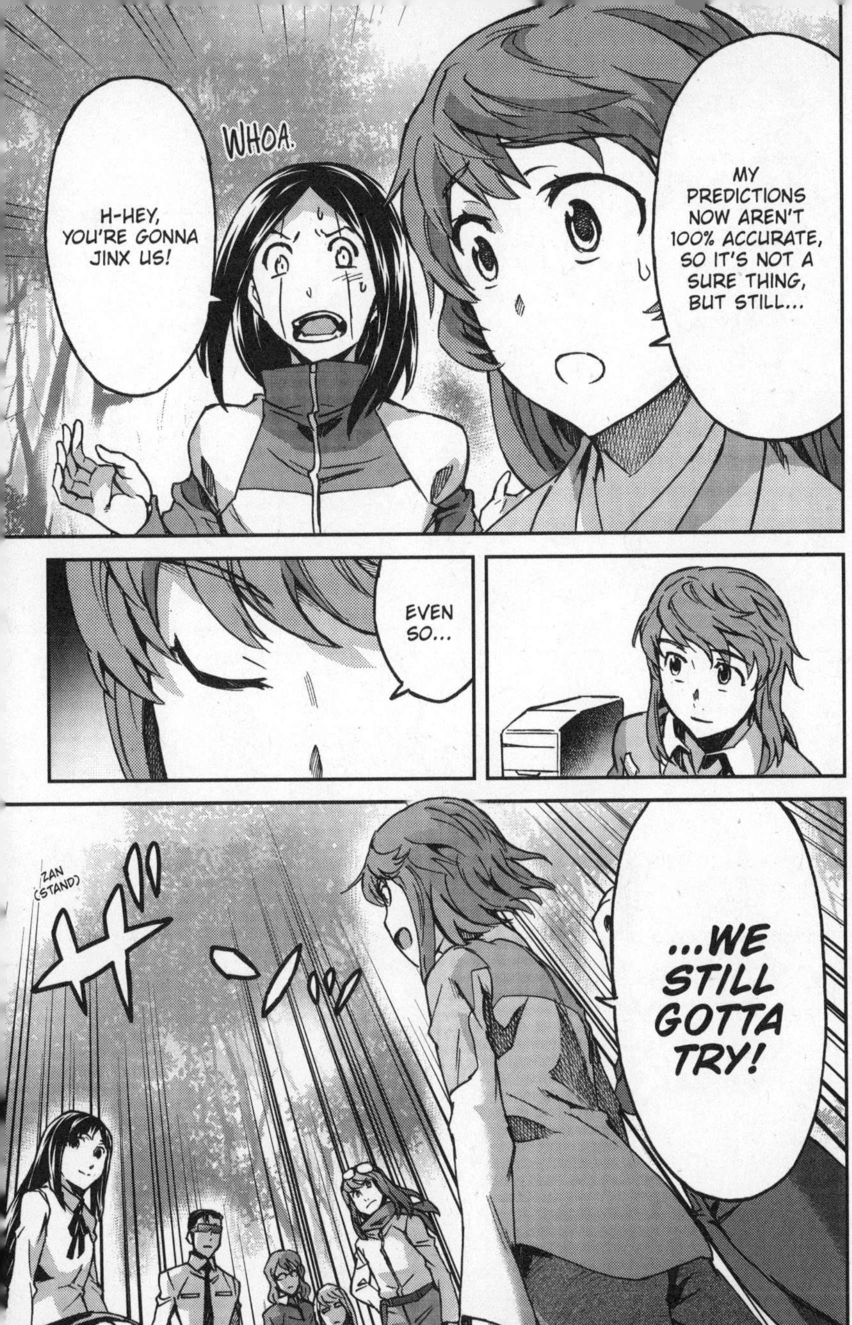
MY PREDICTIONS NOW AREN'T 100% ACCURATE, SO IT'S NOT A SURE THING, BUT STILL...
WHOA.
H-HEY, YOU'RE GONNA JINX US!
EVEN SO...
...WE STILL GOTTA TRY!
ZAN (STAND)

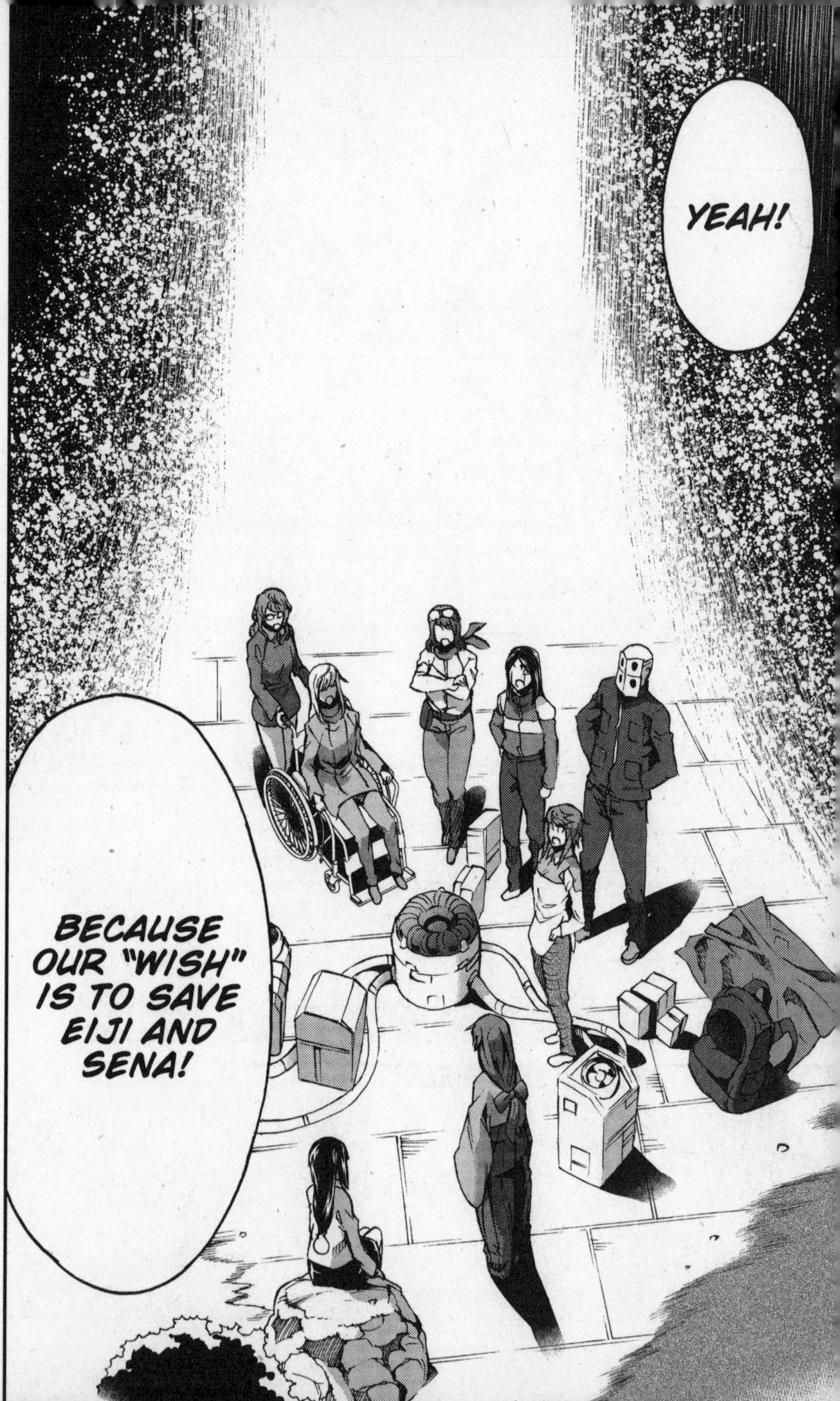
YEAH!
BECAUSE OUR "WISH" IS TO SAVE EIJI AND SENA!

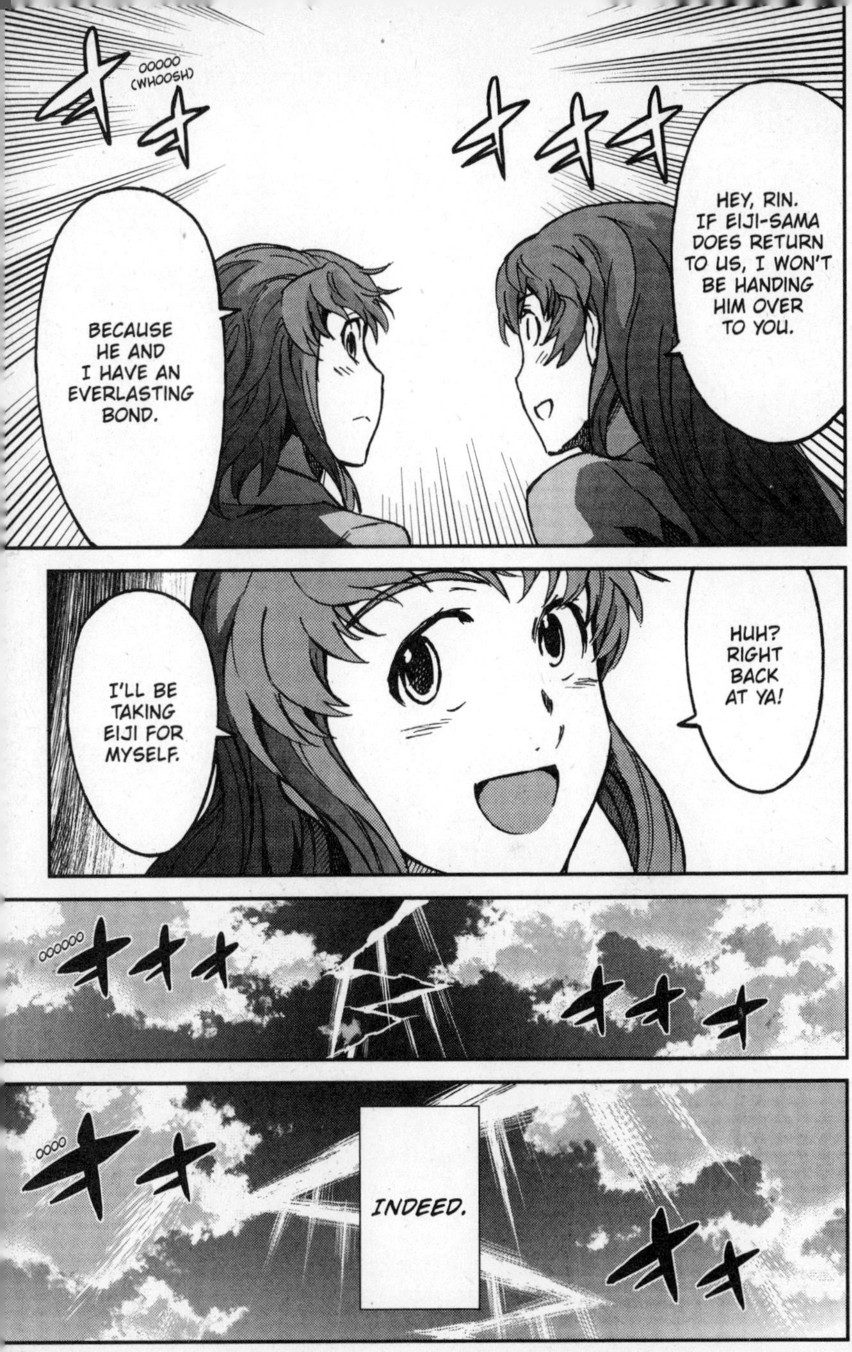
OOOOO (WHOOSH)
HEY, RIN. IF EIJI-SAMA DOES RETURN TO US, I WON'T BE HANDING HIM OVER TO YOU.
BECAUSE HE AND I HAVE AN EVERLASTING BOND.
HUH? RIGHT BACK AT YA!
I'LL BE TAKING EIJI FOR MYSELF.
OOOOOO
OOOO
INDEED.

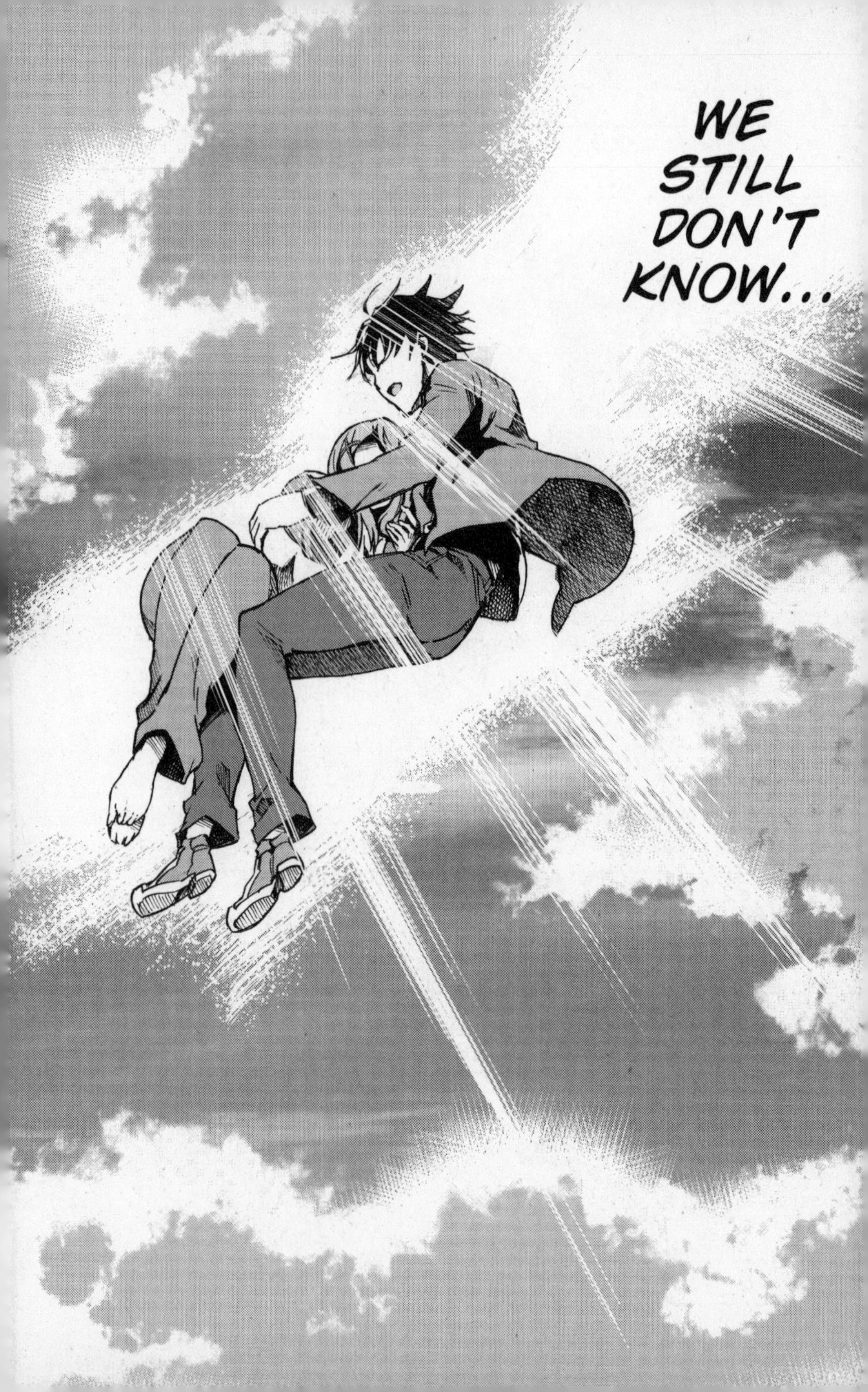
WE STILL DON'T KNOW...

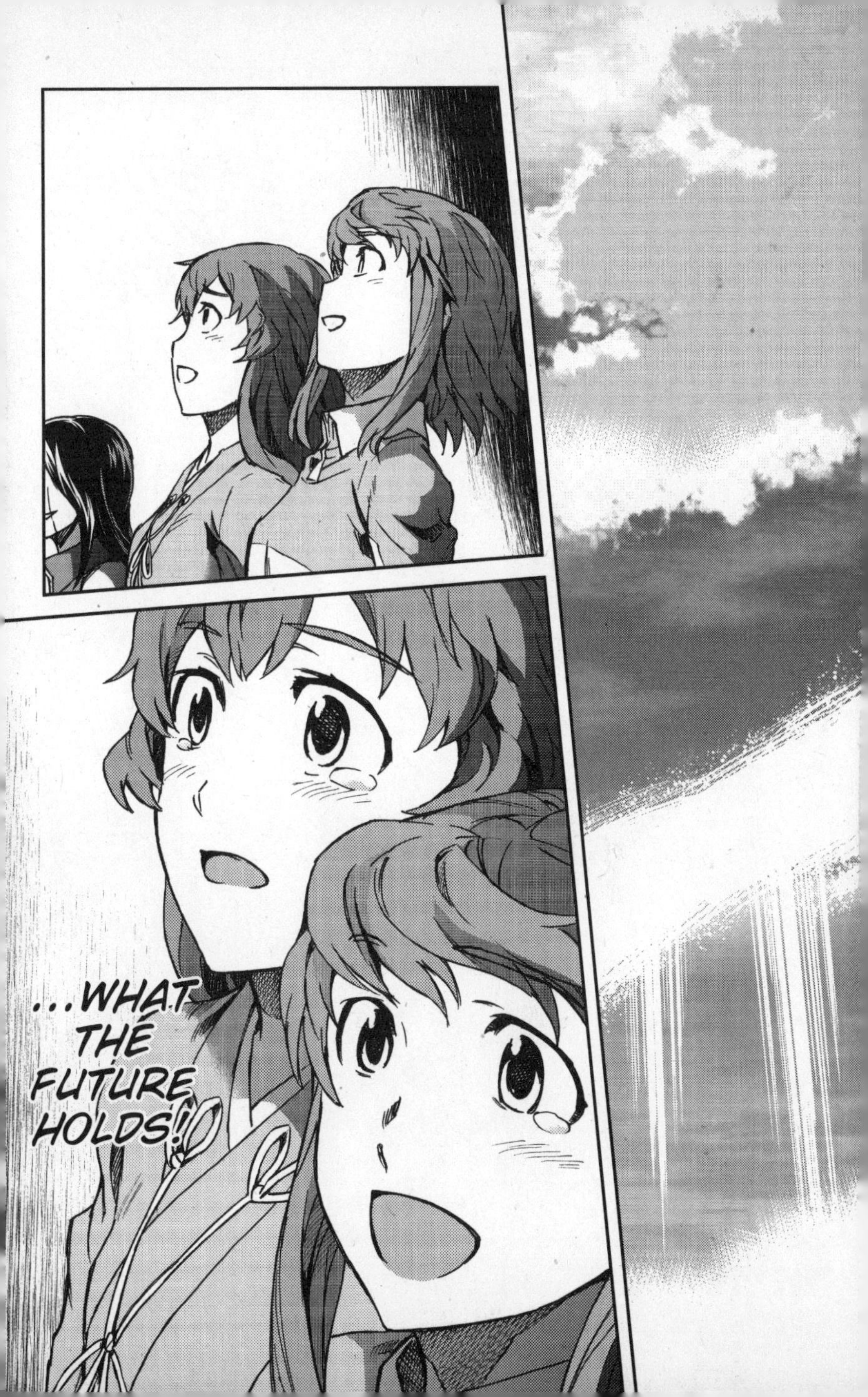
...WHAT THE FUTURE HOLDS!!

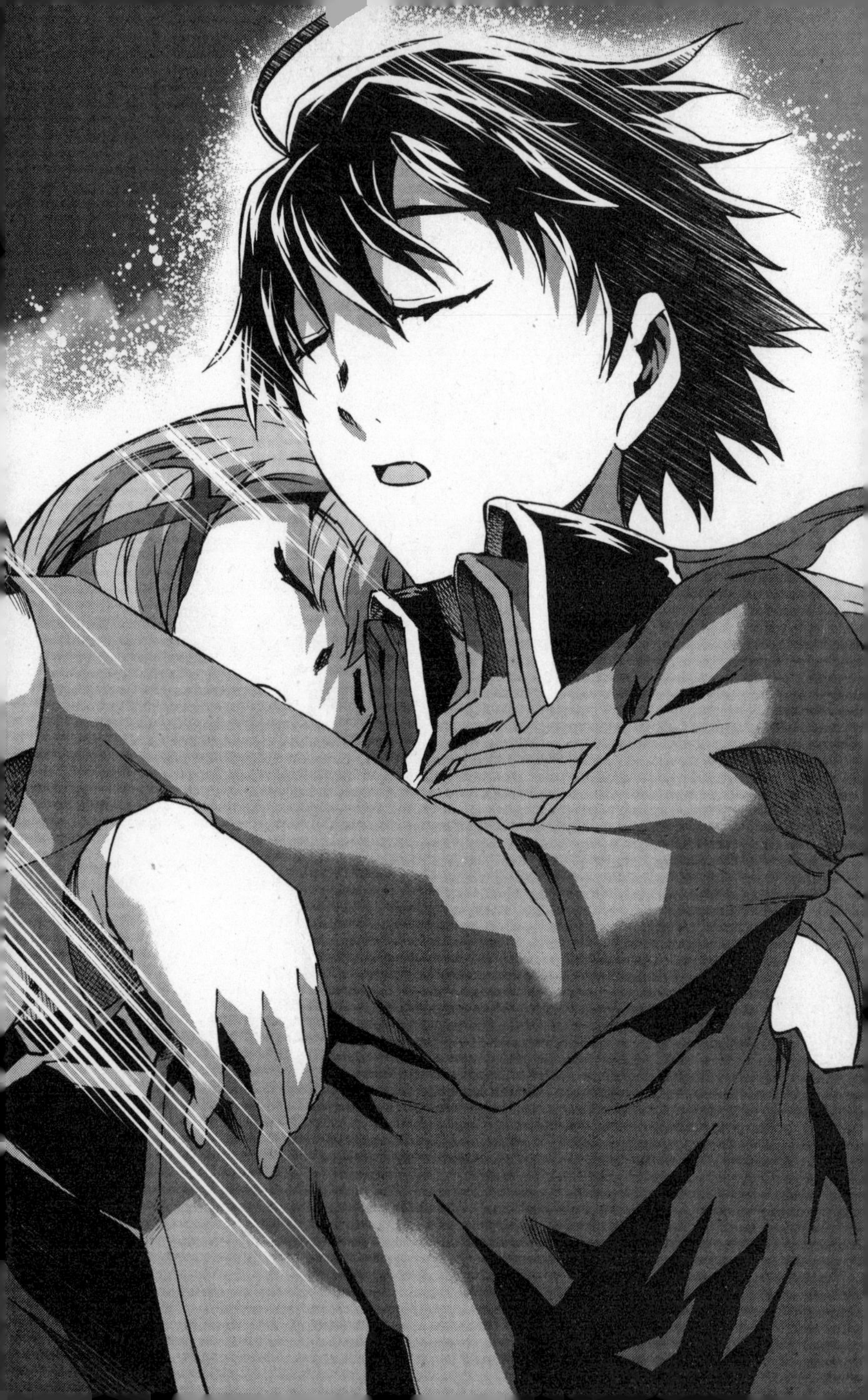

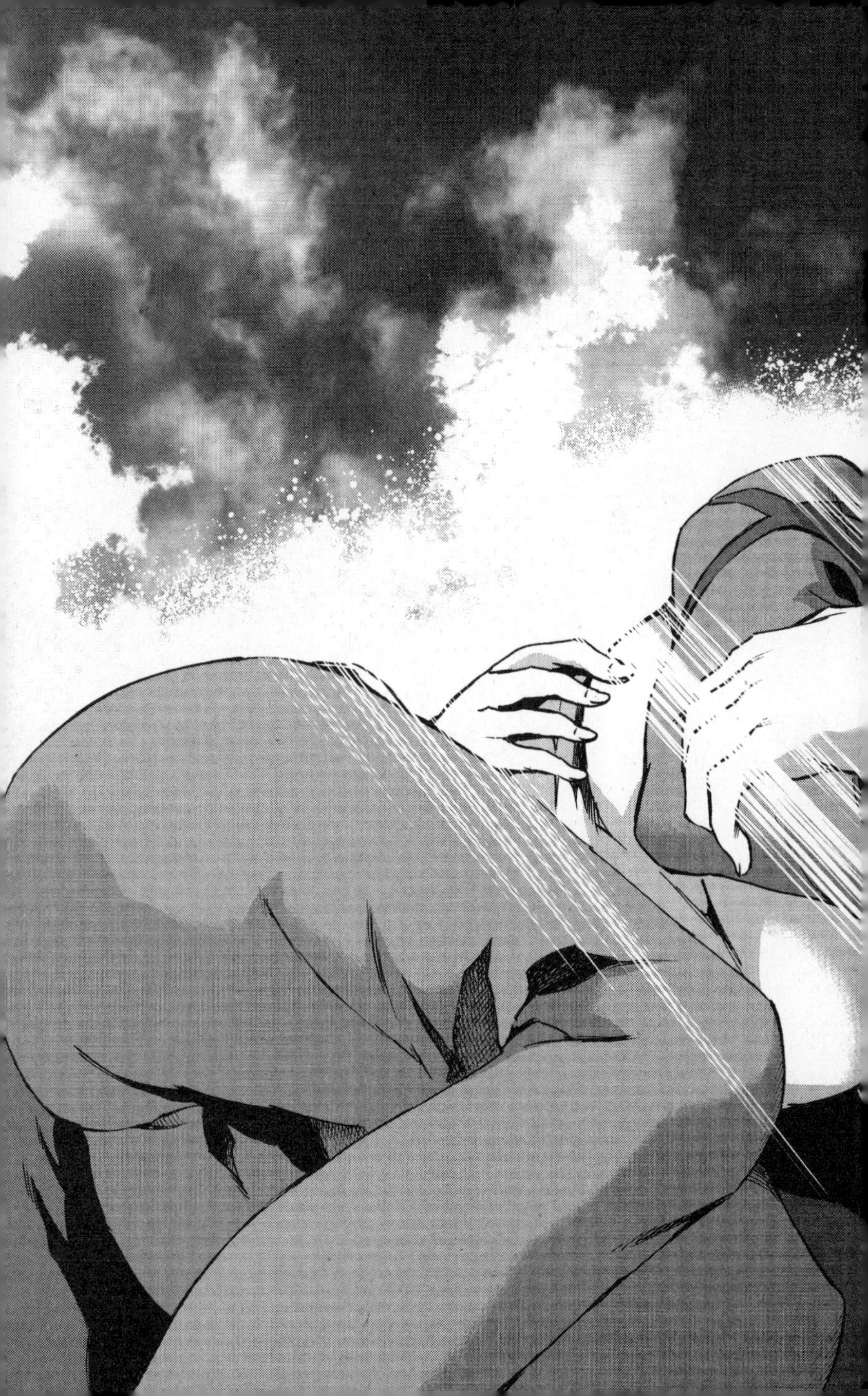

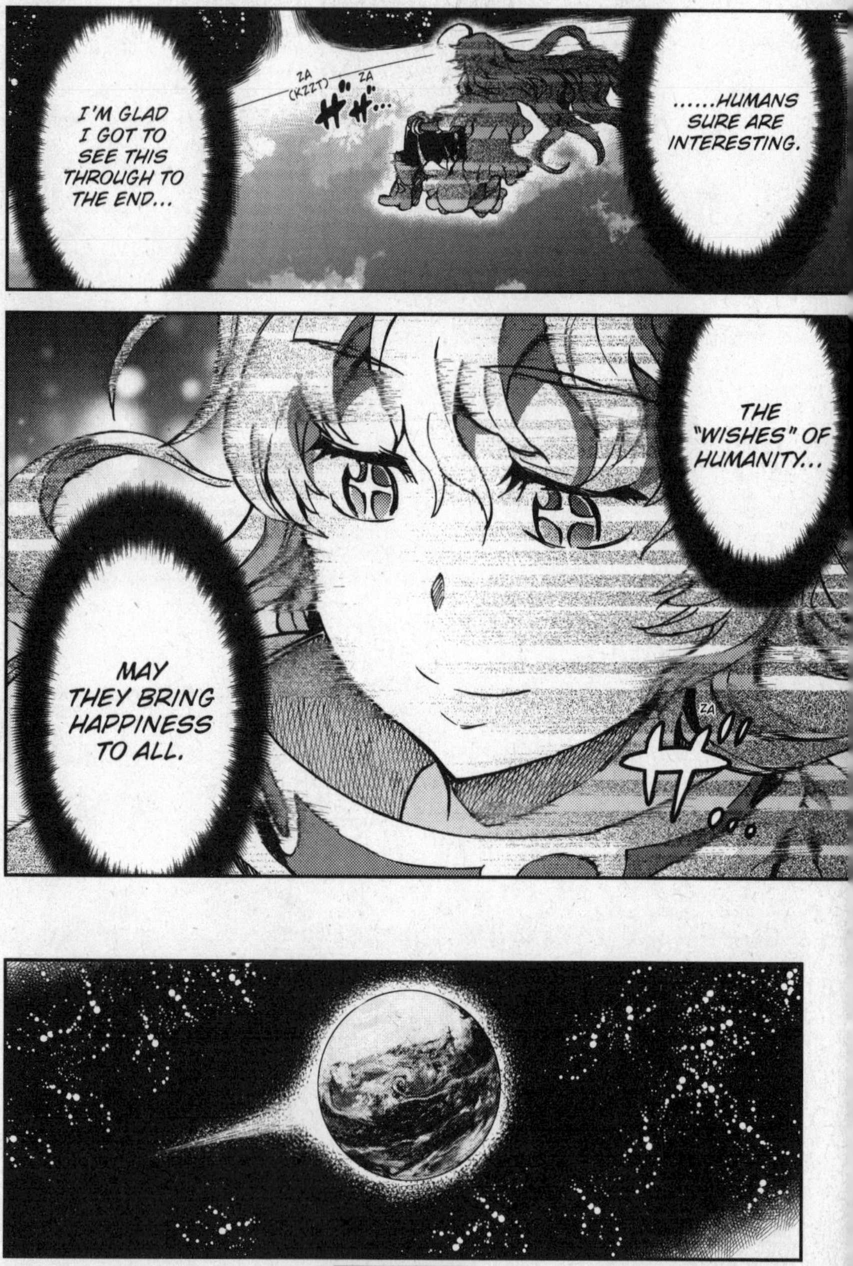

......HUMANS SURE ARE INTERESTING.
ZA (KZZT) ZA
I'M GLAD I GOT TO SEE THIS THROUGH TO THE END...
THE "WISHES" OF HUMANITY...
MAY THEY BRING HAPPINESS TO ALL.
ZA

THE END

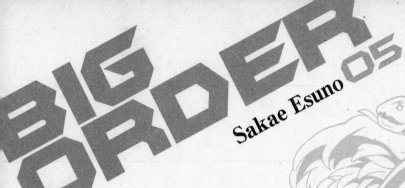

BIG ORDER 05

Sakae Esuno

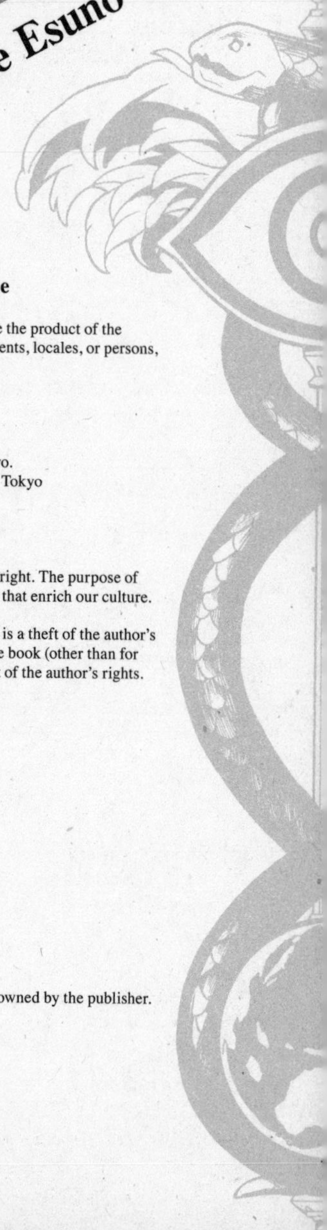

Translation: Caleb Cook • Lettering: Phil Christie

This book is a work of fiction. Names, characters, places, and incidents are the product of the author's imagination or are used fictitiously. Any resemblance to actual events, locales, or persons, living or dead, is coincidental.

First published in Japan in 2016 by KADOKAWA CORPORATION, Tokyo.
English translation rights arranged with KADOKAWA CORPORATION, Tokyo
through Tuttle-Mori Agency, Inc., Tokyo.

Yen Press
1290 Avenue of the Americas
New York, NY 10104

Visit us at yenpress.com
facebook.com/yenpress
twitter.com/yenpress
yenpress.tumblr.com
instagram.com/yenpress

First Yen Press Edition: June 2018

Yen Press is an imprint of Yen Press, LLC.
The Yen Press name and logo are trademarks of Yen Press, LLC.

The publisher is not responsible for websites (or their content) that are not owned by the publisher.

Library of Congress Control Number: 2016958579

ISBN: 978-0-316-41185-1

10 9 8 7 6 5 4 3 2 1

WOR

Printed in the United States of America